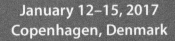

January 12–15, 2017
Copenhagen, Denmark

**Association for
Computing Machinery**

Advancing Computing as a Science & Profession

FOGA'17

Proceedings of the 14th ACM/SIGEVO Conference on
Foundations of Genetic Algorithms

Sponsored by:
ACM SIGEVO

Supported by:
University of Copenhagen

**Association for
Computing Machinery**

Advancing Computing as a Science & Profession

The Association for Computing Machinery
2 Penn Plaza, Suite 701
New York, New York 10121-0701

Notice to Past Authors of ACM-Published Articles
ACM intends to create a complete electronic archive of all articles and/or other material previously published by ACM. If you have written a work that has been previously published by ACM in any journal or conference proceedings prior to 1978, or any SIG Newsletter at any time, and you do NOT want this work to appear in the ACM Digital Library, please inform permissions@acm.org, stating the title of the work, the author(s), and where and when published.

ISBN: 978-1-4503-4651-1 (Digital)

ISBN: 978-1-4503-5452-3 (Print)

Additional copies may be ordered prepaid from:

ACM Order Department
PO Box 30777
New York, NY 10087-0777, USA

Phone: 1-800-342-6626 (USA and Canada)
+1-212-626-0500 (Global)
Fax: +1-212-944-1318
E-mail: acmhelp@acm.org
Hours of Operation: 8:30 am – 4:30 pm ET

Printed in the USA

FOGA 2017 Chairs' Welcome

It is our great pleasure to welcome you to the proceedings of the *14th ACM/SIGEVO Workshop on Foundations of Genetic Algorithms (FOGA XIV)*. Since the first FOGA in 1990, the workshop has established itself as the premier event on the foundations of evolutionary computation. The goal of FOGA is to advance the theoretical understanding of randomised search heuristics and to contribute to making these algorithms more useful in practice. The workshop invites submissions on all kinds of randomised search heuristics, including but not limited to evolutionary algorithms, ant colony optimisation, artificial immune systems, particle swarm optimisation, simulated annealing, Bayesian optimisation, and other Monte Carlo methods for search and optimisation. Contributions bridging theory and practice are particularly encouraged. In addition to rigorous mathematical investigations, experimental studies contributing towards the theoretical foundations of randomised search heuristics are also welcome at FOGA.

FOGA 2017 in Copenhagen, Denmark, was the first to be hosted in a Scandinavian country. We had 23 submissions, out of which 13 papers were accepted for inclusion in these post-conference proceedings. All submissions were thoroughly peer-reviewed, including a second review phase for conditionally accepted manuscripts. We had 23 registrations from 8 different countries from four continents.

The presented papers covered an impressive variety of topics: discrete and continuous optimisation problems, single- and multi-objective optimisation, and various search heuristics, including evolution strategies, evolutionary algorithms, factored evolutionary algorithms, particle swarm optimisation, and estimation-of-distribution algorithms.

We thank Mikkel Thorup giving an inspiring keynote on *Fast and Powerful Hashing using Tabulation* and the University of Copenhagen for providing a spectacular setting in *Festauditoriet*, the picturesque lecture hall in the former Royal Veterinary and Agricultural University.

We are thankful to be given the opportunity to be hosts of FOGA 2017. Many thanks to all the people helping us behind the scenes at SIGEVO, ACM, Sheridan, and the University of Copenhagen. In addition, we would like to thank Christian Gießen and Casper Petersen for their help with the local organisation, and Thomas Jansen for sharing his advice from previous FOGAs.

Most importantly, we'd like to say thanks to the authors and participants of FOGA 2017 who helped make the conference a success. We hope to see you again at FOGA 2019!

Christian Igel
University of Copenhagen, Denmark

Dirk Sudholt
University of Sheffield, United Kingdom

Carsten Witt
Technical University of Denmark, Denmark

Table of Contents

**14th ACM/SIGEVO Workshop on Foundations
of Genetic Algorithms (FOGA XIV)**.. vi

Invited Talk

- **Fast and Powerful Hashing using Tabulation**... 1
  Mikkel Thorup *(University of Copenhagen)*

Regular Papers

- **An Application of Stochastic Differential Equations to Evolutionary Algorithms**............... 3
  Tiago Paixão *(Institute of Science and Technology Austria)*, Jorge Pérez Heredia *(University of Sheffield)*

- **Runtime Analysis of a Discrete Particle Swarm Optimization Algorithm on Sorting
  and OneMax**.. 13
  Moritz Mühlenthaler *(TU Dortmund)*,
  Alexander Raß, Manuel Schmitt, Andreas Siegling, Rolf Wanka *(University of Erlangen-Nuremberg)*

- **Resampling vs Recombination: a Statistical Run Time Estimation**...................... 25
  Tobias Friedrich, Timo Kötzing, Francesco Quinzan, Andrew M. Sutton *(Hasso Plattner Institute)*

- **On the Use of the Dual Formulation for Minimum Weighted Vertex Cover
  in Evolutionary Algorithms**.. 37
  Mojgan Pourhassan *(The University of Adelaide)*, Tobias Friedrich *(Hasso Plattner Institute)*,
  Frank Neumann *(The University of Adelaide)*

- **Analysis of the (1+1) EA on Subclasses of Linear Functions under Uniform
  and Linear Constraints**.. 45
  Tobias Friedrich, Timo Kötzing, Gregor Lagodzinski *(Hasso Plattner Institute)*,
  Frank Neumann *(The University of Adelaide)*, Martin Schirneck *(Hasso Plattner Institute)*

- **Analysis of the Clearing Diversity-Preserving Mechanism**............................... 55
  Edgar Covantes Osuna, Dirk Sudholt *(University of Sheffield)*

- **Lower Bounds on the Run Time of the Univariate Marginal Distribution Algorithm
  on OneMax**.. 65
  Martin S. Krejca *(Hasso Plattner Institute)*, Carsten Witt *(Technical University of Denmark)*

- **Convergence of Factored Evolutionary Algorithms**...................................... 81
  Shane Strasser, John W. Sheppard *(Montana State University)*

- **Hypervolume Subset Selection for Triangular and Inverted Triangular Pareto Fronts
  of Three-Objective Problems**.. 95
  Hisao Ishibuchi, Ryo Imada, Yu Setoguchi, Yusuke Nojima *(Osaka Prefecture Univesity)*

- **Quality Gain Analysis of the Weighted Recombination Evolution Strategy on General
  Convex Quadratic Functions**... 111
  Youhei Akimoto *(Shinshu University)*, Anne Auger, Nikolaus Hansen *(Inria)*

- **On the Statistical Learning Ability of Evolution Strategies**............................ 127
  Ofer M. Shir *(Tel-Hai College, & The Galilee Research Institute - Migal)*,
  Amir Yehudayoff *(Technion - Israel Institute of Technology)*

- **Qualitative and Quantitative Assessment of Step Size Adaptation Rules**........... 139
  Oswin Krause *(University of Copenhagen)*, Tobias Glasmachers *(Ruhr-Universität Bochum)*,
  Christian Igel *(University of Copenhagen)*

- **Linearly Convergent Evolution Strategies via Augmented Lagrangian
  Constraint Handling**.. 149
  Asma Atamna, Anne Auger, Nikolaus Hansen *(Université Paris-Saclay)*

Author Index... 162

14th ACM/SIGEVO Workshop on Foundations of Genetic Algorithms (FOGA XIV)

Organizers: Christian Igel *(University of Copenhagen, Denmark)*
Dirk Sudholt *(University of Sheffield, United Kingdom)*
Carsten Witt *(Technical University of Denmark, Denmark)*

Program Committee: Youhei Akimoto *(Shinshu University, Japan)*
Dirk Arnold *(Dalhousie University, Canada)*
Anne Auger *(INRIA Saclay, France)*
Hans-Georg Beyer *(Vorarlberg University of Applied Sciences, Austria)*
Dimo Brockhoff *(INRIA Lille - Nord Europe, France)*
Maxim Buzdalov *(ITMO University, Russia)*
Francisco Chicano *(University of Málaga, Spain)*
Duc-Cuong Dang *(University of Nottingham, United Kingdom)*
Kenneth De Jong *(George Mason University, USA)*
Carola Doerr *(CNRS and Université Pierre et Marie Curie, France)*
Benjamin Doerr *(École Polytechnique, France)*
Andries Engelbrecht *(University of Pretoria, South Africa)*
Anton Eremeev *(Sobolev Institute of Mathematics, Russia)*
Carlos M. Fonseca *(University of Coimbra, Portugal)*
Tobias Glasmachers *(Ruhr-Universität Bochum, Germany)*
Thomas Jansen *(Aberystwyth University, United Kingdom)*
Timo Kötzing *(Hasso-Plattner-Institut, Germany)*
Oswin Krause *(University of Copenhagen, Denmark)*
Martin Krejca *(Hasso-Plattner-Institut, Germany)*
Marvin Künnemann *(Universität des Saarlandes, Germany)*
William Langdon *(University College London, United Kingdom)*
Per Kristian Lehre *(University of Nottingham, United Kingdom)*
Johannes Lengler *(ETH Zürich, Switzerland)*
Andrei Lissovoi *(University of Sheffield, United Kingdom)*
Alberto Moraglio *(University of Exeter, United Kingdom)*
Samadhi Nallaperuma *(University of Sheffield, United Kingdom)*
Frank Neumann *(The University of Adelaide, Australia)*
Pietro S. Oliveto *(University of Sheffield, United Kingdom)*
Jorge Perez Heredia *(University of Sheffield, United Kingdom)*
Jonathan Rowe *(University of Birmingham, United Kingdom)*
Guenter Rudolph *(TU Dortmund University, Germany)*
Sebastian Stich *(Université Catholique de Louvain, Belgium)*
Andrew Sutton *(Hasso-Plattner-Institut, Germany)*
Sébastien Verel *(Université du Littoral Côte d'Opale, France)*

Program Committee (continued):
Markus Wagner *(The University of Adelaide, Australia)*
Xin Yao *(University of Birmingham, United Kingdom)*
Yang Yu *(Nanjing University, China)*
Christine Zarges *(Aberystwyth University, United Kingdom)*
Zhi-Hua Zhou *(Nanjing University, China)*
Yuren Zhou *(South China University of Technology, China)*

Additional reviewers:
Simon Fong *(University of Birmingham, United Kingdom)*
Luca Manzoni *(University of Milano Bicocca, Italy)*
Chao Qian *(University of Science and Technology of China, China)*
Liangpeng Zhang *(University of Science and Technology of China, China)*

Sponsor:

sigevo

ACM Special Interest Group for
Genetic and Evolutionary Computation

Supporter:

UNIVERSITY OF COPENHAGEN

Fast and Powerful Hashing using Tabulation[*]

[Keynote Talk][†]

Mikkel Thorup
University of Copenhagen, Department of Computer Science
Universitetsparken 5, 2100 Copenhagen East, Denmark
mikkel2thorup@gmail.com

ABSTRACT

Randomized algorithms are often enjoyed for their simplicity, but the hash functions employed to yield the desired probabilistic guarantees are often too complicated to be practical. Here we survey recent results on how simple hashing schemes based on tabulation provide unexpectedly strong guarantees.

Simple tabulation hashing dates back to Zobrist [1970]. Keys are viewed as consisting of c characters and we have precomputed character tables $h_1, ..., h_q$ mapping characters to random hash values. A key $x = (x_1, ..., x_c)$ is hashed to $h_1[x_1] \oplus h_2[x_2] ..... \oplus h_c[x_c]$. This schemes is very fast with character tables in cache. While simple tabulation is not even 4-independent, it does provide many of the guarantees that are normally obtained via higher independence, e.g., linear probing and Cuckoo hashing.

Next we consider *twisted tabulation* where one character is "twisted" with some simple operations. The resulting hash function has powerful distributional properties: Chernoff-Hoeffding type tail bounds and a very small bias for min-wise hashing.

Finally, we consider *double tabulation* where we compose two simple tabulation functions, applying one to the output of the other, and show that this yields very high independence in the classic framework of Carter and Wegman [1977]. In fact, w.h.p., for a given set of size proportional to that of the space consumed, double tabulation gives fully-random hashing.

While these tabulation schemes are all easy to implement and use, their analysis is not.

This keynote talk surveys results from the papers in the reference list.

---

[*]This talk is based on the survey [7].

[†]This keynote talk abstract also appears in *Proceedings of the 36th IARCS Annual Conference on Foundations of Software Technology and Theoretical Computer Science (FSTTCS)*, pages 1.1–2, 2016

1. ACKNOWLEDGMENTS

Author's research is partly supported by Advanced Grant DFF-0602-02499B from the Danish Council for Independent Research.

2. REFERENCES

[1] T. Christiani, R. Pagh, and M. Thorup. From independence to expansion and back again. In *Proceedings of the 47th ACM Symposium on Theory of Computing (STOC)*, pages 813–820, 2015.

[2] S. Dahlgaard, M. B. T. Knudsen, E. Rotenberg, and M. Thorup. Hashing for statistics over k-partitions. In *Proceedings of the 56th IEEE Symposium on Foundations of Computer Science (FOCS)*, pages 1292–1310, 2015.

[3] S. Dahlgaard, M. B. T. Knudsen, E. Rotenberg, and M. Thorup. The power of two choices with simple tabulation. In *Proceedings of the 27th ACM-SIAM Symposium on Discrete Algorithms (SODA)*, pages 1631–1642, 2016.

[4] S. Dahlgaard and M. Thorup. Approximately minwise independence with twisted tabulation. In *Proc. 14th Scandinavian Workshop on Algorithm Theory (SWAT)*, pages 134–145, 2014.

[5] M. Pătraşcu and M. Thorup. The power of simple tabulation-based hashing. *Journal of the ACM*, 59(3):Article 14, 2012. Announced at STOC'11.

[6] M. Pătraşcu and M. Thorup. Twisted tabulation hashing. In *Proc. 24th ACM/SIAM Symposium on Discrete Algorithms (SODA)*, pages 209–228, 2013.

[7] M. Thorup. Fast and powerful hashing using tabulation. *CoRR*, abs/1505.01523, 2015. Invited as a Research Highlight to *Communications of the ACM*.

[8] M. Thorup. Simple tabulation, fast expanders, double tabulation, and high independence. In *Proc. 54th IEEE Symposium on Foundations of Computer Science (FOCS)*, pages 90–99, 2013.

An Application of Stochastic Differential Equations to Evolutionary Algorithms

Tiago Paixão
Institute of Science and Technology Austria
Am Campus 1, 3400 Klosterneuburg, Austria

Jorge Pérez Heredia
University of Sheffield
Sheffield S1 4DP, United Kingdom

ABSTRACT

There has been renewed interest in modelling the behaviour of evolutionary algorithms (EAs) by more traditional mathematical objects, such as ordinary differential equations or Markov chains. The advantage is that the analysis becomes greatly facilitated due to the existence of well established methods. However, this typically comes at the cost of disregarding information about the process. Here, we introduce the use of stochastic differential equations (SDEs) for the study of EAs. SDEs can produce simple analytical results for the dynamics of stochastic processes, unlike Markov chains which can produce rigorous but unwieldy expressions about the dynamics. On the other hand, unlike ordinary differential equations (ODEs), they do not discard information about the stochasticity of the process. We show that these are especially suitable for the analysis of fixed budget scenarios and present analogs of the additive and multiplicative drift theorems for SDEs. We exemplify the use of these methods for two model algorithms ((1+1) EA and RLS) on two canonical problems (ONEMAX and LEADINGONES).

Keywords

theory; stochastic differential equations; drift; fixed budget; evolutionary algorithms

1. INTRODUCTION

Recently, there has been renewed interest in using mathematical models to explain the behaviour of evolutionary algorithms. The aim is to try to describe the dynamics of the algorithm via some mathematical tool such as a Markov chains, a discrete dynamical system or an ordinary differential equation, and then analyse this model of the algorithm. The appeal of this approach is that these mathematical objects have the advantage of being well established and hence having a number of analysis tools at their disposal, affording easy analysis.

One of the first approaches was Goldberg's work on genetic algorithms (GAs) using a deterministic approach and considering an infinite population to obtain the next expected generation [11]. Vose extended Goldberg's results modelling the GA as a Markov Chain and considering a finite population. Vose's work was focused in the analysis of the fixed points of the Markov Chain [34]. Further work regarding fixed points was carried out by Wright and Rowe using a dynamical system approach for steady state GAs [36].

Other approaches can be grouped in the so called stochastic approximation or ordinary differential equation method [35], which considers the EA as a noisy version of an ODE that tracks the average behaviour of the algorithm, thereby disregarding the stochasticity inherent to EAs. Apart from the deterministic approximation of a stochastic process, ODE methods also approximate the time dynamics of these algorithms by a continuous process, resulting in yet another approximation. However, this can easily be calibrated so that every integral time point corresponds to an iteration of the discrete dynamical system. The ODE method was first used in evolutionary computation (EC) by Yin, Rudolph and Schwefel to analyse the asymptotic properties of some recursive algorithms [37] and later for the analysis of the $(1,\lambda)$ evolution strategy [38]. More recent work in this direction has been done by Akimoto, Auger and Hansen analysing the convergence of the continuous time trajectories of evolutionary strategies [1]. Another method based in stochastic differential equations was used by Schaul to analysed convergence analysis of evolution strategies in the continuous domain, however the results were not better than other existing methods [31].

Here, we recover stochastic differential equations for other purposes. In the same spirit as dynamical systems or the stochastic approximation we will describe the evolution of the algorithm by the average performance. However, we will not neglect the stochastic behaviour of the algorithm by including a noisy term that will allow us to take into account the variance of the process. Yielding statements not just about the average behaviour of the algorithm but also for its dispersal around the mean.

Stochastic differential equations have proven to be a powerful tool when dealing with stochastic processes [25]. SDEs have accomplished great achievements in physics, starting with the explanation of Brownian motion by Einstein in 1905 [9], and finance specially for Black and Scholes' work on options prices that yielded a Nobel Prize in Economics in 1997 [3]. Our work also contributes to the new interest towards bridging EC and the related field of Population Genetics (PG) [26, 27, 28, 29]. SDEs have been used in

FOGA '17, January 12 - 15, 2017, Copenhagen, Denmark

© 2017 Copyright held by the owner/author(s). Publication rights licensed to ACM.
ISBN 978-1-4503-4651-1/17/01...$15.00

DOI: http://dx.doi.org/10.1145/3040718.3040729

PG to track the frequency of genes in a population. This approach was first pioneered by Kimura and has ever since been an integral part of the so-called modern synthesis [19]. Many classical results were obtained through this approach including the steady state distribution of gene frequencies of a finite population under mutation and selection [20], and the probability of fixation of a gene [21].

Here, we aim at translating and adapting this powerful approach to the analysis of EAs. The work we present here has several specific aims:

- Improving the understating of EA dynamics without neglecting the stochastic behaviour.

- Introducing SDE to the field of EC.

- Translation of drift theorems from runtime analysis to fixed budget analysis.

The problem in fixed budget analysis is to compute the state of the algorithm after some given time [17], as opposed to the time to reach some specific state (runtime analysis). Fixed budget analysis is quite new and only a few results have been obtained towards this perspective [5, 7, 17, 22, 24].

We will provide a general SDE for the dynamics of EAs which for some scenarios we will be able to solve analytically and obtain equivalent statements to the well known additive and multiplicative drift theorems for runtime analysis.

The main drawback of this approach is that it is still an approximation. Although stochastic, our approach is differential therefore there is a time-continuous assumption underlying this method. More importantly, we will cast the EA as a Gaussian process, i.e. we will only consider the first two moments of its distribution neglecting higher moments. This approximation was already used by Beyer to analyse the rate of progress of evolutionary strategies [2]. But despite this deviation from the rigour of theoretical runtime analysis, we will show by experiments that the precision loss is small within the approximation range.

The paper is structured as follows. First, we start with a brief summary of the SDE techniques required and a measurement of the error of this approximation. Then we present a translation of drift theorems for a fixed budget perspective and finally we conclude with an application for two typical algorithms in two simple problems.

2. PRELIMINARIES

2.1 Stochastic differential equations

This subsection contains the minimal knowledge of SDEs to be able to understand this paper. For more extended and rigorous details of this field we refer the reader to Øksendal's book [25].

Stochastic differential equations are equations that deal with the behaviour of stochastic processes. We can define these processes as a collection of random variables in $\mathbb{R}$ over time t (i.e. $\{X_t\}_{t \geq 0}$), together with an underlying probability space (Ω, F, P) that from now on we will take for granted.

The simplest stochastic process is probably the well known white noise W_t. Its signal integrated over time will produce another famous process $B_t = \int W_t dt$ known as Brownian motion or Wiener process. Some of the characteristics of

these processes are that they have 0 mean and their increments are independent and stationary. Furthermore all the moments higher than the second are 0 (see e.g. [30]).

In this document we will focus on SDEs of the form

$$dX_t = b(t, X_t)dt + \sigma(t, X_t)W_t dt$$
$$= b(t, X_t)dt + \sigma(t, X_t)dB_t. \qquad (1)$$

This equation represents a process where the state change (derivative) depends on both the time and the current position (which can also depend on the time) through b and σ which are usually referred as the drift and diffusion terms or coefficients. We can say that b tracks the expected evolution of the process and σ collects the random behaviour by amplifying a white noise or Brownian motion term.

After applying the usual integration rules one obtains a simple expression for the state after t iterations [25].

$$X_t = X_0 + \int_0^t b(s, X_s)ds + \int_0^t \sigma(s, X_s)dB_s. \qquad (2)$$

The challenge now is to prove the existence of an integral over an stochastic process $\int f dB_s$ and develop its integration rules. This was done by Itô between the years 1944 and 1951: he proved the existence of this integral, worked on stochastic integral equations of the type (2) and applied his developments to the already existing field of SDE [13, 14, 15, 16]. The key idea of Itô's work is a stochastic extension of the Riemann-Stieltjes integral [32] which is itself an extension of the standard Riemann integral for when a function is integrated with respect to another function. The other traditional formulation was given by Stratonovich in 1966 [33].

In this work we will focus on stochastic processes that fit into the following definition of an Itô process (Definition 4.1.1 in [25]).

DEFINITION 1 (1-DIMENSIONAL ITÔ PROCESS).
A 1-dimensional Itô process is a stochastic process X_t on (Ω, F, P) of the form

$$\frac{dX_t}{dt} = b(t, X_t) + \sigma(t, X_t)W_t \qquad (3)$$

where W_t denotes a white noise process, b is absolute integrable in t and σ is square integrable in t.

In the following we will refer as Itô integrals to integrals over a Brownian process $\int f dB_s$ (a formal definition can be found in e.g. [25]). These integrals will have the following properties (taken from Theorem 3.2.1 in [25]).

THEOREM 1 (PROPERTIES OF THE ITÔ INTEGRAL). *Let $f, g \in V(0, T)$ and let $0 \leq S < U < T$. Then*

(i) $\int_S^T f dB_t = \int_S^U f dB_t + \int_U^T f dB_t$

(ii) $\int_S^T (cf + g) dB_t = c \cdot \int_S^T f dB_t + \int_S^T g dB_t$ *(c constant)*

(iii) $E\left(\int_S^T f dB_t\right) = 0$

When dealing with stochastic integrals the usual integration rules do not apply. Here is where Itô's work comes into play providing us with new rules, specially when dealing with changes of variables. The following theorem is taken from Theorem 4.1.2 in [25].

THEOREM 2 (ITÔ FORMULA). *Let X_t be a Itô process given by*

$$dX_t = b(t, X_t)dt + \sigma(t, X_t)dB_t.$$

Let $g(t, x)$ be twice continuously differentiable on $x \in \mathbb{R}$ and once in $t \in \mathbb{R}^+$. Then $Y_t = g(t, X_t)$ is again an Itô process, and

$$dY_t = \frac{\partial g}{\partial t}dt + \frac{\partial g}{\partial x}dX_t + \frac{1}{2}\frac{\partial^2 g}{\partial x^2} \cdot (dX_t)^2, \qquad (4)$$

where $(dX_t)^2 = (dX_t) \cdot (dX_t)$ is computed according to the rules

$$dt \cdot dt = dt \cdot dB_t = dB_t \cdot dt = 0, \quad dB_t \cdot dB_t = dt. \qquad (5)$$

2.2 The diffusion approximation

We refer to the diffusion or SDE approximation as the joint application of a time continuous and Gaussian approximation.

The time evolution of the probability density $p(x, t)$ of any stochastic process X_t can be described by the Chapman-Kolmogorov equation (see e.g. [10])

$$p(x, t + \Delta t) = \int \Delta(\delta \mid x) \cdot p(x - \delta, t) \cdot d\delta \qquad (6)$$

where $\Delta(\delta \mid x)$ is the transition probability of reaching x from $x - \delta$. Let us consider the left hand term: after performing a first order Taylor expansion around $\Delta t = 0$ we obtain

$$p(x, t + \Delta t) \approx p(x, t) + \Delta t \cdot \frac{\partial p(x, t)}{\partial t} \qquad (7)$$

and by Taylor's theorem we know that the error of this approximation will be of order $O(\Delta t)$. Since we are dealing with time-discrete algorithms the time counter is increased every generation by just one unit hence $\Delta t = 1$.

Similarly, for the right hand term of (6) we can write the second order Taylor expansion of $p(x - \delta, t)$ around $\delta = 0$ yielding

$$p(x - \delta, t) \approx p(x, t) - \delta \cdot \frac{\partial p(x, t)}{\partial x} + \frac{\delta^2}{2} \cdot \frac{\partial^2 p(x, t)}{\partial x^2}. \qquad (8)$$

Again, by Taylor's theorem we can estimate the error by $O(\delta^2)$. This approximation will give good results when δ is small i.e. when the system usually moves between close by states in the search space.

Introducing both approximations in (6) and noticing that p no longer depends on δ we can write

$$p(x, t) + \Delta t \cdot \frac{\partial p(x, t)}{\partial t} \approx p(x, t) \cdot \underbrace{\int \Delta(\delta \mid x)d\delta}_{1}$$
$$- \frac{\partial}{\partial x}p(x, t) \cdot \underbrace{\int \delta \cdot \Delta(\delta \mid x)d\delta}_{E(\Delta)}$$
$$+ \frac{1}{2} \cdot \frac{\partial^2}{\partial x^2}p(x, t) \cdot \underbrace{\int \delta^2 \cdot \Delta(\delta \mid x)d\delta}_{E(\Delta^2)}$$

As outlined in the equation above, we can identify these integrals with the statistical moments of Δ leading to the well known diffusion equation

$$\Delta t \cdot \frac{\partial p(x, t)}{\partial t} \approx -\frac{\partial}{\partial x}p(x, t) \cdot \mathrm{E}(\Delta) + \frac{1}{2} \cdot \frac{\partial}{\partial x^2}p(x, t) \cdot \mathrm{E}(\Delta^2). \qquad (9)$$

This equation is known as the Fokker-Planck equation or the Forward Kolmogorov equation [18]. Notice that the first moment $E(\Delta)$ corresponds to the drift as used in runtime analysis. This is an equation for the time evolution of the probability density $p(x, t)$ of the random variable X_t. In principle, one could solve this equation to obtain a probability distribution at any particular time point. However, this is often impossible in practice. Instead, we deal directly with the SDE associated with the Fokker-Planck equation and take that as a model of our EA. The SDE corresponding to equation 9 will be a Itô process of the form [25]:

$$dX_t \approx \mathrm{E}(\Delta)dt + \sqrt{\mathrm{E}(\Delta^2)}dB_t$$

This is the central equation in this paper. We will use it to describe the dynamics of the state of an EA (X_t) by computing its drift coefficient $\mathrm{E}(\Delta)$, second moment or diffusion coefficient $\sqrt{\mathrm{E}(\Delta^2)}$ and applying the Itô formula (Theorem 2) to solve the equation.

3. DRIFT THEOREMS FOR FIXED BUDGET ANALYSIS

As discussed in the previous sections we will approximate the stochastic process underlying an EA as an Itô process of the form

$$dX_t = b(t, X_t)dt + \sigma(t, X_t)dB_t$$
$$= \mathrm{E}(\Delta)dt + \sqrt{\mathrm{E}(\Delta^2)}dB_t \qquad (10)$$

where

$$\mathrm{E}(\Delta) = \mathrm{E}(X_{t+1} - X_t \mid X_t)$$
$$\mathrm{E}(\Delta^2) = \mathrm{E}\left((X_{t+1} - X_t)^2 \mid X_t\right)$$

In general, due to the mathematical expression of the drift b and diffusion σ coefficients it will be impossible to analytically solve this equation for X_t. However there are two simple scenarios from where we can obtain equivalent results to drift theorems for runtime analysis.

The methods to solve SDEs are similar to those to solve ODE but we have to use the Itô formula (Theorem 2) when performing a change of variables. In the following two subsections our approach is to use *a priori* knowledge to find another process Y_t described by a simpler function $g(x, t)$ that we know is the solution of the equivalent ODE ($\sigma = 0$). For example, if our process is of the form $dX_t = X_tdt + X_tdB_t$ our candidate solution for the expectation will be $Y_t = \ln(X_t)$. When the coefficients are more complex we will try to find a variable change that leads to an already known SDE.

3.1 Additive drift

The simplest case is when the drift b does not depend on the time t or the current state X_t (as in the additive drift [12]), under this scenario the expected progress of the algorithm will be linear in time with slope the drift.

THEOREM 3. *Let X_t be an Itô process of the form*

$$dX_t = bdt + \sigma dB_t$$

where B_t is a Brownian process and $b \in \mathbb{R}$ and $\sigma \in \mathbb{R}^+$. Then the following statements are true

$$X_t = X_0 + bt + \sigma B_t$$

$$E(X_t) = E(X_0) + bt$$

$$Var(X_t) = Var(X_0) + \sigma^2 t$$

PROOF. This is a trivial case that can be solved by directly integrating

$$\int_0^t dX_s = \int_0^t b\,ds + \int_0^t \sigma\,dB_s \tag{11}$$

$$X_t = X_0 + bt + \sigma B_t \quad (B_0 = 0). \tag{12}$$

Taking expectations in equation (11) we can compute the expected value

$$\mathrm{E}(X_t) = \mathrm{E}(X_0) + \mathrm{E}\left(\int_0^t b\,ds\right) + \mathrm{E}\left(\int_0^t \sigma\,dB_s\right)$$

due to property (iii) from Theorem 1 the last term averages out yielding

$$\mathrm{E}(X_t) = \mathrm{E}(X_0) + \int_0^t \mathrm{E}(b)\,ds = \mathrm{E}(X_0) + bt. \tag{13}$$

Finally, to compute the variance we use equation (12) in the following way

$$\begin{aligned}
\mathrm{Var}(X_t) &= \mathrm{E}(X_t^2) - \mathrm{E}(X_t)^2 \\
&= \mathrm{E}((X_0 + bt + \sigma B_t)^2) - \mathrm{E}(X_t)^2 \\
&= \mathrm{E}(X_0^2 + (bt)^2 + (\sigma B_t)^2) \\
&\quad + \mathrm{E}(2X_0\sigma B_t + 2bt\sigma B_t + 2X_0 bt) - \mathrm{E}(X_t)^2
\end{aligned}$$

the expectations with linear B_t terms average out yielding

$$\begin{aligned}
\mathrm{Var}(X_t) &= \mathrm{E}(X_0^2) + \mathrm{E}(b^2 t^2) + \mathrm{E}(\sigma^2 B_t^2) \\
&\quad + \mathrm{E}(2X_0 bt) - \mathrm{E}(X_t)^2
\end{aligned}$$

introducing $\mathrm{E}(X_t)$ from equation (13) leads to

$$\begin{aligned}
\mathrm{Var}(X_t) &= \mathrm{E}(X_0^2) + \mathrm{E}(\sigma^2 B_t^2) - \mathrm{E}(X_0)^2 \\
&= \mathrm{Var}(X_0) + \sigma^2 \cdot \mathrm{E}(B_t^2).
\end{aligned}$$

Considering a normalised Brownian motion ($\mathrm{E}(B_t^2) = t$) yields the claimed statement. □

As in runtime analysis it is not typically the case that we know exactly the drift's value, but we can bound it in some range. It follows directly that knowing those bounds we will be able to bound the expected progress after t iterations.

COROLLARY 4. *In the context of Theorem 3, if $b_l \leq b \leq b_u$ and $\sigma_l \leq \sigma \leq \sigma_u$, with $b_l, b_u \in \mathbb{R}$ and $\sigma_l, \sigma_u \in \mathbb{R}^+$. Then*

$$X_0 + b_l t + \sigma_l B_t \leq X_t \leq X_0 + b_u t + \sigma_u B_t$$

$$E(X_0) + b_l t \leq E(X_t) \leq E(X_0) + b_u t$$

$$Var(X_0) + \sigma_l^2 t \leq Var(X_t) \leq Var(X_0) + \sigma_u^2 t.$$

3.2 Multiplicative drift

Analogous to runtime analysis, the assumption of additive drift is in general too loose since it does not take into account the current state of the process. This is solved by the multiplicative drift theorem [8] when the drift is proportional to the current state X_t.

As discussed in the introduction SDEs are a well established method in other research fields, allowing us to recycle already existing results. We will make use of a simplified

version of the Cox-Ingersoll-Ross (CIR) model [4, 23] which describes the evolution of interest rates and has the form

$$dX_t = b(\theta - X_t)dt + \sigma\sqrt{X_t}\,dB_t. \tag{14}$$

The coefficient b specifies the speed (drift) at which the process approaches its expected value θ provoking a mean reversion effect. The noise due to the market dB_t is amplified by a term $\sigma\sqrt{X_t}$ to ensure that there are not negative interest rates (note that this effect is also obtained with any diffusion coefficient that goes to 0 when $X_t = 0$). We will use a simplified version without the mean reversion effect ($\theta = 0$), which resembles an elitist multiplicative drift process.

THEOREM 5 (CIR WITHOUT MEAN REVERSION [4]). *Let $X_t > 0$ be an Itô process of the form*

$$dX_t = -bX_t dt + \sigma\sqrt{X_t}\,dB_t$$

where B_t is a Brownian process and $b, \sigma \in \mathbb{R}^+$. Then the following statements are true

$$E(X_t) = E(X_0) \cdot e^{-bt}$$

$$Var(X_t) = E(X_0)\frac{\sigma^2}{b} \cdot e^{-bt}\left(1 - e^{-bt}\right)$$

PROOF. The results for the expectation and variance of the original CIR process (14) are (equation (19) in [4])

$$\mathrm{E}(X_t) = \mathrm{E}(X_0) \cdot e^{-bt} + \theta\left(1 - e^{-t}\right)$$

$$\begin{aligned}
\mathrm{Var}(X_t) &= \mathrm{E}(X_0)\frac{\sigma^2}{b} \cdot e^{-bt}\left(1 - e^{-bt}\right) \\
&\quad + \theta\frac{\sigma^2}{2b}\left(1 - e^{-t}\right)^2
\end{aligned}$$

Our statement is just the special case when $\theta = 0$. □

Once more, if we can only compute bounds rather than exact values it follows straightforward the next corollary. Notice that the result for the expectation is similar to a previous fixed-budget multiplicative drift developed by Lengler and Spooner (Theorem 1 in [22]).

COROLLARY 6. *In the context of Theorem 5, if $b_l \leq b \leq b_u$ and $\sigma_l \leq \sigma \leq \sigma_u$ with $b_l, b_u, \sigma_l, \sigma_u \in \mathbb{R}^+$ Then*

$$E(X_0) \cdot e^{b_l t} \leq E(X_t) \leq E(X_0) \cdot e^{b_u t}$$

$$Var(X_t) \geq E(X_0)\frac{\sigma_l^2}{b_l}e^{-b_l t}\left(1 - e^{-b_l t}\right)$$

$$Var(X_t) \leq E(X_0)\frac{\sigma_u^2}{b_u}e^{-b_u t}\left(1 - e^{-b_u t}\right)$$

4. APPLICATIONS

Since this is a preliminary work towards introducing SDE to EC we have only considered two simple EAs, namely Randomised Local Search (RLS) and (1+1) EA and two simple functions: ONEMAX and LEADINGONES.

Algorithm 1 RLS

Initialise $x \in \{0, 1\}^n$
repeat
    $y \leftarrow$ choose u.a.r. one bit of x and flip it
    if $f(y) \geq f(x)$ **then**
        $x \leftarrow y$
    end if
until stop

Algorithm 2 (1+1) EA

Initialise $x \in \{0,1\}^n$
repeat
    $y \leftarrow$ flip each bit of x indep. with prob. $1/n$
    if $f(y) \geq f(x)$ **then**
        $x \leftarrow y$
    end if
until stop

4.1 LeadingOnes

As in runtime analysis, LeadingOnes is a good candidate for the additive drift whereas results for OneMax are more accurate using the multiplicative drift.

Definition 2 (LeadingOnes).

$$f(x) = \sum_{i=1}^{n} \prod_{j=1}^{i} x_j$$

Our formulation of additive drift does not consider boundaries on the process but the LeadingOnes problem obviously has two boundaries ($0 \leq x \leq n$). SDEs can cope with boundary conditions but this will highly increase the complexity and extension of the paper and since this is preliminary work we will not consider the boundaries. To circumvent this problem we will add a clause in the statement excluding our results after the optimum is reached similarly as done by Nallaperuma et al. in [24].

Application 7. *Under the SDE approximation, after t iterations, RLS on* LeadingOnes *will find the optimum or reach an expected value and variance of:*

$$E(X_t) = E(X_0) + \frac{2}{n}t$$

$$Var(X_t) = Var(X_0) + \frac{4}{n}t$$

where X_0 is the number of leading ones of the initial search point.

The result for the expectation is in concordance with Theorem 7 in [17] where Jansen and Zarges obtained $1 + 2t/n - 2^{-\Omega((1-\beta)n)} \leq E(X_t) \leq 1 + 2t/n - 2^{-n}$, for a time budget $t = (1-\beta)n^2$ with $1/2 + c < \beta < 1$ and random initialisation. Note that both approaches lead to the same growth term of $2t/n$.

Proof of Application 7. Let us denote by X_t the number of leading ones in the bitstring at time t, and assume that the SDE (10) is a good approximation of the dynamics of X_t (this claim will be supported later by experiments).

As explained in the introduction, the drift and diffusion coefficients will be the first and second moments of the rate of change of the process. Or mathematically speaking

$$b = E(X_{t+1} - X_t \mid X_t)$$
$$= \sum_x x \cdot p(X_{t+1} - X_t = x \mid X_t)$$
$$\sigma^2 = E((X_{t+1} - X_t)^2 \mid X_t)$$
$$= \sum_x x^2 \cdot p((X_{t+1} - X_t)^2 = x \mid X_t)$$

Since RLS uses local mutations it can only produce points in the Hamming neighbourhood, with only 1 out of these n

points (flipping the first 0-bit) leading to an improvement. Noticing that this event will in fact increase X_t in more than 1, actually the impact will be almost 2 due to the geometric distribution followed by the free riders (bits after the leading ones). Therefore the expression for the drift coefficient b is reduced to

$$b \approx \frac{1}{n} \cdot 2$$

Note that the impact will be exactly 2 for an infinite problem size, as in runtime analysis we are interested in big values of the problem size so the approximation is very accurate.

To compute the diffusion coefficient σ we use the same rationale but raising the impact to the power of 2, therefore

$$\sigma^2 \approx \frac{1}{n} \cdot 2^2$$

Now we can say that X_t is described by an SDE of the form

$$dX_t = \frac{2}{n}dt + \frac{2}{\sqrt{n}}dB_t,$$

which fits in our additive drift description (Theorem 3), using this theorem with the previously computed coefficients directly leads to the claimed results. $\square$

The application to the (1+1) EA is equivalent but we have to deal with global mutations, which makes computing the exact value for the drift and diffusion coefficients harder. Instead, we will make use of bounds for these terms.

Application 8. *Under the SDE approximation after t iterations the (1+1) EA on* LeadingOnes *will find the optimum or reach an expected value and variance of:*

$$E(X_0) + \frac{1}{en}t \leq E(X_t) \leq E(X_0) + \frac{2}{n}t$$

$$Var(X_0) + \frac{1}{en}t \leq Var(X_t) \leq Var(X_0) + \frac{4}{n}t$$

where X_0 is the number of leading ones of the initial search point.

Contrasting with the literature as before, we find $E(X_t) = 1 + 2t/n - o\left(\frac{t}{n}\right)$ for a time budget $t = \frac{(1-\beta)n^2}{\alpha(n)}$ with $1/2 + c < \beta < 1$, $\alpha(n) = w(1)$ and random initialisation (Theorem 8 in [17]). Again, the growing term for both results is $2t/n$.

Proof of Application 8. Let us denote by X_t the number of leading ones in the bitstring at time t, and assume that the SDE (10) is a good approximation of the dynamics of X_t.

As in the previous application, the drift can be expressed with two terms: the probability of having a positive drift and its impact. It can be shown that this impact is $2 - 2^{-(n-1-X_t)}$ leading to

$$b(X_t) = \frac{1}{n}\left(1 - \frac{1}{n}\right)^{X_t} \cdot \left(2 - 2^{-(n-1-X_t)}\right).$$

To obtain the bounds for the drift we will consider the extreme cases $X_t = 0$ and $X_t = n - 1$ for the mutational term and bound the impact in the range $[1, 2)$ yielding

$$b \leq \frac{1}{n} \cdot 2 = b_u$$

$$b \geq \frac{1}{n}\left(1 - \frac{1}{n}\right)^{n-1} \cdot 1 \geq \frac{1}{en} = b_l$$

For the diffusion coefficient we can recycle the previous probabilities but we have to raise the impact to the power of 2 to obtain the second moment of the process

$$\sigma_l^2 = \frac{1}{en} \cdot 1^2 \le \sigma^2 \le \frac{1}{n} \cdot 2^2 = \sigma_u^2$$

Finally, introducing these calculations in Corollary 4 proves the result. $\square$

4.2 OneMax

Secondly we apply the multiplicative drift for the same algorithms but for the OneMax problem which is ideal for this drift theorem.

DEFINITION 3 (ONEMAX).

$$f(x) = \sum_{i=1}^{n} x_i$$

In this case the boundary conditions are not a problem since our multiplicative drift bounds can not push the system out of the interval $[0, n]$. Notice that the drift is always increasing the number of ones and vanishes when approaching the optimum.

APPLICATION 9. Under the SDE approximation the expected fitness reached by RLS in ONEMAX after t iterations is

$$E(X_t) = n \left(1 - e^{-\frac{t}{n}}\right) + E(X_0) \cdot e^{-\frac{t}{n}}$$

$$Var(X_t) = (n - E(X_0)) \cdot e^{-\frac{t}{n}} \left(1 - e^{-\frac{t}{n}}\right)$$

where $E(X_0)$ is the expected number of ones of the initial search point.

This result is in accordance with Theorems 4 and 5 in [17] where the authors obtained $E(X_t) = n \left(1 - (1 - 1/n)^t\right)$ for RLS starting in the all zeros bitstring $X_0 = 0^n$ and $E(X_t) = n - n/2 (1 - 1/n)^t$ for random initialisation. Both results can be recovered from our method noticing that $e^{-t/n} = (e^{-1/n})^t \approx (1 - 1/n)^t$ which is a good approximation for large n.

PROOF OF APPLICATION 9. Let us denote by Z_t the number of zeros in the bitstring at time t, and assume that the SDE (10) is a good approximation of the dynamics of Z_t (this claim will be supported later by experiments).

The drift coefficient, as always, will be the first moment (expectation) of the process and the diffusion coefficient will be the second moment.

$$b(Z_t) = E(Z_{t+1} - Z_t \mid Z_t)$$
$$= \sum_z z \cdot p(Z_{t+1} - Z_t = z \mid Z_t)$$
$$\sigma^2(Z_t) = E((Z_{t+1} - Z_t)^2 \mid Z_t)$$
$$= \sum_z z^2 \cdot p((Z_{t+1} - Z_t)^2 = z \mid Z_t)$$

In the ONEMAX problem at state Z_t there are Z_t bit-flips out of n that lead to an improvement, with each of these events reducing the number of zeros by 1, therefore

$$b(Z_t) = -\frac{Z_t}{n}.$$

For the diffusion coefficient we just have to repeat the calculations raising to 2 the impact of each event $(-1)^2$, yielding

$$\sigma^2(Z_t) = (-1)^2 \frac{Z_t}{n} = \frac{Z_t}{n}.$$

Therefore the approximated SDE for this process is of the form $dZ_t = b(Z_t)dt + \sigma \left(\sqrt{Z_t}\right) dB_t$, which fits in our multiplicative drift (Theorem 5). Applying this theorem with $b = -1/n$ and $\sigma = 1/\sqrt{n}$ we obtain the following results

$$E(Z_t) = E(Z_0) \cdot e^{-\frac{t}{n}}$$

$$Var(Z_t) = E(Z_0) \cdot e^{-\frac{t}{n}} \left(1 - e^{-\frac{t}{n}}\right)$$

Finally translating to the number of ones $X_t = n - Z_t$ leads to the theorem's statement. $\square$

The next application is regarding the (1+1) EA, again in this case we have computed bounds on the coefficients rather than exact values due to the difficulty to obtain exact results with global mutations.

APPLICATION 10. Under the SDE approximation the expected fitness reached by the (1+1) EA in ONEMAX after t iterations is bounded by

$$E(X_t) \ge n \left(1 - e^{-\frac{t}{en}}\right) + E(X_0) \cdot e^{-\frac{t}{en}}$$

$$E(X_t) \le n \left(1 - e^{-\frac{3.1t}{n}}\right) + E(X_0) \cdot e^{-\frac{3.1t}{n}}$$

$$Var(X_t) \ge (n - E(X_0)) \cdot e^{-\frac{t}{en}} \left(1 - e^{-\frac{t}{en}}\right)$$

$$Var(X_t) \le (n - E(X_0)) \cdot e^{-3.1\frac{t}{n}} \left(1 - e^{-3.1\frac{t}{n}}\right)$$

where $E(X_0)$ is the expected number of ones of the initial search point.

Once more the comparison with the literature is successful, Theorem 5 in [22] Lengler and Spooner shows similar bounds of $n - \frac{1}{2}ne^{-t/(en)} \le E(X_t) \le n - \frac{1}{2}ne^{-t/n} - O(t/n)$ for random initialisation.

PROOF OF APPLICATION 10. Let us denote by Z_t the number of zeros in the bitstring at time t, and assume that the SDE (10) is a good approximation of the dynamics of Z_t.

The drift and diffusion coefficients (first and second statistic moments of the process) can be expressed as

$$b(Z_t) = \sum_{j=1}^{Z_t} -j \cdot \mathrm{mut}(Z_t, Z_t - j)$$

$$\sigma^2(Z_t) = \sum_{j=1}^{Z_t} (-j)^2 \cdot \mathrm{mut}(Z_t, Z_t - j)$$

where $\mathrm{mut}(Z_t, Z_t - j)$ is the probability of a mutation moving the process from Z_t to $Z_t - j$ zeros, given by the following expression

$$\sum_{j=0}^{n} \binom{Z_t}{j} \binom{n - Z_t}{k + j} \left(\frac{1}{n}\right)^{k+2j} \left(1 - \frac{1}{n}\right)^{n-k-2j}.$$

The drift coefficient can be lower bounded using only the case when $j = 1$ leading

$$b(Z_t) \ge -\frac{Z_t}{n} \left(1 - \frac{1}{n}\right)^{n-1} \ge -\frac{Z_t}{ne}.$$

For the upper bound we can make use of Lemma 3 from [28] to upper bound $\text{mut}(Z_t, Z_t + j)$ by $\left(\frac{Z_t}{n}\right)^j \cdot \left(1 - \frac{1}{n}\right)^{n-j} \cdot \frac{1.14}{j!}$ yielding

$$b(Z_t) = -\sum_{j=1}^{Z_t} \left(\frac{Z_t}{n}\right)^j \cdot \left(1 - \frac{1}{n}\right)^{n-j} \cdot \frac{1.14}{j!} \cdot j$$

$$\leq -1.14 \cdot \frac{Z_t}{n} \cdot \sum_{j=1}^{\infty} \frac{j}{j!} = -1.14 \cdot \frac{Z_t}{n} \cdot e \leq -3.1 \cdot \frac{Z_t}{n}.$$

Analogous calculations lead to the following bounds on the diffusion coefficient

$$\frac{Z_t}{en} \leq \sigma^2(Z_t) \leq 3.1 \cdot \frac{Z_t}{n}$$

Calling Corollary 6 with $-1/en \leq b \leq -3.1/n$ and $1/en \leq \sigma^2 \leq 3.1/n$ leads to

$$\mathrm{E}\left(Z_0\right) \cdot e^{-\frac{1}{en}t} \leq \mathrm{E}\left(Z_t\right) \leq \mathrm{E}\left(Z_0\right) \cdot e^{-\frac{3.1}{n}t}$$

$$\mathrm{Var}\left(Z_t\right) \geq \mathrm{E}\left(Z_0\right) \cdot e^{-\frac{t}{en}}\left(1 - e^{-\frac{t}{en}}\right)$$

$$\mathrm{Var}\left(Z_t\right) \leq \mathrm{E}\left(Z_0\right) \cdot e^{-3.1\frac{t}{n}}\left(1 - e^{-3.1\frac{t}{n}}\right)$$

Finally translating to the number of ones $X_t = n - Z_t$ leads to the claimed results. $\square$

5. EXPERIMENTS

Finally, since this approach is an approximation we have performed some experiments to validate this theory. We can observe that for RLS this approach is very precise whereas for the (1+1) EA the precision is smaller. Nevertheless the bounds for the (1+1) EA properly represent the evolution of the algorithm and the deviation is due to the difficulty of computing good bounds for the drift which is a problem intrinsic to this field and not due to the use of our method.

The next figures represents both the experimental and theoretical results from the applications of the previous section. The experimental results are represented by blue dots in the case of the expectation and a wrinkled shadowed region that deviates from the expectation in one standard deviation, analogously theoretical results are represented by a black line and a smooth shadowed region. In the case of the (1+1) EA for the sake of clarity we have not included our variance estimations to not overload the plot with an excess of shadowed zones.

The parameters of the simulation were chosen accordingly to preliminary experiments to represent the process specially before the optimum was reached. For simplicity we have partly removed the randomness in the initialisation - we have randomly generated a search point X_0 but we have reused it for all the runs. This way the variance of the process is not distorted at the beginning of the experiment due to the initialisation, furthermore the theoretical comparison becomes easier by using $\mathrm{E}\left(X_0\right) = X_0$ and $\mathrm{Var}\left(X_0\right) = 0$.

Figure 1 shows that our method can explain with high precision both the expectation and variance evolution of RLS in LEADINGONES. The only significant difference appears when the system approaches the optimum, this was expected since we did not consider the boundary $X_t \leq n$ in our calculations. This effects affects both the expectation and the variance that should decrease as the process approaches the optimum, unlike the Itô process used as model.

In the case of the (1+1) EA (Figure 2) we can see that our bounds collects the behaviour of the process but there is a gap between the theory and the experiments, this is due to applying an additive drift technique when in reality the drift varies with the current state, but our aim in this is paper is to introduce this new method and do a translation of results from runtime to fixed-budget rather than obtaining sharp bounds.

Finally, we compare these two algorithms on the ONEMAX problem obtaining similar results. The comparison between experiments and theory for RLS is excellent (Figure 3), even better than in LEADINGONES due to the absence of the boundary problem. Again for the (1+1) EA our bounds collects the exponential decrease of the process and although the lower bound has some precision the upper bound is quite loose. Obviously, if we were aiming for precision we could have recycled already known and better bounds for the drift such us $b(Z_t) \leq -\frac{Z_t}{en}\left(1 + \frac{16Z_t}{n}\right)$ from Doerr et al. [6], but then it will become a variable drift and our aim is just to use it as an application example of the multiplicative drift.

The reader might notice that our problem size is not too big ($n = 100$), this is intentional since the SDE method becomes more precise the bigger the problem size is (see subsection 2.2).

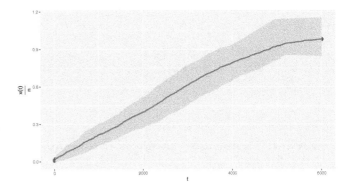

Figure 1: Normalised fitness vs. time for RLS on LEADINGONES. Problem size = 100, runs = 50 and time budget = 6000.

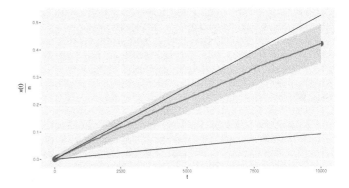

Figure 2: Normalised fitness vs. time for the (1+1) EA on LEADINGONES. Problem size = 100, runs = 50 and time budget = 10000.

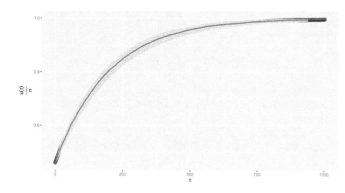

Figure 3: Normalised fitness vs. time for RLS on OneMax. **Problem size = 200, runs = 50 and time budget = 1000.**

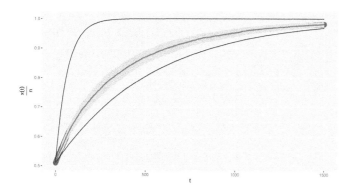

Figure 4: Normalised fitness vs. time for the (1+1) EA on OneMax. **Problem size = 200, runs = 50 and time budget = 1500.**

6. CONCLUSIONS

For the last decade rigorous runtime analysis has become immensely popular, in part due to the emergence of the so-called "drift theorems" that inform about the time to reach a particular state or set of states. However, these results are not directly translatable for fixed budget scenarios which ask about the opposite question: how much improvement can be obtained in a fixed number of fitness evaluations. This problem is relevant in practice: in real problems it is usually impossible to know whether the optimum has been found. In this case, it is arguably more useful to know how much improvement an algorithm can achieve in a fixed number of steps.

Here, we have introduced the use of SDEs to the study of EAs which seem particularly suited to obtain results for fixed budget scenarios. Even though SDEs are approximations of the dynamics of EAs, they can produce analytical insight which is not possible with other tools, such as Markov chains. At the same time, SDEs do not discard the stochasticity of the dynamics and allow for the estimation of the variance of relevant quantities, such as the state at which the algorithm will find itself after t iterations.

Here we made a simple preliminary exploration of the potential of these tools for the study of EAs. We did not make

use of other techniques for the study of SDEs that allow for greater insight into the dynamics of a stochastic process. For example, the Fokker-Planck equation associated with a SDE can be used to track the full probability distribution of the process. Even though this is, in many instances, impossible to solve analytically it can reveal what are the crucial parameters of a stochastic process. Furthermore, it is often solvable for the steady state, allowing for the characterization of the stationary distribution of the process. In fact, these techniques are commonly used in the related field of population genetics where they have been used to provide foundational results. The results we presented here are in themselves interesting, especially when applied to fixed budget analysis, but they also hold the promise that SDEs can become a standard tool in EC.

7. ACKNOWLEDGMENTS

The authors would like to thank Dirk Sudholt and Srdjan Sarikas for valuable input and discussions on this manuscript. The research leading to these results has received funding from the European Union Seventh Framework Programme (FP7/2007-2013) under grant agreement no 618091 (SAGE).

8. REFERENCES

[1] Y. Akimoto, A. Auger, and N. Hansen. Convergence of the continuous time trajectories of isotropic evolution strategies on monotonic $\mathcal{C}^2$-composite functions. In *Parallel Problem Solving from Nature - PPSN XII: 12th International Conference, Taormina, Italy, September 1-5, 2012, Proceedings, Part I*, pages 42–51. Springer Berlin Heidelberg, 2012.

[2] H. Beyer. Towards a theory of 'evolution strategies'. some asymptotical results from the $(1,+\lambda)$-theory. *Evolutionary Computation*, 1:165–188, 1993.

[3] F. Black and M. Scholes. The pricing of options and corporate liabilities. *Journal of Political Economy*, 81(3):637–654, 1973.

[4] J. C. Cox, J. E. Ingersoll, and S. A. Ross. A Theory of the Term Structure of Interest Rates. *Econometrica*, 53(2):385–407, 1985.

[5] B. Doerr, C. Doerr, and J. Yang. Optimal parameter choices via precise black-box analysis. In *Proceedings of the Genetic and Evolutionary Computation Conference 2016*, GECCO '16, pages 1123–1130, New York, NY, USA, 2016. ACM.

[6] B. Doerr, M. Fouz, and C. Witt. Sharp bounds by probability-generating functions and variable drift. In *Proceedings of the 13th Annual Conference on Genetic and Evolutionary Computation*, GECCO '11, pages 2083–2090, New York, NY, USA, 2011. ACM.

[7] B. Doerr, T. Jansen, C. Witt, and C. Zarges. A method to derive fixed budget results from expected optimisation times. In *Proceeding of the fifteenth annual conference on Genetic and evolutionary computation (GECCO '13)*, pages 1581–1588. ACM, 2013.

[8] B. Doerr, D. Johannsen, and C. Winzen. Multiplicative drift analysis. *Algorithmica*, 64(4):673–697, 2012.

[9] A. Einstein. Über die von der molekularkinetischen theorie der wärme geforderte bewegung von in

ruhenden flüssigkeiten suspendierten teilchen. *Annalen der Physik*, 322(8):549–560, 1905.

[10] W. Feller. On the theory of stochastic processes, with particular reference to applications. In *Proceedings of the [First] Berkeley Symposium on Mathematical Statistics and Probability*, pages 403–432, Berkeley, Calif., 1949. University of California Press.

[11] D. Goldberg. Simple genetic algorithms and the minimal, deceptive problem. In L. Davis, editor, *Genetic algorithms and simulated annealing*, pages 74–88. 1987.

[12] J. He and X. Yao. Drift analysis and average time complexity of evolutionary algorithms. *Artificial Intelligence*, 127:57–85, 2001.

[13] K. Ito. Stochastic integral. In *Proceedings of the Imperial Academy*, 1944.

[14] K. Ito. On a stochastic integral equation. In *Proceedings of the Japan Academy*, 1946.

[15] K. Ito. Stochastic differential equations in a differentiable manifold. *Nagoya Mathematical Journal*, 1950.

[16] K. Ito. Diffusion processes and their sample paths. *Nagoya Mathematical Journal*, 1951.

[17] T. Jansen and C. Zarges. Fixed budget computations: a different perspective on run time analysis. In *Proceedings of the Genetic and Evolutionary Computation Conference (GECCO '12)*, pages 1325–1332. ACM, 2012.

[18] S. Karlin and H. M. Taylor. *A Second Course in Stochastic Processes*. Academic Press, New York, 1 edition edition, May 1981.

[19] M. Kimura. Some Problems of Stochastic Processes in Genetics. *The Annals of Mathematical Statistics*, 28(4):882–901, Dec. 1957.

[20] M. Kimura. Diffusion Models in Population Genetics. *Journal of Applied Probabilitiy*, 1(2):177–232, 1964.

[21] M. Kimura. Genetic Variability Maintained in a Finite Population Due to Mutational Production of Neutral and Nearly Neutral Isoalleles. *Genetics Research*, 11(03):247–270, 1968.

[22] J. Lengler and N. Spooner. Fixed budget performance of the (1+1) EA on linear functions. In *Proceedings of the 2015 ACM Conference on Foundations of Genetic Algorithms XIII*, FOGA '15, pages 52–61, New York, NY, USA, 2015. ACM.

[23] Y. Maghsoodi. Solution of the Extended Cir Term Structure and Bond Option Valuation. *Mathematical Finance*, 6(1):89–109, Jan. 1996.

[24] S. Nallaperuma, F. Neumann, and D. Sudholt. A fixed budget analysis of randomized search heuristics for the traveling salesperson problem. In *Proceedings of the Genetic and Evolutionary Computation Conference (GECCO '14)*, pages 807–814. ACM, 2014.

[25] B. Øksendal. *Stochastic Differential Equations: An Introduction with Applications*. University of Michigan Press, 2003.

[26] P. S. Oliveto, T. Paixão, J. Pérez Heredia, D. Sudholt, and B. Trubenová. When non-elitism outperforms elitism for crossing fitness valleys. In *Proceedings of the Genetic and Evolutionary Computation Conference 2016*, GECCO '16, pages 1163–1170, New York, NY, USA, 2016. ACM.

[27] T. Paixão, G. Badkobeh, N. Barton, D. Corus, D.-C. Dang, T. Friedrich, P. K. Lehre, D. Sudholt, A. M. Sutton, and B. Trubenová. Toward a unifying framework for evolutionary processes. *Journal of Theoretical Biology*, 383:28 – 43, 2015.

[28] T. Paixão, J. Pérez Heredia, D. Sudholt, and B. Trubenová. Towards a runtime comparison of natural and artificial evolution. *Algorithmica*, 2016. (To appear).

[29] J. Pérez Heredia, B. Trubenová, D. Sudholt, and T. Paixão. Selection limits to adaptive walks on correlated landscapes. *Genetics*, 2016. (To appear).

[30] S. Ross. *Stochastic Processes*. John Wiley & Sons, 1996.

[31] T. Schaul. Natural evolution strategies converge on sphere functions. In *Proceedings of the 14th Annual Conference on Genetic and Evolutionary Computation*, GECCO '12, pages 329–336, New York, NY, USA, 2012. ACM.

[32] T. J. Stieltjes. Recherches sur les fractions continues. In *Annales de la Faculté des sciences de Toulouse: Mathématiques*, pages 68–71. 1894.

[33] R. Stratonovich. A new representation for stochastic integrals and equations. *SIAM Journal on Control*, 1966.

[34] M. D. Vose. Modeling simple genetic algorithms. *Evol. Comput.*, 3(4):453–472, Dec. 1995.

[35] N. C. Wormald. Differential equations for random processes and random graphs. *Ann. Appl. Probab.*, 5(4):1217–1235, 11 1995.

[36] A. H. Wright and J. E. Rowe. Continuous dynamical system models of steady-state genetic algorithms. In W. N. Martin and W. M. Spears, editors, *Foundations of Genetic Algorithms 6*, pages 209 – 225. Morgan Kaufmann, San Francisco, 2001.

[37] G. Yin, G. Rudolph, and H.-P. Schwefel. Exploiting the connections of evolutionary algorithms and stochastic approximation, 1994.

[38] G. Yin, G. Rudolph, and H.-P. Schwefel. Analyzing $(1,\lambda)$ evolution strategy via stochastic approximation methods. *Evol. Comput*, pages 473–489, 1995.

11

Runtime Analysis of a Discrete Particle Swarm Optimization Algorithm on Sorting and OneMax

Moritz Mühlenthaler*
moritz.muehlenthaler
@math.tu-dortmund.de

Alexander Raß**
alexander.rass@fau.de

Manuel Schmitt**
manuel.schmitt@fau.de

Andreas Siegling**
andreas.siegling@fau.de

Rolf Wanka**
rolf.wanka@fau.de

**Department of Computer Science
University of Erlangen-Nuremberg, Germany

*Fakultät für Mathematik
TU Dortmund, Germany

ABSTRACT

We present the analysis of a discrete particle swarm optimization (PSO) algorithm that works on a significantly large class of discrete optimization problems. Assuming a black-box setting, we prove upper and lower bounds on the expected number of function evaluations required by the proposed algorithm to solve the sorting problem and the problem of maximizing the number of ones in a bitstring, i.e., the function ONEMAX. We show that depending on the probability of moving towards the attractor, the expected optimization time may be polynomial or exponential. The cornerstone of our analysis are Θ-bounds on the expected time it takes until the PSO returns to the attractor. We obtain these bounds by solving linear recurrence equations with constant and non-constant coefficients. We also introduce a useful *indistinguishability* property of states of a Markov chain in order to obtain lower bounds on the expected optimization time of our proposed PSO algorithm.

Keywords

Particle swarm optimization; Discrete Optimization; Runtime analysis; Markov chains

1. INTRODUCTION

The investigation of runtime properties of meta-heuristics, such as evolutionary algorithms (EAs) [4, 6, 25], ant colony optimization (ACO) [2, 12], and particle swarm optimization (PSO) [18, 22], is an ongoing effort in the scientific community. The purpose is to get some understanding of how these algorithms perform in a black-box setting, where the content of the black-box, the objective function, is known to the researcher (and to her or him only). The vast majority of meta-heuristic algorithms uses randomness. So the runtime

FOGA '17, January 12 - 15, 2017, Copenhagen, Denmark

© 2017 Copyright held by the owner/author(s). Publication rights licensed to ACM.
ISBN 978-1-4503-4651-1/17/01... $15.00

DOI: http://dx.doi.org/10.1145/3040718.3040721

behavior of such an algorithm can be considered desirable if, in expectation, it solves a problem efficiently whenever the problem is easy to solve in a non-black-box setting. Runtime analysis can be useful for instance to rule out algorithm variants and parameter choices that lead to excessive runtime even on easy problems. In the present work we propose a simple PSO algorithm for optimizing over discrete domains and provide upper and lower runtime bounds on the sorting problem and ONEMAX, the problem of maximizing the number of ones in a bitstring. It turns out that, depending on the choice of the algorithm parameter, the runtime can be polynomial or exponential.

PSO, introduced by Kennedy and Eberhart [5, 9], is a popular meta-heuristic for solving continuous optimization problems. It is inspired by the social interaction in bird flocks. A PSO algorithm manages a collection (*swarm*) of particles. Each particle consists of an (admissible) solution together with a velocity vector. Information between particles is shared via a common reference solution called *attractor*, which is the best solution found so far. In each iteration of the algorithm, the solution of each particle is updated according to certain movement equations, which yield a hybridization of the following two search strategies: i) looking for better solutions close to the attractor (*exploitation*), and ii) *exploration* of new territory in the search domain. Fields of successful application are, among many others, Biomedical Image Processing [20, 24], Geosciences [13], Agriculture [26], and Materials Science [16].

Although PSO has originally been proposed to solve optimization problems over a — typically rectangular — domain $X \subseteq \mathbb{R}^n$, $n \geq 1$, several authors have adapted PSO to discrete domains. A discrete setting requires a fundamental reinterpretation of the PSO movement equation because corresponding mathematical operations may be lacking in the discrete setting; for example, think of multiplying the difference of two points of the search space with a real number. An early discrete PSO variant is the *binary PSO* proposed in [10], which optimizes over the n-dimensional search space $X = \{0, 1\}^n$. A more general approach optimizing over $X = \{0, \dots, M\}^n$ has been proposed in [23].

In order to reason about the runtime behavior of meta-heuristics, they are typically cast in terms of stochastic processes, in particular random walks. For the binary PSO, the authors of [21, 22] provide various runtime results, e.g., a general lower bound of $\Omega(n/\log n)$ on every function with a unique global optimum and a bound of $\Theta(n\log n)$ on the function ONEMAX, defined as

$$\text{ONEMAX}((x_1,\ldots,x_n)) = \sum_{i=1}^{n} x_i \ .$$

For another set of discrete optimization problems, including many classical problems such as the traveling salesperson problem (TSP) and the sorting problem, the task is to optimize over the set of permutations of n items. In [1], a PSO variant for solving permutation problems has been proposed, which has been evaluated on the TSP. This approach has been refined in [8], where the authors empirically and theoretically investigate an improved PSO variant with a better convergence property.

In this paper we suggest a PSO variant, the ONEPSO, that works in a very general discrete setting: The task is to optimize a function $f : X \to \mathbb{R}$, where X is the set of vertices of a finite, strongly connected graph. A distinguishing feature of the original PSO algorithm as well as the proposed ONEPSO is the attractor. The proposed algorithm balances exploration and exploitation by choosing at random whether to move towards the attractor or to move to a random neighbor of the solution graph. The probability $c \in [0,1]$ of moving towards the attractor is given as a parameter of the algorithm. The choice of c sets the algorithm's bias for moving towards the attractor. For our runtime analysis we assume a swarm size of one, similar to the runtime results on EAs and ACO in [22].

We now give a precise statement of the problems that we employ for the runtime analysis of the ONEPSO algorithm and their search spaces. By the *sorting problem* we refer to the task of arranging n items in non-decreasing order using transpositions. Therefore, the search space is the following (undirected) graph: The vertices are the permutations on $\{1, 2, \ldots, n\}$ and two vertices x, y are adjacent iff there is a transposition t such that $x \circ t = y$. The objective function is the transposition distance to the identity permutation. Figure 1 shows the search space for the problem of sorting items $\{1, 2, 3, 4\}$ using transpositions. Any two permutations drawn in the same layer have the same objective value. For the problem ONEMAX, the search space is the n-dimensional hypercube: A solution is a binary string of length n and two solutions are adjacent iff they differ by exactly one bitflip. The objective function counts the number of ones in a bitstring. So, for the sorting problem and ONE-MAX, the objective function is the distance to the optimum in the respective graph.

Results and Techniques.

Our main results are upper and lower bounds on the expected time taken by the proposed discrete PSO algorithm for solving the sorting problem and ONEMAX in a black-box setting using just elementary methods. The results are summarized in Table 1. For $c = 0$, the algorithm behaves like a random walk on the search space, and for $c = 1$, the algorithm behaves essentially like the $(1 + 1)$-EA variants from [4, 17]. Therefore, for $c = 1$ we refer to these runtime results. However, note that the proof of the lower bound $\Omega(n^2 \log n)$ on sorting claimed in [17, Thm. 4] does not apply to the transposition distance-based objective function which we use in our analysis. Please refer to the discus-

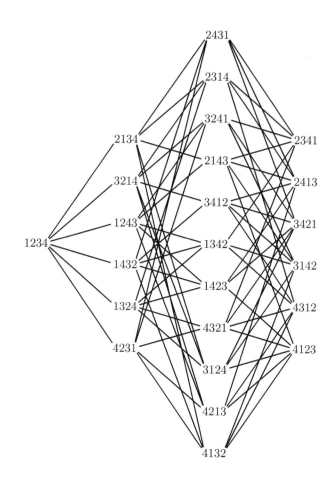

Figure 1: Search space for the problem of sorting four items by transpositions. Two permutations x, y on $\{1, 2, 3, 4\}$ are adjacent iff there is a transposition t such that $x \circ t = y$.

sion in Section 5.1 for details. We show that for $c \geq 1/2$ the expected optimization time for sorting and ONEMAX is polynomial, and for $c \in (0, 1/2)$ the expected optimization time is exponential since for c in this range we provide lower bounds on the base of the exponential expression by $\alpha(c)$ for sorting (see Lemma 15) and $\beta(c)$ for ONEMAX (see Lemma 16) such that $1 < \beta(c) < \alpha(c) < 2$ (see Figure 3). For the case $c = 1/2$ we have maximal exploration while keeping the expected runtime polynomial.

In order to obtain the bounds shown in Table 1, we use a Markov-model which captures the behavior of the ONEPSO algorithm between two consecutive updates of the current best solution, i.e., the attractor. Depending on whether we seek upper or lower bounds on the runtime, the model is instantiated in a slightly different way. The relevant quantity we extract from the Markov-model is the expected number of steps taken until the PSO returns to the attractor. We determine Θ-bounds on the expected return time by an analysis of appropriate recurrence equations with constant and non-constant coefficients. Similar recurrences occur, for example, in the runtime analysis of randomized algorithms for the satisfiability problem [14, 19]. Thus, our analysis of the Markov-model presented in Section 3 may be of general interest.

Table 1: Summary of upper and lower bounds on the expected time taken by the algorithm OnePSO to solve the sorting problem and OneMax for $c \in [0,1]$. The functions $\alpha(c)$ and $\beta(c)$ are given in Lemma 15 and Lemma 16, respectively. Note that $1 < \beta(c) < \alpha(c) < 2$.

	sorting		OneMax	
	lower bound	upper bound	lower bound	upper bound
$c = 1$	$\Omega(n^2)$ [17, Thm. 1]	$O(n^2 \log n)$ [17, Thm. 2]	$\Theta(n \log n)$ [4, Thm. 12]	
$c \in (\frac{1}{2}, 1)$	$\Omega(n^2)$	$O(n^2 \log n)$	$\Theta(n \log n)$	
$c = \frac{1}{2}$	$\Omega(n^{\frac{8}{3}})$	$O(n^3 \log n)$	$\Omega(n^{\frac{3}{2}})$	$O(n^{\frac{3}{2}} \log n)$
$c \in (0, \frac{1}{2})$	$\Omega(\alpha(c)^n \cdot n^2)$	$O\left(\left(\frac{1-c}{c}\right)^n n^2 \log n\right)$	$\Omega(\beta(c)^n \cdot n)$	$O\left(\left(\frac{1-c}{c}\right)^n n \log n\right)$
$c = 0$	$\Theta(n!)$		$\Theta(2^n)$	

Note that our analysis of the expected runtime is essentially tight with respect to the chosen Markov-model. The gaps between upper and lower bounds on the expected runtimes shown in Table 1 are a result of choosing best-case or worst-case bounds on the transition probabilities in the Markov-model, which are problem dependent. Since our bounds on the transition probabilities are essentially tight, see Section 4 in particular, the gap between the expected runtime bounds can only be closed by using a more elaborate model.

Upper Bounds. To obtain the upper bounds shown in Table 1 we use the established *fitness level method* (e.g., see [25]). We instantiate our Markov-model such that improvements of the attractor are only accounted for if the current position is at the attractor. The main difficulty is to determine the expected number of steps needed to return to the attractor. We obtain this quantity from the analysis of the corresponding recurrences.

Lower Bounds. The runtime of the PSO is dominated by the time required for the last improvement of the attractor, after which the global optimum has been found. We again use the Markov-model and observe that in this situation, the global optimum can be reached only when the Markov-model is in a specific state. We argue that the optimal solution is included in a certain set $\overline{Y}$ of indistinguishable states. Therefore, in expectation, this set needs to be hit $\Omega(|\overline{Y}|)$ times until the optimum has been found. By appropriately truncating the states and then bounding the transition probabilities we obtain a lower bound on the expected number of steps required to return to $\overline{Y}$.

Search Space Structure. In Section 4 we consider a partition of the set of permutations on $\{1, 2, \ldots, n\}$ into layers, such that layer i contains all permutations of transposition distance i to a reference permutation. To aid our analysis of the PSO algorithm, we determine tight upper and lower bounds on the number of transpositions that decrease the transposition distance to the first layer. These results apply in any setting where transpositions act on permutations and may therefore also be of general interest. The layer structure of the permutations of $\{1, 2, 3, 4\}$, having the identity as reference permutation, is shown in Figure 1.

2. THE DISCRETE PSO ALGORITHM

The main goal of this paper is to determine the runtime behavior of a simple PSO algorithm that optimizes discrete functions. Since we have just one single particle the algo-

rithm is referred to as OnePSO. Note that the algorithm is different from the 1-PSO studied in [22], which is tailored to optimization over bitstrings. The OnePSO algorithm samples items from a countable set X in order to determine some $x^* \in X$ that minimizes a given *objective function* $f : X \longrightarrow \mathbb{R}$. In order to have a discrete PSO that remains true to the principles of the original PSO for optimization in the domain $\mathbb{R}^n$ from [5, 9], we need some additional structure on X: For each $x \in X$ we have a set of *neighbors* $\mathcal{N}_X(x)$. If the set X is clear from the context we may drop the subscript. The neighborhood structure induces a solution graph with nodes X and arcs $\{xy \mid x, y \in X, y \in \mathcal{N}(x)\}$. The *distance* $d(x, y)$ of solutions $x, y \in X$ is the length of a shortest (directed) xy-path in this graph. We assume that the solution graph is strongly connected, so the PSO cannot get "trapped" in a particular strongly connected component.

The OnePSO algorithm performs the steps shown in Algorithm 1 below. The initial position of the particle is chosen uniformly at random (u.a.r.) from X. The parameter c determines the importance of the attractor a. In each iteration we move towards the attractor with probability c and otherwise move to a random neighbor. Note that the attractor a is updated in line 3 whenever a better solution has been found. We consider the PSO to be an infinite process so we do not give a termination criterion. We refer to the number of function evaluations performed to reach a global optimum $x^* \in X$ as *optimization time*. For practical purposes, efficient sampling of x' in lines 1 and 2 is a requirement. Since we are interested in the optimization time only, efficient sampling is not relevant for our analysis.

Algorithm 1: OnePSO

---

input : Function $f : X \to \mathbb{R}$, $c \in [0,1]$

---

pick position $x \in X$ u.a.r.
$a \longleftarrow x$ /* initialize the attractor */
while *True* **do**
    pick $q \in [0,1]$ u.a.r.
    if $x = a$ *or* $q > c$ **then** /*pick new position x' */
1   pick $x' \in \mathcal{N}(x)$ u.a.r.
    else:
2   pick $x' \in \{y \in \mathcal{N}(x) \mid d(y, a) < d(x, a)\}$ u.a.r.
    $x \longleftarrow x'$ /* update position */
    if $f(x) < f(a)$ **then**   /* update attractor */
3         $a \longleftarrow x$

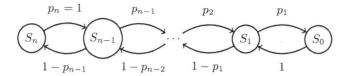

Figure 2: State diagram of the Markov-model

3. THE MODEL

We present a simple Markov-model that captures the behavior of the ONEPSO algorithm between two consecutive updates of the attractor. Using this model we can infer upper and lower bounds on the expected optimization time of the ONEPSO algorithm on suitable discrete functions. For our analysis, we assume that the objective function $f : X \to \mathbb{R}$ has the property that every local optimum is a global one. This includes the class of unimodal functions. This implies that the function is either constant or any non-optimum solution x has a neighbor $y \in \mathcal{N}(x)$ such that $f(x) > f(y)$. This certainly narrows down the class of objective functions to which our analysis applies. However, the class seems still appreciably large.

Assume that the attractor $a \in X$ is fixed and a is not a minimizer of f. Under which conditions can a new "best" solution be found? Certainly, if the current position x is equal to a, then, by the unimodality of f we get an improvement with positive probability. If $x \neq a$ then the attractor may still be improved. However, for the purpose of upper bounding the expected optimization time of the ONEPSO we dismiss the possibility that the attractor is updated if $x \neq a$. As a result, we obtain a reasonably simple Markov-model of the ONEPSO behavior. Quite surprisingly, using the same Markov-model, we are also able to get good lower bounds on the expected optimization time of the ONEPSO (see Section 5.3 for the details).

3.1 Model Specification

Let n be the diameter of the search space X. We partition the search space according to the distance to the attractor $a \in X$. That is, for $0 \leq i \leq n$, let $X_i = \{x \in X \mid d(x, a) = i\}$. Note that this partition does not depend on the objective function. The model consists of $n + 1$ states $S_0, S_1, \ldots, S_n$. Being in state S_i indicates that the current solution x of the ONEPSO is in X_i. For $1 \leq i \leq n$ we denote by p_i the transition probability from S_i to S_{i-1}. The probabilities p_i in turn depend on the parameter c, which is the probability that the ONEPSO explicitly moves towards the attractor. If the current position x is in X_i and the algorithm moves towards the attractor, then the new position is in X_{i-1}. On the other hand, if the PSO updates x to any neighbor chosen u.a.r. from $\mathcal{N}(x)$, then the new position is in X_{i-1} with probability at least $\min_{x \in X_i} |\mathcal{N}(x) \cap X_{i-1}|/|\mathcal{N}(x)|$. So for upper bounds we set

$$p_i = c + (1 - c) \cdot \min_{x \in X_i} \frac{|X_{i-1} \cap \mathcal{N}(x)|}{|\mathcal{N}(x)|} \ .$$

The probability of moving from X_i to X_{i+1} is at most $1 - p_i$. We assume in this model that equality holds for all $1 \leq i < n$, so the probability of moving from S_i to a state S_j, $j \notin \{i - 1, i + 1\}$, is zero. This assumption holds for both problems we investigate in Section 5. Furthermore, if the

ONEPSO is at position $x \in X_n$ then any move brings us closer to the reference solution; so $p_n = 1$.

Let p_a be the probability to improve the attractor if we are currently in state S_0, hence at the attractor. Then the probability p_a depends on f and the choice of a. We have that p_a is positive since f is unimodal. Figure 2 shows the state diagram of the model. By $\mathcal{M}((p_i)_{1 \leq i \leq n})$ we denote an instance of the Markov-model with states $S_0, S_1, \ldots, S_n$ and p_i, $1 \leq i \leq n$.

Our goal is to determine the expected number of steps needed to hit a solution which is better than the attractor after starting in S_0. In order to reach a better solution from S_0 we need in expectation $1/p_a$ tries. If we are unsuccessful in some try, then the ONEPSO moves to S_1. For upper bounds we can ignore the chance to improve the attractor through other states. Thus we need to determine the expected number of steps it takes until we can perform the next try, that is, the expected first hitting time for the state S_0, starting in S_1. The expected number h_i of steps needed to move from S_i to S_0 is given by the following recurrence:

$$
\begin{aligned}
h_n &= 1 + h_{n-1} \\
h_i &= 1 + p_i \cdot h_{i-1} + (1 - p_i) \cdot h_{i+1} \ , \quad 1 \leq i < n \quad (1) \\
h_0 &= 0 \ .
\end{aligned}
$$

Observe that in our applications the probabilities p_i are not constant. If we assume that $p_1 = p_2 = \ldots = p_n = p$ then we get a non-homogeneous recurrence of order two with constant coefficients. In this case, standard methods can be used to determine h_1 as a function of n [7, Ch. 7]. Note also that for $p = 1/k$ this is exactly the recurrence that occurs in the analysis of a randomized algorithm for k-SAT [14, 19] and [11, pp. 160f.]. If p_i is a non-constant function of i, then the recurrence can in some cases be solved, see e.g., [7, Ch. 7] and [15]. Here, due to the structure of the recurrence, we can use a more pedestrian approach, which is outlined in the next subsection.

3.2 Solving the Recurrence

We first present a reformulation of the recurrence given in Equation (1). Let H_i be the expected number of steps needed to move from state S_i to state S_{i-1}. Then H_i can be determined from H_{i+1} as follows: In expectation, we need $1/p_i$ trials to get from S_i to S_{i-1}, and each trial, except for the successful one, requires $1 + H_{i+1}$ steps. The successful trial requires only a single step, so H_i is captured by the following recurrence:

$$H_i = \frac{1}{p_i} (1 + H_{i+1}) - H_{i+1}, \qquad 1 \leq i \leq n \quad (2)$$

$$H_n = 1 \ . \quad (3)$$

In the following, assume that the probabilities p_i are determined by some function $P(n, i)$ depending on n and i. Rearranging Equation (2) gives $H_i = 1/p_i + (1 - p_i)/p_i \cdot H_{i+1}$.

Unfolding this recurrence k times, $1 \le k \le n$, with initial value (3) followed by some rearrangement of the terms yields

$$H_1 = \sum_{i=1}^{k-1} \left(\frac{1}{p_i} \cdot \prod_{j=1}^{i-1} \frac{1-p_j}{p_j} \right) + H_k \cdot \prod_{j=1}^{k-1} \frac{1-p_j}{p_j} \; . \quad (4)$$

Thus, for $k = n$ we obtain the following expression for H_1:

$$H_1 = \sum_{i=1}^{n} \left(\frac{1}{p_i} \cdot \prod_{j=1}^{i-1} \frac{1-p_j}{p_j} \right) - \prod_{j=1}^{n} \frac{1-p_j}{p_j} \; , \quad (5)$$

where the second term is a correction term which is required whenever $P(n,n) = p_n < 1$ in order to satisfy the initial condition given in Equation (3). Equation (5) has also been mentioned in [3, Lemma 3] in the context of the analysis of a $(1+1)$-EA.

In the next two subsections we derive closed-form expressions and asymptotic properties of $H_1 = h_1$ from Equations (4) and (5) for various choices of probabilities p_i.

3.3 Constant Probabilities

If the probabilities $p_i = p$ for some constant $p \in [0, 1]$ and $1 \le i < n$, then recurrences (2) become linear recurrence equations with constant coefficients. Standard methods can be used to determine closed-form expressions for h_i and H_i. However, we are mainly interested in H_1 and are able to determine closed-form expressions directly from Equation (5).

THEOREM 1. *Let $0 < p < 1$. Then the expected return time H_1 to S_0 is*

$$H_1 = h_1 = \begin{cases} \dfrac{1 - 2p \left(\dfrac{1-p}{p} \right)^n}{2p - 1} & \text{if } p \ne \frac{1}{2} \\ 2n - 1 & \text{otherwise} \; . \end{cases} \quad (6)$$

PROOF. By setting $p_i = p$ in Equation (5) and performing some rearrangements the claim is proved. $\square$

It is easily verified that this expression for h_1 satisfies Equation (1). So, with $p_i = p$ we have that the time it takes to return to the attractor is constant, linear, or exponential in n if $p < 1/2$, $p = 1/2$, or $p > 1/2$, respectively.

3.4 Nonconstant Probabilities

Motivated by the runtime analysis of OnePSO applied to optimization problems such as sorting and OneMax, we are particularly interested in the expected time it takes to improve the attractor if the probabilities p_i are *slightly* greater than $1/2$. By *slightly* we mean $p_i = 1/2 + i/(2A(n))$ and $p_i = 1/2 + \binom{i}{2}/(2A(n))$, where $A : \mathbb{N} \to \mathbb{N}$ is some non-decreasing function of n such that $\lim_{n \to \infty} A(n) = \infty$. Clearly, in this setting we cannot hope for a recurrence with constant coefficients. Our goal in this section is to obtain the asymptotics of H_1 as $n \to \infty$ for $A(n) = n$ and $A(n) = \binom{n}{2}$. We show that, surprisingly, for $A(n) = n$ the return time to the attractor is $\Theta(\sqrt{n})$, while for $A(n) = \binom{n}{2}$ the return time is $\Theta(n)$. In the following $\Gamma(z)$ refers to the Gamma-function, which generalizes the factorial to arbitrary complex arguments.

LEMMA 2. *Let $A(n) = n$. Then*

$$H_1 = \frac{\sqrt{\pi} \cdot \Gamma(n+1)}{\Gamma(n + \frac{1}{2})} - 1 \sim \sqrt{\pi n} = \Theta(\sqrt{n}) \; .$$

PROOF. We have $p_n = 1$ so the correction term in Equation (5) is zero. We rearrange the remaining terms of Equation (5) and find that

$$H_1 = \sum_{i=1}^{n} \frac{2n}{n+i} \prod_{j=1}^{i-1} \frac{n-j}{n+j} = 2 \sum_{i=1}^{n} \frac{\prod_{j=0}^{i-1} n-j}{\prod_{j=1}^{i} n+j}$$

$$= 2 \sum_{i=1}^{n} \frac{n! \, n!}{(n-i)! \cdot (n+i)!} = \frac{2(n!)^2}{(2n)!} \sum_{i=1}^{n} \frac{(2n)!}{(n-i)! \cdot (n+i)!}$$

$$= \frac{2}{\binom{2n}{n}} \sum_{i=1}^{n} \binom{2n}{n-i} = \frac{2}{\binom{2n}{n}} \sum_{i=0}^{n-1} \binom{2n}{i}$$

$$= \binom{2n}{n}^{-1} \left(\left(\sum_{i=0}^{2n} \binom{2n}{i} \right) - \binom{2n}{n} \right)$$

$$= \frac{4^n}{\binom{2n}{n}} - 1 \; .$$

Using the identity $\Gamma(n + \frac{1}{2}) = \frac{\sqrt{\pi} \, (2n)!}{4^n \, n!}$ we obtain the first part of the claimed statement and by Stirling's approximation of the factorial we have

$$H_1 = \frac{4^n (n!)^2}{(2n)!} - 1 \sim \sqrt{\pi n} = \Theta(\sqrt{n}) \; .$$

$\square$

THEOREM 3. *Let $M = \mathcal{M}((p_i)_{1 \le i \le n})$, where $p_i = 1/2 + i/(2A(n))$. Then $H_1 = \Theta(\min(\sqrt{A(n)}, n))$ with respect to M.*

PROOF. Let $A(n) = O(n^2)$ and let $n' \in \mathbb{N}$ be the smallest number such that $p_{n'} = 1/2 + n'/(2A(n)) \ge 1$. First, assume that $n' \le n$ and consider the "truncated" model $M' = \mathcal{M}((p_i)_{1 \le i \le n'})$. By Lemma 2 we have $H_1 = \Theta(\sqrt{A(n)})$ with respect to M', which is by the construction of M' also valid for M. On the other hand, assume that $n' > n$ and consider the "extended" model $\tilde{M} = \mathcal{M}((p_i)_{1 \le i \le n'})$. Let $\tilde{H}_1$ be the expected return time to state S_1 with respect to M'. By Lemma 2 we have $\tilde{H}_1 = \Theta(\sqrt{A(n)})$ and since $\tilde{H}_1 \ge H_1$ we obtain $H_1 = O(\sqrt{A(n)})$.

To obtain a lower bound on H_1 for the case $n' > n$ we consider the model $\hat{M} = \mathcal{M}((\hat{p}_i)_{1 \le i \le N})$, where $N = \sqrt{A(n)}$ and $\hat{p}_i = 1/2 + 1/N$ for $1 \le i < N$, and $\hat{p}_N = 1$. Let $\hat{H}_1$ denote the expected return time to state S_1 in $\hat{M}$. Since $\hat{p}_i > p_i$ for $1 \le i \le N$, $\hat{H}_1$ is a lower bound on H_1. Since $\hat{p}_i =: p$ is constant for $1 \le i < N$ we get from Theorem 1 that

$$\hat{H}_1 = \frac{1 - 2p \left(\dfrac{1-p}{p} \right)^N}{2p - 1} \; .$$

Substituting $p = 1/2 + 1/N$ gives

$$\hat{H}_1 = \frac{1}{2} \left(N - (N+2) \cdot \left(\frac{N-2}{N+2} \right)^N \right)$$

$$= \frac{1}{2} \left(N - \frac{(N+2)^3}{(N-2)^2} \cdot \left(1 - \frac{4}{N+2} \right)^{N+2} \right)$$

$$\ge \frac{1}{2} \left(N - \frac{(N+2)^3}{(N-2)^2} \cdot e^{-4} \right) = \Omega(N) \; .$$

Therefore $H_1 = \Omega(N) = \Omega(\sqrt{A(n)})$.

It remains to show that the statement holds if $A(n) \notin O(n^2)$. In this case, $H_1 = O(n)$ is obtained by setting $p_i = 1/2$ for $1 \le i < n$ and invoking Theorem 1. On the other hand, setting $A(n) = n^2$ gives a lower bound on H_1. As discussed above, for $A(n) = n^2$, the expected return time to S_1 is $\Omega(\sqrt{A(n)})$. Therefore, $H_1 = \Omega(n)$, which completes the proof. $\square$

For our applications, ONEMAX and sorting, the following two special cases of Theorem 3 will be of interest:

COROLLARY 4. *Let* $M = \mathcal{M}((1/2 + i/2n)_{1 \le i \le n})$ *and let* $M' = \mathcal{M}((1/2 + i/\binom{n}{2})_{1 \le i \le n})$. *Then* $H_1 = \Theta(\sqrt{n})$ *with respect to* M *and* $H_1 = \Theta(n)$ *with respect to* M'.

We will now consider a slightly different class of instances of the Markov-model in order to obtain a lower bound on the ONEPSO runtime for sorting in Section 5. For this purpose we consider transition probabilities p_i that increase quadratically in i which suits our fitness level analysis of the sorting problem in Section 4. There we will prove that this class of models is relevant for the analysis of the *best case* behavior of the ONEPSO algorithm for sorting n items (see Theorem 9). Although we will only make use of a lower bound on H_1 in this setting later on, we give the following Θ-bounds:

THEOREM 5. *Let* $M = \mathcal{M}\left(\left(\frac{1}{2}\left(1 + \binom{i+1}{2}/\binom{n}{2}\right)\right)_{1 \le i \le n-1}\right)$. *Then* $H_1 = \Theta(n^{2/3})$ *with respect to* M.

PROOF. Consider the expression for H_1 given in Equation (4). Since $p_i > 1/2$ for $1 \le i \le n$ the products are at most 1 and $1/p_i$ is at most 2. Therefore $H_1 \le 2k + H_k$. For H_k the states S_0 to S_{k-2} are irrelevant since they are never visited. We truncate the model to states $S_{k-1}, \ldots, S_n$. For these states the minimal probability of moving towards the attractor is p_{k-1}. Therefore we can set $p_i = p_{k-1}$ for $i \in \{k, \ldots, n\}$ to receive an upper bound on the return time. By reindexing the states we obtain the model $M^* = \mathcal{M}((p_{k-1})_{1 \le k \le n-k+1})$ and, because of the truncation, H_1^* is an upper bound on H_k, where H_1^* is the expected number of steps to move from state S_1 to S_0 in model M^*. To simplify calculations we consider the model $M' = \mathcal{M}((p_{k-1})_{1 \le i \le n})$, which is M^* extended to n states. Let H_1' be the expected number of steps to move from state S_1 to S_0 in model M'. In M' we have the constant probabilities p_{k-1} and can therefore apply Theorem 1 to determine H_1'. Therefore

$$H_k \le H_1^* \le H_1' = \frac{1 - 2p_{k-1}\left(\frac{1-p_{k-1}}{p_{k-1}}\right)^n}{2p_{k-1} - 1}$$

$$\le \frac{1}{2p_{k-1} - 1} = \frac{\binom{n}{2}}{\binom{k}{2}} \; .$$

Altogether we have $H_1 \le 2k + \frac{n(n-1)}{k(k-1)}$. With $k = n^{2/3}$ we get

$$H_1 \le 2n^{\frac{2}{3}} + \frac{n(n-1)}{n^{\frac{2}{3}}(n^{\frac{2}{3}} - 1)}$$

$$= n^{\frac{2}{3}}\left(2 + \frac{1 - n^{-1}}{1 - n^{-\frac{2}{3}}}\right) = O(n^{\frac{2}{3}}) \; ,$$

which certifies that $H_1 = O(n^{2/3})$. Using Equation (4) we

have the following lower bound on H_1:

$$H_1 \ge \sum_{i=1}^{n^{2/3}} \frac{1}{p_i} \prod_{j=1}^{i-1} \frac{1 - p_j}{p_j} \ge n^{\frac{2}{3}} \prod_{j=1}^{n^{2/3}-1} \frac{1 - p_j}{p_j}$$

$$= n^{\frac{2}{3}} \prod_{j=1}^{n^{2/3}-1} \frac{\binom{n}{2} - \binom{j+1}{2}}{\binom{n}{2} + \binom{j+1}{2}} = n^{\frac{2}{3}} \prod_{j=1}^{n^{2/3}-1} 1 - \frac{2\binom{j+1}{2}}{\binom{n}{2} + \binom{j+1}{2}}$$

$$\ge n^{\frac{2}{3}}\left(1 - \sum_{j=1}^{n^{2/3}-1} \frac{2\binom{j+1}{2}}{\binom{n}{2} + \binom{j+1}{2}}\right)$$

$$\ge n^{\frac{2}{3}}\left(1 - \sum_{j=1}^{n^{2/3}-1} \frac{2\binom{j+1}{2}}{\binom{n}{2}}\right)$$

$$= n^{\frac{2}{3}}\left(1 - \frac{2}{\binom{n}{2}} \sum_{j=1}^{n^{2/3}-1} \binom{j+1}{2}\right)$$

$$= n^{\frac{2}{3}}\left(1 - \frac{2}{\binom{n}{2}} \binom{n^{\frac{1}{3}} + 1}{3}\right) = n^{\frac{2}{3}}\left(1 - \frac{2 - 2n^{-\frac{4}{3}}}{3 - 3n^{-1}}\right)$$

$$= \Omega(n^{\frac{2}{3}}) \; .$$

$\square$

4. FITNESS LEVELS FOR SORTING

Sorting is a classical task in computer science. Our motivation to use the ONEPSO algorithm for this task is twofold: First, since sorting can be performed efficiently in a non-black-box setting, our goal is to show that the ONEPSO is able to perform this task efficiently in a black-box setting. Second, we are interested in the effect of using an attractor on the runtime in comparison to the $(1 + 1)$-EA from [17], which uses the concept of *elitism*.

Our goal is to get good bounds on the transition probabilities in our Markov-model of the ONEPSO sorting n items. The search space X is the set of permutations of $\{1, 2, \ldots, n\}$. We will provide insights about the structure of sets X_i of permutations with distance i to the attractor a. Based on these observations we obtain tight best-case and worst-case bounds on the number of transpositions that let the ONEPSO move from X_i to X_{i-1}. The notion of *distance* $d(x, y)$ of two permutations x and y employed here is the minimum number of transpositions needed to transform x into y. As a motivating example, consider the case that the attractor is at the global optimum. Then $\{X_i\}_{1 \le i \le n}$ is a partition of the search space into *fitness levels*. Fitness levels are used heavily for analyzing the expected optimization time of nature-inspired optimization algorithms [17, 22, 25].

In the following we denote by T_n the set of all transpositions on $\{1, 2, \ldots, n\}$, that is, $T_n = \{(i\ j) \mid i, j \in \{1, \ldots, n\}, i \ne j\}$. We first observe that in our setting the sets X_i have the following structure[1]:

PROPOSITION 6. *Let* $X_0 = \{\mathrm{id}_n\}$, *where* id_n *is the permutation on* $\{1, 2, \ldots, n\}$ *consisting of* n *singleton cycles. Then for* $0 \le i \le n-1$, *the set* X_i *consists of the permutations on* $\{1, 2, \ldots, n\}$ *with precisely* $n - i$ *disjoint cycles.*

PROOF. X_0 contains only the attractor, and for each $1 \le i \le n-1$, an item $x \in X_i$ has distance i to the attractor.

---

[1]This was already mentioned in [17], but no proof was given.

Assume that the claimed statement holds for each X_j, $0 \leq j \leq i$ for some $0 \leq i \leq n-1$. Let $\pi \in X_i$ and let $t = (a, b)$ be a transposition. Then $\pi' = t \circ \pi$ is a neighbor of π. We show that π' is either in X_{i-1} or X_{i+1}. If a and b are contained in a common cycle c of π then t splits c into two disjoint cycles. Therefore, π' has $n - (i-1)$ disjoint cycles and, by assumption, $\pi' \in X_{i-1}$. On the other hand, if a and b are contained in two distinct cycles c_1, c_2, then t combines c_1 and c_2 into a single cycle, hence the distance to the attractor increases by one. This is the case for each neighbor of any permutation $\pi \in X_i$. Therefore X_{i+1} contains precisely the permutations consisting of $n - (i+1)$ disjoint cycles. $\square$

By relabeling $\{1, 2, \ldots, n\}$ it is always possible to choose $X_0 = \{\mathrm{id}_n\}$. It follows that $|X_i| = s(n, n-i)$, where $s(n, k)$ denotes the unsigned Stirling numbers of the first kind. Our next goal is to bound the worst case and best case probabilities of moving closer to the attractor. Let $\pi \in X_i$, $1 \leq i \leq n$, and let

$$L_i(\pi) = |\{\tau \in T_n \mid \tau \circ \pi \in X_{i-1}\}|$$

be the number of transpositions that bring the OnePSO from π closer to the attractor. We characterize the cycle structure of the permutations that minimize or maximize L_i:

PROPOSITION 7. *Let $\pi, \pi' \in X_i$, $1 \leq i \leq n$, such that $L_i(\pi) = \min_{x \in X_i}\{L_i(x)\}$ and $L_i(\pi') = \max_{x \in X_i}\{L_i(x)\}$. Then the cycle decomposition of π contains only cycles of length $r = n/i$ if i divides n and otherwise the cycle lengths differ by at most one. Furthermore, the cycle decomposition of π' contains of $n - i - 1$ singleton cycles and one $(i+1)$-cycle.*

PROOF. There are $\binom{k}{2}$ transpositions that split a k-cycle into two smaller cycles. We assume that for $0 \leq i \leq n$ the cycle structure of the permutations in X_i is according to Proposition 6. Let $\pi \in X_i$ such that the cycle decomposition of π contains a cycle c_1 of length $k > 2$ and a cycle c_2 of length $k + \ell$, $\ell \geq 1$. Furthermore, consider a permutation $\pi' \in X_i$ whose cycle decomposition is identical to that of π, except that the items permuted by c_1 and c_2 are permuted by two cycles c_1' and c_2' of lengths $k + 1$ and $k + \ell - 1$, respectively. We count the number of transpositions that split up c_1, c_2, c_1', and c_2', and find that

$$\binom{k}{2} + \binom{k+\ell}{2} \geq \binom{k+1}{2} + \binom{k+\ell-1}{2} \quad (7)$$

holds whenever $k \geq 1$. By iterating this argument the first statement is proved. Similarly, since Equation (7) holds for $k \geq 1$ we deduce that any permutation $\pi \in X_i$ that maximizes $L_i(\pi)$ consists of $n - i - 1$ singleton cycles and one $(i+1)$-cycle. $\square$

We are now ready to give a closed-form expression for the number of transpositions that bring us from state i closer to the attractor. We consider the worst case over all permutations in X_i.

PROPOSITION 8. *For $1 \leq i \leq n-1$,*

$$\min_{x \in X_i}\{L_i(x)\} = (B \cdot (n-i) - i) \cdot \binom{B}{2}$$
$$+ (n - B \cdot (n-i)) \cdot \binom{B+1}{2} ,$$

where $B = \lfloor \frac{n}{n-i} \rfloor$.

PROOF. By Proposition 7, any permutation that minimizes L_i consists of m cycles of length B and m' cycles of length $B + 1$ for some $m \geq 1$, $m' \geq 0$, $B \geq 1$. B is given by $\lfloor \frac{n}{n-i} \rfloor$ and m, m' satisfy the following set of equations:

$$n = m \cdot B + m' \cdot (B+1)$$
$$m + m' = n - i .$$

Solving for m, m' we obtain:

$$m = B \cdot (n-i) - i$$
$$m' = n - B \cdot (n-i) ,$$

which completes the proof. $\square$

Next, we bound the number of transpositions in T_n that let the OnePSO move from X_i to X_{i-1}. We consider the minimum and maximum over all permutations in X_i.

THEOREM 9. *Let $1 \leq i \leq n$. Then*

1. *$\min_{\pi \in X_i}\{L_i(\pi)\} \geq i$ and equality holds for $1 \leq i \leq \lfloor n/2 \rfloor$, and*

2. *$\max_{\pi \in X_i}\{L_i(\pi)\} = \binom{i+1}{2}$.*

PROOF. For brevity, let $f(i) := \min_{\pi \in X_i}\{L_i(\pi)\}$. Proposition 8 gives a closed-form expression for f. We bound this expression to obtain the claimed lower bound on $f(i)$ in the worst-case. For $1 \leq i < n/2$ we have that $B = \lfloor n/(n-i) \rfloor = 1$ and therefore the expression for $f(i)$ given in Proposition 8 simplifies to i. We consider the missing case that n is even and $i = n/2$. It is easy to check that $f(i)$ simplifies to $n/2$ in this case as required. Now assume that $\lfloor n/2 \rfloor < i \leq n-1$. Let $\pi \in X_i$, let c be a longest cycle of π and let k be the length of c. Since $\lfloor n/2 \rfloor < i \leq n-1$ we have that $k \geq 3$. Let $t \in T_n$ such that $t \circ \pi \in X_{i-1}$ and t splits c into a cycle of length $k - 1$ and a singleton cycle. We bound $L_{i-1}(t \circ \pi)$ as follows

1. $L_{i-1}(t \circ \pi) \geq f(i-1)$, and

2. $L_{i-1}(t \circ \pi) + k - 1 \geq f(i)$.

Therefore, $f(i) - f(i-1) \geq k - 1 \geq 2$ and the worst-case bound is proved.

Now the best-case upper bound remains to be proved. By Proposition 7, any permutation $\pi \in X_i$ that maximizes $L_i(\pi)$ consists of $n - i - 1$ singleton cycles and one $(i+1)$-cycle. There are exactly $\binom{i+1}{2}$ transpositions that split up the $(i+1)$-cycle and therefore $\max_{\pi \in X_i}\{L_i(\pi)\} = \binom{i+1}{2}$, which completes the proof. $\square$

5. RUNTIME ANALYSIS

We present a runtime analysis of OnePSO for two combinatorial problems, the sorting problem and OneMax. Our analysis is based on the *fitness level method* [25], in particular its application to the runtime analysis of a $(1+1)$-EA for the sorting problem in [17]. Consider a (discrete) search space X and an objective function $f : X \to \mathbb{R}$, where f assigns m distinct values $f_1 < f_2 < \ldots < f_m$ on X. Let $S_i \subseteq X$ be the set of solutions with value f_i. Assuming that some algorithm $\mathcal{A}$ optimizing f on X leaves fitness level i at most once then the expected runtime of $\mathcal{A}$ is bounded from above by $\sum_{i=1}^{m} 1/s_i$, where s_i is a lower bound on the probability of $\mathcal{A}$ leaving S_i. The method has also been applied successfully, e.g., in [22] to obtain bounds on the expected runtime of a binary PSO proposed in [10].

5.1 Related Results

We first discuss the relevant results from [17, 22]. In [22], general upper bounds on the runtime of the binary PSO for unimodal functions are given, as well as a detailed analysis of its runtime for OneMax. Note that the binary PSO studied in [22] has been designed for optimizing over $\{0, 1\}^n$ and it is different from our proposed OnePSO, which can be applied to a much wider range of discrete problems.

THEOREM 10 ([22, THM. 3]). *Under certain assumptions on the algorithm parameters, the expected number of generations performed by the binary PSO for optimizing $f : \{0, 1\}^n \to \mathbb{R}$ is $O(mn \log n) + \sum_{i=1}^{m-1} 1/s_i$.*

Essentially, this runtime result reflects the fact that the binary PSO converges to the attractor in expected time $O(n \log n)$ unless the attractor has been updated meanwhile. This happens once for each fitness level. For OneMax, this result yields a runtime of $O(n^2 \log n)$. By a more detailed analysis of the behavior of the binary 1-PSO on OneMax, the following improved bound is established:

THEOREM 11 ([22, THM. 5]). *The expected optimization time of the binary 1-PSO on OneMax is $O(n \log n)$.*

In [17], bounds are given for the expected optimization time of a $(1 + 1)$-EA sorting n items. Various choices of objective functions (e.g., Hamming distance, transposition distance,...) as well as mutation operators (e.g., transpositions, reversing keys in a certain range, ...) are considered. A general lower bound of $\Omega(n^2)$ is proved, which holds for all permutation problems having objective functions with a unique optimum [17, Thm. 1]. The most relevant runtime result for a comparison with our OnePSO is the following:

THEOREM 12 ([17, THM. 2]). *The expected optimization time of the $(1+1)$-EA for sorting n items is $O(n^2 \log n)$ if the objective function is the transposition distance to the sorted sequence and mutations are transpositions.*

In the same setting, a lower bound of $\Omega(n^2 \log n)$ is claimed in [17, Thm. 4]. However, there is an error in the proof, since it is implicitly assumed that, in the *best case*, the probability of moving from S_k to S_{k-1} is $O(k/n^2)$, as for the Hamming distance objective function. Recall that we provided a *tight* upper bound of $O(k^2/n^2)$ for this probability in Theorem 9. The correct bound yields an expected optimization time of $\Omega(n^2)$ for the $(1 + 1)$-EA, which offers no advantage over the lower bound given in [17, Thm. 1]. The mode of operation of the $(1 + 1)$-EA considered in [17] is reminiscent of stochastic hill climbing: In each iteration, a random solution is sampled and the current solution is replaced if and only if the solution is better. In order to escape local optima the distance between the current solution and the new one is determined according to Poisson distributed random variables. A bound on the expected runtime is obtained by determining the expected number of trials required to improve the current solution on each fitness level. In contrast, the PSO studied in [22] allows for non-improving solutions, but it converges to the attractor exactly once per fitness level. After the convergence occurred, the PSO behaves essentially like the $(1 + 1)$-EA.

5.2 Upper Bounds

Similar to [17, 22], we use the fitness-level method to prove upper bounds on the expected optimization time of the OnePSO. In contrast to the former, we allow non-improving solutions and return to the attractor as often as needed in order to sample a neighbor of the attractor that belongs to a better fitness level. Therefore, the time needed to return to the attractor contributes a multiplicative term to the expected runtime, which depends on the choice of the algorithm parameter c.

THEOREM 13. *The expected optimization time $T_{\text{sort}}(n)$ of the OnePSO sorting n items is bounded from above by*

$$T_{\text{sort}}(n) = \begin{cases} O(n^2 \log n) & \text{if } c \in (\frac{1}{2}, 1] \\ O(n^3 \log n) & \text{if } c = \frac{1}{2} \\ O\left(\left(\frac{1-c}{c}\right)^n \cdot n^2 \log n\right) & \text{if } c \in (0, \frac{1}{2}) \end{cases}.$$

PROOF. Recall that Theorem 9 supplies the worst-case bound $s_i \geq i/\binom{n}{2}$ over all permutations in X_i. Consider the situation that the attractor has just been updated. Whenever the OnePSO fails to update the attractor in the next iteration it will take in expectation H_1 iterations until the attractor is reached again and then it is improved with probability at least $i/\binom{n}{2}$. Again, if the OnePSO fails to improve the attractor we have to wait H_1 steps, and so on. Since we do not consider the case that the attractor has been improved meanwhile, the general fitness level method yields an expected runtime of at most $\sum_{i=1}^{n}(H_1 + 1)(1/s_i - 1) + 1 = H_1 \cdot O(n^2 \log n)$.

We now bound H_1. Let $c \in (\frac{1}{2}, 1]$ and recall that p_i is the probability of moving from state S_i to state S_{i-1}. Then $1 \geq p_i > c > \frac{1}{2}$. Then the expression for H_1 given in Theorem 1 is bounded from above by the constant $1/(2c-1)$, so $T_{\text{sort}}(n) = O(n^2 \log n)$. Now let $c = \frac{1}{2}$, so $p_i \geq \frac{1}{2} + i/\binom{n}{2}$ by Theorem 9. Then, by Corollary 4, we have $H_1 = O(n)$, so $T_{\text{sort}}(n) = O(n^3 \log n)$. Finally, let $c \in (0, \frac{1}{2})$. Then $p_i > c > 0$, and by Theorem 1, H_1 is bounded from above by

$$H_1 \leq \frac{2c}{1-2c}\left(\frac{1-c}{c}\right)^n = O\left(\left(\frac{1-c}{c}\right)^n\right),$$

so $T_{\text{sort}}(n) = O\left(\left(\frac{1-c}{c}\right)^n \cdot n^2 \log n\right)$. □

Concerning OneMax, we again apply the fitness level method and use the return times from Section 3.

THEOREM 14. *The expected optimization time $T_{\text{OneMax}}(n)$ of the OnePSO solving OneMax is bounded from above by*

$$T_{\text{OneMax}}(n) = \begin{cases} O(n \log n) & \text{if } c \in (\frac{1}{2}, 1] \\ O(n^{\frac{3}{2}} \log n) & \text{if } c = \frac{1}{2} \\ O\left(\left(\frac{1-c}{c}\right)^n \cdot n \log n\right) & \text{if } c \in (0, \frac{1}{2}) \end{cases}.$$

PROOF. The argument is along the lines of the proof of Theorem 13. We observe that on fitness level $0 \leq i \leq n$ there are i bit flips that increase the number of ones in the current solution. Therefore, $s_i = i/n$ and the fitness level method yields an expected runtime of at most $\sum_{i=1}^{n}(H_1 + 1)(1/s_i - 1) + 1 = H_1 \cdot O(n \log n)$. The bounds on H_1 for $c \neq \frac{1}{2}$ are as in the proof of Theorem 13. For $c = \frac{1}{2}$ we invoke Corollary 4 and have $H_1 = O(\sqrt{n})$, which completes the proof. □

We remark that in the case $c = \frac{1}{2}$ it is not sufficient to use the lower bound $p_i \geq \frac{1}{2} + \frac{1}{n}$ in order to obtain the runtime bound given in Theorem 14.

5.3 Lower Bounds

We will show how the model from Section 3 can be used to prove good lower bounds on the expected optimization time of the ONEPSO algorithm in. For this purpose, we will restrict our attention to the *last* improvement of the attractor, which dominates the runtime, both for sorting and ONEMAX.

We first provide lower bounds on the expected return time to the attractor for $c \in (0, \frac{1}{2})$.

LEMMA 15. *Let* $c \in (0, \frac{1}{2})$. *For the sorting problem on* n *items, assume that the attractor has transposition distance one to the identity permutation. Then the expected return time* H_1 *to the attractor is bounded from below by* $H_1 = \Omega(\alpha(c)^n)$, *where*

$$\alpha(c) = \left(\frac{7 - 6c}{1 + 6c}\right)^{\frac{1}{2} \cdot \sqrt{\frac{1-2c}{2(1-c)}}} > 1 \ .$$

PROOF. Let $k = \frac{n}{2} \cdot \sqrt{\frac{1-2 \cdot c}{2-2 \cdot c}}$. The probability of decreasing the distance to the attractor in state $S_{\lfloor k \rfloor - 1}$ can be bounded above by $p = c + (1-c)\binom{\lfloor k \rfloor}{2}/\binom{n}{2}$ using Theorem 9. Furthermore, for $1 \leq i < \lfloor k \rfloor$ we bound

$$p_i \leq c + (1-c) \cdot \frac{\binom{\lfloor k \rfloor}{2}}{\binom{n}{2}} = c + (1-c) \cdot \frac{\lfloor k \rfloor \cdot (\lfloor k \rfloor - 1)}{n(n-1)}$$

$$\leq c + (1-c) \cdot \frac{k(k-1)}{n(n-1)} = c + \frac{1-2c}{8} \cdot \left(\frac{n - 2\sqrt{\frac{2-2c}{1-2\cdot c}}}{n-1}\right)$$

$$\leq \frac{3}{4} \cdot c + \frac{1}{8} \ .$$

We truncate the model to states $S_0, S_1, \ldots, S_{\lfloor k \rfloor}$ and set $p_i = \frac{3}{4} \cdot c + \frac{1}{8}$ for each $1 \leq i < \lfloor k \rfloor$, and set $p_{\lfloor k \rfloor} = 1$. This does not increase return time to the state S_1. We obtain a lower bound on the expected return time H_1 to S_1 in the truncated model by Theorem 1:

$$H_1 \geq \frac{1 - 2 \cdot (\frac{3}{4} \cdot c + \frac{1}{8}) \cdot \left(\frac{1 - (\frac{3}{4} \cdot c + \frac{1}{8})}{\frac{3}{4} \cdot c + \frac{1}{8}}\right)^{\lfloor k \rfloor}}{2 \cdot (\frac{3}{4} \cdot c + \frac{1}{8}) - 1}$$

$$= \frac{(\frac{3}{2} \cdot c + \frac{1}{4}) \cdot \left(\frac{7 - 6 \cdot c}{1 + 6 \cdot c}\right)^{\lfloor k \rfloor} - 1}{\frac{3}{4} - \frac{3}{2} \cdot c}$$

$$= \Omega\left(\left(\frac{7 - 6 \cdot c}{1 + 6 \cdot c}\right)^{\frac{1}{2} \cdot \sqrt{\frac{1-2 \cdot c}{2(1-c)}} \cdot n}\right) = \Omega(\alpha(c)^n)$$

and since $c < \frac{1}{2}$ we have that $\alpha(c) > 1$. $\square$

LEMMA 16. *Let* $c \in (0, \frac{1}{2})$. *For* ONEMAX, *assume that the attractor has Hamming distance one to the optimum* 1^n. *Then the expected return time* H_1 *to the attractor is bounded from below by* $H_1 = \Omega(\beta(c)^n)$, *where*

$$\beta(c) = \left(\frac{3 - 2 \cdot c}{1 + 2 \cdot c}\right)^{\frac{1-2 \cdot c}{4 \cdot (1-c)}} > 1 \ .$$

PROOF. Let $k = \frac{n}{4} \cdot \frac{1-2 \cdot c}{1-c}$. The probability of decreasing the distance to the attractor in state $S_{\lfloor k \rfloor - 1}$ is $p_{\lfloor k \rfloor - 1} =$

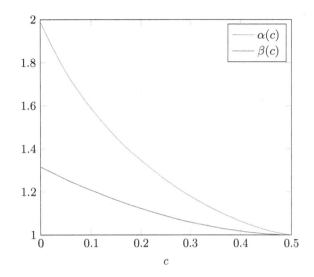

Figure 3: The functions $\alpha(c)$ and $\beta(c)$ for $c \in (0, \frac{1}{2})$

$c + (1-c) \cdot (\lfloor k \rfloor - 1)/n$. Furthermore, for $1 \leq i < \lfloor k \rfloor$ we bound $p_i \leq c + (1-c) \cdot k/n = \frac{c}{2} + \frac{1}{4}$. By truncating the model to states $S_0, S_1, \ldots, S_{\lfloor k \rfloor}$, setting $p_i = \frac{c}{2} + \frac{1}{4}$ for all $1 \leq i < \lfloor k \rfloor$, and setting $p_{\lfloor k \rfloor} = 1$, we obtain a lower bound on H_1 in the original model using Theorem 1:

$$H_1 \geq \frac{1 - 2 \cdot (\frac{c}{2} + \frac{1}{4}) \cdot \left(\frac{1 - (\frac{c}{2} + \frac{1}{4})}{\frac{c}{2} + \frac{1}{4}}\right)^{\lfloor k \rfloor}}{2 \cdot (\frac{c}{2} + \frac{1}{4}) - 1}$$

$$= \frac{(c + \frac{1}{2}) \cdot \left(\frac{3 - 2 \cdot c}{1 + 2 \cdot c}\right)^{\lfloor k \rfloor} - 1}{\frac{1}{2} - c}$$

$$= \Omega\left(\left(\frac{3 - 2 \cdot c}{1 + 2 \cdot c}\right)^{\frac{1-2 \cdot c}{4 \cdot (1-c)} \cdot n}\right) = \Omega(\beta(c)^n)$$

and since $c < \frac{1}{2}$ we have that $\beta(c) > 1$. $\square$

We now introduce a useful notion of *indistinguishability* of certain states of a Markov chain. We will later use this notion to prove lower bounds on the expected optimization time of ONEPSO for sorting and ONEMAX as follows: We show that the optimum is contained in a set $\overline{Y}$ of indistinguishable states. Therefore, in expectation, the states $\overline{Y}$ have to be visited $\Omega(|\overline{Y}|)$ times to hit the optimum with positive constant probability.

DEFINITION 17 (INDISTINGUISHABLE STATES). *Let* M *be a Markov process with a finite set of states* Y *and let* $\overline{Y} \subseteq Y$. *Furthermore, let* $(Z_i)_{i \geq 0}$ *be the sequence of visited states of* M *and let* $T = \min\{t > 0 \mid Z_t \in \overline{Y}\}$. *Then* $\overline{Y}$ *is called* indistinguishable *with respect to* M *if*

1. *the initial state* Z_0 *is uniformly distributed over* $\overline{Y}$, *i. e., for all* $y \in Y$:

$$\Pr[Z_0 = y] = \mathbb{1}_{y \in \overline{Y}}/|\overline{Y}| := \begin{cases} 1/|\overline{Y}| & \text{if } y \in \overline{Y} \\ 0 & \text{if } y \notin \overline{Y} \end{cases} \ .$$

2. *and the probabilities to reach states in* $\overline{Y}$ *from states in* $\overline{Y}$ *are symmetric, i. e., for all* $y_1, y_2 \in \overline{Y}$:

$$\Pr[Z_T = y_2 \mid Z_0 = y_1] = \Pr[Z_T = y_1 \mid Z_0 = y_2] \ .$$

Now we can prove a lower bound on the expected time for finding a specific state.

THEOREM 18. *Let M be a Markov process as in Definition 17 and let $\overline{Y}$ be indistinguishable with respect to M. Let $h(M)$ be a positive real value such that $\mathrm{E}[T] \geq h(M)$, then the expected time to reach a fixed $y \in \overline{Y}$ is bounded below by $h(M) \cdot \Omega(|\overline{Y}|)$.*

PROOF. Let T_i be the stopping time such that $\overline{Y}$ is visited the i-th time.

$$T_i = \min\{t \geq 0 \mid |\{k \mid 0 \leq k \leq t \wedge Z_k \in \overline{Y}\}| \geq i\} .$$

With statement 1 of Definition 17 Z_0 is uniformly distributed over $\overline{Y}$. Therefore $T_1 = 0$ and $T_2 = T$. Statement 2 of Definition 17 implies that $\Pr[Z_{T_i} = y] = \mathbb{1}_{y \in \overline{Y}}/|\overline{Y}|$ for all $i \geq 1$ by the following induction. The base case for $i = 1$ and $T_i = 0$ is ensured by the statement 1 of Definition 17. The induction hypothesis is $\Pr[Z_{T_{i-1}} = y] = \mathbb{1}_{y \in \overline{Y}}/|\overline{Y}|$. The inductive step is verified by the following series of equations.

$$\Pr[Z_{T_i} = y] = \sum_{y' \in \overline{Y}} \Pr[Z_{T_{i-1}} = y'] \cdot \Pr[Z_{T_i} = y \mid Z_{T_{i-1}} = y']$$

$$\stackrel{\text{ind. hyp.}}{=} \sum_{y' \in \overline{Y}} 1/|\overline{Y}| \cdot \Pr[Z_{T_i} = y \mid Z_{T_{i-1}} = y']$$

$$\stackrel{\text{Def.17 st.2}}{=} 1/|\overline{Y}| \cdot \sum_{y' \in \overline{Y}} \Pr[Z_{T_i} = y' \mid Z_{T_{i-1}} = y]$$

$$= 1/|\overline{Y}| .$$

It follows that for all $i > 0$ the difference $T_{i+1} - T_i$ of two consecutive stopping times has the same distribution as T and also

$$\mathrm{E}[T_{i+1} - T_i] = \mathrm{E}[T] \geq h(M) .$$

Now let $y \in \overline{Y}$ be fixed. The probability to reach y within the first $T_{\lfloor |\overline{Y}|/2 \rfloor}$ steps is bounded above by

$$1 - \sum_{i=1}^{\lfloor |\overline{Y}|/2 \rfloor} \Pr[Z_{T_i} = y] \geq 1/2$$

and therefore the expected time to reach the fixed $y \in \overline{Y}$ is bounded below by $\frac{1}{2} \cdot \mathrm{E}[T_{\lfloor |\overline{Y}|/2 \rfloor}] = \frac{1}{2} \cdot \sum_{i=2}^{\lfloor |\overline{Y}|/2 \rfloor} \mathrm{E}[T_i - T_{i-1}] \geq \frac{1}{2} \cdot \sum_{i=2}^{\lfloor |\overline{Y}|/2 \rfloor} h(M) = h(M) \cdot \Omega(|\overline{Y}|)$. $\square$

The following two theorems supply lower bounds on the expected optimization time of the ONEPSO optimizing the sorting problem and ONEMAX.

THEOREM 19. *The expected optimization time $T_{\mathrm{sort}}(n)$ of the ONEPSO sorting n items is bounded from below by*

$$T_{\mathrm{sort}}(n) = \begin{cases} \Omega(n^2) & \text{if } c \in (\frac{1}{2}, 1] \\ \Omega(n^{\frac{8}{3}}) & \text{if } c = \frac{1}{2} \\ \Omega\left(\alpha(c)^n \cdot n^2\right) & \text{if } c \in (0, \frac{1}{2}) . \end{cases}$$

PROOF. Consider the situation that the attractor has just been updated to a solution that has distance one to the optimum. Without loss of generality, we assume that the attractor is the identity permutation and the optimum is the transposition $(0\,1)$. The number of steps required for the next (hence final) improvement of the attractor is a lower

bound on the optimization time for the ONEPSO. We determine a lower bound on this number for various choices of c.

For all $c \in (0, 1]$ we apply Theorem 18. We use all permutations as set of states Y in the Markov process M. Let $\overline{Y} = X_1$ be the subset of states which are a single swap away from the attractor. Therefore the optimal solution is contained in $\overline{Y}$, but up to the point when the ONEPSO reaches the optimal solution it is indistinguishable from all other permutations in $\overline{Y}$. We will immediately prove that $\overline{Y}$ is actually indistinguishable with respect to M. Initially the particle is situated on the attractor and after a single step it is situated at a permutation in $\overline{Y}$, where each permutation has equal probability. We use the permutation after the first step as the initial state of the Markov process Z_0 and all other Z_i are the successive permutations. Therefore statement 1 of Definition 17 is fulfilled. Let $T = \min\{t > 0 \mid Z_t \in \overline{Y}\}$ the stopping time of Theorem 18. For each sequence of states $Z_0, \ldots, Z_T$ there is a one to one mapping to a sequence $\tilde{Z}_0 = Z_T, \tilde{Z}_1, \ldots, \tilde{Z}_{T-1}, \tilde{Z}_T = Z_0$ which has equal probability to appear. The sequence $\tilde{Z}_0, \ldots, \tilde{Z}_T$ is not the reversed sequence, because the forced steps would then lead to the wrong direction, but the sequence can be received by renaming the permutation indices. The renaming is possible because the permutations Z_0 and Z_T are both single swaps. As this one to one mapping exists also the statement 2 of Definition 17 is fulfilled. Finally we need a bound on the expectation of T. If we are in $X_1 = \overline{Y}$ we can either go to the attractor by a forced move or random move and return to X_1 in the next step or we can go to X_2 by a random move and return to X_1 in expectation after H_2 steps. $\mathrm{E}[T] = \left(c + (1-c)/\binom{n}{2}\right) \cdot 2 + (1-c) \cdot \left(1 - 1/\binom{n}{2}\right)(1 + H_2) = \Omega(H_2) =: h(M)$. Theorem 18 provides the lower bound $\Omega(|\overline{Y}| \cdot H_2)$ for the runtime to find the fixed permutation $(0, 1) \in \overline{Y}$ which is the optimal solution. From Equation 2 we get $H_2 = (p_1 \cdot H_1 - 1)/(1 - p_1) \geq (c \cdot H_1 - 1)/(1 - c)$. As $H_1 = \Omega(n^{2/3})$ for $c = \frac{1}{2}$ (see Theorem 5) and $H_1 = \Omega(\alpha(c)^n)$ for $c \in (0, \frac{1}{2})$ (see Lemma 15) also $H_2 = \Omega(H_1)$ for $c \in (0, \frac{1}{2}]$ which results in the lower bounds $T_{\mathrm{sort}}(n) = \Omega(|\overline{Y}| \cdot H_1) = \Omega(\binom{n}{2} \cdot n^{2/3}) = \Omega(n^{8/3})$ for $c = \frac{1}{2}$ and $T_{\mathrm{sort}}(n) = \Omega(|\overline{Y}| \cdot H_1) = \Omega(\binom{n}{2} \cdot \alpha(c)^n) = \Omega(n^2 \cdot \alpha(c)^n)$ for $c \in (0, \frac{1}{2})$. Trivially the return time to X_1 in M can be bounded by 2, which results in the lower bound $T_{\mathrm{sort}}(n) = \Omega(n^2)$ for the case $c \in (\frac{1}{2}, 1]$. $\square$

THEOREM 20. *The expected optimization time $T_{\mathrm{ONEMAX}}(n)$ of the ONEPSO for solving ONEMAX is bounded from below by*

$$T_{\mathrm{ONEMAX}}(n) = \begin{cases} \Omega(n \log n) & \text{if } c \in (\frac{1}{2}, 1] \\ \Omega(n^{\frac{3}{2}}) & \text{if } c = \frac{1}{2} \\ \Omega\left(\beta(c)^n \cdot n\right) & \text{if } c \in (0, \frac{1}{2}) . \end{cases}$$

PROOF. First, let $c \in (\frac{1}{2}, 1]$. Then, with probability at least $\frac{1}{2}$, the initial solution contains at least $k = \lfloor n/2 \rfloor = \Omega(n)$ zeros. Each zero is flipped to one with probability $1/n$ in a random move, and none of the k entries is set to one in a move towards the attractor. The expected time required to sample the k distinct bit flips is bounded from below by the expected time it takes to obtain all coupons in the following instance of the coupon collector's problem: There are k coupons and each coupon is drawn independently with probability $1/k$. The expected time to obtain all coupons is

$\Omega(k \log k)$ [11, Section 5.4.1]. It follows that the expected optimization time is $\Omega(n \log n)$ as claimed.

For $c \in (0, \frac{1}{2}]$ we use the same approach as in the proof of Theorem 19. Consider the situation that the attractor has just been updated to a solution that has distance one to the optimum. We use the set of all bit strings as set of states Y in the Markov process M. Let $\overline{Y} = X_1$ the subset of bit strings which is a single bit flip away from the attractor, hence $\overline{Y}$ contains the optimum. Z_i and T are instantiated as in the proof of Theorem 19. Therefore statement 1 of Definition 17 is fulfilled. Again for each sequence of states $Z_0, \ldots, Z_T$ we have a one to one mapping to a sequence $\tilde{Z}_0 = Z_T, \tilde{Z}_1, \ldots, \tilde{Z}_{T-1}, \tilde{Z}_T = Z_0$ which has equal probability to appear. This sequence is again received by renaming the indices plus some bit changes according to the shape of the attractor. Hence also statement 2 of Definition 17 is fulfilled. Hence $\overline{Y}$ is indistinguishable with respect to M. $E[T] = \Omega(H_2) =: h(M)$. Theorem 18 provides the lower bound $\Omega(|\overline{Y}| \cdot H_2)$ for the runtime to find the optimal solution. $H_2 \geq (c \cdot H_1 - 1)/(1 - c)$. As $H_1 = \Omega(n^{1/2})$ for $c = \frac{1}{2}$ (see Theorem 3) and $H_1 = \Omega(\beta(c)^n)$ for $c \in (0, \frac{1}{2})$ (see Lemma 16) also $H_2 = \Omega(H_1)$ for $c \in (0, \frac{1}{2}]$ which results in the lower bounds $T_{\text{OneMax}}(n) = \Omega(|\overline{Y}| \cdot H_1) = \Omega(n \cdot n^{1/2}) = \Omega(n^{3/2})$ for $c = \frac{1}{2}$ and $T_{\text{OneMax}}(n) = \Omega(|\overline{Y}| \cdot H_1) = \Omega(n \cdot \beta(c)^n) = \Omega(n \cdot \beta(c)^n)$ for $c \in (0, \frac{1}{2})$. $\square$

REMARK 21. *The bounds shown for $c = 0$ in Table 1 can also be derived from the indistinguishability property: In each case, let $\overline{Y} = Y$. It is readily verified that the initial state is uniformly distributed over $\overline{Y}$. Furthermore, any $\overline{Y}$-$\overline{Y}$-path can be reversed and has the same probability to occur. Therefore, condition 2 of Definition 17 is satisfied and the lower runtime bound follows from Theorem 18 by choosing $h(M) = 1$. The upper bound follows from a similar argument.*

6. CONCLUSION

We proposed a PSO algorithm for a broad class of discrete optimization problems. We further provided upper and lower bounds on its expected optimization time for the sorting problem and OneMax. Depending on the algorithm parameter c, which is the probability of moving towards the attractor, the expected optimization time may be polynomial ($c \geq 1/2$) or exponential ($c < 1/2$). The cornerstone of our analysis are Θ-bounds on the expected time it takes until the PSO returns to the attractor. We obtain these bounds by solving linear recurrence equations with constant and non-constant coefficients. We also establish a useful general property of indistinguishability (Definition 17) of a Markov process for obtaining lower bounds on the expected runtime of our proposed PSO.

There are several open problems for future work. First of all, it would be interesting to see if the upper and lower bounds on the expected optimization time for OneMax given in theorems 14 and 20 are valid for any linear function $f : \{0, 1\}^n \to \mathbb{R}, f(x_1, x_2, \ldots, x_n) = \sum_i w_i x_i$? Furthermore, we conjecture that the upper bounds on the sorting problem and $c \geq 1/2$ are tight, as well as the upper bound for OneMax and $c = 1/2$. Finally, it would be interesting to determine the return time to the state S_0 in a more general Markov model $\mathcal{M}((p_i)_{1 \leq i \leq n})$, where $p_i = 1/2 + z(i, n)$ such that $z(i, n) = \text{poly}(i)/\text{poly}(n)$ and $z(i, n)$ is non-decreasing for $1 \leq i \leq n$. This would generalize Theorems 3 and 5, and shed some light on the relation between $z(i, n)$ and the return time to state S_0. Here, we conjecture that for $z(i, n)$ as defined above the return time is in $\text{poly}(n)$.

7. REFERENCES

[1] M. Clerc. Discrete particle swarm optimization, illustrated by the Traveling Salesman Problem. In *New Optimization Techniques in Engineering*, chapter 8, pages 219–239. 2004.

[2] B. Doerr, F. Neumann, D. Sudholt, and C. Witt. On the runtime analysis of the 1-ANT ACO algorithm. In *Proc. 9th ACM Genetic and Evolutionary Computation Conference (GECCO)*, pages 33–40, 2007.

[3] S. Droste, T. Jansen, and I. Wegener. Dynamic parameter control in simple evolutionary algorithms. In *Proc. 6th Workshop on Foundations of Genetic Algorithms (FOGA)*, pages 275–294, 2001.

[4] S. Droste, T. Jansen, and I. Wegener. On the analysis of the (1+1) evolutionary algorithm. *Theoretical Computer Science*, 276(1):51–81, 2002.

[5] R. C. Eberhart and J. Kennedy. A new optimizer using particle swarm theory. In *Proc. 6th International Symposium on Micro Machine and Human Science*, pages 39–43, 1995.

[6] O. Giel and I. Wegener. Evolutionary algorithms and the maximum matching problem. In *Proc. 20th Symp. on Theoretical Aspects of Computer Science (STACS)*, pages 415–426, 2003.

[7] R. L. Graham, D. E. Knuth, and O. Patashnik. *Concrete Mathematics: A Foundation for Computer Science*. Addison-Wesley Longman, 2nd edition, 1994.

[8] M. Hoffmann, M. Mühlenthaler, S. Helwig, and R. Wanka. Discrete particle swarm optimization for TSP: Theoretical results and experimental evaluations. In *Proc. 2nd Int. Conf. on Adaptive and Intelligent Systems (ICAIS)*, pages 416–427, 2011.

[9] J. Kennedy and R. C. Eberhart. Particle swarm optimization. In *Proc. IEEE International Conference on Neural Networks*, volume 4, pages 1942–1948, 1995.

[10] J. Kennedy and R. C. Eberhart. A discrete binary version of the particle swarm algorithm. In *Proc. IEEE Int. Conf. on Systems, Man, and Cybernetics*, volume 5, pages 4104–4108, 1997.

[11] M. Mitzenmacher and E. Upfal. *Probability and Computing*. Cambridge University Press, 2005.

[12] F. Neumann and C. Witt. Runtime analysis of a simple ant colony optimization algorithm. *Algorithmica*, 54(2):243–255, 2007.

[13] J. E. Onwunalu and L. J. Durlofsky. Application of a particle swarm optimization algorithm for determining optimum well location and type. *Computational Geosciences*, 14:183–198, 2010.

[14] C. H. Papadimitriou. On selecting a satisfying truth assignment. In *Proc. 32nd IEEE Symp. on Foundations of Computer Science (FOCS)*, pages 163–169, 1991.

[15] M. Petkovšek. Hypergeometric solutions of linear recurrences with polynomial coefficients. *Journal of Symbolic Computation*, 14(2):243–264, 1992.

[16] K. Ramanathan, V. M. Periasamy, M. Pushpavanam, and U. Natarajan. Particle swarm optimisation of hardness in nickel diamond electro composites. *Archives of Computational Materials Science and Surface Engineering*, 1:232–236, 2009.

[17] J. Scharnow, K. Tinnefeld, and I. Wegener. The analysis of evolutionary algorithms on sorting and shortest paths problems. *Journal of Mathematical Modelling and Algorithms*, 3(4):349–366, 2004.

[18] B. I. Schmitt. Convergence analysis for particle swarm optimization. Doctoral thesis, University of Erlangen-Nuremberg, Germany, 2015.

[19] U. Schöning. A probabilistic algorithm for k-SAT and constraint satisfaction problems. In *Proc. 40th IEEE Symp. on Foundations of Computer Science (FOCS)*, pages 410–414, 1999.

[20] L. Schwab, M. Schmitt, and R. Wanka. Multimodal medical image registration using particle swarm optimization with influence of the data's initial orientation. In *Proc. 12th IEEE Conf. on Computational Intelligence in Bioinformatics and Computational Biology (CIBCB)*, pages 403–410, 2015.

[21] D. Sudholt and C. Witt. Runtime analysis of binary PSO. In *Proc. 10th ACM Genetic and Evolutionary Computation Conf. (GECCO)*, pages 135–142, 2008.

[22] D. Sudholt and C. Witt. Runtime analysis of a binary particle swarm optimizer. *Theoretical Computer Science*, 411(21):2084–2100, 2010.

[23] K. Veeramachaneni, L. Osadciw, and G. Kamath. Probabilistically driven particle swarms for optimization of multi valued discrete problems: Design and analysis. In *Proc. IEEE Swarm Intelligence Symposium (SIS)*, pages 141–149, 2007.

[24] M. P. Wachowiak, R. Smolíková, Y. Zheng, J. M. Zurada, and A. S. Elmaghraby. An approach to multimodal biomedical image registration utilizing particle swarm optimization. *IEEE Transactions on Evolutionary Computation*, 8:289–301, 2004.

[25] I. Wegener. *Evolutionary Optimization*, chapter Methods for the Analysis of Evolutionary Algorithms on Pseudo-Boolean Functions, pages 349–369. Springer US, Boston, MA, 2002.

[26] Q. Yang, J. Wu, Y. Li, W. Li, L. Wang, and Y. Yang. Using the particle swarm optimization algorithm to calibrate the parameters relating to the turbulent flux in the surface layer in the source region of the Yellow River. *Agricultural and Forest Meteorology*, 232:606–622, 2017.

Resampling vs Recombination:
a Statistical Run Time Estimation

Tobias Friedrich
Hasso Plattner Institute
University of Potsdam
Potsdam, Germany

Timo Kötzing
Hasso Plattner Institute
University of Potsdam
Potsdam, Germany

Francesco Quinzan
Hasso Plattner Institute
University of Potsdam
Potsdam, Germany

Andrew M. Sutton
Hasso Plattner Institute
University of Potsdam
Potsdam, Germany

ABSTRACT

Noise is pervasive in real-world optimization, but there is still little understanding of the interplay between the operators of randomized search heuristics and explicit noise-handling techniques, such as statistical resampling. In this paper, we report on several statistical models and theoretical results that help to clarify this reciprocal relationship for a collection of randomized search heuristics on noisy functions.

We consider the optimization of pseudo-Boolean functions under additive posterior Gaussian noise and explore the trade-off between noise reduction and the computational cost of resampling. We first perform experiments to find the optimal parameters at a given noise intensity for a mutation-only evolutionary algorithm, a genetic algorithm employing recombination, an estimation of distribution algorithm (EDA), and an ant colony optimization algorithm. We then observe how the optimal parameter depends on the noise intensity for the different algorithms. Finally, we locate the point where statistical resampling costs more than it is worth in terms of run time. We find that the EA requires the highest number of resamples to obtain the best speed-up, whereas crossover reduces both the run time and the number of resamples required. Most surprisingly, we find that EDA-like algorithms require no resampling, and can handle noise implicitly.

Keywords

Evolutionary Algorithm; Genetic Algorithm; Crossover; Estimation of Distribution Algorithm; Ant Colony Optimization; Robustness; Noise

FOGA '17, January 12 - 15, 2017, Copenhagen, Denmark

© 2017 Copyright held by the owner/author(s). Publication rights licensed to ACM.
ISBN 978-1-4503-4651-1/17/01...$15.00

DOI: http://dx.doi.org/10.1145/3040718.3040723

1. INTRODUCTION

In many practical optimization problems, the objective function has some kind of stochastic component that arises out of different factors, such as measurement error, simulation nonlinearities, the finite precision of Monte Carlo sampling, or other environmental effects. In these scenarios, the direct evaluation of the objective function is not very reliable, and optimization algorithms must employ some kind of noise-handling strategy.

The most common type of noise-handling technique is statistical resampling. In this scenario, an algorithm estimates the true value of a function at a specific point by repeatedly sampling the corresponding value, to increase the signal to noise ratio. This approach comes at a computational cost, as the extra function evaluations must count toward the total run time of the algorithm. The idea of statistical resampling to address noise in the context of genetic algorithms has been studied as far back as 1988. In a paper by Fitzpatrick and Grefenstette [9], it was argued that the implicit parallelism of a GA is a sufficient mechanism for handling noise. They found that the amount of explicit resampling can be reduced in a GA by increasing the population size.

In the context of Evolution Strategies (ES) Arnold and Beyer [3] also found that increased population sizes are preferable to resampling as long as mutation strength is optimally adapted. Goldberg et al. [12] studied the influence of GA population size in the presence of noisy functions, but also with more general sources of noise (such as noisy operators). Arnold and Beyer [4] also noticed that the same algorithm may react in different ways to different types of posterior noise distributions.

The issue of resampling as a noise-handling technique has been approached from many different perspectives over the last few decades. Aizawa and Wah [1] proposed a detailed adaptive strategy for modelling the underlying noise, in order to determine the appropriate number of samples to be drawn from each individual. Stagge [23] recognized that noise can be reduced by repeated sampling, even at the cost of a higher number of function evaluations. However, he argues that computational effort can be saved by focusing only on resampling for the *best* individuals in the population. Many other detailed sampling frameworks have been proposed, such as ones based on *selection races* from the machine learning community [15, 22].

Branke and Schmidt [5, 6] also recognised that resampling strategies produce a trade-off between noise reduction and computational effort. They consider a number of different sampling procedures that attempt to characterize the error probability during the selection step. They also raise the interesting point that sometimes noise can be *beneficial* to stochastic search algorithms (e.g., for promoting objective space exploration), and therefore attempting to eliminate noise completely may not always be the best strategy.

Akimoto et al. [2] explicitly study the run time effect of resampling on various noise models to derive the extra cost incurred by performing enough resampling to ensure the underlying optimization algorithm "sees" a noiseless function. For Gaussian noise, they show the existence of a resampling scheme such that any optimization algorithm that requires $r(\delta)$ function evaluations to optimize a noise-free function f with probability $1 - \delta$ requires $\mathcal{O}(r(\delta) \max\{1, \sigma^2 \log(r\delta)/\delta\})$ evaluations to optimize $f + \mathcal{N}(0, \sigma^2)$ with probability $(1-\delta)^2$ under their resampling scheme.

Recently, Friedrich et al. [10] proved that an Estimation of Distribution Algorithm (EDA) called the Compact Genetic Algorithm (cGA) can *scale gracefully* with noise: its runtime on a noisy OneMax function is bounded by a polynomial in the variance, regardless of noise intensity. The cGA does not explicitly keep a population in memory, but only an array of so-called *allele frequencies* that represent the product distribution of alleles in an implicit population (cf. Goldberg et al. [14]). Offspring are then generated by drawing from this product distribution, and this has the same effect as *gene pool recombination*: all members of the population participate in recombination (rather than, e.g., two) to produce an offspring. On the other hand, they also proved that a mutation-only evolutionary algorithm exhibits superpolynomial runtime due to its reliance on hill-climbing a gradient that becomes obscured in the presence of heavy noise.

The array of allele frequencies employed by the cGA is similar to the pheromone values stored by Ant Colony Optimization (ACO) algorithms. In the latter, the update rule is distinct, but we should still expect similar protection against noise, which has also been recently noted [11].

None of these cases employ resampling, but instead rely on the implicit mechanisms of the GA/EDA/ACO to somehow "filter" the noise. Prügel-Bennett, Rowe and Shapiro [20] proved that a generational evolutionary algorithm using uniform crossover finds the optimum in $\mathcal{O}(\sigma^2 \log^2(\sigma^2))$ fitness evaluations, on OneMax with additive Gaussian noise of standard deviation σ. This result is in line with various studies on the effectiveness of population-based heuristics to deal with noise (Hellwig [17]). Dang and Lehre observe that for some cumulative distributions, the 2-tournament EA gives positive result on OneMax and LeadingOnes with additive posterior noise (cf. Dang [7]). Similarly, Hellwig and Beyer experimentally show that a population size controlled ES performs well in noisy environments. On the other hand, it has been argued that for some instances constant resampling operators are not useful in dealing with additive posterior gaussian noise (cf. Qian [21]).

In the context of continuous optimization, Hansen et. al. developed a heuristic to adapt the resampling based on the noise level of the rank (cf. Hansen [13]). They argue that if there are many rank changes when reevaluating a point, than the number of resampling should be geometrically increased. This suggests that in some cases non-constant resampling is beneficial. A similar idea has been discussed more formally in the form of Bernstein-Races (cf. Heidrich-Meisner [16]). However, the trade-off between resampling, recombination, and implicit methods is still not clear.

In this paper we want to take a first look at the interplay between resampling and implicit noise-handling exhibited by genetic algorithms employing crossover and estimation of distribution algorithms. We perform extensive statistical analysis on the run time of two genetic algorithms and two EDAs, to determine their asymptotic behavior.

2. SETTING AND ALGORITHMS

2.1 The test function

All tests are carried out by performing a global optimum search of the following function:

$$\text{OneMax}\colon (x_1, \ldots, x_n) \longmapsto \sum_{i=1}^{n} x_i$$

with $x_i \in \{0, 1\}$ for all $i = 1, \ldots n$, and with objective space consisting of all pseudo-Boolean strings of fixed size n. We add posterior Gaussian noise in order to simulate an environment where errors of controlled standard deviation are produced. In other words, if we denote with σ the posterior noise standard deviation, the fitness function is

$$\text{OneMax} + \mathcal{N}(0, \sigma^2)$$

with $\mathcal{N}(0, \sigma^2)$ the centered Gaussian distribution. In some cases we simulate a resampling operator: we compute the fitness function r times, and take the average. Thus the test function in its generic form is:

$$\frac{1}{r} \sum_{j=1}^{r} \left(\text{OneMax} + \mathcal{N}(0, \sigma^2) \right)$$

$$= \text{OneMax} + \frac{1}{r} \sum_{j=1}^{r} \mathcal{N}(0, \sigma^2)$$

for a given $r > 0$. The OneMax function has the advantage of being symmetric, well-understood, and extensively studied. The goal of the hereby presented experiments is to statistically infer the asymptotic trend of some algorithms in view of a broader theoretical setting.

2.2 Algorithms

We consider four algorithms, namely $(\mu + 1)$-EA, $(\mu + 1)$-GA, cGA, and λ-MMASib. $(\mu + 1)$-EA and $(\mu + 1)$-GA are search heuristics inspired by the process of natural selection (cf. Algorithm 1 and Algorithm 2).

Typically, they require as input a *population* of strings of fixed length n. After an *offspring* is generated, a mutation factor is introduced, to ensure full objective space exploration. The fitness is then computed, and the less desirable result is discarded. The $(\mu + 1)$-EA and the $(\mu + 1)$-GA differ in how the offspring is generated. In the first case, the offspring is selected u.a.r. from the input population, while in the latter case a crossover operation is performed on two

---

Algorithm 1: $(\mu + 1)$-EA

1   $t \leftarrow 0$;
2   Choose a population $P_0 \subseteq \{0,1\}^n$ s.t. $|P_0| = \mu$ u.a.r;
3   **while** *convergence criterion not met* **do**
4   Select a parent $x \in P_t$ u.a.r;
5   Generate offspring y by flipping each bit of x w/p $\frac{1}{n}$;
6   Choose $z \in P_t \cup \{y\}$ s.t. $f(z) = \max_{x \in P_t} f(x)$;
7   Define population $P_{t+1} \leftarrow (P_t \cup \{y\}) \setminus \{z\}$;
8     $t \leftarrow t + 1$;

Algorithm 2: $(\mu + 1)$-GA

1   $t \leftarrow 0$;
2   Choose population $P_0 \subseteq \{0,1\}^n$ s.t. $|P_0| = \mu$ u.a.r;
3   **while** *convergence criterion not met* **do**
4   Select parents $x_1, x_2 \in P_t$ u.a.r;
5   Generate offspring y by recombining x_1 and x_2 u.a.r;
6   Choose $z \in P_t \cup \{y\}$ s.t. $f(z) = \max_{x \in P_t} f(x)$;
7   Define population $P_{t+1} \leftarrow (P_t \cup \{y\}) \setminus \{z\}$;
8     $t \leftarrow t + 1$;

Algorithm 3: cGA

1   $t \leftarrow 0$;
2   $p_{1,t} \leftarrow p_{2,t} \leftarrow \cdots \leftarrow p_{n,t} \leftarrow 0.5$;
3   **while** *convergence criterion not met* **do**
4   **for** $i = 1 \ldots n$ **do**
5       $x_i \leftarrow 1$ w/ prob. $p_{i,t}$, $x_i \leftarrow 0$ w/ prob. $1 - p_{i,t}$;
6       $y_i \leftarrow 1$ w/ prob. $p_{i,t}$, $y_i \leftarrow 0$ w/ prob. $1 - p_{i,t}$;
7   **if** $f(x_1, \ldots, x_n) < f(y_1, \ldots, y_n)$ **then**
8   Swap $(x_1, \ldots, x_n)$ with $(y_1, \ldots, y_n)$;
9   **for** $i = 1 \ldots n$ **do**
10   **if** $x_i > y_i$ **then**
11       $p_{i,t+1} \leftarrow \min\left(\max\left(p_{i,t} + \frac{1}{K}, \frac{1}{n}\right), 1 - \frac{1}{n}\right)$;
12   **else if** $x_i < y_i$ **then**
13       $p_{i,t+1} \leftarrow \min\left(\max\left(p_{i,t} - \frac{1}{K}, \frac{1}{n}\right), 1 - \frac{1}{n}\right)$;
14   **else**
15       $p_{i,t+1} \leftarrow p_{i,t}$;
16     $t \leftarrow t + 1$;

Algorithm 4: λ-MMASib

1   $t \leftarrow 0$;
2   $p_{1,t} \leftarrow p_{2,t} \leftarrow \cdots \leftarrow p_{n,t} \leftarrow 0.5$;
3   **while** *convergence criterion not met* **do**
4   **for** $i = 1 \ldots \lambda$ **do**
5   Generate x_i w/ prob. $p_t = (p_{1,t}, \ldots, p_{n,t})$
6   Choose $z \in \{x_1, \ldots, x_\lambda\}$ s.t. $f(z) = \min_i\{f(x_i)\}$;
7   **for** $i = 1 \ldots n$ **do**
8   **if** $z_i = 1$ **then**
9       $p_{i,t+1} \leftarrow \min\left(p_{t,i}(1 - \rho) + \rho, 1 - \frac{1}{n}\right)$;
10   **else**
11       $p_{i,t+1} \leftarrow \max\left(p_{t,i}(1 - \rho), \frac{1}{n}\right)$;
12     $t \leftarrow t + 1$;

---

u.a.r. chosen parents. We use uniform crossover, which consists of assembling a new element by choosing coefficients of one parent or the other with probability $p = 0.5$.

The cGA is a search heuristic similar to $(\mu + 1)$-EA and $(\mu + 1)$-GA. As shown in Algorithm 3, this process consists of sampling two *individuals* with given probability distribution, and swapping them according to the fitness evaluation. At each step, the distribution by which individuals are chosen is updated according to the fitness gain, and proportionally to a parameter K. The offspring generation procedure of the Compact Genetic Algorithm is equivalent to a concrete population with the same allele frequencies engaging in *gene pool recombination* introduced by Mühlenbein and Paaß [19]. In gene pool recombination, all members of the population participate as parents in uniform recombination. The correspondence between EDAs and models of sexually recombining populations has already been noted (cf. Mühlenbein and Paaß [18]).

The λ-MMASib is an ant colony optimization method (cf. Algorithm 4). Algorithms of this kind can be described in terms of λ ants exploring given *paths*, which correspond to pseudo-Boolean arrays of length n. The probability distribution by which ants choose one path over another is called *pheromone* vector, and it is updated at each step according to the fitness evaluation, and proportionally to a parameter ρ. Both cGA and λ-MMASib are an estimation of distribution algorithms (EDAs).

2.3   Statistical and experimental setting

For each set of experiments we look at the sample mean, sample standard deviation, and infer the trend toward asymptotic behaviour via model regression. All samples considered are of size $N \geq 10^2$; the exact size and relevant information is given in the description of each experiment. Statistical models with different properties are considered:

- polynomial models: $X \sim \alpha x^k + \beta$;
- rational models: $X \sim \frac{1}{\alpha x^k + \beta}$;
- square-root models: $X \sim \alpha \sqrt{x} + \beta$;
- square-root exponential models: $X \sim \alpha e^{\beta \sqrt{x}}$;
- any linear combination of the above;

In all cases, tests on the predictions made by the fitting models are performed. For a given experiment described by pairs $\{(x_i, y_i)\}_{i \in I}$, denote with $\bar{y}$ the sample mean, and let $\{f_i\}_{i \in I}$ be the predictions of a given model. Consider the quantities

$$SS_{res} := \sum_{i \in I} (y_i - f_i)^2$$

$$SS_{tot} := \sum_{i \in I} (f_i - \bar{y})^2$$

and consider the coefficient of determination

$$R^2 := 1 - \frac{SS_{res}}{SS_{tot}}$$

We assume that the model is valid if $R^2 > 0.95$. This choice is intuitively motivated by the fact that R^2 is the "percent of variance explained" by the model.

We perform a Student's t-Test on the each model, to determine whether it outperforms "random noise" as a predictor. We look at the corresponding p-value, and consider the

algorithm	parameter	description
cGA	K	distribution parameter
$(\mu + 1)$-EA	μ	population size
$(\mu + 1)$-GA	μ	population size
λ-MMASib	ρ	evaporation factor
λ-MMASib	λ	number of ants

Table 1: Parameters for the four algorithms.

model valid only for p-value < 0.05. We accept variables such that the probabilities $p_{|t|}$ of obtaining a corresponding value outside the confidence interval are $p_{|t|} < 10^{-5}$. Thus all variables have a very high level of significance.

All tests are carried out on MacBook Pro (13" Retina, Beginning 2015), with operating system Mac OS X Version 10.11.1, processor 2.7GHz dual-core Intel Core i5 (Turbo Boost up to 3.1GHz) with 3MB shared L3 cache, and memory 8GB of 1866MHz LPDDR3. All algorithms are implemented in C++ on Xcode Version 7.3.1 (7D1014), and implemented as OSX command line executables. The fitting was performed using least-square methods implemented by the 'lm' command of R 3.2.2 GUI 1.66 Mavericks build (6996). Code is available upon request.

Pseudo-random numbers are generated with the Mersenne Twister generator (64 bit) with a state size of 19937 bits, implemented with the 'std::mt19937_64' template instantiation in the <random> library of C++11. The engine has an internal state sequence of n integer elements, which is filled with a pseudo-random series generated on construction or by calling member function seed. The internal state sequence becomes the source for n elements: when the state is advanced, the engine alters the state sequence by twisting the current value. The random numbers thusly generated have a period equivalent to the Mersenne number $2^{(n-1)*w} - 1$.

3. EXPERIMENTAL RESULTS

3.1 Parameter tuning

Each algorithm depends on one or two parameters, as shown in Table 1. The goal of parameter tuning is to reduce the expected number of fitness evaluations until the optimum search point is found. We refer to the optimal configuration by which the expected number of fitness evaluations is minimal as the *sweet spot*.

For every algorithm, parameter tuning is performed by brute force. We go through a list of possible input parameters and count the number of fitness calls that the algorithm needs with a given parameter; we make 10^2 independent runs and take the arithmetic mean. Note that since we count fitness evaluations and not wall clock time, this tuning is independent of the underlying machine. To perform parameter calibration for λ-MMASib, pairs of optimal choices for ρ, λ are tested, thus taking into account a possible correlation between the two. We give exemplary plots for the case of $\sigma^2 = 10$ in this section. The problem size is always fixed at $n = 10^2$.

Figure 1 shows the dependence of the optimization time of the $(\mu+1)$-EA and $(\mu+1)$-GA on the parameter μ. Note that both axes use a logarithmic scale. We see that optimization is slow for very small population sizes μ, quickly improves to best performance, and then slowly worsens again. This

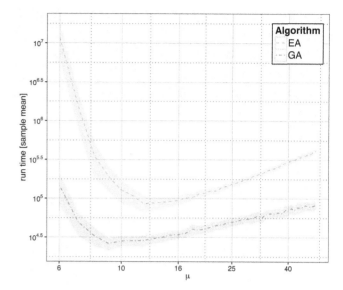

Figure 1: Number of fitness evaluations (run time) for a given parameter choice (μ) for the $(\mu + 1)$-EA and $(\mu + 1)$-GA. The problem size is fixed at $n = 10^2$. The run time is the average over 10^2 runs, and the shading is proportional to the sample standard deviation. Note that both axes follow a logarithmic scale. In both cases we see a unimodal trend. For the $(\mu + 1)$-EA we see a sweet spot for $\mu = 12$, and for the $(\mu + 1)$-GA the sweet spot is $\mu = 9$.

is in contrast to the well-known fact that, in the absence of noise, a choice of $\mu = 1$ is optimal for the $(\mu + 1)$-EA.

In Figure 2 we can see a similar trend for the cGA. In this case, however, we observe a slightly different behaviour. In fact, higher K gives better worst-case and worse average-case. This observation has been already framed theoretically (cf. Droste [8]). For the cGA without boundaries on the distribution adjustment, there is a non-zero probability that the algorithm converges in infinite time ($p(+\infty) > 0$). In our case, we put boundaries on the distribution adjustment (cf. Algorithm 3), and we expect $p(+\infty) = 0$. However, during some runs the algorithm still may take a very long time to reach the optimum.

The case of λ-MMASib is more involved, since we have to optimize two parameters in parallel. Again we approach this problem with brute force and display here only an interesting selection of parameters ρ. As we can see in Figure 3, an evaporation factor slightly below 0.05 with a number of ants of around 5 is optimal.

In all cases there exists a sweet spot for the choice of parameters, at which the algorithm performs best. The difference between the sweet spot and the optimal parameter with absence of noise depends on the algorithm's stability to fitness evaluation errors.

We run statistical analysis on the parameter tuning experiments for the $(\mu + 1)$-EA, and $(\mu + 1)$-GA, as described in Section 2.3. In both cases we find that the parameter tuning trend is best described in term of rational function, as displayed below.

OBSERVATION 1. *Let $\mathcal{A}(\mu)$ be one of $(\mu + 1)$-EA, $(\mu + 1)$-GA, with μ the μ-parameter. Let $\tau_{\mu,\sigma}$ the corresponding random variable that returns the number of fitness evaluations*

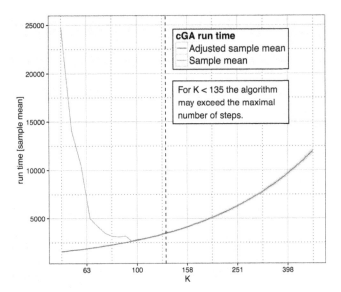

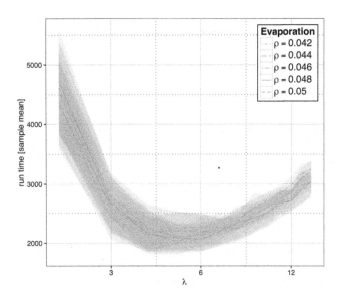

Figure 2: Number of fitness evaluations (run time) for the parameter K for the cGA. The problem size is fixed at $n = 10^2$. The run time is the average over 10^3 runs, and the shading is proportional to the sample standard deviation. We see a unimodal trend, and a sweet spot for $K = 135$. The adjusted sample mean does not consider the points at which the algorithm hits the maximal number of steps allowed, and returns a wrong result.

Figure 3: Number of fitness evaluations (run time) for a given pair of parameters (λ, ρ) for the λ-MMASib. The problem size is fixed at $n = 10^2$. Note that the λ-axis follows a logarithmic scale. The run time is the average over 10^2 runs, and the shading is proportional to the sample standard deviation. We see a unimodal trend, and a sweet spot for $\lambda = 5$ and $\rho = 0.046$.

until convergence, for a given posterior noise standard deviation σ. Consider the map:

$$f_\mathcal{A} : \mu \longmapsto \mathbb{E}[\tau_{\mu,\sigma}]$$

Then there exist $c_1, c_2, c_3 \in \mathbb{R}_{>0}$ s. t.

$$f_\mathcal{A} \sim c_1 - \frac{c_2}{\mu} + \frac{c_3}{\mu^2}$$

We perform nonlinear regression in the case of the cGA. We find that the most suitable model is

$$f_{\mathrm{cGA}} \sim c_2 K^{\frac{2}{3}} + \frac{c_3}{K^7} - c_1$$

for $c_1, c_2, c_3 \in \mathbb{R}_{>0}$. This model seems to be more unnatural than the corresponding one for $(\mu + 1)$-EA or $(\mu + 1)$-GA. This is probably due to the fact that the outcome of the cGA parameter tuning depends on the user-defined maximal number of steps allowed. Thus this model, which is statistically valid, may differ slightly from the underlying true equation. In the case of λ-MMASib we find that the model is

$$f_{\lambda\text{-MMASib}} \sim c_1 + c_2\lambda + c_3\rho + \frac{c_4}{\lambda^2} + \frac{c_5}{\rho^2}$$

with λ the number of ants, ρ the evaporation factor, and $c_1, c_2, c_3, c_4, c_5 \in \mathbb{R}_{>0}$ constants. Again, the model is statistically valid, and all parameters are chosen to be very significant. However, the experimental data for λ-MMASib are a bit more sparse than in the other cases, probably because the parameters are tuned concurrently. Therefore, for the cGA and λ-MMASib sweet spot experiments, we claim a weaker result:

OBSERVATION 2. *Let $\mathcal{A}(x)$ be one of cGA, λ-MMASib, with x a parameter. Let $\tau_{x,\sigma}$ be the corresponding random*

variable that returns the number of fitness evaluation until convergence, and consider the function

$$f_\mathcal{A} : x \longmapsto \mathbb{E}[\tau_{x,\sigma}]$$

Then there exists a parameter choice x_* such that $x_* = \min_{x < +\infty}\{f_\mathcal{A}(x)\}$. Moreover, $f_\mathcal{A}(y) \geq f_\mathcal{A}(y + \epsilon)$ for $y \leq x$ and $f_\mathcal{A}(y) \leq f_\mathcal{A}(y + \epsilon)$ for $y \geq x$, for all $\epsilon > 0$.

The next set of experiments focuses on finding the optimal parameters in dependence on the standard deviation σ of the noise. We exploit the unimodal shape of the dependence on the parameter, and perform a descent with a local search. The performance of this approach depends on finding a good starting value, preferably near the optimum. We increase σ slowly, and start the search where the optimum of the previous σ was found. Since a small change in the standard deviation results only in a small change of optimal parameter, this leads to faster search for the optimum.

The optimal parameters dependent on the noise are depicted in Figure 4 and 5. We can see a polynomial relation (roughly linear) for the $(\mu + 1)$-EA, $(\mu + 1)$-GA, and cGA. The λ-MMASib uses a decreasing evaporation rate while keeping the number of ants constant. In all cases we perform model regression:

OBSERVATION 3. *Let $\mathcal{A}(x)$ be one of the four tested algorithms, with x a parameter, and let $f_\mathcal{A}$ be as above. Consider the function*

$$\min_{x < +\infty}\{f_\mathcal{A}(x)\} : \sigma \longmapsto x_*$$

that returns the optimal parameter for a given posterior noise standard deviation. Then

$$\min_{x < +\infty}\{f_\mathcal{A}(x)\} \sim P(\sigma)$$

for a polynomial P.

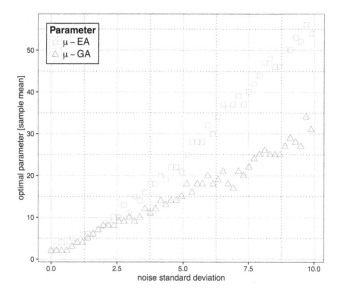

Figure 4: Optimal parameter choice for the $(\mu+1)$-EA and $(\mu+1)$-GA, for a given posterior noise standard deviation σ. The problem size is $n = 10^2$. In both cases, the optimal choice of the μ parameter increases polynomially with respect to the noise standard deviation. Each point is the sample mean of 10^2 runs. The run time for both algorithms with this parameters choice is presented in Figure 7.

3.2 Run time estimation

For each algorithm we approximate the run time function in dependence of the standard deviation and optimal parameter choice. This function returns the number of fitness evaluations to reach the optimum, with optimal parameters tuning, posterior error of fixed standard deviation, and no re-sampling. Let $\mathcal{A}$ be one of cGA, $(\mu+1)$-EA, $(\mu+1)$-GA, λ-MMASib. For a given algorithm and given standard deviation σ, we let

$$\sigma \longmapsto \mathbb{E}[\tau_\sigma]$$

be the expected run time of $\mathcal{A}$ with posterior noise standard deviation σ and optimal parameters choice as in Section 3.1. This set of experiments aims at giving an estimate of $\mathbb{E}[\tau_\sigma]$. The problem size is always fixed at $n = 10^2$, unless otherwise specified. Every observation is the arithmetic mean of 10^2 runs (see Figure 7).

The run time plot in Figure 7 shows that the $(\mu+1)$-EA quickly becomes inefficient, when increasing posterior noise standard deviation. In the case of the $(\mu+1)$-GA, results seem to be slightly better. However, we still can see that this algorithm significantly worsens with increasing posterior noise standard deviation. In the case of the λ-MMASib we see further improvement. The results in Figure 7 show that it reacts much better to increasing posterior noise standard deviation. Still, we observe a polynomial trend, with degree clearly greater than one (cf. Figure 7). We see a similar trend for the cGA.

As in the case of the parameter tuning experiments, we perform statistical regression:

OBSERVATION 4. *Let τ_σ be the runtime of $(\mu+1)$-EA or $(\mu+1)$-GA, for a given posterior noise standard deviation.*

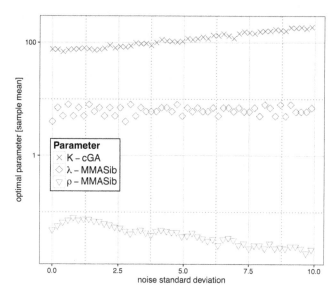

Figure 5: Optimal parameter choice for the cGA and λ-MMASib, for a given posterior noise standard deviation σ. The problem size is fixed at $n = 10^2$. Each point is the sample mean of 10^2 runs. Note that the optimal parameter axis is in logarithmic scale. The K and λ parameters linearly increase for increasing posterior noise standard deviation, while the ρ parameter linearly decreases. The run time for both algorithms with this parameters choice is presented in Figure 7.

Then

$$\mathbb{E}[\tau_\sigma] \sim c_1 e^{c_2\sqrt{\sigma}}$$

for $c_1, c_2 \in \mathbb{R}_{>0}$ constants.

These results confirm the generic fact that, without employing any additional operator, the $(\mu+1)$-EA and $(\mu+1)$-GA perform poorly with noise. According to our statistical models, however, the $(\mu+1)$-GA has coefficient c_2 lower than the $(\mu+1)$-EA, while c_1 is the same for both algorithms. Thus the difference of the runtime in expected value is again exponential. Therefore, it seems that the recombination operator employed by the $(\mu+1)$-GA helps in dealing with posterior noise.

The cGA and λ-MMASib are much more stable under an increase in the posterior noise standard deviation. This is clear when looking at the data (cf. Figure 7), and it can be formalised through statistical analysis:

OBSERVATION 5. *Let τ_σ be the run time for cGA or λ-MMASib, for a given posterior noise standard deviation σ. Then*

$$\mathbb{E}[\tau_\sigma] \sim c_1 \sigma^2 + c_2$$

for $c_1, c_2 \in \mathbb{R}_{>0}$ constants.

Recently, attempts have been made to perform a theoretical analysis of the run time of the hereby presented algorithms, solving OneMax with additive posterior gaussian noise. Particularly useful in this direction was the definition of graceful scaling (cf. Friedrich et al. [10]). Let F be a family of pseudo-Boolean functions $(F_n)_{n \in \mathbb{N}}$, with F_n a set of functions $f : \{0,1\}^n \longrightarrow \mathbb{R}$. Let D be a family of distributions $(D_v)_{v \in \mathbb{R}}$ such that for all $D_v \in D$, $\mathbb{E}[D_v] = 0$. We define F with additive posterior D-noise as the set $F[D] := \{f_n + D_v : f_n \in F_n, D_v \in D\}$.

DEFINITION 1. *An algorithm $\mathcal{A}$ scales gracefully with noise on $F[D]$ if there is a polynomial q such that, for all $g_{n,v} = f_n + D_v \in F[D]$, there exists a parameter setting x such that $\mathcal{A}(x)$ finds the optimum of f_n using at most $q(n, v)$ calls to $g_{n,v}$.*

Even though this definition does not give detailed information regarding the run time, we can safely assume that an algorithm that does not scale gracefully without noise shows experimental run time trend significantly worse than one that scales gracefully with noise. From this point of view, it seems that the $(\mu + 1)$-EA and $(\mu + 1)$-GA do not scale gracefully with noise, while both cGA and λ-MMASib do. In fact, partial theoretical results in this direction have been proven.

THEOREM 1 (THEOREM 11 IN FRIEDRICH ET AL. [10]). *Consider the cGA optimizing* OneMax *with additive posterior Gaussian noise of variance σ^2, and problem size n. If $K = \omega(\sigma^2 \sqrt{n} \log n)$, then the cGA finds the optimum after $\mathcal{O}(K\sigma^2\sqrt{n}\log Kn)$ steps, with probability $1 - o(1)$.*

This result is consistent with the model given in Observation 5. A similar, negative result holds for $(\mu + 1)$-EA. In this case, if we look at the μ parameter, it can be proven that it does not scale polynomially with respect to the problem size. Since our unit of measurement is the number of fitness evaluations, this implies that the $(\mu + 1)$-EA does not scale gracefully with noise.

THEOREM 2 (THEOREM 5 IN FRIEDRICH ET AL. [10]). *Let $\mu \geq 1$ and let D be a distribution on R. Let Y be the random variable describing the minimum over μ independent copies of D. Suppose*

$$Pr(Y > D + n) \geq \frac{1}{2(\mu + 1)}$$

Consider optimisation of OneMax *with reevaluated additive posterior noise from D by $(\mu + 1)$-EA. Then, for μ bounded from above by a polynomial, the optimum will not be evaluated after polynomially many iterations w.h.p.*

Again, this result validates the exponential trend given in Observation 4. Weather the $(\mu + 1)$-GA or the λ-MMASib scale gracefully with noise is still an open question. Based on Theorem 1 and Theorem 2, it has been argued that recombination helps dealing with additive posterior Gaussian noise. This generic idea is confirmed by our observations: the $(\mu + 1)$-GA, which employs recombination, performs better then the $(\mu + 1)$-EA. The fact, however, that they both perform significantly worse than the EDA counterparts, leads us to claim that there are other structural elements which come into play when dealing with posterior noise.

We conclude with a description of the run time trend for the cGA and λ-MMASib, for increasing problem size and posterior noise standard deviation fixed at $\sigma = \sqrt{10}$. The results are displayed in Figure 6. The experiments show that both algorithms have very similar run time. The cGA seems to perform slightly better then the λ-MMASib, probably due to the fact that it uses an implicit recombination operator,

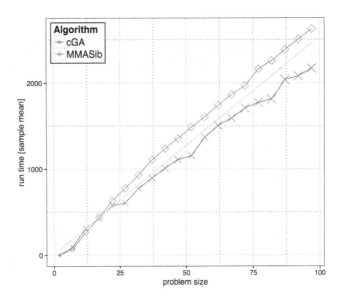

Figure 6: Number of fitness evaluations (run time) for a given problem size, taken to be the arithmetic mean of 10^2 runs, with optimally tuned parameters. Posterior noise standard deviation is fixed at $\sigma = \sqrt{10}$. The size of each point is proportional to the standard deviation. We see that the cGA performs slightly better then the λ-MMASib, even though they give very similar results. A linear approximation of the midpoint between the respective run time functions is highlighted in gray.

that may positively affect its performance in the presence of posterior gaussian noise. As in the other cases, we perform statistical analysis on the hereby presented data:

OBSERVATION 6. *The run time of the cGA, solving* OneMax $+ \mathcal{N}(0, \sigma^2)$, *for a fixed posterior noise standard deviation σ is $\tau_n = \mathcal{O}(n \log(n))$. Similarly, the run time of the λ-MMASib is $\tau_n = \mathcal{O}(n^2 \log(n))$. Moreover, the difference between the respective run times is at least linear for increasing n.*

Note that the run time of the cGA is consistent with the results presented in Theorem 1.

3.3 Resampling

We show that there exists a sweet spot for the resampling operator, as in the case of the parameter tuning experiments, for fixed problem size $n = 10^2$. This time, we do not need to compute directly the optimal setting for the resampling operator: there exists a clear relationship between the run time with and without resampling, which can be effectively described theoretically. In fact, the following equations hold:

$$\mathrm{Var}\left(\frac{1}{r}\sum_{k=1}^{r}\mathcal{N}(0,\sigma^2)\right) = \frac{1}{r^2}\mathrm{Var}\left(\mathcal{N}(0,r\sigma^2)\right) = \frac{\sigma^2}{r}$$

Let $\tau_{\sigma,r}$ be the random variable that returns the run time of an algorithm $\mathcal{A}$, for a given posterior noise standard deviation and number of resampling r. Due to the property of the noise variance mentioned above, we can approximate

$$\mathbb{E}[\tau_{\sigma,r}] = r\mathbb{E}\left[\tau_{\frac{\sigma}{\sqrt{r}}}\right] \qquad (1)$$

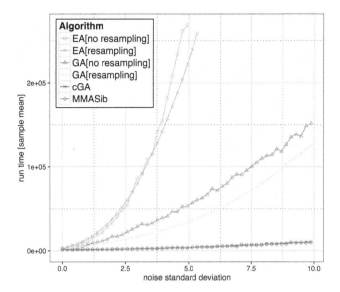

Figure 7: Number of fitness evaluations (run time) for the $(\mu+1)$-EA and $(\mu+1)$-GA with optimal resampling, and the cGA, $(\mu+1)$-EA, $(\mu+1)$-GA and λ-MMASib with no resampling, for a given posterior noise standard deviation. The problem size is fixed at $n = 10^2$. The $(\mu+1)$-EA and $(\mu+1)$-GA with optimal number of samples are derived from Equation 2, while in the other cases we performed direct experiments, with optimal parameter choice as in Figure 4 and Figure 5, and run time given by the arithmetic mean of a sample of 10^2 runs.

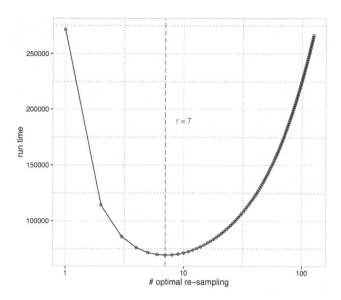

Figure 8: Number of fitness evaluations (run time) for a given number of samples. The problem size is fixed at $n = 10^2$. Posterior noise standard deviation is fixed at $\sigma = 5.0$, and optimal parameter choice is implicitly given in Equation 2. Note that the axis for the optimal number of samples is in logarithmic scale. We observe a unimodal trend, with sweet spot at $r = 7$. In Figure 9 we display the trend of the optimal r for a given posterior noise standard deviation.

from which we obtain the following result:

$$r_\sigma = \min_{1 \le r < +\infty} \left\{ r\mathbb{E}\left[\tau_{\frac{\sigma}{\sqrt{r}}}\right] \right\} \tag{2}$$

with r_σ the optimal amount of resampling for a given posterior noise standard deviation σ.

Using Equation 2, we can readily visualise the behaviour and trend of the optimal r_σ. We only consider the case of the $(\mu+1)$-EA: due to the fact that this algorithm performs poorly and the trend of r_σ is clearer than in other cases, even for low σ. Much like all of the other parameters, we see a unimodal trend and a sweet spot $r_\sigma < +\infty$. In Figure 9 we see the trend of the optimal number of samples for a given posterior noise standard deviation, and we can observe a linear increase in σ.

In Figure 7 we compare the run time trend of the $(\mu+1)$-EA, with the run time trend of $(\mu+1)$-GA, both given when the resampling operator is used and when it is not. The $(\mu+1)$-EA and $(\mu+1)$-GA with resampling are given by means of the regression model described in Observation 4. For both algorithms we observe improvement. However, for posterior noise standard deviation $\sigma \le 10$, it seems that the $(\mu+1)$-EA with resampling still performs worse than the $(\mu+1)$-GA without resampling.

Additional experiments show that the resampling sweet-spot for the cGA and λ-MMASib is $r_\sigma = 1$. In Figure 7, we compare the $(\mu+1)$-EA and $(\mu+1)$-GA with resampling, with the cGA, and λ-MMASib without resampling. We see that the cGA and λ-MMASib perform better then the $(\mu+1)$-EA and $(\mu+1)$-GA with resampling. This confirms the fact that the benefit of resampling is limited, and noticeable

only with algorithms that perform particularly bad under noisy environments. We can frame these ideas rigorously:

LEMMA 1. *Let $\tau_{\sigma,r}$ be the run time of an algorithm $\mathcal{A}$, for a given posterior noise standard deviation σ, and number of samples r. Define $\tau_\sigma = \tau_{\sigma,1}$ and let r_σ be the optimal number of samples. Suppose that*

$$\mathbb{E}[\tau_\sigma] \sim c_1 e^{c_2\sqrt{\sigma}}$$

for $c_1, c_2 \in \mathbb{R}_{>0}$. Then for σ sufficiently large, we have that

$$\mathbb{E}[\tau_{\sigma,r_\sigma}] \sim c_3 \left(\frac{16\sigma}{c_2^2}\right)^2$$

for a constant $c_3 \in \mathbb{R}$.

PROOF. We know from Equation 2 that

$$r_\sigma = \min_{1 \le r < +\infty} \left\{ r\mathbb{E}\left[\tau_{\frac{\sigma}{\sqrt{r}}}\right] \right\}$$

Thus we study the minima of $r\mathbb{E}\left[\tau_{\frac{\sigma}{\sqrt{r}}}\right]$. To do so, we consider the natural extension of this function over the non-negative real numbers, which is continuous and differentiable at each point. The derivative in r is

$$\frac{d}{dr}\left(r\mathbb{E}[\tau_{\frac{\sigma}{\sqrt{r}}}]\right) = \frac{e^{c_2\sqrt{\frac{\sigma}{\sqrt{r}}}+c_1}\left(4\sqrt{r}\sqrt{\frac{\sigma}{\sqrt{r}}} - c_2\sigma\right)}{4\sqrt{r}\sqrt{\frac{\sigma}{\sqrt{r}}}}$$

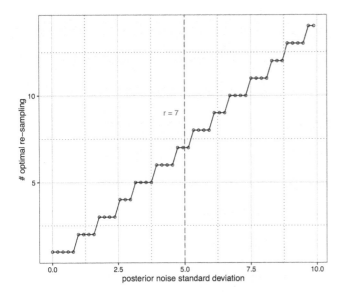

Figure 9: Optimal number of samples for a given posterior noise standard deviation. The optimal parameter choice is given implicitly in Equation 2. We observe a linear increase. For noise standard deviation $\sigma = 5.0$, we obtain the sweet spot displayed in Figure 8 ($r = 7$).

Therefore, all local optima of $r\mathbb{E}\left[\tau_{\frac{\sigma}{\sqrt{r}}}\right]$ in $(0, +\infty) \subseteq \mathbb{R}_{\geq 0}$ satisfy the equation

$$\frac{e^{c_2\sqrt{\frac{\sigma}{\sqrt{r}}}+c_1}\left(4\sqrt{r}\sqrt{\frac{\sigma}{\sqrt{r}}}-c_2\sigma\right)}{4\sqrt{r}\sqrt{\frac{\sigma}{\sqrt{r}}}} = 0$$

Standard calculations give us only one non-negative solution, namely $r_* = \frac{c_2^4\sigma^2}{4^4}$. Moreover,

$$\frac{d}{dr}\left(r\mathbb{E}[\tau_{\frac{\sigma}{\sqrt{r}}}]\right) < 0 \text{ for } 0 < r < r_*$$

$$\frac{d}{dr}\left(r\mathbb{E}[\tau_{\frac{\sigma}{\sqrt{r}}}]\right) > 0 \text{ for } r > r_*$$

Therefore, r_* is the absolute minimum of $r\mathbb{E}[\tau_{\frac{\sigma}{\sqrt{r}}}]$ for $r \in (0, +\infty)$. The sweet-spot for the resampling operator is given by the integer that best approximates this value, i.e.

$$r_\sigma \sim r_* = \frac{c_2^4\sigma^2}{4^4}$$

It follows that

$$\frac{\sigma}{\sqrt{r_\sigma}} \sim \left(\frac{4}{c_2}\right)^2$$

from which it follows that $\mathbb{E}\left[\tau_{\sigma, r_\sigma}\right] = c_3$, for $c_3 \in \mathbb{R}$ constant. Therefore, we obtain that

$$\mathbb{E}\left[\tau_{\sigma, r_\sigma}\right] = r_\sigma\mathbb{E}\left[\tau_{\frac{\sigma}{\sqrt{r_\sigma}}}\right] \sim c_3\left(\frac{16\sigma}{c_2^2}\right)^2$$

where we used the approximation given in Equation 1. $\square$

From Lemma 1 it follows that, if we consider valid the statistical models given in Observation 4 and Observation 5,

algorithm	run time no resampling	resampling sweet spot	run time w/ resampling
$(\mu+1)$-EA	$\mathcal{O}(e^{c\sqrt{\sigma}})$	$\mathcal{O}(\sigma^2)$	$\mathcal{O}(\sigma^2)$
$(\mu+1)$-GA	$\mathcal{O}(e^{c\sqrt{\sigma}})$	$\mathcal{O}(\sigma^2)$	$\mathcal{O}(\sigma^2)$
cGA	$\mathcal{O}(\sigma^2)$	$\mathcal{O}(1)$	$\mathcal{O}(\sigma^2)$
λ-MMASib	$\mathcal{O}(\sigma^2)$	$\mathcal{O}(1)$	$\mathcal{O}(\sigma^2)$

Table 2: Run time with and without resampling for the four algorithms, with respect to posterior noise standard deviation σ.

then the $(\mu+1)$-EA and $(\mu+1)$-GA with resampling have a run time $\mathcal{O}(\sigma^2)$. Therefore, for very large σ, $(\mu+1)$-EA and $(\mu+1)$-GA with resampling perform at least as well as cGA and λ-MMASib without resampling. It is, thus, interesting to understand weather with the latter algorithms we can further improve performance. In this sense, the following lemma holds:

LEMMA 2. *Let τ_σ, $\tau_{\sigma,r}$, and r_σ be as above. Suppose that*

$$\mathbb{E}[\tau_\sigma] \sim c_1\sigma^2 + c_2$$

for $c_1, c_2 \in \mathbb{R}_{>0}$ constants. Then the optimal configuration for the resampling operator is always $r_\sigma = 1$.

PROOF. The proof is very similar to the one given in Lemma 1: we study the minima of the function

$$r\mathbb{E}\left[\tau_{\frac{\sigma}{\sqrt{r}}}\right]$$

We observe, however, that this function is linear in r, and

$$\frac{d}{dr}\left(r\left(c_1\left(\frac{\sigma}{\sqrt{r}}\right)^2 + c_2\right)\right) = c_2$$

for a constant $c_2 > 0$. Therefore, the function $r\mathbb{E}\left[\tau_{\frac{\sigma}{\sqrt{r}}}\right]$ is strongly monotonic non-decreasing and

$$r_\sigma = \min_{1 \leq r < +\infty}\left\{r\mathbb{E}\left[\tau_{\frac{\sigma}{\sqrt{r}}}\right]\right\} = 1$$

$\square$

Combining this result together with Theorem 1 we obtain the following

COROLLARY 1. *The resampling operator is redundant for the cGA optimizing OneMax with additive posterior gaussian noise $\mathcal{N}(0, \sigma^2)$. In particular, the cGA reaches the optimum in $\mathcal{O}(\sigma^2)$ fitness evaluations.*

If we assume that the models presented in Observation 5 are correct, then we conclude that the resampling operator is redundant for λ-MMASib as well, regardless of the posterior noise standard deviation. Therefore, when optimizing OneMax with additive posterior gaussian noise $\mathcal{N}(0, \sigma^2)$, we cannot hope to achieve a run time with order of complexity smaller than $\mathcal{O}(\sigma^2)$, for any of the hereby tested algorithms (cf. Table 2). These results are not in contrast with the experiments displayed in Figure 7. In fact, the resampling operator gives a faster run time for $(\mu+1)$-GA and $(\mu+1)$-EA, but its effect is noticeable only for very large posterior noise standard deviation σ. In the case of $\sigma \leq 10$, the benefit of recombination overwhelms the effect of the resampling operator. Nevertheless, for very large σ, we expect the $(\mu + 1)$-EA with resampling to give better performance then the $(\mu + 1)$-GA without resampling.

4. CONCLUSIONS

We compare empirically the run time behavior of four different bio-inspired search heuristics: $(\mu+1)$-EA, $(\mu+1)$-GA, cGA, and λ-MMASib. Our testbed is the fitness function OneMax + $\mathcal{N}(0,\sigma^2)$, which is a simple unimodal function with posterior noise. All algorithms have local parameters (cf. Table 1), which influence their run time (cf. Figures 1–2). We study the dependence of the parameter on the amount of noise σ and empirically determine for each algorithm the optimal parameter setting depending on σ (cf. Figures 4–5). We give statistical predictions for each parameter's asymptotic behavior.

We are then able to compare the algorithms with optimal parameter settings depending on the level of noise. We observe a strict hierarchy in how well the algorithms can deal with noise (cf. Figure 7). From worst to best this is $(\mu+1)$-EA, $(\mu+1)$-GA, λ-MMASib, and cGA. We show statistically that the $(\mu + 1)$-EA and $(\mu + 1)$-GA have run time trend of $\mathcal{O}(e^{c\sqrt{\sigma}})$, and that the λ-MMASib and cGA have run time trend of $\mathcal{O}(\sigma^2)$. We observe that cGA and λ-MMASib have very similar run time, depending on the problem size.

A common technique to deal with noisy fitness functions is resampling. We therefore also study the optimal number of samples for a given noise level (cf. Figures 8–9). With optimal resampling we observe improved run times for the $(\mu + 1)$-EA and $(\mu + 1)$-GA, which scaled least graceful with noise. However, with optimal resampling both of them have run time $\mathcal{O}(\sigma^2)$. We prove that resampling is redundant for any algorithm with run time $\mathcal{O}(\sigma^2)$, thus showing that cGA and λ-MMASib do not benefit from this operator (cf. Lemma 1-2). Therefore, all four algorithms reach run time complexity of $\mathcal{O}(\sigma^2)$ at most (cf. Table 2).

Overall, this study shows that resampling is more beneficial than crossover, for algorithms that perform poorly in noisy environments. By far the best scaling behaviour was achieved with EDAs, suggesting that such algorithms can handle noise implicitly. We plan to validate all hereby presented statistical models analytically in the future.

Acknowledgements

The research leading to these results has received funding from the European Union Seventh Framework Programme (FP7/2007-2013) under grant agreement no. 618091 (SAGE) and from the German Science Foundation (DFG) under grant agreement FR 2988 (TOSU).

References

[1] A. Aizawa and B. W. Wah. Scheduling of genetic algorithms in a noisy environment. *Evolutionary Computation*, 2(2):97–122, 1994.

[2] Y. Akimoto, S. Astete-Morales, and O. Teytaud. Analysis of runtime of optimization algorithms for noisy functions over discrete codomains. *Theoretical Computer Science*, 605:42–50, 2015.

[3] D. Arnold and H. G. Beyer. Efficiency and mutation strength adaptation of the (μ, μ_I, λ)-ES in a noisy environment. In *Proc. of PPSN '00*, pages 39–48, 2000.

[4] V. D. Arnold and G. H. Beyer. A general noise model and its effects on evolution strategy performance. *IEEE Trans. Evolutionary Computation*, 10(4):380–391, 2006.

[5] J. Branke and C. Schmidt. Selection in the presence of noise. In *Proc. of GECCO '03*, pages 766–777, 2003.

[6] J. Branke and C. Schmidt. Sequential sampling in noisy environments. In *Proc. of PPSN '04*, pages 202–211, 2004.

[7] D.-C. Dang and P. K. Lehre. Efficient optimisation of noisy fitness functions with population-based evolutionary algorithms. In *Proc. of FOGA '15*, pages 62–68, 2015.

[8] S. Droste. A rigorous analysis for the compact genetic algorithm for linear functions. *Natural Computing*, 5(4):257–283, 2006.

[9] M. J. Fitzpatrick and J. J. Grefenstette. Genetic algorithms in noisy environments. *Machine Learning*, 3(2):101–120, 1988.

[10] T. Friedrich, T. Kötzing, M. S. Krejca, and A. M. Sutton. The benefit of recombination in noisy evolutionary search. In *Proc. of ISAAC '15*, pages 140–150, 2015.

[11] T. Friedrich, T. Kötzing, M. S. Krejca, and A. M. Sutton. Robustness of ant colony optimization to noise. In *Proc. of GECCO '15*, pages 17–24, 2015.

[12] D. E. Goldberg, K. Deb, and J. H. Clark. Genetic algorithms, noise, and the sizing of populations. *Complex Systems*, 6:333–362, 1992.

[13] N. Hansen, A. S. P. Niederberger, L. Guzzella, and P. Koumoutsakos. A method for handling uncertainty in evolutionary optimization with an application to feedback control of combustion. *IEEE Trans. Evolutionary Computation*, pages 180–197, 2009.

[14] G. R. Harik, F. G. Lobo, and D. E. Goldberg. The compact genetic algorithm. pages 523–528, 1998.

[15] V. Heidrich-Meisner and C. Igel. Hoeffding and bernstein races for selecting policies in evolutionary direct policy search. In *Proc. of ICML '09*, pages 401–408, 2009.

[16] V. Heidrich-Meisner and C. Igel. Hoeffding and bernstein races for selecting policies in evolutionary direct policy search. In *Proc. of ICML '09*, pages 401–408, 2009.

[17] M. Hellwig and H.-G. Beyer. Evolution under strong noise: A self-adaptive evolution strategy can reach the lower performance bound - the pccmsa-es. In *Proc. of PPSN '16*, pages 26–36, 2016.

[18] H. Mühlenbein and G. Paaß. From recombination of genes to the estimation of distributions I. Binary parameters. In *Proc. of PPSN '96*, pages 178–187. Springer-Verlag, 1996.

[19] H. Mühlenbein and H. Voigt. Gene pool recombination in genetic algorithms. In *Meta-Heuristics*, pages 53–62. Springer US, 1996.

[20] A. Prügel-Bennett, J. Rowe, and J. Shapiro. Run-time analysis of population-based evolutionary algorithm in noisy environments. In *Proc. of FOGA '15*, pages 69–75. ACM, 2015.

[21] C. Qian, Y. Yu, Y. Jin, and Z.-H. Zhou. On the effectiveness of sampling for evolutionary optimization in noisy environments. In *Proc. of PPSN '14*, pages 302–311, 2014.

[22] P. Rolet and O. Teytaud. Bandit-based estimation of distribution algorithms for noisy optimization: Rigorous runtime analysis. In *Proc. of LION '10*, pages 97–110, 2010.

[23] P. Stagge. Averaging efficiently in the presence of noise. In *Proc. of PPSN '98*, pages 188–200, 1998.

On the Use of the Dual Formulation for Minimum Weighted Vertex Cover in Evolutionary Algorithms

Mojgan Pourhassan
Optimisation and Logistics
School of Computer Science
The University of Adelaide
Adelaide, Australia

Tobias Friedrich
Algorithm Engineering
Hasso Plattner Institute
Potsdam, Germany

Frank Neumann
Optimisation and Logistics
School of Computer Science
The University of Adelaide
Adelaide, Australia

ABSTRACT

We consider the weighted minimum vertex cover problem and investigate how its dual formulation can be exploited to design evolutionary algorithms that provably obtain a 2-approximation. Investigating multi-valued representations, we show that variants of randomized local search and the (1+1) EA achieve this goal in expected pseudo-polynomial time. In order to speed up the process, we consider the use of step size adaptation in both algorithms and show that RLS obtains a 2-approximation in expected polynomial time while the (1+1) EA still encounters a pseudo-polynomial lower bound.

1. INTRODUCTION

The theoretical understanding of bio-inspired computing techniques lags far behind their practical success. These algorithms are very popular with practitioners from various domains such as engineering and economics. Having a good understanding of the working principles of evolutionary algorithms and other bio-inspired algorithms helps to increase the trust in these methods and leads to the design of new high performing algorithms. The area of runtime analysis of bio-inspired computing algorithms has contributed significantly to the theoretical understanding of these methods [2, 22, 27].

One of the most prominent NP-hard combinatorial optimization problems that has been studied in this context is the minimum vertex cover problem. Node-based approaches have been studied for this problem in the single-objective and multi-objective setting [18, 25]. Friedrich et al. [18] have shown that in expected polynomial time, the single-objective (1+1) EA cannot achieve a better than trivial approximation ratio. Further investigations regarding the approximation behaviour of evolutionary algorithms for the vertex cover problem have been carried out in [17, 30]. Furthermore, edge-based encodings have been investigated in [23], where an evolutionary algorithm finds a maximal matching from which a 2-approximation vertex cover can be induced.

Inspired by their approach, we investigate a different way of approximating the minimum vertex cover problem by evolutionary algorithms. While Jansen et al. [23] considered the classical vertex

FOGA '17, January 12 - 15, 2017, Copenhagen, Denmark

© 2017 Copyright held by the owner/author(s). Publication rights licensed to ACM.
ISBN 978-1-4503-4651-1/17/01...\$15.00

DOI: http://dx.doi.org/10.1145/3040718.3040726

cover problem, we analyse the weighted version of the problem. We study an edge-based encoding together with a multi-valued representation that works on the dual of the minimum vertex cover formulation. Our investigations can be seen as a generalization of the approach based on matchings investigated by Jansen et al. [23], although no direct connection to the use of dual formulations was made in that paper. We are only aware of four previous theoretical works with multi-valued representations. Doerr et al. [11, 13] regard the optimization of multi-valued linear functions via a variant of the (1+1) EA. More recently, static and dynamically changing variants of multi-valued OneMax functions have been considered [9, 24].

We analyze edge-based approaches generalizing the edge-based encoding in conjunction with a fitness function obtaining maximal matchings investigated in [23]. Our edge-based approaches consider the dual formulation of the weighted vertex cover problem. Working with the dual formulation an encoding assigns a weight to each edge. During the evolutionary process the weight of the edges may be increased or decreased and vertices whose constraints become tight are selected as vertices for the cover. We first study the situation where each weight can only increase or decrease by 1 at each step and present pseudo-polynomial upper bounds on the expected time until our approaches have obtained a 2-approximation for the minimum vertex cover problem.

In order to deal with potentially large weights of the given graph, we incorporate *step size adaptation* into our algorithms. Step size adaptation is a popular mechanism to steer the progress of an evolutionary algorithm to the right level. Step size adaptation is a form of *parameter control* [15], where a parameter is changed during the execution of the algorithm. Adaptive parameters are very essential in continuous search spaces [4] and popularly used for covariance-matrix adaptation [19]. There are only few theoretical studies on adaptive parameters in discrete spaces. Known results are that changing the mutation rate [5, 7] and the population size [8] can reduce the asymptotic runtime. Moreover, dynamically choosing the number of parallel instances in parallel evolutionary algorithms is studied in [26], and self-adjusting of the number of bits to be flipped instead of a standard bit mutation is shown to improve the performance of the optimization process [10].

In this paper, defining $c_1 > 1$ and $c_2 > 1$ as two constants, we show that the use of step size adaptation where the step size is multiplied by c_1 in the case of a success and multiplied by $1/c_2$ in case of failure, leads to a polynomial upper bound on the expected runtime of the RLS algorithm to achieve a 2-approximation. Furthermore, we present a pseudo-polynomial lower bound for the (1+1) EA using this step size adaptation. The proof uses the insight that the considered (1+1) EA is not able to achieve a sufficiently

Algorithm 1: RLS

1 Initialize $s := 0^m$ and $\sigma := 1^m$;
2 **while** *termination condition not satisfied* **do**
3 $\quad$ $s' := s$;
4 $\quad$ Choose $i \in \{1, \cdots, m\}$ uniformly at random;
5 $\quad$ Choose $b \in \{0, 1\}$ uniformly at random;
6 $\quad$ **if** $b = 0$ **then**
7 $\quad\quad$ $s'_i := s'_i + \sigma_i$;
8 $\quad$ **else**
9 $\quad\quad$ $s'_i := \max(s'_i - \sigma_i, 0)$;
10 $\quad$ **if** $\sum_{i=1}^m s_i < \sum_{i=1}^m s'_i$ *and*
$\quad\quad$ $\sum_{j \in \{1,\cdots,m\} | e_j \cap \{v\} \neq \emptyset} s'_j \leq w(v), \ \forall v \in V$ **then**
11 $\quad\quad$ $s := s'$;
12 **return** $C := \{v \in V \mid w(v) = \sum_{j \in \{1,\cdots,m\} \mid e_j \cap \{v\} \neq \emptyset} s_j\}$;

Algorithm 2: (1+1) EA

1 Initialize $s := 0^m$ and $\sigma := 1^m$;
2 **while** *termination condition not satisfied* **do**
3 $\quad$ $s' := s$;
4 $\quad$ **for** $i := 1$ **to** m **do**
5 $\quad\quad$ **with probability** $1/m$ **do**
6 $\quad\quad\quad$ Choose $b \in \{0, 1\}$ uniformly at random;
7 $\quad\quad\quad$ **if** $b = 0$ **then**
8 $\quad\quad\quad\quad$ $s'_i := s'_i + \sigma_i$;
9 $\quad\quad\quad$ **else**
10 $\quad\quad\quad\quad$ $s'_i := \max(s'_i - \sigma_i, 0)$;
11 $\quad$ **if** $\sum_{i=1}^m s_i < \sum_{i=1}^m s'_i$ *and*
$\quad\quad$ $\sum_{j \in \{1,\cdots,m\} | e_j \cap \{v\} \neq \emptyset} s'_j \leq w(v), \ \forall v \in V$ **then**
12 $\quad\quad$ $s := s'$;
13 **return** $C := \{v \in V \mid w(v) = \sum_{j \in \{1,\cdots,m\} \mid e_j \cap \{v\} \neq \emptyset} s_j\}$;

large step size during the optimization process in order to reach a 2-approximation.

This paper is structured as follows. In Section 2, we present our edge-based approach based on a dual formulation for solving the minimum vertex cover problem. We analyze RLS and (1+1) EA with a step size of 1 in Section 3. Afterwards, we show a polynomial upper bound for RLS with Step Size Adaptation in Section 4 and a pseudopolynomial lower bound for (1+1) EA with Step Size Adaptation in Section 5. Finally, we finish with some concluding remarks.

2. PRELIMINARIES

The weighted vertex cover problem is defined as follows. Given a graph $G = (V, E)$ with vertex set $V = \{v_1, \ldots, v_n\}$ and edge set $E = \{e_1, \ldots, e_m\}$, and a positive weight function $w \colon V \to \mathbb{N}^+$ on the vertices, the goal is to find a subset of nodes, $V_C \subseteq V$, that covers all edges and has minimum weight, i.e. $\forall e \in E, e \cap V_C \neq \emptyset$ and $\sum_{v \in V_C} w(v)$ is minimized.

Consider the standard node-based representation, in which a solution $x = (x_1, \ldots, x_n)$ is a bitstring of size n, where $x_i = 1$ iff the node v_i is chosen. With this representation, the Integer Linear Programming (ILP) formulation for this problem is:

$$\min \sum_{i=1}^n w(v_i) \cdot x_i$$
$$s.t. \quad x_i + x_j \geq 1 \quad \forall (i, j) \in E$$
$$x_i \in \{0, 1\} \quad \forall i \in \{1, \cdots, n\}$$

In the linear programming relaxation of the problem, the Fractional Weighted Vertex Cover Problem, the constraint $x \in \{0, 1\}$ is relaxed to $x \in [0, 1]$. We denote the cost of the optimal solution for the original problem and the relaxed version of the problem by OPT and OPT^* respectively. Observe that $OPT^* \leq OPT$.

Any LP problem (which we refer to as the primal problem) has a dual form, which is also an LP problem. When the primal problem is a minimization problem, the dual problem helps with finding lower bounds of the optimal solution of the primal problem (or upper bounds in case the primal form is a maximization problem). Consider the following standard LP problem in which the goal is to minimize the objective function.

$$\min \sum_{i=1}^n c_i x_i$$
$$s.t. \quad \sum_{i=1}^n a_{ji} x_i \geq b_j \quad j = 1, \cdots, m$$
$$x_i \geq 0, \quad i = 1, \cdots, n$$

where c_i, a_{ji} and b_j are given rational numbers. The dual form of the above LP problem can be formulated as the following, where y_i is a variable for the ith inequality. For more explanations on primal and dual forms of an LP problem, and how to derive the dual form from the primal form refer to [31].

$$\max \sum_{j=1}^m b_j y_j$$
$$s.t. \quad \sum_{j=1}^m a_{ji} y_j \leq c_i \quad i = 1, \cdots, n$$
$$y_j \geq 0, \quad j = 1, \cdots, m$$

Considering these formulations, the Weak Duality Theorem described below, helps in finding lower bounds of any feasible solution of the primal problem. The reader can find the proof of this theorem in [31].

Theorem 1 (The Weak Duality Theorem). *If $x = (x_1, \cdots, x_n)$ and $y = (y_1, \cdots, y_m)$ are feasible solutions for the primal and dual problem respectively, then*

$$\sum_{i=1}^n c_i x_i \geq \sum_{j=1}^m b_j y_j.$$

Using the concept of duality and the Weak Duality Theorem, 2-approximations of the vertex cover problem can be obtained. The dual of the relaxed covering problem is a packing problem formulated as the following, where $s_j \in \mathbb{N}^+$ denotes a weight on the edge e_j:

$$\max \sum_{j=1}^m s_j$$
$$s.t. \quad \sum_{j \in \{1,\cdots,m\} | e_j \cap \{v\} \neq \emptyset} s_j \leq w(v) \quad \forall v \in V$$

Algorithm 3: RLS with Step Size Adaptation

1 Initialize $s := 0^m$ and $\sigma := 1^m$;
2 **while** *termination condition not satisfied* **do**
3     $s' := s$;
4     $I := \emptyset$;
5   Choose $i \in \{1, \cdots, m\}$ uniformly at random;
6   Choose $b \in \{0, 1\}$ uniformly at random;
7   **if** $b = 0$ **then**
8        $s'_i := s'_i + \sigma_i$;
9   **else**
10       $s'_i := \max(s'_i - \sigma_i, 0)$;
11    $I := I \cup \{i\}$;
12   **if** $\sum_{i=1}^{m} s_i < \sum_{i=1}^{m} s'_i$ and
      $\sum_{j \in \{1, \cdots, m\} | e_j \cap \{v\} \neq \emptyset} s'_j \leq w(v),\ \forall v \in V$ **then**
13       $s := s'$;
14       $\sigma_i := c_1 \cdot \sigma_i,\ \forall i \in I$;
15   **else**
16       $\sigma_i := \max\left(\frac{\sigma_i}{c_2}, 1\right),\ \forall i \in I$;
17 **return** $C := \{v \in V \mid w(v) = \sum_{j \in \{1, \cdots, m\} \mid e_j \cap \{v\} \neq \emptyset} s_j\}$;

Algorithm 4: (1+1) EA with Step Size Adaptation

1 Initialize $s := 0^m$ and $\sigma := 1^m$;
2 **while** *termination condition not satisfied* **do**
3     $s' := s$;
4     $I := \emptyset$;
5   **for** $i := 1$ **to** m **do**
6   **with probability** $1/m$ **do**
7   Choose $b \in \{0, 1\}$ uniformly at random;
8   **if** $b = 0$ **then**
9              $s'_i := s'_i + \sigma_i$;
10   **else**
11             $s'_i := \max(s'_i - \sigma_i, 0)$;
12          $I := I \cup \{i\}$;
13   **if** $\sum_{i=1}^{m} s_i < \sum_{i=1}^{m} s'_i$ and
      $\sum_{j \in \{1, \cdots, m\} | e_j \cap \{v\} \neq \emptyset} s'_j \leq w(v),\ \forall v \in V$ **then**
14       $s := s'$;
15       $\sigma_i := c_1 \cdot \sigma_i,\ \forall i \in I$;
16   **else**
17       $\sigma_i := \max\left(\frac{\sigma_i}{c_2}, 1\right),\ \forall i \in I$;
18 **return** $C := \{v \in V \mid w(v) = \sum_{j \in \{1, \cdots, m\} \mid e_j \cap \{v\} \neq \emptyset} s_j\}$;

In other words, the dual problem is to maximize the sum of weights on all edges, provided that for each vertex, the sum of weights of edges incident to that vertex is at most equal to the weight of that vertex.

Let $s = (s_1, \cdots, s_m)$, be a maximal feasible solution for the dual problem with a cost of $Cost_D$. Since s is a maximal solution, none of the edges can be assigned a greater weight without violating a constraint. Therefore, for at least one vertex of each edge, v, we have

$$w(v) = \sum_{j \in \{1, \cdots, m\} | e_j \cap \{v\} \neq \emptyset} s_j$$

As a result, the set of nodes for which the above equality holds, $C = \{v \in V \mid w(v) = \sum_{j \in \{1, \cdots, m\} \mid e_j \cap \{v\} \neq \emptyset} s_j\}$, is a vertex cover. The cost of this vertex cover, $Cost_P$, is at most twice the weight of all edges in the dual solution. Therefore, $Cost_P \leq 2 \cdot Cost_D$. Moreover, since s is a feasible solution, according to Weak Duality Theorem (Theorem 1), $Cost_D \leq OPT$, which results in $Cost_P \leq 2 \cdot OPT$, i.e. set C is a 2-approximation for the weighted vertex cover problem.

Constructing maximal solutions for the dual problem has been used in a number of algorithms for finding 2-approximations of the weighted vertex cover problem, e.g. Bar-Yehuda and Evan's greedy algorithm [3] and Clarkson's greedy algorithm [6]. A formal proof of the approximation ratio of the solution obtained by this approach can be found in Theorem 8.4 in [14] (represented in Theorem 2 below). There, the output of a specific algorithm is studied as the maximal dual solution, but the presented proof is valid for Theorem 2 with any given maximal solution s.

Theorem 2. *Consider s, a maximal feasible solution for the dual problem of the relaxed weighted vertex cover problem. The vertex set*

$$C = \{v \in V \mid w(v) = \sum_{j \in \{1, \cdots, m\} \mid e_j \cap \{v\} \neq \emptyset} s_j\}$$

is a 2-approximation for the original weighted vertex cover problem.

In this paper, we analyse the behaviour of four evolutionary algorithms which find a 2-approximation for the weighted vertex cover

problem by means of finding a maximal solution for the dual form of the problem. A simple Randomized Local Search (RLS) is presented in Algorithm 1, where a solution $s = (s_1, \cdots, s_m)$, is represented by a string of m integers, denoting the weights of the m edges of the input graph. This algorithm starts with the initial solution $s = 0^m$, and selects one edge at each step to increase or decrease the weight corresponding to that by one. The new solution replaces the old one, if the sum of weights of edges is increased, and the weight constraint of the packing problem is not violated for any of the vertices. At the end, the algorithm returns the set of nodes for which the constraint has become tight.

One other algorithm that we analyse in this paper is the (1+1) EA, presented in Algorithm 2, which is quite similar to the RLS of Algorithm 1 except for selecting the edges for mutation. In (1+1) EA, at each step a mutation happens on the weight of all edges with probability $1/m$ for each of them, while in RLS one edge is selected and the mutation takes place on the weight of that edge. Note that in (1+1) EA more than one mutation may happen on the current solution.

In both RLS and (1+1) EA (Algorithms 1 and 2) the increment size of one on the weights of the edges might be too small and make the algorithm slow. Motivated by step size adaptation in evolution strategies [4] in RLS with Step Size Adaptation and (1+1) EA with Step Size Adaptation (Algorithms 3 and 4), a step size for each edge is kept in an auxiliary vector $\sigma = (\sigma_1, \cdots, \sigma_m)$. The initial step size for all edges is set to 1. The algorithms work with two constant parameters $c_1 > 1$ and $c_2 > 1$. If a mutation with that size is accepted, the step size is increased by a factor of c_1; otherwise, it is decreased by a factor of c_2 with a minimum accepted size of one.

Analysing the runtime of our algorithms, we find the number of iterations of the while loop, until a maximal packing solution is found, which induces a complete vertex cover. We call this the expected time of obtaining the desired goal by the considered algorithm. It should be noted that the edge-based approach for the unweighted minimum vertex cover investigated by Jansen et al. [23] can be seen as a special case of our formulation as the use of maxi-

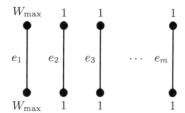

Figure 1: G, **a hard instance for RLS and (1+1) EA**

mal matchings is equivalent to the dual problem if all edges have a weight of 1.

3. RLS AND (1+1) EA

In this section, we present the analysis on finding 2-approximations for the weighted vertex cover problem by RLS and (1+1) EA.

Theorem 3. *The expected time of RLS and (1+1) EA (Algorithms 1 and 2) to find a 2-approximation is $\mathcal{O}(m \cdot OPT)$.*

Proof. In order to prove this theorem, we show that the algorithms find a maximal solution for the dual problem in expected time $\mathcal{O}(m \cdot OPT)$. Having achieved that maximal solution, the algorithms return the set

$$C := \{v \in V \mid w(v) = \sum_{j \in \{1, \cdots, m\} \mid e_j \cap \{v\} \neq \emptyset} s_j\}$$

as the solution for the weighted vertex cover problem which, according to Theorem 2, is a 2-approximation of the optimal solution.

If a solution s is not a maximal solution for the dual problem, then there exists at least one edge for which the assigned weight can be increased. The probability of selecting only that edge for mutation and choosing $b = 0$ is at least $\frac{1}{2 \cdot m}$ for RLS and $\frac{1}{2 \cdot e \cdot m}$ for (1+1) EA at each step, and according to the Weak Duality Theorem (Theorem 1), the cost of any maximal solution is upper bounded by OPT. Therefore, using the method of Fitness Based Partitions [32], we find the expected time $\mathcal{O}(m \cdot OPT)$ for finding a maximal solution for the dual problem by both algorithms. □

Note that the presented upper bound in Theorem 3 is a pseudo polynomial time, because OPT can be exponentially large with respect to the input size. In the remainder of this section, we introduce an instance of the problem for which a pseudo polynomial time is required for finding a 2-approximation. This instance is also used in Section 5, as a hard instance for the (1+1) EA with Step Size Adaptation.

The hard instance of the problem, G, illustrated in Figure 1, contains m edges, $e_1, \cdots, e_m$, none of which share a node with another. One of the edges, e_1, is adjacent to two nodes of weight $W_{\max}$ while all other edges are adjacent to vertices of weight 1. The dual problem of this instance has only one maximal solution: $s_1 = W_{\max}$ and $s_i = 1$, $2 \leq i \leq m$. In this instance, we assume that $W_{\max} > 2^m$.

Theorem 4. *With probability $1 - e^{-\Omega(2^m)}$, the required time for RLS and the (1+1) EA (Algorithm 1 and 2) to find a 2-approximation of G is lower bounded by $\Omega(m \cdot W_{\max})$.*

Proof. Consider a phase of $\frac{m \cdot W_{\max}}{4}$ steps. Let X be the number of times that e_1 is selected for mutation by RLS or (1+1) EA in this phase. Since the probability of selecting e_1 is $\frac{1}{m}$ for both algorithms, the expected value of X is $\frac{W_{\max}}{4}$. As these probabilities

are independent of each other at each step, by Chernoff bounds we get

$$\Pr(X > \frac{W_{\max}}{2}) \leq e^{-\frac{W_{\max}}{12}} = e^{-\Omega(2^m)}$$

At each step that e_1 is selected for mutation, s_1 can be increased by at most 1. Therefore, with probability $1 - e^{-\Omega(2^m)}$, in a phase of $\frac{m \cdot W_{\max}}{4} = \Omega(m \cdot W_{\max})$ steps, we have $s_1 \leq \frac{W_{\max}}{2}$, i.e. s_1 does not reach its maximal value of $W_{\max}$. Therefore, with probability $1 - e^{-\Omega(2^m)}$, the RLS and the (1+1) EA find a 2-approximation of G in time $\Omega(m \cdot W_{\max})$. □

4. RLS with Step Size Adaptation

In this section, we analyse the behaviour of RLS with Step Size Adaptation for finding 2-approximations of the weighted vertex cover problem. We prove that the RLS with Step Size Adaptation finds a 2-approximation for the weighted vertex cover problem in expected polynomial time with respect to the input size, provided that $c_1 = c_2$. This also holds for $c_1 \geq c_2$, which is stated in Corollary 8. The two lemmata below are used in the proof of the main result stated later.

Lemma 5. *If $c_1 = c_2$, the step size σ_i for each edge e_i in RLS with Step Size Adaptation, can only take a value from*

$$\{c_1{}^k \mid 0 \leq k \leq \lceil \log_{c_1} W_{\max} \rceil\},$$

where $W_{\max}$ is the largest weight assigned to any vertex.

Proof. The algorithm starts with initial value of $\sigma_i = 1$ for all edges. This value is increased by a factor of c_1 each time a mutation is accepted for edge e_i, and is divided by the same factor with a minimum accepted value of one if the mutation is rejected (lines 14 and 16 of Algorithm 3). Therefore σ_i is always a power of c_1. Moreover, in order to fulfil the constraints on the vertices, none of the edges can be assigned a weight larger than $W_{\max}$. Therefore, any mutation that increases the current weight of an edge by at least $W_{\max}$, is rejected. Therefore, σ_i can be increased to at most c_1^k where $k = \lceil \log_{c_1} W_{\max} \rceil$. □

Lemma 6. *For an edge e_i, let $D(s_i) = MAX_i - s_i$ where s is the solution obtained so far by the algorithm and MAX_i is the maximum acceptable value for s_i in the current solution s. In expected time $\mathcal{O}(m \log_{c_1}^2 W_{\max})$ a solution s' with $D(s'_i) \leq \frac{c_1 \cdot D(s_i)}{c_1 + 1}$ is found by RLS with Step Size Adaptation when $c_1 = c_2$.*

Proof. Note that since at any step only one mutation happens, for any solution s' obtained after s, we have $D(s'_i) \leq D(s_i)$, otherwise the algorithm would have rejected s'. We divide the analysis into two phases. The first phase, consists of all steps until the algorithm reaches a situation in which s_i is selected for an increasing mutation and $\sigma_i \leq D(s_i)$. In this phase σ_i decreases. The second phase begins when σ_i starts increasing. We show that by the end of the second phase, we have reached a solution s' with $D(s'_i) \leq c_1 \cdot D(s_i)/(c_1 + 1)$.

In the first phase, whenever s_i is selected for an increase, we have $\sigma_i > D(s_i)$; therefore, σ_i is decreased. If $\sigma_i \leq D(s_i)$ at a step in which s_i is selected for an increase, then we are already in the second phase and σ_i is added to s_i, resulting in decreasing $D(s_i)$. Note that it is not only increasing s_i that decreases $D(s_i)$. Instead, increasing the weight of other edges that are adjacent to e_i can also decrease $D(s_i)$. If we reach a solution s' where $D(s'_i) = 0$ in Phase 1, then we already have $D(s'_i) \leq \frac{c_1 \cdot D(s_i)}{c_1 + 1}$ (stated in the lemma) without going to Phase 2.

40

Here we show that Phase 1 is over in expected time $\mathcal{O}(m \cdot \log_{c_1} W_{\max})$. At each step, with probability $\frac{1}{m}$, s_i is mutated. Since $\sigma_i > D(s_i)$, increasing mutations on s_i are rejected as well as decreasing mutations, and σ_i is divided by c_1 with each rejection. This needs to be done at most $\log_{c_1} W_{\max}$ times until we reach $\sigma_i \leq D(s_i)$, which in expectation takes $\mathcal{O}(m \cdot \log_{c_1} W_{\max})$.

The second phase starts when we reach a step with an increasing mutation on s_i in which $1 \leq \sigma_i \leq D(s_i)$. This move is accepted and σ_i is increased by a factor of c_1. Note that $D(s_i)$ might be far larger than σ_i. Since σ_i is always a power of c_1, we define $a \in \mathbb{N}^+$ as $a = \log_{c_1} \sigma_i$ to make the proof easier. Due to Lemma 5, we have $0 \leq a \leq \lceil \log_{c_1} W_{\max} \rceil$. Here, an increase on s_i is accepted by the algorithm and a is increased to $a + 1$, while a decrease is rejected and a is decreased to $a - 1$. The increase and decrease happen with equal probability; therefore, a fair random walk happens for a on integer values in $[0, \lceil \log_{c_1} W_{\max} \rceil]$, with initial value of at least 0.

It is proved that the expected number of required steps for a fair random walk to visit all vertices in a graph with v vertices and e edges is bounded by $2e(v-1)$ [1]. In the fair random walk that happens on a, there are $\lceil \log_{c_1} W_{\max} \rceil + 1$ vertices to visit with $\lceil \log_{c_1} W_{\max} \rceil$ edges between them. This gives us the expected number of steps $k = 2\lceil \log_{c_1} W_{\max} \rceil^2 = \mathcal{O}(\log_{c_1}^2 W_{\max})$ for our random walk, to reach any possible value of a. As a result, as long as $\sigma_i \leq D(s_i)$ holds, in k mutations on s_i, a reaches its maximal possible value which is upper bounded by $\lceil \log_{c_1} W_{\max} \rceil$ after which the inequality does not hold. This implies that k is an upper bound on the number of mutations that can happen on s_i before this phase ends, which is in expectation done in time $\mathcal{O}(m \cdot \log_{c_1}^2 W_{\max})$. At the end of this phase, $\sigma_i > D(s_i')$, whereas the last accepted mutation has increased s_i' by at least $\frac{1}{c_1}\sigma_i$. This implies that

$$D(s_i') \leq D(s_i) - \frac{1}{c_1}\sigma_i \leq \frac{c_1}{c_1 + 1}D(s_i),$$

which completes the proof. $\qquad\square$

Theorem 7. *The RLS with Step Size Adaptation with $c_1 = c_2$ and the initial solution $s = 0^m$, finds a vertex cover that is at least a 2-approximation in expected time $\mathcal{O}(m \cdot \log_{c_1}^3 W_{\max})$.*

Proof. Similar to the proof of Theorem 3, we show that the algorithm finds a maximal solution for the dual problem in expected time $\mathcal{O}(m \cdot \log_{c_1}^3 W_{\max})$.

For each edge e_i, the distance of s_i to its maximal value, D_i, is decreased by at least $\frac{D_i}{c_1+1}$ by RLS with Step Size Adaptation, in expected time $O(m \log_{c_1}^2 W_{\max})$ according to Lemma 6. Since the initial value of D_i is upper bounded by $W_{\max}$, according to Multiplicative Drift Theorem [12], s_i reaches its maximal value in expected time $O(m \log_{c_1}^3 W_{\max})$. $\qquad\square$

In the proof of Lemma 6, setting $c_1 > c_2$, is in favour of increasing the value of σ_i; therefore, the lemma holds in that situation as well, resulting in the following corollary.

Corollary 8. *The RLS with Step Size Adaptation with $c_1 \geq c_2$ and the initial solution $s = 0^m$, finds a vertex cover that is a 2-approximation in expected time $\mathcal{O}(m \cdot \log_{c_1}^3 W_{\max})$.*

5. (1+1) EA with Step Size Adaptation

In this section we prove a pseudo polynomial lower bound on the time that (1+1) EA with Step Size Adaptation requires for finding a 2-approximation of the weighted vertex cover problem, when $c_1 \leq c_2$. To prove this lower bound, we investigate the behaviour

of (1+1) EA with Step Size Adaptation on G (Figure 1), the hard instance of the problem presented in Section 3, with the assumption that $W_{\max} \geq c_1^m$. We show that with high probability, the (1+1) EA with Step Size Adaptation needs exponential time with respect to the input size for finding a maximal dual solution for G.

In the following, $A(s) = \{s_i \mid s_i = 1, 2 \leq i \leq m\}$. Moreover, Phase 1 indicates the steps starting from the initial step until finding a solution s, with $|A(s)| \geq \frac{3m}{4}$, and Phase 2 consists of $c_1^{m^{\varepsilon/2}}$ steps, where $0 < \varepsilon \leq \frac{1}{3}$, starting by the end of Phase 1. We also define Property 9 below, which is used in Lemmata 12 and 14, and Theorem 16.

Property 9. *For current solution s, we have $|A(s)| \geq \frac{m}{2}$.*

In order to prove the main theorem of this section, we make use of Lemmata 10, 12, 13 and 14, which follow.

Lemma 10. *For sufficiently large m, with probability $1 - e^{-\Omega(m^\varepsilon)}$, Phase 1 needs at most $m^{1+\varepsilon}$ steps, where $\varepsilon > 0$ is a constant.*

Proof. Let $Z(s) = \{s_i \mid s_i = 0, 2 \leq i \leq m\}$. Note that $|Z(s)| + |A(s)| = m - 1$. At each step, if one of the edges of set $Z(s)$ is selected for a mutation of increase, and no other mutations happen, the new solution is accepted by the algorithm. Therefore, the probability of producing a solution s' with $|A(s')| = |A(s)| + 1$ is at least

$$\frac{|Z(s)|}{2 \cdot e \cdot m} = \frac{m - 1 - |A(s)|}{2 \cdot e \cdot m}.$$

This implies that, the positive drift on $|A(s)|$, denoted by Δ_+, is at least $\frac{m-1-|A(s)|}{2 \cdot e \cdot m}$ at each step.

Moreover, to obtain a solution s' with $|A(s')| = |A(s)| - k$ from s, k mutations should happen on edges of A, and in order to make these changes acceptable, a mutation of increase should happen on s_1. The probability of increasing s_1 at each step is $\frac{1}{2m}$, and the probability of k other mutations to happen at the same step is upper bounded by

$$\binom{m-1}{k} \cdot \left(\frac{1}{m}\right)^k \left(1 - \frac{1}{m}\right)^{m-1-k} \leq \frac{1.06}{k!e},$$

for sufficiently large m. Here, it suffices if we assume $m \geq 20$. Overall, the probability of finding a solution s' with $|A(s')| = |A(s)| - k$ is at most $\frac{1.06}{k!e \cdot 2m}$. As a result, for the negative drift on $|A(s)|$, denoted by Δ_-, we have

$$
\begin{aligned}
\Delta_- &\leq \sum_{k=1}^{|A(s)|} k \cdot \frac{1.06}{k! e \cdot 2m} \\
&= \frac{1.06}{e \cdot 2m} \sum_{k=1}^{|A(s)|} \frac{1}{(k-1)!} \\
&\leq \frac{1.06}{e \cdot 2m} \cdot 3 = \frac{3.18}{e \cdot 2m}.
\end{aligned}
$$

Summing up, the total drift on $|A(s)|$ is

$$\Delta = \Delta_+ - \Delta_- \geq \frac{m - 4.18 - |A(s)|}{2 \cdot e \cdot m}.$$

We now analyse the time to find a solution with $|A(s)| \geq \frac{3m}{4}$. For any solution s with $|A(s)| < \frac{3m}{4}$, we have $\Delta \geq \frac{\frac{m}{4} - 4}{2 \cdot e \cdot m} \geq 0.0075$, since we have assumed $m > 20$. By additive drift argument [21], we can see that a solution with $|A(s)| \geq \frac{3m}{4}$ is found in expected time $\frac{1}{0.0075} \cdot \frac{3m}{4} = 100m$. By Markov's inequality, with probability at least $\frac{1}{2}$, the time until finding that solution is at most $200m$. Therefore, in a phase of $m^{1+\varepsilon}$ steps, the probability of not finding that solution is $(\frac{1}{2})^{\frac{m^{\varepsilon}}{200}} = e^{-\Omega(m^{\varepsilon})}$. $\qquad\square$

In the proof of the next lemma, we use the Simplified Drift Theorem (Theorem 11) presented in [28, 29]. In this theorem, F_t denotes a filtration on states. In the proof of Lemma 12, we analyse the changes on the size of $A(s)$, and no filtration is applied on the steps.

Theorem 11. *(Simplified Drift Theorem [29]) Let X_t, $t \geq 0$, be real-valued random variables describing a stochastic process over some state space. Suppose there exist an interval $[a, b] \subseteq \mathbb{R}$, two constants $\delta, \varepsilon > 0$ and, possibly depending on $l := b - a$, a function $r(l)$ satisfying $1 \leq r(l) = o(l/\log(l))$ such that for all $t \geq 0$ the following two conditions hold:*
1. $E[X_{t+1} - X_t \mid F_t \wedge a < X_t < b] \geq \varepsilon$,
2. $\Pr(|X_{t+1} - X_t| \geq j \mid F_t \wedge a < X_t) \leq \frac{r(l)}{(1+\delta)^j}$ *for $j \in \mathbb{N}$.*

Then there is a constant $c^* > 0$ such that for $T^* := min\{t \geq 0 : X_t \leq a | F_t \wedge X_0 \geq b\}$ it holds $\Pr(T^* \leq 2^{c^* l/r(l)}) = 2^{-\Omega(l/r(l))}$.

Lemma 12. *For sufficiently large m, with probability $1 - e^{-\Omega(m)}$, Property 9 holds during Phase 2.*

Proof. Phase 2 starts with the solution s with $|A(s)| \geq \frac{3m}{4}$, found by the end of Phase 1. Using Simplified Drift Theorem (Theorem 11) with parameters $\delta = 1$, $r(l) = 1$ and interval $[a, b] = [\frac{m}{2}, \frac{3m}{4}]$, we show that with high probability, a solution s' with $|A(s')| \leq \frac{m}{2}$ is not found by the algorithm until end of Phase 2.

Let $X_t = |A(s)|$, where s is the solution obtained at time t. The total drift on the value of X_t is Δ of the proof of Lemma 10, which is at least 0.0075 when $X_t \leq \frac{3m}{4}$. Therefore, the two conditions of the Simplified Drift Theorem hold:

1. $\mathrm{E}(X_{t+1} - X_t \mid a \leq X_t \leq b) = \mathrm{E}(X_{t+1} - X_t \mid \frac{m}{2} \leq X_t \leq \frac{3m}{4}) \geq 0.0075$, and

2. $\Pr(|X_{t+1} - X_t| \geq j \mid a \leq X_t) \leq \frac{1}{j!e} \leq \frac{1}{2^j} = \frac{r(l)}{(1+\delta)^j}$

The inequality regarding the second condition holds, because the probability of mutating j edges at one step follows the Poisson distribution and is $\frac{1}{j!e}$. Having these two conditions satisfied, the Simplified Drift Theorem says that the probability of finding a solution with $|A(s)| \leq \frac{m}{2}$ in time $2^{\frac{c^* m}{4}}$, $c^* > 0$ a constant, is at most $2^{-\Omega(\frac{m}{4})}$. This implies that with probability $1 - e^{-\Omega(m)}$, such a solution is not found by the end of Phase 2 which consists of $c_1{}^{m^{\varepsilon/2}} = 2^{\log_2 c_1 \cdot m^{\varepsilon/2}}$ steps. $\qquad\square$

Lemma 13. *Let $\varepsilon \leq 1/3$ be a positive constant. In Phase 1, with probability $1 - e^{-\Omega(m^{\varepsilon})}$, the (1+1) EA with Step Size Adaptation does not reach a solution where $s_1 > 2 \cdot m^{\varepsilon} \cdot c_1{}^{2 \cdot m^{\varepsilon}}$. Moreover, the step size of s_1 does not exceed $c_1{}^{2 \cdot m^{\varepsilon}}$, i.e. $\sigma_1 \leq c_1{}^{2 \cdot m^{\varepsilon}}$.*

Proof. From Lemma 10, we know that this phase is at most $m^{1+\varepsilon}$ steps. Let X be the number of times that the first edge is selected for mutation during Phase 1. Since the probability of selecting each edge at each step is $\frac{1}{m}$, the expected value of X is at most m^{ε}. Moreover, since probability of selecting edges are independent of each other, by Chernoff bounds we have:

$$\Pr(X \geq 2 \cdot m^{\varepsilon}) \leq e^{-m^{\varepsilon}/3}.$$

Therefore, with probability $1 - e^{-\Omega(m^{\varepsilon})}$ the first edge is not selected for mutation more than $2 \cdot m^{\varepsilon}$ times, which means that the step size for that edge is at most $c_1{}^{2 \cdot m^{\varepsilon}}$ after that phase. This implies that $2 \cdot m^{\varepsilon} \cdot c_1{}^{2 \cdot m^{\varepsilon}}$ is an upper bound for the value of s_1 by the end of Phase 1. Note that s_1 and σ_1 have not reached their maximal values, since $\varepsilon \leq 1/3$. $\qquad\square$

In the following lemma, we show that when $|A(S)| \geq m/2$, the probability of decreasing the step size σ_1 is larger than the probability of increasing it. This lemma is used in Theorem 16 to show that we do not reach large values of σ_1 in polynomial time.

Lemma 14. *Assuming that Property 9 holds, and also assuming that $\sigma_1 > m$ and $s_1 \leq W_{\max}$, at any step where σ_1 is changed by (1+1) EA with Step Size Adaptation, it is increased with probability $P_{inc} < 0.4$ and decreased with probability $P_{dec} > 0.6$.*

Proof. The value of σ_1 changes at the steps where e_1 is selected for mutation. All other steps make no change on σ_1. Here we only consider the steps at which e_1 is selected for a mutation.

The value of σ_1 increases when a mutation on e_1 is accepted. Since $\sigma_1 > m$ and $s_1 \leq W_{\max}$, any mutation that decreases the value of e_1 is rejected. Since we have assumed that Property 9 holds, there are at least $\frac{m}{2}$ edges other than e_1, with a weight of one. A mutation of increase on these edges is rejected. Therefore, an increase on e_1 is also rejected if one of those edges is selected for an increase in addition to e_i at the same step. The probability that an increase is selected to be done on e_1, while none of those edges are selected for increase, is:

$$\frac{1}{2} \cdot \left(1 - \frac{1}{2m}\right)^{m - \frac{m}{2}} \leq \frac{1}{2} \cdot \left(\frac{1}{e}\right)^{\frac{1}{4}} < 0.4$$

This probability is an upper bound for the probability that an acceptable increase on e_1 happens, which is denoted by P_{inc}. In other words:

$$P_{inc} < 0.4$$

Since $P_{inc} + P_{dec} = 1$ at steps where a mutation happens on e_1, we have $P_{dec} > 0.6$. $\qquad\square$

In order to prove the main theorem of this section, we use the Gambler's Ruin Theorem, introduced by Feller [16]. We use the parameter settings of a variant of this theorem (Theorem 15) presented in [20].

Theorem 15 (Gambler's Ruin Theorem). *[20]*
Let p be the probability of winning one dollar and $q = 1 - p$ be the probability of loosing one dollar in a single bet and let $\delta = q/p$. Starting with x dollars, the probability of reaching $z > x$ dollars before attaining zero dollars is

$$P_x = \frac{\delta^x - 1}{\delta^z - 1}$$

Theorem 16. *For sufficiently large m and a positive constant $\varepsilon \leq \frac{1}{3}$, with probability $1 - e^{-\Omega(m^{\varepsilon/2})}$, the required time for (1+1) EA with Step Size Adaptation (Algorithm 4) to find a 2-approximation on G with $W_{\max} = c_1{}^m$ is lower bounded by $2^{m^{\varepsilon/2}}$, when $c_1 = c_2$.*

Proof. According to Lemma 13, during Phase 1, with probability $1 - e^{-\Omega(m^{\varepsilon})}$, we have $\sigma_1 \leq c_1{}^{2 \cdot m^{\varepsilon}}$. Using Lemma 14 and the Gambler's Ruin Theorem, we prove that with high probability, in Phase 2, we always have $\sigma_1 \leq c_1{}^{m^{2\varepsilon}}$.

Due to Lemma 12, with probability $1 - e^{-\Omega(m)}$, Property 9 holds during Phase 2 which is a requirement of Lemma 14. However, Lemma 14 can only be used for the steps where $\sigma_1 > m$, while Phase 2 may start with $\sigma_1 \leq m$. Nevertheless, in order to reach large values of $c_1^{m^{2\varepsilon}}$ or greater, at some point of Phase 2, we need to deal with a situation where $m < \sigma_1 \leq c_1 m$, since σ_1 increases at each step at most by a factor of c_1. According to Lemma 14, at the steps in which e_1 is selected for mutation, the probability of increasing σ_1 is $p \leq 0.4$ and the probability of decreasing it is $q \geq 0.6$.

Let σ_1^0 be the value of σ_1 at the first point in Phase 2 where $m < \sigma_1 \leq c_1 m$. If $\sigma_1 \leq c_1 m$ holds, then for sufficiently large m we also have $\sigma_1 \leq c_1^{2 \cdot m^\varepsilon}$. Starting from that point where $m < \sigma_1 \leq c_1^{2 \cdot m^\varepsilon}$, we investigate whether the algorithm reaches a situation where $\sigma_1 \leq m$ earlier than a situation where $\sigma_1 \geq c_1^{m^{2\varepsilon}}$.

Every time σ_1 is increased, it is increased by a factor of c_1 and every time that it is decreased, it is decreased by a factor of c_2. Since we have assumed that $c_1 = c_2$, one increasing step and one decreasing step cancel each other and the problem can be mapped to the problem of Gambler's Ruin Theorem (Theorem 15) with parameters p and q described above and $\delta = \frac{q}{p} \geq \frac{0.6}{0.4} > 1$. The number of times that $\sigma_1 = \sigma_1^0$ needs to be decreased to reach $\sigma_1 \leq m$ is at most

$$\lceil \log_{c_2}(\sigma_1^0/m) \rceil \leq \log_{c_2}\left(\frac{c_1^{2 \cdot m^\varepsilon}}{m}\right) + 1 \leq 2 \cdot m^\varepsilon + 1$$

Also, the number of times that $\sigma_1 \leq m$ needs to be increased to reach $\sigma_1 \geq c_1^{m^{2\varepsilon}}$ is at least

$$\lceil \log_{c_1}(c_1^{m^{2\varepsilon}}/m) \rceil \geq m^{2\varepsilon} - \lfloor \log_{c_1} m \rfloor$$

Therefore, other parameters of the Gambler's Ruin Theorem would be $x \leq 2 \cdot m^\varepsilon + 1$ and $z \geq m^{2\varepsilon} - \lfloor \log_{c_1} m \rfloor$. Using that theorem, we get P_x, the probability of reaching a state where $\sigma_1 \geq c_1^{m^{2\varepsilon}}$ before reaching a state where $\sigma_1 \leq m$ as:

$$P_x = \frac{(\delta)^x - 1}{(\delta)^z - 1} \leq \frac{(\delta)^{2 \cdot m^\varepsilon + 1} - 1}{(\delta)^{m^{2\varepsilon} - \lfloor \log_{c_1} m \rfloor} - 1} = e^{-\Omega(m^\varepsilon)}.$$

Consider a phase of $2^{m^{\varepsilon/2}}$ steps. We here show that with probability $e^{-\Omega(m^{\varepsilon/2})}$, $\sigma_1 \geq c_1^{m^{2\varepsilon}}$ during this phase.

We saw that with probability $1 - e^{-\Omega(m^\varepsilon)}$ we reach a state where $\sigma_1 \leq m$ before a state where $\sigma_1 \geq c_1^{m^{2\varepsilon}}$. If σ_1 never increases to $c_1^{m^\varepsilon}$ after that, then we never reach a state where $\sigma_1 \geq c_1^{m^{2\varepsilon}}$. Otherwise, it spends at least

$$\lceil \log_{c_1}(c_1^{m^\varepsilon}/m) \rceil = m^\varepsilon - \lfloor \log_{c_1} m \rfloor$$

steps to reach $c_1^{m^\varepsilon}$. In a phase of $2^{m^{\varepsilon/2}}$ steps, there are at most

$$k = \frac{2^{m^{\varepsilon/2}}}{m^\varepsilon - \lfloor \log_{c_1} m \rfloor}$$

times that σ_1 increases to $c_1^{m^\varepsilon}$, and probability of reaching $c_1^{m^{2\varepsilon}}$ from there is only $e^{-\Omega(m^\varepsilon)}$. Therefore, the probability of σ_1 to reach $c_1^{m^{2\varepsilon}}$ at least once in a phase of $2^{m^{\varepsilon/2}}$ steps, is at most

$$k \cdot e^{-\Omega(m^\varepsilon)} = e^{-\Omega(m^{\varepsilon/2})}.$$

So far we have proved that with probability $1 - e^{-\Omega(m^{\varepsilon/2})}$, $\sigma_1 \leq c_1^{m^{2\varepsilon}}$ during Phase 2 which consists of $c_1^{m^{\varepsilon/2}}$ steps. Moreover, according to Lemma 13, with probability $1 - e^{-\Omega(m^\varepsilon)}$, we have

$s_1 \leq 2 \cdot m^\varepsilon \cdot c_1^{2m^\varepsilon}$ by the end of Phase 1. Therefore, the value of s_1 during both phases is always upper bounded by

$$2 \cdot m^\varepsilon \cdot c_1^{2m^\varepsilon} + c_1^{m^{\varepsilon/2}} \cdot c_1^{m^{2\varepsilon}}$$

which is less than $W_{\max}$, since $\varepsilon \leq 1/3$. Therefore, with probability $1 - e^{-\Omega(m^{\varepsilon/2})}$, the (1+1) EA with Step Size Adaptation does not find a 2-approximation in time $2^{m^{\varepsilon/2}}$. $\square$

Note that for $c_1 < c_2$, the probability of reaching a situation where $\sigma_1 \geq c_1^{m^{2\varepsilon}}$ before reaching $\sigma_1 < m$ is even smaller, since the number of increasing steps that are required to cancel one decreasing step is greater than one. Therefore, this situation is in favour of reaching $\sigma_1 \leq m$, resulting in the following corollary.

Corollary 17. *For sufficiently large m and a positive constant $\varepsilon \leq \frac{1}{3}$, with probability $1 - e^{-\Omega(m^{\varepsilon/2})}$, the required time for (1+1) EA with Step Size Adaptation (Algorithm 4) to find a 2-approximation of G is lower bounded by $2^{m^{\varepsilon/2}}$, when $c_1 \leq c_2$.*

6. CONCLUSION

In this paper, we have considered how to solve the minimum vertex cover problem by its dual formulation based on a multi-valued edge-based encoding. We have proven pseudo-polynomial upper bounds for RLS and the (1+1) EA until they have achieved a 2-approximation. Furthermore, we have investigated the use of step-size adaptation in both algorithms and shown that RLS with step size adaptation obtains a 2-approximation in expected polynomial time; whereas the corresponding (1+1) EA still encounters a pseudo-polynomial lower bound.

Acknowledgments

This research has been supported through Australian Research Council grants DP140103400 and DP160102401.

References

[1] R. Aleliunas, R. M. Karp, R. J. Lipton, L. Lovász, and C. Rackoff. Random walks, universal traversal sequences, and the complexity of maze problems. In *Proceedings of the 20th Annual Symposium on Foundations of Computer Science (FOCS '79)*, pages 218–223. IEEE Press, 1979.

[2] A. Auger and B. Doerr. *Theory of Randomized Search Heuristics: Foundations and Recent Developments*. World Scientific Publishing Co., Inc., 2011.

[3] R. Bar-Yehuda and S. Even. A linear-time approximation algorithm for the weighted vertex cover problem. *Journal of Algorithms*, 2(2):198–203, 1981.

[4] H. Beyer and H. Schwefel. Evolution strategies - A comprehensive introduction. *Natural Computing*, 1(1):3–52, 2002.

[5] S. Böttcher, B. Doerr, and F. Neumann. Optimal fixed and adaptive mutation rates for the leadingones problem. In *Conference on Problem Solving from Nature (PPSN)*, pages 1–10, 2010.

[6] K. L. Clarkson. A modification of the greedy algorithm for vertex cover. *Inf. Process. Lett.*, 16(1):23–25, 1983.

[7] D.-C. Dang and P. K. Lehre. Self-adaptation of mutation rates in non-elitist populations. In *Conference on Problem Solving from Nature (PPSN)*, 2016.

[8] B. Doerr and C. Doerr. Optimal parameter choices through self-adjustment: Applying the 1/5-th rule in discrete settings. In *Genetic and Evolutionary Computation Conference (GECCO)*, pages 1335–1342, 2015.

[9] B. Doerr, C. Doerr, and T. Kötzing. The right mutation strength for multi-valued decision variables. In *Genetic and Evolutionary Computation Conference (GECCO)*, 2016.

[10] B. Doerr, C. Doerr, and J. Yang. k-bit mutation with self-adjusting k outperforms standard bit mutation. In *Parallel Problem Solving from Nature – PPSN XIV: 14th International Conference, Edinburgh, UK, September 17-21, 2016, Proceedings*, pages 824–834. Springer International Publishing, 2016.

[11] B. Doerr, D. Johannsen, and M. Schmidt. Runtime analysis of the (1+1) evolutionary algorithm on strings over finite alphabets. In *Workshop on Foundations of Genetic Algorithms (FOGA)*, pages 119–126, 2011.

[12] B. Doerr, D. Johannsen, and C. Winzen. Multiplicative drift analysis. *Algorithmica*, 64(4):673–697, 2012.

[13] B. Doerr and S. Pohl. Run-time analysis of the (1+1) evolutionary algorithm optimizing linear functions over a finite alphabet. In *Genetic and Evolutionary Computation Conference (GECCO)*, pages 1317–1324, 2012.

[14] D.-Z. Du, K.-I. Ko, and X. Hu. *Design and Analysis of Approximation Algorithms*. Springer Publishing Company, Incorporated, 2011.

[15] A. E. Eiben, Z. Michalewicz, M. Schoenauer, and J. E. Smith. Parameter control in evolutionary algorithms. In *Parameter Setting in Evolutionary Algorithms*, volume 54 of *Studies in Computational Intelligence*, pages 19–46. Springer, 2007.

[16] W. Feller. *An Introduction to Probability Theory and Its Applications*, volume 1. Wiley, 3rd edition, 1968.

[17] T. Friedrich, J. He, N. Hebbinghaus, F. Neumann, and C. Witt. Analyses of simple hybrid algorithms for the vertex cover problem. *Evolutionary Computation*, 17(1):3–19, 2009.

[18] T. Friedrich, J. He, N. Hebbinghaus, F. Neumann, and C. Witt. Approximating covering problems by randomized search heuristics using multi-objective models. *Evolutionary Computation*, 18(4):617–633, 2010.

[19] N. Hansen, S. D. Müller, and P. Koumoutsakos. Reducing the time complexity of the derandomized evolution strategy with covariance matrix adaptation (CMA-ES). *Evolutionary Computation*, 11(1):1–18, 2003.

[20] E. Happ, D. Johannsen, C. Klein, and F. Neumann. Rigorous analyses of fitness-proportional selection for optimizing linear functions. In *Conference on Genetic and Evolutionary Computation (GECCO)*, pages 953–960, 2008.

[21] J. He and X. Yao. Drift analysis and average time complexity of evolutionary algorithms. *Artificial Intelligence*, 127(1):57–85, 2001.

[22] T. Jansen. *Analyzing Evolutionary Algorithms – The Computer Science Perspective*. Natural Computing Series. Springer, 2013.

[23] T. Jansen, P. S. Oliveto, and C. Zarges. Approximating vertex cover using edge-based representations. In *Workshop on Foundations of Genetic Algorithms (FOGA)*, pages 87–96, 2013.

[24] T. Kötzing, A. Lissovoi, and C. Witt. (1+1) EA on generalized dynamic onemax. In *Workshop on Foundations of Genetic Algorithms (FOGA)*, pages 40–51, 2015.

[25] S. Kratsch and F. Neumann. Fixed-parameter evolutionary algorithms and the vertex cover problem. *Algorithmica*, 65(4):754–771, 2013.

[26] J. Lässig and D. Sudholt. Adaptive population models for offspring populations and parallel evolutionary algorithms. Technical report, https://arxiv.org/abs/1102.0588, 2011.

[27] F. Neumann and C. Witt. *Bioinspired Computation in Combinatorial Optimization:Algorithms and Their Computational Complexity*. Springer-Verlag New York, Inc., New York, NY, USA, 1st edition, 2010.

[28] P. Oliveto and C. Witt. Simplified drift analysis for proving lower bounds in evolutionary computation. *Algorithmica*, 59(3):369–386, 2011.

[29] P. Oliveto and C. Witt. Erratum: Simplified drift analysis for proving lower bounds in evolutionary computation. *arXiv*, abs/1211.7184, 2012.

[30] P. S. Oliveto, J. He, and X. Yao. Analysis of the (1+1) -ea for finding approximate solutions to vertex cover problems. *IEEE Trans. Evolutionary Computation*, 13(5):1006–1029, 2009.

[31] V. V. Vazirani. *Approximation Algorithms*. Springer-Verlag New York, Inc., New York, NY, USA, 2001.

[32] I. Wegener. *Methods for the Analysis of Evolutionary Algorithms on Pseudo-Boolean Functions*, pages 349–369. Springer US, Boston, MA, 2002.

Analysis of the (1+1) EA on Subclasses of Linear Functions under Uniform and Linear Constraints

Tobias Friedrich
Hasso Plattner Institute
Potsdam, Germany

Timo Kötzing
Hasso Plattner Institute
Potsdam, Germany

Gregor Lagodzinski
Hasso Plattner Institute
Potsdam, Germany

Frank Neumann
School of Computer Science
The University of Adelaide
Adelaide, Australia

Martin Schirneck
Hasso Plattner Institute
Potsdam, Germany

ABSTRACT

Linear functions have gained a lot of attention in the area of run time analysis of evolutionary computation methods and the corresponding analyses have provided many effective tools for analyzing more complex problems. In this paper, we consider the behavior of the classical (1+1) Evolutionary Algorithm for linear functions under linear constraint. We show tight bounds in the case where both the objective and the constraint function is given by the ONEMAX function and present upper bounds as well as lower bounds for the general case. We also consider the LEADINGONES fitness function.

Categories and Subject Descriptors

F.2 [**Theory of Computation**]: Analysis of Algorithms and Problem Complexity

Keywords

Run time analysis, evolutionary algorithm, knapsack, constraints.

1. INTRODUCTION

Evolutionary algorithms have been used in a wide range of application domains such as water distribution network [27, 30], renewable energy [21], supply chain management [20], and software engineering [9, 18]. Their easy application and adaptation to a wide range of engineering problems qualify them for research even without a deep algorithmic background.

Although evolutionary computation is very popular in a large variety of application domains, the theoretical understanding lacks behind its practical success. Over the last 20

FOGA '17, January 12 - 15, 2017, Copenhagen, Denmark

© 2017 Copyright held by the owner/author(s). Publication rights licensed to ACM.
ISBN 978-1-4503-4651-1/17/01...$15.00

DOI: http://dx.doi.org/10.1145/3040718.3040728

years a lot of progress in understanding evolutionary computing techniques has been achieved by studying the run time behavior of evolutionary algorithms which are simpler than the ones used in practice, but still capture the main aspects of the algorithms [1, 12, 23].

At the heart of these investigations have been studies of the classical (1+1) EA for the class of linear functions [6]. Initial investigations considered ONEMAX [22] as the simplest non-trivial pseudo-Boolean function. Later investigations have been generalized to the whole class of linear functions for which it has been shown in [6] that the (1+1) EA optimizes them in expected time $\Theta(n \log n)$. Further studies investigated the (1+1) EA and linear functions, giving simpler proofs and a more precise analysis by giving the constants hidden in the Θ-notation [4, 29]. Furthermore, linear functions, especially ONEMAX, have been investigated in dynamic [16] and stochastic settings [5, 8] as well as for other evolutionary computing techniques such as particle swarm optimization [28], ant colony optimization [17] and estimation of distribution algorithms [3].

Maximizing a linear function under a linear constraint is equivalent to the well-known NP-hard knapsack problem. Beyond the worst case, the knapsack problem has been well-studied from an average case and smooth complexity perspective and it has been found that this problem can be solved in (expected) polynomial time for a wide range of these settings [2, 26].

It has been shown in [31] that the expected optimization time of the (1+1) EA on a specific deceptive knapsack instance is exponential. We investigate several subclasses of linear functions under linear constraints where the objective function or the given constraint are of type ONEMAX. We call a constraint given by ONEMAX a uniform constraint. The goal of our investigations is to gain an understanding on the working principles of the (1+1) EA for these subclasses. The reader should note that the subclasses under investigation can be solved to optimality in polynomial time by deterministic (greedy) algorithms.

Our findings are summarized in Table 1. We start our investigations by considering ONEMAX together with a uniform constraint of B (that is, only bit strings with at most B 1-bits are feasible) and show that the (1+1) EA is able to find an optimal solution efficiently (in time $O(n \log n)$, but depending on B potentially faster). Note that ONEMAX

Constraint	Problem	Expected Optimization Time	
uniform	finding a feasible solution	$O(n \log(n/B))$	Lemma 3
	OneMax	$\Theta(\sqrt{n})$, if $\|B - n/2\| < \sqrt{n}$ $\Theta(\|B - n/2\|)$, if $\sqrt{n} \leq \|B - n/2\| < n/4$ $\Theta(n \log(n/B_{\min}))$, if $n/4 \leq \|B - n/2\|$	Theorem 4
	$(1 + \varepsilon) \sum_{i=1}^{B} x_i + \sum_{i=B+1}^{n} x_i$	$O(n^2)$	Theorem 7
	linear functions	$\Omega(n^2)$	Theorem 5
		$O(n^2 \log(B\, w_{\max}))$	Theorem 6
	LeadingOnes	$O(n^2 \log B)$	Theorem 8
linear	OneMax	exponential	Theorem 9

Table 1: Overview of Results. The expected optimization times of the (1+1) EA on linear functions and LeadingOnes on bit strings of length n under uniform or linear constraint B. In the extreme case of $B = 0$, $O(n \log(n/B))$ is to be read as $O(n \log n)$. $B_{\min} = \min\{B, n - B\}$, $0 < \varepsilon < 1/n$ is a positive real number, $w_{\max} \geq 1$ is the largest weight of the linear function. The table shows that the optimization time on OneMax under uniform constraint is never larger than in the unconstrained case and that there are ranges of B in which it is significantly smaller. On the contrary, there is a general linear function and a uniform constraint B such that the optimization time is in $\Omega(n^2)$. There is a linear constraint such that the (1+1) EA needs exponential time even on OneMax.

with uniform constraints has many global optima: any bit string with B 1-bits is optimal. We modify OneMax by increasing the weight of the first B bit positions to $1 + \varepsilon$, for a very small value of ε. This ensures that there is only one global optimum. We show that this function requires $O(n^2)$ fitness evaluations to optimize: after reaching the bound of B bits, lighter bits have to be exchanged for more valuable bits; while still k valuable bits are missing, an improving exchange of bits has a probability of $\Theta(k^2/n^2)$. Thus, the Variable Drift Theorem gives us the overall run time of $O(n^2)$.

Investigating more general functions with a uniform constraint, we show that a general upper bound of $O(n^3)$ holds for all linear objective functions. Furthermore, we show that there is a linear function for which the (1+1) EA takes $\Omega(n^2)$ fitness evaluations. We conjecture a general upper bound of $O(n^2)$ for all linear functions, but for now we content ourselves with showing this bound for the $(1 + \varepsilon)$-test function mentioned above.

Finally, we show that LeadingOnes can be optimized in time $O(n^2 \log B)$ and that OneMax with a specific linear constraint implies an exponential run time for the (1+1) EA.

We proceed in Section 2 by introducing the algorithm and the class of constrained optimization problems that is subject to our investigations. We consider uniform constraints in Section 3 and linear constraints in Section 4. Finally, we conclude in Section 5.

2. PRELIMINARIES

We consider as search space the collection $\{0, 1\}^n$ of bit strings $x = x_1 x_2 \ldots x_n$ of fixed length n and examine the class of linear functions

$$f(x) = \sum_{i=1}^{n} w_i x_i.$$

We assume all weights w_i to be positive real numbers that are w.l.o.g at least 1 and denote by $w_{\max} = \max_i w_i$ the maximal weight.

We investigate the optimization of f under a linear constraint given by

$$b(x) = \sum_{i=1}^{n} b_i x_i \leq B$$

where the weights b_i are positive reals and B is a positive upper bound. We call a function f to be under *uniform constraint* if all b_i are equal to 1; otherwise, we say that it is under *linear constraint*. In order to optimize f under the constraint $b(x) \leq B$ we employ the (1+1) Evolutionary Algorithm ((1+1) EA) as given in Algorithm 1.

Algorithm 1: (1+1) EA
---
1 Choose $x \in \{0, 1\}^n$ uniformly at random;
2 **while** *stopping criterion not met* **do**
3 $y \leftarrow$ flip each bit of x ind. with prob. $1/n$;
4   **if** $z(y) \geq z(x)$ **then** $x \leftarrow y$;

Here, x denotes the best search point found so far. We also use the symbol x' for the (possibly mutated) offspring *after* selection; $x^{(0)}$ denotes the initial bit string drawn in Step 1.

During the optimization we use a penalty approach for dealing with infeasible solutions by

$$z(x) = f(x) - (n\, w_{\max} + 1) \cdot \max\{0, b(x) - B\}.$$

In this manner we ensure that infeasible solutions have negative fitness value, which guides the search towards the feasible region of the search space. In particular, Algorithm 1 will *never* adopt an infeasible solution in Step 4 after sampling the first feasible bit string.

We study the number of iterations the (1+1) EA needs until it samples an optimal solution for the first time. This is called the *optimization time* of the algorithm; we usually denote this random variable as T. The expected value of this variable $E[T]$ is called the *expected optimization time*.

In order to study the expected optimization time of the (1+1) EA we apply drift analysis as introduced by He and Yao [11]. An auxiliary function called the *potential* maps a bit string to the real axis allowing us to evaluate the expected progress between consecutive rounds. Usually the potential is chosen such that its minimization corresponds to maximizing the fitness. In particular, the potential reaches its minimal value just in case the bit string is optimal. Depending on the type of expected potential decrease we apply one of several drift theorems [4, 11, 13, 15, 25, 29] with the following being the most general.

Theorem 1 (Variable Drift Theorem [13]). *Let $(X^{(t)})_{t \geq 0}$ be a sequence of random variables over a finite state space $\{0\} \subsetneq S \subsetneq \mathbb{R}_0^+$. Define $s_{\min} = \min\{x \in S \mid x > 0\}$ and $s_{\max} = \max\{x \in S\}$. Furthermore, let T be the random variable denoting the first point in time $t \in \mathbb{N}$ for which $X^{(t)} = 0$. Suppose that there exist a monotonically increasing function $h \colon \mathbb{R}^+ \to \mathbb{R}^+$ such that $1/h$ is integrable on $[s_{\min}, s_{\max}]$ and, for all $t < T$ and $0 \neq s \in S$,*

$$E\left[X^{(t)} - X^{(t+1)} \mid X^{(t)} = s\right] \geq h(s).$$

Then, for all $0 \neq s_0 \in S$,

$$E\left[T \mid X^{(0)} = s_0\right] \leq \frac{s_{\min}}{h(s_{\min})} + \int_{s_{\min}}^{s_0} \frac{1}{h(s)} \, \mathrm{d}s.$$

As the potential usually is based on properties of the current best solution x, we define some notation regarding bit strings. Let $1 \leq i \leq j \leq n$ be two indices. We let $\overline{x_i}$ denote the negation of the bit x_i, $x_{[i,j]} = x_i x_{i+1} \ldots x_j$ is the substring of all bits from position i to j (including). The number of 1-bits in x is denoted $|x|_1 = \sum_{i=1}^{n} x_i$; conversely, $|x|_0 = n - |x|_1$ is the number of 0-bits. We sometimes also use the term *Hamming weight* for the number of 1s.

During the analysis in the sections below we frequently bound an expected value by some conditional expectation. This technique is justified by the following observation from the law of total expectation.

Lemma 2. *Suppose X is a discrete random variable taking values in $\mathbb{R}_0^+$ and $\mathcal{E}$ an arbitrary event with $0 < P[\mathcal{E}] < 1$. Then, $E[X] \geq E[X \mid \mathcal{E}] P[\mathcal{E}]$. If additionally $X > 0$ implies $\mathcal{E}$, equality holds.*

Proof. The conditional expectation $E[X \mid \neg\mathcal{E}]$ exists and cannot be negative due to X being non-negative. Hence,

$$E[X] = E[X \mid \mathcal{E}] P[\mathcal{E}] + E[X \mid \neg\mathcal{E}] P[\neg\mathcal{E}]$$
$$\geq E[X \mid \mathcal{E}] P[\mathcal{E}].$$

If the second condition is met, then $E[X \mid \neg\mathcal{E}] = 0$. $\qquad\square$

3. UNIFORM CONSTRAINT

We start with investigating uniform constraints, i.e., $b_i = 1$ for all $1 \leq i \leq n$. This only restricts the total number of 1-bits in a feasible solution. Hence, we assume the weight bound B to be an integer between 0 and n.

In the following lemma we derive a general bound on the time the (1+1) EA on any pseudo-Boolean function under

uniform constraint needs to sample a feasible solution. This will ease the later analysis. We reduce the problem at hand to the well-known case of the (1+1) EA on the ONEMAX function defined as

$$\text{ONEMAX}(x) = \sum_{i=1}^{n} x_i.$$

We would like to point out that throughout this paper run time estimates of the form $\mathrm{O}(n \log(n/B))$ should be read as $\mathrm{O}(n \log n)$ in the extreme case of $B = 0$.

Lemma 3. *Consider the (1+1) EA optimizing an arbitrary non-negative pseudo-Boolean function under uniform constraint B. Then, the expected number of iterations until the algorithm samples a feasible solution for the first time is in $\mathrm{O}(n \log(n/B))$.*

Proof. In the infeasible range the (1+1) EA strictly prefers bit strings with fewer 1-bits due to the large penalty term of $(n w_{\max} + 1)$. Hence, the optimization process equals that on an unconstrained ONEMAX function considered as a minimization problem, a mutation is accepted if and only if it does not increase the total number of 1-bits $|x|_1$. A standard argument gives an expected drift of at least

$$E[|x|_1 - |x'|_1 \mid |x|_1 > B] \geq \frac{|x|_1}{n}\left(1 - \frac{1}{n}\right)^{n-1} \geq \frac{|x|_1}{en}.$$

by flipping any of the $|x|_1$ 1-bits and nothing else. The Multiplicative Drift Theorem [4] now yields an expected waiting time of

$$E[T] \leq en\left(\ln\left(\frac{n}{B}\right) + 1\right)$$

until $|x|_1$ is reduced from at most n below the cardinality constraint B. $\qquad\square$

As we will see in the next section the bound established above is not always tight. The importance of this result lies elsewhere. By employing Lemma 3, we will often be able to assume the optimization starts with a feasible solution without affecting the asymptotic run time.

3.1 OneMax

In the infeasible region of the search space any pseudo-Boolean function behaves like a ONEMAX problem. To complement this, we now examine the optimization process of the (1+1) EA on ONEMAX as the objective function. The run time turns out to be heavily dependent on the size of the cardinality bound B relative to the length n of the bit string. The following theorem shows that the time needed is never worse than in the unconstrained case. Furthermore, ONEMAX can be maximized even in sub-linear time if B is close to $n/2$.

The analysis of the optimization benefits extensively from symmetries inherent to the underlying random process. For ONEMAX The fitness function is invariant under permutations and the mutation operator of the (1+1) EA is indifferent towards the position and the value of the bits. Additionally, the number of 1-bits and the number of 0-bits in the initial solution are identically distributed, where this distribution is symmetric around its mean value $n/2$.

Theorem 4. *Let $B_{\min}$ denote $\min\{B, n-B\}$. The expected optimization time of the (1+1) EA on ONEMAX under uniform constraint B is in*

$$
\begin{aligned}
&\Theta(\sqrt{n}), &&\text{if } \left|B - \frac{n}{2}\right| < \sqrt{n};\\
&\Theta\left(\left|B - \frac{n}{2}\right|\right), &&\text{if } \sqrt{n} \leq \left|B - \frac{n}{2}\right| < \frac{n}{4};\\
&\Theta\left(n\log\left(\frac{n}{B_{\min}}\right)\right), &&\text{otherwise.}
\end{aligned}
$$

Proof. In this proof we identify the three main quantities that affect the expected run time of the (1+1) EA on constrained ONEMAX: the expected drift, the distance between the initial number of 1-bits and the cardinality bound B, and how far B is away from the central value $n/2$. Intuitively, the distance of the initial solution to B marks the ground we have to cover until we reach an optimal solution and the drift is the speed we travel with. The difference $|B - n/2|$ partitions the range of all possible values of B into regions corresponding to different asymptotic run times.

The first part of this proof is presented as a series of claims giving bounds on these quantities. While the drift can be inferred from standard arguments (Claim 1 below), the analysis of the influence of the two distance measures is more involved. The initial bit string has Hamming weight $n/2$ in expectation. Counter-intuitively, we show that the initial solution has an expected lack/surplus of roughly $\sqrt{n}$ 1-bits compared to any optimal solution even if B is arbitrarily close to $n/2$(Claims 2 & 4). This discrepancy grows linearly when B moves further away from the center $n/2$ (Claim 3).

The second part of the proof consists of deriving bounds on the expected optimization time from these claims.

First, we observe that the problem is equal to unconstrained ONEMAX (considered as a minimization problem or a maximization problem, respectively), if the cardinality bound is set to the extreme values $B = 0$ or $B = n$. Hence, the well-known $\Theta(n\log n)$ bound [6] carries over to this setting. We assume $B \notin \{0, n\}$ in the following. The upper bound also holds for the uniformly constrained case. We find a feasible solution in time $O(n\log n)$ (Lemma 3) and from there improve it until $B < n$ bits are set to 1. This can be done in an additional phase of $O(n\log n)$ rounds by a Coupon Collector's argument. We proceed in showing that for values of B which are closer to $n/2$ the optimization succeeds much faster.

For the drift analysis it is convenient to use either $|x|_1 = $ ONEMAX(x) itself or $|x|_0 = n - |x|_1$ as the potential function, depending on whether the current search string is feasible or not. Our first claim bounds the expected drift with respect to this potential. The results are well-known, we only state them here for completeness. A detailed discussion can be found in [4] and [29].

Claim 1. While the current solution x is feasible, the expected drift is bounded by

$$
\frac{|x|_0}{en} \leq E\big[\,|x|_0 - |x'|_0 \mid |x|_1 < B\,\big] \leq \frac{|x|_0}{n}.
$$

Similarly, if x is infeasible, $E[|x|_1 - |x'|_1] = \Theta(|x|_1/n)$.

Next, we give estimates on the second of the above quantities: the distance between the initial number of 1-bits $|x^{(0)}|_1$ and the constraint B. To ease notation, we employ

$d_B(x^{(0)}) = |B - |x^{(0)}|_1|$ to denote this distance and note that this is a random variable. Furthermore, we denote by $B_{\text{cen}} = |B - n/2|$ the absolute difference between B and the central value $n/2$, the third quantity.

Claim 2. The expected distance is bounded below by

$$
E\big[d_B(x^{(0)})\big] = \Omega(\sqrt{n}).
$$

Suppose $B \leq n/2$, then $|x^{(0)}|_1 \geq (n + \sqrt{n})/2$ is sufficient for $d_B(x^{(0)}) \geq \sqrt{n}/2$. The random variable $|x^{(0)}|_1$ is the sum of n i.i.d. Bernoulli trials and thus has expected value $n/2$ and standard deviation $\sqrt{n}/2$. An application of Lemma 6 in [24] now gives

$$
P\left[|x^{(0)}|_1 \geq \frac{n}{2} + \frac{\sqrt{n}}{2}\right] = \Omega(1).
$$

If $B > n/2$, we apply the same argument to the random variable $|x^{(0)}|_0$ (having the same distribution) and the event $|x^{(0)}|_0 \geq (n + \sqrt{n})/2$. By Lemma 2 we obtain in both cases

$$
E\big[d_B(x^{(0)})\big] \geq \Omega(1) \cdot \frac{\sqrt{n}}{2} = \Omega(\sqrt{n}).
$$

Claim 3. The expected distance is bounded below by

$$
E\big[d_B(x^{(0)})\big] \geq \frac{B_{\text{cen}}}{2}.
$$

The median of the random variable $|x^{(0)}|_1$ is $n/2$. Hence, if $B \leq n/2$, with probability $P[|x^{(0)}|_1 \geq n/2] \geq 1/2$ the distance is at least B_{cen}. The same holds if $B > n/2$ as also $P[|x^{(0)}|_1 \leq n/2] \geq 1/2$. The lower bound again is due to Lemma 2.

Claim 4. The expected distance is bounded above by

$$
E\big[d_B(x^{(0)})\big] \leq B_{\text{cen}} + \frac{e}{4\pi}\sqrt{n}.
$$

The Triangle Inequality yields $d_B(x^{(0)}) \leq B_{\text{cen}} + ||x^{(0)}|_1 - n/2|$. By the monotonicity and linearity of expectations we deduce

$$
\begin{aligned}
E\big[d_B(x^{(0)})\big] &\leq E\left[B_{\text{cen}} + \left||x^{(0)}|_1 - \frac{n}{2}\right|\right]\\
&= B_{\text{cen}} + E\left[\left||x^{(0)}|_1 - \frac{n}{2}\right|\right].
\end{aligned}
$$

The latter expected value is known as the *mean deviation* of a binomially distributed random variable. For the special case of success probability $1/2$ the mean deviation equals $\binom{n}{\lceil n/2\rceil}\lceil n/2\rceil 2^{-n}$, cf. e.g. [7]. Applying Stirling's approximations of the factorial, we obtain

$$
\begin{aligned}
E\left[\left||x^{(0)}|_1 - \frac{n}{2}\right|\right] &= \frac{n}{2^{n+1}}\binom{n}{\frac{n}{2}} = \frac{n}{2^{n+1}} \cdot \frac{n!}{\left(\frac{n}{2}!\right)^2}\\
&\leq \frac{n}{2^{n+1}} \cdot \frac{e\sqrt{n}\left(\frac{n}{e}\right)^n}{\left(\sqrt{2\pi}\sqrt{\frac{n}{2}}\left(\frac{n}{2e}\right)^{\frac{n}{2}}\right)^2} = \frac{e}{2\pi}\sqrt{n}.
\end{aligned}
$$

Claims 2, 3 and 4 together show that if $B_{\text{cen}} < \sqrt{n}$, the initial solution has distance $E[d_B(x^{(0)})] = \Theta(\sqrt{n})$; otherwise, it is in $\Theta(B_{\text{cen}})$.

The last claim states a useful technical property of the first feasible solution found during the optimization, as described in Lemma 3.

Claim 5. If the initial solution was infeasible, with probability superpolynomially close to 1 the first feasible solution sampled by the (1+1) EA has Hamming weight at least $B - \ln n$.

Consider the iteration in which the optimization process enters the feasible region. In order to jump from more than B bits set to 1 to less than $B - \ln n$, at least $\ln n$ bits must flip at once. We get the following bound on the probability,

$$P\big[\,|x'|_1 < B - \ln n \mid |x|_1 > B\,\big] \leq \sum_{i=\ln n}^{n} \binom{n}{i} \frac{1}{n^i}$$

$$\leq n \binom{n}{\ln n} \frac{1}{n^{\ln n}} \leq n \left(\frac{e}{\ln n}\right)^{\ln n} = \frac{1}{n^{\ln \ln n - 2}}.$$

In the remainder of this proof we infer bounds on the expected optimization time from the claims above. We commence with proving an universal lower bound. Claim 1 states that the drift during the whole optimization is at most 1, regardless of feasibility. We recall that T is the random variable denoting the number of rounds the (1+1) EA needs to sample an optimal solution for the first time. Its expected value $E[T \mid d_B(x^{(0)})]$ conditional on the distance of the initial solution to the bound B is again a random variable. Suppose this distance $d_B(x^{(0)})$ is equal to some natural number $0 \leq d \leq n$. The Additive Drift Theorem for lower bounds [11] asserts, for all such d,

$$E\big[T \mid d_B(x^{(0)}) = d\big] \geq d.$$

Utilizing Claim 2, we bound the expectation of the *derived* variable and, in turn, the expected optimization time,

$$E[T] = E\big[E\big[T \mid d_B(x^{(0)})\big]\big] \geq E\big[d_B(x^{(0)})\big] = \Omega(\sqrt{n}).$$

Note that this bound holds for any uniform constraint B.

According to Chernoff bounds, the initial solution has at least $n/3$ and at most $2n/3$ bits set to 1 with probability $1 - 2^{-\Omega(n)}$. We recall that the upper bound of $O(n \log n)$ rounds holds for all values of B. Hence, conditioning on $x^{(0)}$ to contain a linear number of both 1s and 0s affects the expected run time only by a sub-constant number of iterations. We omit this condition in the notation below.

Suppose $B_{\text{cen}} < \sqrt{n}$. While the currently best search point is infeasible, the number of 1-bits cannot increase. However, undershooting the target cardinality bound B by more than $\ln n$ is also unlikely (Claim 5). Conversely, the number of 1-bits cannot decrease while the search point is feasible. In summary, we can assume that the maintained solution x observes $n/3 \leq |x|_1 \leq 2n/3$ during the whole optimization. By Claim 1, the expected drift is at least $1/3e$. The Additive Drift Theorem for upper bounds [11] now yields

$$E\big[T \mid d_B(x^{(0)})\big] \leq 3e \cdot d_B(x^{(0)}).$$

Applying Claim 4 and the same technique as above, we obtain

$$E[T] = E\big[E\big[T \mid d_B(x^{(0)})\big]\big] \leq 3e \cdot E\big[d_B(x^{(0)})\big]$$

$$\leq 3e \left(B_{\text{cen}} + \frac{e}{2\pi}\sqrt{n}\right) = O(\sqrt{n}).$$

In the case of B_{cen} to be between $\sqrt{n}$ and $n/4$, the expected optimization time is in $\Theta(B_{\text{cen}})$. The argument is analogue to above involving Claim 3 (instead of Claim 2) as well as Claim 4. The main observation is that the drift can still assumed to be a constant in this range of B. Note that now $O(B_{\text{cen}} + \sqrt{n}) = O(B_{\text{cen}})$.

Finally, we turn the investigation to the case where the distance B_{cen} is larger than $n/4$. The main difference is that the expected drift can now become sub-constant during the optimization. We use a multiplicative drift argument to handle this issue.

First, we treat the case $B \geq 3n/4$. This implies $B_{\min} = \min\{B, n - B\} = n - B$. Furthermore, by the Chernoff argument shown above, the initial solution is feasible (with probability exponentially close to 1). We employ the number of 0-bits as the potential, which can be at most n. In order to optimize OneMax, the (1+1) EA has to generate an offspring with potential $B_{\min}$. By Claim 1 the expected drift is at least $|x|_0/en$. The Multiplicative Drift Theorem for upper bounds [4] now yields

$$E[T] \leq en \left(\ln\left(\frac{n}{B_{\min}}\right) + 1\right) = O\left(n \log\left(\frac{n}{B_{\min}}\right)\right).$$

Regarding the lower bound, we can assume that the initial solution is not only feasible but has at least $B_{\min} + n/12$ bits set to 0. This implies that the number of 0-bits cannot increase in the optimization. We only measure the time until this number is lower than $B_{\min} + \ln n$. Suppose the current potential is $|x|_0 = k$. Then, the expected drift is at most $k/n =: \delta k$ (Claim 1). Additionally, large jumps are unlikely. More formally, in order to have a progress of at least $k/2 =: \beta k$, between $k/2$ and k bits must flip simultaneously. The probability for such a mutation is at most

$$\sum_{i=k/2}^{k} \binom{n}{i}\frac{1}{n^i} \leq \sum_{i=k/2}^{k} \left(\frac{e}{i}\right)^i \leq \frac{k}{2}\left(\frac{2e}{k}\right)^{\frac{k}{2}}.$$

Since $k \geq B_{\min} + \ln n > \ln n$, we obtain

$$P\left[|x|_0 - |x'|_0 \geq \frac{k}{2} \;\middle|\; |x|_0 = k\right] < \frac{\ln n}{2}\left(\frac{2e}{\ln n}\right)^{\frac{\ln n}{2}}$$

$$\leq \frac{1}{2n\ln k} = \frac{\beta\delta}{\ln k}$$

for n sufficiently large. Hence, the conditions for the Multiplicative Drift Theorem for lower bounds [29] with parameters $\delta = 1/n$ and $\beta = 1/2$ are satisfied and we obtain

$$E[T] \geq \frac{1}{\delta} \, \ln\left(\frac{B_{\min} + n/12}{B_{\min} + \ln n}\right) \frac{1-\beta}{1+\beta}$$

$$\geq \frac{n}{3} \ln\left(\frac{n/12}{B_{\min} + \ln n}\right) \geq \frac{n}{6} \ln\left(\frac{n}{12\,B_{\min}}\right)$$

$$= \Omega\left(n \log\left(\frac{n}{B_{\min}}\right)\right).$$

The proofs of the run time bounds in case of $B \leq n/4$ are similar, but somehow simpler. Note that now $B_{\min} = B$.

For the analysis we invert the roles of 0- and 1-bits. With probability exponentially close to 1 the initial solution is *infeasible* and has a linear surplus of *1-bits*. A reduction below $B_{\min} + \ln n$ is necessary to optimize the bit string. By the same arguments as above this needs an expected number of $\Omega(n \log(n/B))$ iterations. To derive an upper bound, we argue that the search for a feasible solution, which takes time $O(n \log(n/B))$ in expectation (Lemma 3), dominates the run time. Once the (1+1) EA enters the feasible region, by Claim 5 we only need to collect $\ln n$ additional 1-bits with probability superpolynomially close to 1. Since $B \leq n/4$, the currently best solution x yields $|x|_0 \geq 3n/4$. Thus, we again observe a constant drift. Summarizing the two phases yields

$$E[T] = O\!\left(n \log\!\left(\frac{n}{B}\right)\right) + O(\log n) = O\!\left(n \log\!\left(\frac{n}{B_{\min}}\right)\right). \quad \square$$

3.2 Linear Functions

We move to the general case of linear objective functions under uniform constraint. The weights $w_i \geq 1$ are now chosen arbitrarily, whereas every b_i still is equal to 1. Contrary to our results on ONEMAX, the introduction of constraints increases the optimization time of linear functions in general. The reason is that during the optimization the increase of 1-bits stalls at the cardinality bound B. From there, progress is only possible by swapping a 1-bit to a position with larger weight, currently set to 0. This requires a simultaneous flip of both bits.

Theorem 5. *There is a linear function f and a bound B such that the optimization time of the (1+1) EA on f under uniform constraint B is in $\Omega(n^2)$, not only in expectation but even with high probability.[1]*

Proof. Let $\varepsilon > 0$ be an arbitrary positive quantity, possibly even dependent on n. We set the bound $B = 3n/4$ and define function f as

$$f(x) = \sum_{i=1}^{B} (1 + \varepsilon) x_i + \sum_{j=B+1}^{n} x_j.$$

The slight weight increase in the first B bits results in f to having its *unique* global optimum at $x^* = 1^{3n/4} 0^{n/4}$, contrary to the $\binom{n}{B}$ optima in the case of ONEMAX. The main idea of this proof is to show that during the optimization of f under constraint B the (1+1) EA w.h.p. samples a point with constant Hamming distance d_H from the optimum and with exactly B 1-bits. Then, the only way to reach the optimum is to exchange a 0 in the first $3n/4$ bit positions, the *first block*, with a 1 in the last $n/4$ bits, the *second block*. This event has a waiting time in $\Omega(n^2)$.

First, we prove that the (1+1) EA (again w.h.p.), before finding x^*, either samples a search point with Hamming distance between 4 and 8 from the optimum or runs for $\Omega(n^2)$ iteration regardless. We then show that, given such a feasible solution with constant Hamming distance, the algorithm finds another bit string with exactly B 1-bits prior to the optimal one. Finally, a union bound over the polynomially small error probabilities for these events implies the theorem.

[1]We use the term *with high probability* (w.h.p.) for a success probability of at least $1 - n^{-c}$ for some constant $c > 0$.

By Chernoff bounds the initial solution has no more than $2n/3$ bits set to 1 with probability exponentially close to 1. Thus, we observe a linear Hamming distance from x^*. In order to maximize function f the (1+1) EA must decrease this distance below any positive constant. We argue that the algorithm does not jump directly from an individual with distance greater than 8 to one with distance less than 4. To this end, let $d > 8$ be the number of wrongly set bits of the current search point x. We pessimistically assume that every mutation decreasing the distance is accepted. For this mutation at most 3 of these d bits are allowed to not flip at once. The probability for this event is

$$P\big[d_H(x', x^*) < 4 \mid d_H(x, x^*) = d\big] \leq \sum_{i=0}^{3} \binom{d}{d-i} \frac{1}{n^{d-i}}$$

$$\leq 4 \binom{d}{3} \frac{1}{n^{d-3}} \leq \frac{d^3}{n^{d-3}} = O\!\left(\frac{1}{n^6}\right).$$

The last estimate is due to the observation that the upper bound is maximal when $d = 9$. Therefore, for a suitable constant $c > 0$ this jump does not occur in the first cn^2 steps of the optimization with probability at least $1 - 1/n^4$.

We now assume that we are given a feasible solution x with $4 \leq d_H(x, x^*) \leq 8$ and continue the analysis from this point on. If x has exactly B 1-bits, the theorem follows immediately. The reason is as follows. Due to the Hamming distance x can have at most 8 0-bits in the first block and at most 8 1-bits in the second one. Every mutation must flip at least one of these misplaced 0s and 1s in B simultaneously to improve on the fitness value. The probability for this to happen is at most $8^2/n^2$.

What is left is the case where x has Hamming distance between 4 and 8, and strictly less than B 1-bits. However, again due to the distance, $|x|_1 \geq B - 8$ must hold. Consider a run of the (1+1) EA for $t^* = \ln n$ steps. Employing drift analysis, we show that during this phase the current best search point collects B 1s in total but still does not reach x^* w.h.p. A standard argument provides a lower bound of $E[|x'|_1 - |x|_1 \mid |x|_1 < B] \geq 1/4e =: \delta$ on the expected drift since x has more than $\bar{B} = n/4$ bits set to 0 and flipping any of them is accepted as a fitness increase. Furthermore, observe that no mutation incrementing the number of 1s by more than $8 =: s$ is accepted as this would violate the constraint. A tail bound for the Additive Drift Theorem [15] with parameters $\delta = 1/4e$ and $s = 8$ yields that the probability of the (1+1) EA to remove the surplus of 0s within t^* rounds is at least

$$1 - \exp\!\left(-\frac{t^* \delta^2}{8 s^2}\right) = 1 - \exp(-\Omega(\log n)) = 1 - \frac{1}{n^{\Omega(1)}}.$$

We are allowed to assume that the Hamming distance to the optimum does not increase beyond 8 during these t^* steps as otherwise the argument presented above still gives a quadratic lower bound on the run time. On the other hand, in order to reach x^* in this phase all $d \geq 4$ wrongly set bits would have to flip at least once. It is left to prove that this does not happen with high probability: A specific bit position does not flip during t^* rounds with probability $(1 - 1/n)^{t^*}$. Hence, all d bits flip during this phase with probability $(1 - (1 - 1/n)^{t^*})^d$. Therefore, the (1+1) EA does not sample the optimum during the t^* rounds with probability at least

$$1-\left(1-\left(1-\frac{1}{n}\right)^{t^*}\right)^d \geq 1-\left(\frac{t^*}{n}\right)^d \geq 1-\left(\frac{\ln n}{n}\right)^4 \geq 1-\frac{1}{n^2}.$$

The estimate is due to Bernoulli's Inequality and the observation that $\ln n \leq \sqrt{n}$ for n large enough. □

Theorem 6. *For arbitrary values of B, the expected optimization time of the (1+1) EA on any linear function under uniform constraint B is in $O(n^2 \log(B w_{max}))$.*

Proof. We start the analysis with a feasible solution due to Lemma 3. This implies that the (1+1) EA will never sample an infeasible solution from this point on. W.l.o.g. the weights of function f are in descending order starting with the left-most bit, i.e. $w_{max} = w_1 \geq w_2 \geq \cdots \geq w_n$. f under uniform constraint B has a maximum objective value of $f_{max} = \sum_{i=1}^{B} w_i$. For a search point x we assign the potential function $g(x) = f_{max} - f(x)$. This potential is non-negative and attains its minimum value 0 just in case $f(x)$ is optimal.

We again refer to the first B bits as the first block and the remaining $n - B$ bits as the second block and recall that $\overline{x_i}$ denote the negation of the bit at position i. We define two auxiliary functions

$$\text{loss}(x) = \sum_{i=1}^{B} w_i \overline{x_i}; \quad \text{surplus}(x) = \sum_{j=B+1}^{n} w_j x_j.$$

Thus, $\text{loss}(x)$ measures the total weights of the missing positions in the first block, while $\text{surplus}(x)$ is the sum of weights of the superfluous ones in the second block. We can reformulate the potential as

$$g(x) = \text{loss}(x) - \text{surplus}(x).$$

Suppose the current best solution x is non-optimal, let $k \geq 1$ denote the number of 0-bits in the first block of x. We pessimistically assume that $|x|_1$ reached the cardinality bound B. In this case the expected drift with respect to the above potential is minimal, since for $|x|_1 < B$ already a mutation flipping a single 0-bit could improve on the fitness value. Hence, there are exactly k corresponding 1-bits in the second block. Let $\mathcal{A}_{1,2}$ denote the event that one 0 in the first block, one 1 in the second and no other position flips in this round. By the law of total expectation, we bound the expected drift of $g(x)$ with the conditional drift under $\mathcal{A}_{1,2}$. Any of the k 0s in the first block are equally likely to flip and together they make up for the whole value of $\text{loss}(x)$. Thus, the average weight increase by flipping one of them is $\text{loss}(x)/k$. An analogue argument regarding $\text{surplus}(x)$ applies to the weight decrease by flipping one of the k 1s in the second block. We sum these by Lemma 2 on the expected drift of g and the event $\mathcal{A}_{1,2}$:

$$E[g(x) - g(x')] \geq E[g(x) - g(x') \mid \mathcal{A}_{1,2}] P[\mathcal{A}_{1,2}]$$
$$\geq \left(\frac{\text{loss}(x)}{k} - \frac{\text{surplus}(x)}{k}\right) \frac{k^2}{en^2} = g(x) \frac{k}{en^2} \geq \frac{g(x)}{en^2}.$$

We recall that $g(x)$ on feasible solutions is never larger than $f_{max} = \sum_{i=1}^{B} w_i$. The Multiplicative Drift Theorem [4] implies

$$E[T] \leq en^2 (\ln(f_{max}) + 1) \leq en^2 (\ln(B w_{max}) + 1). \quad \square$$

Consider the BinVal-function defined by $\text{BinVal}(x) = \sum_{i=1}^{n} 2^{n-i} x_i$. It serves as one extreme example of a linear function where any weight is strictly larger than the sum of all smaller weights. Hence, we can assume $w_{max} \leq 2^n$ and Theorem 6 implies a worst-case expected optimization time in $O(n^3)$ for all linear functions and arbitrary uniform constraint B. However, we suspect the log-factor appearing in the above bound to be an artifact of the analysis and consequently conjecture that every linear function can be optimized in time $O(n^2)$. As an example we return to the class of functions used in the proof of Theorem 5.

Theorem 7. *Let $0 < \varepsilon < 1/n$ be a positive real. Then, the expected optimization time of the (1+1) EA on the function $f(x) = \sum_{i=1}^{B} (1+\varepsilon) x_i + \sum_{j=B+1}^{n} x_j$ under uniform constraint B is in $O(n^2)$.*

Proof. Due to Lemma 3 the assumption of a feasible search point x as start for our investigation does not affect the asymptotic run time. The key observation of this proof is that any mutation of a feasible solution that reduces the number of 1-bits is rejected, implying a process similar to OneMax. In order for the offspring to be accepted, the fitness cannot be worse than the parents. Hence, any 1-bit deleted from the last $n - B$ bits (the second block) must be balanced by the gain of an additional 1-bit in the first B bits (the first block). Note that due to $\varepsilon < 1/n$ no fewer number of 1-bits suffice. Conversely, if a mutation reduces the number of 1-bits in the first block, one even needs a strict increase of 1-bits in the second block to compensate for that due to $\varepsilon > 0$.

The first statement of Theorem 4 asserts that in expectation within some $O(n \log n)$ iterations we sample a string x with $|x|_1 = B$. We also stay at the cardinality bound until the optimization is finished. We define the potential of a partial solution as the number of missing bits in the first block or, more formally, $g(x) = \sum_{i=1}^{B} \overline{x_i}$. Suppose the current potential is $g(x) = k$. Since we have reached the bound, the second block contains exactly k bits set to 1. Focusing on mutations which flip a single 0-bit in the first block and a single 1-bit in the second block, we bound the expected drift by

$$E[g(x) - g(x') \mid g(x) = k] \geq \frac{k^2}{n^2} \left(1 - \frac{1}{n}\right)^{n-2} \geq \frac{k^2}{en^2} =: h(k).$$

Let T_1 be the random variable denoting the number of iterations until the (1+1) EA reaches the optimum $x^* = 1^B 0^{n-B}$ starting from a solution with B 1-bits. The Variable Drift Theorem (Theorem 1, [13, 25]) applied to function h with $k_0 \leq B$ and $k_{min} = 1$ yields a bound on the expected value

$$E[T_1] \leq \frac{k_{min}}{h(k_{min})} + \int_{k_{min}}^{k_0} \frac{1}{h(k)} \, dk$$
$$= en^2 \left(1 + \int_1^B \frac{1}{k^2} \, dk\right) \leq 2en^2.$$

Together with the bound on finding a solution with exactly B 1-bits, this implies the theorem. □

3.3 LeadingOnes

Another well-studied but *non*-linear pseudo-Boolean function, admits a similar run time bound as in Theorem 6. LeadingOnes is defined as

$$\text{LeadingOnes}(x) = \sum_{i=1}^{n} \prod_{j=1}^{i} x_j$$

and counts the number of consecutive 1-bits starting from the left-most bit. Under uniform constraint B, the unique optimum is the string $1^B 0^{n-B}$.

Theorem 8. *For arbitrary values of B, the expected optimization time of the (1+1) EA on* LeadingOnes *under uniform constraint B is in* $O(n^2 \log B)$.

Proof. Again we can assume the optimization to start with a feasible solution without affecting the asymptotic run time due to Lemma 3. For a given search point x we assign the potential function $g(x)$ by

$$g(x) = B - \text{LeadingOnes}(x).$$

It suffices to bound the expected drift of $g(x)$ in the worst case, where the current solution x is non-optimal and has exactly B bits set to 1. Suppose x has potential $g(x) = k$, then the structure of x is as follows. Starting with the left-most bit there is a consecutive substring of $B - k$ 1-bits followed by a single 0, the remaining $n - B + k - 1$ bits form a substring in which exactly k positions are set to 1. In order to reduce the current potential, it suffices that the prominent first 0 as well as exactly one 1 among the later bits flip. This results in an expected drift of at least

$$E[g(x) - g(x') \mid g(x) = k] \geq \frac{1}{n} \frac{k}{n} \left(1 - \frac{1}{n}\right)^{n-2} \geq \frac{k}{en^2}.$$

Due to the Multiplicative Drift Theorem [4] we derive the bound for the expected time to reduce the potential of any feasible solution to 0

$$E[T] \leq en^2 (\ln(\max g(x)) + 1) = en^2 (\ln B + 1). \qquad \square$$

4. LINEAR CONSTRAINT

We now investigate linear functions under linear constraint, i.e. arbitrary $b_i > 0$ for the constraint function. The resulting optimization problem for bit strings is capable of encoding the NP-complete KnapSack problem, cf. [14]. Thus, it is not surprising that the (1+1) EA needs exponential run time already on the restricted case of OneMax as the objective function. Furthermore, it is well known that there are trap-like problem instances fitting the general knapsack formulation that can not be solved efficiently by simple evolutionary algorithms [10] working with the problem formulation considered in this paper. The reason for this is that they get trapped in a local optimum which has a large Hamming distance to the globally optimal solution. The class instances investigated in [10] consists of $n-1$ items having a weight and profit of 1 and one item having a large weight and profit. We show that even OneMax under a particular linear constraint can not be optimized efficiently by the (1+1) EA.

Theorem 9. *There is a linear function $b(x)$ and a bound B such that the optimization time of the (1+1) EA on* One-Max *under linear constraint $b(x) \leq B$ is in $2^{\Omega(n)}$, not only in expectation but even with overwhelming probability.*[2]

Proof. We define the constraint function $b(x)$ as

$$b(x) = \sum_{i=1}^{2n/3} n x_i + \sum_{i=2n/3+1}^{n} (n+1) x_i$$

together with the bound $B = 2n^2/3$. Therefore, we ensure that every bit string x with $|x|_1 < 2n/3$ is feasible while the ones with $|x|_1 \geq 2n/3$ are infeasible. The *sole exception* is the optimal solution $x^* = 1^{2n/3} 0^{n/3}$. In other words, the collection of strings with exactly $2n/3 - 1$ bits set to 1 form a large plateau of equal but non-optimal fitness. We condition the following analysis on the initial solution being feasible, which happens with overwhelming probability due to Chernoff bounds. After that, the (1+1) EA never adopts an infeasible search point as the current best.

We prove an *unbiasedness* property [19] of the underlying random process. Informally, as long as the optimum has not been found, the probability of a bit string to be sampled in round t depends only on the number of the bits set to 1, not on their position. In order to state this more formally, we first need some additional notation highlighting the effect of selection in the optimization. Let $(X^{(t)})_{t \geq 0}$ be the series of random variables denoting the search points adopted *after* the selection in round t. For $t > 0$ $Y^{(t)}$ denotes the offspring (of individual $X^{(t-1)}$) created in round t *before* any selection takes place, whereas $Y^{(0)} = X^{(0)}$ is the initial solution. For a permutation $\pi \colon \{1, \ldots n\} \to \{1, \ldots n\}$ and bit string $x \in \{0,1\}^n$ let $\pi(x) = x_{\pi(1)} x_{\pi(2)} \ldots x_{\pi(n)}$ be the string obtained from x by deranging its positions according to π.

While x^* has not yet been found the search behaves like the (1+1) EA on unconstrained OneMax with a rejection of solutions with Hamming weight at least $2n/3$. We claim that for any $t > 0$, permutation π and bit string $y \in \{0,1\}^n$

$$P[Y^{(t)} = y \mid X^{(t-1)} \neq x^*] = P[Y^{(t)} = \pi(y) \mid X^{(t-1)} \neq x^*].$$

We prove this by induction over t. Lehre and Witt have characterized the mutation operator of the (1+1) EA as an *unary, unbiased variation operator* [19]; in particular, it is invariant under permutation, that is

$$P[Y^{(t)} = y \mid X^{(t-1)} = x] = P[Y^{(t)} = \pi(y) \mid X^{(t-1)} = \pi(x)].$$

For the initial $X^{(0)}$ every bit string is equally likely to be chosen satisfying the claim.

The search point $X^{(t-1)}$ is equal to the offspring $Y^{(t^*)}$ of the round $t^* < t$ in which it was selected. By the induction hypothesis the claim holds for t^*. The selection itself is also unbiased as the objective function OneMax (with the additional rejection rule) is invariant under bit permutation. This implies that we can apply the law of total probability to express $P[Y^{(t)} = y \mid X^{(t-1)} \neq x^*]$ as a sum over all conditional probabilities that the current best (feasible, non-optimal) solution is x and its offspring is y. We conclude

---

[2]We use the term *with overwhelming probability* for a success probability of at least $1 - 2^{-cn}$ for some constant $c > 0$.

$$P[Y^{(t)} = y \mid X^{(t-1)} \neq x^*]$$

$$= \sum_{|x|_1 < \frac{2}{3}n} P[Y^{(t)} = y \mid X^{(t-1)} = x]\, P[X^{(t-1)} = x]$$

$$= \sum_{|x|_1 < \frac{2}{3}n} P[Y^{(t)} = \pi(y) \mid X^{(t-1)} = \pi(x)]\, P[X^{(t-1)} = \pi(x)]$$

$$= P[Y^{(t)} = \pi(y) \mid X^{(t-1)} \neq x^*].$$

There are $\binom{n}{n/3}$ bit strings with weight $2n/3$, but only one of them is optimal. The unbiasedness regarding permutation implies that for any t the probability of finding x^* in round t is at most

$$P[Y^{(t)} = x^* \mid X^{(t-1)} \neq x^*] \leq \binom{n}{n/3}^{-1} \leq 3^{-\frac{n}{3}},$$

which yields an exponential waiting time. Moreover, a union bound shows that for a suitably small constant $c > 0$ the probability of finding the optimum within the first 2^{cn} iterations is exponentially small. $\qquad\square$

5. CONCLUSION

Studying the run time behavior of linear functions has provided many new tools for analyzing evolutionary computing techniques and set the basis for run time studies for more complex problems. With this paper we have contributed to the area of run time analysis of evolutionary computing by studying classes of linear functions under a given linear constraint. This is equivalent to special classes of the well-known knapsack problem. Central to the area of run time analysis for linear functions is the function ONEMAX. In our study we have focused on problem classes where the objective function or the constraint function is given by ONEMAX.

Our theoretical investigations show that the (1+1) EA can handle uniform constraints efficiently, but fails for more general constraints even on ONEMAX. The constraint handling we employed directs the search within the infeasible region towards the feasible region by adding a penalty dependent on the distance to the constraint. However, the search within the feasible region is not guided by any knowledge about the constraint. Therefore, it is interesting to investigate whether additional information can help direct the search such that ONEMAX with non-uniform constraint can be handled efficiently.

Acknowledgments

The research leading to these results has received funding from the European Union Seventh Framework Programme (FP7/2007-2013) under grant agreement no. 618091 (SAGE) and from the Australian Research Council under grant agreements DP140103400 and DP160102401.

6. REFERENCES

[1] A. Auger and B. Doerr. *Theory of Randomized Search Heuristics: Foundations and Recent Developments.* World Scientific Publishing, 2011.

[2] R. Beier. *Probabilistic Analysis of Discrete Optimization Problems.* PhD thesis, Universität des Saarlandes, 2005.

[3] D. Dang and P. K. Lehre. Simplified Runtime Analysis of Estimation of Distribution Algorithms. In *Proc. of GECCO'15*, pages 513–518, 2015.

[4] B. Doerr, D. Johannsen, and C. Winzen. Multiplicative Drift Analysis. *Algorithmica*, 64:673–697, 2012.

[5] S. Droste. Analysis of the (1+1) EA for a Noisy OneMax. In *Proc. of GECCO'04*, pages 1088–1099, 2004.

[6] S. Droste, T. Jansen, and I. Wegener. On the Analysis of the (1+1) Evolutionary Algorithm. *Theoretical Computer Science*, 276:51–81, 2002.

[7] J. S. Frame. Mean Deviation of the Binomial Distribution. *The American Mathematical Monthly*, 52:377–379, 1945.

[8] C. Gießen and T. Kötzing. Robustness of Populations in Stochastic Environments. *Algorithmica*, 75:462–489, 2016.

[9] M. Harman. Software Engineering Meets Evolutionary Computation. *IEEE Computer*, 44:31–39, 2011.

[10] J. He, B. Mitavskiy, and Y. Zhou. A theoretical assessment of solution quality in evolutionary algorithms for the knapsack problem. In *Proceedings of the IEEE Congress on Evolutionary Computation, CEC 2014, Beijing, China, July 6-11, 2014*, pages 141–148. IEEE, 2014.

[11] J. He and X. Yao. A study of drift analysis for estimating computation time of evolutionary algorithms. *Natural Computing*, 3:21–35, 2004.

[12] T. Jansen. *Analyzing Evolutionary Algorithms - The Computer Science Perspective.* Natural Computing Series. Springer, 2013.

[13] D. Johannsen. *Random Combinatorial Structures and Randomized Search Heuristics.* PhD thesis, Universität des Saarlandes, 2010.

[14] H. Kellerer, U. Pferschy, and D. Pisinger. *Knapsack Problems.* Springer, 2004.

[15] T. Kötzing. Concentration of First Hitting Times Under Additive Drift. *Algorithmica*, 75:490–506, 2016.

[16] T. Kötzing, A. Lissovoi, and C. Witt. (1+1) EA on Generalized Dynamic OneMax. In *Proc. of FOGA'15*, pages 40–51, 2015.

[17] T. Kötzing, F. Neumann, D. Sudholt, and M. Wagner. Simple Max-Min Ant Systems and the Optimization of Linear Pseudo-Boolean Functions. In *Proc. of FOGA'11*, pages 209–218, 2011.

[18] C. Le Goues, T. Nguyen, S. Forrest, and W. Weimer. GenProg: A Generic Method for Automatic Software Repair. *IEEE Transaction on Software Engineering*, 38:54–72, 2012.

[19] P. K. Lehre and C. Witt. Black-Box Search by Unbiased Variation. *Algorithmica*, 64:623–642, 2012.

[20] X. Li, M. R. Bonyadi, Z. Michalewicz, and L. Barone. Solving a Real-world Wheat Blending Problem Using a Hybrid Evolutionary Algorithm. In *Proc. of CEC'13*, pages 2665–2671, 2013.

[21] D. Lückehe, M. Wagner, and O. Kramer. On Evolutionary Approaches to Wind Turbine Placement with Geo-Constraints. In *Proc. of GECCO'15*, pages 1223–1230, 2015.

[22] H. Mühlenbein. How Genetic Algorithms Really Work: Mutation and Hillclimbing. In *Proc. of PPSN'92*, pages 15–26, 1992.

[23] F. Neumann and C. Witt. *Bioinspired Computation in Combinatorial Optimization:Algorithms and Their Computational Complexity*. Springer, 2010.

[24] P. S. Oliveto and C. Witt. Improved Time Complexity Analysis of the Simple Genetic Algorithm. *Theoretical Computer Science*, 605:21–41, 2015.

[25] J. E. Rowe and D. Sudholt. The Choice of the Offspring Population Size in the $(1,\lambda)$ EA. In *Proc. of GECCO'12*, pages 1349–1356, 2012.

[26] D. A. Spielman and S. Teng. Smoothed analysis: an attempt to explain the behavior of algorithms in practice. *Communications of the ACM*, 52:76–84, 2009.

[27] C. S. Stokes, A. R. Simpson, and H. R. Maier. A Computational Software Tool for the Minimization of Costs and Greenhouse Gas Emissions Associated with Water Distribution Systems. *Environmental Modelling and Software*, 69:452–467, 2015.

[28] D. Sudholt and C. Witt. Runtime Analysis of a Binary Particle Swarm Optimizer. *Theoretical Computer Science*, 411:2084–2100, 2010.

[29] C. Witt. Tight Bounds on the Optimization Time of a Randomized Search Heuristic on Linear Functions. *Combinatorics, Probability and Computing*, 22:294–318, 2013.

[30] F. Zheng, A. R. Simpson, and A. C. Zecchin. Improving the Efficiency of Multi-objective Evolutionary Algorithms Through Decomposition: An Application to Water Distribution Network Design. *Environmental Modelling and Software*, 69:240–252, 2015.

[31] Y. Zhou and J. He. A Runtime Analysis of Evolutionary Algorithms for Constrained Optimization Problems. *IEEE Transactions on Evolutionary Computation*, 11:608–619, 2007.

Analysis of the Clearing Diversity-Preserving Mechanism

Edgar Covantes Osuna
University of Sheffield
Sheffield, S1 4DP,
United Kingdom
ecovantes1@sheffield.ac.uk

Dirk Sudholt
University of Sheffield
Sheffield, S1 4DP,
United Kingdom
d.sudholt@sheffield.ac.uk

ABSTRACT

Clearing is a niching method inspired by the principle of assigning the available resources among a subpopulation to a single individual. The clearing procedure supplies these resources only to the best individual of each subpopulation: the winner. So far, its analysis has been focused on experimental approaches that have shown that clearing is a powerful diversity mechanism. We use empirical analysis to highlight some of the characteristics that makes it a useful mechanism and runtime analysis to explain how and why it is a powerful method. We prove that a (μ+1) EA with large enough population size and a phenotypic distance function always succeeds in optimising all functions of unitation for small niches in polynomial time, while a genotypic distance function requires exponential time. Finally, we prove that a (μ+1) EA with phenotypic and genotypic distances is able to find both optima in TwoMax for large niches in polynomial expected time.

Keywords

Clearing, diversity-preserving mechanisms, evolutionary algorithm, runtime analysis

1. INTRODUCTION

One of the major difficulties in a population-based evolutionary algorithm (EA) is the premature convergence toward a sub-optimal individual before the fitness landscape is explored properly. Diversity-preserving mechanisms provide the ability to visit many and/or different unexplored regions of the search space and generate solutions that differ in various significant ways from those seen before [7, 8, 12].

A diverse population can deal with multimodal functions and can explore several hills in the fitness landscape simultaneously, so they can therefore support global exploration and help to locate several local and global optima. The algorithm can offer several good solutions to the user, a feature desirable in multiobjective optimisation. Also, it provides higher chances to find dissimilar individuals and to create

good offspring with the possibility of enhancing the performance of other procedures such as crossover [5].

Most analyses and comparisons made between diversity-preserving mechanisms are assessed by means of empirical investigations [2, 19] or theoretical runtime analyses [3, 4, 6, 9, 13, 14]. There are examples where empirical investigations are used to support theoretical runtime analyses and close the gap between both fields [5, 15]. Both approaches are important to understand how these mechanisms impact the EA runtime and if they enhance the search for obtaining good individuals. These different expectations imply where EAs and which diversity-preserving mechanism should be used and, perhaps even more important, where they should not be used.

In this sense, we use empirical investigations to get insights into the behaviour of the clearing diversity mechanism and we use theoretical runtime analyses to provide foundations of the behaviour of this mechanism. *Clearing* is a niching method inspired by the principle of sharing limited resources within subpopulations of individuals characterised by some similarities. Instead of evenly sharing the available resources among the individuals of a subpopulation, the clearing procedure supplies these resources only to the best individual of each subpopulation: the winner. The winner takes all rather than sharing resources with the other individuals of the same niche (subspace suitable for a small group of the same or similar type of individuals) as is done with fitness sharing [16].

Like in fitness sharing, the clearing algorithm uses a dissimilarity measure given by a threshold called *clearing radius* σ (or sharing radius in the context of fitness sharing) between individuals to determine if they belong to the same subpopulation or not.

The basic idea is to preserve the fitness of the individual that has the best fitness called dominant individual, while it resets the fitness of all the other individuals of the same subpopulation to zero[1]. With such a mechanism, two approaches can be considered. For a given population the set of winners is unique. The winner and all the individuals that it dominates are then fictitiously removed from the population. Then we proceed in the same way with the new population which is then obtained. Thus, the list of all the winners is produced after a certain number of steps.

---

[1] We tacitly assume that all fitness values are larger than 0 for simplicity. In case of a fitness function f with negative fitness values we can change clearing to reset fitness to $f_{\min} - 1$, where $f_{\min}$ is the minimum fitness value of f, such that all reset individuals are worse than any other individuals.

FOGA '17, January 12 - 15, 2017, Copenhagen, Denmark

© 2017 Copyright held by the owner/author(s). Publication rights licensed to ACM.
ISBN 978-1-4503-4651-1/17/01...$15.00

DOI: http://dx.doi.org/10.1145/3040718.3040731

On the other hand, the population can be dominated by several winners. It is also possible to generalise the clearing algorithm by accepting several winners chosen among the *niche capacity* κ (best individuals of each niche defined as the maximum number of winners that a niche can accept). Thus, choosing niching capacities between one and the population size offers intermediate situations between the maximum clearing ($\kappa = 1$) and a standard EA ($\kappa \geq \mu$).

Empirical investigations made in [16, 18] mention that clearing surpasses all other niching methods because of its ability to produce a great quantity of new individuals by randomly recombining elements of different niches, controlling this production by resetting the fitness of the poor individuals in each different niche. Furthermore, an elitist strategy prevents the rejection of the best individuals.

As in past research, we test the clearing diversity mechanism to confirm if the mechanism is able to provide good solutions by means of experiments, and we include theoretical runtime analysis to prove how and why an EA is able to obtain good solutions depending on how the population size, σ, κ, and the dissimilarity measure are chosen.

In the remainder of this paper, we first present the algorithmic approach, functions of unitation, including a bimodal test function of unitation called TwoMax, and the dissimilarity measures used in Section 2. Section 3 contains the experimental approach and results that gave rise to the theoretical analysis presented in Sections 4 and 5 for small and large niches, respectively. In Section 4 we show how the clearing mechanism is able to solve, for small niches and the right distance function, all functions of unitation, and in Section 5 we show how clearing solves TwoMax with the most natural distance function: Hamming distance. We present our conclusions in Section 6, where we mention how well the empirical results match with our theoretical results, giving additional insight into the dynamic behaviour of the algorithm.

2. PRELIMINARIES

We focus our analysis on the simple EA with a finite population called (μ+1) EA. Our aim is to develop rigorous runtime bounds of (μ+1) EA with the clearing diversity mechanism. We want to study how diversity helps to escape local optima. The basic (μ+1) EA has already been investigated in [20]. We incorporate the clearing method into the basic algorithm, resulting in Algorithm 1.

The idea behind Algorithm 1 is: once a population with μ individuals is generated, an individual y is selected and changed according to mutation. A temporary population P_t^* is created from population P_t and the individual y, then the fitness of each individual in P_t^* is updated according to the clearing procedure shown in Algorithm 2. Each individual is compared with the winner(s) of each niche in order to check if it belongs to a certain niche or not and to check if its a winner or if it is cleared. Here $d(x_i, x_j)$ is any dissimilarity measure (distance function) between two individuals x_i and x_j of population P. Finally, we keep control of the *niche capacity* defined by κ.

For the sake of clarity, the replacement policy will be the one defined in [20]: the individuals with best fitness are selected (set of winners) and individuals coming from the new generation are preferred if their fitness values are at least as good as the current ones (novelty is rewarded).

Algorithm 1 (μ+1) EA with clearing

1: Let $t := 0$ and initialise P_0 with μ individuals chosen uniformly at random.
2: **while** optimum not found **do**
3:   Choose $x \in P_t$ uniformly at random.
4:   Create y by flipping each bit in x independently with probability $1/n$.
5:   Let $P_t^* := P_t \cup \{y\}$.
6:   Update $f(P_t^*)$ with the clearing procedure.
7:   Choose $z \in P_t^*$ with worst fitness uniformly at random.
8:   **if** $f(y) \geq f(z)$ **then**
9:     Let $P_{t+1} = P_t^* \setminus \{z\}$.
10:   **else**
11:     Let $P_{t+1} = P_t^* \setminus \{y\}$.
12:   **end if**
13:   $t := t + 1$.
14: **end while**

Algorithm 2 Clearing

1: Sort P according to fitness of individuals by decreasing values.
2: **for** $i = 0$ to $|P|-1$ **do**
3:   **if** $f(x_i) > 0$ **then**
4:     $nbwinners := 1$
5:     **for** $j = i + 1$ to $|P|-1$ **do**
6:       **if** $f(x_j) > 0$ **and** $d(x_i, x_j) < \sigma$ **then**
7:         **if** $nbwinners < \kappa$ **then**
8:           $nbwinners := nbwinners + 1$
9:         **else**
10:           $f(x_j) := 0$
11:         **end if**
12:       **end if**
13:     **end for**
14:   **end if**
15: **end for**

We consider functions of unitation—functions defined over the number of 1-bits contained in a string—for the analysis of small niches and a particular bimodal function of unitation called TwoMax$(x) := \max\{\sum_{i=1}^{n} x_i, n - \sum_{i=1}^{n} x_i\}$ (see Figure 1) for the analysis of large niches, respectively. The function TwoMax consists of two different symmetric branches ZeroMax and OneMax with 0^n and 1^n as global optima, respectively, and has already been investigated for the analysis of the effectiveness of diversity-preserving mechanisms [5, 14].

Since we aim at analysing the global exploration capabilities of Algorithm 1, we analyse the expected time until both optima have been reached. TwoMax is an ideal benchmark function for clearing as it is simply structured, hence facilitating a theoretical analysis, and it is hard for evolutionary algorithms to find both optima as they have the maximum possible Hamming distance. Its choice further allows comparisons with previous approaches such as avoiding genotype or phenotype duplicates [5], deterministic crowding [5], and fitness sharing [5, 14].

Finally, as dissimilarity measures, we have considered two distances, genotypic (Hamming distance) and phenotypic (usually defined as Euclidean distance between two phenotypes). As TwoMax is a function of unitation, we have

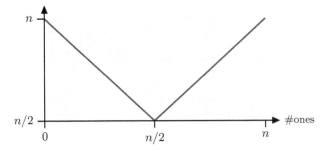

Figure 1: Sketch of the function TWOMAX.

adopted the same approach as in [5, 14], allowing the distance function d to depend on the number of ones: $d(x, y) := ||x|_1 - |y|_1|$.

3. EXPERIMENTS AND THEORY

The experimental approach is focused on the analysis of Algorithm 1 and its behaviour when the parameters σ, κ, and μ are changed and how these parameters can be set. The main objective is to find out general behaviours in order to provide foundations for our theoretical analysis.

In [5, 14] it has been proved that fitness sharing and deterministic crowding allow $(\mu+1)$ EA to find both optima for TWOMAX with high probability. We are interested in observing if clearing has the same capacity, so we consider exponentially increasing population sizes $\mu = 2, 4, 8, \ldots, 1024$ for just one size of $n = 30$ (but a theoretical analysis that holds for all n) and perform 100 runs with different settings of parameters σ and κ, so for this experimental framework, we have defined $\sigma = \{1, 2, \sqrt{n}, n/2\}$, $\kappa = \{1, \sqrt{\mu}, \mu/2, (\mu/2 + \sqrt{\mu}), \mu\}$ with phenotypic distance.

Since we are interested in proving how good/bad clearing is, we define the following outcomes and stopping criteria for each run. *Success*, both branches of TWOMAX have been reached, i.e., the run is stopped if the population contains both 0^n and 1^n in the population. *Failure*, when the population only consists of copies of the same genotype or when a run was stopped manually when after 2000 generations stagnation was detected.

3.1 Empirical Analysis and Results

Before starting to define the results, it is better to define overall behaviours, then to focus on specific results in order to understand how the mentioned parameters work together.

Regarding the *niche capacity* κ, it is mentioned in [16] that while the value of κ approaches the size of the population, the clearing effect vanishes and the search becomes a standard EA. This effect is verified in the present experimental approach. With $\kappa \geq \mu/2$ the capability of the method to explore both branches of TWOMAX is reduced. With a small population $\mu \leq 64$ and $\sigma \leq 2$, one branch takes over, removing the individuals on the other branch achieving at least 0.84 success rate. The only way to compensate this is to increase σ between $\sqrt{n}$ and $n/2$ in order to let more individuals participate in the niche, with $\mu \leq 32$ to achieve 0.80 success rate. A reduced niching capacity seems to have a better effect exploring both branches. The best cases were $1 \leq \kappa \leq \sqrt{\mu}$ for maintaining a set of winners, avoiding takeover or extinction.

For small values of $\sigma = \{1, 2\}$ and $\kappa = 1$, with sufficiently many individuals, $\mu = (n/2 + 1) \cdot \kappa$, every individual can creates its own niche, and since only one individual is allowed to be the winner, the individuals are spread in the search space reaching both optima with 1.0 success and 0.0 failure rate. In this scenario, since we are allowing sufficiently many individuals in the population, individuals can be initialised in both branches, reaching their respective peak as shown in Figure 2 (in this case we only show the behaviour of the population with $\mu = \{8, 16, 32\}$, higher values for μ have the same behaviour).

In this scenario we are making use of small differences between individuals rather than using problem-specific knowledge, such as the minimum distance, that allows us to discriminate between the two branches or optima. Instead, it seems that it is the population size that provides enough pressure to solve it. Also, we use the size of the population to have individuals on both branches or occupy all niches as we will show in Section 4.1. In this scenario, using genotypic distance $(\mu+1)$ EA fails with 1.0 rate because of this metric, since we have defined a small *clearing radius* individuals with the same phenotype will result in a large Hamming distance, creating winners with the same fitness (as will be proved in Section 4.2).

Second, the *clearing radius* σ, defining a small *clearing radius* $\sigma = \{1, 2\}$ with a small *niche capacity* $\kappa < \sqrt{\mu}$ and $\mu \leq 4$ can create takeover or extinction of a certain branch with 1.0 failure rate because one branch may evolve faster. In order to avoid this, it is necessary to increase μ. With $\mu \geq 8$ and a small κ, every niche can have a reduced number of winners, cleared individuals are eliminated as soon as new and better individuals are created (with their respective niches). Also, as we increase μ the spread of the individuals is such that individuals in one branch can reach the other branch as a result of this behaviour with a success rate of 1.0.

For $\sigma = \{\sqrt{n}, n/2\}$ and $\kappa \leq \mu/2$ the behaviour of the algorithm is the opposite. In the case of larger niches it is possible to divide the search space in fewer niches with more winners in each niche. Here the individuals have the opportunity to move, change inside the niche, reach other niches allowing the movement between branches, reaching the opposite optimum with success rate of at least 0.97.

With $\sigma = \sqrt{n}$, $1 \leq \kappa \leq \mu/2$ and $\mu \geq 8$, the method was able to reach both optima with at least 0.97 success rate and 0.03 failure rate. In Figure 3 the effect of κ can be seen with sufficiently many individuals. With restrictive niche capacities (Figure 3a), the population is scattered in the search space while this capacity is reduced as we allow more individuals to be part of each niche (Figure 3c). This behaviour can be generalised and is more evident for larger values of μ.

With $\mu \geq 8$ it is possible to overcome takeover and extinction if σ and κ are chosen appropriately. For example, if $\kappa > \sqrt{\mu}$ and $\sigma = n/2$ it will be necessary to provide $\mu \geq 64$ in order to compensate the takeover of a niche in a certain branch due to the number of winners allowed by κ and the large set up of σ and finally achieve 1.0 success rate.

Finally, for $\sigma = n/2$, $\kappa = 1$, and sufficiently large μ, the algorithm was able to reach both optima with 1.0 success rate. As shown in Figure 4, the search space is divided in 2 niches by σ. Even if all the individuals are initialised in one branch it is possible to climb down. Once there is a winner

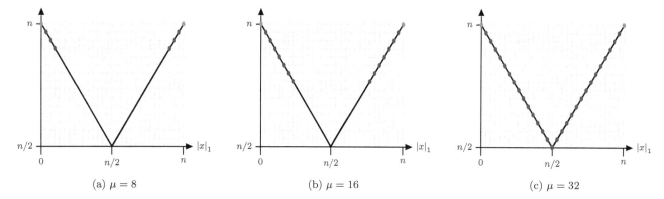

(a) $\mu = 8$ (b) $\mu = 16$ (c) $\mu = 32$

Figure 2: Snapshot of a typical population at the time both optima were reached, showing the spread of individuals in branches of TwoMax for $n = 30$, $\sigma = 1$ and $\kappa = 1$. Where the red (extreme) points represent optimal individuals, blue points represent niche winners. The rows on the grid represents the fitness value of an individual and its position on TwoMax and the columns represent the partitioned search space (niches) created by the parameter σ.

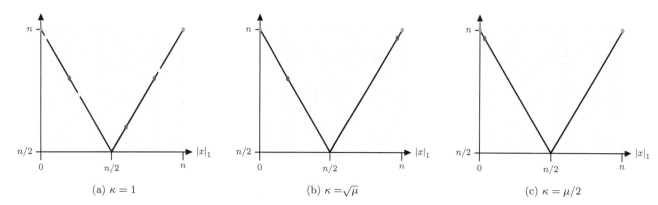

(a) $\kappa = 1$ (b) $\kappa = \sqrt{\mu}$ (c) $\kappa = \mu/2$

Figure 3: Snapshot of a typical population at the time both optima were reached, showing the spread of individuals in branches of TwoMax for $n = 30$, $\sigma = \sqrt{n}$ and $\mu = 8$. Where the red (extreme) points represent optimal individuals, blue points represent niche winners, and the green points represent cleared individuals. The rows on the grid represents the fitness value of an individual and its position on TwoMax and the columns represent the partitioned search space (niches) created by the parameter σ.

in the other branch, this individual will climb up until it reaches the opposite optimum that includes the creation of individuals in the branch as proved in our theoretical analysis for large niches in Section 5.

The last two scenarios have the property of dividing the search space in niches in which the individuals are able to spread, move, climb down a branch; this behaviour allows those individuals to reach different niches, until the opposite branch and optima is reached. In this sense, extreme points always survive, a desirable property in this method.

4. SMALL NICHES

In this section we prove that $(\mu+1)$ EA with phenotypic clearing and a small niche capacity is not only able to achieve both optima of TwoMax but is also able to optimise all functions of unitation with a large enough population, while genotypic clearing fails in achieving such a task.

4.1 Phenotypic Clearing

First it is necessary to define a very important property of clearing, which is its capacity of preventing the rejection of the best individuals in $(\mu+1)$ EA, and once μ is defined

large enough, clearing and the population size pressure will always optimise any function of unitation.

Lemma 4.1 *Consider* $(\mu+1)$ EA *with phenotypic clearing and* $\sigma = 1$, $\mu \geq (n + 1) \cdot \kappa$ *on any fitness function. Then, winners are never removed from the population, i.e., if* $x \in P_t$ *is a winner then* $x \in P_{t+1}$.

Proof. After the first evaluation with clearing, individuals dominated by other individuals are cleared and the dominant individuals are declared as winners. Cleared individuals are removed from the population when new winners are created and occupy new niches. Once an individual becomes a winner, it can only be removed if the size of the population is not large enough to maintain it, as the worst winner is removed if a new winner reaches a new better niche. Since there are at most $n + 1$ niches, each having at most κ winners, if $\mu \geq (n+1) \cdot \kappa$ then there must be a cleared individual amongst the $\mu + 1$ parents and offspring considered for deletion at the end of the generation. Thus, a cleared individual will be deleted, so winners cannot be removed from the population. □

The behaviour described above means, that with the defined parameters and sufficiently large μ to occupy all the

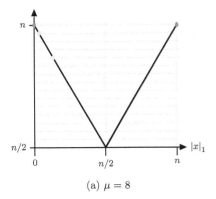

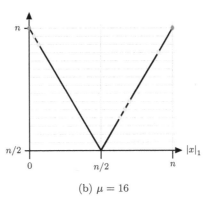

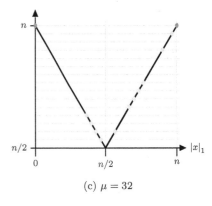

| (a) $\mu = 8$ | (b) $\mu = 16$ | (c) $\mu = 32$ |

Figure 4: Snapshot of a typical population at the time both optima were reached, showing the spread of individuals in branches of TWOMAX for $n = 30$, $\sigma = n/2$ and $\kappa = 1$. Where the red (extreme) points represent optimal individuals, blue points represent niche winners, and the green points represent cleared individuals. The rows on the grid represents the fitness value of an individual and its position on TWOMAX and the columns represent the partitioned search space (niches) created by the parameter σ.

niches, we have enough conditions for the furthest individuals (individuals with the minimum and maximum number of ones in the population) to reach the opposite edges.

Lemma 4.2 *Let f be a function of unitation and $\sigma = 1$, $\mu \geq (n+1)\cdot\kappa$. Then, the expected time for finding the search points 0^n and 1^n with $(\mu+1)$ EA with phenotypic clearing on f is $O(\mu n \log n)$.*

Proof. Now that we know that a winner cannot be removed from the population by Lemma 4.1, it is just a matter of finding the expected time until 0^n and 1^n are found. Because of the elitist approach of $(\mu+1)$ EA, winners will never be replaced if we assume a large enough population size, the winners with the minimum and maximum number of ones in the population will never be removed, we can apply a level-based argument as follows. First, we will focus on estimating the time until the 1^n individual is found (by symmetry, the same analysis apply for the 0^n individual). If the current farthest niche is i, it has a probability of being selected at least of $1/\mu$. In order to create a niche $j > i$, it is just necessary that one of the $n - i$ zeroes is flipped into 1-bit and the other bits remains unchanged. Each bit flip has a probability of being changed (mutated) of $1/n$ and the remaining bits remains unchanged is $(1-1/n)^{n-1}$. Hence, the probability of creating niche j from i with $j > i$ is bounded as follows

$$\frac{1}{\mu} \cdot \frac{n-i}{n} \cdot \left(1 - \frac{1}{n}\right)^{n-1} \geq \frac{n-i}{\mu e n}.$$

The expected time for increasing the best niche i is hence at most $(\mu e n)/(n - i)$ and the expected time for finding 1^n is at most

$$\sum_{i=0}^{n-1} \frac{\mu e n}{n-i} = \mu e n \sum_{i=1}^{n} \frac{1}{i} \leq \mu e n \ln n = O(\mu n \log n).$$

Adding the same time for finding 0^n proves the claim. $\square$

Once the search points 0^n and 1^n have been found, we can focus on the time required for the algorithm until all intermediate niches are discovered.

Lemma 4.3 *Let f be any function of unitation, $\sigma = 1$, $\mu \geq (n + 1) \cdot \kappa$, and assume that the search points 0^n and 1^n are contained in the population. Then, the expected time until all niches are found with $(\mu+1)$ EA with phenotypic clearing on f is $O(\mu n)$.*

Proof. According to Lemma 4.1 and the elitist approach of $(\mu+1)$ EA, winners will never be replaced if we assume a large enough population size and by assumption we already have found both search points 0^n and 1^n. First, we will focus on estimating the time until all niches with $i \geq n/2$ are found (by symmetry, the same analysis applies to $< n/2$ niches). Now, let us divide the search space into $n/2$, if there is an empty niche with $i \geq n/2$ ones, then there must be niche i such that $i \geq n/2$ and $i + 1$ exists. So the probability of selecting this $i + 1$ niche is at least $1/\mu$, and since it is just necessary to flip one of at least $n/2$ 0-bits with probability $1/n$, we have a probability of at least $1/2$ to do so, and a probability of leaving the remaining bits untouched of $(1 - 1/n)^{n-1} \geq 1/e$, all together the probability is bounded from below by $1/(2\mu e)$. Using the level-based argument used before, the expected time to occupy all niches $\geq n/2$ is bounded by

$$\sum_{i=n/2}^{n-1} \frac{2\mu e}{1} \leq 2\mu e n = O(\mu n). \quad \square$$

Theorem 4.4 *Let f be a function of unitation and $\sigma = 1$, $\mu \geq (n + 1) \cdot \kappa$. Then, the expected optimisation time of $(\mu+1)$ EA with phenotype clearing on f is $O(\mu n \log n)$.*

Proof. Now that we have defined and proved all conditions where the algorithm is able to maintain every winner in the population (Lemma 4.1), to find the extreme search points (Lemma 4.2) and intermediate niches (Lemma 4.3) of the function f, we can conclude that the total time required to optimise the function of unitation f is $O(\mu n \log n)$. $\square$

4.2 Genotypic Clearing

In the case of genotypic clearing, $(\mu+1)$ EA behaves like the diversity-preserving mechanism called *no genotype duplicates* already analysed in [5]. $(\mu+1)$ EA with no genotype duplicates rejects the new offspring if the genotype is already contained in the population. The same happens for (μ+1) EA with genotypic clearing and $\sigma = 1$ if the population is initialised with μ mutually different genotypes (which happens with probability at least $1 - \binom{\mu}{2}2^{-n}$). In other words, conditional on the population being initialised with mutually different search points, both algorithms are identical. In [5, Theorem 2], it was proved that (μ+1) EA with no genotype duplicates and $\mu = o(n^{1/2})$ is not powerful enough to explore the landscape and can be easily trapped in one optimum of TWOMAX. Adapting [5, Theorem 2] to the goal of finding both optima and noting that $\binom{\mu}{2}2^{-n} = o(1)$ for the considered μ yields the following.

Corollary 4.5 *The probability that* (μ+1) EA *with genotypic clearing,* $\sigma = 1$ *and* $\mu = o(n^{1/2})$ *finds both optima on* TWOMAX *in time* n^{n-2} *is at most* $o(1)$. *The expected time for finding both optima is* $\Omega(n^{n-1})$.

As mentioned before, the use of a proper distance is really important in the context of clearing. In our case, we use phenotypic distance for functions of unitation, which has been proved to provide more significant information at the time it is required to define small differences (in our case small niches) among individuals in a population, so the use of that knowledge can be taken into consideration at the time the algorithm is set up. Otherwise, if there is no more knowledge related to the specifics of the problem, genotypic clearing can be used but with larger niches as shown in the following section.

5. LARGE NICHES

While small niches work with phenotypic clearing, Theorem 4.5 showed that with genotypic clearing small niches are ineffective. This makes sense as for phenotypic clearing with $\sigma = 1$ a niche with i ones covers $\binom{n}{i}$ search points, whereas a niche in genotypic clearing with $\sigma = 1$ only covers one search point. In this section we turn our attention to larger niches, where, according to our empirical observations from Section 3, cleared search points are likely to spread, move, and climb down a branch.

We first present general insights into these population dynamics with clearing. These results capture the behaviour of the population in the presence of only one winning genotype x^* (of which there may be κ copies). We estimate the time until in this situation the population evolves a search point of Hamming distance d from said winner, for any $d \le \sigma$, or for another winner to emerge (for example, in case an individual of better fitness than x^* is found).

These time bounds are very general as they are independent of the fitness function. This is possible since, assuming the winners are fixed at x^*, all other search points within the clearing radius receive a fitness of 0 and hence are subject to a random walk.

We demonstrate the usefulness of our general method by an application to TWOMAX with a clearing radius of $\sigma = n/2$, where all winners are copies of either 0^n or 1^n. The results hold both for genotypic clearing and phenotypic clearing as the phenotypic distance of any point x to 0^n (1^n, resp.) equals the Hamming distance of x to 0^n (1^n, resp.).

5.1 Population Dynamics with Clearing

We assume that the population contains only one winner genotype x^*, of which there are κ copies. For any given

integer $0 \le d \le \sigma$, we analyse the time for the population to reach a search point of Hamming distance at least d from x^*, or for a winner different from x^* to emerge.

To this end, we will study a potential function φ that measures the dynamics of the population. Let

$$\varphi(P_t) = \sum_{x \in P_t} H(x, x^*)$$

be the sum of all Hamming distances of individuals in the population to the winner x^*. The following lemma shows how the potential develops in expectation.

Lemma 5.1 *Let* P_t *be the current population of* (μ+1) EA *with genotypic clearing on any fitness function such that the only winners are* κ *copies of* x^* *and* $H(x, x^*) < \sigma$ *for all* $x \in P_t$. *Then the expected change of the potential is*

$$\mathrm{E}(\varphi(P_{t+1}) - \varphi(P_t) \mid P_t) = 1 - \frac{\varphi(P_t)}{\mu}\left(\frac{2}{n} + \frac{\kappa - 1}{\mu + 1 - \kappa}\right)$$

unless a winner different from x^* *is created.*

Before proving the lemma, let us make sense of this formula. Ignore the term $\frac{\kappa - 1}{\mu + 1 - \kappa}$ for the moment and consider the formula $1 - \frac{\varphi(P_t)}{\mu} \cdot \frac{2}{n}$. Note that $\varphi(P_t)/\mu$ is the average distance to the winner in P_t. If the population has spread such that is has reached an average distance of $n/2$ then the expected change would be $1 - \frac{\varphi(P_t)}{\mu} \cdot \frac{2}{n} = 1 - \frac{n}{2} \cdot \frac{2}{n} = 0$. Moreover, a smaller average distance will give a positive drift (expected value in the decrease of the distance after a single function evaluation) and an average distance larger than $n/2$ will give a negative drift. This makes sense as a search point performing an independent random walk will attain an equilibrium state around Hamming distance $n/2$ from x^*.

The term $\frac{\kappa - 1}{\mu + 1 - \kappa}$ reflects the fact that losers in the population do not evolve in complete isolation. The population always contains κ copies of x^* that may create offspring and may prevent the population from venturing far away from x^*. In other words, there is a constant influx of search points descending from winners x^*. As the term $\frac{\kappa - 1}{\mu + 1 - \kappa}$ indicates, this effect grows with κ, but (as we will see later) it can be mitigated by setting the population size μ sufficiently large.

Proof of Lemma 5.1. If an individual $x \in P_t$ is selected as parent, the expected distance of its mutant to x^* is

$$H(x, x^*) + \frac{n - H(x, x^*)}{n} - \frac{H(x, x^*)}{n}$$
$$= H(x, x^*) + 1 - \frac{2H(x, x^*)}{n}.$$

Hence after a uniform parent selection and mutation, the expected distance in the offspring is

$$\sum_{x \in P_t} \frac{1}{\mu} \cdot \left(H(x, x^*) + 1 - \frac{2H(x, x^*)}{n}\right) = \frac{\varphi(P_t)}{\mu} + 1 - \frac{2\varphi(P_t)}{\mu n}.$$

After mutation and clearing procedure, there are $\mu + 1$ individuals in P_t with κ copies of x^*. As all $\mu + 1 - \kappa$ non-winner individuals in P_t have fitness 0, one of these will be selected uniformly at random for deletion. The expected distance to x^* in the deleted individual is

$$\sum_{x \in P_t \setminus \{x^*\}} \frac{1}{\mu + 1 - \kappa} \cdot H(x, x^*)$$

$$= \sum_{x \in P_t} \frac{1}{\mu + 1 - \kappa} \cdot H(x, x^*)$$

$$= \frac{\varphi(P_t)}{\mu + 1 - \kappa}.$$

Together, the expected change of the potential is

$$\mathrm{E}(\varphi(P_{t+1}) - \varphi(P_t) \mid P_t) = \frac{\varphi(P_t)}{\mu} + 1 - \frac{2\varphi(P_t)}{\mu n} - \frac{\varphi(P_t)}{\mu + 1 - \kappa}.$$

Using that

$$\frac{\varphi(P_t)}{\mu} - \frac{\varphi(P_t)}{\mu + 1 - \kappa} = \frac{(\mu + 1 - \kappa)\varphi(P_t)}{\mu(\mu + 1 - \kappa)} - \frac{\mu \varphi(P_t)}{\mu(\mu + 1 - \kappa)}$$

$$= -\frac{(\kappa - 1)\varphi(P_t)}{\mu(\mu + 1 - \kappa)}$$

the above simplifies to

$$\mathrm{E}(\varphi(P_{t+1}) - \varphi(P_t) \mid P_t) = 1 - \frac{2\varphi(P_t)}{\mu n} - \frac{(\kappa - 1)\varphi(P_t)}{\mu(\mu + 1 - \kappa)}$$

$$= 1 - \frac{\varphi(P_t)}{\mu}\left(\frac{2}{n} + \frac{\kappa - 1}{\mu + 1 - \kappa}\right).$$

$\square$

The potential allows us to conclude when the population has reached a search point of distance at least d from x^*. The following lemma gives a sufficient condition.

Lemma 5.2 *If P_t contains κ copies of x^* and $\varphi(P_t) > (\mu - \kappa)(d-1)$ then P_t must contain at least one individual x with $H(x, x^*) \geq d$.*

Proof. There are at most $\mu - \kappa$ individuals different from x^*. By the pigeon-hole principle, at least one of them must have at least distance d from x^*. $\square$

In order to bound the time for reaching a high potential given in Lemma 5.2, we will use the following drift theorem, a straightforward extension of the variable drift theorem [11] towards reaching any state smaller than some threshold a. It can be derived with simple adaptations to the proof in [17].

Theorem 5.3 (Generalised variable drift theorem)
Consider a stochastic process $X_0, X_1, \ldots$ on $\mathbb{N}_0$. Suppose there is a monotonic increasing function $h : \mathbb{R}^+ \to \mathbb{R}^+$ such that the function $1/h(x)$ is integrable on $[1, m]$, and with

$$\mathrm{E}(X_t - X_{t+1} \mid X_t = k) \geq h(k)$$

for all $k \in \{a, \ldots, m\}$. Then the expected first hitting time of any state from $\{0, \ldots, a-1\}$ for $a \in \mathbb{N}$ is at most

$$\frac{a}{h(a)} + \int_a^m \frac{1}{h(x)} \, dx.$$

The following lemma now gives an upper bound on the first hitting time (the random variable that denotes the first point in time to reach a certain point) of a search point with distance at least d to the winner x^*.

Lemma 5.4 *Let P_t be the current population of $(\mu+1)$ EA with genotypic clearing and $\sigma \leq n/2$ on any fitness function such that P_t contains κ copies of a unique winner x^* and $H(x, x^*) < d$ for all $x \in P_t$. For any $0 \leq d \leq \sigma$, if $\mu \geq$*

$\kappa \cdot \frac{dn-2d+2}{n-2d+2}$ *then, the expected time until a search point x with $H(x, x^*) \geq d$ is found, or a winner different from x^* is created, is $O(\mu n \log \mu)$.*

Proof. We pessimistically assume that no other winner is created and estimate the first hitting time of a search point with distance at least d. As φ can only increase by at most n in one step, $h_{\max} := (\mu - \kappa)(d - 1) + n$ is an upper bound on the maximum potential that can be achieved in the generation where a distance of d is reached or exceeded for the first time.

In order to apply drift analysis, we define a distance function that describes how close the algorithm is to reaching a population where a distance d was reached. We consider the random walk induced by $h_{\max} - \varphi(P_t)$, stopped as soon as a Hamming distance of at least d from x^* is reached. Due to our definition of $h_{\max}$, the random walk only attains values in $\mathbb{N}_0$ as required by the variable drift theorem.

By Lemma 5.1, abbreviating $\alpha := \frac{1}{\mu}\left(\frac{2}{n} + \frac{\kappa-1}{\mu+1-\kappa}\right)$, provided $h(P_t) > 0$, h decreases in expectation by

$$1 - \alpha\varphi(P_t) = 1 - \alpha h_{\max} + \alpha h(P_t).$$

By definition of h and Lemma 5.2, the population reaches a distance of at least d once the distance $h_{\max} - \varphi(P_t)$ has dropped below n. Using the generalised variable drift theorem, the expected time till this happens is at most

$$\frac{n}{1 - \alpha h_{\max} + \alpha n} + \int_n^{h_{\max}} \frac{1}{1 - \alpha h_{\max} + \alpha x} \, dx$$

Using $\int \frac{1}{ax+b} \, dx = \frac{1}{a} \ln |ax + b|$ [1, Equation 3.3.15], we get

$$\frac{n}{1 - \alpha h_{\max} + \alpha n} + \left[\frac{1}{\alpha} \ln(1 - \alpha h_{\max} + \alpha x)\right]_n^{h_{\max}}$$

$$= \frac{n}{1 - \alpha h_{\max} + \alpha n} + \frac{1}{\alpha} \cdot (\ln(1) - \ln(1 - \alpha h_{\max} + \alpha n))$$

$$= \frac{n}{1 - \alpha h_{\max} + \alpha n} + \frac{1}{\alpha} \ln((1 - \alpha h_{\max} + \alpha n)^{-1}).$$

We now bound the term $1 - \alpha h_{\max} + \alpha n$ from below as follows.

$$1 - \alpha h_{\max} + \alpha n$$

$$= 1 - (\mu - \kappa)(d - 1) \cdot \frac{1}{\mu}\left(\frac{2}{n} + \frac{\kappa - 1}{\mu + 1 - \kappa}\right)$$

$$\geq 1 - (\mu - \kappa)(d - 1) \cdot \frac{1}{\mu}\left(\frac{2}{n} + \frac{\kappa}{\mu - \kappa}\right)$$

$$= 1 - \frac{2(\mu - \kappa)(d - 1) + \kappa(d - 1)n}{\mu n}$$

$$= 1 - \frac{\mu n - 2\mu d + 2\kappa d - \kappa dn + 2\mu - 2\kappa + \kappa n}{\mu n}$$

$$= \frac{\kappa}{\mu} + \frac{n - 2d + 2}{n} - \frac{\kappa dn - 2\kappa d + 2\kappa}{\mu n}$$

$$\geq \frac{\kappa}{\mu} + \frac{n - 2d + 2}{n} - \frac{n - 2d + 2}{n}$$

$$= \frac{\kappa}{\mu}$$

where in the penultimate step we used the assumption $\mu \geq \kappa \cdot \frac{dn-2d+2}{n-2d+2}$. Along with $\alpha \geq 2/(\mu n)$, the expected time bound simplifies to

$$\frac{n}{1 - \alpha h_{\max} + \alpha n} + \frac{1}{\alpha} \ln((1 - \alpha h_{\max} + \alpha n)^{-1})$$
$$\leq \frac{n}{\kappa/\mu} + \frac{\mu n}{2} \ln(\mu/\kappa) = O(\mu n \log \mu). \qquad \square$$

The minimum threshold for μ, $\kappa \cdot \frac{dn-2d+2}{n-2d+2}$, contains a factor of κ. The reason is that the fraction of winners in the population needs to be small enough to allow the population to escape from the vicinity of x^*. The population size hence needs to grow proportionally to the number of winners κ the population is allowed to store.

Note that the restriction $d \leq \sigma \leq n/2$ is necessary in Lemma 5.4. Individuals evolving within the clearing radius, but at a distance larger than $n/2$ to x^* will be driven back towards x^*. If d is significantly larger than $n/2$, we conjecture that the expected time for reaching a distance of at least d from x^* becomes exponential in n.

5.2 An Upper Bound for TwoMax

It is now easy to apply Lemma 5.4 in order to achieve a running time bound on TwoMax. Putting $d = \sigma = n/2$, the condition on μ simplifies to

$$\mu \geq \kappa \cdot \frac{dn - 2d + 2}{n - 2d + 2} = \kappa \cdot \frac{n^2/2 - n + 2}{2}$$

which is implied by $\mu \geq \kappa n^2/4$. Lemma 5.4 then implies the following. Recall that for $x^* \in \{0^n, 1^n\}$, genotypic distances $H(x, x^*)$ equal phenotypic distances, hence the result applies to both genotypic and phenotypic clearing.

Corollary 5.5 *Consider $(\mu+1)$ EA with genotypic or phenotypic clearing, $\kappa \in \mathbb{N}, \mu \geq \kappa n^2/4$ and $\sigma = n/2$ on TwoMax with a population containing κ copies of 0^n (1^n). Then the expected time until a search point with at least (at most) $n/2$ ones is found is $O(\mu n \log \mu)$.*

Theorem 5.6 *The expected time for $(\mu+1)$ EA with genotypic or phenotypic clearing, $\mu \geq \kappa n^2/4$, $\mu \leq \text{poly}(n)$ and $\sigma = n/2$ finding both optima on TwoMax is $O(\mu n \log n)$.*

Proof. We first estimate the time to reach one optimum, 0^n or 1^n. The population is elitist as it always contains a winner with the best-so-far fitness. Hence we can apply a fitness-level argument as follows. If the current best fitness is i, it can be increased by selecting an individual with fitness i (probability at least $1/\mu$) and flipping only one of $n - i$ bits with the minority value (probability at least $(n - i)/(en)$). The expected time for increasing the best fitness i is hence at most $\mu \cdot en/(n-i)$ and the expected time for finding some optimum $x^* \in \{0^n, 1^n\}$ is at most

$$\sum_{i=n/2}^{n-1} \mu \cdot \frac{en}{n - i} = e\mu n \sum_{i=1}^{n/2} \frac{1}{i} \leq e\mu n \ln n.$$

In order to apply Corollary 5.5, we need to have κ copies of x^* in the population. While this isn't the case, a generation picking x^* as parent and not flipping any bits creates another winner x^* that will remain in the population. If there are j copies of x^*, the probability to create another winner is at least $j/\mu \cdot (1 - 1/n)^n \geq j/(4\mu)$ (using $n \geq 2$). Hence the time until the population contains κ copies of x^*

is at most

$$\sum_{j=1}^{\kappa} \frac{4\mu}{j} = O(\mu \log \kappa) = O(\mu \log n)$$

as $\kappa \leq \mu \leq \text{poly}(n)$.

By Corollary 5.5, the expected time till a search point on the opposite branch is created is $O(\mu n \log \mu) = O(\mu n \log n)$. Since the best individual on the opposite branch is a winner in its own niche, it will never be removed. This allows the population to climb this branch as well. Repeating the arguments from the first paragraph of this proof, the expected time till the second optimum is found is at most $e\mu n \ln n$.

Adding up all expected times proves the claim. $\quad \square$

Note that, in contrast to previous analyses of fitness sharing [5, 14], the above analysis does not make use of the specific fitness values of TwoMax. The main argument of how to escape from one local optimum only depends on the size of its basin of attraction. Our results therefore easily extend to more general function classes that can be optimised by leaving a basin of attraction of width at most $n/2$ (e.g. variants of TwoMax with different slopes as defined in Theorem 1 of [10], or asymmetric variants with a suboptimal branch having a smaller basin of attraction).

One limitation of Theorem 5.6 is the steep requirement on the population size: $\mu \geq \kappa n^2/4$. Experiments suggest that smaller population sizes are effective as well, so the quadratic dependence on n could be an artefact of our approach. The condition on μ was chosen to ensure a positive drift of the potential for all populations that haven't reached distance d yet, including the most pessimistic scenario of all losers having distance $d-1$ to x^*. Such a scenario is unlikely: experiments suggest that the population tends to spread out, covering a broad range of distances (see Figure 4). With such a spread, a distance of d can be reached with a much smaller potential than that indicated by Lemma 5.2. For such populations, a smaller μ might still guarantee a positive drift. We conjecture that $(\mu+1)$ EA is still efficient on TwoMax if $\mu = O(n)$. However, proving this may require new arguments on the distribution of losers inside the population.

6. CONCLUSIONS

The present empirical and theoretical investigation has shown that clearing possesses desirable and powerful characteristics. We have used these empirical investigations to get an insight into the behaviour of this diversity-preserving mechanism and to rigorously prove its ability to explore the landscape in two cases, small and large niches.

In the case of small niches, we have proved that clearing can exhaustively explore the landscape when the proper distance and parameters like *clearing radius*, *niche capacity* and population size are set. Also, we have proved that clearing is powerful enough to optimise all functions of unitation. In the case of large niches, clearing has been proved to be as strong as other diversity-preserving mechanisms like deterministic crowding and fitness sharing since it is able to find both optima of the test function TwoMax.

Our theoretical results have also shown that the present analysis can be extended to more general function classes. Also, further theoretical analysis is necessary related to the dynamics of the population (including the distribution of the losers inside the population) since the experiments suggest that smaller population sizes are effective in the case of large niches for TwoMAX.

7. ACKNOWLEDGEMENTS

The authors would like to thank the anonymous reviewers of the pre-conference reviews for their many valuable suggestions which improved the paper. And to the Consejo Nacional de Ciencia y Tecnología — CONACYT (the Mexican National Council for Science and Technology) for the financial support under the grant no. 409151 and registration no. 264342. The research leading to these results has received funding from the European Union Seventh Framework Programme (FP7/2007-2013) under grant agreement no. 618091 (SAGE).

8. REFERENCES

[1] M. Abramowitz and I. A. Stegun. *Handbook of Mathematical Functions with Formulas, Graphs, and Mathematical Tables*. Dover, ninth Dover printing, tenth GPO printing edition, 1964.

[2] N. Chaiyaratana, T. Piroonratana, and N. Sangkawelert. Effects of diversity control in single-objective and multi-objective genetic algorithms. *Journal of Heuristics*, 13(1):1–34, 2007.

[3] B. Doerr, W. Gao, and F. Neumann. Runtime Analysis of Evolutionary Diversity Maximization for OneMinMax. In *Proceedings of the Genetic and Evolutionary Computation Conference 2016*, GECCO '16, pages 557–564. ACM, 2016.

[4] T. Friedrich, N. Hebbinghaus, and F. Neumann. Rigorous Analyses of Simple Diversity Mechanisms. In *Proceedings of the 9th Annual Conference on Genetic and Evolutionary Computation*, GECCO '07, pages 1219–1225. ACM, 2007.

[5] T. Friedrich, P. S. Oliveto, D. Sudholt, and C. Witt. Analysis of diversity-preserving mechanisms for global exploration. *Evolutionary Computation*, 17(4):455–476, 2009.

[6] W. Gao and F. Neumann. Runtime analysis for maximizing population diversity in single-objective optimization. In *Proceedings of the 2014 Annual Conference on Genetic and Evolutionary Computation*, GECCO '14, pages 777–784. ACM, 2014.

[7] M. Gendreau and J.-Y. Potvin. Tabu Search. In *Handbook of Metaheuristics*, pages 41–59. Springer US, 2010.

[8] F. Glover and M. Laguna. *Tabu Search*. Kluwer Academic Publishers, 1997.

[9] T. Jansen and I. Wegener. Real royal road functions—where crossover provably is essential. *Discrete Applied Mathematics*, 149(1–3):111–125, 2005.

[10] T. Jansen and C. Zarges. Example landscapes to support analysis of multimodal optimisation. In *14th International Conference on Parallel Problem Solving from Nature (PPSN XIV)*, pages 792–802. Springer International Publishing, 2016.

[11] D. Johannsen. *Random Combinatorial Structures and Randomized Search Heuristics*. PhD thesis, Universität des Saarlandes, Saarbrücken, Germany and the Max-Planck-Institut für Informatik, 2010.

[12] M. Lozano and C. García-Martínez. Hybrid metaheuristics with evolutionary algorithms specializing in intensification and diversification: Overview and progress report. *Computers & Operations Research*, 37(3):481–497, 2010.

[13] P. S. Oliveto and D. Sudholt. On the Runtime Analysis of Stochastic Ageing Mechanisms. In *Proceedings of the 2014 Annual Conference on Genetic and Evolutionary Computation*, GECCO '14, pages 113–120. ACM, 2014.

[14] P. S. Oliveto, D. Sudholt, and C. Zarges. On the runtime analysis of fitness sharing mechanisms. In *13th International Conference on Parallel Problem Solving from Nature (PPSN 2014)*, volume 8672 of *LNCS*, pages 932–941. Springer, 2014.

[15] P. S. Oliveto and C. Zarges. Analysis of diversity mechanisms for optimisation in dynamic environments with low frequencies of change. *Theoretical Computer Science*, 561, Part A:37–56, 2015.

[16] A. Pétrowski. A clearing procedure as a niching method for genetic algorithms. In *Proceedings of IEEE International Conference on Evolutionary Computation*, pages 798–803, 1996.

[17] J. E. Rowe and D. Sudholt. The choice of the offspring population size in the $(1,\lambda)$ evolutionary algorithm. *Theoretical Computer Science*, 545:20–38, 2014.

[18] B. Sareni and L. Krahenbuhl. Fitness sharing and niching methods revisited. *IEEE Transactions on Evolutionary Computation*, 2(3):97–106, 1998.

[19] R. K. Ursem. Diversity-Guided Evolutionary Algorithms. In *Parallel Problem Solving from Nature – PPSN VII*, pages 462–471. Springer Berlin Heidelberg, 2002.

[20] C. Witt. Runtime analysis of the $(\mu + 1)$ EA on simple pseudo-boolean functions. *Evolutionary Computation*, 14(1):65–86, 2006.

Lower Bounds on the Run Time of the Univariate Marginal Distribution Algorithm on OneMax

Martin S. Krejca
Hasso Platter Institute
Postdam, Germany

Carsten Witt
DTU Compute
Technical University of Denmark
Kongens Lyngby, Denmark

ABSTRACT

The Univariate Marginal Distribution Algorithm (UMDA), a popular estimation of distribution algorithm, is studied from a run time perspective. On the classical OneMax benchmark function, a lower bound of $\Omega(\mu\sqrt{n} + n \log n)$, where μ is the population size, on its expected run time is proved. This is the first direct lower bound on the run time of the UMDA. It is stronger than the bounds that follow from general black-box complexity theory and is matched by the run time of many evolutionary algorithms. The results are obtained through advanced analyses of the stochastic change of the frequencies of bit values maintained by the algorithm, including carefully designed potential functions. These techniques may prove useful in advancing the field of run time analysis for estimation of distribution algorithms in general.

Keywords

Estimation of distribution algorithm; run time analysis; lower bound

1. INTRODUCTION

Traditional algorithms in the field of Evolutionary Computation optimize problems by sampling a certain amount of solutions from the problem's domain, the so-called *population*, and transforming them, such that the new population is closer to an optimum. *Estimation of distribution algorithms* (EDAs; [13]) have a very similar approach but do not store an explicit population of sample solutions. Instead, they store a probability distribution over the problem's domain and update it via an algorithm-specific rule that learns from samples drawn from said distribution.

Although many different variants of EDAs (cf. [12]) and many different domains are possible, theoretical analysis of EDAs in discrete search spaces often considers run time analysis over $\{0,1\}^n$. Further, the focus is on EDAs that store a Poisson binomial distribution, i. e., EDAs that store a probability vector p of n independent probabilities, each compo-

nent p_i denoting the probability that a sampled bit string will have a 1 at position i.

The first theoretical analysis in this setting was conducted by Droste [6], who analyzed the *compact Genetic Algorithm* (cGA), an EDA that only samples two solutions each iteration, on linear functions. Papers considering other EDAs, like, e. g., analysis of an iteration-best *Ant Colony Optimization* (ACO) algorithm by Neumann et al. [15] followed.

Recently, the interest in the theoretical analysis of EDAs has increased [5, 10, 11, 18]. Most of these works derive upper bounds for a specific EDA on the popular OneMax function, which counts the number of 1s in a bit string and is considered to be one of the easiest functions with a unique optimum [17, 20]. The only exceptions are Friedrich et al. [10], who look at general properties of EDAs, and Sudholt and Witt [18], who derive *lower bounds* on OneMax for the aforementioned cGA and iteration-best ACO.

In this paper, we follow the ideas of Sudholt and Witt [18] and derive a lower bound of $\Omega(n \log n)$ for the *Univariate Marginal Distribution Algorithm* (UMDA; [14]) on OneMax, which is a typical lower bound for many evolutionary algorithms on this function. The UMDA is an EDA that samples λ solutions each iteration, selects $\mu < \lambda$ best solutions, and then sets p_i to the relative occurrence of 1s among these μ individuals. The algorithm has already been analyzed some years ago for several artificially designed example functions [1, 2, 3, 4]. However, none these papers considers the most important benchmark function in theory, the OneMax function. In fact, the run time analysis of the UMDA on the simple OneMax function has turned out to be rather challenging; the first such result, showing the upper bound $O(n \log n \log \log n)$ on its expected run time for certain settings of μ and λ, was not published until 2015 [5]. Specific lower bounds for the UMDA were to date missing; the previous best result $\Omega(n/\log n)$ on the expected run time followed from general black box complexity theory [7] and did not shed light on the working principles of the UMDA.

The concepts of the proofs in this paper are based on the prior work from Sudholt and Witt [18]. However, analyzing the UMDA is much more difficult than analyzing the cGA or iteration-best ACO, since the update of the latter algorithms is bounded by an algorithm-specific parameter and the algorithms only have up to three distinct successor states for each value p_i. The UMDA, on the other hand, can change each of its p_i to any value x/μ with a certain probability, where $x \in \{0, \dots, \mu\}$, due to the nature of the UMDA's update rule. This makes analyzing the UMDA far more involved, because every single update has to be

FOGA '17, January 12–15, 2017, Copenhagen, Denmark.

© 2017 Copyright held by the owner/author(s). Publication rights licensed to ACM.
ISBN 978-1-4503-4651-1/17/01... $15.00

DOI: http://dx.doi.org/10.1145/3040718.3040724

bounded probabilistically. Further, the simple update rules for the cGA and iteration-best ACO allow for a distinction into two cases that determines whether a value p_i will increase or decrease; a fact that is heavily exploited in the analyses in [18]. For the UMDA, no such simple case distinction can be made.

This paper is structured as follows: In Section 2, we shortly introduce the setting we are going to analyze and go into detail about the UMDA's update rule, that is, we explain and analyze a property of the algorithm that leads to the lower bound when optimizing OneMax.

Then in Section 3, we state our main result and prove it step by step. The rough outline of the proof follows the ones presented in [18], however, we think that our style of presentation is more accessible, due to dissecting our proof into many different (and often independent) lemmas.

Finally, we conclude and discuss our results and future work in the Conclusions section.

We think that our results can be generalized to all functions with unique optimum with moderate effort.

2. PRELIMINARIES

We consider the *Univariate Marginal Distribution Algorithm* (UMDA [14]; Algorithm 1) maximizing the pseudo-Boolean function OneMax, where, for all $x \in \{0,1\}^n$,

$$\text{OneMax}(x) = \sum_{i=1}^n x_i .$$

Note that the function's unique maximum is the all-ones bit string. However, a more general version can be defined by choosing an arbitrary optimum $a \in \{0,1\}^n$ and defining, for all $x \in \{0,1\}^n$,

$$\text{OneMax}_a(x) = n - d_{\text{H}}(x,a) ,$$

where $d_{\text{H}}(x,a)$ denotes the Hamming distance of the bit strings x and a. Note that OneMax_{1^n} is equivalent to the original definition of OneMax. Our analyses hold true for any function OneMax_a, with $a \in \{0,1\}^n$, due to symmetry of the UMDA's update rule.

Algorithm 1: Univariate Marginal Distribution Algorithm (UMDA)

$t \leftarrow 0$;
$p_{1,t} \leftarrow p_{2,t} \leftarrow \cdots \leftarrow p_{n,t} \leftarrow \frac{1}{2}$;
while termination criterion not met **do**
   $P_t \leftarrow \emptyset$;
   for $j \in \{1,\ldots,\lambda\}$ **do**
      for $i \in \{1,\ldots,n\}$ **do**
         $x_{i,t}^{(j)} \leftarrow 1$ with prob. $p_{i,t}$, $x_{i,t}^{(j)} \leftarrow 0$ with prob. $1 - p_{i,t}$;
      $P_t \leftarrow P_t \cup \{x_t^{(j)}\}$;
   Sort individuals in P descending by fitness, breaking ties uniformly at random;
   for $i \in \{1,\ldots,n\}$ **do**
      $p_{i,t+1} \leftarrow \frac{\sum_{j=1}^{\mu} x_{i,t}^{(j)}}{\mu}$;
      Restrict $p_{i,t+1}$ to be within $[\frac{1}{n}, 1 - \frac{1}{n}]$;
   $t \leftarrow t + 1$;

We call bit strings *individuals* and their respective OneMax values *fitness*.

The UMDA does not store an explicit population but does so implicitly, which makes it an *Estimation of distribution algorithm* (EDA). For each of the n different bit positions, it stores a rational number p_i, which we call *frequency*, determining how likely it is that a hypothetical individual would have a 1 at this position. In other words, the UMDA stores a probability distribution over $\{0,1\}^n$. The starting distribution is the uniform distribution.

In each iteration, the UMDA samples λ individuals such that each individual has a 1 at position i ($i \in \{1,\ldots,n\}$) with probability p_i, independent of all the other frequencies. Thus, individuals are sampled according to a Poisson binomial distribution with probability vector $(p_i)_{i \in \{1,\ldots,n\}}$.

After sampling λ individuals, μ of them with highest fitness are chosen, breaking ties uniformly at random (so-called *selection*). Then, for each position, the respective frequency is set to the relative occurrence of 1s in this position. That is, if the chosen μ best individuals have x 1s among them, the frequency p_i will be updated to x/μ for the next iteration. Note that such an update allows large jumps like, e.g., from $(\mu - 1)/\mu$ to $1/\mu$, spanning almost the entire interval of a frequency!

If a frequency is either 0 or 1, it cannot change anymore, since then all bits at this position will be either 0 or 1. To prevent the UMDA from getting stuck in such a way, we narrow the interval of possible frequencies down to $[1/n, 1 - 1/n]$. This way, there is always a chance of sampling 0s and 1s for each position. This is a common approach used by other EDAs as well, such as the cGA or ACO algorithms (mentioned in the introduction).

Overall, we are interested in a lower bound of the UMDA's expected number of *function evaluations* on OneMax until the optimum is sampled. Note that this is the expected number of iterations until the optimum is sampled times λ.

In all of our calculations, we always assume that $\lambda = (1 + \beta)\mu$, for some constant $\beta > 0$. Of course, we could also choose $\lambda = \omega(\mu)$ but then each iteration would be even more expensive. Choosing $\lambda = \Theta(\mu)$ lets us basically focus on the minimal number of function evaluations per iteration, as μ of them are at least needed to make an update.

2.1 Selecting Individuals

To optimize a function efficiently, the UMDA needs to evolve its frequencies into the right direction, making it more likely to sample an optimum. In the setting of OneMax, this means that each frequency should be increased (toward a value of $1 - 1/n$). This is where selection comes into play.

By selecting μ best individuals every iteration w.r.t. their fitness, we hope that many of them have correctly set bits at each position, such that the respective frequencies increase. However, even in the simple case of OneMax, where a 1 is always better than a 0, there is a flaw in the update process that prevents the UMDA from optimizing OneMax too fast. To see why this flaw occurs, consider an arbitrary position j in the following.

When selecting individuals for an update to p_j, the UMDA does so by always considering the fitness of each *entire* individual. That is, although each frequency is independently updated from the others, selection is done w.r.t. *all* positions at once. Thus, when looking at position j, it can happen that we have many 0s, because the individuals chosen for the update may have many 1s in their remaining positions, which can lead to a decrease of p_j.

Since having a 1 at a position is always better than a 0 when considering OneMax, selection is biased, pushing for more 1s at each position. However, this bias is not necessarily too large: Consider that for each individual each bit but bit j has already been sampled. When looking at selection w.r.t. to only $n-1$ bits in each individual, some individuals may already be so good that they are determined to be chosen for selection, whereas others may be so bad that they definitely cannot be chosen for selection, regardless of the outcome of bit j.

Consider the fitness of all individuals sampled during one iteration of the UMDA w.r.t. $n-1$ bits, i.e., all bits but bit j, called *level*. Assume that the individuals are sorted decreasingly by their level; each individual having a unique index. Let w^+ be the level of the individual with rank μ, and let w^- be the level of the individual with rank $\mu+1$. Since bit j has not been considered so far, its value can potentially increase each individual's level by 1. Now assume that $w^+ = w^- + 1$. Then, individuals from level w^- can end up with the same fitness as individuals from level w^+, once bit j has been sampled. Thus, individuals from level w^+ were still prone to selection.

Among the μ individuals chosen during selection, we distinguish between two different types: 1st-class and 2nd-class individuals. 1st-class individuals are those which are chosen during selection no matter which value bit j has. The remaining of the μ individuals are the 2nd-class individuals; they had to compete with other individuals for selection. Therefore, their bit value j is biased toward 1 compared to 1st-class individuals. Note that 2nd-class individuals can only exist if $w^+ \leq w^- + 1$, since in this case, individuals from level w^- can still be as good as individuals from level w^+ after sampling bit j.

Let X_t be the number of 1s at position j sampled in iteration t of the UMDA, and let C^* denote the number of 2nd-class individuals in iteration $t+1$. Note that the number of 1s of 1st-class individuals during iteration $t+1$ follows a binomial distribution with success probability X_t/μ. Since we have $\mu - C^*$ 1st-class individuals, the distribution of the number of 1s of these follows $\mathrm{Bin}(\mu - C^*, X_t/\mu)$. Note that the actual frequency in iteration $t+1$ might be set to either $1/n$ or $1-1/n$ if the number of 1s in the μ selected individuals is too close to 0 or μ, respectively. We will be able to ignore this fact in our forthcoming analyses since all considerations are stopped when a frequency drops below $1/n$ or exceeds $1-1/n$.

2.2 The Number of 2nd-Class Individuals

As in the previous section, consider again a bit position j. In this section, we again speak of levels as defined in the previous section. Level $n-1$ is the topmost, and level 0 is the lowermost. For all $i \in \{0, \ldots, n-1\}$, let C_i denote the cardinality of level i, i.e., the number of individuals in level i during an arbitrary iteration of the UMDA, and let $C_{\geq i} = \sum_{a=i}^{n-1} C_a$.

Let M denote the index of the first level from the top such that the number of sampled individuals is greater than μ when including the following level, i.e.,

$$M = \max\{i \mid C_{\geq i-1} > \mu\}.$$

Note that M can never be 0, and only if $M = n-1$, C_M can be greater than μ. Note further that C_M can be 0.

Due to the definition of M, if $M \neq n-1$, level $M-1$ contains the individual of rank $\mu+1$, as described in the previous section. Thus, levels M, $M-1$, and $M-2$ contain all of the individuals that are prone to selection (if such exist at all). Hence, individuals in levels at least $M+1$ are definitely 1st-class individuals. 2nd-class individuals, if any, have to come from level M, $M-1$, or $M-2$. We call the individuals from these three levels *2nd-class candidates*. Note that the actual number of 2nd-class individuals is bounded from above by $\mu - C_{\geq M+1} = \mu - C_{\geq M} + C_M$, since exactly μ individuals are selected.

Since the 2nd-class individuals are the only ones that are prone to selection and thus the only ones that actively help in progressing a single frequency toward 1, it is of utmost importance to understand the distribution of $C^* := \mu - C_{\geq M+1}$, that is, the biased impact to an update. Moreover, we will also need a bound on the number of 2nd-class candidates.

Before we get to analyzing the 2nd-class individuals, we introduce several auxiliary statements. We start with a very useful lemma on conditional binomially distributed random variables.

Lemma 1. *Let X be a binomially distributed random variable with arbitrary parameters. Then for any $x, y \geq 0$, it holds*

$$\Pr(X \geq x + y \mid X \geq x) \leq \Pr(X \geq y).$$

Proof. Let n and p be the parameters of the underlying binomial distribution. The event $X \geq x + y \mid X \geq x$ is equivalent to the following: given some index $k \leq n$ such that there are exactly x successes in k trials, there are at least y successes among the $n-k$ remaining trials. Note that the number of successes in the last set of trials follows a binomial distribution with parameters $n-k$ and p. Hence, the probability of collecting at least y successes is no greater than the probability of at least y successes in n independent trials with success probability p, i.e., a binomial distribution with parameters n and p. $\qquad\square$

Moreover, we are going to use a corollary that is based on Lemma 8 from [18], the proof of which can be seen in [19, Lemma 9]. Also, the idea behind the corollary is given in [19] but not presented as an independent statement.

Lemma 2. *Let S be the sum of m independent Poisson trials with probabilities $p_i \in [1/6, 5/6]$ for all $i \in \{1, \ldots, m\}$. Then, for all $0 \leq s \leq m$, $\Pr(S = s) = O(1/\sqrt{m})$.*

Corollary 3. *Let X be the sum of n independent Poisson trials with probabilities p_i, $i \in \{1, \ldots, n\}$. Further, let $\Theta(n)$ many p_i-s be within $[1/6, 5/6]$. Then, for all $0 \leq x \leq n$, $\Pr(X = x) = O(1/\sqrt{n})$.*

Proof. Let $m = \Theta(n)$ denote the number of p_i-s that are within $[1/6, 5/6]$. When sampling X, assume w.l.o.g. that the first m trials are the ones with $p_i \in [1/6, 5/6]$. Let S denote the sum of these trials, and let Y denote the sum of the remaining $n-m$ trials. Since the trials are independent, we get $\Pr(X = x) = \sum_{s=0}^{x} \Pr(S = s) \Pr(Y = x - s)$.

We can upper-bound $\Pr(S = s) = O(1/\sqrt{m}) = O(1/\sqrt{n})$ by using Lemma 2 and $m = \Theta(n)$. Thus, we have $\Pr(X =$

$x) = O(1/\sqrt{n}) \sum_{s=0}^{x} \Pr(Y = x - s)$. Bounding the sum by 1 concludes the proof. $\qquad\square$

The corollary lets us easily get upper bounds for the probability that a sampled individual has a certain (and arbitrary) fitness (w.r.t. to either all n positions or all positions but j). To apply it, we have to make sure that $\Theta(n)$ frequencies are still within $[1/6, 5/6]$. Thus, we assume from now on that this assumption holds. In Section 3.2, we will prove under which circumstances this assumption holds.

Note that all statements from now on regarding a specific position j hold regardless of the bits at any other of the $\Theta(n)$ positions that do not stay within $[1/6, 5/6]$. This means that the statements are even true if the bits at those other positions are chosen by an adversary.

We are now ready to analyze C^* and the number of 2nd-class candidates.

Lemma 4. *Consider the UMDA with $\lambda = (1+\beta)\mu$ optimizing OneMax, and let $\widetilde{Z}$ be a random variable that takes values in $\{1, \ldots, \lambda\}$ only with probability at most $2e^{-(\varepsilon^2/(3+3\varepsilon))\mu} = e^{-\Omega(\mu)}$ and is 0 otherwise, where $\varepsilon > 0$ is a constant such that $\varepsilon < 1 - 1/(1 + \beta)$. If there are $\Theta(n)$ frequencies in $[1/6, 5/6]$, then the distribution of C^* is stochastically dominated by $\mathrm{Bin}\bigl(\lambda, O(1/\sqrt{n})\bigr) + \widetilde{Z}$ and the distribution of $C_M + C_{M-1} + C_{M-2}$ is stochastically dominated by $1 + \mathrm{Bin}\bigl(\lambda, O(1/\sqrt{n})\bigr) + \widetilde{Z}$.*

Proof. The proof carefully investigates and then reformulates the stochastic process generating the λ individuals (before selection), restricted to $n - 1$ bits. Each individual is sampled by a Poisson binomial distribution for a vector of probabilities $p' = (p'_1, \ldots, p'_{n-1})$ obtained from the frequencies of the UMDA by leaving one entry out. Counting its number of 1s, each of the λ individuals then falls into some level i, where $0 \le i \le n - 1$, with some probability q_i depending on the vector p'. Since the individuals are created independently, the number of individuals in level i is binomially distributed with parameters $n - 1$ and q_i.

Next, we take an alternative view on the process putting individuals into levels, using the principle of deferred decisions. We imagine that the process first samples all individuals in level 0 (through λ trials, all of which either hit the level or not), then (using the trials which did not hit level 0) all individuals in level $1, \ldots$, up to level $n - 1$.

The number of individuals C_0 in level 0 is still binomially distributed with parameters λ and q_0. However, after all individuals in level 0 have been sampled, the distribution changes. We have $\lambda - C_0$ trials left, each of which can hit one of the levels 1 to $n - 1$. In particular, such a trial will hit level 1 with probability $q_1/(1 - q_0)$, by the definition of conditional probability since level 0 is excluded. This holds independently for all of the $\lambda - C_0$ trials so that C_1 follows a binomial distribution with parameters $\lambda - C_0$ and $q_1/(1 - q_0)$. Inductively, also all C_i for $i > 1$ are binomially distributed; e.g., C_{n-1} is distributed with parameters $\lambda - C_{n-2} - \cdots - C_0$ and 1. Note that this model of the sampling process can also be applied for any other permutation of the levels; we will make use of this fact.

We first focus on $C^* = \mu - C_{\ge M+1}$ and will later use bounds on its distribution to analyze $C_M + C_{M-1} + C_{M-2}$. Formally, by applying the law of total probability, the dis-

tribution of C^* looks as follows for $k \in \{0, \ldots, \lambda\}$:

$$\Pr(C^* \ge k) = \sum_{i=1}^{n-1} \Pr(M = i) \cdot \Pr(\mu - C_{\ge i+1} \ge k \mid M = i).$$
(1)

We will bound the terms of the sum differently with respect to the index i. First, we look into a particular value i^* such that $\Pr(M \ge i^*)$ is exponentially unlikely, and then make a case distinction via i^*.

Let X be the number of 1s in a single individual sampled (without conditioning on certain levels being hit). Choose i^* such that $\Pr(X \ge i^* - 1) \le 1/\bigl((1+\varepsilon)(1+\beta)\bigr)$ and $\Pr(X \ge i^* - 1) \ge 1/\bigl((1 + \varepsilon)(1 + \beta)\bigr) - O(1/\sqrt{n})$. Such an i^* must exist, since every level is hit with probability $O(1/\sqrt{n})$ when sampling an individual, according to Corollary 3. Clearly, we also have $i^* \le n - 1$.

A crucial observation is that $\Pr(M \ge i^*) = e^{-\Omega(\mu)}$, since the expected number of individuals sampled with at least $i^* - 1$ 1s is at most $\lambda/\bigl((1+\varepsilon)(1+\beta)\bigr) = \mu/(1+\varepsilon)$, and the probability of sampling at least $(1+\varepsilon) \cdot \mu/(1+\varepsilon) = \mu$ is at most $e^{-\varepsilon^2 \cdot \mu/(3(1+\varepsilon))} = e^{-\Omega(\mu)}$ by Chernoff bounds. Note that we have considered level $i^* - 1$ since $C_{\ge i^* - 1} < \mu$ implies $M < i^*$.

In Equation (1), considering the partial sum for all $i \ge i^*$, we therefore immediately estimate

$$\sum_{i=i^*}^{n-1} \Pr(M = i) \cdot \Pr(\mu - C_{\ge i+1} \ge k \mid M = i) \le \Pr(M \ge i^*)$$

$$\le e^{-\Omega(\mu)},$$

as shown just before.

For the terms with $i < i^*$ (in particular, the case $i = n - 1$ is excluded), we take a view on the final expression in Equation (1) and focus on $\Pr(\mu - C_{\ge i+1} \ge k \mid M = i)$, in which we want to reformulate the underlying event appropriately. Here we note that

$$(\mu - C_{\ge i+1} \ge k) \mid (M = i)$$

is equivalent to

$$(C_{\le i} \ge \lambda - \mu + k) \mid (M = i),$$

where $C_{\le i} = \sum_{j=0}^{i} C_j$, and, using the definition of M, this is also equivalent to

$$(C_{\le i} \ge \lambda - \mu + k) \mid (C_{\le i-2} < \lambda - \mu \cap C_{\le i-1} \ge \lambda - \mu).$$

We now take the above-mentioned view on the stochastic process and assume that levels 0 to $i - 2$ have been sampled and a number of experiments in a binomial distribution is carried out to determine the individuals from level $i - 1$. Hence, given some $C_{\le i-2} = a < \lambda - \mu$, our event is equivalent to that the event

$$E^* := \bigl(C_i + C_{i-1} \ge (\lambda - \mu - a) + k\bigr) \mid (C_{i-1} \ge \lambda - \mu - a)$$

happens.

Recall from our model above that C_{i-1} follows a binomial distribution with $\lambda - a$ trials and with a certain success probability s; similarly, C_i follows a binomial distribution with parameters $\lambda - a - C_{i-1}$ and s'. As we are interested in a cumulative distribution, we may pessimistically upper-bound the total number of trials for C_{i-1} by λ. Regarding s, note that it denotes the probability to sample an individual with $i - 1$ 1s, given that it cannot have less than $i - 1$ 1s. Note further that $\Pr(X \geq i^* - 1)$, where X again denotes the level of the individual sampled in a trial, is a lower bound for all probabilities $\Pr(X \geq i - 1)$, since $i < i^*$. To upper-bound s, we use Corollary 3, which tells us that the unconditional probability to hit a level is in $O(1/\sqrt{n})$, regardless of the level hit. However, we have to condition on the event that certain levels (namely $0, \ldots, i-2$, where $i < i^*$) cannot be hit anymore. We pessimistically exclude even some more levels than possible, more precisely, we exclude the levels from 0 up to $i^* - 2$. This means that we condition on $\Pr(X \geq i^* - 1)$. By the definition of conditional probability, the probability of $O(1/\sqrt{n})$ from Corollary 3 thus gets increased by a factor of $1/\Pr(X \geq i^* - 1)$, which is constant. Hence, C_{i-1} is stochastically dominated by a binomial distribution with parameters λ and $O(1/\sqrt{n})$.

Similarly, assuming that also level $i-1$ has been sampled, C_i is dominated by a binomial distribution with parameters $\lambda - C_{i-1}$ and $O(1/\sqrt{n})$.

To finally bound $\Pr(E^*)$, which involves a condition on the outcome on C_{i-1}, we apply Lemma 1, where we let $X := C_{i-1}$ and $x = \lambda - \mu - a$ as well as $y = k$. Since we have bounded C_{i-1} (without the condition on $C_{i-1} \geq x$) by a binomial distribution with success probability $O(1/\sqrt{n})$, we get from the lemma that $\Pr(C_{i-1} - x \geq k \mid C_{i-1} \geq x) \leq \Pr(\text{Bin}(\lambda, O(1/\sqrt{n})) \geq k)$. Note that the right-hand side is a bound independent of $C_0, \ldots, C_{i-1}$. With respect to C_i, we do not consider an additional condition on its outcome but use the result $\Pr(C_i \geq k) \leq \Pr(\text{Bin}(\lambda - C_{i-1}, O(1/\sqrt{n})) \geq k)$ derived in the last paragraph directly. Hence, both $C_{i-1} - x$, conditioned on $C_{i-1} \geq x$, and C_i have been bounded by binomial distributions with second parameter $O(1/\sqrt{n})$. In E^*, we are confronted with the sum of these two random variables and study the distribution of the sum. Together, $\Pr(E^*) \leq \Pr(\text{Bin}(\lambda, O(1/\sqrt{n})) \geq k)$, since we consider at most λ trials. Pulling this term in front of the sum over i for the terms $i < i^*$ in (1) and estimating this sum with 1 (since we sum over mutually disjoint events) leaves us with an additional term of $\Pr(\text{Bin}(\lambda, O(1/\sqrt{n})) \geq k)$ for $\Pr(\mu - C_{\geq M+1} \geq k)$. This proves the lemma's statement on the distribution of C^*.

We are left with analyzing $C^{**} := C_M + C_{M-1} + C_{M-2}$. We handle the very unlikely case $M = n-1$, whose probability is upper-bounded by $\Pr(M \geq i^*)$, separately and cover it by adding the random variable $\widetilde{Z}$ to our result. By a symmetrical argument to the above, for some index i^{**} such that $\Pr(X < i^{**}) = 1 - 1/((1-\varepsilon)(1+\beta)) + O(1/\sqrt{n}))$, we obtain that $M \leq i^{**}$ also happens with probability at most $e^{-\varepsilon^2 \cdot \mu/(2(1-\varepsilon))} \leq e^{-\varepsilon^2 \cdot \mu/(3+3\varepsilon)}$, for $\varepsilon < 1 - 1/(1+\beta)$. This unlikely case is also included in $\widetilde{Z}$. From now on, we assume $i^{**} < M < n-1$. We note that by definition of M, we then have $C_{\geq M} \leq \mu$ and $C_{\geq M-1} \geq \mu + 1$ and thus $C_{M-1} \geq 1$. Hence, we have to investigate the distribution of C^{**} conditional on $C^{**} \geq 1 + (\mu - C_{\geq M+1})$, i.e., $C^{**} \geq 1 + C^*$.

We take the same view on the stochastic process as above but imagine now that the levels are sampled in the order from $n-1$ down to 0. Conditioning on that levels $n-1, \ldots, M+1$ have been sampled, levels M, $M-1$ and $M-2$ are still hit with probability $O(1/\sqrt{n})$ each, since $\Pr(X < i^{**})$ is a constant. Hence, we can use Lemma 1 similarly as above and get

$$\Pr(C_{M-1} \geq 1 + C^* + k) \leq \Pr(\text{Bin}(\lambda - C_M, O(1/\sqrt{n})) \geq k).$$

Note that the right-hand side of the inequality is independent of C^*. Applying the argumentation once more for level $M - 2$ (where no conditions on the size exist), we get $\Pr(C_{M-2} \geq k) \leq \Pr(\text{Bin}(\lambda - C_M - C_{M-1}, O(1/\sqrt{n})) \geq k)$. Using our stochastic bound on C^* from above, we altogether obtain that C^{**} is stochastically dominated by the sum of 1, three binomially distributed random variables with a total number of λ trials and success probability $O(1/\sqrt{n})$ each, and the variable $\widetilde{Z}$. $\square$

Now that we understand how C^* is distributed, we can look at the distribution of both the 1st- and 2nd-class individuals. We even can take a finer-grained view on the number of 1s contributed by them.

Lemma 5. *Consider the UMDA optimizing* OneMax. *Consider further that $\Theta(n)$ frequencies are within $[1/6, 5/6]$ and that we are in iteration t. Let j be any position, and let X_t denote the number of 1s at position j in iteration t.*

The distribution Z_1 of the number of 1s of 1st-class individuals is stochastically dominated by $\text{Bin}(\mu, X_t/\mu)$, and the distribution Z_2 of the number of 1s of 2nd-class individuals is stochastically dominated by C^*, where C^* is distributed as seen in Lemma 4. In particular, the expected value of Z_2 is at most $O(\mu/\sqrt{n}) + e^{-\Omega(\mu)}$.

Further the expected value of Z_2, given X_t, is at most $O(X_t/\mu + X_t/\sqrt{n}) + e^{-\Omega(\mu)}$.

Proof. The distribution of Z_1 has already been described in Section 2.1 as $\text{Bin}(\mu - C^*, X_t/\mu)$, which is dominated by $\text{Bin}(\mu, X_t/\mu)$. We also know that the number of 2nd-class individuals is bounded from above by C^*, and their number of 1s is trivial bounded by this cardinality too. The first statement on the expected value of Z_2 follows by taking the expected value of the binomial distribution and noting that $\text{E}(\widetilde{Z}) \leq \lambda e^{-\Omega(\mu)} = e^{-\Omega(\mu)}$, using $\lambda = O(\mu)$.

To show the second statement on the expected value of Z_2, we recall our definition of 2nd-class candidates from above. These candidates have not been subject to selection yet. Each of these candidates samples a 1 at position j independently of the others with probability X_t/μ, so the expected total number of 1s in 2nd-class candidates is the expected number of candidates multiplied with X_t/μ, by Wald's identity. By Lemma 4, there is an expected number of at most $1 + O(\mu/\sqrt{n}) + e^{-\Omega(\mu)}$ of candidates, using again $\lambda = O(\mu)$. Since the 2nd-class individuals are only selected from the candidates, the claim on the expected value of Z_2 follows. $\square$

3. LOWER BOUND ON ONEMAX

In the following, we derive a lower bound on the UMDA's run time on OneMax. First, we state the main theorem.

Theorem 6. *Let $\lambda = (1 + \beta)\mu$ for some constant $\beta > 0$. Then the expected optimization time of the UMDA on* OneMax *is $\Omega(\mu\sqrt{n} + n \log n)$.*

To prove the theorem, we will distinguish between different cases for λ: small, medium, and large. We will cover the lemmas we use to prove the different cases in different sections. The first and the last case are fairly easy to prove, hence we discuss them first, leaving the second case of medium λ – the most difficult one – to be discussed last.

In each of the following sections, we will introduce the basic idea behind each of the proofs.

3.1 Small Population Sizes

In this section, we consider a population size of $\lambda \leq (1 - c_1) \log_2 n$, for some constant $c_1 > 0$. If the population size is that small, the probability that a frequency reaches $1/n$ is rather high, and thus the probability to sample the optimum will be quite small.

If enough frequencies drop to $1/n$, we can bound the expected number of fitness evaluations until we sample the optimum by $\Omega(n \log n)$. The following lemma and its proof closely follow [19, Lemma 13].

Lemma 7. *Assume that $\Omega(n^{c_1})$ frequencies, $c_1 > 0$ being a constant, are at $1/n$. Then the UMDA will need with high probability and in expectation still $\Omega(n \log n)$ function evaluations to optimize any function with a unique global optimum.*

Proof. Due to symmetry, we can w.l.o.g. assume that the global optimum is the all-ones string.

We look at $(c_2 n \ln n)/(2\lambda)$ iterations, where $c_2 < c_1$ is a positive constant, and show that it is very unlikely to sample the all-ones string during that time. Note that this translates to $\Omega(n \log n)$ function evaluations until the optimum is sampled, as the UMDA samples λ offspring every iteration.

Consider a single position with frequency at $1/n$. The probability that this position never samples a 1 during our time of $(c_2 n \ln n)/(2\lambda)$ iterations is at least

$$\left(1 - \frac{\lambda}{n}\right)^{\frac{c_2 n \ln n}{2\lambda}} \geq (1 - o(1)) e^{-\frac{c_2}{2} \ln n} \geq n^{-c_2}$$

if n is large enough.

Given $\Omega(n^{c_1})$ frequencies at $1/n$, the probability that all of these positions sample at least one 1 during $(c_2 n \ln n)/(2\lambda)$ iterations is at most

$$\left(1 - n^{-c_2}\right)^{\Omega(n^{c_1})} \leq e^{-\Omega(n^{c_1 - c_2})} ,$$

which is exponentially small in n, since $c_1 > c_2$, due to our assumptions.

Hence, with high probability, the UMDA will need at least $\Omega(n \log n)$ function evaluations to find the optimum.

Since the expected value of function evaluations is finite (due to the bound of $1 - 1/n$ and $1/n$ for the frequencies) and it is $\Omega(n \log n)$ with high probability, it follows that the expected number of fitness evaluations is $\Omega(n \log n)$ as well. □

We can now prove our lower bound for small population sizes.

Theorem 8. *Let $\lambda \leq (1 - c_1) \log_2 n$ for some arbitrarily small constant $c_1 > 0$. Then, the UMDA will need with high probability and in expectation $\Omega(n \log n)$ function evaluations to optimize any function with a unique global optimum.*

Proof. Due to symmetry, we can w.l.o.g. assume that the global optimum is the all-ones string. We consider an arbitrary position i and study the first iteration of the UMDA. The probability that all λ bits at position i are sampled as 0 equals $2^{-\lambda} \geq n^{-(1-c_1)}$. In this case, the frequency of the position is set to $1/n$. The expected number of such positions is n^{c_1}, and by Chernoff bounds, with high probability $\Omega(n^{c_1})$ such positions exist (noting that c_1 is a positive constant by assumption).

Applying Lemma 7 yields the result, since we already have $\Omega(n^{c_1})$ frequencies at $1/n$ after a single iteration of the UMDA with high probability. □

3.2 Large Population Sizes

Here, we are going to show that a population size of $\lambda = \Omega(\sqrt{n} \log n)$ lead to a run time of $\Omega(n \log n)$. To prove this, we first show that it is unlikely that too many frequencies leave the interval $[1/6, 5/6]$ quickly in this scenario. Thus, it is also unlikely to sample the optimum.

We start by proving that a single frequency does not leave $[1/6, 5/6]$ too quickly, for $\mu = \omega(1)$. We make use of Corollary 3 and the lemmas following from it, all of which make use of the lemmas we prove here themselves. At the end of this section, we will discuss why this seemingly contradictory approach is feasible.

Lemma 9. *Consider an arbitrary frequency of the UMDA with $\lambda = \omega(1)$ optimizing* OneMax. *During at least $\gamma \cdot \min\{\mu, \sqrt{n}\}$ iterations, for a sufficiently small constant γ, this frequency will not leave $[1/6, 5/6]$ with a probability of at least a constant greater than 0.*

Proof. We consider the expected change of an arbitrary position's frequency p_t over time t. Let X_t, again, denote the number of 1s of the μ selected individuals. Note that $p_{t+1} = X_t/\mu$.

Due to Lemma 5, we know that X_t is the sum of two random variables $Z_{1,t}$ and $Z_{2,t}$, where $Z_{1,t} \prec \text{Bin}(\mu, X_{t-1}/\mu)$ corresponds to the number of 1s due to the 1st-class individuals, and $Z_{2,t} \prec \text{Bin}(\lambda, O(1/\sqrt{n})) + \widetilde{Z}_t$ corresponds to the 2nd-class individuals' number of 1s, pessimistically assuming that each 2nd-class individual contributes a 1.

First, we are going to upper-bound the probability of p_t reaching $5/6$ during $\gamma \cdot \min\{\mu, \sqrt{n}\}$ iterations. Then, we do the same for reaching $1/6$. Taking the converse probability of a union bound over both cases yields the result.

Since $Z_{1,t}$ is dominated by a martingale which we want to account for in the process, we analyze $\phi_{t+1} := (X_t/\mu)^2$, with $\phi_0 = (1/2)^2$. Note that the square function is injective in this case because both X_t and μ are nonnegative. The original process of p_t reaching $5/6$ translates into the new process p_t^2 reaching $5/6^2$.

We bound the expected change during one step:

$$\begin{aligned}
\text{E}(\phi_{t+1} - \phi_t \mid \phi_t) &= \frac{1}{\mu^2}\left(\text{E}(X_t^2 \mid \phi_t) - X_{t-1}^2\right) \\
&= \frac{1}{\mu^2}\left(\text{E}\left((Z_{1,t} + Z_{2,t})^2 \mid \phi_t\right) - X_{t-1}^2\right) \\
&= \frac{1}{\mu^2}\left(\text{E}(Z_{1,t}^2 \mid \phi_t) + \text{E}(Z_{2,t}^2 \mid \phi_t) \right. \\
&\qquad \left. + 2\text{E}(Z_{1,t} \cdot Z_{2,t} \mid \phi_t) - X_{t-1}^2\right) .
\end{aligned}$$

As discussed before, we will look at the dominating distributions of $Z_{1,t}$ and $Z_{2,t}$. Further, note that $Z_{1,t}$ and $Z_{2,t}$ are not independent, but their dominating distributions are.

We calculate the different terms separately:

$$\text{E}(Z_{1,t}^2 \mid \phi_t) \leq \mu \frac{X_{t-1}}{\mu} + \mu(\mu-1)\frac{X_{t-1}^2}{\mu^2} \leq X_{t-1} + X_{t-1}^2 ,$$

i.e., the second moment of a binomially distributed random variable, as seen by noting that $\text{E}(Z_{1,t}^2 \mid \phi_t) = \text{Var}(Z_{1,t} \mid \phi_t) + \text{E}(Z_{1,t} \mid \phi_t)^2$.

For $Z_{2,t}$, let $Z_t^* \sim \mathrm{Bin}\left(\lambda, \mathrm{O}(1/\sqrt{n})\right)$, and recall that $\widetilde{Z}$ is a random variable that takes values in $\{1,\dots,\lambda\}$ with probability $\mathrm{e}^{-\Omega(\mu)}$ and is 0 otherwise. Using, again, the second moment of a binomially distributed random variable, we get

$$
\begin{aligned}
\mathrm{E}(Z_{2,t}^2 \mid \phi_t) &\leq \mathrm{E}\left((Z_t^*)^2 \mid \phi_t\right) + \mathrm{E}\left((\widetilde{Z}_t)^2 \mid \phi_t\right) \\
&\quad + 2\mathrm{E}(Z_t^* \mid \phi_t)\mathrm{E}(\widetilde{Z}_t \mid \phi_t) \\
&\leq \mathrm{O}\left(\frac{\mu}{\sqrt{n}}\right) + \mathrm{O}\left(\frac{\mu^2}{n}\right) + \mu^2 \mathrm{e}^{-\Omega(\mu)} + \mathrm{O}\left(\frac{\mu^2}{\sqrt{n}}\mathrm{e}^{-\Omega(\mu)}\right) \\
&\leq \max\left\{\mathrm{O}\left(\frac{\mu}{\sqrt{n}}\right), \mathrm{O}\left(\frac{\mu^2}{n}\right), \mu^2\mathrm{e}^{-\Omega(\mu)}\right\} ,
\end{aligned}
$$

because the term $\mathrm{O}(\mu^2/(\sqrt{n}\mathrm{e}^{\Omega(\mu)}))$ is always dominated by another term. Note that $\mathrm{O}(\mu/\sqrt{n})$ dominates if the constant in the $\Omega(\mu)$ of $\mathrm{e}^{-\Omega(\mu)}$ is at least $1/2$ and if $\mu = \mathrm{o}(\sqrt{n})$. For $\mu = \Omega(\sqrt{n})$, the term $\mathrm{O}(\mu^2/n)$ dominates. In the remaining cases (when μ is logarithmic), the term $\mu^2 \mathrm{e}^{-\Omega(\mu)}$ dominates.

For the first moment of $Z_{2,t}$, we can get a similar bound:

$$
\mathrm{E}(Z_{2,t} \mid \phi_t) \leq \max\left\{\mathrm{O}\left(\frac{\mu}{\sqrt{n}}\right), \mu\mathrm{e}^{-\Omega(\mu)}\right\} ,
$$

where the term $\mu\mathrm{e}^{-\Omega(\mu)}$ only dominates if the constant in the $\Omega(\mu)$ is less than $1/2$.

Using our prior calculations and independence of the dominating distributions, we can bound

$$
2\mathrm{E}\left(Z_{1,t}\cdot Z_{2,t} \mid \phi_t\right) \leq X_{t-1}\cdot \max\left\{\mathrm{O}\left(\frac{\mu}{\sqrt{n}}\right), \mu\mathrm{e}^{-\Omega(\mu)}\right\} .
$$

Thus, we get

$$
\begin{aligned}
&\mathrm{E}(\phi_{t+1} - \phi_t \mid \phi_t) \\
&\leq \frac{1}{\mu^2}\left(X_{t-1} + X_{t-1}^2 + \max\left\{\mathrm{O}\left(\frac{\mu}{\sqrt{n}}\right), \mathrm{O}\left(\frac{\mu^2}{n}\right), \mu^2\mathrm{e}^{-\Omega(\mu)}\right\}\right. \\
&\qquad \left. + X_{t-1}\cdot\max\left\{\mathrm{O}\left(\frac{\mu}{\sqrt{n}}\right), \mu\mathrm{e}^{-\Omega(\mu)}\right\} - X_{t-1}^2\right) \\
&\leq \frac{1}{\mu^2}\left(\max\left\{\mathrm{O}\left(\frac{\mu}{\sqrt{n}}\right), \mathrm{O}\left(\frac{\mu^2}{n}\right), \mu^2\mathrm{e}^{-\Omega(\mu)}\right\}\right. \\
&\qquad \left. + X_{t-1}\left(1 + \max\left\{\mathrm{O}\left(\frac{\mu}{\sqrt{n}}\right), \mu\mathrm{e}^{-\Omega(\mu)}\right\}\right)\right) \\
&\overset{X_{t-1}\leq\mu}{\leq} \frac{1}{\mu^2}\mu\left(1 + \max\left\{\mathrm{O}\left(\frac{\mu}{\sqrt{n}}\right), \mu\mathrm{e}^{-\Omega(\mu)}\right\}\right) \\
&\leq \mathrm{O}\left(\max\left\{\frac{1}{\mu}, \frac{1}{\sqrt{n}}\right\}\right) .
\end{aligned}
$$

Let P_T describe the Markov process $p_t^2 = \phi_t$ starting at $(1/2)^2$ and then progressing by $\phi_{t+1} - \phi_t$ for T iterations. Due to our bounds, we get

$$
\begin{aligned}
\mathrm{E}(P_T) &= \left(\frac{1}{2}\right)^2 + \sum_{t=0}^{T-1} \mathrm{E}(\phi_{t+1} - \phi_t \mid \phi_t) \\
&\leq \frac{1}{4} + \zeta T \cdot \max\left\{\frac{1}{\mu}, \frac{1}{\sqrt{n}}\right\} ,
\end{aligned}
$$

for a sufficiently large constant ζ.

Using Markov's inequality gives us, for $k > 1$,

$$
\mathrm{Pr}\left(P_T \geq k\left(\frac{1}{4} + \zeta T\cdot\max\left\{\frac{1}{\mu}, \frac{1}{\sqrt{n}}\right\}\right)\right) \leq \mathrm{Pr}\left(P_T \geq k\mathrm{E}(P_T)\right)
$$

$$
\leq \frac{1}{k} .
$$

We want that $(5/6)^2 \geq k(1/4 + \zeta T \cdot \max\{1/\mu, 1/\sqrt{n}\})$, since then $\mathrm{Pr}(P_T \geq 25/36)$ is upper-bounded by $\mathrm{Pr}(P_T \geq k(1/4 + \zeta T \cdot \max\{1/\mu, 1/\sqrt{n}\})) \leq 1/k$. We get

$$
\begin{aligned}
\frac{25}{36} &\geq k\left(\frac{1}{4} + \zeta T\cdot\max\left\{\frac{1}{\mu}, \frac{1}{\sqrt{n}}\right\}\right) \\
&\Leftrightarrow T \leq \left(\frac{25}{36k} - \frac{1}{4}\right)\frac{\min\{\mu, \sqrt{n}\}}{\zeta} ,
\end{aligned}
$$

which is positive as long as $k < 25/9$. Thus, we can bound $k \in (1, 25/9)$.

Hence, if $T \leq \gamma \cdot \min\{\mu, \sqrt{n}\}$, for a constant γ sufficiently small, then the probability of an arbitrary frequency exceeding $5/6$ is at most a constant less than $1/2$ (for $k > 2 \in (1, 25/9)$).

We now analyze how likely it is that p_t hits $1/6$ in a similar amount of time. For this case, we define a slightly different potential $\phi_{t+1}' := (1 - X_t/\mu)^2 = 1 - 2X_t/\mu + (X_t/\mu)^2$, i.e., we mirror the process at $1/2$ and then use the same potential as before.

Looking at the difference during one step, we see that

$$
\begin{aligned}
\phi_{t+1}' - \phi_t' &= 1 - 2\frac{X_t}{\mu} + \left(\frac{X_t}{\mu}\right)^2 - 1 + 2\frac{X_{t-1}}{\mu} - \left(\frac{X_{t-1}}{\mu}\right)^2 \\
&= \frac{2}{\mu}(X_{t-1} - X_t) + \phi_{t+1} - \phi_t ,
\end{aligned}
$$

where we only have to determine the expected value of $X_{t-1} - X_t$, because we already analyzed $\phi_{t+1} - \phi_t$ before.

Considering just the 1st-class individuals, it holds that $\mathrm{E}(X_t) = \mathrm{E}(X_{t-1})$, because we then have a martingale. But due to the elitist selection of the UMDA, actually $\mathrm{E}(X_t) \geq \mathrm{E}(X_{t-1})$ holds, because of the bias of the 2nd-class individuals, which prefer 1s over 0s. Thus, $\mathrm{E}(X_{t-1} - X_t \mid \phi_t') \leq 0$, and we get

$$
\mathrm{E}(\phi_{t+1}' - \phi_t' \mid \phi_t') \leq \mathrm{E}(\phi_{t+1} - \phi_t \mid \phi_t) ,
$$

which we already analyzed.

Hence, we can argue analogously as before and get, again, a probability of at most a constant less than $1/2$ to reach $1/6$ during at most $\gamma \cdot \min\{\mu, \sqrt{n}\}$ iterations.

Taking a union bound over both cases finishes the proof. $\square$

We now expand the case from a single frequency to all frequencies.

Lemma 10. *During at least $\gamma \cdot \min\{\mu, \sqrt{n}\}$ iterations of the UMDA optimizing* OneMax, *for a sufficiently small constant γ, $\Theta(n)$ frequencies stay in the interval $[1/6, 5/6]$ with at least constant probability.*

Proof. We look at $T \leq \gamma \cdot \min\{\mu, \sqrt{n}\}$ iterations. Thus, the probability for a single frequency to leave $[1/6, 5/6]$ is at most a constant $c < 1$, according to Lemma 9. In expectation, there are at most cn frequencies outside of $[1/6, 5/6]$, and due to Markov's inequality, the probability that there are at least $(1+\delta)cn$ such frequencies, for a constant $\delta > 0$ with $(1+\delta)c < 1$, is at most $1/(1+\delta)$. This means that with at least constant probability, at least $(1 - c(1+\delta))n = \Theta(n)$ frequencies are still within $[1/6, 5/6]$. $\square$

Note that the proof of Lemma 9 relies on Corollary 3, and the proof of Corollary 3 also relies on Lemma 9. Formally, this cyclic dependency can be solved by proving both propositions in conjunction via induction over the number of iterations up to $\gamma \cdot \min\{\mu, \sqrt{n}\}$, for a sufficiently small constant γ. For the base case, all frequencies are at $1/2 \in [1/6, 5/6]$, and both propositions hold. For the inductive step, assuming that $t < \gamma \cdot \min\{\mu, \sqrt{n}\}$, we already now that both propositions hold up to iteration t. Thus, the requirements for the proofs of Corollary 3 and Lemma 9 are fulfilled, and the proofs themselves pass.

We now prove an easy lower bound.

Corollary 11. *Consider the UMDA optimizing OneMax with $\mu = \Omega(\sqrt{n}\log n)$. Its run time is then in $\Omega(n \log n)$ in expectation and with probability at least $1 - \mathrm{e}^{-\Omega(n)}$.*

Proof. Since we assume $\mu = \Omega(\sqrt{n}\log n)$, Lemma 10 yields that within at most $\gamma \cdot \min\{\mu, \sqrt{n}\} = \gamma\sqrt{n}$ iterations, γ sufficiently small, at least $\Theta(n)$ frequencies are at most $5/6$ with probability $\Omega(1)$. Hence, assuming this to happen, the probability to sample the optimum is at most $(5/6)^{\Theta(n)} \leq \mathrm{e}^{-\Theta(n)}$, and, thus, the expected run time is in $\gamma\sqrt{n}\lambda = \Omega(n \log n)$. $\square$

3.3 Medium Population Sizes

In this section, we consider the remaining population sizes of $\mu = \mathrm{O}(\sqrt{n}\log n)$ (and $\mu = \Omega(\log n)$), where we recall that $\lambda = (1+\beta)\mu$. Basically, we lower-bound the probability that a single frequency hits $1/n$. To do so, we analyze the one-step change of the number of 1s at the frequency's position and approximate it via a normal distribution. For this, we are going to use a general form of the central limit theorem (CLT), along with a bound on the approximation error.

Lemma 12 (CLT with Lyapunov condition, Berry-Esseen inequality [9, p. 544]). *Let $X_1, \ldots, X_m$ be a sequence of independent random variables, each with finite expected value μ_i and variance σ_i^2. Define*

$$s_m^2 := \sum_{i=1}^{m} \sigma_i^2 \quad and \quad C_m := \frac{1}{s_m}\sum_{i=1}^{m}(X_i - \mu_i) .$$

If there exists a $\delta > 0$ such that

$$\lim_{m \to \infty} \frac{1}{s_m^{2+\delta}}\sum_{i=1}^{m} \mathrm{E}\left(|X_i - \mu_i|^{2+\delta}\right) = 0$$

(assuming all the moments of order $2 + \delta$ to be defined), then C_m converges in distribution to a standard normally distributed random variable.

Moreover, the approximation error is bounded as follows: for all $x \in \mathbb{R}$,

$$|\mathrm{Pr}(C_m \leq x) - \Phi(x)| \leq C \cdot \frac{\sum_{i=1}^{m} \mathrm{E}\left(|X_i - \mu_i|^3\right)}{s_m^3}$$

where C is an absolute constant and $\Phi(x)$ denotes the cumulative distribution function of the standard normal distribution.

To make use of Lemma 12, we need to study the stochastic process on the X_t values (which again denotes the number of 1s of an arbitrary position) and determine the accumulated expectations and variances of every single one-step change. Using the notation from Lemma 5, we note that the X_t value

in expectation changes very little from one step to the next since $\mathrm{E}(Z_1) = 0$ and also $\mathrm{E}(Z_2)$ is close to 0. However, considerable variances are responsible for changes of the X_t value, and it turns out that the variances are heavily dependent on the current state. We get $\mathrm{Var}(Z_1) = X_t(1 - X_t/\mu)$, i.e., if $X_t \leq \mu/2$, then the 1st-class individuals are responsible for a typical deviation of $\sqrt{X_t}$. This dependency of $\mathrm{Var}(Z_1)$ on X_t makes a direct application of Lemma 12 difficult.

To make the CLT applicable, we define a potential function that transforms X_t such that the expected difference between two points in time is still close to 0, but the variance is independent of the state. This potential function is inspired by the approach used in [18] to analyze two very simple EDAs. Since the standard deviation of Z_1 is $\Theta(\sqrt{X_t})$, we work with a potential function whose slope at point X_t is $\Theta(1/\sqrt{X_t})$, so that the dependency of the variance on the state cancels out.

We proceed with the formal definition. Let g denote the potential function, defined over $\{0, \ldots, \mu\}$. Our definition is simpler than the one from [18], as we do not need g to be centrally symmetric around $\mu/2$. We define

$$g(x) := \sqrt{\mu}\sum_{j=x}^{\mu-1}\frac{1}{\sqrt{j+1}} .$$

We will often use the following bounds on the change of potential. For $0 \leq y < x \leq \mu$, we get

$$g(y) - g(x) = \sqrt{\mu}\sum_{j=y}^{x-1}\frac{1}{\sqrt{j+1}} \leq \sqrt{\mu}\frac{x-y}{\sqrt{y+1}} , \text{ and} \quad (2)$$

$$g(y) - g(x) = \sqrt{\mu}\sum_{j=y}^{x-1}\frac{1}{\sqrt{j+1}} \geq \sqrt{\mu}\frac{x-y}{\sqrt{x+1}} . \quad (3)$$

Let $\Delta_t = g(X_{t+1}) - g(X_t)$.

3.3.1 Bounding the Expected Change of Potential

We start by bounding the expected value of Δ_t and see that also the transformed process moves very little in expectation (however, its variance will be large, as shown in the following subsection). Because of the Lyapunov condition, which we will address in Section 3.3.3, we do so in both directions.

Lemma 13. *Let $\mu = \mathrm{O}(\sqrt{n}\log n)$. Then, for all t and all $X_t \in \{1, \ldots, \mu - 1\}$,*

$$\mathrm{E}(\Delta_t \mid X_t) \geq -\left(\mathrm{e}^{-\Omega(\mu)} + \mathrm{O}\left(\frac{X_t}{\mu} + \frac{X_t}{\sqrt{n}}\right)\right)\sqrt{\frac{\mu}{X_t + 1}}$$

$$and \; \mathrm{E}(\Delta_t \mid X_t) \leq 111\sqrt{\frac{\mu}{X_t}} .$$

Proof. We abbreviate $X_t = x$. Further, we always condition on x without denoting this explicitly.

First, we derive the lower bound. We have $\mathrm{E}(\Delta_t) = \mathrm{E}(g(X_{t+1})) - g(x)$. Because g is convex we get by Jensen's inequality that $\mathrm{E}(g(X_{t+1})) - g(x) \geq g(\mathrm{E}(X_{t+1})) - g(x) \geq g(x + \mathrm{e}^{-\Omega(\mu)} + \mathrm{O}(x/\mu + x/\sqrt{n})) - g(x)$, where we used that

$$\mathrm{E}(X_{t+1}) \leq x + \mathrm{e}^{-\Omega(\mu)} + \mathrm{O}\left(\frac{x}{\mu} + \frac{x}{\sqrt{n}}\right) ,$$

which follows from Lemma 5 by studying the expected number of 1s contributed by the two classes of individuals.

Applying (2), gives us the desired result of

$$g\left(x + e^{-\Omega(\mu)} + O\left(\frac{x}{\mu} + \frac{x}{\sqrt{n}}\right)\right) - g(x)$$

$$\geq -\left(e^{-\Omega(\mu)} + O\left(\frac{x}{\mu} + \frac{x}{\sqrt{n}}\right)\right)\sqrt{\frac{\mu}{x+1}}.$$

The upper bound will be shown by ignoring 2nd-class individuals, since they are biased toward increasing x and, therefore, decreasing Δ_t. Hence, we now assume that X_{t+1} follows a binomial distribution with parameters μ and x/μ, i.e., $E(X_{t+1} - x) = 0$. In a delicate analysis, we will estimate how much $E(\Delta_t)$ is shifted away from 0 due to the nonlinearity of the potential function. We use the inequalities

$$g(i) \leq g(x) + \frac{\sqrt{\mu}(x-i)}{\sqrt{i+1}} \quad \text{for } i < x, \text{ and}$$

$$g(i) \leq g(x) + \frac{\sqrt{\mu}(x-i)}{\sqrt{i+1}} \quad \text{for } i > x,$$

which are just rearrangements of (2) and (3), noting that $x - i$ is negative in the second inequality.

$$E(\Delta_t) = \sum_{i=0}^{\mu} \big(g(i) - g(x)\big) \Pr(X_{t+1} = i)$$

$$\leq \sum_{i=0}^{x-1} \left(g(x) + \frac{\sqrt{\mu}(x-i)}{\sqrt{i+1}} - g(x)\right) \Pr(X_{t+1} = i)$$

$$+ \sum_{i=x+1}^{\mu} \left(g(x) + \frac{\sqrt{\mu}(x-i)}{\sqrt{i+1}} - g(x)\right) \Pr(X_{t+1} = i)$$

$$= \sum_{i=0}^{\infty} \left(\frac{\sqrt{\mu}(x-i)}{\sqrt{i+1}} \Pr(X_{t+1} = i)\right).$$

We now split the set of possible outcomes of i into intervals of length $\sqrt{x}$. More precisely $I_k := [x - (k+1)\sqrt{x}, x - k\sqrt{x}]$ for $k \in \mathbb{Z}$, i.e., also negative indices are allowed, leading to intervals lying above x. We get

$$E(\Delta_t) \leq \sum_{k=0}^{\infty} \sum_{i \in I_k} \left(\frac{\sqrt{\mu}(x-i)}{\sqrt{i - (k+1)\sqrt{x} + 1}} \Pr(X_{t+1} = i)\right.$$

$$\left. - \frac{\sqrt{\mu}(x-i)}{\sqrt{i + (k+1)\sqrt{x} + 1}} \Pr(X_{t+1} = 2x - i)\right),$$

noting that both i and $2x-i$ have a distance of $x-i$ to x. We take special care of intervals where $x - (k+1)\sqrt{x} \leq x/2$ (i.e., $k \geq \sqrt{x}/2 - 1$) and handle them directly. The maximum increase in potential is observed when $X_{t+1} = 0$ and equals

$$\sqrt{\mu}\sum_{j=0}^{x-1}\frac{1}{\sqrt{j+1}} \leq \sqrt{\mu}\left(1 + \int_1^x \frac{1}{\sqrt{z}}\,dz\right)$$

$$= \sqrt{\mu}(1 + 2\sqrt{x} - 2\sqrt{1}) \leq \sqrt{4\mu x}.$$

By Chernoff bounds, the probability of $X_{t+1} \leq x/2$ is at most $e^{-x/24}$. Hence, the intervals of index at least $k_{\max} := \sqrt{x}/2 - 1$ contribute only a term of $S^* := \sqrt{4\mu x}e^{-x/24} \leq 100\sqrt{\mu/x}$ to $E(\Delta_t)$.[1]

---
[1] The inequality $2xe^{-x/24} \leq 100/\sqrt{x}$ for $x \geq 1$ can be checked using elementary calculus.

For smaller k, we argue more precisely. Since

$$\frac{\sqrt{x + (k+1)\sqrt{x} + 1}}{\sqrt{x - (k+1)\sqrt{x} + 1}}$$

$$= 1 + \frac{\sqrt{x + (k+1)\sqrt{x} + 1} - \sqrt{x - (k+1)\sqrt{x} + 1}}{\sqrt{x - (k+1)\sqrt{x} + 1}}$$

$$\leq 1 + \frac{\frac{2(k+1)\sqrt{x}}{2\sqrt{x-(k+1)\sqrt{x}+1}}}{\sqrt{x - (k+1)\sqrt{x} + 1}} = 1 + \frac{(k+1)\sqrt{x}}{x - (k+1)\sqrt{x} + 1},$$

(where the last inequality follows from $a - b \leq (a^2 - b^2)/2b$ for $a \geq b > 0$), we have

$$E(\Delta_t) \leq \sum_{k=0}^{k_{\max}} \sum_{i \in I_k} \left(\frac{\sqrt{\mu}(x-i)}{\sqrt{x + (k+1)\sqrt{x} + 1}}\right. \tag{4}$$

$$\cdot \left(1 + \frac{(k+1)\sqrt{x}}{x - (k+1)\sqrt{x} + 1}\right) \Pr(X_{t+1} = i)$$

$$\left. - \frac{\sqrt{\mu}(x-i)}{\sqrt{x + (k+1)\sqrt{x} + 1}} \Pr(X_{t+1} = 2x - i)\right) + S^*.$$

We now look more closely into the inner sum and work with the abbreviation

$$E_k^* := \sum_{i \in I_k} \Big((x-i) \cdot \Pr(X_{t+1} = i)$$

$$- (x-i)\Pr(X_{t+1} = 2x - i)\Big).$$

Coming back to (4), this enables us to estimate the inner sum for arbitrary k:

$$\sum_{i \in I_k} \left(\frac{\sqrt{\mu}(x-i)}{\sqrt{x + (k+1)\sqrt{x} + 1}}\left(1 + \frac{(k+1)\sqrt{x}}{x - (k+1)\sqrt{x} + 1}\right)\right.$$

$$\cdot \Pr(X_{t+1} = i)$$

$$\left. - \frac{\sqrt{\mu}(x-i)}{\sqrt{x + (k+1)\sqrt{x} + 1}} \Pr(X_{t+1} = 2x - i)\right)$$

$$\leq E_k^* \cdot \frac{\sqrt{\mu}}{\sqrt{x + (k+1)\sqrt{x} + 1}}$$

$$+ \sum_{i \in I_k} \frac{\sqrt{\mu}(x-i)}{\sqrt{x + (k+1)\sqrt{x} + 1}} \frac{(k+1)\sqrt{x}}{x - (k+1)\sqrt{x} + 1} \Pr(X_{t+1} = i)$$

$$\leq \frac{E_k^*\sqrt{\mu}}{\sqrt{x + (k+1)\sqrt{x} + 1}} + \sum_{i \in I_k} \frac{\sqrt{\mu}(x-i)(k+1)}{x - (k+1)\sqrt{x} + 1}$$

$$\cdot \Pr(X_{t+1} = i),$$

where the last inequality estimated $\sqrt{x}/\sqrt{x + (k+1)\sqrt{x} + 1} \leq 1$. Since $k \leq k_{\max}$, i.e., $(k+1)\sqrt{x} \leq \sqrt{x}/2$, the last bound is easily bounded from above by

$$\frac{E_k^*\sqrt{\mu}}{\sqrt{x + (k+1)\sqrt{x} + 1}} + \sum_{i \in I_k} \frac{\sqrt{\mu}(x-i)(k+1)}{\frac{x}{2}} \Pr(X_{t+1} = i).$$

We proceed by bounding the sum over I_k, noting that we have $\Pr(X_{t+1} \in I_k) \leq \Pr(X_{t+1} \leq x - k\sqrt{x}) \leq e^{-k^2/3}$ by Chernoff bounds. Hence, since $x - i \leq (k+1)\sqrt{x}$ for $i \in I_k$, we get

$$\sum_{i \in I_k} \frac{\sqrt{\mu}(x-i)(k+1)}{\frac{x}{2}} \Pr(X_{t+1} = i)$$

$$\leq \frac{2\sqrt{\mu}}{x} \sum_{i \in I_k} (k+1)\sqrt{x}\, \mathrm{Pr}(X_{t+1} = i)$$

$$\leq \frac{2\sqrt{\mu}(k+1)}{\sqrt{x}} \sum_{i \in I_k} \mathrm{Pr}(X_{t+1} = i) \leq \frac{2\sqrt{\mu}(k+1)e^{-\frac{k^2}{3}}}{\sqrt{x}} .$$

Altogether, we have obtained from (4) the simpler inequality

$$\mathrm{E}(\Delta_t) \leq \sum_{k=0}^{k_{\max}} \frac{E_k^* \sqrt{\mu}}{\sqrt{x + (k+1)\sqrt{x} + 1}} + \frac{2\sqrt{\mu}(k+1)e^{-\frac{k^2}{3}}}{\sqrt{x}} + S^*,$$

(5)

which we will bound further. The idea is to exploit that

$$\sum_{k \geq 0} E_k^* = 0 , \qquad (6)$$

which is a reformulation of $\mathrm{E}(X_{t+1}) = x$. Using similar calculations as above, we manipulate the sum

$$\sum_{k \geq 0} \frac{E_k^* \sqrt{\mu}}{\sqrt{x + (k+1)\sqrt{x} + 1}} ,$$

stemming from the upper bound (5), and recognize that it equals

$$\sum_{k \geq 0} \frac{E_k^* \sqrt{\mu}}{\sqrt{x + \sqrt{x} + 1}}$$

$$\cdot \left(1 + \frac{\sqrt{x + \sqrt{x} + 1} - \sqrt{x + (k+1)\sqrt{x} + 1}}{\sqrt{x + (k+1)\sqrt{x} + 1}} \right)$$

$$\leq \sum_{\substack{k \geq 0 \\ E_k^* < 0}} \frac{E_k^* \sqrt{\mu}}{\sqrt{x + \sqrt{x} + 1}} \left(1 \right.$$

$$\left. - \frac{k\sqrt{x}}{2\sqrt{x + (k+1)\sqrt{x} + 1}\sqrt{x + \sqrt{x} + 1}} \right)$$

$$+ \sum_{\substack{k \geq 0 \\ E_k^* \geq 0}} \frac{E_k^* \sqrt{\mu}}{\sqrt{x + \sqrt{x} + 1}} \cdot 1 ,$$

where we again used $a - b \leq (a^2 - b^2)/2b$ for $a \geq b > 0$.

Similarly as above, we get, using Chernoff bounds,

$$E_k^* \geq \sum_{i=x+k\sqrt{x}}^{x+(k+1)\sqrt{x}} (x - i)\, \mathrm{Pr}(X_{t+1} = i) \geq -2(k+1)e^{-\frac{k^2}{3}}\sqrt{x} .$$

Combining this with (6), we arrive at the inequality

$$\sum_{k \geq 0} \frac{E_k^* \sqrt{\mu}}{\sqrt{x + (k+1)\sqrt{x} + 1}} \leq \sum_{k \geq 0} \frac{2(k+1)e^{-\frac{k^2}{3}}\sqrt{x}\sqrt{\mu}}{\sqrt{x + \sqrt{x} + 1}}$$

$$\cdot \frac{k\sqrt{x}}{2\sqrt{x + (k+1)\sqrt{x} + 1}\sqrt{x + \sqrt{x} + 1}} ,$$

which is at most $\sum_{k \geq 0} \left(k(k+1)e^{-k^2/3}\sqrt{\mu} \right)/\sqrt{x}$.

Substituting this into (5), we finally obtain

$$\mathrm{E}(\Delta_t) \leq \sum_{k \geq 0} \frac{2(k+1)e^{-\frac{k^2}{3}}\sqrt{\mu}}{\sqrt{x}} + \frac{k(k+1)e^{-\frac{k^2}{3}}\sqrt{\mu}}{\sqrt{x}} + S^*$$

$$\leq 11\frac{\sqrt{\mu}}{\sqrt{x}} + \frac{100\sqrt{\mu}}{\sqrt{x}} = 111\frac{\sqrt{\mu}}{\sqrt{x}} ,$$

which finally proves the upper bound. $\qquad \square$

3.3.2 Lower Bound on the Variance of the Potential Change

Before we analyze the variance of Δ_t, we introduce a lemma that we are going to use.

Lemma 14 ([16, Lemma 6]). *Let* $X \sim \mathrm{Bin}(\mu, r/\mu)$ *with* $r \in [0, \mu]$, *let* $\ell = \min\{r, \mu - r\}$, *and let* $\zeta > 0$ *be an arbitrary constant. Then* $\mathrm{Pr}(X \geq \mathrm{E}(X) + \zeta\sqrt{\ell}) = \Omega(1)$. *Note that if* $r \leq \mu/2$, *we get* $\mathrm{Pr}(X \geq \mathrm{E}(X) + \zeta\sqrt{\mathrm{E}(X)}) = \Omega(1)$.

In [16], the lemma is only stated for $\zeta = 1$. However, introducing the constant factor does not change the lemmas's proof at all.

With Lemma 14 in place, we now lower-bound the variance of Δ_t. Note that the following lemma only applies up to $X_t \leq (5/6)\mu$, which will be guaranteed in its application.

Lemma 15. *Let* $\mu = \omega(1)$ *and* $\mu = O(\sqrt{n}\log n)$. *Then, for all* t *and* $X_t \in \{1, \ldots, (5/6)\mu\}$,

$$\mathrm{Var}(\Delta_t \mid X_t) = \Omega(\mu) .$$

Proof. Again, we abbreviate $X_t = x$ and always condition on x without denoting so. Let $E^* := -\left(1 + \gamma(x/\sqrt{n}+1)\right) \cdot \sqrt{\mu/(x+1)}$ be a lower bound on $\mathrm{E}(\Delta_t)$ from Lemma 13, where we pessimistically estimated $e^{-\Omega(\mu)} \leq 1$, $x/\mu \leq 1$ because $x \leq \mu$, and where γ is a sufficiently large constant that captures the implicit constant in the O-notation. We estimate

$$\mathrm{Var}(\Delta_t) = \mathrm{E}\left(\left(\Delta_t - \mathrm{E}(\Delta_t) \right)^2 \right)$$

$$\geq \mathrm{E}\left(\left(\Delta_t - \mathrm{E}(\Delta_t) \right)^2 \cdot \mathbb{1}\{\Delta_t < E^*\} \right)$$

$$\geq \mathrm{E}\left(\left(\Delta_t - E^* \right)^2 \cdot \mathbb{1}\{\Delta_t < E^*\} \right) .$$

Note that we can ignore 2nd-class individuals, as they would only increase X_{t+1} even further, leading to a greater difference of Δ_t and E^*.

We derive a sufficient condition for $\Delta_t < E^*$. For this, we introduce the constant ζ and claim that $g(x + \zeta\sqrt{x}) \leq g(x) + E^*$ if ζ is sufficiently large. This claim is equivalent to $g(x) - g(x + \zeta\sqrt{x}) \geq -E^*$.

We lower-bound the left-hand side as follows: $g(x) - g(x + \zeta\sqrt{x}) \geq \sqrt{\mu} \cdot \zeta\sqrt{x}/(\sqrt{x + \zeta\sqrt{x} + 1}) \geq \sqrt{\mu} \cdot \zeta\sqrt{x}/\sqrt{2\zeta x} = \sqrt{\mu\zeta/2}$ (if ζ is sufficiently large), according to Inequality (3), which should be at least $-E^*$.

The inequality $\sqrt{\mu\zeta/2} \geq -E^*$ is equivalent to $\sqrt{\zeta/2} \cdot \sqrt{x+1} - 1 \geq \gamma(x/\sqrt{n} + 1)$. We prove this inequality by lower-bounding the left-hand side as follows: $\sqrt{\zeta/2} \cdot \sqrt{x+1} - 1 \geq \sqrt{\zeta x}/2$ if ζ is sufficiently large.

It is now evident that $\sqrt{\zeta x}/2 \geq \gamma(x/\sqrt{n} + 1) \Leftrightarrow \sqrt{\zeta}/2 \geq \gamma(\sqrt{x/n} + 1/\sqrt{x})$ holds (for $x \neq 0$) if ζ is sufficiently large, i.e., if $\zeta \geq (4\gamma)^2$, because $x \leq \mu$ and we assume $\mu = O(\sqrt{n}\log n)$, thus, $\sqrt{x/n} + 1/\sqrt{x} \leq 1 + o(1)$. For $x = 0$, the inequality trivially holds.

Using the inequality derived above, we get:

$$\Delta_t < E^* \Leftrightarrow g(X_{t+1}) - g(x) < E^* \Leftrightarrow g(X_{t+1}) < g(x) + E^*$$

$$\Leftarrow g(X_{t+1}) < g(x + \zeta\sqrt{x}) \Leftrightarrow X_{t+1} > x + \zeta\sqrt{x} ,$$

where we used the definition of g and that it is a decreasing function.

We proceed by estimating the expected value. First, we see that, assuming $X_{t+1} > x + \zeta\sqrt{x}$,

$$\Delta_t - E^* = g(X_{t+1}) - \left(g(x) + E^*\right) \leq g(X_{t+1}) - g(x + \zeta\sqrt{x})$$

$$= -\sqrt{\mu} \sum_{j=x+\zeta\sqrt{x}}^{X_{t+1}-1} \frac{1}{\sqrt{j+1}} \ ,$$

by using the same bounds as before. Note that we derive an upper bound of $\Delta_t - E^*$, because we only consider $\Delta_t < E^*$, i.e., $\Delta_t - E^* < 0$. Thus, its square gets minimized for an upper bound.

Using Jensen's inequality and that $X_{t+1} > x+\zeta\sqrt{x}$ implies $\Delta_t < E^*$, we get

$$\mathrm{E}\Big((\Delta_t - E^*)^2 \cdot \mathbb{1}\{\Delta_t < E^*\}\Big)$$
$$\geq \mathrm{E}\Big((\Delta_t - E^*)^2 \cdot \mathbb{1}\{X_{t+1} > x+\zeta\sqrt{x}\}\Big)$$
$$\geq \mathrm{E}\Big((g(X_{t+1}) - g(x+\zeta\sqrt{x})) \cdot \mathbb{1}\{X_{t+1} > x+\zeta\sqrt{x}\}\Big)^2$$
$$= \Bigg(\sum_{i=0}^{\mu} (-\sqrt{\mu}) \sum_{j=x+\zeta\sqrt{x}}^{i-1} \frac{1}{\sqrt{j+1}} \cdot \mathbb{1}\{i > x+\zeta\sqrt{x}\}$$
$$\cdot \Pr(X_{t+1} = i)\Bigg)^2$$
$$= \mu\Bigg(\sum_{i=x+\zeta\sqrt{x}+1}^{\mu} \sum_{j=x+\zeta\sqrt{x}}^{i-1} \frac{1}{\sqrt{j+1}} \Pr(X_{t+1}=i)\Bigg)^2 \ .$$

We now derive a lower bound for the second sum. Using Inequality (3), we get

$$\sum_{j=x+\zeta\sqrt{x}}^{i-1} \frac{1}{\sqrt{j+1}} \geq \frac{i-x-\zeta\sqrt{x}}{\sqrt{i}} \ .$$

Substituting this back into the expectation gives us

$$\mu\Bigg(\sum_{i=x+\zeta\sqrt{x}+1}^{\mu} \sum_{j=x+\zeta\sqrt{x}}^{i-1} \frac{1}{\sqrt{j+1}} \Pr(X_{t+1}=i)\Bigg)^2$$
$$\geq \mu\Bigg(\sum_{i=x+\zeta\sqrt{x}+1}^{\mu} \frac{i-x-\zeta\sqrt{x}}{\sqrt{i}} \Pr(X_{t+1}=i)\Bigg)^2$$
$$\geq \mu\Bigg(\sum_{i=x+2\zeta\sqrt{x}+1}^{\mu} \frac{i-x-\zeta\sqrt{x}}{\sqrt{i}} \Pr(X_{t+1}=i)\Bigg)^2 \ ,$$

where we narrowed the range for i. In this new range, $(i-x-\zeta\sqrt{x})/\sqrt{i}$ is monotonically increasing with respect to i and hence minimal for $i = x+2\zeta\sqrt{x}+1$:

$$\frac{x+2\zeta\sqrt{x}+1-x-\zeta\sqrt{x}}{\sqrt{x+2\zeta\sqrt{x}+1}} = \frac{\zeta\sqrt{x}+1}{\sqrt{x+2\zeta\sqrt{x}+1}} \geq \frac{\zeta\sqrt{x}+1}{\sqrt{3\zeta x}}$$
$$= \sqrt{\frac{\zeta}{3}} + \frac{1}{\sqrt{3\zeta x}} = \Omega(1) \ .$$

Hence, we finally have

$$\mathrm{Var}(\Delta) \geq \Omega(\mu)\Bigg(\sum_{i=x+2\zeta\sqrt{x}+1}^{\mu} \Pr(X_{t+1}=i)\Bigg)^2$$
$$\geq \Omega(\mu) \Pr(X_{t+1} \geq x+2\zeta\sqrt{x}+1)^2 \geq \Omega(\mu) \ .$$

The last inequality used Lemma 14 to lower-bound the probability. The lemma can be used immediately for $x \leq \mu/2$. Otherwise, we still have $x \leq (5/6)\mu$ by assumption. Then

Lemma 14 gives us a bound on $\Pr(X_{t+1} \geq x+\zeta\sqrt{\mu-x})$, which only changes everything by a constant factor, since $\sqrt{x}/\sqrt{\mu-x} \leq \sqrt{(5\mu/6)/(\mu/6)} = \mathrm{O}(1)$. $\quad\square$

3.3.3 Establishing the Lyapunov Condition

To establish the Lyapunov condition w. r. t. the sequence Δ_t, it is by Lemma 12 crucial to bound the individual variances and the $2+\delta$-th central absolute moment. The variances have already been studied in Lemma 15. Using $\delta = 1$, we are left with the analysis of the third central moment. This is dealt with in the following lemma.

Lemma 16. *If $\mu = \omega(1)$ and $\mu = \mathrm{O}(\sqrt{n}\log n)$, then*

$$\mathrm{E}\big(|\Delta_t - \mathrm{E}(\Delta_t)|^3 \mid X_t\big) = \mathrm{O}(\mu^{3/2}) \ .$$

Proof. We bound $\mathrm{E}\big(|\Delta_t - \mathrm{E}(\Delta_t)|^3 \mid X_t\big)$ by

$$\mathrm{E}\Big((|\Delta_t| + |\mathrm{E}(\Delta_t)|)^3 \mid X_t\Big) \ ,$$

aiming at reusing the bounds on $\mathrm{E}(\Delta_t \mid X_t)$ we know from Lemma 13.

To treat the binomial expression raised to the third power, we use the simple bound

$$(a+b)^3 = a^3 + 3ab^2 + 3a^2b + b^3 \leq 4a^3 + 4b^3$$

for $a, b \geq 0$.

Thus,

$$\mathrm{E}\big(|\Delta_t - \mathrm{E}(\Delta_t)|^3 \mid X_t\big) \leq 4\mathrm{E}(|\Delta_t|^3 \mid X_t) + 4|\mathrm{E}(\Delta_t \mid X_t)|^3 \ ,$$

and we already have the bounds $-\mathrm{O}(\sqrt{\mu}) \leq \mathrm{E}(\Delta_t \mid X_t) = \mathrm{O}(\sqrt{\mu})$, which follow from Lemma 13 for all $X_t \in \{1, \ldots, \mu-1\}$ and $x = \mathrm{O}(\sqrt{n}\log n)$.

The main task left is to bound $\mathrm{E}(|\Delta_t|^3 \mid X_t)$. We claim that $\mathrm{E}(|\Delta_t|^3 \mid X_t) = \mathrm{O}(\mu^{3/2})$. To show this, we assume an arbitrary X_t value. To bound the third moment, we analyze the distribution of $g(X_{t+1}) - g(X_t)$. We recall from Lemma 5 that X_{t+1} (i. e., the new value before applying the potential function) is given by the sum of two distributions, both of which are binomial or 'almost-binomial'. More precisely $X_{t+1} = Z_1 + Z(C^*)$, where Z_1 is the number of 1s sampled through 1st-class individuals, C^* is the number of 2nd-class individuals and $Z(C^*)$ is the number of 1s sampled through them. We note, using Lemmas 4 and 5, that $Z(C^*) \prec C^* \prec C^* \prec \mathrm{Bin}(\lambda, c/\sqrt{n}) + \widetilde{Z}$, for some constant $c > 0$, and $\widetilde{Z}$ takes some value from $1, \ldots, \lambda$ only with probability at most $e^{-\Omega(\mu)}$. Moreover, $Z_1 \sim \mathrm{Bin}(\mu - C^*, X_t/\mu)$,

To overestimate $|\Delta_t| = |g(X_{t+1}) - g(X_t)|$, we observe that

$$|X_{t+1} - X_t| = |Z_1 + Z(C^*) - X_t| \cdot \mathbb{1}\{Z_1 + Z(C^*) < X_t\}$$
$$+ |Z_1 + Z(C^*) - X_t| \cdot \mathbb{1}\{Z_1 + Z(C^*) \geq X_t\} \ .$$

Hence, to bound $|\Delta_t|$, it is enough to take the maximum of the two values

- $\Psi_1 := \Big|g\Big(\mathrm{Bin}\big(\mu, \frac{X_t}{\mu}\big)\Big) - g(X_t)\Big|$ and

- $\Psi_2 := \Big|g\Big(\mathrm{Bin}\big(\mu, \frac{X_t}{\mu}\big) + \mathrm{Bin}\big(\lambda, \frac{c}{\sqrt{n}}\big) + \widetilde{Z}\Big) - g(X_t)\Big|$

and analyze it. The first expression covers the case that $Z_1 + Z(C^*) < X_t$. Then, we transform C^* random variables whose success probability is greater than X_t/μ (since 2nd-class individuals are biased towards 1s) into variables with success probability exactly X_t/μ, which increases the probability of $Z_1 + Z(C^*)$ being less than X_t. On the other hand, if $Z_1 + Z(C^*) \geq X_t$, we get an even larger value by including C^* additional experiments.

We claim that $\mathrm{E}(|\Psi_1|^3 \mid X_t) = \mathrm{O}(\mu^{3/2})$. To show this, we proceed similarly as in computing the first moment of Δ_t and define intervals of length $\sqrt{x}$, where $x := X_t$ (hereinafter, we implicitly condition on this outcome). More precisely $I_k := [x - (k+1)\sqrt{x}, x - k\sqrt{x}]$ for $k \in \mathbb{Z}$, i.e., also negative indices are allowed, leading to intervals lying above x. We get

$$\mathrm{E}(|\Psi_1|^3 \mid x) \leq \sum_{k=0}^{\infty} \sum_{i \in I_k \cup I_{-k}} \left(\frac{\sqrt{\mu}(|i-x|)}{x - (k+1)\sqrt{x}} \right)^3 \Pr(|\Psi_1| = |i|)$$

$$\leq \sum_{k=0}^{\infty} \left(\frac{\sqrt{\mu}(|i-x|)}{x - (k+1)\sqrt{x}} \right)^3 \Pr(|\Psi_1| \geq k\sqrt{x}) ,$$

by applying (2) to bound $g(x) - g(y)$ for $y < x$. Note that for $k \leq \sqrt{x}$, we have by Chernoff bounds that $\Pr(X_{t+1} \in I_k) \leq \Pr(X_{t+1} \leq x - k\sqrt{x}) \leq \mathrm{e}^{-k^2/3}$ and $\Pr(X_{t+1} \in I_{-k}) \leq \Pr(X_{t+1} \geq x + k\sqrt{x}) \leq \mathrm{e}^{-k^2/4}$. Moreover, $\Pr(X_{t+1} \leq x/2) \leq \mathrm{e}^{-x/24}$. Using the standard form of Chernoff bounds, we also bound the probability $\Pr(X_{t+1} \geq (1+j/2)x) \leq \left(\mathrm{e}^{j/2}/(1+j/2)^{1+j/2} \right)^x \leq \mathrm{e}^{-jx/10}$ for $j \geq 1$.

Using these different estimates while distinguishing between $k \leq \sqrt{x}/2 - 1$ and $k \geq \sqrt{x}/2$, we get for $x \geq 1$ that

$\mathrm{E}(|\Psi_1|^3 \mid x)$

$$\leq \sum_{k=0}^{\frac{\sqrt{x}}{2}-1} \left(\frac{\sqrt{\mu}(k+1)\sqrt{x}}{\frac{x}{2}} \right)^3 2\mathrm{e}^{-\frac{k^2}{4}}$$

$$+ \left(g(0) - g(x) \right)^3 \Pr\left(X_{t+1} \leq \frac{x}{2} \right)$$

$$+ \sum_{j=1}^{\infty} \left(g(x) - g\left(x\left(1 + \frac{j}{2}\right) \right) \right)^3 \Pr\left(X_{t+1} \geq x + j\frac{x}{2} \right)$$

$$\leq \mathrm{O}\left(\mu^{\frac{3}{2}}\right) + (x\sqrt{\mu})^3 \mathrm{e}^{-\frac{x}{24}} + \sum_{j=1}^{\infty} \left(j\frac{x}{2}\sqrt{\mu} \right)^3 \mathrm{e}^{-j\frac{x}{10}} = \mathrm{O}\left(\mu^{\frac{3}{2}}\right) ,$$

where we use the trivial bound $g(x) - g(y) \leq \sqrt{\mu}|x-y|$ and pessimistically assume $X_{t+1} = 0$ in the case $X_{t+1} \leq x/2$.

With respect to Ψ_2, we observe that

$$\Psi_2 \prec \left| g\left(\mathrm{Bin}\left(\mu, \frac{x}{\mu}\right) \right) - g(x) \right|$$

$$+ \mathrm{O}(\mu)\Pr(\widetilde{Z} \neq 0) + \left(g(0) - g\left(\mathrm{Bin}\left(\lambda, \frac{c}{\sqrt{n}}\right) \right) \right)$$

by using $g(x+a+b) - g(x) = \left(g(x+a) - g(x) \right) + \left(g(x+a+b) - g(x+a) \right)$, for arbitrary $a, b \in \mathbb{R}$, and pessimistically estimating the contribution of $Z(C^*)$ to occur at point 0, where the potential function is steepest. Moreover, we pessimistically assume that the event $\widetilde{Z} \neq 0$ leads to the maximum possible change of g-value, which is $g(0) - g(\mu) = \mathrm{O}(\mu)$. Hence,

$$\mathrm{E}(|\Psi_2|^3 \mid x) \leq 4\mathrm{E}\left(\left| g\left(\mathrm{Bin}\left(\mu, \frac{x}{\mu}\right) \right) - g(x) \right|^3 \right) \quad (7)$$

$$+ 4\mathrm{E}\left(\left(g(0) - g\left(\mathrm{Bin}\left(\lambda, \frac{c}{\sqrt{n}}\right) \right) \right)^3 \right) + \mathrm{O}(\mu^3) \cdot \Pr(\widetilde{Z} \neq 0) .$$

We recall that $\Pr(\widetilde{Z} \neq 0) \leq \mathrm{e}^{-\Omega(\mu)}$, so that $\mathrm{O}(\mu^3) \cdot \Pr(\widetilde{Z} \neq 0) = \mathrm{O}(\mu^3) \cdot \mathrm{e}^{-\Omega(\mu)} = o(1) = \mathrm{O}(\mu^{3/2})$, for $\mu = \omega(1)$. Hence, the last term from Lemma 7 has already been bounded as desired, and we only have to show bounds on the first two terms of (7).

We recognize that the first term of (7) is $\mathrm{O}(\mu^{3/2})$ since, up to constant factors, it is the same as $\mathrm{E}(|\Psi_1|^3 \mid X_t)$. Hence, we are left with the claim

$$\mathrm{E}\left(\left(g(0) - g\left(\mathrm{Bin}\left(\lambda, \frac{c}{\sqrt{n}}\right) \right) \right)^3 \right) = \mathrm{O}\left(\mu^{\frac{3}{2}}\right) ,$$

which (as the derivative of $-g$ is at most $\sqrt{\mu}$) will be proved by establishing the stronger claim

$$\sqrt{\mu} \cdot \mathrm{E}\left(\mathrm{Bin}\left(\lambda, \frac{c}{\sqrt{n}}\right)^3 \right) = \mathrm{O}\left(\mu^{\frac{3}{2}}\right) .$$

To show this, we let $Z \sim \mathrm{Bin}(\lambda, c/\sqrt{n})$ and consider different intervals I_k, $k \geq 0$, that Z can fall into. The definition of intervals distinguishes two cases.

Case 1: $\lambda \geq \sqrt{n}/(2ec)$. We define $I_0 := [0, 2ec\lambda/\sqrt{n}]$ and $I_k := [(1+k)ec\lambda/\sqrt{n}, (2+k)ec\lambda/\sqrt{n}]$ for $k \geq 1$. Then (similar to the analysis of $\mathrm{E}(|\Psi_1|^3 \mid x)$), we get

$$\mathrm{E}\left(\mathrm{Bin}\left(\lambda, \frac{c}{\sqrt{n}}\right)^3 \right) \leq \left(\frac{2ec\lambda}{\sqrt{n}} \right)^3$$

$$+ \sum_{k=1}^{\infty} \left(\frac{(2+k)ec\lambda}{\sqrt{n}} \right)^3 \Pr(Z \in I_k) .$$

We use the Chernoff bound $\Pr(X \geq t) \leq 2^{-t}$ for $t \geq 2e\mathrm{E}(X)$. This gives us $\Pr(Z \in I_k) \leq \mathrm{e}^{-(2+k)e\lambda/\sqrt{n}} \leq \mathrm{e}^{-k/2}$ by our assumption on λ. We get

$$\mathrm{E}\left(\mathrm{Bin}\left(\lambda, \frac{c}{\sqrt{n}}\right)^3 \right) \leq \mathrm{O}\left(\frac{\lambda^3}{n^{\frac{3}{2}}} \right) + \mathrm{O}\left(\frac{\lambda^3}{n^{\frac{3}{2}}} \right) \sum_{k=1}^{\infty} (2+k)^3 \mathrm{e}^{-\frac{k}{2}}$$

$$= \mathrm{O}\left(\frac{\lambda^3}{n^{\frac{3}{2}}} \right) = \mathrm{O}\left(\frac{\mu^3}{n^{\frac{3}{2}}} \right) ,$$

hence $\sqrt{\mu} \cdot \mathrm{E}\left(\mathrm{Bin}(\lambda, c/\sqrt{n})^3 \right) = \mathrm{O}(\mu^{7/2}/n^{3/2})$. Since $\mu = \mathrm{O}(\sqrt{n}\log n)$ by assumption of the lemma, the bound is at most $\mathrm{O}\left(n^{1/4}(\log n)^{7/2} \right)$, and this is clearly $\mathrm{O}(\mu^{3/2})$ since $\mu = \Omega(\sqrt{n})$ in this case.

Case 2: $\lambda < \sqrt{n}/2e$. Then $I_k := [k, k+1]$ for $k \geq 0$. We note that $\mathrm{E}(Z) = \mathrm{O}(1)$ since $\mu = \mathrm{O}(\lambda) = \mathrm{O}(\sqrt{n})$. Hence, by Chernoff bounds for $k > \mathrm{E}(Z)$, $\Pr(Z \geq k) = \mathrm{e}^{-\alpha k}$ for some constant $\alpha > 0$. We get

$$\mathrm{E}\left(\left(g(0) - g(Z) \right)^3 \right)$$

$$\leq (\sqrt{\mu})^3 \cdot \mathrm{E}(Z^3) \leq \mu^{3/2} \cdot \mathrm{E}(Z)^3 + \sum_{k > \mathrm{E}(Z)}^{\infty} (\mu k)^3 2^{-\alpha k} .$$

Thus, using $\mu = \mathrm{O}(\sqrt{n})$,

$$\mathrm{E}\left(\left(g(0) - g(Z) \right)^3 \right) \leq \mathrm{O}\left((\sqrt{\mu})^3 \right) + (\sqrt{\mu})^3 \sum_{k=1}^{\infty} k^3 2^{-\alpha k}$$

$$= \mathrm{O}\left(\mu^{\frac{3}{2}} \right) ,$$

which completes the proof. $\qquad \square$

Using Lemmas 15 and 16, we now establish the Lyapunov condition, assuming $X_t \leq (5/6)\mu$ for all $t \geq 0$. Using

Lemma 12, we get for $s_t^2 := \sum_{j=0}^{t-1} \mathrm{Var}(\Delta_j \mid X_j)$ that

$$\frac{1}{s_t^3} \sum_{j=0}^{t-1} \mathrm{E}\big(|\Delta_j - \mathrm{E}(\Delta_j)|^3 \mid X_j\big) = \mathrm{O}\left(\frac{\mu^{1.5}t}{\mu^{1.5}t^{1.5}}\right) = \mathrm{O}(1/\sqrt{t}),$$

which is $\mathrm{o}(1)$ for $t = \omega(1)$. The sum of the Δ_j can then be approximated as stated in the following lemma.

Lemma 17. *Let $Y_t := \sum_{j=0}^{t-1} \Delta_j$ and $t = \omega(1)$. Then*

$$\frac{Y_t - \mathrm{E}(Y_t \mid X_0)}{\sqrt{\sum_{j=0}^{t-1} \mathrm{Var}(\Delta_j \mid X_j)}}$$

converges in distribution to $\mathrm{N}(0,1)$. The absolute error of this approximation is $\mathrm{O}(1/\sqrt{t})$.

3.3.4 Likelihood of a Frequency Getting Very Small

We will now apply Lemma 17 to prove how likely it is for a single frequency to either get close to $1/n$ or exceed $5/6$. For this, we will use the following estimates for $\Phi(x)$. More precise formulas exist, but they do not yield any benefit in our analysis.

Lemma 18 ([8, p. 175]). *For any $x > 0$,*

$$\left(\frac{1}{x} - \frac{1}{x^3}\right)\frac{1}{\sqrt{2\pi}}e^{-\frac{x^2}{2}} \leq 1 - \Phi(x) \leq \frac{1}{x}\frac{1}{\sqrt{2\pi}}e^{-\frac{x^2}{2}},$$

and for $x < 0$,

$$\left(\frac{-1}{x} - \frac{-1}{x^3}\right)\frac{1}{\sqrt{2\pi}}e^{-\frac{x^2}{2}} \leq \Phi(x) \leq \frac{-1}{x}\frac{1}{\sqrt{2\pi}}e^{-\frac{x^2}{2}}.$$

Lemma 19. *Consider a bit of the UMDA on OneMax and let p_t be its frequency in iteration t. We say that the process breaks a border at time t if $\min\{p_t, 1-p_t\} \leq 1/n$. Given $s < 0$ and any starting state $p_0 \leq 5/6$, let T_s be the smallest t such that $p_t - p_0 \leq s$ holds or a border is broken.*

Assume that $\Omega(n)$ other frequencies stay within $[1/6, 5/6]$ until time T_s. Choosing $0 < \alpha < 1$, where $1/\alpha = \mathrm{o}(\mu)$ and $\alpha = \mathrm{O}(\sqrt{n}/\mu)$, and $-1 < s < 0$ constant, we then have for some constant $\kappa > 0$ that

$$\Pr\big(T_s \leq \alpha s^2 \mu \text{ or } p_t \text{ exceeds } \tfrac{5}{6} \text{ before } T_s\big)$$

$$\geq \left(\frac{(|s|\alpha)^{\frac{1}{2}}}{\kappa} - \frac{(|s|\alpha)^{\frac{3}{2}}}{\kappa^3}\right)\frac{1}{\sqrt{2\pi}}e^{-\frac{\kappa^2}{2|s|\alpha}} - \mathrm{O}\left(\frac{1}{\sqrt{\alpha\mu}}\right).$$

Proof. Throughout the analysis, we assume $X_t \leq (5/6)\mu$, since all considerations are stopped when the frequency exceeds $5/6$, i.e., when $X_t \geq (5/6)\mu$. By Lemma 13, we have $\mathrm{E}(\Delta_j \mid X_j) \geq -\sqrt{\mu/(X_j+1)}\big(e^{-\Omega(\mu)} + \gamma_1(X_j/\sqrt{n} + X_j/\mu)\big)$ for all $j \geq 0$ and $1 \leq X_j \leq \mu - 1$, where $\gamma_1 > 0$ is a sufficiently large constant. Moreover, according to Lemma 15, $\mathrm{Var}(\Delta_j \mid X_j) \geq c\mu$ for some constant $c > 0$. Since the Lyapunov condition has been established for $Y_t := \sum_{j=0}^{t-1} \Delta_j$ in Lemma 17, we know that $(Y_t - \mathrm{E}(Y_t \mid X_0))/s_t$ converges in distribution to $\mathrm{N}(0,1)$ if $t = \omega(1)$. The lemma chooses $t = \alpha s^2 \mu$, which is $\omega(1)$ since $\alpha = \omega(1/\mu)$ by assumption.

For $s_t^2 := \sum_{j=0}^{t-1} \mathrm{Var}(\Delta_j \mid X_j)$, we obtain $s_t^2 \geq \alpha s^2 c\mu^2$. Hence, recalling that $s < 0$ is assumed, we get $s_t \geq \sqrt{\alpha c}|s|\mu$. The next task is to bound $\mathrm{E}(Y_t)$. Using our bound on $\mathrm{E}(\Delta_j \mid X_j)$ and recalling that $0 \leq X_t \leq (5/6)\mu$ and $\mu = \omega(1)$, we have

$$\mathrm{E}(\Delta_t \mid X_t) \geq -\left(e^{-\Omega(\mu)}\sqrt{\frac{\mu}{1}} + \gamma_1 \frac{\frac{5}{6}\mu}{\sqrt{\frac{5}{6}\mu+1}}\left(\frac{\sqrt{\mu}}{\sqrt{n}} + \frac{1}{\sqrt{\mu}}\right)\right)$$

$$\geq -\left(\mathrm{O}(1) + \gamma_2 \frac{\mu}{\sqrt{n}}\right),$$

for some constant $\gamma_2 > 0$.

This implies $\mathrm{E}(Y_t) \geq -t\big(\mathrm{O}(1) + \gamma_2\mu/\sqrt{n}\big) = -\alpha s^2 \mu\big(\mathrm{O}(1) + \gamma_2\mu/\sqrt{n}\big)$. Therefore,

$$\frac{\mathrm{E}(Y_t)}{s_t} \geq -\frac{(\alpha s^2 \mu)\big(\mathrm{O}(1) + \gamma_2\frac{\mu}{\sqrt{n}}\big)}{\sqrt{\alpha c}|s|\mu} \geq -\gamma_3\sqrt{\frac{1}{c\alpha}},$$

for some constant $\gamma_3 > 0$ depending on α, using the assumptions $|s| \leq 1$ along with both $\alpha \leq 1$ and $\alpha = \mathrm{O}(\sqrt{n}/\mu)$.

To bound $\Pr(Y_t \geq r)$ for arbitrary r, we note that

$$Y_t \geq r \iff \frac{Y_t}{s_t} - \frac{\mathrm{E}(Y_t \mid X_0)}{s_t} \geq \frac{r}{s_t} - \frac{\mathrm{E}(Y_t \mid X_0)}{s_t},$$

and recall that the distribution of $Y_t/s_t - \mathrm{E}(Y_t \mid X_0)/s_t$ converges to $\mathrm{N}(0,1)$ with absolute error $\mathrm{O}(1/\sqrt{t})$. Hence,

$$\Pr(Y_t \geq r) \geq 1 - \Phi\left(\frac{r}{\sqrt{c\alpha}|s|\mu} + \gamma_3\sqrt{\frac{1}{c\alpha}}\right) - \mathrm{O}\left(\frac{1}{\sqrt{t}}\right) \quad (8)$$

for any r such that the argument of Φ is positive, where Φ denotes the cumulative distribution function of the standard normal distribution.

We focus on the event E^* that $Y_t \geq 2\mu\sqrt{|s|}$, recalling that $s < 0$ and $X_t \geq X_0 \iff Y_t \leq Y_0$. Note that E^* means $g(X_t) - g(X_0) \geq 2\mu\sqrt{|s|}$, and this implies an upper bound on the negative $X_t - X_0$ as follows: Function g is steepest at point 0, and from the definition for any $y \geq 1$,

$$g(y) - g(0) \leq \sum_{j=0}^{y-1}\sqrt{\frac{\mu}{j+1}} \leq \sqrt{\mu}\left(1 + \int_1^y \frac{1}{\sqrt{j}}\,\mathrm{d}j\right)$$

$$= \sqrt{\mu}(1 + 2\sqrt{y} - 2\sqrt{1}) \leq 2\sqrt{y\mu}.$$

Thus, the event $g(X_t) - g(X_0) \geq a$ for $a > 0$ is only possible if $X_t \leq X_0 - a^2/(4\mu)$. In other words, event E^* implies $X_t - X_0 \leq s\mu$, which is equivalent to $p_t - p_0 \leq s$. Hence, to complete the proof, we only need a lower bound on the probability of E^*. Setting $r := 2\mu\sqrt{|s|}$ in (8), we bound the argument of Φ according to

$$\frac{r}{\sqrt{c\alpha}|s|\mu} + \frac{\gamma_3}{\sqrt{c\alpha}} \leq \frac{2}{\sqrt{c|s|\alpha}} + \frac{\gamma_3}{\sqrt{c\alpha}} \leq \frac{\gamma_4}{\sqrt{c|s|\alpha}},$$

for some constant $\gamma_4 > 0$, since $|s| \leq 1$.

By Lemma 18,

$$1 - \Phi\left(\frac{\gamma_4}{\sqrt{c|s|\alpha}}\right)$$

$$\geq \left(\frac{\sqrt{c|s|\alpha}}{\gamma_4} - \frac{(\sqrt{c|s|\alpha})^3}{\gamma_4^3}\right)\frac{1}{\sqrt{2\pi}}e^{-\frac{\gamma_4^2}{2c s\alpha}}$$

$$=: p(\alpha, s),$$

which means that the frequency changes by s (which is negative) until iteration $\alpha s^2 \mu$ with probability at least $p(\alpha, s) - \mathrm{O}(1/\sqrt{t}) = p(\alpha, s) - \mathrm{O}(1/\sqrt{\alpha\mu})$, where the last term stems from the bound on the absolute error of the approximation by the Normal distribution. Choosing $\kappa := \gamma_4/\sqrt{c}$ in the statement of the lemma completes the proof. $\square$

3.4 Proof of the Lower Bound

Finally, we put all previous lemmas together to prove our main theorem: Theorem 6.

Proof of Theorem 6. As outlined above, we distinguish between three regimes for λ. The case of small λ ($\lambda < (1 - c_1)\log_2 n$) is covered by Theorem 8, noting that $\Omega(n\log n)$ dominates the lower bound for the considered range of μ. The case of large λ ($\mu = \Omega(\sqrt{n}\log n)$) is covered by Corollary 11. We are left with the medium case ($\mu = \Omega(\log n)$ and $\mu = o(\sqrt{n}\log n)$), which is the most challenging one to prove.

In the following, we consider a phase consisting of $T := s^2\gamma \cdot \min\{\mu, \sqrt{n}\}$ iterations, for the constant $\gamma > 0$ from Lemma 10; without loss of generality, $\gamma < 1$ is assumed. We conceptually split individuals (i.e., bit strings) of the UMDA into two substrings of length $n/2$ each and apply Lemma 10 w.r.t. the first half of the bits. In the following, we condition on the event that $\Omega(n)$ frequencies from the first half are within the interval $[1/6, 5/6]$ throughout the phase.

We show next that some frequencies from the second half are likely to walk down to the lower border. Let j be an arbitrary position from the second half. First, we apply Lemma 9. Hence, p_j does not exceed $5/6$ within the phase with probability $\Omega(1)$. In the following, we condition on this event.

We then revisit bit j and apply Lemma 19 to show that, under this condition, the random walk on its frequency p_j achieves a negative displacement. Note that the event of not exceeding a certain positive displacement (more precisely, the displacement of $5/6 - 1/2 = 1/3$) is positively correlated with the event of reaching a given negative displacement (formally, the state of the conditioned stochastic process is always stochastically smaller than of the unconditioned process). We can therefore apply Lemma 19 for a negative displacement of $s := -5/6$ within T iterations. Note that the condition of the lemma that demands $\Omega(n)$ frequencies to be within $[1/6, 5/6]$ is satisfied by our assumption concerning the first half of the bits. Choosing $\alpha = T/(s^2\mu)$, we get $1/\alpha = o(\log n)$ (since $\mu = o(\sqrt{n}\log n)$ and $T = \Theta(\min\{\mu, \sqrt{n}\})$), whereby we easily satisfy the assumption $1/\alpha = o(\mu)$. As $T = O(\sqrt{n})$ and s constant, we also satisfy the assumption $\alpha = O(\sqrt{n}/\mu)$. Moreover, $\alpha \leq \gamma < 1$ by definition. Now Lemma 19 states that the probability of the random walk on p_j reaching a total displacement of $-5/6$ (or hitting the lower border before) within the phase of length T is at least

$$\left(\frac{(|s|\alpha)^{\frac{1}{2}}}{\kappa} - \frac{(|s|\alpha)^{\frac{3}{2}}}{\kappa^3}\right)\frac{1}{\sqrt{2\pi}}e^{-\frac{\kappa^2}{2\cdot|s|\alpha}} - O\left(\frac{1}{\sqrt{\alpha\mu}}\right). \quad (9)$$

To bound the last expression from below, we distinguish between two cases. If $\mu \leq \sqrt{n}$, then $\alpha = \Omega(1)$ and (9) is at least

$$\Omega(1) - O\left(\frac{1}{\sqrt{\mu}}\right) = \Omega(1)$$

since $T = \Omega(\mu) = \Omega(\log n) = \omega(1)$. If $\mu \geq \sqrt{n}$, then we have $T = \Omega(\sqrt{n})$. Since $1/\alpha = o(\log n)$, we estimate (9) from below by

$$\Omega\left(\frac{1}{o(\sqrt{\log n})} \cdot e^{-o(\ln n)}\right) - O\left(\frac{\log n}{n^{1/4}}\right) \geq n^{-\eta},$$

for some $\eta = \eta(n) = o(1)$. Combining this with the probability of not exceeding $5/6$, the probability of p_j hitting the lower border within T iterations is, in any case, $\Omega(n^{-\eta})$. Note that this argumentation applies to every of the last $n/2$

bits, and, as explained in Section 2.2, the bounds derived hold independently for all these bits. Hence by Chernoff bounds, with probability $1 - 2^{-\Omega(n^{1-\eta})}$, the number of frequencies from the second half that hit the lower border within T iterations is $\Omega(n^{1-\eta})$.

A frequency that has hit the lower border $1/n$ somewhere in the phase may recover (i.e., reach a larger value) by the end of the phase. However, for each bit the probability of not recovering is at least

$$\left(1 - \frac{1}{n}\right)^{T\lambda} \geq e^{-o(\log n)} = n^{-\eta'}$$

for some $\eta' = o(1)$, since we consider $T = O(\sqrt{n})$ iterations and $\lambda = o(\sqrt{n}\log n)$ samples per iteration. Again applying Chernoff bounds leaves $\Omega(n^{1-\eta-\eta'})$ bits at the lower border at iteration T with probability $1 - 2^{-\Omega(n^{1-\eta-\eta'})}$.

Now, making use of Lemma 7 gives us the desired run time bound. □

Conclusions

We have analyzed the UMDA on OneMax and obtained the general bound $\Omega(\mu\sqrt{n} + n\log n)$ on its expected run time for combinations of μ and λ such that $\lambda = O(\mu)$. This lower bound analysis is the first of its kind and contributes advanced techniques, including potential functions.

We also think that our lower bound for the UMDA is tight and that an expected run time of $O(n\log n)$ can be achieved on OneMax for carefully chosen parameters μ and λ. As the best upper bound to date is $O(n\log n\log\log n)$ [5], a formal proof of an improved upper bound would be interesting. We also note that our results assume $\lambda = O(\mu)$. However, we do not think that larger λ can be beneficial; if $\lambda = \alpha\mu$, for $\alpha = \omega(1)$, the progress due to 2nd-class individuals can be by a factor of at most α bigger; however, also the computational effort per generation would grow by this factor. Still, we have not presented a formal proof in this case.

Further run time analyses of the UMDA or other EDAs for other classes of functions are an obvious subject for future research. In this respect, we hope that our technical contributions are useful and can be extended towards a more general lower bound technique at some point.

Acknowledgments.
Financial support by the Danish Council for Independent Research (DFF–FNU 4002–00542) is gratefully acknowledged.

The authors would like to thank the anonymous reviewers for their comments, which greatly improved the quality of this paper.

References

[1] Tianshi Chen, Per Kristian Lehre, Ke Tang, and Xin Yao. When is an estimation of distribution algorithm better than an evolutionary algorithm? In *Proc. of CEC '09*, pages 1470–1477, 2009.

[2] Tianshi Chen, Ke Tang, Guoliang Chen, and Xin Yao. On the analysis of average time complexity of estimation of distribution algorithms. In *Proc. of CEC '07*, pages 453–460, 2007.

[3] Tianshi Chen, Ke Tang, Guoliang Chen, and Xin Yao. Rigorous time complexity analysis of univariate

marginal distribution algorithm with margins. In *Proc. of CEC '09*, pages 2157–2164, 2009.

[4] Tianshi Chen, Ke Tang, Guoliang Chen, and Xin Yao. Analysis of computational time of simple estimation of distribution algorithms. *IEEE Transactions on Evolutionary Computation*, 14(1):1–22, 2010.

[5] Duc-Cuong Dang and Per Kristian Lehre. Simplified runtime analysis of estimation of distribution algorithms. In *Proc. of GECCO '15*, pages 513–518, 2015.

[6] Stefan Droste. A rigorous analysis of the compact genetic algorithm for linear functions. *Natural Computing*, 5(3):257–283, 2006.

[7] Stefan Droste, Thomas Jansen, and Ingo Wegener. Upper and lower bounds for randomized search heuristics in black-box optimization. *Theory of Computing Systems*, 39:525–544, 2006.

[8] William Feller. *An Introduction to Probability Theory and Its Applications*, volume 1. Wiley, 1968.

[9] William Feller. *An Introduction to Probability Theory and Its Applications*, volume 2. Wiley, 1971.

[10] Tobias Friedrich, Timo Kötzing, and Martin S. Krejca. EDAs cannot be balanced and stable. In *Proc. of GECCO '16*, pages 1139–1146, 2016.

[11] Tobias Friedrich, Timo Kötzing, Martin S. Krejca, and Andrew M. Sutton. The benefit of recombination in noisy evolutionary search. In *Proc. of ISSAC '15*, pages 140–150, 2015.

[12] Mark Hauschild and Martin Pelikan. An introduction and survey of estimation of distribution algorithms. *Swarm and Evolutionary Computation*, 1(3):111–128, 2011.

[13] Pedro Larrañaga and Jose A. Lozano, editors. *Estimation of Distribution Algorithms: A New Tool for Evolutionary Computation*, volume 2 of *Genetic Algorithms and Evolutionary Computation*. Springer, 2002.

[14] Heinz Mühlenbein and Gerhard Paass. From Recombination of Genes to the Estimation of Distributions I. Binary Parameters. In *Proc. of PPSN IV*, pages 178–187, 1996.

[15] Frank Neumann, Dirk Sudholt, and Carsten Witt. A few ants are enough: ACO with iteration-best update. In *Proc. of GECCO '10*, pages 63–70, 2010.

[16] Pietro S. Oliveto and Carsten Witt. Improved time complexity analysis of the simple genetic algorithm. *Theoretical Computer Science*, 605:21–41, 2015.

[17] Dirk Sudholt. A new method for lower bounds on the running time of evolutionary algorithms. *IEEE Transactions on Evolutionary Computation*, 17(3):418–435, 2013.

[18] Dirk Sudholt and Carsten Witt. Update strength in EDAs and ACO: How to avoid genetic drift. In *Proc. of GECCO '16*, pages 61–68, 2016.

[19] Dirk Sudholt and Carsten Witt. Update strength in EDAs and ACO: How to avoid genetic drift. *ArXiv e-prints, http://arxiv.org/abs/1607.04063*, July 2016.

[20] Carsten Witt. Tight bounds on the optimization time of a randomized search heuristic on linear functions. *Combinatorics, Probability and Computing*, 22(2):294–318, 2013.

Convergence of Factored Evolutionary Algorithms

Shane Strasser
Gianforte School of Computing
357 Barnard Hall
Montana State University
Bozeman, MT 59717
shane.strasser@msu.montana.edu

John W. Sheppard
Gianforte School of Computing
357 Barnard Hall
Montana State University
Bozeman, MT 59717
john.sheppard@montana.edu

ABSTRACT

Factored Evolutionary Algorithms (FEA) have been found to be an effective way to optimize single objective functions by partitioning the variables in the function into overlapping subpopulations, or factors. While there exist several works empirically evaluating FEA, there exists very little literature exploring FEA's theoretical properties. In this paper, we prove that the final solution returned by FEA will be the results of converging to a single point. Additionally, we show how the convergence of FEA to a single point in the search space could be to a suboptimal point in space. However, we demonstrate empirically that when using specific factor architectures, the probability of converging to these suboptimal points in space approaches zero. Finally, where hybrid versions Cooperative Coevolutionary Algorithms have been proposed as a means to escape these suboptimal points, we show how FEA is able to outperform its hybrid version.

Keywords

Particle Swarm Optimization, Factored Evolutionary Algorithms, Convergence

1. INTRODUCTION

Many important problems involve function optimization, including bin packing, the traveling salesman problem, job shop scheduling, neural network training, and Bayesian network inference [26]. Often, stochastic search algorithms are used to solve such problems because the randomness used in the algorithms helps to escape local optima. One of the best-known families of stochastic search algorithms is the Evolutionary Algorithm (EA).

An example of an EA is the Genetic Algorithm (GA) which is inspired by the idea of Darwinian Evolution. Each individual in a GA acts like a chromosome and is modified in a manner that mimics genetics [9]. During each iteration, candidate solutions undergo search operations such as crossover and mutation. Another popular EA that has been found to perform well on a variety of optimization problems

FOGA '17, January 12–15, 2017, Copenhagen, Denmark.

© 2017 ACM. ISBN 978-1-4503-4651-1/17/01...$15.00

DOI: http://dx.doi.org/10.1145/3040718.3040727

is Differential Evolution (DE) [1]. The DE algorithm is similar to GA in that individuals undergo mutation, crossover, and selection, but differs in how those operations are performed.

Another population-based approach is called Particle Swarm Optimization (PSO) [12]. While GA and DE use a population of individuals that reproduce with one another, PSO uses a swarm of particles that "fly" around the search space. In addition to a vector that represents a candidate solution, particles use a velocity vector to control how the particles move through the space.

While GA and DE have been applied successfully to a wide range of problems, they are susceptible to hitchhiking, which is when poor values become associated with good schemata [15, 25]. Similarly, PSO can be prone to what is called "two steps forward and one step back," which happens when near optimal parts of an individual's current position may be thrown away if the rest of the individual's position causes the individual to have low fitness [30]. The consequences of hitchhiking and two steps forward and one step back is that the algorithm will often converge to suboptimal solutions [23].

One way to mitigate hitchhiking and "two steps forward and one step back" in GA, DE, and PSO is by generating subpopulations that optimize over subsets of variables [20]. Potter and De Jong presented one of the earliest such algorithms called the Cooperative Coevolutionary Genetic Algorithm (CCGA) that subdivided the problem by creating an individual GA that optimized over a single variable at a time. Other methods similar to CCGA have been presented, such as the Cooperative Particle Swarm Optimization (CPSO), which uses PSO as the underlying search algorithm and allows subpopulations to optimize over larger groups of variables [31]. However, one drawback to both of these methods is that they assume disjoint subpopulations.

Factored Evolutionary Algorithms (FEA) are a generalization of CCGA and CPSO that allow for subpopulations to overlap with one another [27]. The idea behind FEA is similar to how polynomials can be decomposed into a product of factors. FEA decomposes the optimization problem into a set of factors that when put together, represent full solutions to the problem. Additionally, FEA encourages the factors to overlap, which allows the factors to compete with one another for inclusion in a full solution Another unique property of FEA is that it allows for any population based algorithm to be used as the underlying optimization algorithm. [5]. Consequently, subpopulations or subswarms are associated with each factor, and the desired search algorithm is used to search the subspace covered by that factor.

Strasser *et al.* demonstrated that FEA is able to outperform other Cooperative Coevolutionary algorithms on a wide range of problems [27]. While FEA has been found to perform well, there is still little known about its convergence properties. For example, in previous work, the final solution returned by FEA always converged to a single point; however, it was unknown whether this would always be the case. Additionally, it was unknown if the final solution returned would be located at a global or local minimum. In this paper, we prove that FEA does converge to a single point, but that this point may not be a local or global minimum. We are also able to show that individual factors in FEA may become stuck at points in the search space called pseudominima. A pseudominimum is a point in the search space that appears as a local minimum in each subset of a configuration of subsets for the optimization problem, but is not a true local minimum for that problem as a whole.

Given these results, we demonstrate that, while FEA may theoretically not reach a local minimum, the likelihood of this occurring is often very small. To do so, we compare FEA with a hybrid version of CPSO that is guaranteed to reach a local minimum, called CPSO-H, which alternates between CPSO and PSO. By allowing a regular PSO to modify individuals in the subswarms in CPSO, CPSO-H is able to escape instances when subswarms become stuck at pseudominima. Additionally, we present a version of FEA called FEA-H, which alternates between FEA and the full EA. In doing so, we discover that while CPSO-H outperforms CPSO, the performance of FEA-H was usually equal or even worse than FEA.

There are several contributions made in this work. First, we prove under what conditions FEA will converge to a single solution. Second, we prove that FEA may converge to suboptimal solutions called pseudominima. Third, we define a hybrid FEA algorithm that combines FEA with a full population algorithm, called FEA-H. Finally, we present experimental results showing that while FEA may theoretically become stuck in pseudominima, the probability of this occurring is often very small.

The remainder of the paper is organized as follows. We first discuss relevant related work in Section 2 and then provide a detailed description of FEA in Section 3. In Section 4, we present our theoretical results that the full solution returned by FEA will converge to a single point if the factors also converge. Additionally, we show that this convergence may be to a pseudominimum. Next, in Section 5 we present a hybrid version of FEA, called FEA-H, that allows FEA to escape pseudominimum by alternating between FEA and a full single population EA. Finally, we compare FEA to Cooperative Coevolutionary algorithms as well as Cooperative Coevolutionary algorithms hybridized with single population algorithms in Section 6 and provide our conclusions and future work in Section 7.

2. RELATED WORK

Factored Evolutionary Algorithms (FEA) were first proposed by Strasser *et al.* as a framework for decomposing a single objective optimization problem into a set of subproblems that can be optimized by any evolutionary or swarm-based algorithm [27]. When put together, solutions to these subproblems (i.e., factors) represent full solutions to the problem. Additionally, FEA encourages the factors to overlap with one another, which allows the factors to compete for inclusion in the full solution [5, 27]. Strasser *et al.* demonstrated that FEA versions of Particle Swarm Optimization, Genetic Algorithms, Differential Evolution, and even simple Hill climbing outperformed single population and Cooperative Coevolutionary versions of the same algorithms. The authors also compared several different methods for deriving subpopulations for FEA and found that the architecture derived from a variable's Markov blanket outperformed the competing approaches. We make note that FEA has a similar name to the Fast Evolutionary Algorithm, which is a genetic algorithm that uses a fitness approximation routine to calculate the fitness of children based on the fitness of the parents, reducing the number of fitness evaluations [22].

One of the earliest versions of FEA was the Cooperative Coevolutionary Genetic Algorithm (CCGA) proposed by Potter and De Jong [20]. CCGA uses *subspecies* to represent non-overlapping subcomponents of a potential solution. Complete solutions are then built by assembling the current best subcomponents in a process called *collaboration*. The paper showed that, in most cases, CCGA significantly outperformed traditional GAs. Only in cases where the optimization function had high interdependence between the function variables (i.e., epistasis) did CCGA struggle because relationships between these variables were ignored.

More dynamic versions of CCGA have been proposed that allow for subpopulations to evolve over time [21]. When stagnation is detected in the population, a new subpopulation is initialized randomly and added to the set of subpopulations. Similarly, a subpopulation is removed if it makes small contributions to the overall fitness. Because of the dynamic subpopulations, there does exist the possibility that two subpopulations may overlap one another. However, this overlap is not guaranteed, and the algorithm does not have a means to resolve discrepancies between these overlapping subpopulations. The authors were able to demonstrate that their algorithm could evolve an effective number of subpopulations and was competitive with domain-specific algorithms on training cascade networks [21].

This idea of Cooperative Coevolutionary Evolutionary Algorithms (CCEA) was also applied by Van den Bergh and Engelbrecht when using PSO to train neural networks [30]. In their paper, the authors tested four fixed subswarm architectures of their own design. Comparing these four different architectures, the success of the algorithms was highly dependent on the architecture used, again due to the interdependence between the variables. By keeping variables with interdependencies together, the algorithm was more effective at exploring the search space [30]; however the subswarm architecture still did not allow for overlap.

Later, Van den Bergh and Engelbrecht extended their work by applying it to a wider range of optimization problems [31]. Cooperative PSO (CPSO) was introduced as a generalization of the authors' prior work, which was able to get around the problem of losing good values since each dimension is optimized by a single subpopulation. However, one drawback to CPSO is that it can become trapped in what the authors call *pseudominima*, which are places that are minima when looking at a single dimension but over the entire search space are not local minima. To avoid this problem, the authors introduce a hybrid algorithm that alternates between CPSO and PSO. The result was an algorithm that always outperformed PSO and was competitive with but more robust than CPSO.

Cooperative Coevolutionary (CC) algorithms have also been applied to Differential Evolution. Shi et al. proposed a simple and direct application of CCGA to DE, which they called CCDE [25]. Other adaptations have been more complex, such as those presented by Yang et al., where the authors developed a weighted cooperative algorithm that used DE to optimize problems over 100 dimensions [34]. In particular, their weighting scheme allowed for evolving subpopulations. The authors' algorithm was found to outperform regular CC algorithms on most of the test functions explored [34].

Another variation of CCEA that used evolving subpopulations was proposed by Li and Yao [14]. Here, the subpopulation sizes were allowed to grow or to shrink when stagnation was detected, creating a wider range of variable groups. The authors showed that their algorithm performed better than others on functions that had complex multimodal fitness landscapes, but performed slightly worse than PSO on unimodal functions. They noted that, while groups of random variables perform well, there should exist more intelligent ways of creating subpopulations.

CPSO was first adapted to allow explicitly for overlapping variables by Haberman and Sheppard in 2012 [8]. Here the authors developed an algorithm called Particle-based Routing with Overlapping Swarms for Energy Efficiency (PROSE), which used PSO as the underlying optimization algorithm. PROSE was presented as a method to develop energy-aware routing protocols for sensor networks that ensure reliable path selection while minimizing energy consumption during message transmission. Each subswarm in PROSE represented a sensor and all of the sensors' immediate neighbors in the network. PROSE was shown to be able to extend the life of the sensor networks and to perform significantly better than current energy-aware routing protocols.

Subsequently, PROSE was adapted by Ganesan Pillai and Sheppard to learn the weights of deep artificial neural networks [19]. In that work, the authors developed an algorithm called Overlapping Swarm Intelligence (OSI) where each swarm represents a unique path starting at an input node and ending at an output node. A common vector of weights, called the full global solution, is also maintained across all swarms to describe a global view of the network, which is created by combining the weights of the best particles in each of the swarms. The authors showed that OSI outperformed several other PSO-based algorithms, as well as standard backpropagation, on deep networks.

A distributed version of OSI was developed subsequently by Fortier et al. called Distributed Overlapping Swarm Intelligence (DOSI) [7]. In that paper, a communication and sharing algorithm was defined so that swarms could share values while also competing with one another. The key distinction from OSI was that a global solution was not used for fitness evaluation. The authors were able to show that DOSI's performance was close to that of OSI's on several different networks but there were instances when OSI outperformed DOSI. DOSI never outperformed OSI but was generally competitive.

OSI and DOSI have also been applied to the full and partial abductive inference problems in Bayesian networks, where the task is to find the most probable set of states for a set of nodes in the network given a set of observations [3, 5]

The authors were able to show that OSI and DOSI outperformed several other population-based and traditional algorithms, such as PSO, GA, simulated annealing, stochastic local search, and mini-bucket elimination.

Other applications of OSI and DOSI include learning the parameters or structure of Bayesian networks. For example, Fortier et al. adapted OSI to learn the structure of Bayesian classifiers by allowing subswarms to learn the links for each variable in the network [4]. Here each variable represents an attribute in the data, and for each variable, two subswarms were created—one for the incoming links and one for the outgoing links. The authors were able to show that in most cases OSI was able to significantly outperform competing structure learning approaches.

When learning Bayesian networks, latent or unobserved variables are often introduced, and Fortier et al. used OSI to learn the parameters of these latent variables [6]. A subswarm was created for each node with unknown parameters and all of the variables in that node's Markov blanket. The authors were able to show that OSI outperformed the competing approaches, including the traditionally-applied expectation-maximization algorithm, and that the amount of overlap between the subswarms can impact the performance of OSI.

There has been a limited number of papers published that have attempted to analyze theoretically the convergence of CCEAs, most of which have focused on collaboration in CCGA to evaluate individuals in a subpopulation [16]. For example, when evaluating an individual, which values should be pulled from other subpopulations to allow for calculating the fitness of the individual?

One of the earliest was by Wiegand et al., who developed a framework to analyze convergence properties of CCEA using evolutionary game theory to model the interaction of two subpopulations [32]. The authors calculated the next generation by using a payoff matrix A and proved that when trajectories converge to a fixed point, the populations become homogeneous. Additionally, the authors showed that subpopulations may converge to points with "suboptimal fitness values." Finally, the authors used their framework to investigate empirically the effects of uniform crossover and bit flip mutation.

One of the drawbacks to this approach was that the authors assumed infinite population in each of the subpopulations and that an individual's fitness is given as the average fitness using all individuals from the other subpopulation during collaboration [17]. Panait et al. relax this requirement by modeling the fitness evaluation of an individual as the average fitness of N randomly chosen individuals from the other subpopulation. Additionally, the authors use evolutionary game theory as a way to visualize different convergence properties of CCEA [17].

Later work by Panait argued that the primary reason for poor performance in CCGAs is caused by poor selection of individuals during collaboration [16]. The authors go on to use a refined evolutionary game theory model and show that a CCGA will converge to globally optimal solution when the collaboration process is set properly. Additionally, Panait showed that a collaboration process that uses the best individuals from subpopulations outperforms a collaboration process that uses the average or worst individuals.

Other theoretical work involved with CCGAs has been to investigate its robustness. Wiegand and Potter first defined a framework for characterizing robustness in evolutionary algorithms [33]. Using this framework, the authors were able to show that CCGAs exploit this robustness during search and demonstrate empirically how this is done [33].

As described elsewhere, Van den Bergh and Engelbrecht also presented work looking at the convergence of CCEAs [31], especially within the context of pseudominima. The authors present an extension to CPSO called CPSO-H, that avoids the problem of convergence to pseudominimum by iterating between CPSO and a full PSO algorithm, allowing the algorithm to escape pseudominima during the PSO portion of the algorithm. Because the CPSO-H iterates between CPSO and a regular PSO, the authors claim that any convergence results that are applicable to the full PSO are also applicable to CPSO-H [29].

Finally, we make note of some of the similarities between FEA and the Sequential Subspace Optimization (SESOP) algorithm [2]. SESOP is a gradient descent method that determines the next update based on a set of subspaces spanned by the current gradient and all previous steps. This is similar to FEA in that during each update, only a subset of variables may be updated. SESOP is different than FEA in that during each update, any subset of variables may be updated whereas in FEA, an individual is only able to update the same set of variables. Because SESOP is able to update any combination of variables, it is also less likely to become trapped in in pseudominima.

There are several different ways our theoretical work presented here differs from the previous work. The first is that prior work does not consider the overlap between factors (subpopulations). Second, we are currently not interested in the optimal way to evaluate an individual in a factor. Because there are multiple factors, the complexity to evaluate an individual with a large set of randomly selected values from other factors becomes intractable. FEA handles this problem by performing a local search during the competition step to generate a full global solution to allow for individuals to evaluate themselves. Finally, our work differs in that we enable any optimization algorithm to be used. All previous work assumes a particular algorithm, such as CPSO using PSO.

3. THE FACTORED EVOLUTIONARY ALGORITHM

In this section, we describe FEA. Note that a full specification of FEA can be found in [27]. There are three major subfunctions in FEA: update, competition and sharing. The update function is the simplest and allows each factor to optimize over its set of variables. The competition function creates a full solution that is used by factors to evaluate a partial solution, while the sharing step uses the full solution to inject information in the factors. Before giving the pseudocode for these steps, we first formally define factors in FEA.

3.1 Factors

Given a function $f : \boldsymbol{D}^N \to \mathbb{R}$ with domain $\boldsymbol{D}^N$ to be optimized with parameters $\boldsymbol{X} = \langle X_1, X_2, \ldots, X_N \rangle$, let $\boldsymbol{S}_i$ be a subset of $\boldsymbol{X}$. Let K be the average size of all subsets $\boldsymbol{S}_i$. Without loss of generality, assume that all subsets $\boldsymbol{S}_i$ are the same size. A subpopulation or *factor* $\boldsymbol{P}_i$ can then be defined over the variables in $\boldsymbol{S}_i$ that are optimizing f.

Algorithm 1 FEA Compete

Input: Function f to optimize, factors $\boldsymbol{S}$, full global solution $\boldsymbol{G}$

Output: Full solution $\boldsymbol{G}$

1: $randVarPerm \leftarrow$ RandomPermutation(N)
2: **for** $ranVarIndex = 1$ **to** N **do**
3: $i \leftarrow randVarPerm[ranVarIndex]$
4: $bestFit \leftarrow f(\boldsymbol{G})$
5: $bestVal \leftarrow \boldsymbol{P}_1[X_i]$
6: $\boldsymbol{S}_i \leftarrow \{\boldsymbol{S}_k | X_i \in \boldsymbol{S}_k\}$
7: $randPopPerm \leftarrow$ RandomPermutation($|\boldsymbol{S}_i|$)
8: **for** $ranPopIndex = 1$ **to** $|\boldsymbol{S}_i|$ **do**
9:    $\boldsymbol{P}_j \leftarrow \boldsymbol{S}_i[randPopPerm[ranPopIndex]]$
10:    $\boldsymbol{G}[X_i] \leftarrow \boldsymbol{P}_j[X_i]$
11:    **if** $f(\boldsymbol{G})$ is better than $bestFit$ **then**
12:      $bestVal \leftarrow \boldsymbol{P}_j[X_i]$
13:      $bestFit \leftarrow f(\boldsymbol{G})$
14:    **end if**
15: **end for**
16: $\boldsymbol{G}[X_i] \leftarrow bestVal$
17: **end for**
18: **return G**

Note that f can still be optimized over the variables in $\boldsymbol{S}_i$ by holding variables $\boldsymbol{R}_i = \boldsymbol{X} \setminus \boldsymbol{S}_i$ constant. We refer to $\boldsymbol{R}_i$ as factor $\boldsymbol{S}_i$'s *remaining values*. An algorithm that uses a set of subpopulations to optimize a problem is called a multi-population algorithm. We denote the set of s factor in a multi-population algorithm as $\boldsymbol{S} = \cup_{i=1}^s \boldsymbol{P}_i$.

When $s = 1$ and $\boldsymbol{S}_1 = \boldsymbol{X}$, then $\boldsymbol{S}$ will have just a single population that results in a traditional application of the population-based algorithm, such as PSO, DE, or GA. However, when $s > 1$, $\boldsymbol{S}_i \subset \boldsymbol{X}$, and $\bigcup \boldsymbol{S}_i = \boldsymbol{X}$ for all populations, the algorithm becomes a multi-population algorithm. We define FEA to be an algorithm where the factors that are proper subsets of $\boldsymbol{X}$ and at least one factor overlaps with another factor.

Because each population is only optimizing over a subset of values in $\boldsymbol{X}$, the factor defined for $\boldsymbol{S}_i$ needs to know the values of $\boldsymbol{R}_i$ for local fitness evaluations. Given a factor $\boldsymbol{P}_i$ and its remaining values $\boldsymbol{R}_i$, fitness for a partial solution in factor $\boldsymbol{P}_i$ can be calculated as $f(\boldsymbol{S}_i \cup \boldsymbol{R}_i)$. The values for $\boldsymbol{R}_i$ are derived from the other factors, which thereby allows $\boldsymbol{P}_i$ to use values optimized by other factors. The algorithm accomplishes this through competition and sharing as follows.

3.2 Competition

The goal of competition in FEA is to find the factors with the state assignments that have the best fitness for each dimension. Here, we present the competition algorithm described by Strasser *et al.* [27] (Algorithm 1). FEA constructs a *full global solution* $\boldsymbol{G} = \langle X_1, X_2, \ldots, X_N \rangle$ that evaluates the optimized values from factors. For every $X_i \in \boldsymbol{X}$, the algorithm iterates over every factor containing X_i and finds the best value from those factors.

The algorithm first iterates over a random permutation of all of the variables in $\boldsymbol{X}$, shown in line 2. Note that this permutation changes each time the algorithm is run. Lines 4 and 5 initialize variables that are used for the competition. Next, the algorithm iterates over another random permutation of all the factors that are optimizing the variable X_i. Lines 10-14 then compare the individual values of variable

Algorithm 2 FEA Share

Input: Full global solution G, factors $\mathcal{S}$
Output: Updated factors $\mathcal{S}$

1: **for all** $P_i \in \mathcal{S}$ **do**
2:      **for all** $X_j \in R_i$ **do**
3:          $R_i[X_j] \leftarrow G[X_j]$
4:      **end for**
5:      $p_w \leftarrow P_i.\text{worst}()$
6:      **for all** $X_j \in S_i$ **do**
7:          $p_w[X_j] \leftarrow G[X_j]$
8:      **end for**
9:      $p_w.fitness \leftarrow f(p_w \cup R_i)$
10: **end for**
11: **return** $\mathcal{S}$

Algorithm 3 Factored Evolutionary Algorithm

Input: Function f to optimize, optimization algorithm A
Output: Full solution G

1: $\mathcal{S} \leftarrow \text{initializeFactors}(f, X, A)$
2: $G \leftarrow \text{initializeFullGlobal}(\mathcal{S})$
3: **repeat**
4:      **for all** $P_i \in \mathcal{S}$ **do**
5:          **repeat**
6:              $P_i.\text{updateIndividuals}()$
7:          **until** Termination criterion is met
8:      **end for**
9:      $G \leftarrow \text{Compete}(f, \mathcal{S}, G)$
10:      $\mathcal{S} \leftarrow \text{Share}(G, \mathcal{S})$
11: **until** Termination criterion is met
12: **return** G

X_i by substituting the factors' values into G. In our implementation, the factor uses the best value found during the entire search process as its candidate value to be evaluated in lines 10-14. Note that this means changes are only made when the new fitness is strictly greater than the previous fitness. The values yielding the best fitness from the overlapping factors are saved and then inserted into G. Once the algorithm has iterated over all variables in X, the algorithm exits and returns G.

Note that competition is not guaranteed to find the best combination of values from each factor, nor does it guarantee the combination of values is better than the previous G. However, by iterating over random permutations of X and $\mathcal{S}$, the algorithm is able to explore different combinations and is still able to find good combinations of values.

3.3 Sharing

The sharing step serves two purposes. First it allows overlapping factors to inject their current knowledge into other factors. Previous work by Fortier *et al.* discovered that this is one of the largest contributors to the FEA's performance [5]. Second, it sets each factor's R_i values to those in the full global solution G so that each factor P_i can evaluate its partial solution on f. The sharing algorithm is provided in Algorithm 2.

The share algorithm iterates over all the factors and updates each factor's remaining values by setting each variable $X_j \in R_i$ to the value in G (lines 2-4). Next, the algorithm injects information from G into factor P_i. To accomplish this, the algorithm finds the individual with the worst fitness in P_i (line 5). Then, the share algorithm sets the worst individual p_w's current position to the values in G (lines 6 - 8). Finally, the fitness for p_w is recalculated in line 9.

3.4 FEA

Now that the share and competition algorithms have been defined, we can give the full FEA (Algorithm 3). The algorithm works as follows. First, all of the subpopulations are initialized according to the optimization algorithm being used and the subpopulation architecture (line 1). The full global solution G is randomly initialized in line 2.

Next, the algorithm begins inter-factor optimization, which consists of three steps (lines 3-11). First, the algorithm iterates over each factor and optimizes the values using the corresponding search algorithm until some stopping criterion is met (line 6). The optimization of each individual factor is called the intra-population optimization step. Following

intra-population optimization of all factors, competition occurs between factors in the Compete function on line 9. Finally, the Share function on line 10 shares the updated best states between the factors. These three inter-population optimization steps are repeated until the stopping criterion is met.

4. CONVERGENCE OF FEA

One open question concerning FEA is its convergence behavior. Previous work with FEA has found that the full global solution G always converged to a single solution; however, no one has analyzed under what conditions convergence will occur. Here, we present work showing that the full global solution G in FEA will converge to a single solution if the individual factors also converge. Additionally, we show that FEA may converge to suboptimal solutions that are not local minima.

4.1 Convergence to Single Solutions

First, we will prove under what conditions the full global solution G converges to a single solution. The following assumes the function being optimized is a minimization problem. We begin with some definitions.

DEFINITION 1. *Let Δ_i^t be the change in factor S_i's best position at time t where $S_i^t = [s_{(i,1)}^t, s_{(i,2)}^t, \ldots, s_{(i,k)}^t]$ is the best position for factor S_i at time t, where each position $s_{(i,j)}$ corresponds to a parameter in the function $f : D^N \to \mathbb{R}$ with domain D^N and parameters X. The change in the position for a single factor S_i is calculated as*

$$\Delta_i^t = d(S_i^{t-1}, S_i^t) = \sqrt{\sum_{j=1}^{K}(s_{(i,j)}^{t-1} - s_{(i,j)}^t)^2}$$

where K is the size of the factor.

DEFINITION 2. *Let $df(S_i)^t$ be the change in fitness in factor S_i's at time t, where*

$$df(S_i)^t = f(S_i^{t-1} \cup R_i^{t-1}) - f(S_i^t \cup R_i^t).$$

where R_i^t are the set of values from G.

Because S_i is only updated if the fitness is strictly less than the previous fitness, we know $df(S_i)^t \geq 0$.

DEFINITION 3. *Let $\Delta_{\boldsymbol{G}}^t$ be the change in position for $\boldsymbol{G}$ where*

$$\Delta_{\boldsymbol{G}}^t = d(\boldsymbol{G}^{t-1}, \boldsymbol{G}^t) = \sqrt{\sum_{i=1}^N (g_i^{t-1} - g_i^t)^2}$$

and $\boldsymbol{G}^t = [g_1^t, g_2^t, \ldots, g_N^t]$.

DEFINITION 4. *Let $df(\boldsymbol{G})^t$ be the change in fitness of $\boldsymbol{G}$ at time t where*

$$df(\boldsymbol{G})^t = f(\boldsymbol{G}^{t-1}) - f(\boldsymbol{G}^t)$$

DEFINITION 5. *Let $\boldsymbol{D}_f$ represent the search space for the function f. Similarly, Let $\boldsymbol{D}_{Comp}^t$ be the search space for the competition algorithm at time t. Note that $\boldsymbol{D}_{Comp}^t$ is a discrete search space and is given by the set of best positions from all factors,*

$$\boldsymbol{D}_{Comp}^t = [D_1^t, D_2^t, \ldots, D_N^t]$$

where D_i^t is the set of values a variable X_i in $\boldsymbol{G}$ can assume at time t,

$$D_i^t = [s_{(1,i)}^t, s_{(2,i)}^t, \ldots, s_{(K,i)}^t]$$

and $s_{(1,i)}^t$ is the best position at time t for the first factor $\boldsymbol{S}_1$ that optimizes parameter X_i.

DEFINITION 6. *Let $\boldsymbol{C}^t$ be the set of all points in which $\boldsymbol{G}$ can assume at time t. The set $\boldsymbol{C}^t$ is determined by $\boldsymbol{D}_{Comp}^t$ and consists of*

$$\boldsymbol{C}^t = \{D_1^t \times D_2^t \times \cdots \times D_N^t\},$$

where

$$C_i^t = [s_{(a,1)}^t, s_{(b,2)}^t, \ldots, s_{(z,N)}^t]$$

and $s_{(a,1)}^t$ is a value for variable X_1 from a factor a. We denote the size of $\boldsymbol{C}^t$ as L.

DEFINITION 7. *A factor $\boldsymbol{S}_i$ converges when*

$$\lim_{t \to \infty} \Delta_i^t = 0.$$

Similarly, $\boldsymbol{G}$ is said to have converged when

$$\lim_{t \to \infty} \Delta_{\boldsymbol{G}}^t = 0.$$

THEOREM 4.1. *Assume that at time $t - 1$, $\boldsymbol{G}$ is at a local optimum in $\boldsymbol{D}_{Comp}^{t-1}$. If $df(\boldsymbol{S}_i)^t = 0$ for all factors i, then $\Delta_{\boldsymbol{G}}^t = 0$ and $df(\boldsymbol{G})^t = 0$.*

PROOF. If $df(\boldsymbol{S}_i)^t = 0$, then no factors were updated and $\Delta_i^t = 0$ for all i. This indicates that the search space remain unchanged from $t-1$ to t and $\boldsymbol{C}^{t-1} = \boldsymbol{C}^t$. Since $\boldsymbol{G}$ was at a local optimum in $\boldsymbol{C}^{t-1}$, $\boldsymbol{G}$ is also at a local optimum in $\boldsymbol{C}^t$. Because there are no single changes that the competition algorithm can make to improve the fitness of $\boldsymbol{G}$, $\Delta_{\boldsymbol{G}}^t = 0$. Finally, because $\boldsymbol{G}$ remains unchanged, so does its fitness $df(\boldsymbol{G})^t = 0$. $\square$

The above theorem shows that if the full global solution is locally optimal and the search space $\boldsymbol{D}_{Comp}^t$ does not change, then there are no changes that the competition algorithm can make to increase the fitness of $\boldsymbol{G}$. This leads us to the next theorem, which relates the convergence of factors to the convergence of $\boldsymbol{G}$.

THEOREM 4.2. *If $\boldsymbol{G}$ is at a local optimum in $\boldsymbol{D}_{Comp}^t$ and all factors have converged, then $\boldsymbol{G}$ has also converged.*

PROOF. By definition of convergence for a factor $\boldsymbol{S}_i$,

$$d(\boldsymbol{S}_i^{t-1}, \boldsymbol{S}_i^t) = 0$$
$$\boldsymbol{S}_i^{t-1} = \boldsymbol{S}_i^t.$$

Therefore,

$$f(\boldsymbol{S}_i^{t-1}) = f(\boldsymbol{S}_i^t)$$
$$f(\boldsymbol{S}_i^{t-1}) - f(\boldsymbol{S}_i^t) = 0$$
$$df(\boldsymbol{S}_i)^t = 0$$

for all factors i. By Theorem 4.1, $\boldsymbol{G}$ will not change and therefore has converged. $\square$

The above theorem requires that all of the factors have already converged to guarantee the full global solution also converges. We relax this constraint in the next Theorem by only assuming that at some point in time the factors converge.

THEOREM 4.3. *If all the factors $\boldsymbol{S}_i$ in FEA converge at some point in time during FEA's optimization of f, then the full global solution $\boldsymbol{G}$ will also converge.*

PROOF. By definition of convergence for each factor $\boldsymbol{S}_i$,

$$\lim_{t \to \infty} \Delta_{\boldsymbol{S}_i}^t = 0.$$

Thus,

$$\lim_{t \to \infty} \sqrt{\sum_{j=1}^N (s_{i,j}{}^{t-1} - s_{i,j}{}^t)^2} = 0.$$

Because the distance function is positive semidefinite,

$$\lim_{t \to \infty} (s_{i,j}{}^{t-1} - s_{i,j}{}^t)^2 = 0$$

for all j in i. Let Δ_C^t be the change in $\boldsymbol{A}$ at time t,

$$\Delta_C^t = \frac{\sum_{i=1}^L d(C_i^{t-1}, C_i^t)}{L}$$

where C_i^t is the ith point in $\boldsymbol{C}$ at time t, and d is the Euclidean distance. Because $C_{i,j}^{t-1}$ is factor k's value for variable j, we know that the sequence of values will converge

$$\lim_{t \to \infty} (S_{k,j}{}^{t-1} - S_{k,j}{}^t)^2 = 0$$

therefore,

$$\lim_{t \to \infty} (C_{i,j}^{t-1} - C_{i,j}^t)^2 = 0.$$

for all j given i. Additionally,

$$\lim_{t \to \infty} d(C_i^{t-1}, C_i^t) = 0$$

for all factors i. Putting this together gives us

$$\lim_{t \to \infty} \frac{\sum_{i=1}^M d(\boldsymbol{C}_i^{t-1}, \boldsymbol{C}_i^t)}{M} = 0.$$

So,

$$\lim_{t \to \infty} \Delta_C^t = 0.$$

Recalling that this is a discrete search space with a finite number of points for the competition algorithm to explore, this shows that the search space $\boldsymbol{D}_{Comp}^{t}$ also converges to a set of discrete points. Eventually, the competition algorithm, which is a local search algorithm (i.e., Hill Climbing), will either reach a local optimum or hit all points. Therefore, $\boldsymbol{G}$ will converge. $\square$

The above theorem requires that all of the factors in FEA have converged. However, it is possible for the full global solution in FEA to converge even if not all of the factors have converged. Instead, we only require that $\boldsymbol{G}$ is a local optimum in all subsequent search spaces, which allows for some of the factors to not converge.

THEOREM 4.4. *If $\boldsymbol{G}$ is a local optimum in all spaces $\boldsymbol{D}_{Comp}^{t}$ $\forall t > t_0$, then $\boldsymbol{G}$ has converged.*

PROOF. Since $\boldsymbol{G}$ was at a local optimum in $\boldsymbol{C}^{t}$ for all future time past t_0, there are no single changes that the competition algorithm can make to improve the fitness of $\boldsymbol{G}$ during each FEA iteration. Therefore, $\Delta_{\boldsymbol{G}}^{t} = 0$, which by definition is the convergence of $\boldsymbol{G}$. $\square$

4.2 Pseudominimum Convergence

The previous section showed that if the search space for the competition algorithm converges or if $\boldsymbol{G}$ is at a local optimum, then the full global solution $\boldsymbol{G}$ will converge to a single point. However, it is unknown to what kind of solutions the full global solution will converge. Additionally, while $\boldsymbol{G}$ may be located at a local optimum in $\boldsymbol{D}_{Comp}^{t}$, it may not be a local optimum in $\boldsymbol{D}_{f}^{t}$. Here, we prove that $\boldsymbol{G}$ may become stuck in suboptimal points in the search space known as pseudominima.

DEFINITION 8. *A local minimum is a point*

$$\boldsymbol{x}^{*} = (x_1, x_2, \dots, x_N)$$

if there exists some $\epsilon > 0$ such that $f(\boldsymbol{x}^{*}) < f(\boldsymbol{x})$ for all points within a distance ϵ from $\boldsymbol{x}^{*}$.

DEFINITION 9. *Given a subspace $\mathcal{S}$ in $\mathbb{R}^{K}$ where $K < N$, a pseudominimum is a point*

$$\boldsymbol{x}_p = (x_1, x_2, \dots, x_N)$$

such that $\mathbf{x}_p$ is a local minimum in the subspace $\mathcal{S}$ but is not a local minimum for f.

DEFINITION 10. *Given a subspace $\mathcal{S}$ in $\mathbb{R}^{K}$ where $K < N$, a global pseudominimum is a point*

$$\boldsymbol{x}_p = (x_1, x_2, \dots, x_N)$$

such that $\mathbf{x}_p$ is a global minimum in the subspace $\mathcal{S}$ but is not a local or global minimum for f.

EXAMPLE 1. *An example of a global pseudominimum is the point $(0,0)$ for the function*

$$f(\mathbf{X}) = g(h(\mathbf{X})) \tag{1}$$

where

$$g(\mathbf{X}) = X_1^2 + X_2^2 -$$
$$(\tanh(10X_1) + 1)(\tanh(-10X_2) + 1) \exp\left(\frac{X_1 + X_2}{3}\right)$$

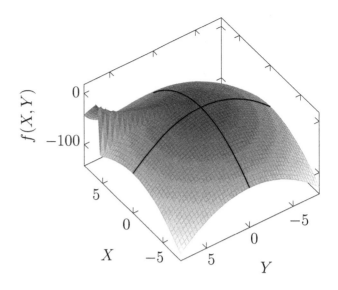

Figure 1: **An inverse plot of Equation 1. Point $(0,0)$ is an example of a global pseudominimum.**

and $\mathbf{h}(\mathbf{X}, \theta)$ is a rotation operator defined as

$$\mathbf{h}(\mathbf{X}, \theta) = \begin{bmatrix} \cos(\theta) & -\sin(\theta) \\ \sin(\theta) & \cos(\theta) \end{bmatrix} \begin{bmatrix} X_1 \\ X_2 \end{bmatrix}.$$

To highlight the shape of the function, we plot the inverse in Figure 1. The point $(0,0)$ is a global pseudominimum in the subspace defined by the y axis at $X = 0$ because moving in any direction in the y-axis, the function increases in value. However, the point is not a local minimum since the function can be decreased in the x and y axes simultaneously.

We also make note of a special set of pseudominima, called, maximal pseudominima, which are defined as follows.

DEFINITION 11. *Given a subspace $\mathcal{S}$ in $\mathbb{R}^{K}$ where $K < N$, a maximal pseudominimum is a point*

$$\mathbf{x}_p = (x_1, x_2, \dots, x_N)$$

such that $\mathbf{x}_p$ is a local minimum in the subspace $\mathcal{S}$ but is not a local minimum for $\mathcal{S} \cup X_i$ for all variables in $\mathbb{R}^{N}$.

Definition 11 differs from Definition 9 in a key way. A pseudominimum in subspace $\mathcal{S}$ may also be a pseudominimum $\mathcal{S} \cup X_i$ where X_i is some dimension not in $\mathcal{S}$. The definition of a pseudominimum only requires that a point not be a local minimum for all dimensions. For example, a point may be a pseudominimum in two dimensions X_1 and X_2 for a function with 5 variables X_1, X_2, X_3, X_4, X_5. But it may also be a pseudominimum in the dimensions X_1, X_2, and X_3. If the point is not a pseudominimum in the subspaces X_1, X_2, X_3, X_4 and X_1, X_2, X_3, X_5, then it is a maximal pseudominimum.

We note that pseudominima are similar to saddle points. While saddle points are pseudominima, not all pseudominima are saddle points. For example, $(0,0)$ in Figure 1 is a pseudominimum but is not a saddle point.

With these definitions, we can now give the following theorems. First, we show that there exist global pseudominima that will trap FEA. The second theorem generalizes this existence theorem by showing under what conditions FEA will become trapped by global pseudominima.

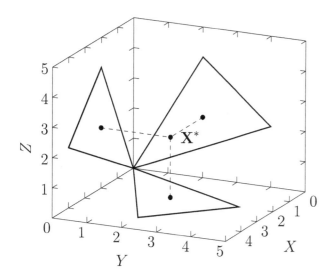

Figure 2: Three-dimensional function with a pseudominimum when projected into primary planes.

THEOREM 4.5. *There exist global pseudominima that will trap FEA.*

PROOF. We prove this by example. Assume we are given a function $f : \boldsymbol{D}^N \rightarrow \mathbb{R}$ with domain $\boldsymbol{D}^N$, that the output of the function is greater than 0, and the function is strictly increasing when moving in any direction from the origin. Additionally, there exists a simplex with a point at the origin where the rest of the points that define the simplex are strictly greater than 0. At the the tip of simplex, the output of f is equal to the origin, and within the simplex, the fitness decreases from all of the points that define the simplex to a local minimum $\boldsymbol{X}^* = (X_1^*, X_2^*, \ldots, X_N^*)$.

An example function with 3 dimensions is shown in Figure 2 with the sides of the triangle region projected onto the primary planes. In this example, the function for three variables X, Y and Z, is equal to $f(\boldsymbol{X}) = ||\boldsymbol{X}||$. The only exception is in a triangle shaped region where $f(\boldsymbol{X}) < 0$. Let B be the simplex region. We represent the function as

$$f(\boldsymbol{X}) = \begin{cases} g(\boldsymbol{X}) & \text{if } B \text{ contains } \boldsymbol{X} \\ \sqrt{X^2 + Y^2 + Z^2} & \text{else} \end{cases}$$

where

$$g(\boldsymbol{X}) = (X - X^*)^2 + (Y - Y^*)^2 + (Z - Z^*)^2 - C.$$

C is a constant value to ensure that all values of the function g within the simplex are negative.

Suppose an FEA is applied with factors $S_1, S_2, \ldots S_M$ where each factor S_i optimizes over a pair of variables X_j, X_k. Note that the origin $(0, 0 \ldots, 0)$ is a global pseudominimum defined by the FEA's factors since moving in only two directions causes f to increase in value. However, the origin is not a local minimum since f decreases in value by moving in all N directions simultaneously. thereby moving into the simplex with negative values.

Suppose the FEA has a full global solution G at the origin $(0, 0, \ldots, 0)$. If during factor $\boldsymbol{S}_1$'s solve step it evaluates the point X_1^*, X_2^*, the fitness will be some value L. By definition of f, the output is strictly increasing when moving away from the origin, and therefore, L is greater than 0. This is

because FEA uses the full global solution $\boldsymbol{G}$ to evaluate the values X_1^*, X_2^*.

In the example shown in Figure 2, this would equate to three factors: $\boldsymbol{S}_1, \boldsymbol{S}_2$, and $\boldsymbol{S}_3$, each of which optimizes over variables XY, YZ and XZ, respectively. Additionally, $\boldsymbol{G} = (0, 0, 0)$. Factor $\boldsymbol{S}_1$ would evaluate the point X^*, Y^* as

$$f(X^*, Y^*, 0) = \sqrt{(X^*)^2 + (Y^*)^2}.$$

Note that this point is not within the simplex because all points that define the simplex are strictly greater than 0.

Because the fitness of X^*, Y^* is greater than 0 and the current best fitness of the factor, the factor discards this point and X_1^*, X_2^* will not be used in the competition and sharing steps. Consequently, the full global solution is unable to move from the origin to $(X^*, Y^*, 0, \ldots, 0)$. This same phenomenon will also occur for all factors; therefore, FEA will be stuck at the global pseudominimum. □

THEOREM 4.6. *Given an FEA, let $\boldsymbol{S}$ be a set of subspaces $\mathbb{R}^K$ as defined by the set of factors in the FEA. If FEA's full global solution reaches a point $\boldsymbol{p}$ that is a global pseudominimum in all subspaces $\mathcal{S}_i \in \boldsymbol{S}$, then FEA will be unable to escape $\boldsymbol{p}$.*

PROOF. Assume we are given a function $f : \boldsymbol{D}^N \rightarrow \mathbb{R}$ with domain $\boldsymbol{D}^N$ and that the FEA has a set of factors $S_1, S_2, \ldots S_M$. Also, assume that the full global solution $\boldsymbol{G} = (X_1^*, X_2^*, \ldots X_N^*)$ is at a point $\boldsymbol{p}$ that is a global pseudominimum. By definition of a global pseudominimum, each factor $\boldsymbol{S}_i$ will be unable to move to a better position because all other points in the subspace that factor $\boldsymbol{S}_i$ is searching over will have fitness greater than the current fitness of $\boldsymbol{S}_i$ at $\boldsymbol{p}$. Since each factor will be unable to locate a position with better fitness than its current position, the factor will not use other values different than those in $\boldsymbol{G}$ during the competition and sharing steps of FEA. Because no other values are used during competition, the full global solution is unable to move from the global pseudominimum; therefore, FEA will be unable to escape from the global pseudominimum. □

While this shows that FEA may become stuck, the factors must be optimizing over the variables that induce the pseudominimum. For example, if a factor is optimizing over all 3 variables in Figure 2, then the factor using hill climbing as the algorithm will not be trapped by the point (0,0,0). This suggests that if it is known where a pseudominimum occurs, then there should exist a factor that optimizes over a superset of variables that induce the pseudominimum. Note also that this only works if the pseudominimum is maximal.

Another consequence of this result is that it may provide another explanation of the results presented by Strasser *et al.* as to why certain factor architectures outperform others [27]. In that work, the authors hypothesized that the best factor architecture performed better than the other architecture because the better performing architecture minimized hitchhiking. However, the performance of the better factor architecture may also be due to fact that the factors have less chance of becoming trapped in pseudominima.

5. HYBRID FEA

In the previous section, we showed that the full global solution $\mathbf{G}$ in FEA will converge to a single solution. However, similar to CPSO, FEA may converge to suboptimal

Algorithm 4 Hybrid Factored Evolutionary Algorithm

Input: Function f to optimize, optimization algorithm A
Output: Full solution G

1: $\boldsymbol{S} \leftarrow$ initializeFactors($f, \boldsymbol{X}, A$)
2: $\boldsymbol{G} \leftarrow$ initializeFullGlobal($\boldsymbol{S}$)
3: **repeat**
4:     **for all** $\boldsymbol{S}_i \in \boldsymbol{S}$ **do**
5:         **repeat**
6:             $\boldsymbol{S}_i$.updateIndividuals()
7:         **until** Termination criterion is met
8:     **end for**
9:     $\boldsymbol{G} \leftarrow$ Compete($f, \boldsymbol{S}$)
10:    Share($\boldsymbol{G}, \boldsymbol{S}$)
11:    $Full$.seed($\boldsymbol{G}$)
12:    **repeat**
13:       $Full$.updateIndividuals()
14:    **until** Termination criterion is met
15:    **if** $Full$.bestFitness() is better than $f(\boldsymbol{G})$ **then**
16:       $\boldsymbol{G} \leftarrow Full$.bestSolution()
17:    **end if**
18: **until** Termination criterion is met
19: **return** $\boldsymbol{G}$

solutions called pseudominima that regular EA are able to escape. As described earlier, van den Bergh and Engelbrecht proposed an extension to the CPSO algorithm called Hybrid Cooperative Particle Swarm Optimization (CPSO-H). CPSO-H combined the benefits of CPSO and a regular PSO by performing a number of iterations using CPSO followed by running a regular PSO. By performing several iterations with a full PSO, CPSO-H is able to escape pseudominima because an individual is able to modify all variables in one round of updates. Here, we present a similar extension to FEA called FEA-H (Algorithm 4).

FEA-H works as follows. First, it performs the same set of operations as FEA—Update, Compete, and Share—in lines 1–10. Next, FEA-H performs a set of updates to the full EA population, which is denoted as $Full$. First, the position of the individual with the worst fitness from $Full$ is set to the full global solution $\boldsymbol{G}$ (line 11). In line 14, the full population updates its individuals until some stopping criteria is satisfied. Finally, the fitness of the best solution in $Full$ is compared with $\boldsymbol{G}$. If the fitness of the best individual from the full population is better than the full global solution, then the algorithm sets $\boldsymbol{G}$ to solution with the better fitness (line 16). However, if the fitness is not better, then no changes are made to $\boldsymbol{G}$.

By running a set of iterations with a full EA, FEA-H is should be able to escape pseudominima. This is because when $Full$ updates its individuals, each individual has the opportunity to change every variable simultaneously. For example, in Figure 1, the full population is able to move individuals from the origin to the optimal solution by following the incline on the ridge. However, if the factor architecture subsumes the pseudominima in the fitness landscape, then FEA will not become stuck at suboptimal solutions, and FEA-H will provide little to no benefit over FEA.

6. EMPIRICAL ANALYSIS

As shown in Section 4, FEA is still susceptible to pseudominima. However, FEA only becomes stuck at these points

if the factors are optimizing over a subset of variables in $\mathbb{R}^k$. We hypothesize that for certain factor architectures in FEA, the probability of pseudominima becomes low. To test this hypothesis, we compare versions of CPSO and FEA with the hybrid version of CPSO-H presented by Van de Bergh and Englebrecht [31]. In addition, we compare all algorithms with FEA-H presented in Section 5. If FEA does become stuck in pseudominima, then one would expect FEA-H to outperform FEA because the full population in FEA-H allows the algorithm to escape pseudominima. However, if FEA does not become stuck in pseudominima, FEA-H will provide little to no benefit over FEA.

For the test problems we chose NK landscapes, abductive inference in Bayesian Networks, and some common benchmark optimization problems. NK landscapes were included because they represent commonly used functions for evaluating the performance of evolutionary algorithms applied to epistatic functions. We included abductive inference in Bayesian Networks because they are a practical combinatorial optimization problem.

Because the focus in this set of experiments is to analyze the convergence of FEA, we restrict our analysis to using PSO as the underlying search algorithm. Previous work by Strasser *et al.* has already demonstrated the performance of FEA versions with Genetic Algorithms, Differential Evolution, Particle Swarm Optimization, and simple Hill Climbing over single population and Cooperative Coevolutionary versions. On the NK landscapes and abductive inference, we used a modified version of PSO since both problems are functions with a discrete input. To handle these problems, we used the Integer and Categorical Particle Swarm Optimization (ICPSO) algorithm proposed by Strasser *et al* as the underlying search algorithm [28].

6.1 Integer and Categorical PSO

The Integer and Categorical Particle Swarm Optimization (ICPSO) algorithm is a new PSO algorithm developed by Strasser *et al.* that has been shown to outperform other discrete PSO algorithms [28]. The ICPSO algorithm incorporates ideas from Estimation of Distribution Algorithms (EDAs) in that particles in the PSO represent probability distributions rather than solution values, and the PSO update modifies the probability distributions. This differs from other PSO variants, where a particle's position is often a direct representation of the solution values.

In ICPSO, a particle p's position is represented as

$$\boldsymbol{X}_p = [\mathcal{D}_{p,1}, \mathcal{D}_{p,2}, \ldots, \mathcal{D}_{p,n}]$$

where each $\boldsymbol{D}_{p,i}$ denotes the probability distribution for variable X_i. In other words, each entry in the particle's position vector is itself comprised of a set of distributions:

$$\boldsymbol{D}_{p,i} = [d_{p,i}^a, d_{p,i}^b, \ldots, d_{p,i}^k],$$

where $d_{p,i}^j$ corresponds to the probability that variable X_i takes on value j for particle p.

A particle's velocity is a vector of n vectors ϕ, one for each variable in the solution, that adjust the particle's probability distributions.

$$\boldsymbol{V}_p = [\phi_{p,1}, \phi_{p,2}, \ldots, \phi_{p,n}]$$
$$\phi_{p,i} = [\psi_{p,i}^a, \psi_{p,i}^b, \ldots, \psi_{p,i}^k].$$

where $\psi_{p,i}^j$ is particle p's velocity for variable i in state j. The velocity and position update equations are identical to those of traditional PSO and applied directly to the continuous values in the distribution.

$$\begin{aligned} \boldsymbol{V_p} &= \omega \boldsymbol{V_p} + U(0,\phi_1) \otimes (\boldsymbol{pBest} - \boldsymbol{X_p}) \\ &\quad + U(0,\phi_2) \otimes (\boldsymbol{gBest} - \boldsymbol{X_p}) \\ \boldsymbol{X_p} &= \boldsymbol{X_p} + \boldsymbol{V_p} \end{aligned}$$

The difference operator is defined as a component-wise difference between the two position vectors, i.e. for each variable X_i and value $j \in Vals(X_i)$, $d_{(\mathbf{pBest_p} - \mathbf{P_p}),i}^j = d_{pB,i}^j - d_{p,i}^j$. Here, $d_{p_B}^j$ is the personal best position's probability that variable X_i takes value j. The global best equation is identical except $\boldsymbol{pBest_p}$ is replaced with $\boldsymbol{gBest}$ and $d_{pB,i}^j$ with $d_{gB,i}^j$. The addition of the velocity vector to the position vector is similarly component-wise over each value in the distribution. For each probability for variable X_i and possible value j, the addition is $d_{p,i}^j + \psi_{p,i}^j$.

After the velocity and position update, an extra check is performed to ensure that probabilities fall within $[0, 1]$. Additionally, the distribution is normalized to ensure that its values sum to 1.

To evaluate a particle p, its distributions are sampled to create a candidate solution

$$\boldsymbol{S_p} = [s_{p,1}, s_{p,2}, \ldots, s_{p,n}]$$

where $s_{p,j}$ denotes the state of variable X_j.

The fitness function is used to evaluate the sample's fitness, which then is used to evaluate the distribution. When a particle produces a sample that beats the global or local best, both the distributions from that particle's position, $\boldsymbol{P_p}$, and the sample itself, $\boldsymbol{S_p}$, are used to update the best values. Mathematically, for all states $j \in Vals(X_i)$ the global best's probability is updated as

$$d_{gB,i}^j = \begin{cases} \epsilon \times d_{p,i}^j & \text{if } j \neq s_{p,i} \\ d_{p,i}^j + \sum\limits_{\substack{k \in Vals(X_i) \\ \wedge k \neq j}} (1-\epsilon) \times d_{p,i}^k & \text{if } j = s_{p,i} \end{cases}$$

where ϵ, the *scaling factor*, is a user-set parameter that determines the magnitude of the shift in the distribution restricted to $[0, 1)$. This increases the likelihood of the distribution producing samples similar to the best sample, while inherently maintaining a valid probability distribution. The procedure for setting the local best is directly analogous. The global best sample is returned as the solution at the end of optimization.

6.2 Test Problems

6.2.1 NK landscapes

An NK landscape model contains two parameters, N and K, that control the overall size of the landscape and the structure or amount of interaction between each dimension, respectively [11]. It is defined by a function $f : \mathcal{B}^N \to \mathbb{R}^+$ where $\mathcal{B}^N$ is a bit string of length N. K specifies the number of other bits in the string on which a bit is dependent. This interaction is often referred to as epistasis. Given a landscape, the fitness value is calculated as

$$f(\mathbf{X}) = \frac{1}{N} \sum_{i=1}^{N} f_i(X_i, nb_K(X_i))$$

where $nb_K(X_i)$ returns the K bits that are located within X_i's neighborhood. The individual factors f_i are then defined as $f_i : \mathcal{B}^K \to \mathbb{R}^+$ and the values of f_i are generally created randomly.

There are multiple ways to define the neighborhood function. In our work, we used the next K contiguous bits of the string starting at X_i. If the end of the string is reached, then the neighborhood wraps back around to the beginning of the string. We generated NK landscapes with parameters $N = 25, 40, 50$, and $K = 5$. For each set of parameters, we created 30 random landscapes and ran each algorithm 30 times.

6.2.2 Bayesian Networks

A Bayesian network is a directed acyclic graph $G = (\mathbf{V}, \mathbf{E})$ that encodes a joint probability distribution over a set of random variables, where each variable can assume one of an arbitrary number of mutually exclusive values [13, 18]. In a Bayesian network, each random variable X_i is represented by a node, and edges between nodes in the network represent probabilistic relationships between the random variables. Each root node contains a prior probability distribution while each non-root node contains a local probability distribution conditioned on the node's parents.

A common type of query for Bayesian networks is called abductive inference, which finds the most probable state assignment to a set of unobserved variables given a set of observed variables (evidence). To evaluate the fitness of a state assignment in abductive inference, we used the log likelihood ℓ, which is calculated as

$$\ell(\mathbf{x}) = \sum_{i=1}^{n} \log P(x_i | \text{Pa}(x_i))$$

where $\mathbf{x} = \{x_1, x_2 \ldots x_n\}$ is a complete state assignment and $\text{Pa}(x_i)$ corresponds to the assignments for the parents of X_i. However, in all our experiments, we used an empty evidence set to minimize the number of parameters in the experiment. For test networks, we used the Alarm, Andres, Child, Hailfinder, Hepar2, Insurance, and Win95pts Bayesian networks from the Bayesian Network Repository [24].

6.2.3 Benchmark Optimization Problems

For the benchmark functions, we chose the following: Ackley's, Dixon Price, Exponential, Griewank, Rastrigin, Rosenbrock, Schwefel 1.2, and Sphere [10]. All of the problems are minimization problems with optimal finesses of 0.0 except for Exponential, whose optimal fitness is -1.0. All of the problems are scalable, meaning they can be optimized for versions of any dimension. The Sphere function is separable. The remaining functions are non-separable with most functions depending on adjacent, overlapping dimensions such as x_i and x_{i+1}. All functions were tested with 30 dimensions.

6.3 Setup

For the FEA algorithm on the NK landscapes and Bayesian networks, we used the Markov blanket factor architecture proposed by Fortier *et al.* since this was shown by Strasser *et al.* to outperform all other architectures on Bayesian networks and NK landscapes [5, 27]. On the Benchmark functions, we used the Simple Centered (SC) architecture of size two proposed by Strasser *et al.* since SC architecture had the most consistent performance over all functions [27]. The SC architecture creates a factor for each neighboring pairs of variables in an ordered list of variables corresponding to the function definition.

For the CPSO algorithms, we had each subswarm optimize over two variables in the problem. This subswarm size was found to have the most consistent performance during the tuning of the algorithms. Furthermore, even when other subswarm sizes performed better than those used here, the differences were not significant.

Each algorithm was given a total of 400 individuals to divide between their subswarms. For the hybrid algorithms CPSO-H and FEA-H, an additional 10 individuals were used for the full algorithm step of the algorithms. These values were found to perform well for all algorithms during tuning. On the NK landscapes and abductive inference, both versions of CPSO and FEA used ICPSO as the underlying search algorithm. On the benchmark problems, we used canonical PSO. For both PSOs, the ω parameter was set to 0.729, and ϕ_1 and ϕ_2 were both set to 1.49618. In ICPSO, the scaling value ϵ was set to 0.75. These values were found to perform well for all algorithms on all problems during tuning of the algorithms.

6.4 Results

Table 1 shows the results comparing CPSO, CPSO-H, FEA, and FEA-H on maximizing NK landscapes. Results from abductive inference on Bayesian networks are shown in Table 2 Note that both these problems are maximization. Results comparing CPSO, CPSO-H, FEA, and FEA-H on minimizing the benchmark functions are in Table 3. All results are expressed as means over 30 trials with standard errors in parentheses. Bold values indicate a significant difference between the regular CPSO or FEA algorithms with the hybrid versions using Mann-Whitney U test with $\alpha = 0.05$. Note that we did not perform any statistical testing between CPSO and FEA because it has already been shown by Strasser *et al.* that FEA outperforms CPSO.

As we can see in the NK landscape results, CPSO-H outperformed CPSO on two out of the three landscapes, but was only significantly better on $N = 25, K = 5$. Only on the larger problems ($N = 50$) did CPSO-H tie with CPSO-H. However, when looking at the FEA, the hybrid version of FEA was always outperformed by regular FEA, so hybridization provided no benefit and appears to have hurt performance.

The Bayesian network results show a similar trend in comparing regular and hybrid versions of CPSO and FEA. On the Andes, Hailfinder, Insurance, and Win95pts networks, CPSO-H outperformed CPSO significantly. Additionally, it was not outperformed by CPSO on the Alarm and Child networks. Only on the Hepar2 networks did CPSO significantly outperform CPSO-H. FEA outperformed FEA-H significantly on the Andes, Hailfinder, and Win95pts networks. Furthermore, it was only outperformed by FEA-H on the Child and Hepar2 networks. Note that in both of these cases, there was no significant difference between FEA and FEA-H.

On the benchmark functions, CPSO-H outperforms CPSO significantly on Griewank and Schwefel whereas, CPSO performs significantly better than CPSO-H on the Ackleys, Dixon Price, Exponential, Rastrigin and Sphere functions. FEA outperformed FEA-H by a significant margin on all functions except the Griewank function, where FEA-H outperformed FEA. We also note that the trends in the dif-

ferences between CPSO and CPSO-H are similar to that of FEA and FEA-H. Only on the Schwefel function was there a significant difference in the trends of CPSO and CPSO-H with that of FEA and FEA-H.

6.5 Analysis

From the NK landscape, Bayesian network, and benchmark results, we see that the full PSO steps used by FEA-H provided a performance gain only a few times. In particular, FEA-H only significantly outperformed FEA on the Griewank function. Additionally, in many of the problems, the full population steps in FEA-H hurt the performance.

While CPSO-H significantly outperformed CPSO on the majority of the NK landscapes and Bayesian networks, CPSO performed significantly better than CPSO-H on the majority of the benchmark functions. There are two possible reasons for this result. One is that in the majority of the functions, there are fewer pseudominima that trap CPSO; therefore, CPO-H provides fewer benefits than regular CPSO. The other possible reason is that the creation of the subswarms for CPSO leads to the ability to avoid the pseudominima in the search space on the majority of the functions.

Another result we would like to make note of is the similarities between CPSO and FEA on the benchmark functions. We believe that the similarity of these results is due to the subswarm (factor) size for both CPSO and FEA being set to two thus not adequately capturing all of the variable interactions. Even with these similarities, on the Rosenbrock and Schwefel functions, CPSO did not outperform CPSO-H whereas FEA outperformed FEA-H on both these functions. Specifically, with Rosenbrock and Schwefel functions the overlap in FEA appears to allow the subpopulations to capture the majority of the of the variable interactions that CPSO is unable to capture. Again, this is because CPSO subpoulations optimize only disjoint sets of variables.

For the NK landscape and Bayesian networks, we believe that the performance of FEA over FEA-H is because the factors in FEA are less susceptible to pseudominima than the subswarms in CPSO. In the benchmark functions, CPSO was able to escape the majority of the pseudominima. But on the NK landscapes and Bayesian networks, CPSO had a higher liklihood of becoming trapped in pseudominima, which explains why CPSO-H often outperformed CPSO. Meanwhile, the factors in FEA are less prone to get stuck in pseudominima because they are optimizing over larger groups of subspaces that induce the pseudominima; therefore, the full PSO steps are not needed.

We explored this hypothesis further by running an experiment where, during FEA, we checked to see if the factors' best solutions were at a pseudominimum after the compete step. Because the Bayesian networks and NK landscapes are discrete problems, we are able to look at all neighboring states of a factor. For a given factor S_i, if there does not exist a neighboring state with better fitness, then S_i could be at a pseudominimum. However, this point could also be a true local minimum. To see if S_i is in fact at a pseudominimum, we check to see if any neighboring points of $S_i \cup R_i$ have better fitness. If there does exist a neighboring point of $S_i \cup R_i$ with better fitness, then S_i is a true pseudominimum. However, if there are no neighboring points of $S_i \cup R_i$ with better fitness, then S_i is at a local minimum and not a pseudominimum. If the factor is not at a pseudominima or local minima, it is ignored in the calculation. This is because

Table 1: Results from comparing regular and hybrid versions of CPSO and FEA on NK landscapes.

	CPSO	CPSO-H	FEA	FEA-H
N=25, K = 5	1.78E+01(6.06E−02)	**1.83E+01(3.80E−02)**	**1.91E+01(3.15E−02)**	1.89E+01(3.19E−02)
N=40, K = 5	2.81E+01(1.09E−01)	**2.86E+01(7.00E−02)**	**3.05E+01(4.72E−02)**	3.01E+01(5.08E−02)
N=50, K = 5	**3.47E+01(1.31E−01)**	3.47E+01(6.74E−02)	**3.81E+01(3.87E−02)**	3.65E+01(5.11E−02)

Table 2: Results from comparing regular and hybrid versions of CPSO and FEA on Bayesian networks.

	CPSO	CPSO-H	FEA	FEA-H
Alarm	−1.99E+01(2.01E+00)	−1.59E+01(1.49E+00)	−9.12E+00(5.44E−01)	−9.87E+00(6.45E−01)
Andes	−2.01E+02(8.72E+01)	**−1.72E+02(7.12E+00)**	**−7.37E+01(8.34E−01)**	−8.80E+01(1.30E+00)
Child	−9.54E+00(5.08E−01)	−9.06E+00(4.48E−01)	−6.61E+00(3.03E−01)	−6.57E+00(2.98E−01)
Hailfinder	−7.39E+02(1.60E+02)	**−2.28E+02(6.92E+01)**	**−3.43E+01(3.61E−01)**	−3.57E+01(3.18E−01)
Hepar2	**−1.86E+01(4.48E−01)**	−2.14E+01(7.96E−01)	−1.81E+01(4.35E−01)	−1.76E+01(3.04E−01)
Insurance	−3.26E+02(8.56E+01)	**−1.57E+01(9.07E−01)**	−9.65E+00(4.13E−01)	−1.04E+01(2.91E−01)
Win95pts	−2.65E+02(1.10E+02)	**−1.17E+02(3.46E+01)**	**−1.82E+01(5.90E−01)**	−3.26E+01(1.16E+00)

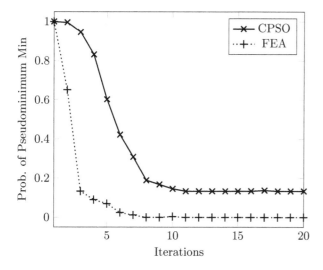

Figure 3: Probability of pseudominimum for NK landscape N = 25, K = 5.

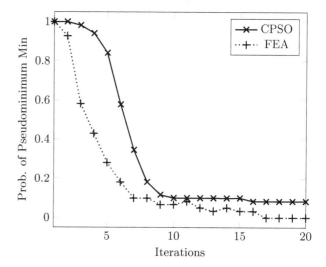

Figure 4: Probability of pseudominimum for Insurance network

a factor not at a local or pseudominimum suggests that the factor is still in the process of moving towards a better area in the search space.

We ran these experiments on the NK landscape with $N = 25$, $K = 5$, and on the Insurance network. Results for both CPSO and FEA are shown in Figures 3 and 4 respectively. In both these figures, the X-axis represents the number of iterations of the evolutionary algorithm. The Y-axis gives the probability of a pseudominimum at each iteration and is calculated as

$$\frac{\#pm}{\#pm + \#lm}$$

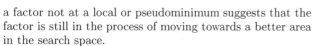

where $\#pm$ is the number of factors at a pseudominimum and $\#lm$ is the number of factors at a local minimum. A value of 1 means that all subswarms and factors are located at pseudominima while 0 indicates that all factors are located at local minima. Note that there is a possibility that the probability of a pseudominimum may become undefined if none of the factors are at a local minima or pseudominima. However, those instances were never encountered in these experiments.

As we can see in the two figures, both CPSO and FEA begin with a high probability of being located at pseudominima. This is likely due to the fact that the subswarms have just begun to locate good areas in the search space and are still moving towards those areas. However, we can see that the probability of factors being located at pseudominima in FEA decreases much faster than CPSO. Additionally, as the number of iterations increase, the probability for FEA becomes closer to zero. While the probability of CPSO does decrease over time, there is approximately a 20% probability of a subswarm being located at a pseudominimum. Finally, we note that the probability of pseudominima never increases because the definition of pseudominimum excludes a local minimum. Once a factor reaches a local minimum, it becomes more difficult for the factor to escape the local minimum, thus reducing the likelihood of a factor moving from a local minimum to a pseudominimum.

These results highlight why CPSO-H sees greater performance gains over CPSO than FEA-H does over FEA. On the NK landscapes and Bayesian networks, CPSO becomes trapped in pseudominima. CPSO-H is able to escape these

Table 3: Results from comparing regular and hybrid versions of CPSO and FEA on benchmark functions.

	CPSO	CPSO-H	FEA	FEA-H
Ackleys	**6.47E−06(3.86E−07)**	5.61E−05(6.24E−06)	**6.12E−06(7.39E−07)**	9.90E−05(1.20E−05)
Dixon Price	**2.22E−02(2.22E−02)**	2.17E−01(1.52E−01)	**4.44E−02(3.09E−02)**	1.56E−01(5.23E−02)
Exponential	**−1.00E+00(2.95E−10)**	−1.00E+00(1.02E−08)	**−1.00E+00(1.47E−10)**	−1.00E+00(7.34E−08)
Griewank	3.17E−02(1.95E−02)	**3.11E−03(1.50E−03)**	4.77E−02(8.32E−03)	**5.33E−03(1.99E−03)**
Rastrigin	**4.34E+00(3.83E−01)**	5.27E+00(3.76E−01)	**3.38E+00(2.96E−01)**	4.51E+00(4.49E−01)
Rosenbrock	2.81E+00(5.77E−01)	2.28E+01(1.40E+01)	**9.29E+00(3.07E+00)**	4.80E+01(7.22E+00)
Schwefel	2.86E+05(5.31E+04)	**1.42E+03(5.08E+02)**	**6.06E+02(5.63E+01)**	1.00E+03(6.96E+01)
Sphere	**2.15E−08(6.64E−09)**	7.48E−07(1.68E−07)	**8.97E−09(1.20E−09)**	3.21E−06(1.15E−06)

pseudominima and continue searching towards better solutions. FEA, on the other hand, has a smaller probability of becoming stuck in a pseudominima; therefore, the full swarm steps in FEA-H provide less benefit because the algorithm is already able to move towards good locations in the search space.

While the results suggest that FEA is less prone to pseudominima, the benchmark results suggest that the architecture is not the best for all functions. This is demonstrated by FEA-H significantly outperforming FEA on the Griewank function. We believe that main cause is that the factor architecture used for the Griewank function is suboptimal, and given a better factor architecture, we may see FEA outperform FEA-H. However, despite a suboptimal factor architectures, FEA is still competitive with both FEA-H and both versions of CPSO.

7. CONCLUSIONS AND FUTURE WORK

In this paper, we proved that the full global solution G found by FEA will converge to a single point if the individual factors also converge. Even so, we also proved that FEA is still susceptible to pseudominima. Despite the fact that FEA can become stuck at pseudominima, we demonstrated that, when using certain factor architectures, the probability of factors becoming stuck at pseudominimum approaches zero. To test this, we compared hybrid versions of CPSO and FEA and demonstrated that FEA-H did not provide significant performance gains on discrete problems. Additionally, we showed that over time, FEA has a lower probability of pseudominimum than CPSO.

There are a variety of areas we wish to explore for future work. The first is further investigation into the different factor architectures for benchmark functions. While previous work by Strasser *et al.* showed the Simple Center factor architecture has consistent performance, the results comparing FEA and FEA-H suggest that it may not be the best architecture for all functions [27]. Strasser *et al.* were also able to show that the Markov architecture was the best for abductive inference in Bayesian networks. One possible way to derive better factor architectures for the benchmark functions would be to map the functions to a Bayesian network and then use the resulting Markov blankets as a way to derive factors for FEA.

Another area of research is a more in depth analysis of FEA's different parameters, such as the number of iterations during the update step. These different parameters could also affect the complexity of FEA. As demonstrated by Strasser *et al*, FEA requires more fitness evaluations than its single-population counterparts [27]. One possible explanation is that this increase in complexity is driven by the number of iterations FEA allows each subpopulation to perform during the Update step. To verify this, we plan to vary the number of iterations allowed during the update step and compare the performance in terms of fitness and number of fitness evaluations.

Finally, we plan to apply FEA to a wider range of problems; for example, additional benchmark test functions and combinatorial optimization problems such as MaxSAT. This will help inform us further regarding to what type of problems FEA is most effective at solving. Additionally, we want to investigate the scalability of FEA by applying it to large optimization problems.

8. REFERENCES
[1] S. Das and P. N. Suganthan. Differential evolution: A survey of the state-of-the-art. *IEEE Transactions on Evolutionary Computation*, 15(1):4–31, 2011.

[2] M. Elad, B. Matalon, and M. Zibulevsky. Coordinate and subspace optimization methods for linear least squares with non-quadratic regularization. *Applied and Computational Harmonic Analysis*, 23(3):346–367, 2007.

[3] N. Fortier, J. Sheppard, and K. G. Pillai. Bayesian abductive inference using overlapping swarm intelligence. In *Proceedings of the IEEE Swarm Intelligence Symposium (SIS)*, pages 263–270. IEEE, 2013.

[4] N. Fortier, J. Sheppard, and S. Strasser. Learning Bayesian classifiers using overlapping swarm intelligence. In *Proceedings of the IEEE Swarm Intelligence Symposium (SIS)*, pages 1–8. IEEE, 2014.

[5] N. Fortier, J. Sheppard, and S. Strasser. Abductive inference in Bayesian networks using distributed overlapping swarm intelligence. *Soft Computing*, 19(4):981–1001, 2015.

[6] N. Fortier, J. Sheppard, and S. Strasser. Parameter estimation in Bayesian networks using overlapping swarm intelligence. In *Proceedings of the Genetic and Evolutionary Computation Conference (GECCO)*, pages 9–16. ACM, 2015.

[7] N. Fortier, J. W. Sheppard, and K. Pillai. DOSI: training artificial neural networks using overlapping swarm intelligence with local credit assignment. In *Joint 6th International Conference on Soft Computing and Intelligent Systems (SCIS) and 13th International Symposium on Advanced Intelligent Systems (ISIS)*, pages 1420–1425. IEEE, 2012.

[8] B. K. Haberman and J. W. Sheppard. Overlapping particle swarms for energy-efficient routing in sensor networks. *Wireless Networks*, 18(4):351–363, 2012.

[9] J. H. Holland. *Adaptation in natural and artificial systems: An introductory analysis with applications to biology, control, and artificial intelligence.* U Michigan Press, 1975.

[10] M. Jamil and X.-S. Yang. A literature survey of benchmark functions for global optimisation problems. *International Journal of Mathematical Modelling and Numerical Optimisation,* 4(2):150–194, 2013.

[11] S. A. Kauffman. *The origins of order: Self-organization and selection in evolution.* Oxford university press, 1993.

[12] J. Kennedy and R. Eberhart. Particle swarm optimization. In *Proceedings of the IEEE International Conference on Neural Networks,* pages 1942–1948, 1995.

[13] D. Koller and N. Friedman. *Probabilistic Graphical Models - Principles and Techniques.* MIT Press, 2009.

[14] X. Li and X. Yao. Cooperatively coevolving particle swarms for large scale optimization. *IEEE Transactions on Evolutionary Computation,* 16(2):210–224, 2012.

[15] M. Mitchell, S. Forrest, and J. H. Holland. The royal road for genetic algorithms: Fitness landscapes and ga performance. In *Proceedings of the first european conference on artificial life,* pages 245–254. Cambridge: The MIT Press, 1992.

[16] L. Panait. Theoretical convergence guarantees for cooperative coevolutionary algorithms. *Evolutionary computation,* 18(4):581–615, 2010.

[17] L. Panait, R. P. Wiegand, and S. Luke. A visual demonstration of convergence properties of cooperative coevolution. In *International Conference on Parallel Problem Solving from Nature,* pages 892–901. Springer, 2004.

[18] J. Pearl. *Probabilistic reasoning in intelligent systems: networks of plausible inference.* Morgan Kaufmann, 1988.

[19] K. G. Pillai and J. Sheppard. Overlapping swarm intelligence for training artificial neural networks. In *Proceedings of the IEEE Swarm Intelligence Symposium (SIS),* pages 1–8. IEEE, 2011.

[20] M. A. Potter and K. A. De Jong. A cooperative coevolutionary approach to function optimization. In *Parallel Problem Solving from Nature?PPSN III,* pages 249–257. Springer, 1994.

[21] M. A. Potter and K. A. De Jong. Cooperative coevolution: An architecture for evolving coadapted subcomponents. *Evolutionary Computation,* 8(1):1–29, 2000.

[22] M. Salami and T. Hendtlass. A fast evaluation strategy for evolutionary algorithms. *Applied Soft Computing,* 2(3):156–173, 2003.

[23] N. N. Schraudolph and R. K. Belew. Dynamic parameter encoding for genetic algorithms. *Machine learning,* 9(1):9–21, 1992.

[24] M. Scutari. Bayesian network repository. http://www.bnlearn.com/bnrepository, 2012.

[25] Y.-j. Shi, H.-f. Teng, and Z.-q. Li. Cooperative co-evolutionary differential evolution for function optimization. In *Advances in natural computation,* pages 1080–1088. Springer, 2005.

[26] J. C. Spall. *Introduction to Stochastic Search and Optimization: Estimation, Simulation, and Control.* John Wiley & Sons, 2005.

[27] S. Strasser, N. Fortier, J. Sheppard, and R. Goodman. Factored evolutionary algorithms. *IEEE Transactions on Evolutionary Computation,* PP(99):1–1, 2016.

[28] S. Strasser, R. Goodman, J. Sheppard, and S. Butcher. A new discrete particle swarm optimization algorithm. In *Proceedings of the Genetic and Evolutionary Computation Conference (GECCO),* pages 53–60. ACM, 2016.

[29] F. Van Den Bergh. *An analysis of particle swarm optimizers.* PhD thesis, University of Pretoria, 2006.

[30] F. Van den Bergh and A. P. Engelbrecht. Cooperative learning in neural networks using particle swarm optimizers. *South African Computer Journal,* (26):p–84, 2000.

[31] F. Van den Bergh and A. P. Engelbrecht. A cooperative approach to particle swarm optimization. *IEEE Transactions on Evolutionary Computation,* 8(3):225–239, 2004.

[32] R. P. Wiegand, W. C. Liles, and K. A. De Jong. Modeling variation in cooperative coevolution using evolutionary game theory. In *FOGA,* pages 203–220, 2002.

[33] R. P. Wiegand and M. A. Potter. Robustness in cooperative coevolution. In *Proceedings of the Genetic and Evolutionary Computation Conference (GECCO),* pages 369–376. ACM, 2006.

[34] Z. Yang, K. Tang, and X. Yao. Large scale evolutionary optimization using cooperative coevolution. *Information Sciences,* 178(15):2985–2999, 2008.

Hypervolume Subset Selection for Triangular and Inverted Triangular Pareto Fronts of Three-Objective Problems

Hisao Ishibuchi, Ryo Imada, Yu Setoguchi, and Yusuke Nojima
Department of Computer Science and Intelligent Systems
Osaka Prefecture University
Sakai, Osaka, 599-8531
Japan
{hisaoi@, ryo.imada@ci., yu.setoguchi@ci., nojima@}cs.osakafu-u.ac.jp

ABSTRACT

Hypervolume subset selection is to find a pre-specified number of solutions for hypervolume maximization. The optimal distribution of solutions on the Pareto front has been theoretically studied for two-objective problems in the literature. In this paper, we discuss hypervolume subset selection for three-objective problems with triangular and inverted triangular Pareto fronts. Our contribution is to show that the effect of the location of a reference point for hypervolume calculation on the optimal distribution of solutions is totally different between triangular and inverted triangular Pareto fronts. When the reference point is far from the Pareto front, most solutions are on the sides of the inverted triangular Pareto front while they are evenly distributed over the entire triangular Pareto front. These properties seem to hold in multiobjective problems with four or more objectives. We also show that the effect of the location of a reference point on the optimal distribution is totally different between maximization and minimization problems with the same triangular Pareto fronts. This property is supported by the fact that maximization problems with triangular Pareto fronts are equivalent to minimization problems with inverted triangular Pareto fronts. The optimal distribution of solutions is also discussed when the reference point is close to the Pareto front (i.e., when its location is between the nadir point and the Pareto front).

CCS Concepts

•Computing methodologies; Optimization algorithms; Search methodologies.

Keywords:Evolutionary multiobjective optimization; Pareto front; solution subset selection; hypervolume maximization.

1. INTRODUCTION

DOI: http://dx.doi.org/10.1145/3040718.3040730Hypervolume [23] has been frequently used to evaluate a set of solutions in the evolutionary multiobjective optimization (EMO) community [24] (i.e., to compare the search ability of different EMO algorithms). This is mainly because the hypervolume is a Pareto compliant performance indicator (e.g., see [22]). It has also been frequently used in indicator-based algorithms such as SMS-EMOA [5] and HypE [3] where multiobjective optimization is handled as single-

FOGA'17, January 12–15, 2017, Copenhagen, Denmark.
© 2017 ACM. ISBN 978-1-4503-4651-1/17/01...$15.00.
DOI: http://dx.doi.org/10.1145/3040718.3040730

objective hypervolume maximization. In those algorithms, a population of solutions is evolved to maximize its hypervolume. Hypervolume maximization needs the convergence of solutions to the Pareto front as well as their diversification over the entire Pareto front. When a two-objective problem has a linear Pareto front, the optimal distribution of solutions for hypervolume maximization is equidistant solutions on the Pareto front [1], [9].

Recently, hypervolume maximization by selecting a pre-specified number of solutions from a large number of candidates has been actively studied in the EMO community [4], [6], [7], [11]-[13], [15], [17], [20]. This task is referred to as hypervolume subset selection. The optimal distribution of solutions for hypervolume maximization has been also theoretically studied in the literature [1], [2], [9], [10], [21]. Almost all of those studies are for two-objective problems. Whereas the optimal distribution of solutions for multiobjective problems with three or more objectives was discussed in [21], a single-dimensional curve was assumed as the Pareto front. In this paper, we discuss hypervolume maximization for multiobjective problems with three or more objectives. We focus on a frequently-used many-objective test problem DTLZ1 [8] and its two variants: inverted DTLZ1 [19] and Max-DTLZ1 [18]. We show that these three problems have different optimal distributions for hypervolume maximization while they have the same (or inverted) Pareto front in the normalized objective space.

In Figure 1, we show solution sets obtained for the three-objective DTLZ1 and inverted DTLZ1 problems by SMS-EMOA [5]. A population of size 50 was evolved for 1,000,000 generations to maximize the hypervolume for the reference point (20, 20, 20). Since the Pareto front of each test problem is included in the cube $[0.0, 0.5]^3$, the reference point (20, 20, 20) is far from the Pareto front. In this paper, we explain why all solutions in Figure 1 (b) are on the sides of the inverted triangular Pareto front whereas well-distributed solutions are obtained over the entire triangular Pareto front in Figure 1 (a).

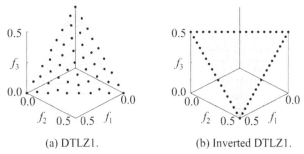

(a) DTLZ1.   (b) Inverted DTLZ1.

Figure 1. Obtained solution sets by SMS-EMOA when the reference point is far from the Pareto front: (20, 20, 20).

The triangular Pareto front of the three-objective DTLZ1 problem is written as follows [8]:

$$PF = \{(f_1, f_2, f_3) \mid f_1 + f_2 + f_3 = 0.5, \ 0 \le f_i \le 0.5 \ \text{for} \ i = 1, 2, 3\}. \quad (1)$$

Thus the nadir point is (0.5, 0.5, 0.5). The three-objective inverted DTLZ1 problem [19] has the same nadir point since its inverted triangular Pareto front is written as follows:

$$PF = \{(f_1, f_2, f_3) \mid f_1 + f_2 + f_3 = 1, \ 0 \le f_i \le 0.5 \ \text{for} \ i = 1, 2, 3\}. \quad (2)$$

In the same manner as in Figure 1, we applied SMS-EMOA to DTLZ1 and its inverted version using the nadir point (0.5, 0.5, 0.5) as the reference point. Figure 2 shows the obtained solution set for each test problem. Whereas the two solution sets in Figure 2 are well distributed over the Pareto fronts, they have a clear difference. No solutions are very close to the sides of the inverted triangular Pareto front in Figure 2 (b) whereas about six solutions in Figure 2 (a) are very close to each side of the triangular Pareto front. In this paper, we explain the reason for this difference.

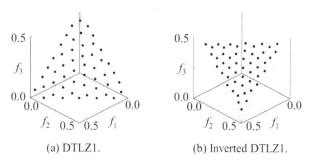

(a) DTLZ1.   (b) Inverted DTLZ1.

Figure 2. Obtained solution sets by SMS-EMOA when the nadir point (0.5, 0.5, 0.5) is used as the reference point.

For comparison, we also examine another variant of DTLZ1 called Max-DTLZ1 [18]. In Max-DTLZ1, all objectives to be minimized in DTLZ1 are maximized. In this paper, we handle DTLZ1, inverted DTLZ1 and Max-DTLZ1 under a special setting where the number of distance variables is always 0 while the number of position variables is $m - 1$ for m-objective problems. In this setting, all feasible solutions of each problem are Pareto optimal. As a result, the DTLZ1 and Max-DTLZ1 problems have the same triangular Pareto front in (1). It should be noted that the ideal point (0, 0, 0) of DTLZ1 is the nadir point of Max-DTLZ1.

In the same manner as in Figure 1 and Figure 2, we applied SMS-EMOA to Max-DTLZ1 using the nadir point (0, 0, 0) as the reference point. We also applied SMS-EMOA to Max-DTLZ1 using (−20, −20, −20) as the reference point. This reference point is far from the Pareto front. The obtained solution set for each reference point is shown in Figure 3.

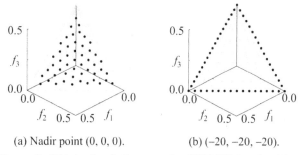

(a) Nadir point (0, 0, 0).   (b) (−20, −20, −20).

Figure 3. Obtained solution sets by SMS-EMOA for Max-DTLZ1 for the reference points (0, 0, 0) and (−20, −20, −20).

From Figures 1-3, we can see that the obtained solution sets for Max-DTLZ1 in Figure 3 are similar to those for the inverted DTLZ1 in Figures 1 and 2. This is because Max-DTLZ1, which is a maximization problem with a triangular Pareto front (see Figure 3), is equivalent to a minimization problem with an inverted triangular Pareto front as we will explain later in this paper.

This paper is organized as follows. In Section 2, first we briefly explain basic concepts in multiobjective optimization such as Pareto optimality, Pareto front, hypervolume, and hypervolume subset selection. Then we explain the Pareto front of each test problem: DTLZ1, inverted DTLZ1 and Max-DTLZ1. We show that the three test problems have exactly the same Pareto front:

$$PF = \{(f_1, f_2, f_3) \mid f_1 + f_2 + f_3 = 1, \ 0 \le f_i \le 1 \ \text{for} \ i = 1, 2, 3\}, \quad (3)$$

in the normalized objective space when the inverted DTLZ1 is handled as the equivalent maximization problem. When the inverted DTLZ1 is handled as a minimization problem in the normalized objective space, its Pareto front can be written as $PF = \{(f_1, f_2, f_3) \mid f_1 + f_2 + f_3 = 2, 0 \le f_i \le 1 \ \text{for} \ i = 1, 2, 3\}$. In Section 3, we discuss hypervolume subset selection for the case where the reference point is far from the Pareto front. We explain why totally different distributions of solutions are obtained in Figure 1 for the three-objective DTLZ1 and inverted DTLZ1 problems. In Section 4, we discuss hypervolume subset selection for the case where the nadir point is used as the reference point. We explain why different solution sets are obtained in Figure 2 for the three-objective DTLZ1 and inverted DTLZ1 problems. We also discuss the optimal distribution of solutions when a reference point is close to the Pareto front (i.e., when its location is between the nadir point and the Pareto front). In this case, different solution sets are obtained by SMS-EMOA for DTLZ1 and Max-DTLZ1 as shown in Figure 4. We explain why obtained solutions for DTLZ1 are in an inverted triangle whereas those for Max-DTLZ1 are triangular. In Section 5, we discuss the effect of the reference point on the hypervolume-based comparison results of different solution sets. Experimental results on other test problems are shown in Section 6. Finally we conclude this paper in Section 7.

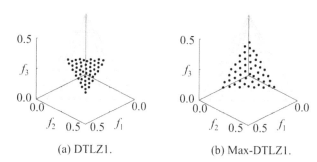

(a) DTLZ1.   (b) Max-DTLZ1.

Figure 4. Obtained solution sets by SMS-EMOA when the reference point is close to the Pareto front, which is specified as (0.25, 0.25, 0.25) in (a) and (0.05, 0.05, 0.05) in (b).

2. MULTIOBJECTIVE TEST PROBLEMS
2.1 Multiobjective Optimization
First we show some basic concepts in multiobjective optimization before explaining hypervolume subset selection and test problems. Let us assume that we have an m-objective minimization problem:

$$\text{Minimize} \ f_1(x), f_2(x), ..., f_m(x) \ \text{subject to} \ x \in X, \quad (4)$$

where x is a decision vector, X is its feasible region, and $f_i(x)$ is the ith objective to be minimized ($i = 1, 2, ..., m$). The m-objective minimization problem in (4) can be rewritten as the following *m*-objective maximization problem by multiplying each objective by (−1):

Maximize $-f_1(\mathbf{x}), -f_2(\mathbf{x}), ..., -f_m(\mathbf{x})$ subject to $\mathbf{x} \in X$.   (5)

Let us assume that $\mathbf{a}$ and $\mathbf{b}$ are two solutions in the objective space of the *m*-objective minimization problem in (4): $\mathbf{a} = (a_1, a_2, ..., a_m)$ and $\mathbf{b} = (b_1, b_2, ..., b_m)$. When the following condition holds, $\mathbf{b}$ is referred to as being dominated by $\mathbf{a}$ (i.e., $\mathbf{a}$ is better than $\mathbf{b}$ in the sense of Pareto dominance): $a_i \le b_i$ for all i's and $a_j < b_j$ for at least one j. This condition can be rewritten as $\mathbf{a} \le \mathbf{b}$ (i.e., $a_i \le b_i$ for all i's) and $\mathbf{a} \ne \mathbf{b}$. When a solution $\mathbf{x}^*$ (i.e., a point $\mathbf{f}(\mathbf{x}^*) = (f_1(\mathbf{x}^*), f_2(\mathbf{x}^*), ..., f_m(\mathbf{x}^*))$ in the objective space) is not dominated by any other solution, $\mathbf{x}^*$ is referred to as a Pareto optimal solution. In general, a multiobjective optimization problem has a number of Pareto optimal solutions. The set of all Pareto optimal solutions is the Pareto optimal solution set. The Pareto optimal solution set in the objective space is referred to as the Pareto front. The Pareto front shows the tradeoff relation among the objectives.

A multiobjective problem has two special points in the objective space. One is the ideal point z_{Ideal}, which is defined by the best value of each objective. The other is the nadir point z_{Nadir}, which is defined by the worst value of each objective in the Pareto optimal solution set. These two points are illustrated in Figure 5 for minimization and maximization problems.

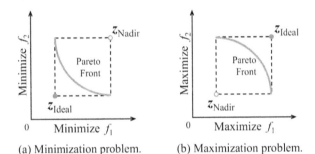

(a) Minimization problem.   (b) Maximization problem.

Figure 5. Ideal point and nadir point for minimization and maximization problems.

2.2 Hypervolume Subset Selection

A reference point for hypervolume calculation is a point in the *m*-dimensional objective space. We denote the reference point by $\mathbf{r} = (r_1, r_2, ..., r_m)$. The hypervolume of a point $\mathbf{a} = (a_1, a_2, ..., a_m)$ is the area ($m = 2$), volume ($m = 3$) or hypervolume ($m \ge 4$) of the dominated region by $\mathbf{a}$ bounded by the reference point $\mathbf{r}$. This region can be written for the *m*-objective minimization problem as follows (see Figure 6 (a)):

$$D(\mathbf{a}, \mathbf{r}) = \{(z_1, z_2, ..., z_m) \mid a_i \le z_i \le r_i \text{ for } i = 1, 2, ..., m\}.   (6)$$

The hypervolume of a set of μ points, $S = \{\mathbf{a}^1, \mathbf{a}^2, ..., \mathbf{a}^\mu\}$, is the area, volume or hypervolume of the union of the dominated region by each point (see Figure 6 (b)):

$$D(S, \mathbf{r}) = D(\mathbf{a}^1, \mathbf{r}) \cup D(\mathbf{a}^2, \mathbf{r}) \cup ... \cup D(\mathbf{a}^\mu, \mathbf{r}).   (7)$$

If the reference point $\mathbf{r}$ is not dominated by any point in the point set S, the hypervolume of S is 0. This is because the dominated region by each point bounded by the reference point is empty.

For the *m*-objective maximization problem, the hypervolume of a single point $\mathbf{a}$ is calculated from the following dominated region by $\mathbf{a}$ bounded by the reference point $\mathbf{r}$ (see Figure 7 (a)):

$$D(\mathbf{a}, \mathbf{r}) = \{(z_1, z_2, ..., z_m) \mid r_i \le z_i \le a_i \text{ for } i = 1, 2, ..., m\}.   (8)$$

The hypervolume of a set of μ points, $S = \{\mathbf{a}^1, \mathbf{a}^2, ..., \mathbf{a}^\mu\}$, is calculated in the same manner as in (7). That is, the hypervolume is the area, volume or hypervolume of the union of the dominated region by each point (see Figure 7 (b)).

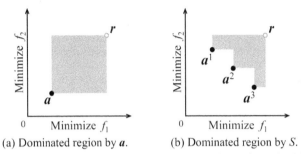

(a) Dominated region by $\mathbf{a}$.   (b) Dominated region by S.

Figure 6. Illustration of the hypervolume of a point a in (a) and the hypervolume of a point set $S = \{a^1, a^2, a^3\}$ in (b) for minimization problems.

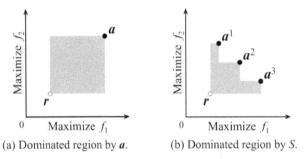

(a) Dominated region by $\mathbf{a}$.   (b) Dominated region by S.

Figure 7. Illustration of the hypervolume of a point a in (a) and the hypervolume of a point set $S = \{a^1, a^2, a^3\}$ in (b) for maximization problems.

The hypervolume contribution of a point $\mathbf{a}^j$ in a point set S ($\mathbf{a}^j \in S$) is the amount of decrease in the hypervolume by removing $\mathbf{a}^j$ from S. That is, the hypervolume contribution of $\mathbf{a}^j$ in S is defined as $HV(S) - HV(S \backslash \{\mathbf{a}^j\})$ where $HV(S)$ is the hypervolume of S and $HV(S \backslash \{\mathbf{a}^j\})$ is the hypervolume of S excluding $\mathbf{a}^j$. Figure 8 shows the hypervolume contribution of $\mathbf{a}^2$ in the point set $S = \{\mathbf{a}^1, \mathbf{a}^2, \mathbf{a}^3\}$.

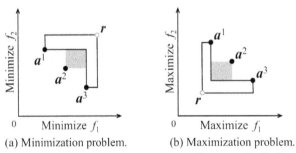

(a) Minimization problem.   (b) Maximization problem.

Figure 8. Hypervolume contribution of a^2 in $S = \{a^1, a^2, a^3\}$.

Hypervolume subset selection for finding μ solutions can be written as the following optimization problem:

$$\text{Maximize } HV(S) \text{ subject to } |S| = \mu.   (9)$$

Hypervolume subset selection is usually formulated as a discrete optimization problem for selecting μ solutions from a number of given non-dominated solutions (i.e., from a pre-specified set of candidate solutions). In this paper, we discuss the selection of μ solutions for hypervolume maximization from all Pareto optimal solutions. That is, the entire Pareto optimal solution set is assumed as the candidate solution set in our hypervolume subset selection.

The optimal μ-distribution is the distribution of μ solutions which maximizes the hypervolume, i.e., the distribution of μ solutions in the optimal solution set S^* of the hypervolume subset selection problem in (9). When the Pareto front of a two-objective problem is linear (i.e., a line), it was shown in the literature (e.g., see [2]) that the hypervolume is maximized by a set of equidistant points on the Pareto front as shown in Figure 9. The two extreme solutions of the Pareto front are included in the optimal solution set S^* when some conditions on the Pareto front and the location of the reference point are satisfied (for details, see [2]).

The optimal solution set S^* (i.e., the optimal μ-distribution) does not depend on the location of the reference point in Figure 9 as long as the following two conditions hold: (i) the two extreme solutions of the Pareto front are included in the optimal solution set S^*, and (ii) the reference point r is dominated by the nadir point as in Figure 9. The second condition (ii) holds when the reference point is far from the Pareto front (see Figure 9). Under these conditions, subset selection is to maximize the hypervolume of $(\mu-2)$ solutions in the shaded region in Figure 10 (since the two extreme solutions are included in the optimal solution set S^*).

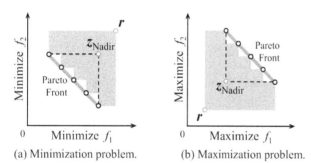

(a) Minimization problem.　(b) Maximization problem.

Figure 9. Optimal solution set S^* with five solutions.

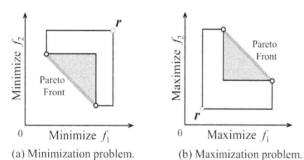

(a) Minimization problem.　(b) Maximization problem.

Figure 10. Hypervolume contribution of all solutions on the Pareto front excluding the two extreme solutions.

2.3 DTLZ1 Test Problem

As a scalable test problem where the number of objectives can be arbitrarily specified, DTLZ1 [8] has been frequently used for evaluating the search ability of many-objective evolutionary algorithms. Each objective in DTLZ1 can be written as

$$\text{Minimize} \quad f_i(\boldsymbol{x}) = (1 + g(\boldsymbol{x}_{\text{dis}}))h_i(\boldsymbol{x}_{\text{pos}}), \ i = 1, 2, ..., m, \quad (10)$$

where the decision vector $\boldsymbol{x} = (x_1, x_2, ..., x_{m+k-1})$ is separable into the first $m-1$ position variables in $\boldsymbol{x}_{\text{pos}} = (x_1, x_2, ..., x_{m-1})$ and the

other k distance variables in $\boldsymbol{x}_{\text{dis}} = (x_m, x_{m+1}, ..., x_{m+k-1})$. The number of decision variables is specified by the parameter k. In (10), $h_i(\boldsymbol{x}_{\text{pos}})$ determines the shape of the Pareto front ($h_i(\boldsymbol{x}_{\text{pos}}) \geq 0$) while $g(\boldsymbol{x}_{\text{dis}})$ specifies the distance from the Pareto front ($g(\boldsymbol{x}_{\text{dis}}) \geq 0$). All decision variables have the same constraint condition: $0 \leq x_j \leq 1$ for $j = 1, 2, ..., m+k-1$.

The Pareto optimal solution set of DTLZ1 is the set of all feasible solutions with $g(\boldsymbol{x}_{\text{dis}}) = 0$. DTLZ1 has no Pareto optimal solution with $g(\boldsymbol{x}_{\text{dis}}) > 0$. Since the decision vector $\boldsymbol{x}$ is separable into $\boldsymbol{x}_{\text{pos}}$ and $\boldsymbol{x}_{\text{dis}}$, the Pareto front of DTLZ1 can be written as

$$f_i(\boldsymbol{x}) = h_i(\boldsymbol{x}_{\text{pos}}), \ i = 1, 2, ..., m, \quad (11)$$

where $0 \leq x_j \leq 1$ for $j = 1, 2, ..., m-1$. It is well known that DTLZ1 has the following linear Pareto front [8]:

$$\{(f_1, f_2, ..., f_m) \mid \sum_{i=1}^{m} f_i = 0.5, 0 \leq f_i \leq 0.5 \text{ for } i = 1, 2, ..., m\}. \quad (12)$$

When we applied SMS-EMOA to DTLZ1 in Section 1, we specified the number of distance variables in $\boldsymbol{x}_{\text{dis}}$ as zero (i.e., $k = 0$) to remove $g(\boldsymbol{x}_{\text{dis}})$ from each objective in (10). Under this setting, all feasible solutions of DTLZ1 are Pareto optimal. This means that SMS-EMOA examined only Pareto optimal solutions in Section 1. We also applied SMS-EMOA to the inverted DTLZ1 and Max-DTLZ1 problems in the same setting (i.e., $k = 0$) in Section 1. This is to focus on hypervolume subset selection from Pareto optimal solutions.

2.4 Variants of DTLZ Test Problems

The inverted DTLZ1 problem was formulated in [19] as a scalable test problem with an inverted triangular Pareto front by modifying each objective function of DTLZ1 as

$$u_i(\boldsymbol{x}) = 0.5(1 + g(\boldsymbol{x}_{\text{dis}})) - f_i(\boldsymbol{x}), \ i = 1, 2, ..., m, \quad (13)$$

where $u_i(\boldsymbol{x})$ is the ith objective of the inverted DTLZ1 problem. As in DTLZ1, the Pareto optimal solution set of the inverted DTLZ1 problem is the set of all feasible solutions with $g(\boldsymbol{x}_{\text{dis}}) = 0$. Using $g(\boldsymbol{x}_{\text{dis}}) = 0$ in the right-hand side of (13) and also in (10), the Pareto front of the inverted DTLZ1 problem can be written as

$$u_i(\boldsymbol{x}) = 0.5 - h_i(\boldsymbol{x}_{\text{pos}}), \ i = 1, 2, ..., m. \quad (14)$$

Since the Pareto front in (12) is generated by $h_i(\boldsymbol{x}_{\text{pos}})$ in (11) using all feasible solutions in $\boldsymbol{x}_{\text{pos}}$, we have the following relation for $u_i(\boldsymbol{x})$ on the Pareto front in (14) from (11) and (12):

$$\sum_{i=1}^{m} u_i(\boldsymbol{x}) = \sum_{i=1}^{m} 0.5 - \sum_{i=1}^{m} h_i(\boldsymbol{x}_{\text{pos}}) = 0.5m - 0.5 = (m-1)/2, \quad (15)$$

where $0 \leq u_i(\boldsymbol{x}) \leq 0.5$ ($i = 1, 2, ..., m$). Since all feasible solutions satisfying (15) are Pareto optimal, the Pareto front of the m-objective inverted DTLZ1 is written as

$$\{(f_1, f_2, ..., f_m) \mid \sum_{i=1}^{m} f_i = (m-1)/2, 0 \leq f_i \leq 0.5 \text{ for } i = 1, 2, ..., m\}. \quad (16)$$

Max-DTLZ1 was formulated in [18] by replacing "Minimize" with "Maximize" in the formulation of DTLZ1 as

$$\text{Maximize} \quad f_i(\boldsymbol{x}) = (1 + g(\boldsymbol{x}_{\text{dis}}))h_i(\boldsymbol{x}_{\text{pos}}), \ i = 1, 2, ..., m. \quad (17)$$

Except for this replacement, Max-DTLZ1 is the same as DTLZ1. Thus these two test problems have the same objective functions, the same decision variables, and the same feasible region.

In general, DTLZ1 and Max-DTLZ1 have different Pareto fronts [18]. However, when $k = 0$ (i.e., the number of distance variables is 0), Max-DTLZ1 has the same linear Pareto front as DTLZ1. That is, the Pareto front of Max-DTLZ1 can be also written by (12). This is because the entire feasible region of DTLZ1, which is the same as the entire feasible region of Max-DTLZ1, is the Pareto front of DTLZ1 when $k = 0$ (i.e., because no feasible solution is dominated by any other feasible solutions when $k = 0$).

For simplicity of explanations, we normalize the objective space of DTLZ1 and Max-DTLZ1 so that the Pareto front in (12) is normalized in $[0, 1]^m$ as follows (i.e., $[0, 0.5]^m \rightarrow [0, 1]^m$):

$$\{(f_1, f_2, ..., f_m) \mid \sum_{i=1}^{m} f_i = 1, 0 \leq f_i \leq 1 \text{ for } i = 1, 2, ..., m\}. \tag{18}$$

We also apply the same normalization to the objective space of the inverted DTLZ1 so that the Pareto front in (16) is normalized in $[0, 1]^m$ as follows (i.e., $[0, 0.5]^m \rightarrow [0, 1]^m$):

$$\{(f_1, f_2, ..., f_m) \mid \sum_{i=1}^{m} f_i = (m-1), 0 \leq f_i \leq 1 \text{ for } i = 1, 2, ..., m\}. \tag{19}$$

Let us explain that the normalized Pareto front in (19) of the inverted DTLZ1 problem can be viewed as being the same as the normalized Pareto front in (18) of Max-DTLZ1. In general, the minimization problem of $f_i(\mathbf{x})$ is equivalent to the maximization problem of $-f_i(\mathbf{x})$. So, we can formulate the following equivalent maximization problem of $q_i(\mathbf{x})$ from the inverted DTLZ1 problem with $f_i(\mathbf{x})$, $i = 1, 2, ..., m$:

$$\text{Maximize } q_i(\mathbf{x}) = -f_i(\mathbf{x}), \ i = 1, 2, ..., m. \tag{20}$$

By replacing $f_i(\mathbf{x})$ with $-q_i(\mathbf{x})$ in (19), we obtain the following Pareto front of the maximization problem in (20):

$$\{(q_1, q_2, ..., q_m) \mid \sum_{i=1}^{m} q_i = (1-m), \ -1 \leq q_i \leq 0 \text{ for } i = 1, 2, ..., m\}. \tag{21}$$

We normalize the objective space of the maximization problem in (20) so that the Pareto front in (21) is normalized in $[0, 1]^m$ as follows (i.e., $[-1, 0]^m \rightarrow [0, 1]^m$: $q_i = f_i - 1$ in (21)):

$$\{(f_1, f_2, ..., f_m) \mid \sum_{i=1}^{m} f_i = 1, 0 \leq f_i \leq 1 \text{ for } i = 1, 2, ..., m\}. \tag{22}$$

This is the same as the normalized Pareto front of Max-DTLZ1 in (18). That is, the normalized inverted triangular Pareto front in (19) of the inverted DTLZ1 problem is equivalent to the normalized triangular Pareto front in (18) of Max-DTLZ1.

In general (i.e., when $k > 0$), the Pareto front of Max-DTLZ1 can be written as

$$\{(f_1, f_2, ..., f_m) \mid \sum_{i=1}^{m} f_i = g_{\max}, 0 \leq f_i \leq g_{\max} \text{ for } i = 1, 2, ..., m\}, \tag{23}$$

where $g_{\max}$ is the maximum value of the distance function $g(\mathbf{x}_{\text{dis}})$. This Pareto front can be normalized to $[0, 1]^m$. Thus we can see that Max-DTLZ1 and DTLZ1 have the same normalized Pareto front, which is also the same as the normalized Pareto front of the inverted DTLZ1 when it is handled as a maximization problem.

Since the inverted triangular Pareto front of the inverted DTLZ1 problem is equivalent to the triangular Pareto front of Max-DTLZ1, we mainly discuss the optimal distribution of solutions on the normalized triangular Pareto front in (22) for minimization and maximization problems in the rest of this paper.

3. FAR REFERENCE POINT

In this section, we discuss the optimal distribution of solutions on the normalized triangular Pareto front in (22) when the reference point for hypervolume calculation is far from the Pareto front. Our main focus in this section is the effect of the location of the reference point on the optimal distribution of solutions.

As we explained in Section 2, the location of the reference point has no effect on the optimal distribution of solutions for two-objective problems under the following conditions: (i) the two extreme solutions of the Pareto front are included in the optimal solution set, and (ii) the reference point is dominated by the nadir point. When these conditions hold, the location of the reference point has no effects on the hypervolume contribution of each solution except for the two extreme solutions as shown in Figure 9 and Figure 10. In this section, we discuss whether the three extreme solutions of the triangular Pareto front of a three-objective problem play the same role as in the case of two objectives. Then we show that the extreme solutions of the triangular Pareto front play different roles between the DTLZ1 problem and the Max-DTLZ1 problem (i.e., between DTLZ1 and the inverted DTLZ1). We will see from our discussions that the extreme solutions of the triangular Pareto front of only DTLZ1 play the same role as those of two-objective problems.

3.1 DTLZ1

The normalized triangular Pareto front of the three-objective DTLZ1 problem is shown by the shaded triangle in Figure 11, which is written as $f_1 + f_2 + f_3 = 1$ and $0 \leq f_i \leq 1$ for $i = 1, 2, 3$. In Figure 11, the nadir point is $(1, 1, 1)$ since DTLZ1 is a minimization problem. We assume that the reference point $\mathbf{r} = (r_1, r_2, r_3)$ is far from the Pareto front (e.g., $\mathbf{r} = (10, 10, 10)$). We also assume that the three extreme solutions A $(1, 0, 0)$, B $(0, 1, 0)$, C $(0, 0, 1)$ of the normalized triangular Pareto front in Figure 11 are included in the optimal solution set S^*.

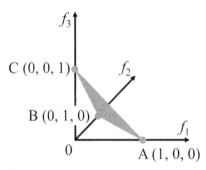

Figure 11. The normalized triangular Pareto front of DTLZ1: $f_1 + f_2 + f_3 = 1$ and $0 \leq f_i \leq 1$ for $i = 1, 2, 3$.

The dominated region by each extreme solution in Figure 11 bounded by the reference point $\mathbf{r} = (r_1, r_2, r_3)$ can be written as

$$D(A, \mathbf{r}) = \{(z_1, z_2, z_3) \mid 1 \leq z_1 \leq r_1, 0 \leq z_2 \leq r_2, 0 \leq z_3 \leq r_3\}, \tag{24}$$

$$D(B, \mathbf{r}) = \{(z_1, z_2, z_3) \mid 0 \leq z_1 \leq r_1, 1 \leq z_2 \leq r_2, 0 \leq z_3 \leq r_3\}, \tag{25}$$

$$D(C, \mathbf{r}) = \{(z_1, z_2, z_3) \mid 0 \leq z_1 \leq r_1, 0 \leq z_2 \leq r_2, 1 \leq z_3 \leq r_3\}. \tag{26}$$

Figure 12 shows the dominated region by the extreme solution A bounded by the reference point $\mathbf{r}$. We can see from Figure 12 that all solutions in the cuboid $[1, r_1] \times [0, r_2] \times [0, r_3]$ (i.e., all solutions with $1 \leq f_1$) are dominated by the extreme solution A. In the same manner as Figure 12, we can show that all solutions in the cuboid

$[0, r_1] \times [1, r_2] \times [0, r_3]$ (i.e., all solutions with $1 \le f_2$) are dominated by the extreme solution B. We can also show that all solutions in the cuboid $[0, r_1] \times [0, r_2] \times [1, r_3]$ (i.e., all solutions with $1 \le f_3$) are dominated by the extreme solution C.

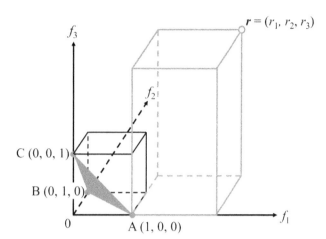

Figure 12. The dominated region by the extreme solution A.

From these discussions, we can see that the dominated region by the triangular Pareto front in the three-dimensional objective space is also dominated by at least one of the three extreme solutions A, B and C except for the inside of the unit cube $[0, 1]^3$ in Figure 12. This situation is the same as the case of two-objective problems in Figure 10. The optimal distribution of solutions except for the three extreme solutions can be specified by maximizing their hypervolume inside the unit cube $[0, 1]^3$. As a result, when the reference point is far from the Pareto front, the location of the reference point has no effect on the optimal distribution of solutions as long as the three extreme solutions are included in the optimal solution set. Thus a set of well-distributed solutions was obtained by SMS-EMOA in Figure 1 (a) when (20, 20, 20) was used as the reference point.

These discussions can be easily extended to the case of four or more objectives. Let us assume that an m-objective minimization problem has the normalized triangular Pareto front defined by (22): $f_1 + f_2 + ... + f_m = 1$ and $0 \le f_i \le 1$. This Pareto front has the m extreme solutions: $(1, 0, 0, ..., 0), (0, 1, 0, ..., 0), ..., (0, 0, ..., 0, 1)$. The dominated region by the first extreme solution A bounded by the reference point $r = (r_1, r_2, ..., r_m)$ can be written as

$$D(A, r) = \{(z_1, ..., z_m) \mid 1 \le z_1 \le r_1, 0 \le z_i \le r_i \text{ for } i = 2, ..., m\}. \quad (27)$$

That is, all solutions in the hyper-cuboid $[1, r_1] \times [0, r_2] \times [0, r_3] \times ... \times [0, r_m]$ are dominated by A. Since the dominated region by each extreme solution can be written in the same manner, we can see that the dominated region by the triangular Pareto front in the m-dimensional objective space is also dominated by at least one of the m extreme solutions except for the inside of the unit hypercube $[0, 1]^m$. This means that the location of the reference point has no effect on the optimal distribution as long as (i) all the m extreme solutions are included in the optimal solution set and (ii) the reference point is far from the Pareto front.

These discussions show that the extreme solutions of the triangular Pareto front of the multiobjective DTLZ1 problem with three or more objectives play the same role in hypervolume calculation as in the case of two-objective problems in Figure 10 when the reference point is far from the Pareto front.

The above-mentioned role of the extreme solutions of the Pareto front in hypervolume calculation can be explained in a different manner using the projection from the three-dimensional objective space to a two-dimensional subspace. Let us assume that a solution set S has the following four solutions L (0, 0.5, 0.5), M (0.5, 0, 0.5), N (0.5, 0.5, 0) and Z (1/3, 1/3, 1/3) on the Pareto front in addition to the three extreme solutions A, B and C in Figure 12. Their projections to the two-dimensional subspace with f_2 and f_3 are shown in Figure 13 (a). Since DTLZ1 is a minimization problem, the extreme solution A dominates all the other solutions in the two-dimensional subspace with f_2 and f_3 in Figure 13 (a). That is, the f_2-f_3 subspace in Figure 13 (a) has only a single non-dominated solution.

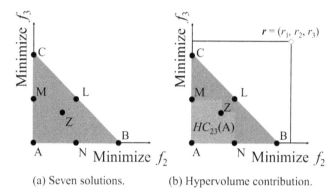

(a) Seven solutions. (b) Hypervolume contribution.

Figure 13. Projection of the Pareto front and the seven solutions to the two-dimensional subspace with f_2 and f_3.

When the extreme solution A is included in a solution set S, no other solution has a positive hypervolume contribution in the f_2-f_3 subspace in Figure 13 (a). Let us denote the hypervolume contribution of A in the f_2-f_3 subspace as $HC_{23}(A)$, which is shown by the red area in Figure 13 (b). When the reference point $r = (r_1, r_2, r_3)$ is far from the Pareto front, the extreme solution A has a large hypervolume contribution calculated as $(r_1 - 1) \times HC_{23}(A)$ in the original three-dimensional objective space, which increases as the value of r_1 increases. Hypervolume contribution of no other solution increases as the value of r_1 increases. These discussions for the extreme solution A (1, 0, 0) on the f_2-f_3 subspace hold for the extreme solution B (0, 1, 0) on the f_1-f_3 subspace and the extreme solution C (0, 0, 1) on the f_1-f_2 subspace. Thus hypervolume contribution of any non-extreme solution in Figure 13 does not depend on the location of the reference point as far as the reference point is dominated by the nadir point.

These discussions can be generalized to the case of m objectives. Let us assume that a solution set S includes some Pareto optimal solutions and all the m extreme solutions $(1, 0, ..., 0), (0, 1, 0, ..., 0), ..., (0, ..., 0, 1)$ of the triangular Pareto front defined by $f_1 + f_2 + ... + f_m = 1$ and $0 \le f_i \le 1$. First we consider the projection to the $(m-1)$-dimensional subspace with $f_2, f_3, ..., f_m$. The extreme solution $(1, 0, ..., 0)$ is projected to $(0, 0, ..., 0)$, which dominates all the other solutions in the f_2-f_3-...-f_m subspace. Thus the increase of r_1 of the reference point $r = (r_1, r_2, ..., r_m)$ increases only the hypervolume contribution of the extreme solution $(1, 0, ..., 0)$. The increase of r_1 has no effect on the hypervolume contribution of any other solution. These discussions hold for the other extreme solutions of the Pareto front and the other $(m-1)$-dimensional subspaces (e.g., for the extreme solution $(0, 1, 0, ..., 0)$ and the f_1-f_3-...-f_m subspace). Thus the hypervolume contribution of any non-extreme solution does not depend on the location of the reference point as far as (i) all the m extreme solutions of the Pareto front are included in the solution set, and (ii) the reference point is dominated by the nadir point.

These discussions show that the optimal distribution of solutions for hypervolume maximization does not depend on the location of a reference point when (i) all the m extreme solutions of the triangular Pareto front of the m-dimensional DTLZ1 problem are included in the optimal solution set and (ii) the reference point is far from the Pareto front.

3.2 Max-DTLZ1 and Inverted DTLZ1

In this subsection, we discuss the optimal distribution of solutions for hypervolume maximization for the Max-DTLZ1 problem and the inverted-DTLZ1 problem.

Let us consider a three-objective maximization problem with the normalized triangular Pareto front in Figure 11. As in Subsection 3.1, we assume that the three extreme solutions A $(1, 0, 0)$, B $(0, 1, 0)$ and C $(0, 0, 1)$ of the normalized triangular Pareto front in Figure 11 are included in a solution set S for hypervolume maximization. We also assume that the reference point $r = (r_1, r_2, r_3)$ is far from the Pareto front: $r_1 \ll 0, r_2 \ll 0$ and $r_3 \ll 0$.

In our maximization problem with the normalized triangular Pareto front, the dominated region by each extreme solution bounded by the reference point $r = (r_1, r_2, r_3)$ can be written as

$$D(A, r) = \{(z_1, z_2, z_3) \mid r_1 \le z_1 \le 1, r_2 \le z_2 \le 0, r_3 \le z_3 \le 0\}, \qquad (28)$$

$$D(B, r) = \{(z_1, z_2, z_3) \mid r_1 \le z_1 \le 0, r_2 \le z_2 \le 1, r_3 \le z_3 \le 0\}, \qquad (29)$$

$$D(C, r) = \{(z_1, z_2, z_3) \mid r_1 \le z_1 \le 0, r_2 \le z_2 \le 0, r_3 \le z_3 \le 1\}. \qquad (30)$$

Figure 14 (and Figure 15) shows the dominated region by the extreme solution A (and C) bounded by the reference point r. From these figures, we can see that some regions outside the unit cube $[0, 1]^3$ are not dominated by any extreme solution whereas they are dominated by the Pareto front. For example, we can see from Figure 14 and Figure 15 that the triangle pole in Figure 16 in the region with $f_2 \le 0$ is not dominated by any extreme solution whereas it is dominated by the Pareto front.

The triangle pole in the region with $f_2 \le 0$ in Figure 16, which is dominated by the Pareto front but not dominated by any extreme solution, can be written as follows:

$$\{(z_1, z_2, z_3) \mid 0 \le z_1 \le 1, r_2 \le z_2 \le 0, 0 \le z_3 \le 1, z_1 + z_3 \le 1\}. \qquad (31)$$

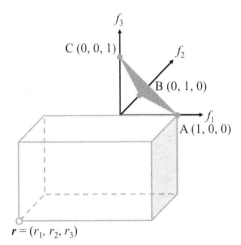

Figure 14. The dominated region by the extreme solution A.

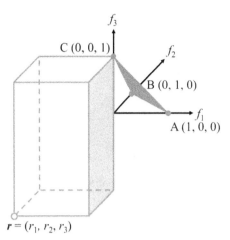

Figure 15. The dominated region by the extreme solution C.

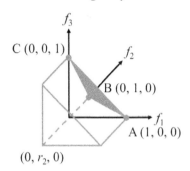

Figure 16. Uncovered region with $f_2 \le 0$ by the three extreme solutions A, B and C.

Similar triangle poles exist in the regions with $f_1 \le 0$ and $f_3 \le 0$. They can be written as

$$\{(z_1, z_2, z_3) \mid r_1 \le z_1 \le 0, 0 \le z_2 \le 1, 0 \le z_3 \le 1, z_2 + z_3 \le 1\}, \qquad (32)$$

$$\{(z_1, z_2, z_3) \mid 0 \le z_1 \le 1, 0 \le z_2 \le 1, r_3 \le z_3 \le 0, z_1 + z_2 \le 1\}. \qquad (33)$$

From (31)-(33) and Figure 16, we can see that the length of each uncovered triangle pole depends on the location of the reference point. The length increases (i.e., its hypervolume increases) by moving the reference point away from the Pareto front. Thus the hypervolume contributions of some non-extreme solutions depend on the location of the reference point. This means that the optimal distribution of solutions for hypervolume maximization also depends on its location.

Since all solutions are on the sides of the triangular Pareto front of the three-objective Max-DTLZ1 problem in Figure 3 (b) when the reference point is far from the Pareto front, one may expect that the hypervolume contribution of a solution on a side of the Pareto front of Max-DTLZ1 increases by moving the reference point away from the Pareto front. One may also expect that the hypervolume contribution of a solution inside the Pareto front does not increase by moving the reference point away from the Pareto front (since no solution exists inside the the triangular Pareto front in Figure 3 (b)). Let us examine these expectations.

In Figure 17, we show the hypervolume contribution of a solution M $(0.5, 0, 0.5)$ in the solution set $\{A, B, C, M\}$ where M is the midpoint of A and C. The hypervolume contribution of M is the volume of the following square pole (which is $|r_2|/4$):

$$\{(z_1, z_2, z_3) \mid 0 \le z_1 \le 0.5, r_2 \le z_2 \le 0, 0 \le z_3 \le 0.5\}. \qquad (34)$$

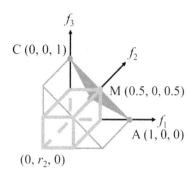

Figure 17. Hypervolume contribution of the solution M (0.5, 0, 0.5) in the solution set {A, B, C, M}.

The square pole dominated by M in Figure 17 covers 1/2 of the uncovered triangle pole with $f_2 \leq 0$. In addition to M, let us include solutions L (0, 0.5, 0.5) and N (0.5, 0.5, 0) to the solution set {A, B, C, M}. The hypervolume contributions of L, M and N in {A, B, C, L, M, N} are $|r_1|/4$, $|r_2|/4$ and $|r_3|/4$, respectively, which are calculated in different regions. In Figure 17, the volume of the square pole is the hypervolume contribution of M.

Now, let us consider the inclusion of a new solution Y (0.25, 0, 0.75) to the solution set {A, B, C, L, M, N} as shown in Figure 18. The hypervolume contribution of Y is the volume of the smaller square pole in Figure 18, which is calculated as $|r_2|/16$.

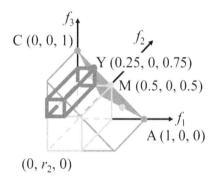

Figure 18. Hypervolume contribution of the solution Y (0.25, 0, 0.75) in the solution set {A, B, C, L, M, N}.

Instead of including the solution Y, let us consider the inclusion of a solution Z = (1/3, 1/3, 1/3), which is at the center of the triangular Pareto front. The hypervolume contribution of Z is calculated as 1/27 (i.e., the volume of the cube $[0, 1/3]^3$) since the outside of the cube $[0, 0.5]^3$ is covered by the solution set {A, B, C, L, M, N}. When the reference point is far from the Pareto front (i.e., $|r_2|$ is large), the hypervolume contribution 1/27 of the solution Z (1/3, 1/3, 1/3) at the center of the Pareto front is much smaller than $|r_2|/16$ of the solution Y (0.25, 0, 0.75) on the line AC. This may explain why all solutions are on the sides of the Pareto front in Figure 3 (b) for hypervolume maximization using 50 solutions for the reference point (−20, −20, −20).

Of course, the solution Z (1/3, 1/3, 1/3) at the center of the Pareto front has a large hypervolume contribution when only the three extreme solutions A, B and C are included in the solution set. That is, the hypervolume contribution of Z in the solution set {A, B, C, Z} is calculated as $|r_1|/9 + |r_2|/9 + |r_3|/9 + 1/27$. The first three terms are the volumes of the three square poles in the three regions with $f_1 \leq 0$, $f_2 \leq 0$ and $f_3 \leq 0$. However, these three parts completely disappear by including the three solutions L, M and N.

It should be noted that the inclusion of Z decreases the hypervolume contribution of each of L, M and N from $|r_i|/4$ to $(|r_i|/4 - |r_i|/9)$, which is still large when $|r_i|$ is large. As shown by these calculations, it is difficult for inside solutions to continue to have a large hypervolume contribution.

Let us assume that all solutions in the solution set are on the sides of the triangular Pareto front. Under this assumption, we discuss the hypervolume maximization in the triangle pole in Figures 16-18 by a pre-specified number of solutions on the line AC. Since the contribution of each solution is always the volume of a pole of the length $|r_2|$, this task is exactly the same as the hypervolume maximization for a two-objective problem with the linear Pareto front between (1, 0) and (0, 1) for the reference point (0, 0). This may explain why equidistant solutions are obtained in Figure 3 (b).

It is difficult to extend these discussions on the three-objective Max-DTLZ1 problem to the case of four or more objectives. However, our experimental results suggest that all solutions are on the sides of the triangular Pareto front in the case of four objectives (i.e., four-objective Max-DTLZ1). In Figure 19, we show 50 solutions obtained after 1,000,000 generations of SMS-EMOA for the four-objective Max-DTLZ1 problem when the reference point is (−20, −20, −20, −20). The obtained solutions in the four-dimensional objective space are shown by projecting them to its two-dimensional subspaces. Figure 19 suggests that all solutions are on the sides of the triangular Pareto front of the four-objective Max-DTLZ1 problem.

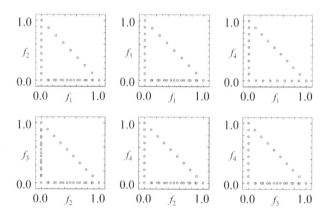

Figure 19. The obtained solutions for the four-objective Max-DTLZ1 problem for the reference point (−20, −20, −20, −20).

As in the previous subsection, let us discuss the effect of the location of the reference point on the optimal distribution of solutions using the projection of solutions of the three-objective Max-DTLZ1 problem to the two-dimensional subspace with f_2 and f_3. We use the solution set including the seven solutions A, B, C, L, M, N and Z in Figure 13 (see Figure 20).

Since our problem in this subsection is a maximization problem, all solutions on the side BC of the triangular Pareto front between solution B (0, 1, 0) and solution C (0, 0, 1) are Pareto optimal in the f_2-f_3 subspace (see Figure 20). In Figure 20, we show the hypervolume contribution of B, C and L on the side BC in the f_2-f_3 subspace. Not only the two extreme solutions B (0, 1, 0) and C (0, 0, 1) but also the solution L (0, 1/2, 1/2) on the side BC has a positive hypervolume contribution in the f_2-f_3 subspace. Thus their hypervolume contributions increase as the absolute value of r_1 increases (i.e., the value of r_1 decreases, e.g., to −20). Since these discussions hold for the f_1-f_2 and f_1-f_3 subspaces, we can see that the hypervolume contributions of solutions on the sides of the triangular Pareto front increase as the distance of the reference point from the Pareto front increases. On the contrary, the hypervolume contributions of solutions inside the triangular Pareto front do not increase (when they are dominated solutions in all two-dimensional subspaces). These discussions explain why all solutions are obtained on the sides of the triangular Pareto front in Figure 3 (b) when the reference point is far from the Pareto front.

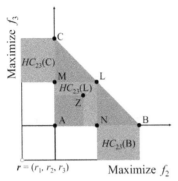

Figure 20. Projection of the Pareto front and the seven solutions to the two-dimensional subspace with f_2 and f_3. Hypervolume contribution of each solution in the subspace is shown by the shaded region in red.

These discussions can be generalized to the case of m objectives. For simplicity of explanation, we specify the reference point r as $r = (r_1, r_2, ..., r_m) = (-r, -r, ..., -r)$ using a positive value r. Let us examine the projection of the triangular Pareto front (which is defined by $f_1 + f_2 + ... + f_m = 1$ and $0 \le f_i \le 1$ for $i = 1, 2, ..., m$ in the m-dimensional objective space) to its subspaces.

First we consider the projection of the Pareto front to the $(m-1)$-dimensional subspace with $f_2, f_3, ..., f_m$. The projected Pareto front can be written as $f_2 + ... + f_m \le 1$ and $0 \le f_i \le 1$ for $i = 2, ..., m$ (e.g., the projected Pareto front in Figure 20 is written as $f_2 + f_3 \le 1$ and $0 \le f_i \le 1$ for $i = 2, 3$). The set of the non-dominated solutions in the f_2-f_3- ... -f_m subspace can be written as $f_2 + ... + f_m = 1$ and $0 \le f_i \le 1$ for $i = 2, 3, ..., m$ (e.g., the set of the non-dominated solutions in Figure 20 is written as $f_2 + f_3 = 1$ and $0 \le f_i \le 1$ for $i = 2, 3$). The hypervolume contribution of each non-dominated solution in the f_2-f_3- ... -f_m subspace increases as the value of r_1 decreases (i.e., as the value of r increases). That is, their hypervolume contributions increase with r.

Next, let us consider the projection to the f_3-f_4- ... -f_m subspace. The projected Pareto front can be written as $f_3 + ... + f_m \le 1$ and $0 \le f_i \le 1$ for $i = 3, 4, ..., m$. The set of the non-dominated solutions in the f_3-f_4- ... -f_m subspace can be written as $f_3 + ... + f_m = 1$ and $0 \le f_i \le 1$ for $i = 3, 4, ..., m$. The hypervolume contribution of each non-dominated solution in the f_3-f_4- ... -f_m subspace increases as the values of r_1 and r_2 decrease (i.e., as the value of r increases). That is, their hypervolume contributions increase with r^2.

In the same manner, we can examine the projection of the m-dimensional objective space to its k-dimensional subspace. As the extreme case, let us examine the case with $k = 1$. The Pareto front in the m-dimensional objective space is projected to the interval [0, 1] in the single-dimensional subspace with f_m. The single point with $f_m = 1$ is the non-dominated solution in the interval [0, 1]. This point is the projection of the extreme solution $(0, 0, ..., 0, 1)$.

Its hypervolume contribution increases with r^{m-1} by increasing the value of r (i.e., by specifying the reference point far away from the Pareto front). This discussion holds for all extreme solutions. Thus, when the reference point is far from the Pareto front, the extreme solutions are likely to be in the optimal solution set. However, this is not always the case (e.g., when the number of solutions in the solution set is one, the Pareto optimal solution at the center of the Pareto front is the optimal selection).

When the triangular Pareto front in the m-dimensional objective space is projected to the 2-dimensional subspace with f_2 and f_3, the projected Pareto front is written as $f_2 + f_3 \le 1$ and $0 \le f_i \le 1$ for $i = 2, 3$ (see Figure 20). The set of the non-dominated solutions in the f_2-f_3 subspace is written as $f_2 + f_3 = 1$ and $0 \le f_i \le 1$ for $i = 2, 3$. The Pareto optimal solutions on the line between the two extreme solutions $(0, 1, 0, ..., 0)$ and $(0, 0, 1, 0, ..., 0)$ are projected to the non-dominated solutions in the f_2-f_3 subspace. Their hypervolume contributions increase with r^{m-2} when we increase the value of r. These discussions hold for all pairs of two extreme solutions. That is, the hypervolume contributions of the Pareto optimal solutions on the lines between any two extreme solutions increase with r^{m-2}. As a result, when the reference point is far from the Pareto front and the size of a solution set is much larger than the number of the extreme solutions, it is likely that some solutions on the line between each pair of the extreme solutions (i.e., some solutions on each edge of the m-dimensional triangular Pareto front) are included in the optimal solution set. These discussions explain why all the obtained solutions in Figure 19 are on the lines of the four extreme solutions (including the four extreme solutions).

3.3 Optimal Solution Sets

From the discussions in Subsection 3.2, we can obtain the following property with respect to the hypervolume contribution of a Pareto optimal solution of an m-objective maximization problem when the reference point $r = (-r, -r, ..., -r)$ moves far away from the Pareto front: The hypervolume contribution of a Pareto optimal solution increases with r^{m-k} when it is a non-overlapping non-dominated solution in at least one k-dimensional subspace and not a non-overlapping non-dominated solution in any $(k-1)$-dimensional subspace. The condition "non-overlapping" is needed since overlapping solutions have no hypervolume contribution. This property also holds for an m-dimensional minimization problem with the reference point $r = (r, r, ..., r)$.

Let us discuss the implication of this property for the case of $m = 3$ (i.e., three-objective problems) and a large value of r. In this case, Pareto optimal solutions in a solution set of a three-objective problem can be categorized into the following three classes:

Class 0: A Class 0 solution has no two-dimensional subspace where it is a non-overlapping non-dominated solution. Its hypervolume contribution does not increase when we increase the value of r.

Class 1: A Class 1 solution has at least one two-dimensional subspace and no single-dimensional subspace where it is a non-overlapping non-dominated solution. Its hypervolume contribution increases with r when we increase the value of r.

Class 2: A Class 2 solution has at least one single-dimensional subspace where it is a non-overlapping non-dominated solution. Its hypervolume contribution increases with r^2 when we increase the value of r.

For example, the Pareto optimal solutions of the normalized three-objective DTLZ1 problem in Subsection 3.1 are categorized as

(i) The three extreme solutions A (1, 0, 0), B (0, 1, 0), C (0, 0, 1):
If the three extreme solutions A, B and C are included in a solution set, they are Class 1 solutions. They are not Class 2 solutions because two of them always overlap at the point of $f_i = 0$ in each single-dimensional subspace.

(ii) All the other Pareto optimal solutions:
They are Class 0 solutions (when the three extreme solutions are included in the solution set). They are not Class 1 solutions because they are always dominated by one of the three extreme solutions in all of the two-dimensional subspaces (e.g., they are dominated by C (0, 0, 1) in the two-dimensional f_1-f_2 subspace).

When r is large, all the three extreme solutions are likely to be included in the optimal solution set. Let us consider a solution set S with μ ($\mu \geq 3$) solutions including two extreme solutions of the three-objective DTLZ1 problem. By adding the other extreme solution, we generate a new solution set S' with ($\mu + 1$) solutions including all the three extreme solutions. Then we generate a new solution set S'' by removing a single solution with the smallest hypervolume contribution from S'. Since the hypervolume contribution of each extreme solution increases with r and that of any other solution does not increase, we can specify a large value of r so that a non-extreme solution has the smallest hypervolume contribution. The obtained solution set S'' by removing such a non-extreme solution has a larger hypervolume than the solution set S for the specified value of r. This means that the solution set S excluding a single extreme solution cannot be the best solution set with μ ($\mu \geq 3$) solutions. Thus, we can say that all the three extreme solutions are included in the optimal solution set with μ ($\mu \geq 3$) solutions when r is large.

These discussions for the three-objective DTLZ1 problem can be generalized to the case of four or more objectives. That is, for the m-objective DTLZ1 problem, it is likely that all the m extreme solutions are included in the optimal solution set with μ ($\mu \geq m$) solutions. If a solution set includes all the m extreme solutions, the hypervolume contribution of any other solution does not increase when we increase the value of r.

Discussions for Max-DTLZ1 are more complicated. For example, the Pareto optimal solutions of the normalized three-objective Max-DTLZ1 problem in Subsection 3.2 are categorized as

(i) The three extreme solutions A (1, 0, 0), B (0, 1, 0), C (0, 0, 1):
If the three extreme solutions A, B and C are included in the solution set, they are Class 2 solutions. This is because each extreme solution is the non-overlapping best solution at $f_i = 1$ in the corresponding single-dimensional subspace with f_i.

(ii) All solutions on the sides of the Pareto front:
They are Class 1 solutions (if all the three extreme solutions are included in a solution set). As explained in Figure 20, each solution on a side of the Pareto front is a non-overlapping non-dominated solution in a two-dimensional subspace. They are not Class 2 solutions because their projections to each single-dimensional subspace with f_i are always dominated by an extreme solution at $f_i = 1$.

(iii) All the other Pareto optimal solutions:
If all the three extreme solutions and all solutions on the sides of the Pareto front are included in a solution set, all the other Pareto optimal solutions are Class 0 solutions. If solutions on a part of a side are not included in a solution set, some inside Pareto optimal solutions around the uncovered part can be Class 1 solutions. By increasing the number of solutions on the sides of the Pareto front, more inside solutions become Class 0 solutions.

When r is large (i.e., when the reference point is far from the Pareto front), all the three extreme solutions of the three-objective Max-DTLZ1 problem are likely to be included in the optimal solution set with μ solutions ($\mu \geq 3$). This can be explained in the same manner as the above discussions for the DTLZ1 problem. When r is large and $\mu > 3$, some Class 1 solutions are included in the optimal solution set. However, it is not likely that any Class 0 solution is included in the optimal solution set. Let us assume that a Class 0 solution is included in a solution set S with μ solutions. We generate a new solution set S' with ($\mu + 1$) solutions by adding a Class 1 solution. For the new solution set S', we can specify a large value of r so that the Class 0 solution has the smallest hypervolume contribution. A new solution set S'' is generated by removing the Class 0 solution with the smallest hypervolume contribution. Since S'' has a larger hypervolume than S, S is not the optimal solution set with μ solutions. That is, no Class 0 solution is included in the optimal solution set of the three-objective Max-DTLZ1 problem when r is large.

4. NEAR REFERENCE POINT
In this section, we discuss hypervolume maximization for the case where the reference point is the same as the nadir point or very close to the Pareto front (i.e., closer than the nadir point).

4.1 DTLZ1
First we discuss the case where the nadir point (1, 1, 1) of the normalized three-objective DTLZ1 problem is used as the reference point (see Figure 21). In this figure, it is clear that the hypervolume contribution of the three extreme solutions A, B and C is zero. Thus they are not included in the optimal solution set as shown in Figure 2 (a). However, solutions on the sides of the Pareto front have positive hypervolume contributions. Thus some solutions are obtained on the sides in Figure 2 (a).

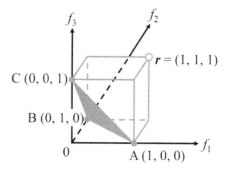

Figure 21. The normalized three-objective DTLZ1 Problem and the reference point (1, 1, 1).

For example, the hypervolume of solution M (0.5, 0, 0.5) at the midpoint between A and C is the volume of the following region:

$$D(M, r) = \{(z_1, z_2, z_3) \mid 0.5 \leq z_1 \leq 1, 0 \leq z_2 \leq 1, 0.5 \leq z_3 \leq 1\}. \quad (35)$$

Thus the hypervolume of M is 1/4, which is 1/4 of the volume of the unit cube $[0, 1]^3$. Whereas M has a large hypervolume, its contribution is decreased by other solutions. Let us consider the solution set {M, Z} where Z (1/3, 1/3, 1/3) is the solution at the center of the Pareto front. In this case, the hypervolume contribution of M is the volume of the following region:

$$\{(z_1, z_2, z_3) \mid 0.5 \leq z_1 \leq 1, 0 \leq z_2 \leq 1/3, 0.5 \leq z_3 \leq 1\}. \quad (36)$$

Thus the hypervolume contribution of M is calculated as 1/12. Let us consider another solution set {M, Y} where Y (0.25, 0, 0.75) is a point on the line AC (see Figure 18). In this case, the hypervolume contribution of M is the volume of the region:

$$\{(z_1, z_2, z_3) \mid 0.5 \le z_1 \le 1, \, 0 \le z_2 \le 1, \, 0.5 \le z_3 \le 0.75\}. \qquad (37)$$

Thus the hypervolume contribution is calculated as 1/8. As shown by these calculations, all Pareto optimal solutions except for the three extreme solutions have positive hypervolume contributions. The hypervolume contribution of a solution on the sides of the triangular Pareto front (and also a solution inside the Pareto front) is decreased by adding other solutions to the solution set. Since the hypervolume contribution of each solution is calculated in the unit cube $[0, 1]^3$, there exists no particular region (e.g., the sides of the triangular Pareto front) where solutions have dominatingly large hypervolume contributions. Thus solutions do not concentrate on a particular region of the Pareto front.

Next let us consider the case where the reference point is close to the Pareto front (more specifically, the reference point dominates the nadir point). For example, let us assume that the reference point is (0.6, 0.6, 0.6) in the normalized objective space with the nadir point (1, 1, 1) and the ideal point (0, 0, 0). Under this setting of the reference point, the hypervolume contribution is zero in the following part of the Pareto front: $0.6 \le f_1$, $0.6 \le f_2$ or $0.6 \le f_3$. This is because any solutions satisfying $0.6 \le f_1$, $0.6 \le f_2$ or $0.6 \le f_3$ do not dominate the reference point. Only solutions on the Pareto front between the three lines $f_1 = 0.6$, $f_2 = 0.6$ and $f_3 = 0.6$ in Figure 22 have positive hypervolume contributions. Figure 22 shows the obtained solutions by SMS-EMOA with 1,000,000 generations for the normalized three-objective DTLZ1 problem with the reference point (0.6, 0.6, 0.6). It should be noted that the hypervolume contribution of any solution on the three lines in Figure 22 is zero. So no solutions are obtained on the three lines. When the reference point is the nadir point (1, 1, 1), the three lines move to the three extreme solutions. In this case, the hypervolume contribution of each extreme solution is zero whereas all the other Pareto optimal solutions have positive hypervolume contributions. When the reference point is (0.5, 0.5, 0.5), the three lines in Figure 22 form the inscribed inverted triangle in the Pareto front. In Figure 4 (a), the reference point is specified as (0.5, 0.5, 0.5) in the normalized objective space. The obtained solutions are inside the inscribed inverted triangle in the Pareto front in Figure 4 (a).

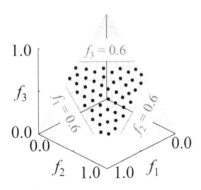

Figure 22. The obtained solutions by SMS-EMOA for the three-objective normalized DTLZ1 problem for the reference point (0.6, 0.6, 0.6).

Almost all discussions in this subsection can be extended to the case of four or more objectives. For example, when the nadir point is used as the reference point, no extreme solution of the triangular Pareto front on the hyperplane $f_1 + f_2 + \ldots + f_m = 1$ has a

positive hypervolume contribution. Thus they are not included in the optimal solution set for hypervolume maximization. However, solutions on the sides of the Pareto front can be included in the optimal solution sets. When the reference point is close to the Pareto front (i.e., the reference point dominates the nadir point), solutions in the optimal solution set are inside an inverted triangular region of the Pareto front since no solutions outside the region have positive hypervolume contributions.

4.2 Max-DTLZ1 and Inverted DTLZ1

First we consider the case where the nadir point (0, 0, 0) is used as the reference point in the normalized three-objective Max-DTLZ1 problem. In this case, it is clear that the hypervolume contribution of all solutions on the sides of the triangular Pareto front is zero. For example, all solutions on the side between A (1, 0, 0) and C (0, 0, 1) in Figure 21 have zero as the value of the second objective. Thus the hypervolume contributions of all points on this line are always zero. As a result, no solutions are obtained on the sides of the triangular Pareto front as shown in Figure 3 (a).

Next let us consider the case where the reference point is very close to the Pareto front (i.e., the reference point dominates the nadir point). For example, let us assume that the reference point is (0.2, 0.2, 0.2) in the normalized objective space with the nadir point (0, 0, 0) and the ideal point (1, 1, 1). Under this setting, only Pareto optimal solutions inside the triangular region satisfying the following condition have positive hypervolume values: $0.2 \le f_1$, $0.2 \le f_2$ and $0.2 \le f_3$. This triangular region is shown in Figure 23 together with the obtained solutions by SMS-EMOA. Since no solutions on the sides of this triangular region have positive hypervolume contributions, no solutions are obtained on the sides of the smaller triangle in Figure 23. It is interesting to observe that solutions are obtained in the triangular region for Max-DTLZ1 (whereas they are obtained in the inverted triangular region for DTLZ1) when the reference point is close to the Pareto front. This observation may be a useful insight when we try to focus the search of an indicator-based algorithm on a small region of the Pareto front using a reference point. When the nadir point (0, 0, 0) is used as the reference point, the small triangle in Figure 23 becomes the same as the triangular Pareto front (see Figure 3 (a)).

Almost all discussions in this subsection can be extended to the case of four or more objectives. For example, when the nadir point (0, 0, ..., 0) is used as the reference point, no solutions on the sides of the triangular Pareto front are obtained in the optimal solution set of Max-DTLZ1 with four or more objectives. We may be able to focus on a small triangular region of the Pareto front by using a reference point close to the Pareto front.

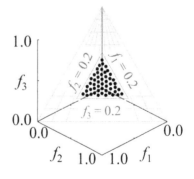

Figure 23. The obtained solutions by SMS-EMOA for the three-objective normalized Max-DTLZ1 problem for the reference point (0.2, 0.2, 0.2).

5. EFFECTS ON COMPARISON RESULTS

In this section, we examine the effect of the location of the reference point for hypervolume calculation on hypervolume-based performance comparison results of multiple solution sets. First we generated four solution sets by applying MOEA/D-PBI to the normalized three-objective DTLZ1 using four settings of the reference point in the PBI function: (0.2, 0.2, 0.2), (0.1, 0.1, 0.1), (0, 0, 0) and (−0.1, −0.1, −0.1). In the PBI function, we used only the distance d_2 from the reference line since all feasible solutions were Pareto optimal under our setting of the number of distance variables (i.e., $k = 0$). The population size was specified as 105. The generated solution sets are referred to as solution sets A, B, C and D as shown in Figure 24. For comparison, we also generated solution set E by uniformly sampling solutions only on the sides of the Pareto front. This solution set is shown in Figure 25.

Then we compared the five solution sets using the hypervolume where five settings of the reference point for hypervolume calculation were examined: (1.0, 1.0, 1.0), (1.1, 1.1, 1.1), (1.2, 1.2, 1.2), (1.5, 1.5, 1.5) and (2.0, 2.0, 2.0). The evaluation result of each solution set is shown as the rank among the five solution sets in Table 1 (1: the best, 5: the worst). Independent of the setting of the reference point for hypervolume calculation, we obtained the same performance comparison results for the five solution sets in Table 1. This observation is consistent with the discussions in Subsection 3.1 where we showed that the optimal distribution of solutions is independent of the reference point as long as the three extreme solutions are included in the solution set and the reference point is dominated by the nadir point.

Table 1. Ranking of the five solution sets when they are compared as solution sets of the normalized three-objective DTLZ1 Problem for each setting of the reference point: Comparison results for the minimization problem.

Reference Point	1.0	1.1	1.2	1.5	2.0
Solution set A	5	5	5	5	5
Solution set B	4	4	4	4	4
Solution set C	1	1	1	1	1
Solution set D	2	2	2	2	2
Solution set E	3	3	3	3	3

We also compared the five solution sets as solution sets of the normalized three-objective Max-DTLZ1 problem. Experimental results are shown in Table 2. When the nadir point (0, 0, 0) is used as the reference point, the solution set B has the largest hypervolume value. This may be because all solutions on the sides of the triangular Pareto front have no hypervolume contribution in this setting. When the reference point is a little bit smaller than the nadir point (i.e., (−0.1, −0.1, −0.1): a little bit away from the Pareto front than the nadir point (0, 0, 0)), the solution set C has the largest hypervolume value. When the reference point is far from the Pareto front (i.e., (−20, −20, −20)), the solution set E has the largest hypervolume value in Table 2. As shown in Table 2, performance comparison results depend heavily on the location of the reference point for hypervolume calculation.

Table 2. Ranking of the five solution sets when they are compared as solution sets of the normalized three-objective Max-DTLZ1 Problem for each setting of the reference point: Comparison results for the maximization problem.

Reference Point	0.0	−0.1	−0.2	−0.5	−20
Solution set A	4	4	5	5	5
Solution set B	1	3	3	4	4
Solution set C	2	1	1	2	3
Solution set D	3	2	2	1	2
Solution set E	5	5	4	3	1

Our experimental results on DTLZ1 (Table 1) and Max-DTLZ1 (Table 2) are consistent with our discussions on the optimal distribution of solutions in Section 3 and Section 4. We also performed computational experiments for the case of four objectives in the same manner as in Table 1 and Table 2. First MOEA/D-PBI with the population size 969 was applied to the normalized four-objective DTLZ1 problem to obtain four solution sets using four settings of the reference point: (0.2, 0.2, 0.2, 0.2), (0.1, 0.1, 0.1, 0.1), (0, 0, 0, 0) and (−0.1, −0.1, −0.1, −0.1). The obtained four solution sets are referred to as solution sets A, B, C and D, respectively. Solution set E with 969 solutions was generated by uniformly sampling solutions on the sides of the triangular Pareto front (i.e., solutions were sampled uniformly on the lines between all pairs of the four extreme solutions (1, 0, 0, 0), (0, 1, 0, 0), (0, 0, 1. 0) and (0, 0, 0, 1)). Then the five solution sets were compared using the hypervolume for different settings of the reference point for hypervolume calculation.

Table 3 shows the performance comparison results when the five solution sets were evaluated as solution sets of the normalized four-objective DTLZ1 problem. As in Table 1, we obtained the same performance comparison results independent of the setting of the reference point for hypervolume calculation in Table 3.

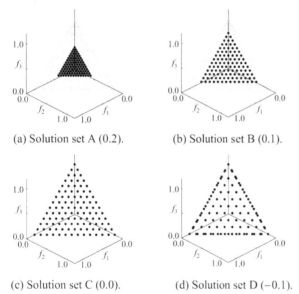

(a) Solution set A (0.2).   (b) Solution set B (0.1).

(c) Solution set C (0.0).   (d) Solution set D (−0.1).

Figure 24. Four solution sets obtained by MOEA/D-PBI.

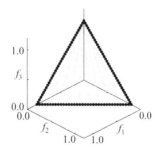

Figure 25. Solution set E.

Table 3. Ranking of the five solution sets when they are compared as solution sets of the normalized four-objective DTLZ1 Problem for each setting of the reference point: Comparison results for the minimization problem.

Reference Point	1.0	1.1	1.2	1.5	2.0
Solution set A	5	5	5	5	5
Solution set B	4	4	4	4	4
Solution set C	1	1	1	1	1
Solution set D	2	2	2	2	2
Solution set E	3	3	3	3	3

We also compared the same five solution sets for the normalized four-objective Max-DTLZ1 problem. Experimental results are shown in Table 4. As in Table 2, the performance comparison results of the five solution sets in Table 4 heavily depend on the setting of the reference point for hypervolume calculation. For example, a different solution set is evaluated as being the best for each of the three similar specifications: 0.0, −0.1 and −0.2.

Table 4. Ranking of the five solution sets when they are compared as solution sets of the normalized four-objective Max-DTLZ1 Problem for each setting of the reference point: Comparison results for the maximization problem.

Reference Point	0.0	−0.1	−0.2	−0.5	−20
Solution set A	4	4	5	5	5
Solution set B	1	3	3	4	4
Solution set C	2	1	2	2	3
Solution set D	3	2	1	1	2
Solution set E	5	5	4	3	1

6. FURTHER EXAMINATIONS
In this section, we examine the property derived in Section 3: The hypervolume contribution of a Pareto optimal solution of an m-objective problem increases with r^{m-k} when it is a non-overlapping non-dominated solution in a k-dimensional subspace and not in any $(k-1)$-dimensional subspace. When it is not a non-overlapping non-dominated solution in any $(m-1)$-dimensional subspace, its hypervolume contribution does not increase with r.

6.1 DTLZ1 with a Constraint on f_3
We added a constraint condition $f_3(x) \leq 0.5$ to the three-objective normalized DTLZ1 problem. Its Pareto front is shown in Figure 26. All solutions on the line with $f_3(x) = 0.5$ (i.e., all solutions on the line ML in Figure 26) are non-overlapping non-dominated solutions in the f_1-f_2 subspace. Computational experiments were performed using SMS-EMOA in the same manner as in Section 1. That is, the objective space was normalized for the original DTLZ1 problem without the constraint condition $f_3(x) \leq 0.5$ as shown in Figure 26.

Experimental results are shown in Figure 27 where we can observe a clear dependence of the obtained solution sets on the location of a reference point $r = (r, r, r)$. This is because all Pareto optimal solutions on the line ML with $f_3(x) = 0.5$ are non-overlapping non-dominated solutions in the f_1-f_2 subspace of the modified DTLZ1 problem in this subsection. By increasing the value of r (i.e., by moving the reference point far from the Pareto front), more solutions are obtained on the line ML (most solutions are on the line ML when $r = 100$).

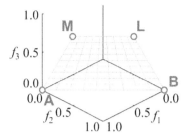

Figure 26. Pareto front of DTLZ1 with $f_3(x) \leq 0.5$.

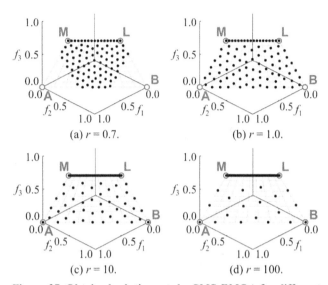

(a) $r = 0.7$.　　(b) $r = 1.0$.

(c) $r = 10$.　　(d) $r = 100$.

Figure 27. Obtained solution sets by SMS-EMOA for different reference points (DTLZ1 with $f_3(x) \leq 0.5$).

6.2 Inverted DTLZ1 with a Constraint on f_3
We added a constraint condition $f_3(x) \geq 0.5$ to the three-objective normalized inverted DTLZ1 problem. Its Pareto front is shown in Figure 28. No Pareto optimal solution on the line ML with $f_3(x) = 0.5$ except for M and L is non-dominated in any two-dimensional subspace (whereas all Pareto optimal solutions on the other sides of the Pareto front are non-overlapping non-dominated solutions in a two-dimensional subspace). Experimental results of SMS-EMOA are shown in Figure 29.

From Figure 29 (and also from Figure 27), we can see that many solutions were obtained on some sides of the Pareto front where the Pareto optimal solutions were non-overlapping non-dominated solutions in a two-dimensional subspace. More solutions were obtained on those sides by increasing the value of r (i.e., by moving the reference point far away from the Pareto front).

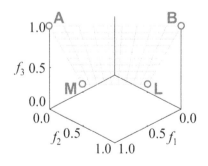

Figure 28. Pareto front of Inverted DTLZ1 with $f_3(x) \geq 0.5$.

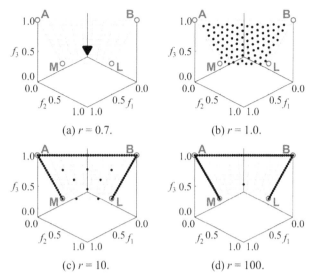

(a) r = 0.7.   (b) r = 1.0.

(c) r = 10.   (d) r = 100.

Figure 29. Obtained solution sets by SMS-EMOA for different reference points (Inverted DTLZ1 with $f_3(x) \geq 0.5$).

6.3 DTLZ1 with Constraints on f_1 and f_2

We added constraint conditions $f_1(x) \leq 0.5$ and $f_2(x) \leq 0.5$ to the three-objective normalized DTLZ1 problem. The Pareto front of this problem is shown in Figure 30. The projections of the Pareto front to the f_1-f_2, f_1-f_3 and f_2-f_3 subspaces are shown in Figure 31. In Figure 31 (a), only a single solution C is Pareto optimal in the f_1-f_2 subspace as in the three-objective normalized DTLZ1 problem. However, in Figure 31 (b), all Pareto optimal solutions on the line with $f_2(x) = 0.5$ (i.e., all Pareto optimal solutions on the line LN) are non-overlapping non-dominated solutions in the f_1-f_3 subspace. In Figure 31 (c), all Pareto optimal solutions on the line MN with $f_1(x) = 0.5$ are non-overlapping non-dominated solutions in the f_2-f_3 subspace. Experimental results of SMS-EMOA are shown in Figure 32. We can see from Figure 32 that many solutions were obtained on the lines LN and MN. By increasing the value of r, more solutions were obtained on the two lines.

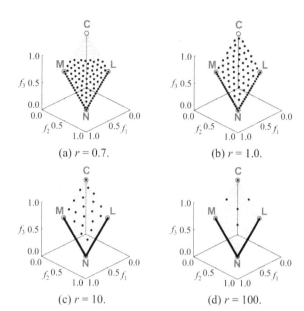

(a) r = 0.7.   (b) r = 1.0.

(c) r = 10.   (d) r = 100.

Figure 32. Obtained solution sets by SMS-EMOA for different reference points (DTLZ1 with $f_1(x) \geq 0.5$ and $f_2(x) \geq 0.5$).

6.4 WFG3

The WFG3 problem [14] was intended to be a test problem with a degenerate Pareto front. However, recently it has been shown in [16] that the WFG3 problem with three or more objectives has a non-degenerate part of the Pareto front in addition to the intended degenerate Pareto front. The Pareto front of the three-objective WFG3 test problem is shown in Figure 33. Its projections to the two-objective subspaces are shown in Figure 34. The line AB in Figure 33 is the originally intended degenerate Pareto front. Figure 34 shows that all solutions on the line AB in (b) and the line CB in (c) are non-overlapping non-dominated solutions in at least one of the three two-dimensional subspaces. In Figure 34 (a), solution A is the best solution (no other non-dominated solutions).

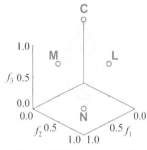

Figure 30. Pareto front of DTLZ1 with $f_1(x) \geq 0.5$ and $f_2(x) \geq$ 0.5.

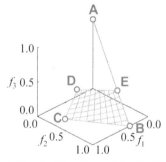

Figure 33. Pareto front of the three-objective WFG3 problem.

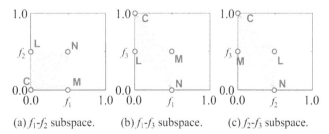

(a) f_1-f_2 subspace. (b) f_1-f_3 subspace. (c) f_2-f_3 subspace.

Figure 31. Projections of the Pareto front in Figure 30 to the two-dimensional subspaces.

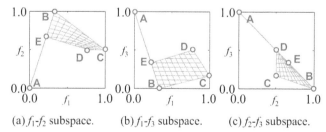

(a) f_1-f_2 subspace. (b) f_1-f_3 subspace. (c) f_2-f_3 subspace.

Figure 34. Projections of the Pareto front in Figure 33 to the two-dimensional subspace (WFG3).

Experimental results by SMS-EMOA are shown in Figure 35. We can see from Figure 35 that (almost) all solutions were obtained on the right and bottom boundaries of the Pareto front (i.e., on the lines AB and BC) when the reference point was far from the Pareto front. We can also see from Figure 35 that many solutions were not obtained inside the Pareto front even when $r = 1.0$ (i.e., even when the reference point was $(1, 1, 1)$). This is because all inside solutions have very small hypervolume contributions. We can also see that more solutions were obtained on an upper part of the line AB with large values of f_3 than its lower part with small values of f_3. This is because the upper part of AB is non-dominated in both the f_2-f_3 and f_1-f_3 subspaces whereas the lower part is non-dominated only in the f_2-f_3 subspace (see Figure 34).

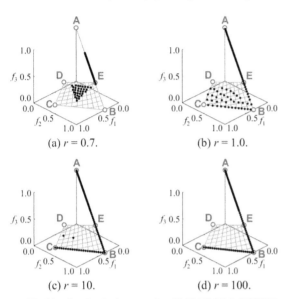

(a) $r = 0.7$. (b) $r = 1.0$.

(c) $r = 10$. (d) $r = 100$.

Figure 35. Obtained solution sets by SMS-EMOA (WFG3).

7. CONCLUDING REMARKS

In this paper, we discussed the optimal distribution of solutions for hypervolume maximization on the triangular Pareto fronts of the three-objective DTLZ1 test problem [8] and its two variants: inverted DTLZ1 [19] and Max-DTLZ1 [18]. Our contribution was to show that the optimal distribution is totally different between three-objective minimization and maximization problems even when they have the same triangular Pareto front. This fact has not necessarily been well recognized in the EMO community because such a large difference does not exist in the case of two objectives. This is also because maximization problems with triangular Pareto fronts and minimization problems with inverted triangular Pareto front have not been used in many studies.

The reason for the large difference in the optimal distribution of solutions between three-objective minimization and maximization problems is that the extreme solutions play different roles. In the case of a three-objective minimization problem with a triangular Pareto front, the optimal distribution of solutions can be discussed within the unit cube $[0, 1]^3$ in the normalized objective space independent of the location of the reference point (when the three extreme solutions are included in a solution set and the reference point is far from the Pareto front). This is because the outside of the unit cube $[0, 1]^3$ is dominated by at least one extreme solution. As a result, a set of the three extreme solutions and well-distributed solutions over the entire Pareto front has a large hypervolume value independent of the location of the reference

point for hypervolume calculation as far as the reference point is far from the Pareto front. However, in the case of a three-objective maximization problem with a triangular Pareto front, the optimal distribution of solutions heavily depends on the location of the reference point. For example, when the reference point is far from the Pareto front, a larger hypervolume value is obtained from a set of solutions on the sides of the Pareto front than a set of well-distributed solutions over the entire Pareto front. This is because the extreme solutions cannot dominate all the regions outside the unit cube $[0, 1]^3$. As a result, every solution on each side of the triangular Pareto front is non-dominated on the corresponding two-dimensional subspace of the three-dimensional objective space. Thus their hypervolume contributions increase as the reference point moves away from the Pareto front.

From our discussions in this paper, one may think that minimization problems with triangular Pareto fronts such as DTLZ1 seem to have a good property as test problems in their performance evaluation: robustness with respect to the location of the reference point. We do not have to examine multiple reference points for hypervolume calculation, which leads to multi-objective solution set optimization [15]. However, minimization problems with triangular Pareto fronts have a somewhat strange property as multiobjective test problems: A single extreme solution of an m-objective problem simultaneously optimizes $(m-1)$ objectives. For example, an extreme solution $(1, 0, 0, 0)$ simultaneously optimizes the second, third and fourth objectives of a four-objective minimization problem with the normalized triangular Pareto front where the ideal point is $(0, 0, 0, 0)$ and the nadir point is $(1, 1, 1, 1)$. If we remove the first objective to formulate a three-objective problem, the formulated three-objective problem has a single optimal solution for all objectives. This strange property is related to the robustness of minimization problems with triangular Pareto fronts with respect to the location of the reference point in hypervolume-based performance comparison results.

On the contrary, performance comparison results of solution sets of maximization problems with triangular Pareto fronts strongly depend on the location of the reference point for hypervolume calculation. In our computational experiments on the three-objective and four-objective Max-DTLZ1 problems, a different solution set had the largest hypervolume for a different reference point. Our experimental results suggest that we should be careful when performance is compared for multiobjective maximization problems with triangular Pareto fronts (and many other test problems with constraint conditions as shown in Section 6). For those test problems, multiple reference points may be needed [15]. Whereas maximization problems with triangular Pareto fronts (i.e., minimization problems with inverted triangular Pareto fronts) do not have robustness with respect to the location of the reference point in hypervolume-based performance comparison, their extreme points do not have the above-mentioned strange property. Each extreme solution optimizes only a single objective. For example, the extreme solution $(1, 0, 0, 0)$ optimizes only the first objective of a four-objective maximization problem while it simultaneously optimizes all the other three objectives of a four-objective minimization problem with a triangular Pareto front.

Whereas we clearly demonstrated the difference in the effect of the reference point on the optimal distribution of solutions between three-objective minimization and maximization problems, we did not theoretically derive any optimal distribution of solutions in a three-dimensional objective space. Derivation of the optimal distributions of solutions for triangular and inverted triangular Pareto fronts is left for future research.

8. REFERENCES

[1] Auger, A., Bader, J., Brockhoff, D., and Zitzler, E. 2009. Theory of the hypervolume indicator: Optimal μ-distributions and the choice of the reference point. In *Proceeding of 10th International Workshop on Foundations of Genetic Algorithms* (Orlando, USA, January 9-11, 2009) 87-102. DOI: http://doi.acm.org/10.1145/1527125.1527138

[2] Auger, A., Bader, J., Brockhoff, D., and Zitzler, E. 2012. Hypervolume-based multiobjective optimization: Theoretical foundations and practical implications. *Theoretical Computer Science* 425 (March 2012) 75-103.

[3] Bader, J. and Zitzler, E. 2011. HypE: An algorithm for fast hypervolume-based many-objective optimization. *Evolutionary Computation* 19, 1 (Spring 2011) 45-76.

[4] Basseur, M., Derbel, B., Goëffon, A., and Liefooghe, A. 2016. Experiments on greedy and local search heuristics for *d*-dimensional hypervolume subset selection. In *Proceedings of 2016 Genetic and Evolutionary Computation Conference* (Denver, USA, July 20-24, 2016) 541-548. DOI: http://doi.acm.org/10.1145/2908812.2908949

[5] Beume, N., Naujoks, B., and Emmerich, M. 2007. SMS-EMOA: Multiobjective selection based on dominated hypervolume. *European Journal of Operational Research* 180, 3 (September 2007) 1653-1669.

[6] Bringmann, K., Friedrich, T., and Klitzke, P. 2014. Generic postprocessing via subset selection for hypervolume and epsilon-indicator. *Lecture Notes in Computer Science 8672: Parallel Problem Solving from Nature - PPSN XIII* (Ljubljana, Slovenia, September 13-17, 2014) 518–527.

[7] Bringmann, K., Friedrich, T., and Klitzke, P. 2014. Two-dimensional subset selection for hypervolume and epsilon-indicator. In *Proceedings of 2014 Genetic and Evolutionary Computation Conference* (Vancouver, Canada, July 12-16, 2014) 589-596. DOI: http://doi.acm.org/10.1145/2576768.2598276.

[8] Deb, K., Thiele, L., Laumanns, M., and Zitzler, E. 2002. Scalable multi-objective optimization test problems. In *Proceedings of 2002 Congress on Evolutionary Computation* (Honolulu, USA, May 12-17, 2002) 825-830.

[9] Emmerich, M. T. M., Deutz, A. H., and Beume, N. 2007. Gradient-based/evolutionary relay hybrid for computing Pareto front approximations maximizing the S-metric. *Lecture Notes in Computer Science 4771: Hybrid Metaheuristics - HM 2007* (Dortmund, Germany, October 8-9, 2007) 140-156.

[10] Friedrich, T., Neumann, F., and Thyssen, C. 2015. Multiplicative approximations, optimal hypervolume distributions, and the choice of the reference point. *Evolutionary Computation* 23, 1 (Spring 2015) 131-159.

[11] Glasmachers, T. 2014. Optimized approximation sets for low-dimensional benchmark Pareto fronts. *Lecture Notes in Computer Science 8672: Parallel Problem Solving from Nature - PPSN XIII.* (Ljubljana, Slovenia, September 13-17, 2014) 569-578.

[12] Guerreiro, A. P., Fonseca, C. M., and Paquete, L. 2015. Greedy hypervolume subset selection in the three-objective case. In *Proceedings of 2015 Genetic and Evolutionary Computation Conference.* (Madrid, Spain, July 11-15, 2015) 671-678. DOI: http://doi.acm.org/10.1145/2739480.2754812

[13] Guerreiro, A. P., Fonseca, C. M., and Paquete, L. 2016. Greedy hypervolume subset selection in low dimensions. *Evolutionary Computation* 24, 3 (Fall 2016) 521-544.

[14] Huband, S., Hingston, P., Barone, L., and While, L. 2006. A review of multiobjective test problems and a scalable test problem toolkit. *IEEE Trans. on Evolutionary Computation* 10, 5 (October 2006) 477-506.

[15] Ishibuchi, H., Masuda, H., and Nojima, Y. 2014. Meta-level multi-objective formulations of set optimization for multi-objective optimization problems: Multi-reference point approach to hypervolume maximization, *Companion of 2014 Genetic and Evolutionary Computation Conference* (Vancouver, Canada, July 12-16, 2014) 89-90.

[16] Ishibuchi, H., Masuda, H., and Nojima, Y. 2016. Pareto fronts of many-objective degenerate test problems. *IEEE Trans. on Evolutionary Computation* 20, 5 (October 2016) 807-813.

[17] Ishibuchi, H., Setoguchi, Y., Masuda, H., and Nojima, Y. 2016. How to compare many-objective algorithms under different settings of population and archive sizes. In *Proceedings of 2016 IEEE Congress on Evolutionary Computation* (Vancouver, July 24-29, 2016) 1149-1156.

[18] Ishibuchi, H., Setoguchi, Y., Masuda, H., and Nojima, Y. 2016. Performance of decomposition-based many-objective algorithms strongly depends on Pareto front shapes. *IEEE Trans. on Evolutionary Computation* (Early Access). http://ieeexplore.ieee.org/xpl/tocresult.jsp?isnumber=4358751

[19] Jain, H. and Deb, K. 2014. An evolutionary many-objective optimization algorithm using reference-point based non-dominated sorting approach, Part II: Handling constraints and extending to an adaptive approach. *IEEE Trans. on Evolutionary Computation* 18, 4 (August 2014) 602-622.

[20] Kuhn, T., Fonseca, C. M., Paquete, L., Ruzika, S., Duarte, M. M., and Figueira, J. R. 2016. Hypervolume subset selection in two dimensions: Formulations and algorithms. *Evolutionary Computation* 24, 3 (Fall 2016) 411-425.

[21] Shukla, P.K., Doll, N., and Schmeck, H. 2014. A theoretical analysis of volume based Pareto front approximations. In *Proceedings of 2014 Genetic and Evolutionary Computation Conference* (Vancouver, Canada, July 12-16, 2014) 1415-1422. http://doi.acm.org/10.1145/2576768.2598348

[22] Zitzler, E., Brockhoff, D., and Thiele, L. 2007. The hypervolume indicator revisited: On the design of Pareto-compliant indicators via weighted integration. *Lecture Notes in Computer Science 4403: Evolutionary Multi-Criterion Optimization - EMO 2007* (Matsushima, Japan, March 5-8, 2007) 862-876.

[23] Zitzler, E. and Thiele, L. 1998. Multiobjective optimization using evolutionary algorithms - A comparative case study. *Lecture Notes in Computer Science 1498: Parallel Problem Solving from Nature - PPSN V* (Amsterdam, Netherlands, September 27-30) 292-301.

[24] Zitzler, E., Thiele, L., Laumanns, M., Fonseca, C.M., and da Fonseca, V.G. 2003. Performance assessment of multiobjective optimizers: An analysis and review. *IEEE Trans. on Evolutionary Computation* 7, 2 (April 2003) 117-132.

Quality Gain Analysis of the Weighted Recombination Evolution Strategy on General Convex Quadratic Functions

Youhei Akimoto
Shinshu University
380-8553 Nagano, Japan
y_akimoto@shinshu-u.ac.jp

Anne Auger
Inria, Research Centre Saclay
91120 Palaiseau, France
anne.auger@inria.fr

Nikolaus Hansen
Inria, Research Centre Saclay
91120 Palaiseau, France
nikolaus.hansen@inria.fr

ABSTRACT

We investigate evolution strategies with weighted recombination on general convex quadratic functions. We derive the asymptotic quality gain in the limit of the dimension to infinity, and derive the optimal recombination weights and the optimal step-size. This work is an extension of previous works where the asymptotic quality gain of evolution strategies with weighted recombination was derived on the infinite dimensional sphere function. Moreover, for a finite dimensional search space, we derive rigorous bounds for the quality gain on a general quadratic function. They reveal the dependency of the quality gain both in the eigenvalue distribution of the Hessian matrix and on the recombination weights. Taking the search space dimension to infinity, it turns out that the optimal recombination weights are independent of the Hessian matrix, i.e., the recombination weights optimal for the sphere function are optimal for convex quadratic functions.

CCS Concepts

•**Mathematics of computing → Bio-inspired optimization;** •**Theory of computation → Theory of randomized search heuristics;**

Keywords

Evolution strategies; recombination weights; optimal step-size; quality gain analysis; general convex quadratic function

1. INTRODUCTION

Evolution Strategies (ES) are bio-inspired, randomized search algorithms to minimize a function $f : \mathbb{R}^N \to \mathbb{R}$ in continuous domain. The most commonly used variant of evolution strategies, namely the covariance matrix adaptation evolution strategy (CMA-ES) [,], is one of the state-of-the-art randomized search algorithms for black-box contin-

FOGA '17, January 12-15, 2017, Copenhagen, Denmark

© 2017 ACM. ISBN 978-1-4503-4651-1/17/01. . . $15.00

DOI: http://dx.doi.org/10.1145/3040718.3040720

uous optimization. It maintains a multivariate normal distribution from which candidate solutions are sampled. The parameters of the multivariate normal distribution are updated using the candidate solutions and their function value ranking. Due to its population-based and comparison-based nature, the algorithm is robust and effective on non-convex and rugged functions.

Often the performance evaluation of evolutionary algorithms is based on empirical studies. One of the reason is that mathematically rigorous analysis of randomized algorithms are often too complicated due to the comparison-based and population-based nature and the complex adaptation mechanisms. To perform a rigorous analysis we often need to simplify some algorithmic components. However, theoretical studies can help our understanding of the behavior of the algorithms, provide optimal scenario that may not be empirically recognized, and reveal the dependency of the performance on the internal parameter settings. For example, the recombination weights in CMA-ES are selected based on the mathematical analysis of an evolution strategy [ ][1]. Moreover, the optimal rate of convergence of the step-size is used to estimate the condition number of the product of the covariance matrix and the Hessian matrix of the objective function, which a recent variant of CMA-ES exploits for online selection of the restricted covariance matrix model [ ].

Analysis based on progress rate or quality gain are among the first theoretical studies of evolution strategies that were carried out (see [ ] for historical results of different variants of evolution strategies). Progress or quality gain measures the *expected progress in one step* (measured in terms of norm for the progress rate and objective function for the quality gain). Simplifying assumptions are then made to be able to derive explicit formula. Typically on spherical functions, it is assumed that the step-size times the dimension divided by the norm of the mean of the sampling distribution is constant. This allows to derive quantitative explicit estimates of the progress rate for the dimension N large that are correct in the limit of N to infinity (see (10)). Those analysis are particularly useful to know the dependency of the expected progress on the parameters of the algorithm such as the population size, number of parents, and recombination weights. Based on these results, one can derive some

---

[1]The weights of CMA-ES were set before the publication [ ] because the theoretical result of optimal weights on the sphere was known before the publication.

optimal parameter setting, in particular the recombination weights [ ].

The progress rate on the sphere is linked to the convergence rate of "real" algorithms, that is implementing a proper step-size or/and covariance matrix adaptation. First, it is directly related to the convergence rate of an "artificial" algorithm where the step-size is set proportionally to the distance to the optimum (see [ ] for instance)[2]. Second, the convergence rate of this artificial algorithm for a proper choice of proportionality constant gives a bound on the convergence rate of step-size adaptive algorithms. For $(1 + \lambda)$ or $(1, \lambda)$ ESs the bound holds on any function with a unique global optimum, that is, a step-size adaptive $(1 \overset{+}{,} \lambda)$-ES optimizing any function f with a unique global optimum will not achieve a convergence rate faster than the convergence rate of the artificial algorithm with step-size proportional to the optimum on the sphere function [, ,][3]. For algorithms implementing recombination, this bound holds not on any f but on spherical functions [,]. While analyzing the convergence and convergence rate of "real" algorithms is generally quite intricate, there is a simple connection between progress rate analysis and convergence analysis of step-size adaptive evolution strategies: on scaling-invariance functions (with optimum in zero without loss of generality (w.l.g.)), the mean vector divided by the step-size is a Markov chain whose stability analysis leads to the linear convergence of the algorithm [ ]. In progress rate analysis the dynamic of this Markov chain is simplified and assumed to be constant.

In this paper, we investigate ESs with weighted recombination on a general convex quadratic function. Since the CMA-ES and most of the recent variants of CMA-ES [, ,] employ weighted recombination, weighted recombination ESs are among the most important categories of ESs. The first analysis of weighted recombination ESs were done in [ ], where the quality gain has been derived on the infinite dimensional sphere function $f : x \mapsto \|x\|^2$. Moreover, the optimal step-size and the optimal recombination weights are derived. The quality gain on a convex quadratic function has been studied in [,] for a variant of weighted recombination ESs called $(\mu/\mu_I, \lambda)$-ES that employs the truncation weights, where the weights for μ best candidate solutions are $1/\mu$ and the other weights are zero. We extend and generalize these results with a mathematically rigorous derivation.

The contributions of this paper are as follows.

First, the asymptotic quality gain of the weighted recombination evolution strategy on a convex quadratic function $f(x) = \frac{1}{2}(x - x^*)^{\mathrm{T}} \mathbf{A}(x - x^*)$ with Hessian $\mathbf{A}$ satisfying $\mathrm{Tr}(\mathbf{A}^2)/\mathrm{Tr}(\mathbf{A})^2 \ll 1$ is derived for the infinite dimensional search space. The recombination weights optimal for the quality gain turn out to be the same values as the ones derived for the infinite dimensional sphere function [ ]. It implies that the optimal weights derived for the infinite dimensional sphere function is optimal independently of the Hessian matrix $\mathbf{A}$ of the objective function and the covariance matrix $\mathbf{C}$ of the sampling distribution. Moreover, we

see the dependency of the quality gain on the eigenvalue distribution of the Hessian matrix. It provides a better understanding of the algorithm than our empirical knowledge that the convergence speed of the algorithm with a fixed covariance matrix is roughly proportional to $1/(N \, \mathrm{Cond}(\mathbf{AC}))$ when $\mathbf{C}$ is fixed, whereas our result reveals the dependency of the convergence speed not only on the condition number of $\mathbf{AC}$ but on the eigenvalue distribution of $\mathbf{AC}$ as long as $\mathrm{Tr}((\mathbf{AC})^2) \ll \mathrm{Tr}(\mathbf{AC})^2$. This may lead to a better algorithm design since such an empirical knowledge is used for algorithm design [ ].

Second, our proof is rather different from the derivations of the quality gain and the progress rate in previous works. On the one hand results derived in for instance [, ,] rely on a geometric intuition of the algorithm in the infinite dimensional search space and on various approximations. On the other hand, the rigorous derivation of the progress rate (or convergence rate of the algorithm with step-size proportional to the optimum) on the sphere function provided for instance in [,] only holds on spherical functions and provides solely a limit without a bound between the finite dimensional convergence rate and its asymptotic limit (see below). In contrast, we provide a novel and mathematically rigorous proof, based on the expression of the expectation of the recombination weights assigned to a given candidate solution as a function of the candidate solution. It is inspired by the previous work [ ].

Third, our result is not only asymptotic for N to infinity as opposed to previous rigorous results deriving progress rate [, ,] (see also [ ] for an overview of those results) but we provide an error bound between the finite dimensional quality gain and its limit. The bound shows the dependency of the convergence speed of the quality gain of the weighted recombination ES solving an arbitrary convex quadratic function to its limit on the recombination weights and the eigenvalue distribution of the Hessian matrix of the objective function. Thanks to the explicit bound, we can treat the population size increasing with the dimension of the search space and provide (for instance) a rigorous sufficient condition on the dependency between population size and N such that the per-iteration convergence rate scaling of $O(\lambda/N)$ holds for algorithms with intermediate recombination [ ].

This paper is organized as follows. In Section 2, we formally define the evolution strategy with weighted recombination. The quality gain analysis on the infinite dimensional sphere function is revisited. In Section 3, we derive the quality gain bound for a finite dimensional convex quadratic function. The asymptotic quality gain is derived as a consequence. We discuss how the eigenvalue distribution of the Hessian matrix of the objective function influences the quality gain and its convergence speed for $N \to \infty$. In Section 4, we conduct simulations to visualize the effect of different Hessian matrices, the dimension, the recombination weights, the learning rate for the mean vector update, and the step-size. In Section 5, we discuss further topics: the tightness of the derived bound, interpretation of the results for a fixed but non-identity covariance matrix, the dynamics of the mean vector on a convex quadratic function, the geometric interpretation of the optimal setting, the linear convergence proof using the quality gain analysis, and further related works.

---

[2]The algorithm is "artificial" in that the distance to the optimum is unavailable in practice.

[3]More precisely, $(1 \overset{+}{,} \lambda)$-ES optimizing any function f (that may have more than one global optimum) can not converge towards a given optimum x^* faster in the search space than the artificial algorithm with step-size proportional to the distance to x^*.

2. FORMULATION

2.1 Evolution Strategy with Weighted Recombination

We consider an evolution strategy with weighted recombination. At each iteration $t \geqslant 0$ it samples candidate solutions $X_1, \ldots, X_\lambda$ from the N-dimensional normal distribution $\mathcal{N}(\boldsymbol{m}^{(t)}, (\sigma^{(t)})^2 \mathbf{I})$, where $\boldsymbol{m}^{(t)} \in \mathbb{R}^N$ is the mean vector and $\sigma^{(t)} > 0$ is the standard deviation, also called the step-size or the mutation strength in the work of Beyer and his co-authors, e.g. [ ], and $\mathbf{I}$ is the identity matrix of dimension N. The candidate solutions are evaluated on a given objective function $f : \mathbb{R}^N \to \mathbb{R}$. W.l.g., we assume f to be minimized. Let $i : \lambda$ be the index of the ith best candidate solution among $X_1, \ldots, X_\lambda$, i.e., $f(X_{1:\lambda}) \leqslant \ldots \leqslant f(X_{\lambda:\lambda})$, and $w_1 \geqslant \cdots \geqslant w_\lambda$ be the weights. W.l.g., we assume $\sum_{i=1}^{\lambda} |w_i| = 1$. Let $\mu_w = 1/\sum_{i=1}^{\lambda} w_i^2$ denote the so-called effective variance selection mass. The mean vector is updated according to

$$\boldsymbol{m}^{(t+1)} = \boldsymbol{m}^{(t)} + c_m \sum_{i=1}^{\lambda} w_i(X_{i:\lambda} - \boldsymbol{m}^{(t)}) \, , \qquad (1)$$

where $c_m > 0$ is the learning rate of the mean vector update, i.e., $\kappa = 1/c_m$ is the ratio between the standard deviation σ and the step-size for the mean update $\sigma \cdot c_m$.

To proceed the analysis with a mathematical rigor, we introduce the weight function as follows

$$W(i; (X_k)_{k=1}^{\lambda}) := \sum_{k=1+l}^{u} \frac{w_k}{u - l}, \qquad (2)$$

where $\mathbb{I}\{\text{condition}\}$ is the indicator function which is 1 if the condition is true and 0 otherwise, and l and u are the numbers of strictly better candidate solutions and equally well or better candidate solutions than X_i, respectively, which are defined as follows

$$l = \sum_{j=1}^{\lambda} \mathbb{I}\{f(X_j) < f(X_i)\} \, , \qquad (3)$$

$$u = \sum_{j=1}^{\lambda} \mathbb{I}\{f(X_j) \leqslant f(X_i)\} \, . \qquad (4)$$

The weight value for X_i is the arithmetic average of the weights w_k for the tie candidate solutions. In other words, all the tie candidate solutions have the same weight values. If there is no tie, the weight value for the ith best candidate solution $X_{i:\lambda}$ is simply w_i. With the weight function, we rewrite the algorithm (1) as follows

$$\boldsymbol{m}^{(t+1)} = \boldsymbol{m}^{(t)} + c_m \sum_{i=1}^{\lambda} W(i; (X_k)_{k=1}^{\lambda})(X_i - \boldsymbol{m}^{(t)}) \, , \qquad (5)$$

or equivalently, letting $Z_k = (X_k - \boldsymbol{m}^{(t)})/\sigma^{(t)} \sim \mathcal{N}(\mathbf{0}, \mathbf{I})$,

$$\boldsymbol{m}^{(t+1)} = \boldsymbol{m}^{(t)} + c_m \sigma^{(t)} \sum_{i=1}^{\lambda} W(i; (\boldsymbol{m}^{(t)} + \sigma^{(t)} Z_k)_{k=1}^{\lambda}) Z_i \, . \qquad (6)$$

The above update (5) (or (6)) is equivalent with the original update (1) if there is no tie among λ candidate solutions. If the objective function is a convex quadratic function, there will be no tie with probability one (w.p.1). Therefore, they are equivalent w.p.1.

The motivation of the new formulation is twofold. One is to well define the update even when there is tie, which happens w.p.0, though. The other is a technical reason. In (1)

the already sorted candidate solutions $X_{i:\lambda}$ are all correlated and they are not anymore normally distributed. However, they are assumed to be normally distributed in the previous work [, ,]. To ensure that such an approximation leads to the asymptotically true quality gain limit, a mathematically involved analysis has to be done. See [, ,] for details. In (5) or (6), the ranking computation is a part of the weight function and X_i are still independent and normally distributed. This allows us in a rigorous and novel approach to derive the quality gain on a convex quadratic function.

In the analysis of this paper, we do not consider the adaptation of step-size $\sigma^{(t)}$. Instead we investigate the response of the progress measure to the input step-size $\sigma^{(t)} = \sigma$.

2.2 Quality Gain Analysis on a Spherical Function

In general, it is too difficult to analyze the Markov chain defined by rank-based stochastic algorithms on the continuous domain. One won't obtain the explicit formula of the convergence rate of an algorithm. Instead, we study the expected amount of the progress in one algorithmic iteration. The quality gain [,] is one of a common measure to evaluate such progress. It is defined as the expectation of the relative decrease of the function value. In this paper we define the quality gain as the conditional expectation of the relative decrease of the function value given the mean vector $\boldsymbol{m}^{(t)} = \boldsymbol{m}$ and the step-size $\sigma^{(t)} = \sigma$ as

$$\phi(\boldsymbol{m}, \sigma) = \frac{\mathbb{E}[f(\boldsymbol{m}^{(t)}) - f(\boldsymbol{m}^{(t+1)}) \mid \boldsymbol{m}^{(t)} = \boldsymbol{m}, \sigma^{(t)} = \sigma]}{f(\boldsymbol{m}^{(t)}) - f(x^*)} \, , \qquad (7)$$

where $x^* \in \mathbb{R}^N$ is (one of) the global minimum of f. Note that the quality gain depends also on the weights $(w_k)_{k=1}^{\lambda}$, the learning rate c_m, and the dimension N. To avoid division by zero, we assume that $\boldsymbol{m} \in \mathbb{R}^N \setminus \{x^*\}$.

In [ ], the algorithm (1) solving a spherical function $f(x) = \|x\|^2$ is analyzed. For this purpose, the *normalized step-size* and the *normalized quality gain* are introduced. The normalized step-size at $\boldsymbol{m}$ is defined as

$$\bar{\sigma} = \frac{\sigma c_m N}{\|\boldsymbol{m}\|} \, , \qquad (8)$$

and the normalized quality gain is defined as the quality gain ϕ scaled by $N/2$, namely,

$$\bar{\phi}(\boldsymbol{m}, \bar{\sigma}) = \frac{N}{2} \phi(\boldsymbol{m}, \sigma = \bar{\sigma}\|\boldsymbol{m}\|/(c_m N)) \, . \qquad (9)$$

It is stated that by taking $N \to \infty$, the normalized quality gain converges to the *asymptotic normalized quality gain*

$$\bar{\phi}_\infty(\bar{\sigma}, (w_k)_{k=1}^{\lambda}) = -\bar{\sigma} \sum_{i=1}^{\lambda} w_i \mathbb{E}[\mathcal{N}_{i:\lambda}] - \frac{\bar{\sigma}^2}{2} \sum_{i=1}^{\lambda} w_i^2 \, , \qquad (10)$$

where $\mathbb{E}[\mathcal{N}_{i:\lambda}]$ is the expected value of the ith smallest order statistics $\mathcal{N}_{i:\lambda}$ from λ independent populations sampled from the standard normal distribution (a formal proof of this result is presented in [ ] with the detailed proof for the uniform integrability done in [ ]). For a sufficiently large N, one can approximate the quality gain as $\phi(\boldsymbol{m}, \sigma) \approx (N/2)\bar{\phi}_\infty(\bar{\sigma} = \sigma c_m N/\|\boldsymbol{m}\|, (w_k)_{k=1}^{\lambda})$.

Consider the optimal parameter setting that maximize $\bar{\phi}_\infty(\bar{\sigma}, (w_k)_{k=1}^{\lambda})$ in (10). Remember $\sum_{i=1}^{\lambda} |w_i| = 1$ and $\mu_w = 1/\sum_{i=1}^{\lambda} w_i^2$. The optimal weights w_i^* are

$$w_i^* = -\frac{\mathbb{E}[\mathcal{N}_{i:\lambda}]}{\sum_{i=1}^{\lambda} |\mathbb{E}[\mathcal{N}_{i:\lambda}]|} \, . \qquad (11)$$

Moreover, given $(w_k)_{k=1}^{\lambda}$, the optimal normalized step-size $\bar{\sigma}^*$ is

$$\bar{\sigma}^*((w_k)_{k=1}^{\lambda}) = -\mu_w \sum_{i=1}^{\lambda} w_i \mathbb{E}[\mathcal{N}_{i:\lambda}] \ . \tag{12}$$

The optimal value of the asymptotic normalized quality gain is $\bar{\phi}_{\infty}(\bar{\sigma}^*((w_k^*)_{k=1}^{\lambda}), (w_k^*)_{k=1}^{\lambda}) = \frac{1}{2}\sum_{i=1}^{\lambda}\mathbb{E}[\mathcal{N}_{i:\lambda}]^2$, which is roughly estimated by $\lambda/2$ if λ is sufficiently large, say $\lambda \geqslant 10^2$. Therefore, the quality gain is approximated by λ/N.

We have three remarks on the optimal normalized quality gain. First, it tells that the quality gain is proportional to $1/N$. Note that we know from [ ] that a comparison-based algorithm can not achieve the convergence rate better than $1/N$. One can not expect a faster convergence except a constant factor. Second, the quality gain is to measure the improvement in one iteration. If we generate and evaluate λ candidate solutions every iteration, the quality gain per evaluation (f-call) is $1/\lambda$ times smaller, i.e., the quality gain per evaluation is $1/N$, rather than λ/N. It implies that the number of iterations to achieve the same amount of the quality gain is inversely proportional to λ, which is ideal when the algorithm is implemented on a parallel computer. The third remark is that the result is obtained in the limit $N \to \infty$ while λ is fixed. Therefore, it is implicitly assumed that $\lambda \ll N$. The second remark above holds only when $\lambda \ll N$. In practice, the quality gain per iteration tends to level out as λ increases.

Figure 1 shows how the asymptotic normalized quality gain divided by λ scales with λ when the optimal step-size $\sigma = \|\boldsymbol{m}\|\bar{\sigma}^*((w_k)_{k=1}^{\lambda})/(c_m N)$ is employed. Four different weights schemes are employed, the optimal weights ($w_k \propto -\mathbb{E}[\mathcal{N}_{k:\lambda}]$), the weights used in the CMA-ES ($w_k \propto \max(\ln\left(\frac{\lambda+1}{2}\right) - \ln(k), 0)$), and the truncation weights ($w_k = 1/\mu$ for $k = 1, \ldots, \mu$ and $w_k = 0$ for $k = \mu+1, \ldots, \lambda$) with $\mu = \lfloor \lambda/4 \rfloor$ and $\mu = \lfloor \lambda/10 \rfloor$. All the weights are scaled so that $\sum_{k=1}^{\lambda}|w_k| = 1$. The expected value of the normal order statistics $\mathcal{N}_{i:\lambda}$ for $i \leqslant \lceil \lambda/2 \rceil$ is approximated by the Blom's formula

$$\mathbb{E}[\mathcal{N}_{i:\lambda}] \approx \Phi^{-1}\left(\frac{i-\alpha}{\lambda-2\alpha+1}\right), \quad \alpha = 0.375 \ , \tag{13}$$

where Φ is the cumulative density function of the standard normal distribution. Note that $\mathbb{E}[\mathcal{N}_{1:\lambda}] < \cdots < \mathbb{E}[\mathcal{N}_{\lambda:\lambda}]$ and $\mathbb{E}[\mathcal{N}_{i:\lambda}] = -\mathbb{E}[\mathcal{N}_{\lambda-i:\lambda}]$. When the optimal weights are used, it goes up to 0.5 as λ increases (implying $\sum_{k=1}^{\lambda}|\mathbb{E}[\mathcal{N}_{i:\lambda}]| \approx \lambda$ for a sufficiently large λ). On the other hand, the quality gain with only nonnegative weights can not be above 0.25, which will be obtained if the first half of the weights are proportional to the optimal setting and the last half of the weights are zero. The CMA type weights well approximate the optimal nonnegative weights.

The optimal step-size (12) depends on $(w_k)_{k=1}^{\lambda}$, in particular, depends on μ. For example, consider the truncation weights with a fixed ratio λ/μ. Then, we find $\bar{\sigma}^* = \sum_{i=1}^{\mu}(-\mathbb{E}[\mathcal{N}_{i:\lambda}]) \in \Theta(\mu)$. It implies that the optimal step-size is roughly proportional to μ. However, since the optimality holds for $N \to \infty$ while λ is fixed, it is implicitly assumed that $\lambda \ll N$. Therefore, $\bar{\sigma}^* \in \Theta(\mu)$ may not hold if $\lambda \not\ll N$.

The asymptotic normalized quality gain (10) can be seen as a quadratic function of $\bar{\sigma}$. Figure 2 shows how the normalized quality gain divided by λ scales with $\bar{\sigma}/\bar{\sigma}^*$. The maximum normalized quality gain is reached when $\bar{\sigma}/\bar{\sigma}^* = 1$. With a smaller step-size, we observe a slower convergence.

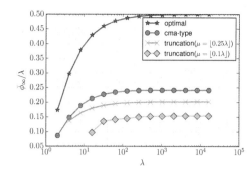

Figure 1: The asymptotic normalized quality gain $\bar{\phi}_{\infty}(\bar{\sigma}^*((w_k)_{k=1}^{\lambda}), (w_k)_{k=1}^{\lambda})$ divided by λ vs λ.

On the other hand, we observe a rapid drop of the normalized quality gain if we increase the step-size. With $\bar{\sigma}/\bar{\sigma}^* = 2$, we see no progress. With a larger step-size, we observe the negative progress, i.e., the divergence of the mean vector.

The normalized quality gain depends only on the normalized step-size $\bar{\sigma}$ and the weights $(w_k)_{k=1}^{\lambda}$. Since the normalized step-size does not change if we multiply c_m by some factor and divide σ by some factor, one can say that c_m doesn't have any impact on the asymptotic normalized quality gain, hence on the quality gain, as long as σc_m is constant. This is unintuitive and not true in a finite dimensional space. The step-size σ realizes the standard deviation of the sampling distribution and it has an impact on the ranking of the candidate solutions. On the other hand, the product σc_m is the step-size of the $\boldsymbol{m}$-update, which must depend on the ranking of the candidate solutions. The asymptotic normalized quality gain provided above tells us that the ranking of the candidate solutions is independent of $\bar{\sigma}$ in the infinite dimensional space.

3. QUALITY GAIN ANALYSIS ON A GENERAL QUADRATIC FUNCTION

In this section we derive the normalized quality gain bound and the asymptotic normalized quality gain of the weighted recombination ES (1) minimizing a quadratic function with its Hessian $\nabla\nabla f(x) = \mathbf{A}$ assumed to be nonnegative definite and symmetric, i.e.,

$$f(x) = \frac{1}{2}(x - x^*)^{\mathrm{T}}\mathbf{A}(x - x^*) \ , \tag{14}$$

where $x^* \in \mathbb{R}^N$ is the global optimal solution[4]. The performance of an algorithm on a quadratic function is essential to understand the local behavior of the algorithm since an arbitrary twice continuously differentiable function can be approximated by a quadratic function locally.

3.1 Normalized Quality Gain and Normalized Step-Size

We introduce the normalized step-size and the normalized quality gain as we did in (8) and (9) for the sphere function. First of all, if the objective function is homogeneous around the optimal solution x^*, the optimal step-size must be a

---

[4]A nonnegative definite matrix $\mathbf{A}$ is a matrix having only nonnegative eigenvalues, i.e., $x^{\mathrm{T}}\mathbf{A}x \geqslant 0$ for all $x \in \mathbb{R}^N$. If $\mathbf{A}$ is not full rank, i.e., it has a zero eigenvalue, the optimum x^* is not unique.

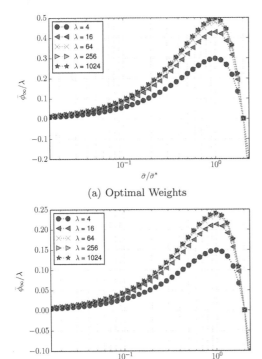

(a) Optimal Weights

(b) CMA Weights

Figure 2: The asymptotic normalized quality gain divided by λ vs the normalized step-size ratio $\bar{\sigma}/\bar{\sigma}^*$. The results for the population size $\lambda = 4^i$ for $i = 1, 2, 3, 4, 5$ are shown.

homogeneous function of degree one with respect to $\boldsymbol{m} - x^*$. This is formally stated in the following proposition. The proof is found in Appendix A.

PROPOSITION 3.1. *Let $f : \mathbb{R}^N \to \mathbb{R}$ be a homogeneous function of degree n, i.e., $f(\alpha \cdot x) = \alpha^n f(x)$ for a fixed integer $n > 0$ for any $\alpha > 0$ and any $x \in \mathbb{R}^N$. Consider the weighted recombination ES (1) minimizing a function $g : x \mapsto f(x - x^*)$. Then, the quality gain is scale-invariant, i.e., $\phi(x^* + (\boldsymbol{m} - x^*), \sigma) = \phi(x^* + \alpha(\boldsymbol{m} - x^*), \alpha\sigma)$ for any $\alpha > 0$. Moreover, the optimal step-size $\sigma^* = \mathrm{argmax}_{\sigma \geq 0} \phi(\boldsymbol{m}, \sigma)$, if it is well-defined, is a function of $\boldsymbol{m} - x^*$. For the sake of simplicity we write the optimal step-size as a map $\sigma^* : \boldsymbol{m} - x^* \mapsto \sigma^*(\boldsymbol{m} - x^*)$. It is a homogeneous function of degree 1, i.e., $\sigma^*(\alpha \cdot (\boldsymbol{m} - x^*)) = \alpha\sigma^*(\boldsymbol{m} - x^*)$ for any $\alpha > 0$.*

Note that the function $\boldsymbol{m} \mapsto \|\nabla f(\boldsymbol{m})\| = \|\mathbf{A}(\boldsymbol{m} - x^*)\|$ is homogeneous of degree one around x^*. However, this function is not invariant to scaling of a function, i.e., scaling of Hessian $\mathbf{A}$. To make it scale invariant, we will divide it by the trace $\mathrm{Tr}(\mathbf{A})$ of Hessian $\mathbf{A}$. Therefore, the function $\boldsymbol{m} \mapsto \|\nabla f(\boldsymbol{m})\|/\mathrm{Tr}(\mathbf{A})$ is our candidate for the optimal step-size. We define the normalized step-size and the scale-invariant step-size for a quadratic function as follows.

DEFINITION 3.2. *For a quadratic function (14), the normalized step-size $\bar{\sigma} > 0$ is defined as*

$$\bar{\sigma} = \frac{\sigma c_m \mathrm{Tr}(\mathbf{A})}{\|\nabla f(\boldsymbol{m})\|} . \tag{15}$$

In other words, the step-size is given by

$$\sigma = \frac{\bar{\sigma}\|\nabla f(\boldsymbol{m})\|}{c_m \mathrm{Tr}(\mathbf{A})} . \tag{16}$$

We call it the scale-invariant step-size *for a quadratic function* (14).

The normalized quality gain of weighted recombination ES with scale-invariant step-size on a quadratic function is then defined as follows.

DEFINITION 3.3. *Let $g : \mathbb{R}^N \to \mathbb{R}$ be the $\boldsymbol{m}$-dependent scaling factor of the normalized quality gain defined by*

$$g(\boldsymbol{m}) = \frac{\|\nabla f(\boldsymbol{m})\|^2}{f(\boldsymbol{m}) \mathrm{Tr}(\mathbf{A})} . \tag{17}$$

The normalized quality gain for a quadratic function is defined as

$$\bar{\phi}(\boldsymbol{m}, \bar{\sigma}) = \frac{\phi(\boldsymbol{m}, \sigma = \bar{\sigma}\|\nabla f(\boldsymbol{m})\|/(c_m \mathrm{Tr}(\mathbf{A})))}{g(\boldsymbol{m})} . \tag{18}$$

In other words,

$$\phi(\boldsymbol{m}, \sigma = \bar{\sigma}\|\nabla f(\boldsymbol{m})\|/(c_m \mathrm{Tr}(\mathbf{A}))) = g(\boldsymbol{m})\bar{\phi}(\boldsymbol{m}, \bar{\sigma}) . \tag{19}$$

Note that the normalized step-size and the normalized quality gain defined above agree with (8) and (9), respectively, if $f(x) = \|x\|^2$, where $\mathbf{A} = 2\mathbf{I}$, $\nabla f(\boldsymbol{m}) = \boldsymbol{m}$ and $g(\boldsymbol{m}) = 2/N$. Moreover, they are equivalent to Eq. (4.104) in [ ] introduced to analyze the $(1+\lambda)$-ES and the $(1, \lambda)$-ES. The same normalized step-size has been used for $(\mu/\mu_I, \lambda)$-ES [12,]. See Section 4.3.1 of [ ] for the motivation of these normalization.

3.2 Theorem: Normalized Quality Gain on Convex Quadratic Functions

The following theorem provides an upper bound of the difference between the normalized quality gain on a finite dimensional convex quadratic function and the asymptotic normalized quality gain derived on the sphere function.

THEOREM 3.4 (NORMALIZED QUALITY GAIN BOUND). *Consider the weighted recombination evolution strategy (6) solving a convex quadratic function (14). Let the normalized step-size and the normalized quality gain defined as (15) and (18). Then,*

$$\sup_{\boldsymbol{m} \in \mathbb{R}^N \setminus \{x^*\}} \left| \bar{\phi}(\boldsymbol{m}, \bar{\sigma}) - \bar{\phi}_\infty(\bar{\sigma}, (w_k)_{k=1}^\lambda) \right|$$

$$\leqslant \frac{3}{(4\pi)^{\frac{1}{3}}} \frac{\bar{\sigma}^{\frac{5}{3}}}{c_m^{\frac{2}{3}}} \lambda(\lambda - 1) \max_{k \in [\![1, \lambda-1]\!]} |w_{k+1} - w_k| \left[\frac{\mathrm{Tr}(\mathbf{A}^2)}{\mathrm{Tr}(\mathbf{A})^2} \right]^{\frac{1}{3}}$$

$$+ \frac{\bar{\sigma}^2}{2^{\frac{1}{2}}} \left[\left[(\lambda^2 - \lambda) \sum_{k=1}^\lambda \sum_{l=k+1}^\lambda w_k^2 w_l^2 \right]^{\frac{1}{2}} \right.$$

$$\left. + \left[\lambda \sum_{k=1}^\lambda w_k^4 \right]^{\frac{1}{2}} \right] \left[\frac{\mathrm{Tr}(\mathbf{A}^2)}{\mathrm{Tr}(\mathbf{A})^2} \right]^{\frac{1}{2}} , \tag{20}$$

where $\bar{\phi}_\infty(\bar{\sigma}, (w_k)_{k=1}^\lambda)$ is the function defined in (10).

The first consequence of Theorem 3.4 is the generalization of the infinite dimensional analysis on the sphere function in [ ] to a convex quadratic function. Let $(\mathbf{A}_N)_{N \in \mathbb{N}}$ be the sequence of Hessian matrices $\mathbf{A}_N$ of a convex quadratic function (14) of dimension $N \in \mathbb{N}_+$. Under the condition

$\mathrm{Tr}(\mathbf{A}_N^2)/\mathrm{Tr}(\mathbf{A}_N)^2 \to 0$ as $N \to \infty$, we can prove that the normalized quality gain defined in (18) converges to the unique limit $\bar{\phi}_\infty(\bar{\sigma}, (w_k)_{k=1}^\lambda)$. In particular, the limit agrees with the one of (10) derived for the sphere function. The following corollary formalizes it, which can be immediately derived from Theorem 3.4.

COROLLARY 3.5 (NORMALIZED QUALITY GAIN LIMIT). *Suppose that* $\mathrm{Tr}(\mathbf{A}_N^2)/\mathrm{Tr}(\mathbf{A}_N)^2 \to 0$ *as* $N \to \infty$. *Then,*

$$\lim_{N\to\infty} \sup_{\boldsymbol{m}\in\mathbb{R}^N\setminus\{x^*\}} \left|\bar{\phi}(\boldsymbol{m},\bar{\sigma}) - \bar{\phi}_\infty(\bar{\sigma},(w_k)_{k=1}^\lambda)\right| = 0 \ . \quad (21)$$

It tells that the quality gain on a convex quadratic function with Hessian $\mathbf{A}$ such that $\mathrm{Tr}(\mathbf{A}^2) \ll \mathrm{Tr}(\mathbf{A})^2$ under the scale-invariant step-size (Definition 3.2) is approximated by the product of the normalization factor $g(\boldsymbol{m})$ and the asymptotical normalized quality gain as

$$\phi(\boldsymbol{m},\sigma) = g(\boldsymbol{m})\bar{\phi}(\boldsymbol{m},\bar{\sigma}) \approx g(\boldsymbol{m})\bar{\phi}_\infty(\bar{\sigma},(w_k)_{k=1}^\lambda)$$
$$= \frac{\|\nabla f(\boldsymbol{m})\|^2}{f(\boldsymbol{m})\,\mathrm{Tr}(\mathbf{A})}\left[-\bar{\sigma}\sum_{i=1}^\lambda w_i\mathbb{E}[\mathcal{N}_{i:\lambda}] - \frac{\bar{\sigma}^2}{2}\sum_{i=1}^\lambda w_i^2\right] . \quad (22)$$

Asymptotically, the quality gain can be decomposed in two parts: the normalization factor $g(\boldsymbol{m})$ that depends on the mean vector and the eigenvalue distribution of $\mathbf{A}$, and the asymptotic normalized quality gain that depends on the normalized step-size and the recombination weights. Note that the RHS of (22) agrees with the limit of the one derived for the $(1,\lambda)$-ES (Eq. (4.108) in [ ]) if $c_m = 1$, $w_1 = 1$ and $w_i = 0$ for $i \geqslant 2$.[5] Moreover, it coincides with the limit of the quality gain for $(\mu/\mu_I,\lambda)$-ES deduced from the results obtained in [,] if $c_m = 1$, $w_i = 1/\mu$ for $i = 1,\ldots,\mu$ and $w_i = 0$ for $i = \mu+1,\ldots,\lambda$.

The second consequence is a further generalization of Corollary 3.5 that allows us to take λ increasing to $+\infty$ as $N \to \infty$. It reflects the practical setting that we often set λ dependently on N. The optimal normalized step-size $\bar{\sigma}^*$ (with a slight abuse of notation) given in (12) depends on $(w_k)_{k=1}^\lambda$ and typically scales up in the order of $O(\lambda)$. Moreover, if $\bar{\sigma} = \beta\bar{\sigma}^*$ for some $\beta \in (0,2)$, the asymptotic normalized quality gain is

$$\bar{\phi}_\infty(\beta\bar{\sigma}^*,(w_k)_{k=1}^\lambda) = (\beta - \beta^2/2)(\bar{\sigma}^*)^2\sum_{i=1}^\lambda w_i^2$$
$$= (\beta - \beta^2/2)\mu_w(\textstyle\sum_{i=1}^\lambda w_i\mathbb{E}[\mathcal{N}_{i:\lambda}])^2,$$

where the right-most side is maximized when $w_i \propto -\mathbb{E}[\mathcal{N}_{i:\lambda}]$ and the maximum value is $(\beta - \beta^2/2)\sum_{i=1}^\lambda|\mathbb{E}[\mathcal{N}_{i:\lambda}]| \in \Theta(\lambda)$ (see (25) below). Since both the normalized step-size and the normalized quality gain typically diverges towards infinity, the convergence of the normalized quality gain pointwise with respect to $\bar{\sigma}$ such as (21) is not sufficient. In the following, we provide a sufficient condition to show the convergence of the error rate between the normalized quality gain and the asymptotic normalized quality gain uniformly for $\bar{\sigma} \in [\epsilon\bar{\sigma}^*, (2-\epsilon)\bar{\sigma}^*]$.

---

[5]In [ ], the author claims that the condition on $\mathbf{A}$ to obtain the limit (22) for $N \to \infty$ is $\bar{\sigma}\,\mathrm{Tr}(\mathbf{A}^2)^{\frac{1}{2}} \ll \mathrm{Tr}(\mathbf{A})$ (Eq. (4.107) in [ ], called the Sphere model condition). It can be satisfied if $\bar{\sigma} \ll 1$ but $\mathrm{Tr}(\mathbf{A}^2)^{\frac{1}{2}} \approx \mathrm{Tr}(\mathbf{A})$, however, $d_1(\mathbf{A}) \ll \mathrm{Tr}(\mathbf{A})$ is assumed to derive Eq. (4.108) and is not satisfied when $\mathrm{Tr}(\mathbf{A}^2)^{\frac{1}{2}} \approx \mathrm{Tr}(\mathbf{A})$. In Theorem 3.4, if we have $\bar{\sigma} \to \infty$ but $\mathrm{Tr}(\mathbf{A}^2)^{\frac{1}{2}} \ll \mathrm{Tr}(\mathbf{A})$, both LHS and RHS of (20) converge to zero, but the RHS converges faster.

COROLLARY 3.6. *Let* λ_N *be the population size for the dimension* N *and* $(w_k^{(N)})_{k=1}^{\lambda_N}$ *be the sequence of weights of length* λ_N. *Let* $\bar{\sigma}_N^*$ *be the optimal normalized step-size defined in* (12) *given* $(w_k^{(N)})_{k=1}^{\lambda_N}$. *Suppose that*

$$\max\left[\lambda^2, \frac{\lambda^6\mu_w^2\max_k|w_{k+1}-w_k|^3}{-\sum_{i=1}^\lambda w_i\mathbb{E}[\mathcal{N}_{i:\lambda}]}\right] \in o\left[\frac{\mathrm{Tr}(\mathbf{A}_N)^2}{\mathrm{Tr}(\mathbf{A}_N^2)}\right] , \quad (23)$$

where $\max_k$ *is taken over* $k \in [\![1, \lambda-1]\!]$. *Then, for any* $\epsilon \in (0,1)$,

$$\lim_{N\to\infty} \sup_{\bar{\sigma}} \sup_{\boldsymbol{m}\in\mathbb{R}^N\setminus\{x^*\}} \frac{\left|\bar{\phi}(\boldsymbol{m},\bar{\sigma}) - \bar{\phi}_\infty(\bar{\sigma},(w_k^{(N)})_{k=1}^{\lambda_N})\right|}{\bar{\phi}_\infty(\bar{\sigma},(w_k^{(N)})_{k=1}^{\lambda_N})} = 0 , \quad (24)$$

where $\sup_{\bar{\sigma}}$ *is taken over* $\bar{\sigma} \in [\epsilon\bar{\sigma}_N^*, (2-\epsilon)\bar{\sigma}_N^*]$.

Consider, for example, the truncation weights with the number of parents μ_N and the sphere function ($\mathbf{A} = 2\mathbf{I}$). Then, the condition reads $\lambda_N^6/(-\sum_{i=1}^{\mu_N}\mathbb{E}[\mathcal{N}_{i:\lambda}]) \in o(N)$. In particular, if λ_N/μ_N is constant (or upper bounded), it reads $\lambda_N^5 \in o(N)$. If μ_N is upper bounded, then the condition reads $\lambda_N^6 \in o(N)$. If we consider the optimal weights (11), using the trivial inequality $|w_{k+1}-w_k| \leqslant |w_\lambda - w_1|$ and the fact (see for example Example 8.1.1 in [ ]) that

$$\lim_{\lambda\to\infty} \frac{\mathbb{E}[\mathcal{N}_{\lambda:\lambda}] - \mathbb{E}[\mathcal{N}_{1:\lambda}]}{2(2\ln(\lambda))^{\frac{1}{2}}} = 1 ,$$
$$\lim_{\lambda\to\infty} \frac{1}{\lambda}\sum_{i=1}^\lambda\mathbb{E}[\mathcal{N}_{i:\lambda}]^2 = 1 , \quad (25)$$
$$\lim_{\lambda\to\infty} \frac{1}{\lambda}\sum_{i=1}^\lambda|\mathbb{E}[\mathcal{N}_{i:\lambda}]| = \left(\frac{2}{\pi}\right)^{\frac{1}{2}} ,$$

the condition reads $\lambda_N^5(\ln(\lambda_N))^{\frac{3}{2}} \in o(N)$. In the state-of-the-art algorithm, namely the CMA-ES, the default population size is $\lambda_N = 4 + \lfloor 3\ln(N)\rfloor$ and the weights are similar to the positive part of the optimal weights and the others are zero. This case fits in Corollary 3.6 as well.

This condition $\lambda_N \in o(N^{1/6})$ is a rigorous (but seemingly not tight) bound for the scaling of λ such that the per-iteration convergence rate of a $(\mu/\mu, \lambda)$-ES with a fixed λ/μ on the sphere function scales like $O(\lambda/N)$ [, Equation 6.140].

Remark that contrary to the spherical case where we can show that for any dimension, the algorithm with scale-invariant step-size $\sigma = \sigma^{\mathrm{opt}}\|x - x^*\|$ (for a proper choice of constant σ^{opt} and optimal weights) is optimal [,], we cannot prove here the optimality of the scale-invariant step-size (16) for a finite dimension. However for a quadratic function with $\mathrm{Tr}(\mathbf{A}^2) \ll \mathrm{Tr}(\mathbf{A})^2$, the algorithm with the scale-invariant step-size (16) achieves the quality gain greater than $1 - \epsilon$ times the optimal quality gain $g(\boldsymbol{m})\bar{\phi}_\infty$, where $\epsilon > 0$ is the right-hand side of (20) divided by $\bar{\phi}_\infty$.

3.3 Effect of the Eigenvalue Distribution of the Hessian Matrix

The theorem tells that the optimal weights are the same on any infinite dimensional quadratic function satisfying the condition $\mathrm{Tr}(\mathbf{A}^2)/\mathrm{Tr}(\mathbf{A})^2 \to 0$. In particular, the optimal weights on such quadratic functions are the same as the optimal weights on the infinite dimensional sphere function. It is a nice feature since we do not need to tune the weight values depending on the function.

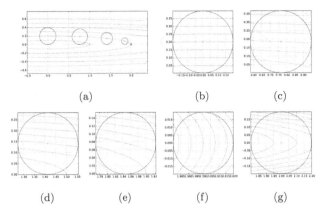

$$(a) \qquad (b) \qquad (c)$$

$$(d) \qquad (e) \qquad (f) \qquad (g)$$

Figure 3: The scale-invariant step-size on $f(x) = x^{\mathrm{T}}\mathbf{A}x/2$ with $\mathbf{A} = \mathrm{diag}(1, 100)$. (a) The circles with radius $\|\nabla f(\boldsymbol{m})\|/\mathrm{Tr}(\mathbf{A})$ centered at $\boldsymbol{m} = 2\mathbf{A}^{-\frac{1}{2}}[\cos(\theta), \sin(\theta)]^{\mathrm{T}}$ with $\theta = \frac{1}{2}\pi, \frac{3}{8}\pi, \frac{1}{4}\pi, \frac{1}{8}\pi, 0$. (b–f) The contour lines focused in each circle. (g) The contour lines focused in the circle with the same radius as (b) centered at the same point as (f).

The optimal normalized step-size and the optimal normalized quality gain are independent of $\mathbf{A}$. However, the step-size and the quality gain depends on it. When the weights and the normalized step-size are fixed, the step-size and quality gain are

$$\sigma = \frac{\bar{\sigma}}{c_m}\frac{\|\nabla f(\boldsymbol{m})\|}{\mathrm{Tr}(\mathbf{A})}, \quad \phi(\boldsymbol{m}, \sigma) = g(\boldsymbol{m})\bar{\phi}_\infty(\bar{\sigma}, (w_k)_{k=1}^\lambda) \ . \quad (26)$$

Since $\nabla f(\boldsymbol{m}) = \mathbf{A}(\boldsymbol{m} - x^*)$, we have

$$\frac{d_N(\mathbf{A})}{\mathrm{Tr}(\mathbf{A})}\|\boldsymbol{m} - x^*\| \leqslant \frac{\|\nabla f(\boldsymbol{m})\|}{\mathrm{Tr}(\mathbf{A})} \leqslant \frac{d_1(\mathbf{A})}{\mathrm{Tr}(\mathbf{A})}\|\boldsymbol{m} - x^*\|$$

$$\frac{d_N(\mathbf{A})}{\mathrm{Tr}(\mathbf{A})} \leqslant \frac{g(\boldsymbol{m})}{2} \leqslant \frac{d_1(\mathbf{A})}{\mathrm{Tr}(\mathbf{A})} \ ,$$

where $d_i(\mathbf{A})$ are the ith greatest eigenvalue of $\mathbf{A}$. The lower and upper equalities for both of the above inequalities hold if and only if $\boldsymbol{m} - x^*$ is parallel to the eigenspace corresponding to the smallest and largest eigenvalues of $\mathbf{A}$, respectively.

On the surface of the hyper ellipsoid centered at the optimum x^*, the optimal step-size can be different by the factor of at most $\mathrm{Cond}(\mathbf{A}) = d_1(\mathbf{A})/d_N(\mathbf{A})$. This is visualized in Figure 3. Each circle corresponds to the equal density line of the normal distribution with the mean $\boldsymbol{m}$ and the standard deviation $\|\nabla f(\boldsymbol{m})\|/\mathrm{Tr}(\mathbf{A})$. If we focus on the area around each circle, which is the right area to look at since the candidate solutions are produced around there, the function landscape looks like a parabolic ridge function.

In the above discussion we assumed that $\mathbf{A}$ is positive definite, i.e., $d_1(\mathbf{A}) \geqslant \ldots \geqslant d_N(\mathbf{A}) > 0$. However, the condition $\mathrm{Tr}(\mathbf{A}^2)/\mathrm{Tr}(\mathbf{A})^2 \to 0$ can be met even if $\mathbf{A}$ is positive semidefinite. Let M be the mathematical rank of $\mathbf{A}$. That is, $d_1(\mathbf{A}) \geqslant \ldots \geqslant d_M(\mathbf{A}) > 0$ and $d_{M+1}(\mathbf{A}) = \cdots = d_N(\mathbf{A})$. In this case, the kernel of $\mathbf{A}$ (the eigenspace corresponding to zero eigenvalue) does not affect the objective function value. The condition $\mathrm{Tr}(\mathbf{A}^2)/\mathrm{Tr}(\mathbf{A})^2 \to 0$ requires the dimension M of the effective search space to tend to the infinity as $N \to \infty$. Let $\boldsymbol{m}^+$ and $\boldsymbol{m}^-$ be the decomposition of $\boldsymbol{m}$ such that $\boldsymbol{m}^-$ is the projection of $\boldsymbol{m}$ onto the subspace through x^* spanned by the eigenvectors of $\mathbf{A}$ corresponding to the

zero eigenvalue, and $\boldsymbol{m}^+ = \boldsymbol{m} - \boldsymbol{m}^-$. Then, we have

$$\frac{d_M(\mathbf{A})}{\mathrm{Tr}(\mathbf{A})} \leqslant \frac{g(\boldsymbol{m})}{2} \leqslant \frac{d_1(\mathbf{A})}{\mathrm{Tr}(\mathbf{A})}$$

$$\frac{d_M(\mathbf{A})}{\mathrm{Tr}(\mathbf{A})}\|\boldsymbol{m}^+\| \leqslant \frac{\|\nabla f(\boldsymbol{m})\|}{\mathrm{Tr}(\mathbf{A})} \leqslant \frac{d_1(\mathbf{A})}{\mathrm{Tr}(\mathbf{A})}\|\boldsymbol{m}^+\| \ .$$

In this case, $g(\boldsymbol{m})$ can be $2/M$ if $d_1(\mathbf{A}) = \cdots = d_M(\mathbf{A}) > 0$ and $d_i(\mathbf{A}) = 0$ for $i \in [\![M+1, N]\!]$. The quality gain is then proportional to $2/M$, instead of $2/N$. That is, the optimal evolution strategy (evolution strategy with the optimal step-size) solves the quadratic function with the effective rank M defined on the N dimensional search space as efficiently as it solves its projection onto the effective search space (hence n dimensional search space).

Table 1 summarizes $d_N(\mathbf{A})/\mathrm{Tr}(\mathbf{A})$ and $d_1(\mathbf{A})/\mathrm{Tr}(\mathbf{A})$, which are the lower and upper bound of $g(\boldsymbol{m})/2$, and $\mathrm{Tr}(\mathbf{A}^2)/\mathrm{Tr}(\mathbf{A})^2$ for different types of $\mathbf{A}$. Note that the lower bound and the upper bound of $g(\boldsymbol{m})$, i.e., the worst and the best possible quality gain coefficients, are $d_N(\mathbf{A})/\mathrm{Tr}(\mathbf{A})$ and $d_1(\mathbf{A})/\mathrm{Tr}(\mathbf{A})$, respectively. The value of the fraction $\mathrm{Tr}(\mathbf{A}^2)/\mathrm{Tr}(\mathbf{A})^2$ tells us how fast the normalized quality gain converges as $N \to \infty$. If the condition number $\alpha = \mathrm{Cond}(\mathbf{A})$ is fixed, the worst case is maximized when the function has a discus type structure ($d_1(\mathbf{A}) = \alpha$ and $d_2(\mathbf{A}) = \cdots = d_N(\mathbf{A}) = 1$), and is minimized when the function has a cigar type structure ($d_1(\mathbf{A}) = \cdots = d_{N-1}(\mathbf{A}) = \alpha$ and $d_N(\mathbf{A}) = 1$). The value of $d_N(\mathbf{A})/\mathrm{Tr}(\mathbf{A})$ will be close to $1/N$ as $N \to \infty$ for the discus type function, whereas it will be close to $1/(N\alpha)$ for the cigar. Therefore, if $N \gg \alpha$, the worst case quality gain on the discus type function is as high as the quality gain on the spherical function, whereas the worst case quality gain on the cigar function is $1/\alpha$ times smaller. On the other hand, the inequality $\mathrm{Tr}(\mathbf{A}^2)/\mathrm{Tr}(\mathbf{A})^2 < 1/(N-1)$ on the cigar type function holds independently of α, while $\mathrm{Tr}(\mathbf{A}^2)/\mathrm{Tr}(\mathbf{A})^2$ depends heavily on α on the discus type function. The fraction will not be sufficiently small and we can not approximate the normalized quality gain by Theorem 3.4 unless $\alpha \ll N$. Therefore, the theorem is not appropriate for functions of discus type if the condition number is higher than the dimension of interest[6].

3.4 Proof of the Theorem

Here we sketch the main line of the proof of Theorem 3.4. First we expand the normalized quality gain. Let

$$\mathbf{e} = \nabla f(\boldsymbol{m})/\|\nabla f(\boldsymbol{m})\| \ . \quad (27)$$

With (15), it is easy to see that

$$f(\boldsymbol{m} + \sigma z) - f(\boldsymbol{m})$$

$$= \frac{\|\nabla f(\boldsymbol{m})\|^2}{\mathrm{Tr}(\mathbf{A})}\left(\frac{\bar{\sigma}}{c_m}\mathbf{e}^{\mathrm{T}}z + \frac{1}{2}\left(\frac{\bar{\sigma}}{c_m}\right)^2\frac{z^{\mathrm{T}}\mathbf{A}z}{\mathrm{Tr}(\mathbf{A})}\right) \ . \quad (28)$$

Using (28) with $z = (\boldsymbol{m}^{(t+1)} - \boldsymbol{m}^{(t)})/\sigma$, the normalized quality gain on a convex quadratic function can be written as

$$\bar{\phi}(\boldsymbol{m}, \bar{\sigma}) = -\left(\bar{\sigma}\sum_{i=1}^\lambda \mathbb{E}[W(i; (X_k)_{k=1}^\lambda)\mathbf{e}^{\mathrm{T}}Z_i] + \right.$$

$$\left. \frac{\bar{\sigma}^2}{2}\sum_{i=1}^\lambda\sum_{j=1}^\lambda \mathbb{E}\left[W(i; (X_k)_{k=1}^\lambda)W(j; (X_k)_{k=1}^\lambda)\frac{Z_i^{\mathrm{T}}\mathbf{A}Z_j}{\mathrm{Tr}(\mathbf{A})}\right]\right) \ , \quad (29)$$

---

[6]However, the worst case scenario on the discus type function, $1/(\alpha+(N-1))$, describes an empirical observation that the convergence speed of evolution strategy with isotropic distribution does not scale up with N for $N \ll \alpha$.

Table 1: Different types of the eigenvalue distributions of $\mathbf{A}$. The second to fourth types (discus: $d_1(\mathbf{A}) = \alpha$ and $d_2(\mathbf{A}) = \cdots = d_N(\mathbf{A}) = 1$, cigar: $d_1(\mathbf{A}) = \cdots = d_{N-1}(\mathbf{A}) = \alpha$ and $d_N(\mathbf{A}) = 1$) have the condition number $\mathrm{Cond}(\mathbf{A}) = d_1(\mathbf{A})/d_N(\mathbf{A}) = \alpha$, while the last type has the condition number αN. The third and the fifth types has the eigenvalues $d_i(\mathbf{A}) = \alpha^{\frac{i-1}{N-1}}$ and $d_i(\mathbf{A}) = \alpha \cdot i$, respectively.

Type	$\frac{d_N(\mathbf{A})}{\mathrm{Tr}(\mathbf{A})}$	$\frac{d_1(\mathbf{A})}{\mathrm{Tr}(\mathbf{A})}$	$\frac{\mathrm{Tr}(\mathbf{A}^2)}{\mathrm{Tr}(\mathbf{A})^2}$
Sphere	$\frac{1}{N}$	$\frac{1}{N}$	$\frac{1}{N}$
Discus	$\frac{1}{(N-1)+\alpha}$	$\frac{\alpha}{(N-1)+\alpha}$	$\frac{(N-1)+\alpha^2}{((N-1)+\alpha)^2}$
$\alpha^{\frac{i-1}{N-1}}$	$\frac{\alpha^{\frac{1}{N-1}}-1}{\alpha^{\frac{N}{N-1}}-1}$	$\frac{\alpha^{\frac{N}{N-1}}-\alpha}{\alpha^{\frac{N}{N-1}}-1}$	$\frac{\left(\alpha^{\frac{2N}{N-1}}-1\right)/\left(\alpha^{\frac{N}{N-1}}-1\right)}{\left(\alpha^{\frac{N}{N-1}}-1\right)^2/\left(\alpha^{\frac{1}{N-1}}-1\right)^2}$
Cigar	$\frac{1}{(N-1)\alpha+1}$	$\frac{\alpha}{(N-1)\alpha+1}$	$\frac{(N-1)\alpha^2+1}{((N-1)\alpha+1)^2}$
$\alpha \cdot i$	$\frac{1}{N(N+1)/2}$	$\frac{1}{(N+1)/2}$	$\frac{\frac{1}{6}N(N+1)(2N+1)}{\left(N(N+1)/2\right)^2}$

where $X_k = \boldsymbol{m}^{(t)} + \sigma^{(t)}Z_k$.

The following lemma provides the expression of the conditional expectation of the weight function.

LEMMA 3.7. *Let $X \sim \mathcal{N}(\boldsymbol{m}, \sigma^2\mathbf{I})$ and $(X_i)_{i=1}^{\lambda}$ be the i.i.d. copies of X. Let $c_f(t) = \Pr[f(X) < t]$ be the cumulative density function of the function value $f(X)$. Then, we have for any $i,j \in [\![1,\lambda]\!]$, $i \neq j$,*

$$\mathbb{E}_{X_k,k\neq i}[W(i;(X_k)_{k=1}^{\lambda}) \mid f(X_i)] = u_1(c_f(f(X_i)))$$

$$\mathbb{E}_{X_k,k\neq i}[W(i;(X_k)_{k=1}^{\lambda})^2 \mid f(X_i)] = u_2(c_f(f(X_i)))$$

$$\mathbb{E}_{X_k,k\neq i,k\neq j}[W(i;(X_k)_{k=1}^{\lambda})W(j;(X_k)_{k=1}^{\lambda}) \mid f(X_i),f(X_j)]$$
$$= u_3(c_f(f(X_i)), c_f(f(X_j))) ,$$

where

$$u_1(p) = \sum_{k=1}^{\lambda} w_k \frac{(\lambda-1)!}{(k-1)!(\lambda-k)!} p^{k-1}(1-p)^{\lambda-k} , \quad (30)$$

$$u_2(p) = \sum_{k=1}^{\lambda} w_k^2 \frac{(\lambda-1)!}{(k-1)!(\lambda-k)!} p^{k-1}(1-p)^{\lambda-k} . \quad (31)$$

$$u_3(p,q) = \sum_{k=1}^{\lambda-1}\sum_{l=k+1}^{\lambda} w_k w_l \frac{(\lambda-2)!}{(k-1)!(l-k-1)!(\lambda-l)!}$$
$$\times \min(p,q)^{k-1}|q-p|^{l-k-1}(1-\max(p,q))^{\lambda-l} . \quad (32)$$

Thanks to Lemma 3.7 and the fact that $(X_k)_{k=1}^{\lambda}$ are i.i.d., we can further rewrite the normalized quality gain by taking the iterated expectation $\mathbb{E} = \mathbb{E}_{X_i}\mathbb{E}_{X_k,k\neq i}$ as

$$\bar{\phi}(\boldsymbol{m},\bar{\sigma})$$
$$= -\bar{\sigma}\lambda\mathbb{E}[u_1(c_f(f(X)))\mathbf{e}^{\mathrm{T}}Z]$$
$$\quad -\frac{\bar{\sigma}^2\lambda}{2}\mathbb{E}\left[u_2(c_f(f(X)))\frac{Z^{\mathrm{T}}\mathbf{A}Z}{\mathrm{Tr}(\mathbf{A})}\right]$$
$$\quad -\frac{\bar{\sigma}^2(\lambda-1)\lambda}{2}\mathbb{E}\left[u_3(c_f(f(X)), c_f(f(\tilde{X})))\frac{Z^{\mathrm{T}}\mathbf{A}\tilde{Z}}{\mathrm{Tr}(\mathbf{A})}\right]$$
$$\qquad\qquad\qquad\qquad\qquad\qquad\qquad (33)$$
$$= -\bar{\sigma}\lambda\mathbb{E}[u_1(c_f(f(X)))\mathbf{e}^{\mathrm{T}}Z] - \frac{\bar{\sigma}^2\lambda}{2}\mathbb{E}[u_2(c_f(f(X)))]$$
$$\quad -\frac{\bar{\sigma}^2\lambda}{2}\mathbb{E}\left[u_2(c_f(f(X)))\left(\frac{Z^{\mathrm{T}}\mathbf{A}Z}{\mathrm{Tr}(\mathbf{A})}-1\right)\right]$$
$$\quad -\frac{\bar{\sigma}^2(\lambda-1)\lambda}{2}\mathbb{E}\left[u_3(c_f(f(X)), c_f(f(\tilde{X})))\frac{Z^{\mathrm{T}}\mathbf{A}\tilde{Z}}{\mathrm{Tr}(\mathbf{A})}\right] .$$

Here Z and $\tilde{Z}$ are independent and N-multivariate normally distributed with zero mean and identity covariance matrix and $X = \boldsymbol{m} + \sigma Z$ and $\tilde{X} = \boldsymbol{m} + \sigma\tilde{Z}$, where $\sigma = \bar{\sigma}\|\nabla f(\boldsymbol{m})\|/(c_m \mathrm{Tr}(\mathbf{A}))$.

The following lemma shows that the second term on the right-most side of (33) depends only on the weights $(w_k)_{k=1}^{\lambda}$.

LEMMA 3.8. $\lambda\mathbb{E}[u_2(c_f(f(X)))] = \sum_{i=1}^{\lambda} w_i^2$.

The following two lemmas show that the third and the fourth terms on the right-most size of (33) fade away as $\mathrm{Tr}(\mathbf{A}_N^2)/\mathrm{Tr}(\mathbf{A}_N)^2 \to 0$.

LEMMA 3.9.

$$\sup_{\boldsymbol{m}\in\mathbb{R}^N}\left|\mathbb{E}\left[u_2(c_f(f(X)))\left(\frac{Z^{\mathrm{T}}\mathbf{A}Z}{\mathrm{Tr}(\mathbf{A})}-1\right)\right]\right|$$
$$\leqslant 2^{\frac{1}{2}}\left(\frac{1}{\lambda}\sum_{k=1}^{\lambda} w_k^4\right)^{\frac{1}{2}}\left(\frac{\mathrm{Tr}(\mathbf{A}^2)}{\mathrm{Tr}(\mathbf{A})^2}\right)^{\frac{1}{2}} .$$

LEMMA 3.10.

$$\sup_{\boldsymbol{m}\in\mathbb{R}^N}\left|\mathbb{E}\left[u_3(c_f(f(X)), c_f(f(\tilde{X})))\frac{Z^{\mathrm{T}}\mathbf{A}\tilde{Z}}{\mathrm{Tr}(\mathbf{A})}\right]\right|$$
$$\leqslant \left(\frac{2}{\lambda(\lambda-1)}\sum_{k=1}^{\lambda}\sum_{l=k+1}^{\lambda} w_k^2 w_l^2\right)^{\frac{1}{2}}\left(\frac{\mathrm{Tr}(\mathbf{A}^2)}{\mathrm{Tr}(\mathbf{A})^2}\right)^{\frac{1}{2}} .$$

Finally we deal with the first term on the right-most side of (33). For this purpose, we introduce an orthogonal matrix $\mathbf{Q}$ such that $\mathbf{Q}\mathbf{e} = (1,0,\ldots,0)$, and let $\mathcal{N} = \mathbf{Q}Z$. Since Z is N-multivariate standard normally distributed, so is its orthogonal transformation $\mathcal{N}$. Hereafter, for any $x \in \mathbb{R}^N$ the ith coordinate of x is denoted by $[x]_i$.

LEMMA 3.11.

$$\sup_{\boldsymbol{m}\in\mathbb{R}^N\setminus\{x^*\}}|\mathbb{E}[u_1(c_f(f(X)))[\mathcal{N}]_1] - \mathbb{E}[u_1(\Phi([\mathcal{N}]_1))[\mathcal{N}]_1]|$$
$$\leqslant 3(\lambda-1)\max_{k\in[\![1,\lambda-1]\!]}|w_{k+1}-w_k|\left[\frac{1}{4\pi}\left(\frac{\bar{\sigma}}{c_m}\right)^2\frac{\mathrm{Tr}(\mathbf{A}^2)}{\mathrm{Tr}(\mathbf{A})^2}\right]^{\frac{1}{3}} .$$

LEMMA 3.12. *Let $\mathcal{N}_{1:\lambda} \leqslant \ldots \leqslant \mathcal{N}_{\lambda:\lambda}$ be the normal order statistics. Then, $\lambda\mathbb{E}[u_1(\Phi([\mathcal{N}]_1))[\mathcal{N}]_1] = \sum_{i=1}^{\lambda} w_i\mathbb{E}[\mathcal{N}_{i:\lambda}]$.*

We finalize the proof of Theorem 3.4. From (33), we have

$$\sup_{\boldsymbol{m}\in\mathbb{R}^N\setminus\{x^*\}}\left|\bar{\phi}(\boldsymbol{m},\bar{\sigma}) - \left(-\bar{\sigma}\sum_{i=1}^{\lambda} w_i\mathbb{E}[\mathcal{N}_{i:\lambda}] - \frac{\bar{\sigma}^2}{2}\sum_{i=1}^{\lambda} w_i^2\right)\right|$$
$$\leqslant \sup_{\boldsymbol{m}\in\mathbb{R}^N\setminus\{x^*\}}\left|-\bar{\sigma}\lambda\mathbb{E}[u_1(c_f(f(X)))\mathbf{e}^{\mathrm{T}}Z] - \left(-\bar{\sigma}\sum_{i=1}^{\lambda} w_i\mathbb{E}[\mathcal{N}_{i:\lambda}]\right)\right|$$
$$+ \sup_{\boldsymbol{m}\in\mathbb{R}^N\setminus\{x^*\}}\left|-\frac{\bar{\sigma}^2\lambda}{2}\mathbb{E}[u_2(c_f(f(X)))] - \left(-\frac{\bar{\sigma}^2}{2}\sum_{i=1}^{\lambda} w_i^2\right)\right|$$
$$+ \sup_{\boldsymbol{m}\in\mathbb{R}^N\setminus\{x^*\}}\left|-\frac{\bar{\sigma}^2\lambda}{2}\mathbb{E}\left[u_2(c_f(f(X)))\left(\frac{Z^{\mathrm{T}}\mathbf{A}Z}{\mathrm{Tr}(\mathbf{A})}-1\right)\right]\right|$$
$$+ \sup_{\boldsymbol{m}\in\mathbb{R}^N\setminus\{x^*\}}\left|-\frac{\bar{\sigma}^2(\lambda-1)\lambda}{2}\mathbb{E}\left[u_3(c_f(f(X)), c_f(f(\tilde{X})))\frac{Z^{\mathrm{T}}\mathbf{A}\tilde{Z}}{\mathrm{Tr}(\mathbf{A})}\right]\right| .$$

In light of Lemmas 3.11 and 3.12, the first term is upper bounded by

$$\frac{3}{(4\pi)^{\frac{1}{3}}}\frac{\bar{\sigma}^{\frac{5}{3}}}{c_m^{\frac{2}{3}}}\lambda(\lambda-1)\max_{k\in[\![1,\lambda-1]\!]}|w_{k+1}-w_k|\left(\frac{\mathrm{Tr}(\mathbf{A}^2)}{\mathrm{Tr}(\mathbf{A})^2}\right)^{\frac{1}{3}} . \quad (34)$$

Thanks to lemma 3.8, the second term is zero. The third term and the fourth term are bounded using Lemmas 3.9 and 3.10, respectively, as

$$\frac{1}{2^{\frac{1}{2}}} \bar{\sigma}^2 \left(\lambda \sum_{k=1}^{\lambda} w_k^4 \right)^{\frac{1}{2}} \left(\frac{\mathrm{Tr}(\mathbf{A}^2)}{\mathrm{Tr}(\mathbf{A})^2} \right)^{\frac{1}{2}} \quad \text{and}$$

$$\frac{1}{2^{\frac{1}{2}}} \bar{\sigma}^2 \left((\lambda-1)\lambda \sum_{k=1}^{\lambda} \sum_{l=k+1}^{\lambda} w_k^2 w_l^2 \right)^{\frac{1}{2}} \left(\frac{\mathrm{Tr}(\mathbf{A}^2)}{\mathrm{Tr}(\mathbf{A})^2} \right)^{\frac{1}{2}} .$$

This completes the proof.

4. SIMULATION

We conduct experiments to see (i) how the empirical normalized quality gain deviates from the asymptotic normalized quality gain (9) on a finite dimensional quadratic function, (ii) how it depends on the Hessian $\mathbf{A}$, and (iii) how it changes when we change c_m while fixing $\bar{\sigma} \times c_m$.

To estimate the normalized quality gain, we run T iterations of the algorithm (1) with scale-invariant step-size (16) and average the empirical quality gain at each iteration, namely,

$$\frac{0.9}{T} \sum_{t=T/10}^{T-1} \bar{\phi}(\boldsymbol{m}^{(t)}, \bar{\sigma}) . \tag{35}$$

We set $T = 10000$ and run 10 trials with the initial mean $\boldsymbol{m}^{(0)}$ taken from the uniform distribution on the unit sphere surface[7]. We plot the median ($\times$) and the 10%- and 90%-tile range (shaded area in same color, always thin and often not even visible) over the trials, along with the asymptotic normalized quality gain $\bar{\phi}_\infty$ ($\times$) and the theoretical bound with $c_m = 1$ (outside shaded area) and $c_m = \infty$ (inside shaded area). The results are summarized in Figure 4. Note that the normalized quality gain is divided by λ, i.e., per-sample normalized quality gain is displayed, and the normalized step-size is divided by the optimal normalized step-size $\bar{\sigma}^* = \bar{\sigma}^*((w_k)_{k=1}^\lambda)$ given in (16) (with a slight abuse of notation) so that the peak of $\bar{\phi}_\infty$ is located at 1 and its value is around 0.5 for the optimal weights and 0.25 for the non-negative CMA-type weights.

Effect of A. We first focus on the results with $c_m = 1$ (the default setting). The empirical normalized quality gain gets closer to the normalized quality gain derived for the infinite dimensional quadratic function as N increases. The approach of the empirical normalized quality gain to the theory is the fastest for the sphere function ($\mathbf{A} = \mathbf{I}$). For convex quadratic functions with the same condition number of $\alpha = 10^6$, the speed of the convergence of the *normalized* quality gain to $\bar{\phi}_\infty$ as $N \to \infty$ is the fastest for the cigar function, and the slowest for the discus function. This reflects the upper bound derived in Theorem 3.4 that depends on the ratio $\mathrm{Tr}(\mathbf{A}^2)/\mathrm{Tr}(\mathbf{A})^2$, whose value is summarized in Table 1 for the functions tested here. For the cigar function the (normalization) ratio is close to $1/(N-1)$, while for the discus function the ratio is very close to 1 for $N \ll \alpha$ and we do not observe significant difference between results on different N.

---

[7] We checked the dependency of the estimated normalized quality gain on the number of iterations T. Comparing the median values over 10 trials obtained with $T = 1000$ and $T = 10000$, the maximum difference was 0.0004 for $\bar{\sigma}/\bar{\sigma}^* \leqslant 0.1$, and 0.009 for $\bar{\sigma}/\bar{\sigma}^* \leqslant 2$ among all settings (all functions, all dimensions, both types of weights, and all values of c_m).

Effect of c_m. On the sphere function, we observe that a larger c_m leads to a better empirical normalized quality gain if $\bar{\sigma} c_m$ is fixed. The reason is as follows. On the sphere function, the negative gradient everywhere points to the global optimum. The function is locally approximated by a linear function whose normal vector is given by the gradient of the function. When c_m is large and hence the step-size is small, the ranking of the candidate solutions tends to admit the ranking of the solutions on the linear function. Then, it tends to provide a good estimate of the gradient. Therefore, a smaller step size, i.e., a larger c_m, leads to better progress. On the other quadratic functions, we observe a similar tendency when $\mathrm{Tr}(\mathbf{A}^2)/\mathrm{Tr}(\mathbf{A})^2$ is small enough. However, if λ is relatively large or $\mathrm{Tr}(\mathbf{A}^2)/\mathrm{Tr}(\mathbf{A})^2$ is relatively large, particularly on the discus function, a large c_m tends to result in a poor convergence performance. On a quadratic function in general, its gradient does not point to the optimum. If σ is sufficiently small but σc_m is relatively large, the mean vector is updated in the negative gradient direction and overshoots since the actual step-size σc_m is too large. Consequently, σ will become even smaller in practice. This behavior will be more emphasized if the condition number of the Hessian is higher.

Effect of w_k. We clearly see the difference between the normalized quality gain response with the optimal weights and the non-negative weights used in the CMA-ES. Compared with the curves for the optimal weights, the curves for the CMA-type weights tend to be closer to the asymptotic normalized quality gain. The difference is emphasized when the learning rate c_m for the mean vector update is smaller than one. Differently from the tendency we observe for the optimal weights, a smaller c_m results in a higher empirical quality gain.

The optimal weights are symmetric around zero, implying that they assume the symmetry of the sorted candidate solutions. Such a symmetry does not hold for a general convex quadratic function in a finite dimensional search space unless the step-size is sufficiently small. Since the symmetry can not be assumed in practice, using the negative part of the weights leads to unpromising behavior when c_m is small, i.e., $\bar{\sigma}$ is large.

5. FURTHER DISCUSSION

Tightness of the Normalized Quality Gain Bound. As we see in Figures 4, the theoretically derived bound (Theorem 3.4) is not tight, in particular for the interesting area where the normalized quality gain has a peak.

The bound (20) has two terms. The first term is mainly from the approximation error of the cumulative density function of $f(X)$ (scaled by the right factor) for $X \sim \mathcal{N}(\boldsymbol{m}, \sigma \mathbf{I})$ by the cumulative density function of the univariate standard normal distribution $\mathcal{N}$. In the proof of Lemma 3.11, we use the Chebyshev's inequality to bound the error. However, since we know the distribution of $\mathcal{N}$ and $f(X)$, we may be able to improve the first term by exploiting the distributions. Since the first term dominates if c_m is fixed, a better bound for the first term will lead to a tighter bound.

The second term of (20) comes from the quadratic terms of (33). It bounds the deviation of the normalized quality gain due to a random walk of $\boldsymbol{m}$ on the equal function

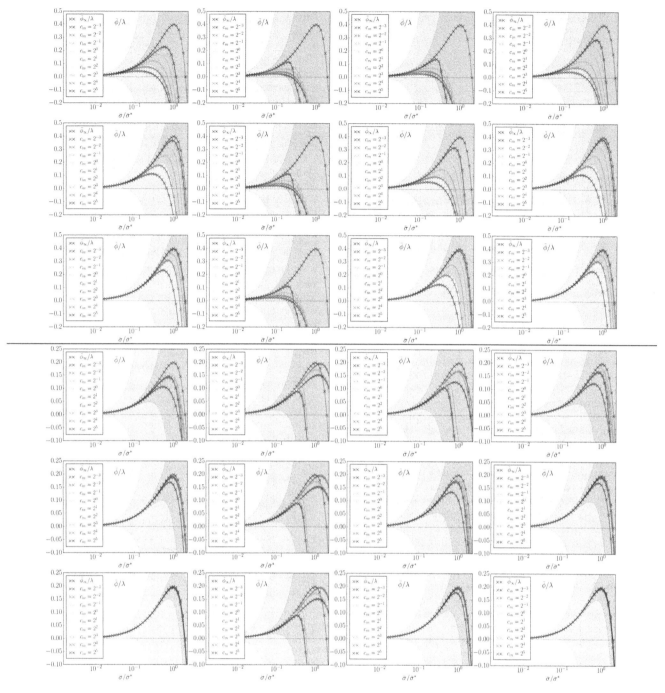

Figure 4: Empirical normalized quality gain on four convex quadratic functions, Sphere, Discus, Ellipsoid and Cigar (from left to right) of dimension $N = 10$, 100 and 1000 (from top to bottom). The optimal weights (top) and the (nonnegative) CMA-type weights are used and $\lambda = 10$.

value surface (hyperellipsoid). It becomes almost independent of selection (ranking) of candidate solutions as N goes sufficiently large. In the proofs of Lemmas 3.9 and 3.10 we simply use the Cauchy-Schwarz inequality to evaluate the effect of selection (weight functions u_2 and u_3) and the noise due to stochastic sampling of candidate solutions separately. The second term gives the best upper bound that is achieved when $c_m \to \infty$, though it is not a realistic setting. Even if $c_m \to \infty$ is considered, we can not yet obtain the $O(\lambda/N)$

scale up of the quality gain for $\lambda \in o(N)$, but we obtain $\lambda \in o(N^{\frac{1}{2}})$ for $(\mu/\mu_I, \lambda)$-ES with fixed μ/λ ratio. To answer the question if we can achieve $O(\lambda/N)$ scale up for $\lambda \in o(N)$, we need to improve both the first and second terms of the bound (20).

Non-Isotropic Gaussian Sampling. The isotropic covariance matrix of the multivariate normal sampling distribution is considered above. We can generalize all of the results in this paper to an arbitrary positive definite symmetric covariance matrix $\mathbf{C}$ by considering the affine transformation of the search space. Let $f : x \mapsto (x - x^*)^{\mathrm{T}} \mathbf{A}(x - x^*)$, and consider the coordinate transformation $x \mapsto y = \mathbf{C}^{-\frac{1}{2}}x$. In the latter coordinate system the function f can be written as $f(x) = \bar{f}(y) = (y - \mathbf{C}^{-\frac{1}{2}}x^*)^{\mathrm{T}}(\mathbf{C}^{\frac{1}{2}}\mathbf{A}\mathbf{C}^{\frac{1}{2}})(y - \mathbf{C}^{-\frac{1}{2}}x^*)$. The multivariate normal distribution $\mathcal{N}(m, \sigma^2\mathbf{C})$ is transformed into $\mathcal{N}(\mathbf{C}^{-\frac{1}{2}}m, \sigma^2\mathbf{I})$ by the same transformation. Then, it is easy to prove that the quality gain on the function f given the parameter $(m, \sigma, \mathbf{C})$ is equivalent to the quality gain on the function $\bar{f}$ given $(\mathbf{C}^{-\frac{1}{2}}m, \sigma^2, \mathbf{I})$. The normalization factor $g(m)$ of the quality gain and the normalized step-size are then rewritten as

$$g(m) = \frac{\|\mathbf{C}^{\frac{1}{2}}\mathbf{A}(m - x^*)\|^2}{f(m)\,\mathrm{Tr}(\mathbf{C}^{\frac{1}{2}}\mathbf{A}\mathbf{C}^{\frac{1}{2}})} \ , \tag{36}$$

$$\bar{\sigma} = \frac{\sigma c_m\,\mathrm{Tr}(\mathbf{C}^{\frac{1}{2}}\mathbf{A}\mathbf{C}^{\frac{1}{2}})}{\|\mathbf{C}^{\frac{1}{2}}\mathbf{A}(m - x^*)\|} \ . \tag{37}$$

Interpretation of Dynamics. The asymptotic quality gain depends on m through $g(m)$. In practice, we observe near worst case performance with $g(m) \approx 2d_N(\mathbf{A})/\mathrm{Tr}(\mathbf{A})$, which implies that $m - x^*$ is almost parallel to the eigenspace corresponding to the smallest eigenvalue $d_N(\mathbf{A})$ of the Hessian matrix. We provide an intuition to explain this behavior, which will be useful to understand the algorithm, even though the argument is not fully rigorous.

We consider the weighted recombination ES (6) with scale-invariant step-size (16). Lemma 3.11 implies that the order of the function values $f(X_i)$ coincide with the order of $[\mathcal{N}_i]_1 = \mathbf{e}^{\mathrm{T}}(X_i - m^{(t)})/\sigma^{(t)}$, where $\mathbf{e} = \nabla f(m^{(t)})/\|\nabla f(m^{(t)})\|$. This is because if $d \sim \mathcal{N}(\mathbf{0}, \mathbf{I})$, then $d^{\mathrm{T}}\mathbf{A}d/\mathrm{Tr}(\mathbf{A})$ in (28) almost surely converges to one by the strong law of large numbers. It means that the function value of the candidate solutions is determined solely by the first component on the right-hand side of (28), that is, $\mathbf{e}^{\mathrm{T}}(X_i - m^{(t)})/\sigma^{(t)}$.

Since the ranking of the function only depends on $\mathbf{e}^{\mathrm{T}}(X_i - m^{(t)})/\sigma^{(t)}$, one can rewrite the update of the mean vector as

$$m^{(t+1)} = m^{(t)} + c_m\sigma^{(t)}\sum_{i=1}^{\lambda} w_i\mathcal{N}_{i:\lambda}(0, 1) \cdot \mathbf{e}$$
$$+ c_m\sigma^{(t)}\mu_w^{-\frac{1}{2}}\mathcal{N}(\mathbf{0}, \mathbf{I} - \mathbf{e}\mathbf{e}^{\mathrm{T}}) \ , \tag{38}$$

where $\mu_w = \left(\sum_{i=1}^{\lambda} w_i^2\right)^{-1}$, $\mathcal{N}_{i:\lambda}(0, 1)$ are the ith order statistics from λ population of $\mathcal{N}(0, 1)$, and $\mathcal{N}(\mathbf{0}, \mathbf{I} - \mathbf{e}\mathbf{e}^{\mathrm{T}})$ is the normal distributed random vector with mean vector $\mathbf{0}$ and the degenerated covariance matrix $\mathbf{I} - \mathbf{e}\mathbf{e}^{\mathrm{T}}$. It implies that the mean vector moves along the gradient direction with the distribution $c_m\sigma^{(t)}\sum_{i=1}^{\lambda} w_i\mathcal{N}_{i:\lambda}(0, 1)$, while it moves randomly in the subspace orthogonal to the gradient with the distribution $c_m\sigma^{(t)}\mu_w^{-\frac{1}{2}}\mathcal{N}(\mathbf{0}, \mathbf{I} - \mathbf{e}\mathbf{e}^{\mathrm{T}})$.

If the function is the spherical function, $\mathbf{A} \propto \mathbf{I}$, the mean vector does a symmetric, unbiased random walk on the surface of a hypersphere while the radius of the hypersphere gradually decreases due to the second term on (38). If the function is a general convex quadratic function, $\mathbf{A} \not\propto \mathbf{I}$, the corresponding random walk on the surface of a hyperellipsoid becomes biased. Then, $m - x^*$ tends to be parallel to the eigenspace corresponding to the smallest eigenvalue

$d_N(\mathbf{A})$, which means that the quality gain is close to the worst case of $d_N(\mathbf{A})/\mathrm{Tr}(\mathbf{A})$[8].

Geometric Interpretation of the Optimal Situation. On the sphere function, we know that the optimal step-size puts the algorithm in the situation where $f(m)$ improves twice as much by m moving towards the optimum as it deteriorates by m moving randomly in the subspace orthogonal to the gradient direction [ ]. On a general convex quadratic function, we find the analogous result. From (33) and lemmas in Section 3.4, the first term of the asymptotic normalized quality gain (10), i.e. $-\bar{\sigma}\sum_{i=1}^{\lambda} w_i\mathbb{E}[\mathcal{N}_{i:\lambda}]$, is due to the movement of m towards the negative gradient direction, and the second term, i.e. $-\frac{\bar{\sigma}^2}{2}\sum_{i=1}^{\lambda} w_i^2$, is due to the random walk in the orthogonal subspaces[9]. The asymptotic normalized quality gain is maximized when the normalized step-size is set such that $-\bar{\sigma}\sum_{i=1}^{\lambda} w_i\mathbb{E}[\mathcal{N}_{i:\lambda}] = \bar{\sigma}^2\sum_{i=1}^{\lambda} w_i^2$. That is, the amount of the decrease of $f(m)$ by m moving into the negative gradient direction is twice greater than the increase of $f(m)$ by m moving in its orthogonal subspace.

Linear Convergence. We can derive the linear convergence of the algorithm where at each iteration, the step-size is proportional to $\|\nabla f(m)\|/c_m\,\mathrm{Tr}(\mathbf{A})$ from our quality gain analysis. Since the algorithm is stochastic, there are several ways to define the linear convergence. Here, we define the linear convergence of the algorithms by

$$\lim_{t \to \infty} -\frac{1}{t}\sum_{i=1}^{t}\mathbb{E}\left[\ln\frac{f(m^{(i+1)})}{f(m^{(i)})}\right] = \mathrm{CR} > 0 \ . \tag{39}$$

If we consider the weighted recombination evolution strategy with the step-size (16), using the normalized log quality gain, we can rewrite the above definition as

$$-\frac{1}{t}\sum_{i=1}^{t}\mathbb{E}\left[\ln\frac{f(m^{(i+1)})}{f(m^{(i)})}\right] = \frac{1}{t}\sum_{i=1}^{t}\mathbb{E}\left[g(m^{(i)})\bar{\phi}_{\ln}(m^{(i)}, \bar{\sigma})\right].$$

The convergence CR is lower bounded by using Theorem 3.4. Using the inequality $g(m) \geqslant 2d_N(\mathbf{A})/\mathrm{Tr}(\mathbf{A})$, we can lower bound each term on the right-hand side of the above equality as

$$g(m^{(t)})\bar{\phi}_{\ln}(m^{(t)}, \bar{\sigma}) \geqslant \frac{2d_N(\mathbf{A})}{\mathrm{Tr}(\mathbf{A})}\bar{\phi}_{\ln}(m^{(t)}, \bar{\sigma}) \ .$$

Then, note that $\bar{\phi}_{\ln}(m, \bar{\sigma}) \geqslant \bar{\phi}(m, \bar{\sigma})$. Letting the right-hand side of the inequality (20) be denoted by $\epsilon(\mathbf{A}, \bar{\sigma}, (w_k)_{k=1}^{\lambda})$, we have

$$\bar{\phi}_{\ln}(m^{(t)}, \bar{\sigma}) \geqslant \bar{\phi}(m, \bar{\sigma}) \geqslant \bar{\phi}_{\infty}(\bar{\sigma}, (w_k)_{k=1}^{\lambda}) - \epsilon(\mathbf{A}, \bar{\sigma}, (w_k)_{k=1}^{\lambda}) \ .$$

---

[8]The reason may be explained as follows. It is illustrated in Figure 3 that the optimal step-size is the largest when m is on the shortest axis of the hyperellipsoid, and the smallest when m is on the longest axis. It implies that the progress in one step is the largest in the short axis direction (parallel to the eigenvector corresponding to the largest eigenvalue of $\mathbf{A}$), and the smallest in the long axis direction (parallel the eigenvector corresponding to the largest eigenvalue of $\mathbf{A}$). It implies the situation quickly becomes closer to the worst case, while it takes longer iterations to escape from near worst situation. Therefore, we observe near worst situation in practice.

[9]More precisely, the second term comes from the quadratic term in (28) that contains the information in the gradient direction as well. However, the above statement is true in the limit $N \to \infty$.

Altogether, we obtain

$$\mathrm{CR} \geqslant \frac{2d_N(\mathbf{A})}{\mathrm{Tr}(\mathbf{A})} \left(\bar{\phi}_\infty(\bar{\sigma}, (w_k)_{k=1}^\lambda) - \epsilon(\mathbf{A}, \bar{\sigma}, (w_k)_{k=1}^\lambda) \right) \ .$$

Therefore, if $\bar{\phi}_\infty(\bar{\sigma}, (w_k)_{k=1}^\lambda) > \epsilon(\mathbf{A}, \bar{\sigma}, (w_k)_{k=1}^\lambda)$, the convergence rate $\mathrm{CR} > 0$ and the algorithm converges. For choices of λ and N that were discussed previously in the paper, we know that $\epsilon(\mathbf{A}, \bar{\sigma}, (w_k)_{k=1}^\lambda)$ goes to zero such that the condition will be satisfied.

Related Work. Reference [ ] studied the $(1+1)$-ES with the one-fifth success rule on a convex quadratic function with Hessian

$$\mathbf{A} = \frac{1}{2} \mathrm{diag}(\underbrace{\alpha, \ldots, \alpha}_{\lfloor N\theta \rfloor}, \underbrace{1, \ldots, 1}_{N - \lfloor N\theta \rfloor}) \ , \qquad (40)$$

where $\alpha \geqslant 1$ is the condition number, $\theta \in [0, 1]$ determines the proportion of the number of short axes of the ellipsoid. To analyze the algorithmic behavior, the so-called *localization parameter*, ζ, that is the distance to the optimum in the last $N - \lfloor N\theta \rfloor$ dimensional subspace divided by the distance to the optimum in the first $\lfloor N\theta \rfloor$ times α. In the reference, it is proved that for $\alpha \in poly(N)$ and $\theta = 1/2$, if the initialization satisfies $\sigma^{(0)} = \Theta(f(\boldsymbol{m})^{\frac{1}{2}}/N/\alpha)$ and $\zeta^{-1} = O(1)$, then the number of iterations to reduce the initial f-value to a 2^{-b}-fraction for $b = poly(N)$ is $\Theta(b\alpha N)$. It translates as that the convergence rate is $\Theta(1/(\alpha N))$. It almost matches the worst case of the quality gain, $\Omega(d_N(\mathbf{A})/\mathrm{Tr}(\mathbf{A})) = \Omega(2/((\alpha + 1)N))$. The convergence rate of $O(1/N)$ is also proved on a general quadratic function with a bounded condition number, $\alpha \in O(1)$. However, the influence of the condition number α to the convergence rate is missing.

References [ ] and [ ] studied ES with intermediate recombination and ES with weighted recombination, respectively, on the same type of quadratic functions with Hessian (40). Their results, progress rate and quality gain, depend on the localization parameter, the steady-state value of which is then analyzed to obtain the steady-state quality gain. References [,] studied the progress rate and the quality gain on the general convex quadratic model as we already mentioned in the paper. Our study is differentiated from these results by a mathematical rigorousness. On the other hands, in these references, the dynamics of the step-size control mechanisms, self-adaptation and cumulative step-size adaptation, is analyzed. These are beyond the scope of this paper and we do not discuss further on this topic.

6. ACKNOWLEDGEMENTS

This work is partially supported by JSPS KAKENHI Grant Number 15K16063.

7. REFERENCES

[1] Y. Akimoto, A. Auger, and N. Hansen. Convergence of the continuous time trajectories of isotropic evolution strategies on monotonic $\mathcal{C}^2$-composite functions. In *Problem Solving from Nature - PPSN XII*, pages 42–51, 2012.

[2] Y. Akimoto and N. Hansen. Online model selection for restricted covariance matrix adaptation. In *Parallel Problem Solving from Nature - PPSN XIV*, pages 3–13, 2016.

[3] Y. Akimoto and N. Hansen. Projection-based restricted covariance matrix adaptation for high dimension. In *Genetic and Evolutionary Computation Conference, GECCO*, pages 197–204, 2016.

[4] D. V. Arnold. Optimal weighted recombination. In *Foundations of Genetic Algorithms*, pages 215–237, 2005.

[5] D. V. Arnold. On the use of evolution strategies for optimising certain positive definite quadratic forms. In *Genetic and Evolutionary Computation Conference, GECCO*, pages 634–641, 2007.

[6] A. Auger. *Analysis of Comparison-based Stochastic Continuous Black-Box Optimization Algorithms.* Habilitation, Universitè Paris-Sud, 2015.

[7] A. Auger, D. Brockhoff, and N. Hansen. Mirrored sampling in evolution strategies with weighted recombination. In *Genetic and Evolutionary Computation Conference, GECCO*, pages 861–868, 2011.

[8] A. Auger and N. Hansen. Reconsidering the progress rate theory for evolution strategies in finite dimensions. In *Genetic and Evolutionary Computation Conference, GECCO*, pages 445–452, 2006.

[9] A. Auger and N. Hansen. Linear convergence of comparison-based step-size adaptive randomized search via stability of markov chains. *SIAM Journal on Optimization*, 26(3):1589–1624, 2016.

[10] H.-G. Beyer. Towards a theory of 'evolution strategies': Results for $(1+, \lambda)$-strategies on (nearly) arbitrary fitness functions. In *Parallel Problem Solving from Nature - PPSN III*, pages 58–67, 1994.

[11] H.-G. Beyer. *The Theory of Evolution Strategies*. Natural Computing Series. Springer-Verlag, 2001.

[12] H.-G. Beyer and M. Hellwig. The dynamics of cumulative step size adaptation on the ellipsoid model. *Evolutionary Computation*, 24(1):25–57, 2016.

[13] H.-G. Beyer and A. Melkozerov. The dynamics of self-adaptive multirecombinant evolution strategies on the general ellipsoid model. *IEEE Transactions on Evolutionary Computation*, 18(5):764–778, 2014.

[14] A. DasGupta. *Asymptotic theory of statistics and probability*. Springer Science & Business Media, 2008.

[15] L. Devroye. *Non-Uniform Random Variate Generation*. Springer New York, 1986.

[16] S. Finck and H.-G. Beyer. Weighted recombination evolution strategy on a class of pdqf's. In *Foundations of Genetic Algorithms, FOGA*, pages 1–12, 2009.

[17] N. Hansen and A. Auger. Principled design of continuous stochastic search: From theory to practice. In Y. Borenstein and A. Moraglio, editors, *Theory and Principled Methods for the Design of Metaheuristics*. Springer, 2014.

[18] N. Hansen and S. Kern. Evaluating the cma evolution strategy on multimodal test functions. In *Parallel Problem Solving from Nature - PPSN VIII*, pages 282–291, 2004.

[19] J. Jägersküpper. How the $(1+1)$ es using isotropic mutations minimizes positive definite quadratic forms. *Theoretical Computer Science*, 361(1):38–56, 2006.

[20] M. Jebalia and A. Auger. Log-linear convergence of the scale-invariant $(\mu/\mu_w, \lambda)$-es and optimal μ for

intermediate recombination for large population sizes. In *Parallel Problem Solving from Nature - PPSN XI*, pages 52–62, 2010.

[21] M. Jebalia and A. Auger. Log-linear convergence of the scale-invariant $(\mu/\mu_w, \lambda)$-ES and optimal mu for intermediate recombination for large population sizes. Research Report RR-7275, Jun 2010.

[22] M. Jebalia, A. Auger, and P. Liardet. Log-linear convergence and optimal bounds for the (1+1)-es. In *Evolution Artificielle (EA '07)*, pages 207–218, 2008.

[23] I. Loshchilov. A computationally efficient limited memory cma-es for large scale optimization. In *Genetic and Evolutionary Computation Conference, GECCO*, pages 397–404, 2014.

[24] I. Rechenberg. *Evolutionsstrategie '94*. Frommann-Holzboog, Stuttgart-Bad Cannstatt, 1994.

[25] R. Ros and N. Hansen. A simple modification in cma-es achieving linear time and space complexity. In *Parallel Problem Solving from Nature - PPSN X*, pages 296–305, 2008.

[26] O. Teytaud and S. Gelly. General lower bounds for evolutionary algorithms. In *Parallel Problem Solving from Nature - PPSN IX*, pages 21–31, 2006.

APPENDIX

A.   PROOFS

In the following, let $H_N = \frac{\bar{\sigma}}{c_m}[\mathcal{N}]_1 + \frac{\bar{\sigma}^2}{2c_m^2}\frac{\mathcal{N}^{\mathrm{T}}\mathbf{QAQ}^{\mathrm{T}}\mathcal{N}}{\mathrm{Tr}(\mathbf{A})}$. Let $\tilde{\mathcal{N}}$, $\tilde{Z}$, $\tilde{X}$, $\tilde{H}_N$ be the i.i.d. copies of $\mathcal{N}$, Z, X, H_N, respectively. Moreover, let c_N be the cumulative density function of H_N.

PROOF OF PROPOSITION 3.1. Let $\boldsymbol{d} = c_m \sum_{i=1}^\lambda W(i; (\boldsymbol{m} + \sigma Z_k)_{k=1}^\lambda) Z_i$, where $(Z_i)_{i=1}^\lambda$ are independent and N-variate standard normally distributed random vectors. Then,

$$\phi(x^* + (\boldsymbol{m} - x^*), \sigma)$$
$$= \phi(\boldsymbol{m}, \sigma)$$
$$= -\frac{\mathbb{E}[g(\boldsymbol{m} + \sigma\boldsymbol{d})] - g(\boldsymbol{m})}{g(\boldsymbol{m})}$$
$$= -\frac{\mathbb{E}[f(\boldsymbol{m} + \sigma\boldsymbol{d} - x^*)] - f(\boldsymbol{m} - x^*)}{f(\boldsymbol{m} - x^*)}$$
$$= -\frac{\alpha^{-n}\mathbb{E}[f(\alpha \cdot (\boldsymbol{m} + \sigma\boldsymbol{d} - x^*))] - \alpha^{-n}f(\alpha \cdot (\boldsymbol{m} - x^*))}{\alpha^{-n}f(\alpha \cdot (\boldsymbol{m} - x^*))}$$
$$= -\frac{\mathbb{E}[f(\alpha \cdot (\boldsymbol{m} + \sigma\boldsymbol{d} - x^*))] - f(\alpha \cdot (\boldsymbol{m} - x^*))}{f(\alpha \cdot (\boldsymbol{m} - x^*))}$$
$$= -\frac{\mathbb{E}[g(x^* + \alpha \cdot (\boldsymbol{m} - x^*) + \alpha\sigma\boldsymbol{d})] - g(x^* + \alpha \cdot (\boldsymbol{m} - x^*))}{g(x^* + \alpha \cdot (\boldsymbol{m} - x^*))}$$
$$= \phi(x^* + \alpha(\boldsymbol{m} - x^*), \alpha\sigma) .$$

That is, the quality gain is scale invariant around $(x^*, 0)$. Moreover, the above equality implies that $\mathrm{argmax}_\sigma \phi(x^* + (\boldsymbol{m} - x^*), \sigma) = \mathrm{argmax}_\sigma \phi(x^* + \alpha(\boldsymbol{m} - x^*), \alpha\sigma)$, i.e., the optimal step-size at $x^* + \alpha(\boldsymbol{m} - x^*)$ is α times greater than the optimal step-size at $x^* + (\boldsymbol{m} - x^*)$. Therefore, the optimal step-size as a function of $\boldsymbol{m} - x^*$ is homogeneous with the exponent 1, i.e., $\sigma^*(\alpha \cdot (\boldsymbol{m} - x^*)) = \alpha\sigma^*(\boldsymbol{m} - x^*)$. $\square$

PROOF OF COROLLARY 3.6. Let $\bar{\sigma} = \beta\bar{\sigma}_w^*$ for some $\beta \in [\epsilon, 2 - \epsilon]$. Two terms depending on $\bar{\sigma}$ on the right-hand side

of (20) divided by $\bar{\phi}_\infty(\bar{\sigma}, (w_k)_{k=1}^\lambda)$ read

$$\frac{\bar{\sigma}^{\frac{5}{3}}}{\bar{\phi}_\infty(\beta\bar{\sigma}_w^*, (w_k)_{k=1}^\lambda)} = \frac{\beta^{\frac{2}{3}}/(1 - \beta/2)}{(\sum_{i=1}^\lambda w_i^2)(\bar{\sigma}_w^*)^{\frac{1}{3}}}$$
$$= \frac{\beta^{\frac{2}{3}}/(1 - \beta/2)}{(\sum_{i=1}^\lambda w_i^2)^{\frac{2}{3}}(-\sum_{i=1}^\lambda w_i\mathbb{E}[\mathcal{N}_{i:\lambda}])^{\frac{1}{3}}} \quad (41)$$

and

$$\frac{\bar{\sigma}^2}{\bar{\phi}_\infty(\bar{\sigma}, (w_k)_{k=1}^\lambda)} = \frac{\beta/(1 - \beta/2)}{(\sum_{i=1}^\lambda w_i^2)} . \quad (42)$$

The three terms depending on λ and $(w_k)_{k=1}^\lambda$ on the right-hand side of (20) are respectively bounded as

$$(\lambda^2 - \lambda) \max_{k \in [\![1, \lambda-1]\!]} |w_{k+1} - w_k| \leqslant \lambda^2 \max_{k \in [\![1, \lambda-1]\!]} |w_{k+1} - w_k| \quad (43)$$

and

$$\left(\lambda \sum_{k=1}^\lambda w_k^4\right)^{\frac{1}{2}} \leqslant \lambda^{\frac{1}{2}} \sum_{k=1}^\lambda w_k^2 \quad (44)$$

$$\left((\lambda - 1)\lambda \sum_{k=1}^\lambda \sum_{l=k+1}^\lambda w_k^2 w_l^2\right)^{\frac{1}{2}} \leqslant \lambda \sum_{k=1}^\lambda w_k^2 . \quad (45)$$

Using the above equalities and inequalities, we obtain

$$\frac{\sup_{\boldsymbol{m} \in \mathbb{R}^N \setminus \{x^*\}} |\bar{\phi}(\boldsymbol{m}, \bar{\sigma}) - \bar{\phi}_\infty(\bar{\sigma}, (w_k)_{k=1}^\lambda)|}{\bar{\phi}_\infty(\bar{\sigma}, (w_k)_{k=1}^\lambda)}$$
$$\leqslant \frac{3\beta^{\frac{2}{3}}}{(4\pi)^{\frac{1}{3}}c_m^{\frac{2}{3}}(1 - \frac{\beta}{2})} \left[\frac{\lambda^6 \max_{k \in [\![1, \lambda-1]\!]} |w_{k+1} - w_k|^3}{(\sum_{i=1}^\lambda w_i^2)^2(-\sum_{i=1}^\lambda w_i\mathbb{E}[\mathcal{N}_{i:\lambda}])}\frac{\mathrm{Tr}(\mathbf{A}^2)}{\mathrm{Tr}(\mathbf{A})^2}\right]^{\frac{1}{3}}$$
$$+ \frac{\beta}{2^{\frac{1}{2}}(1 - \frac{\beta}{2})} \left[(\lambda^{\frac{1}{2}} + \lambda)^2 \frac{\mathrm{Tr}(\mathbf{A}^2)}{\mathrm{Tr}(\mathbf{A})^2}\right]^{\frac{1}{2}} . \quad (46)$$

Under the condition (23), both the first and the second terms on the RHS of (46) converge to zero as $N \to \infty$. This completes the proof. $\square$

PROOF OF LEMMA 3.7. Since $(X_k)_{k=1}^\lambda$ are independently and normally distributed, the conditional probability of an event $\mathbb{I}\{f(X_k) < f(X_i)\} = 1$ for any $k \neq i$ given X_i is $c_f(f(X_i))$. Then, the probability of $\sum_{k=1}^\lambda \mathbb{I}\{f(X_k) \leqslant f(X_i)\}$ being a for $a \in [\![1, \lambda]\!]$ is given by the binomial probability mass

$$\frac{(\lambda - 1)!}{(a - 1)!(\lambda - a)!}p^{a-1}(1 - p)^{\lambda - a} \quad (47)$$

with $p = c_f(f(X_i))$. Note that the sum of the above probabilities over $a \in [\![1, \lambda]\!]$ is one. It implies that $W(i; (X_k)_{k=1}^\lambda)^\alpha$ takes the value of w_a with probability one. Then, for any $\alpha \geqslant 0$,

$$\mathbb{E}_{X_k, k \neq i}[W(i; (X_k)_{k=1}^\lambda)^\alpha \mid f(X_i)]$$
$$= \sum_{k=1}^\lambda w_k^\alpha \frac{(\lambda - 1)!}{(k - 1)!(\lambda - k)!}p^{k-1}(1 - p)^{\lambda - k} .$$

Similarly, the joint probability of $\sum_{k=1}^\lambda \mathbb{I}\{f(X_k) \leqslant f(X_i)\}$ and $\sum_{k=1}^\lambda \mathbb{I}\{f(X_k) \leqslant f(X_j)\}$ is derived. Due to the symmetry of $W(i; (X_k)_{k=1}^\lambda)W(j; (X_k)_{k=1}^\lambda)$, we can assume w.l.g. that $f(X_i) \leqslant f(X_j)$. Then, the conditional joint probability of $\sum_{k=1}^\lambda \mathbb{I}\{f(X_k) \leqslant f(X_i)\} = a$ and $\sum_{k=1}^\lambda \mathbb{I}\{f(X_k) \leqslant$

$f(X_j)\} = b$ for $a, b \in [\![1, \lambda]\!]$ given X_i and X_j is expressed by the trinomial probability mass

$$\frac{(\lambda - 2)!}{(a-1)!(b-a-1)!(\lambda-b)!}p^{a-1}(q-p)^{b-a-1}(1-q)^{\lambda-b} \quad (48)$$

with $p = c_f(f(X_i))$ and $q = c_f(f(X_j))$ if $a < b$, and zero otherwise. Note that the sum of the above probability over $1 \leqslant a < b \leqslant \lambda$ is 1. It implies that $W(i; (X_k)_{k=1}^{\lambda})W(j; (X_k)_{k=1}^{\lambda})$ takes a value of the form $w_a w_b$ with probability one. Hence, we find

$$\mathbb{E}_{X_k, k\neq i, k\neq j}[W(i; (X_k)_{k=1}^{\lambda})W(j; (X_k)_{k=1}^{\lambda}) \mid f(X_i), f(X_j)]$$
$$= \sum_{m=1}^{\lambda-1}\sum_{l=m+1}^{\lambda} w_m w_l \Pr\left[\sum_{k=1}^{\lambda}\mathbb{I}\{f(X_k) \leqslant f(X_i)\} = m \wedge \right.$$
$$\left. \sum_{k=1}^{\lambda}\mathbb{I}\{f(X_k) \leqslant f(X_j)\} = l\right],$$

which reads (32). $\quad\square$

PROOF OF LEMMA 3.8. We first prove that $c_f(f(X_i))$ is uniformly distributed in $[0, 1]$. When X_i follows a N-variate normal distribution with a positive definite covariance matrix, one can immediately see that $\Pr[f(X_i) = \alpha] = 0$ for any $\alpha \in \mathbb{R}$. It implies that $f(X_i)$ has a continuous distribution function c_f. Then, from the well-known fact [, Theorem 2.1], we find that $c_f(f(X))$ is uniformly distributed in $[0, 1]$. This proves the first equality in the lemma statement.

Taking the integral of (31) with respect to $p \in [0, 1]$ and using the formula $\int_0^1 p^{a-1}(1-p)^{\lambda-a}dp = (a-1)!(\lambda - a)!/\lambda!$, we find $\int_0^1 \lambda u_2(x)dx = \sum_{i=1}^{\lambda} w_i^2$. This completes the proof. $\quad\square$

LEMMA A.1.

$$\mathbb{E}[u_2(c_f(f(X_i)))^2] \leqslant \frac{1}{\lambda}\sum_{k=1}^{\lambda} w_k^4$$

$$\mathbb{E}[u_3(c_f(f(X_i)), c_f(f(X_j)))^2] \leqslant \frac{2}{\lambda(\lambda-1)}\sum_{k=1}^{\lambda}\sum_{l=k+1}^{\lambda} w_k^2 w_l^2 .$$

PROOF OF LEMMA A.1. From the first paragraph of the proof of Lemma 3.8, we find that $c_f(f(X_i))$ and $c_f(f(X_j))$ are independent and uniformly distributed on $[0, 1]$.

By using Jensen's inequality to exchange the square and the conditional expectation, we have

$$\mathbb{E}[u_2(c_f(f(X_i)))^2]$$
$$= \mathbb{E}_i[\mathbb{E}_{k\neq i}[W(i; (X_k)_{k=1}^{\lambda}) \mid f(X_i)]^2]$$
$$\leqslant \mathbb{E}_i[\mathbb{E}_{k\neq i}[W(i; (X_k)_{k=1}^{\lambda})^2 \mid f(X_i)]]$$
$$= \mathbb{E}[W(i; (X_k)_{k=1}^{\lambda})^2]$$
$$= \sum_{k=1}^{\lambda} w_k^4 \frac{(\lambda-1)!}{(k-1)!(\lambda-k)!}\int_0^1 p^{k-1}(1-p)^{\lambda-k}dp .$$

Using the formula $\int_0^1 p^{k-1}(1-p)^{\lambda-k}dp = (k-1)!(\lambda-k)!/\lambda!$, the right-most side becomes $\frac{1}{\lambda}\sum_{k=1}^{\lambda} w_k^4$.

Analogously, we obtain

$$\mathbb{E}[u_3(c_f(f(X_i)), c_f(f(X_j)))^2]$$
$$= \mathbb{E}_{i,j}[\mathbb{E}_{k\neq i,j}[W(i; (X_k)_{k=1}^{\lambda})W(j; (X_k)_{k=1}^{\lambda}) \mid f(X_i)f(X_j)]^2]$$
$$\leqslant \mathbb{E}_{i,j}[\mathbb{E}_{k\neq i,j}[W(i; (X_k)_{k=1}^{\lambda})^2 W(j; (X_k)_{k=1}^{\lambda})^2 \mid f(X_i)f(X_j)]]$$
$$= \mathbb{E}[W(i; (X_k)_{k=1}^{\lambda})^2 W(j; (X_k)_{k=1}^{\lambda})^2]$$
$$= \sum_{k=1}^{\lambda-1}\sum_{l=k+1}^{\lambda}\frac{w_k^2 w_l^2(\lambda-2)!}{(k-1)!(l-k-1)!(\lambda-l)!}$$
$$\times \int_0^1\int_0^q 2p^{k-1}(q-p)^{l-k-1}(1-q)^{\lambda-l}dpdq .$$

Using the formula $\int_0^q p^{k-1}(q-p)^{l-k-1}dp = (k-1)!(l-k-1)!/(l-1)!q^{l-1}$ and $\int_0^1 q^{l-1}(1-q)^{\lambda-l}dq = (l-1)!(\lambda-l)!/\lambda!$, the right-most side becomes $\frac{2}{\lambda(\lambda-1)}\sum_{k=1}^{\lambda}\sum_{l=k+1}^{\lambda} w_k^2 w_l^2$. $\quad\square$

LEMMA A.2. The derivative of u_1 is given by

$$\frac{du_1}{dp} = (\lambda-1)\sum_{k=1}^{\lambda-1}(w_{k+1} - w_k)\binom{\lambda-2}{k-1}p^{k-1}(1-p)^{\lambda-k-1} . \quad (49)$$

Hence, u_1 is Lipschitz continuous, i.e., $|u_1(p) - u_1(q)| \leqslant L|p - q|$, with the Lipschitz constant

$$L \leqslant (\lambda-1)\max_{k\in[\![1,\lambda-1]\!]}|w_{k+1} - w_k| .$$

PROOF OF LEMMA A.2. The derivative of u_1 w.r.t. p is $\lambda\sum_{k=0}^{\lambda-1} w_{k+1}\binom{\lambda-1}{k}\frac{d}{dp}[p^k(1-p)^{\lambda-k-1}]$, where

$$\frac{dp^k(1-p)^{\lambda-k-1}}{dp} = kp^{k-1}(1-p)^{\lambda-k-1}$$
$$- (\lambda-k-1)p^k(1-p)^{\lambda-k-2} .$$

Substituting them, we have

$$\frac{du_1(p)}{dp}$$
$$= -w_1(\lambda-1)(1-p)^{\lambda-2} + w_\lambda(\lambda-1)p^{\lambda-2}$$
$$- \sum_{k=2}^{\lambda-1} w_k\binom{\lambda-1}{k-1}(\lambda-k)p^{k-1}(1-p)^{\lambda-k-1}$$
$$+ \sum_{k=2}^{\lambda-1} w_k\binom{\lambda-1}{k-1}(k-1)p^{k-2}(1-p)^{\lambda-k}$$
$$= (\lambda-1)\sum_{k=2}^{\lambda}(w_k - w_{k-1})\binom{\lambda-2}{k-2}p^{k-2}(1-p)^{\lambda-k}$$
$$= (\lambda-1)\sum_{k=1}^{\lambda-1}(w_{k+1} - w_k)\binom{\lambda-2}{k-1}p^{k-1}(1-p)^{\lambda-k-1} .$$

The Lipschitz constant L is the maximum of the absolute value of the above derivative. Note that $\binom{\lambda-2}{k-1}p^{k-1}(1-p)^{\lambda-k-1}$ sums up to one. The absolute value of the right-most side is upper bounded by $(\lambda-1)\max_{k\in[\![1,\lambda-1]\!]}|w_{k+1} - w_k|$. Therefore, $L \leqslant (\lambda-1)\max_{k\in[\![1,\lambda-1]\!]}|w_{k+1} - w_k|$. $\quad\square$

PROOF OF LEMMA 3.9. Since $\mathbf{A}$ is nonnegative definite and symmetric, there exist an orthogonal matrix $\mathbf{E}$ and a nonnegative diagonal matrix $\mathbf{D}$ such that $\mathbf{A} = \mathbf{EDE}^{\mathrm{T}}$, where each diagonal element of $\mathbf{D}$ is an eigenvalue of $\mathbf{A}$. Since the distribution of Z is isotropic, Z and $\mathcal{N} = \mathbf{E}^{\mathrm{T}}Z$

follow the same distribution, i.e., $\mathcal{N} = (\mathcal{N}_1, \ldots, \mathcal{N}_N)$ is N-multivariate standard normally distributed. Using this fact, we obtain

$$\mathbb{E}\left[\left(\frac{Z^{\mathrm{T}}\mathbf{A}Z}{\mathrm{Tr}(\mathbf{A})} - 1\right)^2\right]$$

$$= \mathbb{E}\left[\left(\sum_{i=1}^{N} \frac{[\mathbf{D}]_i}{\mathrm{Tr}(\mathbf{A})}(\mathcal{N}_i^2 - 1)\right)^2\right]$$

$$= \sum_{i=1}^{N}\sum_{j=1}^{N} \frac{[\mathbf{D}]_i[\mathbf{D}]_j}{\mathrm{Tr}(\mathbf{A})^2} \mathbb{E}\left[(\mathcal{N}_i^2 - 1)(\mathcal{N}_j^2 - 1)\right]$$

$$= \sum_{i=1}^{N} \frac{[\mathbf{D}]_i^2}{\mathrm{Tr}(\mathbf{A})^2} \mathbb{E}\left[(\mathcal{N}_i^2 - 1)^2\right]$$

$$+ \sum_{i=1}^{N}\sum_{j=1,j\neq i}^{N} \frac{[\mathbf{D}]_i[\mathbf{D}]_j}{\mathrm{Tr}(\mathbf{A})^2} \mathbb{E}\left[(\mathcal{N}_i^2 - 1)\right]\mathbb{E}\left[(\mathcal{N}_j^2 - 1)\right]$$

$$= \sum_{i=1}^{N} \frac{[\mathbf{D}]_i^2}{\mathrm{Tr}(\mathbf{A})^2} \mathbb{E}\left[(\mathcal{N}_i^2 - 1)^2\right] = 2\frac{\sum_{i=1}^{N}[\mathbf{D}]_i^2}{\mathrm{Tr}(\mathbf{A})^2} = 2\frac{\mathrm{Tr}(\mathbf{A}^2)}{\mathrm{Tr}(\mathbf{A})^2} .$$

Here we used the relation $\mathrm{Tr}(\mathbf{A}^2) = \mathrm{Tr}((\mathbf{EDE})^2) = \mathrm{Tr}(\mathbf{D}^2)$. Applying the Schwarz inequality and using Lemma A.1, we obtain

$$\mathbb{E}\left[\left|u_2(c_f(f(X)))((Z^{\mathrm{T}}\mathbf{A}Z)/\mathrm{Tr}(\mathbf{A}) - 1)\right|\right]^2$$

$$\leqslant \mathbb{E}[|u_2(c_f(f(X)))|^2]\mathbb{E}[((Z^{\mathrm{T}}\mathbf{A}Z)/\mathrm{Tr}(\mathbf{A}) - 1)^2]$$

$$\leqslant 2\left(\frac{1}{\lambda}\sum_{k=1}^{\lambda} w_k^4\right)\frac{\mathrm{Tr}(\mathbf{A}^2)}{\mathrm{Tr}(\mathbf{A})^2} . \quad \square$$

PROOF OF LEMMA 3.10. Let $\mathbf{A} = \mathbf{EDE}^{\mathrm{T}}$ be the eigen decomposition of $\mathbf{A}$ as we do in the proof of Lemma 3.9, and let $\mathcal{N} = \mathbf{E}^{\mathrm{T}}Z_1$ and $\tilde{\mathcal{N}} = \mathbf{E}^{\mathrm{T}}Z_2$. Then,

$$\mathbb{E}\left[\left(\frac{Z_1^{\mathrm{T}}\mathbf{A}Z_2}{\mathrm{Tr}(\mathbf{A})}\right)^2\right]$$

$$= \mathbb{E}\left[\left(\sum_{i=1}^{N} \frac{[\mathbf{D}]_i}{\mathrm{Tr}(\mathbf{A})}[\mathcal{N}]_i[\tilde{\mathcal{N}}]_i\right)^2\right]$$

$$= \sum_{i=1}^{N}\sum_{j=1}^{N} \frac{[\mathbf{D}]_i[\mathbf{D}]_j}{\mathrm{Tr}(\mathbf{A})^2} \mathbb{E}\left[[\mathcal{N}]_i[\tilde{\mathcal{N}}]_i[\mathcal{N}]_j[\tilde{\mathcal{N}}]_j\right]$$

$$= \sum_{i=1}^{N} \frac{[\mathbf{D}]_i^2}{\mathrm{Tr}(\mathbf{A})^2} \mathbb{E}[[\mathcal{N}]_i^2]\mathbb{E}[[\tilde{\mathcal{N}}]_i^2]$$

$$+ \sum_{i=1}^{N}\sum_{j=1,j\neq i}^{N} \frac{[\mathbf{D}]_i[\mathbf{D}]_j}{\mathrm{Tr}(\mathbf{A})^2} \mathbb{E}[[\mathcal{N}]_i]\mathbb{E}[[\tilde{\mathcal{N}}]_i]\mathbb{E}[[\mathcal{N}]_j]\mathbb{E}[[\tilde{\mathcal{N}}]_j]$$

$$= \frac{\sum_{i=1}^{N}[\mathbf{D}]_i^2}{\mathrm{Tr}(\mathbf{A})^2} = \frac{\mathrm{Tr}(\mathbf{A}^2)}{\mathrm{Tr}(\mathbf{A})^2} .$$

Applying the Schwarz inequality and using Lemma A.1,

$$\mathbb{E}\left[|u_3(c_f(f(X_1)), c_f(f(X_2)))(Z_1^{\mathrm{T}}\mathbf{A}Z_2)/\mathrm{Tr}(\mathbf{A})|\right]^2$$

$$\leqslant \mathbb{E}\left[|u_3(c_f(f(X_1)), c_f(f(X_2)))|^2\right]\mathbb{E}\left[((Z_1^{\mathrm{T}}\mathbf{A}Z_2)/\mathrm{Tr}(\mathbf{A}))^2\right]$$

$$\leqslant \left(\frac{2}{\lambda(\lambda-1)}\sum_{k=1}^{\lambda}\sum_{l=k+1}^{\lambda} w_k^2 w_l^2\right)\frac{\mathrm{Tr}(\mathbf{A}^2)}{\mathrm{Tr}(\mathbf{A})^2} . \quad \square$$

LEMMA A.3. $c_f(f(X)) = c_N(H_N)$.

PROOF OF LEMMA A.3. The probability of the i.i.d. copy $f(\tilde{X})$ of $f(X)$ being smaller than $f(X)$ is written as

$$c_f(f(X))$$

$$= \Pr[f(\tilde{X}) < f(X)]$$

$$= \Pr[f(\tilde{X}) - f(\boldsymbol{m}^{(t)}) < f(X) - f(\boldsymbol{m}^{(t)})]$$

$$= \Pr\left[\frac{f(\tilde{X}) - f(\boldsymbol{m}^{(t)})}{\|\nabla f(\boldsymbol{m}^{(t)})\|^2/\mathrm{Tr}(\mathbf{A})} < \frac{f(X) - f(\boldsymbol{m}^{(t)})}{\|\nabla f(\boldsymbol{m}^{(t)})\|^2/\mathrm{Tr}(\mathbf{A})}\right]$$

$$= \Pr\left[\frac{\bar{\sigma}}{c_m}\mathbf{e}^{\mathrm{T}}\tilde{Z} + \frac{\bar{\sigma}^2}{2c_m^2}\frac{\tilde{Z}^{\mathrm{T}}\mathbf{A}\tilde{Z}}{\mathrm{Tr}(\mathbf{A})} < \frac{\bar{\sigma}}{c_m}\mathbf{e}^{\mathrm{T}}Z + \frac{\bar{\sigma}^2}{2c_m^2}\frac{Z^{\mathrm{T}}\mathbf{A}Z}{\mathrm{Tr}(\mathbf{A})}\right]$$

$$= \Pr\left[\frac{\bar{\sigma}}{c_m}(\mathbf{Qe})^{\mathrm{T}}\tilde{\mathcal{N}} + \frac{\bar{\sigma}^2}{c_m^2}\frac{\tilde{\mathcal{N}}^{\mathrm{T}}\mathbf{QAQ}^{\mathrm{T}}\tilde{\mathcal{N}}}{2\mathrm{Tr}(\mathbf{A})}\right.$$

$$\left. < \frac{\bar{\sigma}}{c_m}(\mathbf{Qe})^{\mathrm{T}}\tilde{\mathcal{N}} + \frac{\bar{\sigma}^2}{c_m^2}\frac{\tilde{\mathcal{N}}^{\mathrm{T}}\mathbf{QAQ}^{\mathrm{T}}\tilde{\mathcal{N}}}{2\mathrm{Tr}(\mathbf{A})}\right]$$

$$= \Pr\left[\frac{\bar{\sigma}}{c_m}[\tilde{\mathcal{N}}]_1 + \frac{\bar{\sigma}^2}{c_m^2}\frac{\tilde{\mathcal{N}}^{\mathrm{T}}\mathbf{QAQ}^{\mathrm{T}}\tilde{\mathcal{N}}}{2\mathrm{Tr}(\mathbf{A})}\right.$$

$$\left. < \frac{\bar{\sigma}}{c_m}[\mathcal{N}]_1 + \frac{\bar{\sigma}^2}{c_m^2}\frac{\mathcal{N}^{\mathrm{T}}\mathbf{QAQ}^{\mathrm{T}}\mathcal{N}}{2\mathrm{Tr}(\mathbf{A})}\right]$$

$$= \Pr\left[\tilde{H}_N < H_N\right] = c_N(H_N) .$$

Here we used (28). $\square$

LEMMA A.4. For any $\epsilon > 0$,

$$\Pr\left[\sup_{\boldsymbol{m}\in\mathbb{R}^N\backslash\{x^*\}}\left|H_N - \left[\frac{\bar{\sigma}[\mathcal{N}]_1}{c_m} + \frac{\bar{\sigma}^2}{2c_m^2}\right]\right| \geqslant \epsilon\right]$$

$$\leqslant \frac{\bar{\sigma}^4}{2\epsilon^2 c_m^4}\frac{\mathrm{Tr}(\mathbf{A}^2)}{\mathrm{Tr}(\mathbf{A})^2} .$$

PROOF OF LEMMA A.4. By Chebyshev's inequality, for any $\epsilon > 0$

$$\Pr\left[\sup_{\boldsymbol{m}\in\mathbb{R}^N\backslash\{x^*\}}\left|H_N - \left[\frac{\bar{\sigma}[\mathcal{N}]_1}{c_m} + \frac{\bar{\sigma}^2}{2c_m^2}\right]\right| \geqslant \epsilon\right]$$

$$\leqslant \frac{\bar{\sigma}^4}{4\epsilon^2 c_m^4}\mathbb{E}\left[\sup_{\boldsymbol{m}\in\mathbb{R}^N\backslash\{x^*\}}\left(\frac{\mathcal{N}^{\mathrm{T}}\mathbf{QAQ}^{\mathrm{T}}\mathcal{N}}{\mathrm{Tr}(\mathbf{A})} - 1\right)^2\right] . \quad (50)$$

Analogously to what we have done in the proof of Lemma 3.9, we find

$$\mathbb{E}\left[\sup_{\boldsymbol{m}\in\mathbb{R}^N\backslash\{x^*\}}\left(\frac{\mathcal{N}^{\mathrm{T}}\mathbf{QAQ}^{\mathrm{T}}\mathcal{N}}{\mathrm{Tr}(\mathbf{A})} - 1\right)^2\right]$$

$$= 2\frac{\sup_{\boldsymbol{m}\in\mathbb{R}^N\backslash\{x^*\}}\mathrm{Tr}((\mathbf{QAQ}^{\mathrm{T}})^2)}{\mathrm{Tr}(\mathbf{A})^2} = 2\frac{\mathrm{Tr}(\mathbf{A}^2)}{\mathrm{Tr}(\mathbf{A})^2} .$$

Inserting the above equality to (50), we end the proof. $\square$

LEMMA A.5. For any $\alpha \geqslant 1$,

$$\mathbb{E}\left[\sup_{\boldsymbol{m}\in\mathbb{R}^N\backslash\{x^*\}}|c_N(H_N) - \Phi([\mathcal{N}]_1)|^\alpha\right] \leqslant 3\left[\frac{\bar{\sigma}^2}{4\pi c_m^2}\frac{\mathrm{Tr}(\mathbf{A}^2)}{\mathrm{Tr}(\mathbf{A})^2}\right]^{\frac{1}{3}} .$$

PROOF OF LEMMA A.5. The trivial inequality $|c_N(H_N) - c([\mathcal{N}]_1)| \leqslant 1$ for $\alpha \geqslant 1$ gives that $|c_N(H_N) - c([\mathcal{N}]_1)|^\alpha \leqslant |c_N(H_N) - c([\mathcal{N}]_1)|$. Then, we have $\mathbb{E}[\sup_{\boldsymbol{m}\in\mathbb{R}^N\backslash\{x^*\}}|c_N(H_N) - c([\mathcal{N}]_1)|^\alpha] \leqslant \mathbb{E}[\sup_{\boldsymbol{m}\in\mathbb{R}^N\backslash\{x^*\}}|c_N(H_N) - c([\mathcal{N}]_1)|]$ and it suffices to show the desired inequality for $\alpha = 1$.

Consider the case $\alpha = 1$. For any $\epsilon > 0$ and any $\boldsymbol{m} \in \mathbb{R}^N \setminus \{x^*\}$,

$$|c_N(H_N) - \Phi([\mathcal{N}]_1)|$$
$$= |\Pr[\tilde{H}_N < H_N] - \Pr[[\tilde{\mathcal{N}}]_1 < [\mathcal{N}]_1]|$$
$$= |\Pr[\tilde{H}_N < H_N]$$
$$\quad - \Pr[(\tfrac{\bar{\sigma}}{c_m})[\tilde{\mathcal{N}}]_1 + \tfrac{1}{2}(\tfrac{\bar{\sigma}}{c_m})^2 < (\tfrac{\bar{\sigma}}{c_m})[\mathcal{N}]_1 + \tfrac{1}{2}(\tfrac{\bar{\sigma}}{c_m})^2]|$$
$$= |\mathbb{E}[\mathbb{I}\{\tilde{H}_N < H_N\}]$$
$$\quad - \mathbb{E}[\mathbb{I}\{(\tfrac{\bar{\sigma}}{c_m})[\tilde{\mathcal{N}}]_1 + \tfrac{1}{2}(\tfrac{\bar{\sigma}}{c_m})^2 < (\tfrac{\bar{\sigma}}{c_m})[\mathcal{N}]_1 + \tfrac{1}{2}(\tfrac{\bar{\sigma}}{c_m})^2\}]|$$
$$\leqslant \mathbb{E}[|\mathbb{I}\{\tilde{H}_N < H_N\}$$
$$\quad - \mathbb{I}\{(\tfrac{\bar{\sigma}}{c_m})[\tilde{\mathcal{N}}]_1 + \tfrac{1}{2}(\tfrac{\bar{\sigma}}{c_m})^2 < (\tfrac{\bar{\sigma}}{c_m})[\mathcal{N}]_1 + \tfrac{1}{2}(\tfrac{\bar{\sigma}}{c_m})^2\}|]$$
$$\leqslant \mathbb{E}[\mathbb{I}\{|((\tfrac{\bar{\sigma}}{c_m})[\tilde{\mathcal{N}}]_1 + \tfrac{1}{2}(\tfrac{\bar{\sigma}}{c_m})^2) - ((\tfrac{\bar{\sigma}}{c_m})[\mathcal{N}]_1 + \tfrac{1}{2}(\tfrac{\bar{\sigma}}{c_m})^2)| < \epsilon\}$$
$$\quad + \mathbb{I}\{|H_N - ((\tfrac{\bar{\sigma}}{c_m})[\mathcal{N}]_1 + \tfrac{1}{2}(\tfrac{\bar{\sigma}}{c_m})^2)| \geqslant \tfrac{1}{2}\epsilon\}$$
$$\quad + \mathbb{I}\{|\tilde{H}_N - ((\tfrac{\bar{\sigma}}{c_m})[\tilde{\mathcal{N}}]_1 + \tfrac{1}{2}(\tfrac{\bar{\sigma}}{c_m})^2)| \geqslant \tfrac{1}{2}\epsilon\}]$$
$$= \Pr[|((\tfrac{\bar{\sigma}}{c_m})[\tilde{\mathcal{N}}]_1 + \tfrac{1}{2}(\tfrac{\bar{\sigma}}{c_m})^2) - ((\tfrac{\bar{\sigma}}{c_m})[\mathcal{N}]_1 + \tfrac{1}{2}(\tfrac{\bar{\sigma}}{c_m})^2)| < \epsilon]$$
$$\quad + \mathbb{I}\{|H_N - ((\tfrac{\bar{\sigma}}{c_m})[\mathcal{N}]_1 + \tfrac{1}{2}(\tfrac{\bar{\sigma}}{c_m})^2)| \geqslant \tfrac{1}{2}\epsilon\}$$
$$\quad + \Pr[|\tilde{H}_N - ((\tfrac{\bar{\sigma}}{c_m})[\tilde{\mathcal{N}}]_1 + \tfrac{1}{2}(\tfrac{\bar{\sigma}}{c_m})^2)| \geqslant \tfrac{1}{2}\epsilon]$$
$$= \Pr[|[\tilde{\mathcal{N}}]_1 - [\mathcal{N}]_1| < \epsilon/(\tfrac{\bar{\sigma}}{c_m})]$$
$$\quad + \mathbb{I}\{|H_N - ((\tfrac{\bar{\sigma}}{c_m})[\mathcal{N}]_1 + \tfrac{1}{2}(\tfrac{\bar{\sigma}}{c_m})^2)| \geqslant \tfrac{1}{2}\epsilon\}$$
$$\quad + \Pr[|\tilde{H}_N - ((\tfrac{\bar{\sigma}}{c_m})[\tilde{\mathcal{N}}]_1 + \tfrac{1}{2}(\tfrac{\bar{\sigma}}{c_m})^2)| \geqslant \tfrac{1}{2}\epsilon]$$
$$\leqslant \Pr[|[\tilde{\mathcal{N}}]_1 - [\mathcal{N}]_1| < \epsilon/(\tfrac{\bar{\sigma}}{c_m})]$$
$$\quad + \mathbb{I}\{\sup_{\boldsymbol{m} \in \mathbb{R}^N \setminus \{x^*\}}|H_N - ((\tfrac{\bar{\sigma}}{c_m})[\mathcal{N}]_1 + \tfrac{1}{2}(\tfrac{\bar{\sigma}}{c_m})^2)| \geqslant \tfrac{1}{2}\epsilon\}$$
$$\quad + \Pr[\sup_{\boldsymbol{m} \in \mathbb{R}^N \setminus \{x^*\}}|\tilde{H}_N - ((\tfrac{\bar{\sigma}}{c_m})[\tilde{\mathcal{N}}]_1 + \tfrac{1}{2}(\tfrac{\bar{\sigma}}{c_m})^2)| \geqslant \tfrac{1}{2}\epsilon] ,$$

where the probability and the expectation are taken for $\tilde{H}_N$ and $[\tilde{\mathcal{N}}]_1$. Taking the expectation of the right-most side of the above equality for H_N and $[\mathcal{N}]_1$, we find

$$\mathbb{E}\left[\sup_{\boldsymbol{m} \in \mathbb{R}^N \setminus \{x^*\}}|c_N(H_N) - \Phi([\mathcal{N}]_1)|\right]$$
$$\leqslant \Pr\left[|[\tilde{\mathcal{N}}]_1 - [\mathcal{N}]_1| < \epsilon/(\tfrac{\bar{\sigma}}{c_m})\right]$$
$$\quad + \mathbb{E}\left[\mathbb{I}\left\{\sup_{\boldsymbol{m} \in \mathbb{R}^N \setminus \{x^*\}}\left|H_N - \left(\frac{\bar{\sigma}}{c_m}[\mathcal{N}]_1 + \frac{1}{2}\frac{\bar{\sigma}^2}{c_m^2}\right)\right| \geqslant \frac{1}{2}\epsilon\right\}\right]$$
$$\quad + \Pr\left[\sup_{\boldsymbol{m} \in \mathbb{R}^N \setminus \{x^*\}}\left|\tilde{H}_N - \left(\frac{\bar{\sigma}}{c_m}[\tilde{\mathcal{N}}]_1 + \frac{1}{2}\frac{\bar{\sigma}^2}{c_m^2}\right)\right| \geqslant \frac{1}{2}\epsilon\right]$$
$$= \Pr\left[|[\tilde{\mathcal{N}}]_1 - [\mathcal{N}]_1| < \epsilon/(\tfrac{\bar{\sigma}}{c_m})\right]$$
$$\quad + 2\Pr\left[\sup_{\boldsymbol{m} \in \mathbb{R}^N \setminus \{x^*\}}\left|H_N - \left(\frac{\bar{\sigma}}{c_m}[\mathcal{N}]_1 + \frac{1}{2}\frac{\bar{\sigma}^2}{c_m^2}\right)\right| \geqslant \frac{1}{2}\epsilon\right]$$
$$= \Pr\left[|[\mathcal{N}]_1| < \epsilon/\left(2^{\frac{1}{2}}(\tfrac{\bar{\sigma}}{c_m})\right)\right]$$
$$\quad + 2\Pr\left[\sup_{\boldsymbol{m} \in \mathbb{R}^N \setminus \{x^*\}}\left|H_N - \left(\frac{\bar{\sigma}}{c_m}[\mathcal{N}]_1 + \frac{1}{2}\frac{\bar{\sigma}^2}{c_m^2}\right)\right| \geqslant \frac{1}{2}\epsilon\right] .$$

The first term on the right-most side is upper bounded as

$$\Pr[|[\mathcal{N}]_1| < \epsilon/(2^{\frac{1}{2}}(\tfrac{\bar{\sigma}}{c_m}))] = \int_0^{\epsilon/(2^{\frac{1}{2}}(\frac{\bar{\sigma}}{c_m}))} (2/\pi)^{\frac{1}{2}} \exp(-x^2/2)\mathrm{d}x$$
$$\leqslant (2/\pi)^{\frac{1}{2}}(\epsilon/(2^{\frac{1}{2}}(\tfrac{\bar{\sigma}}{c_m}))) = \epsilon/(\pi^{\frac{1}{2}}(\tfrac{\bar{\sigma}}{c_m})) .$$

The second term is upper bounded by $\frac{\bar{\sigma}^4}{\epsilon^2 c_m^4}\frac{\mathrm{Tr}(\mathbf{A}^2)}{\mathrm{Tr}(\mathbf{A})^2}$ in light of Lemma A.4. Since the above inequality holds for any $\epsilon > 0$,

letting $\epsilon = (2\pi^{\frac{1}{2}}(\tfrac{\bar{\sigma}}{c_m})^5(\mathrm{Tr}(\mathbf{A}^2)/\mathrm{Tr}(\mathbf{A})^2))^{\frac{1}{3}}$, we obtain

$$\mathbb{E}\left[\sup_{\boldsymbol{m} \in \mathbb{R}^N \setminus \{x^*\}}|c_N(H_N) - \Phi([\mathcal{N}]_1)|\right]$$
$$\leqslant \frac{\epsilon c_m}{\pi^{\frac{1}{2}}\bar{\sigma}} + \frac{\bar{\sigma}^4}{\epsilon^2 c_m^4}\frac{\mathrm{Tr}(\mathbf{A}^2)}{\mathrm{Tr}(\mathbf{A})^2} = 3\left(\frac{\bar{\sigma}^2}{4\pi c_m^2}\frac{\mathrm{Tr}(\mathbf{A}^2)}{\mathrm{Tr}(\mathbf{A})^2}\right)^{\frac{1}{3}} . \quad \square$$

PROOF OF LEMMA 3.11. In light of Lemma A.2, we find that the function u_1 is Lipschitz continuous, i.e., $|u_1(x) - u_1(y)| \leqslant L|x - y|$ for any $x, y \in [0, 1]$, with the Lipschitz constant L upper bounded by $(\lambda - 1)\max_{k \in [\![1, \lambda-1]\!]}|w_{k+1} - w_k|$. Then, applying the Schwarz inequality and Lemma A.5, we have

$$\sup_{\boldsymbol{m} \in \mathbb{R}^N \setminus \{x^*\}}|\mathbb{E}[u_1(c_N(H_N))[\mathcal{N}]_1] - \mathbb{E}[u_1(\Phi([\mathcal{N}]_1))[\mathcal{N}]_1]|$$
$$\leqslant \sup_{\boldsymbol{m} \in \mathbb{R}^N \setminus \{x^*\}}\mathbb{E}[|u_1(c_N(H_N)) - u_1(\Phi([\mathcal{N}]_1))||[\mathcal{N}]_1|]$$
$$\leqslant \sup_{\boldsymbol{m} \in \mathbb{R}^N \setminus \{x^*\}}\mathbb{E}[|u_1(c_N(H_N)) - u_1(\Phi([\mathcal{N}]_1))|^2 \mathbb{E}[|[\mathcal{N}]_1|^2]$$
$$= \sup_{\boldsymbol{m} \in \mathbb{R}^N \setminus \{x^*\}}\mathbb{E}[|u_1(c_N(H_N)) - u_1(\Phi([\mathcal{N}]_1))|^2]$$
$$\leqslant \sup_{\boldsymbol{m} \in \mathbb{R}^N \setminus \{x^*\}}L\mathbb{E}[|c_N(H_N) - \Phi([\mathcal{N}]_1)|^2]$$
$$\leqslant L\mathbb{E}\left[\sup_{\boldsymbol{m} \in \mathbb{R}^N \setminus \{x^*\}}|c_N(H_N) - \Phi([\mathcal{N}]_1)|^2\right]$$
$$\leqslant 3L\left(\frac{(\bar{\sigma}/c_m)^2}{4\pi}\frac{\mathrm{Tr}(\mathbf{A}^2)}{\mathrm{Tr}(\mathbf{A})^2}\right)^{\frac{1}{3}}$$
$$\leqslant 3(\lambda - 1)\max_{k \in [\![1, \lambda-1]\!]}|w_{k+1} - w_k|\left(\frac{(\bar{\sigma}/c_m)^2}{4\pi}\frac{\mathrm{Tr}(\mathbf{A}^2)}{\mathrm{Tr}(\mathbf{A})^2}\right)^{\frac{1}{3}} .$$

Note that $c_f(f(X)) = c_N(H_N)$ (Lemma A.3). This completes the proof. $\square$

PROOF OF LEMMA 3.12. Letting $p_{i:\lambda}$ be the pdf of $\mathcal{N}_{i:\lambda}$, we have

$$\lambda \int u_1(\Phi([\mathcal{N}]_1))p([\mathcal{N}]_1)[\mathcal{N}]_1 d[\mathcal{N}]_1$$
$$= \sum_{k=1}^{\lambda} w_k \int p_{i:\lambda}([\mathcal{N}]_1)[\mathcal{N}]_1 d[\mathcal{N}]_1$$
$$= \sum_{k=1}^{\lambda} w_k \mathbb{E}[\mathcal{N}_{i:\lambda}] . \quad \square$$

On the Statistical Learning Ability of Evolution Strategies

Ofer M. Shir
Computer Science Department, Tel-Hai College,
and The Galilee Research Institute - Migal,
Upper Galilee, Israel
ofersh@telhai.ac.il

Amir Yehudayoff
Department of Mathematics
Technion - Israel Institute of Technology,
Haifa, Israel
amir.yehudayoff@gmail.com

ABSTRACT

We explore the ability of Evolution Strategies (ESs) to statistically learn the local landscape. Specifically, we consider ESs operating only with isotropic Gaussian mutations near the optimum and investigate the covariance matrix when constructed out of selected individuals by truncation. Unlike previous studies, we do not assume a Derandomization adaptation scheme, nor do we use Information Geometric Optimization in our proofs. We prove that the statistically constructed covariance matrix over such selected decision vectors has the same eigenvectors as the Hessian matrix. We further prove that when the population size is increased, the covariance becomes proportional to the inverse of the Hessian. We also devise and corroborate an analytic approximation of this covariance matrix. In the framework we consider, this confirms the classical hypothesis that learning the landscape is an inherent property of standard ESs, and that this capability stems only from the usage of isotropic Gaussian mutations and rank-based selection.

Categories and Subject Descriptors

F.2.1 [**Theory of Computation**]: ANALYSIS OF ALGORITHMS AND PROBLEM COMPLEXITY—*Numerical Algorithms and Problems*; G.1.6 [**Mathematics of Computing**]: NUMERICAL ANALYSIS—*Optimization*

Keywords

Theory of evolution strategies; covariance; Hessian; statistical landscape learning; limit distributions of order statistics

1. INTRODUCTION

Evolution Strategies (ESs) are popular heuristics that excel in global optimization of continuous search landscapes [15]. They utilize a Gaussian-based update (mutation) step with an evolving covariance matrix. Since their development, it has been hypothesized that this learned covariance matrix, which defines the mutation operation, approximates

FOGA '17, January 12-15, 2017, Copenhagen, Denmark

© 2017 ACM. ISBN 978-1-4503-4651-1/17/01...$15.00

DOI: http://dx.doi.org/10.1145/3040718.3040722

the inverse Hessian of the search landscape. It was supported by the rationale that locating the optimum by an ES can be accommodated using mutation steps that fit the actual landscape. In other words, that the optimal covariance distribution can offer mutation steps whose *equidensity probability contours* match the *level sets* of the landscape, and so they maximize the progress rate [13]. Altogether, the motivation to hold a covariance matrix reflective of the eigen-directions of the landscape Hessian is well-justified [15]. Nonetheless, it has never been formally proven that the classical ES machinery can indeed learn such a covariance matrix. Rudolph's study on correlated mutations [13] motivated researchers to design ESs that accumulate search information by means of covariance matrices or any other forms of statistically learned algebraic structures [3]. Especially, selected individuals' information is accumulated in practice by Derandomized ESs [10], which have become a successful family of search heuristics, referred herein as modern ESs. Finally, it should be stressed that there exists overwhelming empirical evidence for the hypothesis that ESs can learn such a covariance matrix (see, e.g., [16]).

Recent developments in randomized search heuristics for continuous optimization succeeded in making a link between certain modern ESs (e.g., the renowned CMA-ES [3]) to Information Geometry (IG) [2], which is typically employed in Machine Learning. The high relevance of IG to modern ESs is apparent due to the routinely deployed strategy adaptation by means of the mutation distribution update. This line of research work originated in the release of the so-called Natural ESs [17], and the consequent compilation of the IG Optimization (IGO) philosophy [12] as well as the formulation of the Natural Gradient (NGD) algorithm [1]. In short, the building-block of this class of algorithms is the *natural gradient method* [2]. Importantly, in the context of landscape learning, modern ESs were proven to achieve such learning under certain adaptation mechanisms. Akimoto proved that the NGD algorithm adapts its covariance matrix so it becomes proportional to the inverse landscape Hessian of any monotonic convex-quadratic composite function in the limit of a large population size. More broadly, Beyer [4] showed that implementation of the IGO philosophy leads to a self-adapted covariance matrix that is proportional to the inverse landscape Hessian in the same limit.

The current study "goes back to basics" in the sense that it investigates ESs' capacity to learn the landscape – only by means of isotropic Gaussian mutations and rank-based truncation selection. Its primary goal is thus to investigate the statistical learning potential of an accumulated set of selected individuals (so-called *winners* of each generation) when an ES operates in the vicinity of a landscape optimum, without adaptation. We show that accumulation of such *winners* carries the potential to reveal valuable landscape information, even with isotropic Gaussian mutations.

First, we prove that the statistically-constructed covariance matrix over *winning* decision vectors commutes with the Hessian matrix about the optimum (i.e., the two matrices share the same eigenvectors, and therefore their level sets are positioned along the same axes). This result indicates that in learning a covariance, an ES deduces the sensitive directions for an effective optimization, and may do so even with isotropic mutations. This result, however, holds for all population sizes and is primarily based on the invariance of the Gaussian measure with respect to rotations.

We then prove that the covariance matrix of the winning vectors converges to the inverse of the landscape Hessian, up to a scalar factor, when the population size tends to infinity. This shows that for large populations, ESs indeed unveil a lot of information on the landscape. Furthermore, we provide an explicit analytic approximation of this covariance matrix, which holds for large population sizes.

The remainder of this paper is organized as follows. The framework is formally stated in Section 2, where the assumed model is described in detail. In Section 3 we formulate the covariance matrix, derive the necessary density function, and then prove that the covariance and the Hessian commute both in $(1, \lambda)$- and (μ, λ)-truncation selection. We address in Section 4 the relation between the covariance matrix and the landscape Hessian, subject to a large population size. Section 5 provides an analytical covariance approximation for an ES with $(1, \lambda)$-selection. A simulation study encompassing various landscape scenarios for $(1, \lambda)$ selection is presented in Section 6, constituting a numerical corroboration for all the theoretical outcomes throughout this work. Finally, the results are discussed in Section 7.

2. STATISTICAL LANDSCAPE LEARNING

We outline the *research question* that we target:

> What is the relation between the statistically-constructed covariance matrix over *winners* to the landscape Hessian?

We focus on the *a posteriori* statistical construction of the covariance matrix of the decision variables. Next, we formulate the problem, assume a model and present our notation.

2.1 The Model

Let $J : \mathbb{R}^n \to \mathbb{R}$ denote the objective function subject to minimization. We assume that J is minimized at the location $\vec{x}^*$, which is assumed for simplicity to be the origin. The objective function may be *Taylor-expanded* about the optimum. We model the n-dimensional basin of attraction about $\vec{x}^*$ by means of a quadratic approximation. We assume that this expansion is precise:

$$J\left(\vec{x} - \vec{x}^*\right) = J(\vec{x}) = \vec{x}^T \cdot \mathcal{H} \cdot \vec{x}, \qquad (1)$$

with $\mathcal{H}$ being the landscape Hessian about the optimum.

The classical non-elitist single-parent ES operates in the following manner: λ search-points $\vec{x}_1, \ldots, \vec{x}_\lambda$ are generated in each iteration, based upon Gaussian sampling with respect to the parent point. We are especially concerned with

the canonical ES variation operator, which adds a normally distributed *mutation* $\vec{z} \sim \mathcal{N}(\vec{0}, \mathbf{I})$. That is, $\vec{x}_1, \ldots, \vec{x}_\lambda$ are independent and each is $\mathcal{N}(\vec{0}, \mathbf{I})$. Upon evaluating those λ points with respect to J, the best (minimal) individual is selected and recorded as

$$\vec{y} = \arg \min \left\{ J(\vec{x}_1), \; J(\vec{x}_2), \; \ldots, \; J(\vec{x}_\lambda) \right\}. \qquad (2)$$

Finally, let ω denote the *winning* objective function value,

$$\omega = J(\vec{y}) = \min \left\{ J(\vec{x}_1), \; J(\vec{x}_2), \; \ldots, \; J(\vec{x}_\lambda) \right\}. \qquad (3)$$

We will also consider the case of (μ, λ)-selection, where the truncated subset of μ winners is selected (formal details appear in subsection 3.2).

We mention the difference between the optimization phase, which aims to arrive at the optimum and is not discussed here, to the statistical learning of the basin, which lies in the focus of this study.

The sampling procedure is summarized as Algorithm 1, wherein statCovariance refers to a routine for *statistically* constructing a covariance matrix from raw observations.

---

1   $t \leftarrow 0$
2   $\mathcal{S} \leftarrow \emptyset$
3 **repeat**
4   **for** $k \leftarrow 1$ **to** λ **do**
5      $\vec{x}_k^{(t+1)} \leftarrow \vec{x}^* + \vec{z}_k, \quad \vec{z}_k \sim \mathcal{N}(\vec{0}, \mathbf{I})$
6      $J_k^{(t+1)} \leftarrow \texttt{evaluate}\left(\vec{x}_k^{(t+1)}\right)$
7   **end**
8    $m_{t+1} \leftarrow \arg \min \left(\left\{ J_i^{(t+1)} \right\}_{i=1}^{\lambda} \right)$
9    $\mathcal{S} \leftarrow \mathcal{S} \cup \left\{ \vec{x}_{m_{t+1}}^{(t+1)} \right\}$
10    $t \leftarrow t + 1$
11 **until** $t \geq N_{iter}$
    output: $\mathcal{C}^{\text{stat}} = \texttt{statCovariance}(\mathcal{S})$

Algorithm 1: Statistical sampling by $(1, \lambda)$-selection

---

2.2 Underlying Probability Functions

In the simplest case of an isotropic basin, the Hessian matrix is the identity: $\mathcal{H} = \mathbf{I}$. In this case, $\psi = J(\vec{z})$ is a random variable which obeys the standard χ^2-distribution, possessing the following cumulative distribution function (CDF) accounting for the search-space dimensionality n:

$$F_{\chi^2}(\psi) = \frac{1}{2^{n/2} \Gamma(n/2)} \int_0^\psi t^{\frac{n}{2}-1} \exp\left(-\frac{t}{2}\right) \, \mathrm{d}t, \qquad (4)$$

with $\Gamma(t)$ being the Gamma function. The probability density function (PDF) is given by:

$$f_{\chi^2}(\psi) = \frac{1}{2^{n/2} \Gamma(n/2)} \psi^{n/2-1} \exp\left(-\frac{\psi}{2}\right). \qquad (5)$$

In the general case [11], the Hessian is a positive definite matrix possessing the following eigendecomposition form,

$$\mathcal{H} = \mathcal{U} \mathcal{D} \mathcal{U}^{-1}, \qquad \mathcal{D} = \mathrm{diag}\left[\Delta_1, \ldots, \Delta_n\right],$$

with $\{\Delta_i\}_{i=1}^{n}$ being the eigenvalues. The random variable ψ now obeys a generalized χ^2-distribution, whose *exact distri-*

Term	Description	Notation
landscape Hessian	positive definite matrix defining the landscape structure	$\mathcal{H}$
objective function	subject to minimization, assumed to be minimized at $\vec{x}^*$	$J(\vec{x}) = \vec{x}^T \cdot \mathcal{H} \cdot \vec{x}$
random vector	a normal Gaussian mutation	$\vec{z}$
random vector's function value	representing the objective function's value of $\vec{z}$	$\psi = J(\vec{z})$
population size	number of generated search-points per iteration	λ
offspring	λ independent copies of $\vec{z}$	$\vec{x}_1, \ldots, \vec{x}_\lambda$
parental population size	number of selected search-points per iteration	μ
winner	the recorded best (minimal) individual by selection	$\vec{y}$
winning value	the winning objective function value	$\omega = J(\vec{y})$
ℓ^{th} winner	the recorded ℓ^{th}-best individual by selection	$\vec{y}_{\ell:\lambda}$
ℓ^{th} winning value	the ℓth-best objective function value	$\omega_{\ell:\lambda}$
covariance matrix	covariance matrix over winning decision vectors (Eq. 10)	$\mathcal{C}$
statistical covariance matrix	statistically-constructed matrix (Algorithm 1)	$\mathcal{C}^{\text{stat}}$

Table 1: Nomenclature.

bution function is described as follows [7]:

$$F_{\mathcal{H}\chi^2}(\psi) = \int_0^\infty \frac{2}{\pi} \frac{\sin \frac{t\psi}{2}}{t} \cos \left(-t\psi + \frac{1}{2} \sum_{j=1}^n \tan^{-1} 2\Delta_j t \right)$$
$$\times \prod_{j=1}^n \left(1 + \Delta_j^2 t^2 \right)^{-\frac{1}{4}} \, \mathrm{d}t,$$

$$(6)$$

with an unknown closed form. At the same time, this CDF is known to follow an *approximation* [7],

$$F_{\tau\chi^2}(\psi) = \frac{\Upsilon^\eta}{\Gamma(\eta)} \int_0^\psi t^{\eta-1} \exp(-\Upsilon t) \, \mathrm{d}t, \qquad (7)$$

with Υ and η accounting for the first two moments of $\vec{z}^T \mathcal{H} \vec{z}$ (and the subscript τ marks the transformed distribution):

$$\Upsilon = \frac{1}{2} \frac{\sum_{i=1}^n \Delta_i}{\sum_{i=1}^n \Delta_i^2}, \qquad \eta = \frac{1}{2} \frac{\left(\sum_{i=1}^n \Delta_i \right)^2}{\sum_{i=1}^n \Delta_i^2}. \qquad (8)$$

The density function of this approximation reads:

$$f_{\tau\chi^2}(\psi) = \frac{\Upsilon^\eta}{\Gamma(\eta)} \psi^{\eta-1} \exp(-\Upsilon \psi). \qquad (9)$$

The accuracy of this approximation depends upon the standard deviation of the eigenvalues [7]. Later on, we shall assume that this standard deviation is moderate, and adopt this approximation. For the isotropic case, it can be easily verified that Eq. 9 reduces to Eq. 5.

The notation introduced above is summarized in Table 1.

3. THE COVARIANCE MATRIX

We now describe the covariance matrix and prove it commutes with the landscape Hessian. By construction, the origin is set at the parent search-point, which is located at the optimum. Analytically, the covariance elements are thus reduced to the following *expectation values*:

$$\boxed{\mathcal{C}_{ij} = \int x_i x_j \text{PDF}_{\vec{y}}(\vec{x}) \, \mathrm{d}\vec{x}}, \qquad (10)$$

where $\text{PDF}_{\vec{y}}(\vec{x})$ is an n-dimensional density function characterizing the *winning* decision variables about the optimum. The current study aims at understanding this expression in Eq. 10. To this end, revealing the nature of $\text{PDF}_{\vec{y}}$ is necessary for the interpretation of the covariance matrix. It is important to keep in mind that the ES selection is blind to the location of the candidate solutions in the search space, and its sole criterion is the ranked objective function value.

3.1 A Single Winner: $(1, \lambda)$-Selection

The density function of a single *winning* vector of decision variables $\vec{y}$ is related to the density of the *winning* value ω via the following relation:

$$\boxed{\text{PDF}_{\vec{y}}(\vec{x}) = \text{PDF}_\omega(J(\vec{x})) \cdot \frac{\text{PDF}_{\vec{z}}(\vec{x})}{\text{PDF}_\psi(J(\vec{x}))}}, \qquad (11)$$

with $\text{PDF}_{\vec{z}}$ denoting the density function for generating an individual by *mutation*, and PDF_ψ denoting the density function of the objective function values (Eqs. 5 or 9). A brief justification follows. The density functions satisfy the conditional probability relation:

$$\text{PDF}_{\vec{y}}(\vec{x}) = \text{PDF}_\omega(J(\vec{x})) \cdot \text{PDF}_{\vec{y}|\omega}(\vec{x} \mid J(\vec{x})). \qquad (12)$$

Now consider the distribution of $[\vec{y}; \omega]$ on $\mathbb{R}^{n+1}$. The density of $\vec{y}$ conditioned on the value of $J(\vec{y})$ is that of a normal Gaussian subject to this conditioning, since we may sample $[\vec{y}; \omega]$ by the following construction: First sample $\{J_1, \ldots, J_\lambda\}$ according to PDF_ψ independently. Then sample $\{\vec{x}_1, \ldots, \vec{x}_\lambda\}$ conditioned on the values of $J_1, \ldots, J_\lambda$ independently. Finally, ω is set to the minimum J_ℓ, and $\vec{y}$ is set to $\vec{x}_\ell$. In other words, following selection, a winning value is chosen to be ω, and the corresponding vector becomes the winning vector $\vec{y}$. The winning vector $\vec{y}$ conditioned on $J(\vec{y}) = \omega$ is generated in the same manner as a normally-distributed $\vec{z}$ conditioned on $J(\vec{z}) = \omega$. That is, $\text{PDF}_{\vec{y}|\omega} = \text{PDF}_{\vec{z}|\psi}$. This density therefore reads:

$$\text{PDF}_{\vec{y}|\omega}(\vec{x} \mid J(\vec{x})) = \text{PDF}_{\vec{z}|\psi}(\vec{x} \mid J(\vec{x})) = \frac{\text{PDF}_{\vec{z}}(\vec{x})}{\text{PDF}_\psi(J(\vec{x}))}. \qquad (13)$$

This explicit structure of the winners' density already yields covariance and Hessian matrices that share the same eigenvectors, as stated in the following proposition:

PROPOSITION 1. *The covariance matrix and the Hessian commute and are simultaneously diagonalizable, when the objective function follows the quadratic approximation.*

In a nutshell, the proof follows from the invariance of the Normal distribution under rotations, and from the symmetry of the objective function (for instance, if the Hessian is diagonal, then $J(x_1, x_2, \ldots, x_n) = J(-x_1, x_2, \ldots, x_n)$).

PROOF. Given the density function in Eq. 11, the objective function is assumed to satisfy $J(\vec{x}) = \vec{x}^T \cdot \mathcal{H} \cdot \vec{x}$, and the covariance matrix reads:

$$\mathcal{C}_{ij} = \int x_i x_j \mathrm{PDF}_\omega \left(\vec{x}^T \cdot \mathcal{H} \cdot \vec{x} \right) \cdot \frac{\mathrm{PDF}_{\vec{z}}(\vec{x})}{\mathrm{PDF}_\psi \left(\vec{x}^T \cdot \mathcal{H} \cdot \vec{x} \right)} \mathrm{d}\vec{x}. \quad (14)$$

Consider the orthogonal matrix $\mathcal{U}$, which diagonalizes $\mathcal{H}$ into $\mathcal{D}$ and possesses a determinant of value 1:

$$\mathcal{U}^{-1} \mathcal{H} \mathcal{U} = \mathcal{D} \equiv \mathrm{diag}\,[\Delta_1, \Delta_2, \ldots, \Delta_n],$$

$$\vec{\vartheta} = \mathcal{U}^{-1} \vec{x},$$

$$\mathrm{d}\vec{\vartheta} = \mathrm{d}\vec{x}.$$

We target the integral $\mathcal{T}_{ij} = \left(\mathcal{U}^{-1} \mathcal{C} \mathcal{U} \right)_{ij}$ and apply a change of variables into $\vec{\vartheta}$ (after changing order of summations):

$$\mathcal{T}_{ij} = \frac{1}{\sqrt{(2\pi)^n}} \int_{-\infty}^{+\infty} \int_{-\infty}^{+\infty} \cdots \int_{-\infty}^{+\infty} \vartheta_i \vartheta_j \exp\left(-\frac{1}{2} \vec{\vartheta}^T \vec{\vartheta} \right) \times$$

$$\times \frac{\mathrm{PDF}_\omega \left(\vec{\vartheta}^T \cdot \mathcal{D} \cdot \vec{\vartheta} \right)}{\mathrm{PDF}_\psi \left(\vec{\vartheta}^T \cdot \mathcal{D} \cdot \vec{\vartheta} \right)} \mathrm{d}\vartheta_1 \mathrm{d}\vartheta_2 \cdots \mathrm{d}\vartheta_n.$$

$$(15)$$

$\mathcal{T}_{ij}$ vanishes for any $i \neq j$ due to symmetry considerations: The overall integrand is an *odd* function, because all the terms are *even* functions, except for ϑ_j, ϑ_i when they differ. Therefore, the integration over the entire domain yields zero. Hence, $\mathcal{T}$ is the diagonalized form of $\mathcal{C}$, with $\mathcal{U}$ holding the eigenvectors. □

3.2 (μ, λ)-Truncation Selection

Here, instead of a single winner in each iteration, we select μ winners out of the population of size λ. We denote by $J_{1:\lambda} \leq J_{2:\lambda} \leq \ldots \leq J_{\lambda:\lambda}$ the order statistics obtained by sorting the objective function values. We denote by $\omega_{1:\lambda}, \ldots, \omega_{\mu:\lambda}$ the first μ values from this list, and by $\vec{y}_{1:\lambda}, \ldots, \vec{y}_{\mu:\lambda}$ their corresponding vectors. To study the covariance in this case, we consider the pairwise density of the kth-degree and ℓ^{th}-degree winners ($\ell > k$):

$$\boxed{\begin{aligned} \mathrm{PDF}_{\vec{y}_{k:\lambda}, \vec{y}_{\ell:\lambda}}(\vec{x}_k, \vec{x}_\ell) = \mathrm{PDF}_{\omega_{k:\lambda}, \omega_{\ell:\lambda}}\left(J(\vec{x}_k), J(\vec{x}_\ell) \right) \times \\ \times \left(\frac{\mathrm{PDF}_{\vec{z}}(\vec{x}_k)}{\mathrm{PDF}_\psi \left(J(\vec{x}_k) \right)} \right) \cdot \left(\frac{\mathrm{PDF}_{\vec{z}}(\vec{x}_\ell)}{\mathrm{PDF}_\psi \left(J(\vec{x}_\ell) \right)} \right) \end{aligned}}$$
$$(16)$$

The covariance element, up to a normalization factor, reads:

$$\boxed{\mathcal{C}_{ij} \propto \sum_{k < \ell \leq \mu} \int x_{k,i} x_{\ell,j} \mathrm{PDF}_{\vec{y}_{k:\lambda}, \vec{y}_{\ell:\lambda}}(\vec{x}_k, \vec{x}_\ell)\, \mathrm{d}\vec{x}_k \mathrm{d}\vec{x}_\ell}. \quad (17)$$

A similar argument to the proof of Proposition 1 implies the following generalization:

PROPOSITION 2. *The rank-μ covariance matrix and the Hessian commute and are simultaneously diagonalizable, when the objective function follows the quadratic approximation.*

4. THE INVERSE RELATION

In this section we investigate the relation between the covariance matrix over winning vectors, $\mathcal{C}$, and the landscape Hessian $\mathcal{H}$. For simplicity, we consider $(1, \lambda)$-selection.

In order to formulate the *density* of the *winner*, it is convenient to first characterize the distribution function:[1]

$$\mathrm{CDF}_\omega (v) = \mathbf{Pr}\{\omega \leq v\} = 1 - (1 - \mathrm{CDF}_\psi (v))^\lambda. \quad (18)$$

The density function is obtained upon differentiating:

$$\mathrm{PDF}_\omega (v) = \lambda \cdot (1 - \mathrm{CDF}_\psi (v))^{\lambda - 1} \cdot \mathrm{PDF}_\psi (v). \quad (19)$$

The following shows that for a large population size λ, the covariance matrix is close to being proportional to the inverse of the landscape Hessian:

PROPOSITION 3. *For every invertible $\mathcal{H}$ and $\lambda \in \mathbb{N}$, there exists a constant $\alpha = \alpha(\mathcal{H}, \lambda) > 0$ such that*

$$\lim_{\lambda \to \infty} \alpha \mathcal{C} \mathcal{H} = \mathbf{I}.$$

Before proving this proposition, it seems worth noting that if we slightly changed the construction – by choosing $\tilde{\vec{z}}$ uniformly on the unit sphere (i.e., $\|\tilde{\vec{z}}\| = 1$), rather than $\vec{z} \sim \mathcal{N}(\vec{0}, \mathbf{I})$ – then although $\mathcal{C}$ and $\mathcal{H}$ would still commute, simulations show that $\mathcal{C}^{\mathrm{stat}}$ would not be the inverse of $\mathcal{H}$. This hints that the theorem above is not "universal" and holds only for specific distributions, such as the Normal.

Here is some intuition for the proof. First, Proposition 1 tells us that we may assume that both $\mathcal{H}$ and $\mathcal{C}$ are diagonalizable in the same base. Now, for a large λ, the winner $\vec{y}$ is close to the origin, which in turn implies that $(\mathcal{C}\mathcal{H})_{ii}$ does not actually depend on i.

PROOF. In the following, $\epsilon_1, \epsilon_2, \ldots$ tend to zero as λ tends to infinity.

Let us first assume that $\mathcal{H}$ is diagonal. Proposition 1 implies that $\mathcal{C}$ is diagonal as well, which means that the off-diagonal elements in $\mathcal{C}\mathcal{H}$ are zero, so we only need to argue on the diagonal elements. We already know from Eqs. 10, 11 and 19 that

$$\mathcal{C}_{ii} = \mathbb{E}\left[y_i^2 \right] = \int x_i^2 \lambda (1 - \mathrm{CDF}_\psi (J(\vec{x})))^{\lambda - 1} f(\|\vec{x}\|) \mathrm{d}\vec{x}, \quad (20)$$

where $f = \mathrm{PDF}_{\vec{z}}$. By changing variables from $\vec{x}$ into $\vec{r}$, defined as $r_i = \sqrt{\Delta_i} \cdot x_i$ for all i, one gets

$$\Delta_i \mathcal{C}_{ii} = c_{\mathcal{H}} \int r_i^2 \lambda (1 - \mathrm{CDF}_\psi (\|\vec{r}\|^2))^{\lambda - 1} \exp\left(-\hat{J}(\vec{r}) \right) \mathrm{d}\vec{r}, \quad (21)$$

where $c_{\mathcal{H}} > 0$ is a constant that depends on $\mathcal{H}$, and $\hat{J}$ is a positive definite diagonal quadratic form. We partition the domain of integration into two parts: Let

$$A = \{\vec{r} : \mathrm{CDF}_\psi (\|\vec{r}\|^2) > 1/\sqrt{\lambda}\}, \quad (22)$$

and let $\bar{A}$ denote the complement of A.

First, consider the integral over $\bar{A}$. If $\vec{r} \in \bar{A}$, then $\mathrm{CDF}_\psi (\|\vec{r}\|^2)$ is at most $1/\sqrt{\lambda}$, which means that $\hat{J}(\vec{r}) \leq \epsilon_1$, since CDF_ψ is close to zero only near zero, and $\hat{J}$ is continuous. Let

$$\alpha = \frac{1}{c_{\mathcal{H}} \int_{\bar{A}} r_i^2 \lambda (1 - \mathrm{CDF}_\psi (\|\vec{r}\|^2))^{\lambda - 1} \mathrm{d}\vec{r}}, \quad (23)$$

---

[1] Gupta [9] showed that when the dimension n is *even*, the distribution of the winners for the χ^2 distribution (isotropic case) possesses a simple form:

$$\mathrm{CDF}_\omega^{(n=2m)}(v) = 1 - \exp\left(-\lambda \frac{v}{2} \right) \left(\sum_{j=0}^{\frac{n}{2}-1} \frac{v^j}{j!} \right)^\lambda.$$

which does not depend on i (the norm $\|\vec{r}\|$ is symmetric in i and so is the definition of A). Thus,

$$\frac{1}{\alpha} = c_{\mathcal{H}} \int_{\bar{A}} r_i^2 \lambda (1 - \text{CDF}_\psi(\|\vec{r}\|^2))^{\lambda-1} \mathrm{d}\vec{r}$$

$$\geq c_{\mathcal{H}} \int_{\bar{A}} r_i^2 \lambda (1 - \text{CDF}_\psi(\|\vec{r}\|^2))^{\lambda-1} \exp\left(-\hat{J}(\vec{r})\right) \mathrm{d}\vec{r}$$

$$\geq c_{\mathcal{H}} \int_{\bar{A}} r_i^2 \lambda (1 - \text{CDF}_\psi(\|\vec{r}\|^2))^{\lambda-1} \exp(-\epsilon_1) \mathrm{d}\vec{r} \qquad (24)$$

$$\geq \frac{1-\epsilon_1}{\alpha}.$$

Hence,

$$\alpha \Delta_i \mathcal{C}_{ii} \geq 1 - \epsilon_1, \qquad (25)$$

where we used the fact that $1 - \xi \leq \exp(-\xi)$ for all ξ.

Second, consider the integral over A. We claim that

$$\mathcal{C}_{ii} \geq \frac{c_A}{\lambda^2}, \qquad (26)$$

where $c_A > 0$ is some constant. The reason being that z_i is normally distributed, and so for every $\epsilon > 0$, it takes values in the interval $[-\epsilon, \epsilon]$ with a probability at most 2ϵ. So, by the union bound, $\mathbf{Pr}\{|y_i| < \epsilon\} \leq 2\lambda\epsilon$, and by setting $\epsilon = \frac{1}{4\lambda}$,

$$\mathbf{Pr}\left\{|y_i| < \frac{1}{4\lambda}\right\} \leq \frac{1}{2}. \qquad (27)$$

The claim follows since $\mathbb{E}\left[y_i^2\right] \geq \frac{1}{32\lambda^2}$. The integral over A is therefore at most

$$c_{\mathcal{H}} \int_A r_i^2 \lambda (1 - \text{CDF}_\psi(\|\vec{r}\|^2))^{\lambda-1} \exp\left(-\hat{J}(\vec{r})\right) \mathrm{d}\vec{r}$$

$$\leq c_{\mathcal{H}} \lambda (1 - 1/\sqrt{\lambda})^{\lambda-1} \int_A r_i^2 \exp\left(-\hat{J}(\vec{r})\right) \mathrm{d}\vec{r} \qquad (28)$$

$$\leq \epsilon_2 \Delta_i \mathcal{C}_{ii},$$

where we used the fact that $\int \zeta_i^2 \exp\left(-\hat{J}(\vec{\zeta})\right) \mathrm{d}\vec{\zeta}$ is at most a constant (that may depend on $\mathcal{H}$), and we used Eq. 26.

Therefore, using Eq. 24, $\alpha \Delta_i \mathcal{C}_{ii} \leq 1 + \epsilon_2 \alpha \Delta_i \mathcal{C}_{ii}$, so

$$\alpha \Delta_i \mathcal{C}_{ii} \leq 1 + \epsilon_3,$$

which together with Eq. 25 completes the proof for a diagonal Hessian.

Finally, consider a non-diagonal $\mathcal{H}$. Let $\mathcal{U}$ be the eigenvectors of $\mathcal{H}$, such that $\mathcal{U}^{-1}\mathcal{H}\mathcal{U} = \mathcal{D}$, with $\mathcal{D}$ diagonal. By Proposition 1, $\mathcal{U}^{-1}\mathcal{C}\mathcal{U} = \mathcal{T}$ with $\mathcal{T}$ diagonal as well. Since $\mathcal{N}(\vec{0}, \mathbf{I})$ is invariant under rotations, the argument above shows that $\alpha \mathcal{T}\mathcal{D}$ tends to $\mathbf{I}$ as λ tends to infinity. Hence,

$$\lim_{\lambda \to \infty} \alpha \mathcal{C}\mathcal{H} - \mathbf{I} = \lim_{\lambda \to \infty} \mathcal{U}(\alpha \mathcal{T}\mathcal{D} - \mathbf{I})\mathcal{U}^{-1} = 0. \qquad (29)$$

$\square$

5. ANALYTIC APPROXIMATION

In this section we provide an approximation for $\text{PDF}_\omega(J(\vec{x}))$ and consequently for $\text{PDF}_{\vec{y}}(\vec{x})$ in order to explicitly calculate the covariance matrix in Eq. 10.

Upon substituting the explicit forms into CDF_ψ and PDF_ψ (using either Eqs. (4,5) for the *isotropic* χ^2 or Eqs. (7,9) for the *transformed* χ^2), the desired density function $\text{PDF}_\omega(J(\vec{x}))$ is obtained, however not in a closed form.

Gupta [9] derived explicit order statistic results from the Gamma distribution, to which the χ^2 distribution belongs, comprising the CDF as well as moments of the kth order statistic. Such results could reveal a closed form for $\text{PDF}_\omega(J(\vec{x}))$, which seems far too complex to address when targeting Eq. 10. Next, we will seek an *approximation* for $\text{PDF}_\omega(J(\vec{x}))$, which will enable us to realize the relation of Eq. 11 when large values of λ are assumed.

5.1 Limit Distributions of Order Statistics

We consider the winners' density when the population size λ tends to infinity. We denote the limit of the CDF in Eq. 18, with a subscript λ, as $\mathcal{L}_\lambda(v) = 1 - (1 - \text{CDF}_\psi(v))^\lambda$:

$$\lim_{\lambda \to \infty} \mathcal{L}_\lambda(v) = \begin{cases} 0 & \text{if } \text{CDF}_\psi(v) = 0 \\ 1 & \text{if } \text{CDF}_\psi(v) > 0 \end{cases} .$$

According to the Fisher-Tippett theorem [8], also known as the *extremal types theorem*, the *von-Mises* family of distributions for *minima* (or the minimal generalized extreme value distributions ($\text{GEVD}_{\min}$)) are the only non-degenerate family of distributions satisfying this limit. They are characterized as a unified family of distributions by the following:

$$\mathcal{L}_\kappa(v; \kappa_1, \kappa_2, \kappa_3) = 1 - \exp\left\{-\left[1 + \kappa_3\left(\frac{v - \kappa_1}{\kappa_2}\right)\right]^{1/\kappa_3}\right\}. \qquad (30)$$

Furthermore, since the distribution of the minimum moves toward the origin as λ increases, normalizing constants are needed to avoid degeneracy and to obtain in general

$$\lim_{\lambda \to \infty} \mathcal{L}_\lambda(a_\lambda^* v + b_\lambda^*) =$$
$$\lim_{\lambda \to \infty} 1 - (1 - \text{CDF}_\psi(a_\lambda^* v + b_\lambda^*))^\lambda = \mathcal{L}(v) \quad \forall v . \qquad (31)$$

The location parameter, κ_1, and the scale parameter, κ_2, are clearly interlinked to the aforementioned normalizing constants. The shape parameter, κ_3, determines the identity of the characteristic CDF, namely either Weibull, Gumbell, or Frechét. This parameter is evaluated by means of the following limit, whose existence is a necessary and sufficient condition for a continuous distribution function CDF_ψ to belong to the domain of attraction for minima of $\mathcal{L}_\kappa$:

$$\kappa_3 = \lim_{\varepsilon \to 0} -\log_2 \frac{\text{CDF}_\psi^{-1}(\varepsilon) - \text{CDF}_\psi^{-1}(2\varepsilon)}{\text{CDF}_\psi^{-1}(2\varepsilon) - \text{CDF}_\psi^{-1}(4\varepsilon)}, \qquad (32)$$

where CDF_ψ^{-1} refers to the inverse CDF (the quantile function of $\text{CDF}_\psi(v)$; see Theorem 9.6 in [5] [pp. 204-205]):

- If $\kappa_3 > 0$, CDF_ψ belongs to the Weibull minimal domain of attraction,

- if $\kappa_3 = 0$, CDF_ψ belongs to the Gumbel minimal domain of attraction, and

- if $\kappa_3 < 0$, CDF_ψ belongs to the Frechét minimal domain of attraction.

Note that Rudolph had already taken a related mathematical approach, which he termed *asymptotic theory of extreme order statistics*, to characterize convergence properties of ESs on a class of convex objective functions [14]. Moreover, GEVD is introduced within the broad perspective of Stochastic Global Optimization in [18].[2]

---

[2] This book constitutes by itself a proper mathematical reference for this topic, yet in a slightly different light.

PROPOSITION 4. *For the isotropic χ^2 distribution, the limit for Eq. 32 exists and reads $\kappa_3 = 2/n$.*

PROOF. The limit needs to be evaluated about $\varepsilon \longrightarrow 0$. By inserting an asymptotic expansion of the Gamma function's integrand, F_{χ^2} of Eq. 4 may be written in this limit using Stirling's formula as

$$F_{\chi^2}(\varepsilon) = \frac{1}{2^{n/2}\Gamma(n/2)}\varepsilon^{\frac{n}{2}}\sum_{k=0}^{\infty}\frac{(-1)^k\left(\frac{\varepsilon}{2}\right)^k}{\left(\frac{n}{2}+k\right)k!}$$
$$\approx \frac{2}{n\cdot 2^{n/2}\Gamma(n/2)}\varepsilon^{\frac{n}{2}} \approx \left(\frac{\varepsilon}{4}\frac{e}{n}\right)^{\frac{n}{2}},$$

where we took only the zeroth-order term in the sum into consideration. The quantile (inverse) function has the form:

$$F_{\chi^2}^{-1}(\varepsilon) \approx \frac{4n}{e}\cdot\varepsilon^{\frac{2}{n}}. \tag{33}$$

Targeting the limit in Eq. 32 yields

$$\frac{F_{\chi^2}^{-1}(\varepsilon)-F_{\chi^2}^{-1}(2\varepsilon)}{F_{\chi^2}^{-1}(2\varepsilon)-F_{\chi^2}^{-1}(4\varepsilon)} \approx \frac{\varepsilon^{\frac{2}{n}}\left(2^{\frac{2}{n}}-1\right)}{\varepsilon^{\frac{2}{n}}\left(4^{\frac{2}{n}}-2^{\frac{2}{n}}\right)} = \frac{1}{2^{\frac{2}{n}}}, \tag{34}$$

which allows to conclude with:

$$\kappa_3 = \lim_{\varepsilon\longrightarrow 0}-\log_2\frac{F_{\chi^2}^{-1}(\varepsilon)-F_{\chi^2}^{-1}(2\varepsilon)}{F_{\chi^2}^{-1}(2\varepsilon)-F_{\chi^2}^{-1}(4\varepsilon)} = \frac{2}{n}. \tag{35}$$

$\square$

Since the transformed distribution (Eq. 7) has a similar CDF in the limit $\varepsilon \to 0$,

$$F_{\tau\chi^2}^{-1}(\varepsilon) \approx \frac{4n}{e}\cdot\varepsilon^{\frac{2}{n}}, \tag{36}$$

Eq. 35 holds as is and implies the following generalization:

PROPOSITION 5. *For the transformed χ^2 distribution, the limit for Eq. 32 exists and also reads $\kappa_3 = 2/n$.*

PROPOSITION 6. *For the standard and transformed χ^2 distributions, the normalizing constants*

$$a_\lambda^* = F_{\chi^2}^{-1}\left(\frac{1}{\lambda}\right), \quad b_\lambda^* = \inf\left\{\psi\,|\,F_{\chi^2}(\psi)>0\right\} = 0$$

ensure that the limit distribution of Eq. 31 is not degenerate.

PROOF. Given the constants

$$a_\lambda^* = F_{\chi^2}^{-1}\left(\frac{1}{\lambda}\right) \approx \frac{4n}{e}\left(\frac{1}{\lambda}\right)^{2/n}, \quad b_\lambda^* = 0,$$

the limit becomes (using $F_{\chi^2}(\varepsilon) = F_{\tau\chi^2}(\varepsilon) = \left(\frac{\varepsilon}{4}\frac{e}{n}\right)^{\frac{n}{2}}$):

$$\lim_{\lambda\longrightarrow\infty}1-\left\{1-\mathtt{CDF}_\psi\left[v\frac{4n}{e}\left(\frac{1}{\lambda}\right)^{2/n}\right]\right\}^\lambda =$$
$$\lim_{\lambda\longrightarrow\infty}1-\left[1-r(n)\left(\frac{v^{n/2}}{\lambda}\right)\right]^\lambda = \tag{37}$$
$$1-\exp\left[-r(n)(v)^{n/2}\right],$$

with $r(n) = \left(\frac{e}{4n}\right)^{n/2}$. Hence, the limit distribution exists and is not degenerate, as claimed. $\square$

COROLLARY 1. *Since the shape parameter κ_3 is always positive, the extreme minima of the χ^2-distributions belong to the Weibull domain of attraction. Normalized extreme minima values, $(\omega-b_\lambda^*)/a_\lambda^*$, may be represented by a random variable $\tilde{v}$, which in turn reduces Eq. 30 to the following CDF (importantly, the so-called **tail-index** is $1/\kappa_3 = n/2$):*

$$\mathtt{CDF}_\omega(v)\xrightarrow{\lambda\to\infty}\mathtt{CDF}_\omega^{GEVD}(\tilde{v}) = 1-\exp\left(-\tilde{v}^{n/2}\right). \tag{38}$$

See [5] and [6] for an overview on the family of generalized extreme value distributions and on the limit distributions of order statistics. In particular, see table 9.1 in [5][p. 200] for the relationship between the parameters of the GEVD and the Weibull distribution, which allows the reduction of Eq. 30 to Eq. 38. Also, for the exact determination of the tail index value, see Theorem 2.3 in [18].

COROLLARY 2. *Under the GEVD approximation for treating large populations, $\lambda \to \infty$, upon normalizing the random variable to $\tilde{v} = (v-b_\lambda^*)/a_\lambda^*$ and using the tail-index result, $1/\kappa_3 = \frac{n}{2}$, the CDF and PDF forms for a single winning event read:*

$$\mathtt{CDF}_\omega^{\mathrm{GEVD}}(\tilde{v}) = 1-\exp\left(-\tilde{v}^{\frac{n}{2}}\right)$$
$$\mathtt{PDF}_\omega^{\mathrm{GEVD}}(\tilde{v}) = \frac{n}{2}\tilde{v}^{\frac{n}{2}-1}\exp\left(-\tilde{v}^{\frac{n}{2}}\right). \tag{39}$$

5.2 Covariance Derivation for $(1,\lambda)$-Selection

By setting the *Weibull* form as the characteristic density $\mathtt{PDF}_\omega$, we may rewrite Eq. 10 by utilizing Eq. 11 as follows with the normalized $\tilde{J}(\vec{x}) \equiv (J(\vec{x})-b_\lambda^*)/a_\lambda^*$:

$$\mathcal{C}_{ij} = \int_{-\infty}^{+\infty}\cdots\int_{-\infty}^{+\infty}x_ix_j\frac{n}{2}\tilde{J}(\vec{x})^{\frac{n}{2}-1}\exp\left[-\tilde{J}(\vec{x})^{\frac{n}{2}}\right]\times$$
$$\times\frac{\frac{1}{\sqrt{(2\pi)^n}}\exp\left(-\frac{1}{2}\vec{x}^T\vec{x}\right)}{\frac{\Upsilon^\eta}{\Gamma(\eta)}J(\vec{x})^{\eta-1}\exp(-\Upsilon J(\vec{x}))}dx_1dx_2\cdots dx_n. \tag{40}$$

J is assumed here to satisfy $J(\vec{x}) = \vec{x}^T\cdot\mathcal{H}\cdot\vec{x}$, and must be normalized only for the $\mathtt{PDF}_\omega$ term by means of a_λ^* alone since $b_\lambda^* = 0$; this yields altogether the following approximation (referred to as $\mathcal{C}^{Eq41}$):

$$\boxed{\begin{aligned}\mathcal{C}_{ij} = \Phi_\mathcal{C}\int_{-\infty}^{+\infty}\cdots\int_{-\infty}^{+\infty}x_ix_j\left(\vec{x}^T\mathcal{H}\vec{x}\right)^{\frac{n}{2}-\eta}\times\\\times\exp\left[\Upsilon\vec{x}^T\mathcal{H}\vec{x}-\left(\frac{\vec{x}^T\mathcal{H}\vec{x}}{a_\lambda^*}\right)^{\frac{n}{2}}-\frac{1}{2}\vec{x}^T\vec{x}\right]dx_1dx_2\cdots dx_n,\end{aligned}} \tag{41}$$

with a normalizing constant $\Phi_\mathcal{C} = \frac{n\Gamma(\eta)}{2\Upsilon^\eta\left(a_\lambda^*\right)^{\frac{n}{2}-1}\sqrt{(2\pi)^n}}$.

For the isotropic case, $\mathcal{H} = h_0\mathbf{I}$, the integration is straightforward ($\eta = \frac{n}{2}$, $\Upsilon = \frac{1}{2h_0}$) – the attained covariance is the inverse Hessian multiplied by an explicit factor:

$$\mathcal{C}^{(\mathcal{H}=h_0\mathbf{I})} = \frac{\Gamma\left(\frac{n}{2}\right)\cdot\Gamma\left(1+\frac{2}{n}\right)\cdot\phi(n)\cdot a_\lambda^*}{2\pi^{n/2}}\cdot\mathcal{H}^{-1}, \tag{42}$$

wherein

$$\phi(n) = \begin{cases}\frac{\pi^m}{m!} & n = 2m\\\frac{2^{m+1}\pi^m}{1\cdot3\cdot5\cdots(2m+1)} & n = 2m+1.\end{cases} \tag{43}$$

132

For the general case of any positive-definite Hessian $\mathcal{H}$, the integral in Eq. 41 has an unknown closed form. We note that this form of the covariance also commutes with the Hessian, in line with the results presented above.

6. SIMULATION STUDY

Numerical validation is provided herein for two aspects: Section 6.1 validates Propositions 1 and 3, and Section 6.2 validates the analytic approximation of the covariance matrix. We implemented our model into a numerical procedure, adhering to Algorithm 1, with $\mathcal{C}^{\text{stat}}$ sampled as specified.

6.1 $\mathcal{C}^{\text{stat}}$ versus $\mathcal{H}$

6.1.1 Eigendecomposition and Commutator Errors

We generated a large set of random positive-definite matrices with various dimensions $\{n_j\}$ and with a spectrum of moderate condition numbers (< 10). For each trial j, the numerical procedure generated a random symmetric matrix A_j, diagonalized it into a set of orthonormal eigenvectors U_j, drew n_j random positive numbers in a diagonal matrix D_j, and set $\mathcal{H}_j = U_j D_j U_j^{-1}$. We then applied Algorithm 1 by considering $\{\mathcal{H}_j\}$ as the landscape Hessians. The resultant covariance matrices were diagonalized and compared to the Hessian matrices and their eigendecomposition – which always matched. Given the commutator, and its numerical evaluation using the Frobenius norm ("commutator error"),

$$\text{C.E.:} \quad \|\mathcal{H}_j \mathcal{C}^{\text{stat}} - \mathcal{C}^{\text{stat}} \mathcal{H}_j\|_{\text{frob}} , \quad (44)$$

it was evident that the two matrices always commute over such well-conditioned random Hessians (obtaining a zero matrix to a practical precision, $\|\cdot\|_{\text{frob}} < 10^{-1}$), as proved. As for ill-conditioned Hessians, a systematic evaluation over separable ellipsoids of the form $(\mathcal{H}_{\text{ellipse}})_{ii} = c^{\frac{i-1}{n-1}}$, with condition numbers in the range $c \in [2 \ldots 1000]$, was carried out for $N_{\text{iter}} = 10^5$ iterations. The resultant commutator errors for various settings are depicted in Figure 1, exhibiting a linear pattern as a function of the condition number. The linearity in this error can be explained by the need to learn only the increasingly-stretched eigenvalues (no off-diagonal learning since $\mathcal{H}$ and $\mathcal{C}$ always commute).

6.1.2 The Inverse Relation under a Large Population

We extended the current numerical test to examine the inverse relation in light of increasing the population size. In what follows, we present results for a specific landscape Hessian at dimension $n = 4$ of the form

$$\mathcal{H}_0 = \text{diag} [1.0, \ 3.5, \ 6.0, \ 8.5]. \quad (45)$$

We applied Algorithm 1 with various population sizes, $\lambda = \{20, 100, 500, 1000\}$, over either $N_{\text{iter}} = 10^4$ or $N_{\text{iter}} = 10^5$ iterations. The resultant covariance matrices were multiplied by the Hessian matrix, $\mathcal{H}_0 \mathcal{C}^{\text{stat}}$. The overall deviations from the identity matrix are assessed by the multiplication's condition number, using a so-called "I.D. measure", to reflect the error in Eq. 29 for a finite population size λ:

$$\text{I.D.:} \quad \text{cond} \left(\mathcal{H}_0 \mathcal{C}^{\text{stat}} \right) - 1.0 . \quad (46)$$

They are presented in Table 2 for the various settings alongside the multiplications. Evidently, the best accuracy was obtained for $N_{\text{iter}} = 10^5$, $\lambda = 1000$; see Section 7 for a discussion. Finally, Figure 4 depicts the evaluation of the

separable ellipsoids using this measure, which exhibits a linear pattern as a function of the condition number, similarly to the C.E. measure. This linearity can be explained by the same argument of learning only the eigenvalues.

6.2 $\mathcal{C}^{\text{stat}}$ versus $\mathcal{C}^{Eq41}$

Here, we corroborated the analytic approximation for the covariance matrix. To this end, we considered four quadratic basins of attraction at various search-space dimensions:

(H-1) $n = 3$, $\mathcal{H}_1 = \left[\sqrt{2}/2 \ 0.25 \ 0.1; \ 0.25 \ 1 \ 0; \ 0.1 \ 0 \ \sqrt{2} \right]$

(H-2) $n = 10$, $\mathcal{H}_2 = \text{diag} [1.0, 1.5, \ldots, 5.5]$

(H-3) $n = 30$, $\mathcal{H}_3 = \text{diag} \left[\vec{1}^{10}, 2 \cdot \vec{1}^{10}, 3 \cdot \vec{1}^{10} \right]$

(H-4) $n = 100$, $\mathcal{H}_4 = 2.0 \cdot \mathbf{I}^{100 \times 100}$

6.2.1 Validating the Approximated Density $f_{\tau \chi^2}$

Figure 2 depicts the approximated density functions of the transformed χ^2 distribution, $f_{\tau \chi^2}$ (Eq. 9) for the four Hessian forms (H-1)-(H-4), which evidently constitute sound approximations.

6.2.2 Validating the Densities PDF_ω and $\text{PDF}_\omega^{\text{GEVD}}$

Figures 3 and 5 provide validation for the winners' density, which was exactly described by PDF_ω in Eq. 19, and was later approximated by $\text{PDF}_\omega^{\text{GEVD}}$ in Eq. 39 for large λ. Interestingly, PDF_ω, which is realized here by the approximated transformed χ^2 distribution $F_{\tau \chi^2}$, exhibits decreased accuracy on $\mathcal{H}_1$, $\mathcal{H}_2$ and $\mathcal{H}_3$. Evidently, it is highly sensitive to the approximation error of $F_{\tau \chi^2}$, which is amplified by the exponent λ. At the same time, $\text{PDF}_\omega^{\text{GEVD}}$ exhibits decreased accuracy on $\mathcal{H}_2$, $\mathcal{H}_3$ and $\mathcal{H}_4$, due to its sensitivity to the population size λ. Indeed, improvements for this approximation were evident when λ was increased (see additional settings on Figure 5).

6.2.3 Validating the Approximated Integral

Finally, we compared $\mathcal{C}^{\text{stat}}$ to the obtained analytical approximation, $\mathcal{C}^{Eq41}$. For the isotropic case, the result of Eq. 42 has been successfully corroborated for a range of search-space dimensions n. For instance, $\mathcal{C}^{\text{stat}}$ for the 100-dimensional case (H-4) was constructed using $\lambda = 5000$ and over $5 \cdot 10^5$ iterations to obtain a diagonal with an expected value 0.5617 ± 0.0012; Eq. 42 obtained a value of 0.5680. For the general case, we considered the 3-dimensional case (H-1). $\mathcal{C}^{\text{stat}}$ was constructed using $\lambda = 20$ and over various N_{iter} settings, to be presented side-by-side with the numerical integration of Eq. 41 in Table 3.[3] Additionally, their explicit eigenvectors are provided therein. It is evident that the accuracy of the eigenvectors $\mathcal{U}^{Eq41}$ (which are extracted from the approximated integral $\mathcal{C}^{Eq41}$) is very high when compared to the (known) eigenvectors $\mathcal{U}^{\mathcal{H}_1}$.

7. DISCUSSION

Our analytical work modeled passive evolutionary learning in a manner that no strategy adaptation is conducted when constructing a covariance matrix out of winning decision vectors. This investigation focused on the class of positive quadratic functions in the vicinity of their minima.

We proved that the covariance matrix of winning decision vectors commutes with the landscape Hessian about

---

[3]The integral of Eq. 41 was calculated using MATLAB's **integral3** function with the iterated method.

the optimum when isotropic Gaussian mutations are utilized – both for $(1, \lambda)$- and (μ, λ)-selection. The implication of this result is the capacity of ESs to extract the *sensitive optimization directions* from the learned covariance matrix. This result holds for all population sizes λ. Mathematically, it is quite a general phenomenon. However, this generality may also be interpreted as a weakness in the sense that in practice we would expect accuracy to improve as λ increases. Somewhat surprisingly, this learning capability stems only from two components: (i) isotropic Gaussian mutations, and (ii) rank-based selection. Evidently, learning the landscape is an inherent property of classical ESs. It does not require Derandomization, nor does it require IGO as a proof tool.

A stronger and more useful property of the covariance matrix is that it converges, up to scaling, to the inverse of the landscape Hessian when the population size λ is large. In fact, the proof of Proposition 3, alongside standard probability estimates, essentially allow to get concrete bounds on the necessary number of samples needed to approximate the inverse of the Hessian, up to scaling. This approximation has two parts. One part is in guaranteeing that $\mathcal{C}^{\text{stat}}$ is pointwise ϵ-close to $\mathcal{C}$ with confidence $1 - \delta$. We show that the eigenvalues of $\mathcal{C}$ are at least $\Omega(1/\lambda^2)$, which means that if we want $\mathcal{C}^{\text{stat}}$ to be close to $\mathcal{C}$ in a meaningful way, then it suffices to take $\epsilon \ll 1/\lambda^2$. The number of samples required for this part is polynomial in $\lambda, 1/\epsilon, \ln(n)$ and $\ln(1/\delta)$. The second part is in guaranteeing that $\mathcal{C}$ is pointwise ϵ-close to $\alpha \mathcal{H}^{-1}$ for some constant $\alpha > 0$, which depends on λ and $\mathcal{H}$. The upper bound on the number of samples needed for this part depends on ϵ, λ and on the spectrum of $\mathcal{H}$.

On a different note, when $\mathcal{H}$ is unknown, it may be constructed by a unique least squares estimator [13]. Since $\frac{1}{2}n(n+1)$ unknown elements are to be recovered, it is necessary to make $\frac{1}{2}(n^2 + n + 2)$ objective function calls to ensure that the Gramian matrix is regular.

Finally, we derived an analytical approximation for the covariance matrix, based on two presumptions: (i) the generalized χ^2 density function was approximated, assuming moderate standard deviation of the Hessian eigenvalues, and (ii) the winners' distribution was shown to follow the *Weibull* distribution with a calculated tail-index when the population size λ is large, adhering to the limit distributions of order statistics.

In a concluding simulation study, our results were numerically corroborated at multiple levels.

7.1 Future Work

We outline possible directions for future research:
1. What mechanisms can increase the convergence rates?
2. Proving the analogue phenomena when sampling takes place near a general point, since similar behavior was indeed observed in simulations.

8. ACKNOWLEDGEMENTS

The authors are indebted to Jonathan Roslund, for his significant contributions that ignited this line of work.

9. REFERENCES

[1] Y. Akimoto. Analysis of a natural gradient algorithm on monotonic convex-quadratic-composite functions. In *Proceedings of the 14th Annual Conference on Genetic and Evolutionary Computation*, GECCO '12, pages 1293–1300, New York, NY, USA, 2012. ACM.

[2] S.-I. Amari and H. Nagaoka. *Methods of Information Geometry*, volume 191 of *Translations of Mathematical Monographs*. American Mathematical Society, 2000.

[3] T. Bäck, C. Foussette, and P. Krause. *Contemporary Evolution Strategies*. Natural Computing Series. Springer-Verlag Berlin Heidelberg, 2013.

[4] H.-G. Beyer. Convergence analysis of evolutionary algorithms that are based on the paradigm of information geometry. *Evolutionary Computation*, 22(4):679–709, Dec. 2014.

[5] E. Castillo, A. S. Hadi, N. Balakrishnan, and J. M. Sarabia. *Extreme Value and Related Models with Applications in Engineering and Science*. John Wiley and Sons, 2004.

[6] P. Embrechts, C. Klüppelberg, and T. Mikosch. *Modelling Extremal Events for Insurance and Finance*. Springer-Verlag, 1997.

[7] A. H. Feiveson and F. C. Delaney. The distribution and properties of a weighted sum of chi squares. Technical report, National Aeronautics and Space Administration, 1968.

[8] R. Fisher and L. Tippett. Limiting forms of the frequency distribution of the largest or smallest member of a sample. *Proc. Cambridge Philos. Soc.*, 24:180–190, 1928.

[9] S. S. Gupta. Order Statistics from the Gamma Distribution. *Technometrics*, 2, May 1960.

[10] N. Hansen and A. Ostermeier. Completely Derandomized Self-Adaptation in Evolution Strategies. *Evolutionary Computation*, 9(2):159–195, 2001.

[11] P. Moschopoulos and W. Canada. The distribution function of a linear combination of chi-squares. *Computers & Mathematics with Applications*, 10(4):383–386, 1984.

[12] Y. Ollivier, L. Arnold, A. Auger, and N. Hansen. Information-Geometric Optimization Algorithms: A Unifying Picture via Invariance Principles. arXiv:1106.3708v3, 2014.

[13] G. Rudolph. On Correlated Mutations in Evolution Strategies. In *Parallel Problem Solving from Nature - PPSN II*, pages 105–114, Amsterdam, 1992. Elsevier.

[14] G. Rudolph. Convergence rates of evolutionary algorithms for a class of convex objective functions. *Control and Cybernetics*, 26(3), 1997.

[15] G. Rudolph. *Handbook of Natural Computing: Theory, Experiments, and Applications*, chapter Evolutionary Strategies, pages 673–698. Springer-Verlag, Berlin-Heidelberg, Germany, 2012.

[16] O. M. Shir, J. Roslund, D. Whitley, and H. Rabitz. Efficient retrieval of landscape hessian: Forced optimal covariance adaptive learning. *Physical Review E*, 89:063306, Jun 2014.

[17] D. Wierstra, T. Schaul, T. Glasmachers, Y. Sun, J. Peters, and J. Schmidhuber. Natural evolution strategies. *J. Mach. Learn. Res.*, 15(1):949–980, Jan. 2014.

[18] A. Zhigljavsky and A. Žilinskas. *Stochastic Global Optimization*. Springer Optimization and Its Applications. Springer US, 2007.

Population	$N_{\text{iter}} = 10^4$		$N_{\text{iter}} = 10^5$	
	$\mathcal{H}_0\mathcal{C}^{\text{stat}}$	I.D.	$\mathcal{H}_0\mathcal{C}^{\text{stat}}$	I.D.
$\lambda = 20$	$\begin{pmatrix} 0.4460 & 0.0017 & -0.0003 & -0.0014 \\ 0.0058 & 0.6087 & -0.0039 & -0.0059 \\ -0.0019 & -0.0067 & 0.6768 & 0.0007 \\ -0.0118 & -0.0143 & 0.0010 & 0.7059 \end{pmatrix}$	0.5856	$\begin{pmatrix} 0.4454 & -0.0006 & -0.0005 & -0.0005 \\ -0.0020 & 0.6254 & -0.0019 & -0.0012 \\ -0.0032 & -0.0032 & 0.6707 & 0.0003 \\ -0.0041 & -0.0029 & 0.0004 & 0.6965 \end{pmatrix}$	0.5640
$\lambda = 100$	$\begin{pmatrix} 0.2142 & -0.0006 & -0.0001 & 0.0003 \\ -0.0022 & 0.2469 & 0.0007 & 0.0002 \\ -0.0003 & 0.0013 & 0.2609 & 0.0030 \\ 0.0024 & 0.0005 & 0.0043 & 0.2610 \end{pmatrix}$	0.2353	$\begin{pmatrix} 0.2176 & -0.0004 & -0.0003 & 0.0003 \\ -0.0015 & 0.2522 & 0.0005 & 0.0000 \\ -0.0019 & 0.0009 & 0.2581 & -0.0009 \\ 0.0028 & 0.0001 & -0.0013 & 0.2615 \end{pmatrix}$	0.2038
$\lambda = 500$	$\begin{pmatrix} 0.1021 & -0.0010 & -0.0006 & -0.0003 \\ -0.0034 & 0.1086 & -0.0000 & -0.0004 \\ -0.0034 & -0.0000 & 0.1055 & 0.0003 \\ -0.0027 & -0.0009 & 0.0005 & 0.1055 \end{pmatrix}$	0.0806	$\begin{pmatrix} 0.1009 & 0.0001 & -0.0002 & 0.0001 \\ 0.0003 & 0.1066 & -0.0002 & -0.0001 \\ -0.0012 & -0.0004 & 0.1078 & -0.0001 \\ 0.0006 & -0.0003 & -0.0001 & 0.1079 \end{pmatrix}$	0.0706
$\lambda = 1000$	$\begin{pmatrix} 0.0713 & -0.0008 & -0.0000 & -0.0001 \\ -0.0026 & 0.0762 & -0.0003 & 0.0002 \\ -0.0001 & -0.0005 & 0.0763 & 0.0003 \\ -0.0007 & 0.0006 & 0.0004 & 0.0755 \end{pmatrix}$	0.0839	$\begin{pmatrix} 0.0716 & -0.0001 & -0.0000 & -0.0000 \\ -0.0005 & 0.0750 & -0.0002 & -0.0002 \\ -0.0003 & -0.0003 & 0.0751 & 0.0001 \\ -0.0000 & -0.0005 & 0.0002 & 0.0751 \end{pmatrix}$	0.0548

Table 2: Numerical examination of the inverse relation for the $\mathcal{H}_0$ use-case (Eq. 45). The multiplication $\mathcal{H}_0\mathcal{C}^{\text{stat}}$, and the I.D. measure, $\text{cond}\,(\mathcal{H}_0\mathcal{C}^{\text{stat}}) - 1.0$, are explicitly presented for various population sizes and over either [**LEFT**] $N_{\text{iter}} = 10^4$, or [**RIGHT**] $N_{\text{iter}} = 10^5$ iterations.

$\mathcal{C}^{Eq41} = \begin{pmatrix} 0.1618 & -0.0367 & -0.0107 \\ -0.0367 & 0.1179 & 0.0024 \\ -0.0107 & 0.0024 & 0.0804 \end{pmatrix}$		$\mathcal{U}^{Eq41} = \begin{pmatrix} 0.1692 & -0.4680 & 0.8674 \\ 0.0981 & -0.8677 & -0.4873 \\ 0.9807 & 0.1675 & -0.1010 \end{pmatrix}$	
$\mathcal{C}^{\text{stat}}_{\{N_{\text{iter}}=10^5\}} = \begin{pmatrix} 0.1532 & -0.0350 & -0.0104 \\ -0.0350 & 0.1120 & 0.0026 \\ -0.0104 & 0.0026 & 0.0764 \end{pmatrix}$	error = 0.0115	$\mathcal{U}^{\text{stat}}_{\{N_{\text{iter}}=10^5\}} = \begin{pmatrix} 0.1726 & -0.4704 & 0.8654 \\ 0.0945 & -0.8666 & -0.4899 \\ 0.9805 & 0.1664 & -0.1051 \end{pmatrix}$	error = 0.0077
$\mathcal{C}^{\text{stat}}_{\{N_{\text{iter}}=5\cdot10^5\}} = \begin{pmatrix} 0.1527 & -0.0344 & -0.0102 \\ -0.0344 & 0.1116 & 0.0023 \\ -0.0102 & 0.0023 & 0.0763 \end{pmatrix}$	error = 0.0123	$\mathcal{U}^{\text{stat}}_{\{N_{\text{iter}}=5\cdot10^5\}} = \begin{pmatrix} 0.1716 & -0.4681 & 0.8669 \\ 0.0984 & -0.8674 & -0.4878 \\ 0.9802 & 0.1690 & -0.1028 \end{pmatrix}$	error = 0.0034
$\mathcal{C}^{\text{stat}}_{\{N_{\text{iter}}=5\cdot10^6\}} = \begin{pmatrix} 0.1530 & -0.0346 & -0.0100 \\ -0.0346 & 0.1116 & 0.0023 \\ -0.0100 & 0.0023 & 0.0760 \end{pmatrix}$	error = 0.0121	$\mathcal{U}^{\text{stat}}_{\{N_{\text{iter}}=5\cdot10^6\}} = \begin{pmatrix} 0.1662 & -0.4691 & 0.8674 \\ 0.0942 & -0.8680 & -0.4875 \\ 0.9816 & 0.1627 & -0.1001 \end{pmatrix}$	error = 0.0071
$\mathcal{H}_1\mathcal{C}^{Eq41} = \begin{pmatrix} 0.1042 & 0.0038 & 0.0011 \\ 0.0038 & 0.1087 & -0.0003 \\ 0.0011 & -0.0003 & 0.1126 \end{pmatrix}$	I.D. = 0.1061	$\mathcal{U}^{\mathcal{H}_1} = \begin{pmatrix} 0.1692 & -0.4680 & 0.8674 \\ 0.0981 & -0.8677 & -0.4873 \\ 0.9807 & 0.1675 & -0.1010 \end{pmatrix}$	error = 0.0

Table 3: Numerical integration of Eq. 41 applied to case (H-1), side-by-side with $\mathcal{C}^{\text{stat}}$ of Algorithm 1. The analytic covariance $\mathcal{C}^{Eq41}$ obtained by numerical integration of Eq. 41 and its eigenvectors $\mathcal{U}^{Eq41}$ [**TOP**] *versus* the statistically-constructed covariance matrix $\mathcal{C}^{\text{stat}}$ and its corresponding eigenvectors $\mathcal{U}^{\text{stat}}$ calculated by Algorithm 1 with $\lambda = 20$ over various number of iterations [**MIDDLE 3 rows**]. The deviations ("error"), $\|\mathcal{C}^{Eq41} - \mathcal{C}^{\text{stat}}\|_{\text{frob}}$ or $\|\mathcal{U}^{Eq41} - \mathcal{U}^{\text{stat}}\|_{\text{frob}}$, are also presented within. Finally, the multiplication $\mathcal{H}_1\mathcal{C}^{Eq41}$ is explicitly presented, alongside the eigenvectors of the Hessian matrix, $\mathcal{U}^{\mathcal{H}_1}$ [**BOTTOM**].

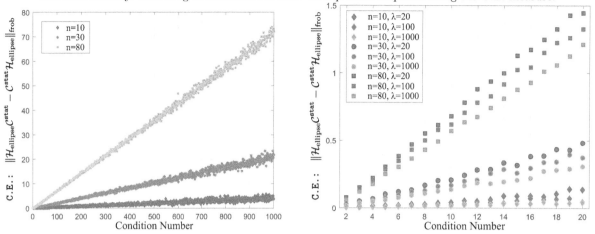

Simulation Study: Assessing the commutator error on separable ellipsoids using the C.E. measure.

Figure 1: **Systematic evaluation of Eq. 44 using $\{10, 30, 80\}$–dimensional separable ellipsoids of the form** $(\mathcal{H}_{\text{ellipse}})_{ii} = c^{\frac{i-1}{n-1}}$ **with** $N_{\text{iter}} = 10^5$. **[LEFT] Condition numbers in the range** $c = 2 \dots 1000$ **using** $\lambda = 100$. **[RIGHT] Condition numbers in the range** $c = 2 \dots 20$ **using various population size settings,** $\lambda = \{20, 100, 1000\}$.

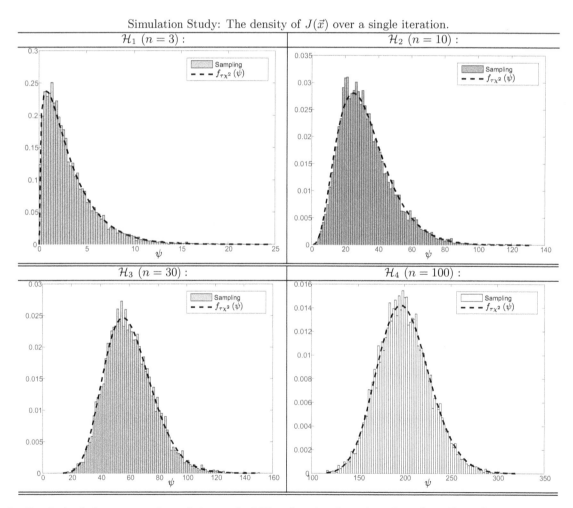

Simulation Study: The density of $J(\vec{x})$ over a single iteration.

Figure 2: **Statistical demonstration of the probability density function that describes the generation of individuals (offspring) over quadratic basins, considering** $\{\mathcal{H}_1, \mathcal{H}_2, \mathcal{H}_3, \mathcal{H}_4\}$ **at** $n = \{3, 10, 30, 100\}$, **respectively, with the exact forms listed in (H-1)-(H-4). The density of** $J(\vec{x})$ **is depicted over a single sample of** 10^4 **individuals: statistical histograms in bars, versus the analytically derived density approximation (dashed curve) according to** $f_{\tau\chi^2}$ **(Eq. 9).**

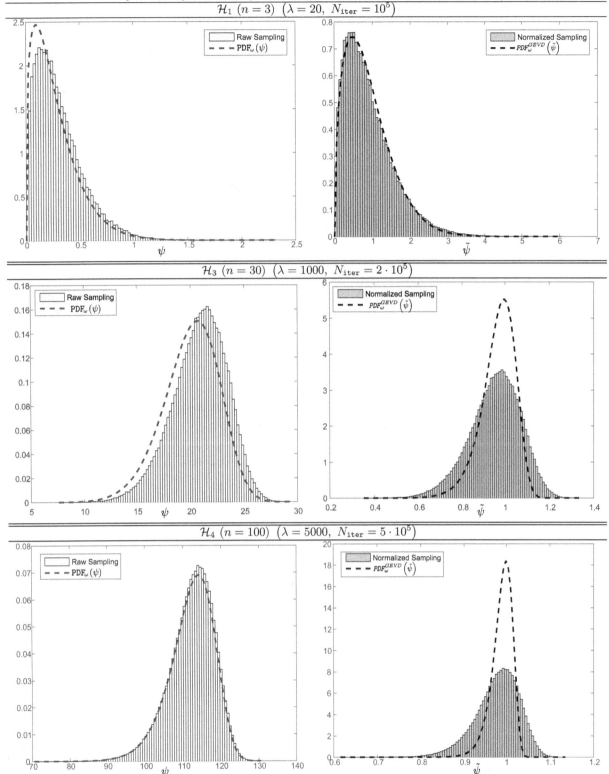

Figure 3: **Statistical demonstration of the probability density functions that describe the winning events of quadratic basin minimization, considering $\{\mathcal{H}_1, \mathcal{H}_3, \mathcal{H}_4\}$ at $n = \{3, 30, 100\}$, respectively, with the exact forms listed in (H-1),(H-3),(H-4). The winners' densities over a population of λ individuals are depicted following N_{iter} iterations: [LEFT column] Statistical histograms of raw samples (bars), versus the analytical density (dashed curve) according to PDF_ω (Eq. 19); [RIGHT column] Statistical histograms of normalized samples (bars), versus the GEVD density approximation (dashed curve) according to $\text{PDF}_\omega^{\text{GEVD}}$ (Eq. 39).**

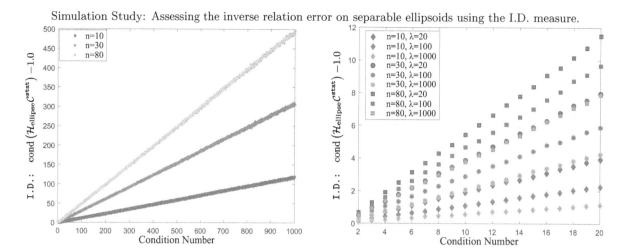

Simulation Study: Assessing the inverse relation error on separable ellipsoids using the I.D. measure.

Figure 4: Systematic evaluation of Eq. 46 using $\{10, 30, 80\}$–dimensional separable ellipsoids of the form $(\mathcal{H}_{\text{ellipse}})_{ii} = c^{\frac{i-1}{n-1}}$ with $N_{\text{iter}} = 10^5$. [LEFT] Condition numbers in the range $c = 2 \dots 1000$ using $\lambda = 100$. [RIGHT] Zooming into $c = 2 \dots 20$ over $\lambda = \{20, 100, 1000\}$.

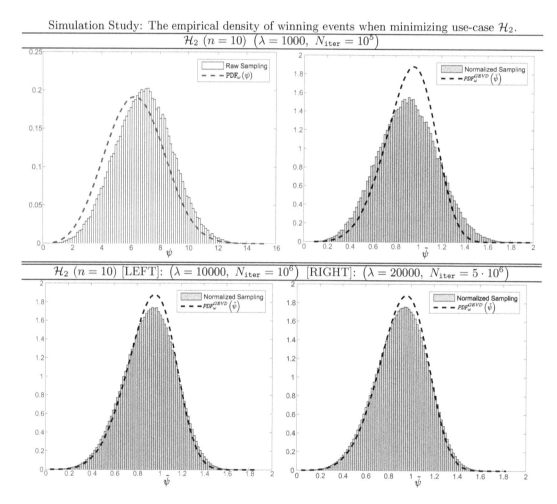

Simulation Study: The empirical density of winning events when minimizing use-case $\mathcal{H}_2$.

Figure 5: Statistical demonstration of the probability density functions that describe the winning events of quadratic basin minimization, considering $\mathcal{H}_2$ [TOP], with two additional GEVD approximations for $\mathcal{H}_2$ featuring different settings [BOTTOM].

Qualitative and Quantitative Assessment
of Step Size Adaptation Rules

Oswin Krause
Department of Computer
Science
University of Copenhagen
Copenhagen, Denmark
oswin.krause@di.ku.dk

Tobias Glasmachers
Institut für Neuroinformatik
Ruhr-Universität Bochum
Bochum, Germany
tobias.glasmachers
@ini.rub.de

Christian Igel
Department of Computer
Science
University of Copenhagen
Copenhagen, Denmark
igel@di.ku.dk

ABSTRACT

We present a comparison of step size adaptation methods for evolution strategies, covering recent developments in the field. Following recent work by Hansen et al. we formulate a concise list of performance criteria: a) fast convergence of the mean, b) near-optimal fixed point of the normalized step size dynamics, and c) invariance to adding constant dimensions of the objective function. Our results show that algorithms violating these principles tend to underestimate the step size or are unreliable when the function does not fit to the algorithm's tuned hyperparameters. In contrast, we find that cumulative step size adaptation (CSA) and two-point adaptation (TPA) provide reliable estimates of the optimal step size. We further find that removing the evolution path of CSA still leads to a reliable algorithm without the computational requirements of CSA.

Categories and Subject Descriptors

[Continuous Optimization]

Keywords

evolution strategies, step size adaptation, comparison

1. INTRODUCTION

We consider minimization of a "black-box" function $f : \mathbb{R}^d \to \mathbb{R}$ defined on a d-dimensional real vector space. For optimization we consider Evolution Strategies (ES) using a normal search distribution $\mathcal{N}(m, \sigma^2 C)$ with mean $m \in \mathbb{R}^d$, covariance matrix $C \in \mathbb{R}^{d \times d}$, and global step size $\sigma > 0$. Adaptation of the step size enables linear convergence on scale invariant functions [2], while covariance matrix adaptation (CMA) [8] renders the asymptotic convergence rate independent of the conditioning number of the Hessian.[1]

---

[1] This statement requires a twice continuously differentiable function with strictly positive definite Hessian in the isolated optimum.

FOGA '17, January 12 - 15, 2017, Copenhagen, Denmark

© 2017 Copyright held by the owner/author(s). Publication rights licensed to ACM.
ISBN 978-1-4503-4651-1/17/01...$15.00

DOI: http://dx.doi.org/10.1145/3040718.3040725

This paper is concerned with the conceptual and empirical comparison of a number of state-of-the-art mechanisms for controlling the algorithm's step size σ.

Step size control mechanisms have been a core component of ESs, dating back to Rechenberg's famous 1/5-rule [16]. Consequently there exists a plethora of step size adaptation (SA) mechanisms [15, 5, 12, 9, 1]

Comparing these algorithms is a problematic task. The traditional approach is to judge the competitors on a set of benchmark problems. However, such a comparison relies heavily on the tuning of the algorithms' hyperparameters. Relying on previously tuned settings of the hyperparameters does not lead to a fair comparison as tuning always involves a trade-off between performance and the stability of the algorithm on unknown functions, which might lead to a much more conservative tuning which can often be improved for specific tasks. Moreover, even assuming well tuned algorithms, in a regime where one algorithm does not dominate all others on every tested benchmark function it is not straightforward to rank the algorithms.

Recently a new, more qualitative approach was proposed. It is based on how the behavior of an algorithm matches a desired reference behavior [7]. Only a small set of simple benchmark functions is used and algorithms are not assessed by their optimization performance alone, but according to *how* they achieve it. Thus it is not only important how fast an algorithm finds a solution of given accuracy. In addition it is judged according to how effective and robust its internal mechanisms work. This type of analysis gives deeper insight into the algorithm's behavior. Consequently, tuning plays a much smaller role than in a purely benchmark function based comparison.

The present comparison study is similar in nature and draws heavily from the approach proposed by [7]. We modify the original catalog of desiderata only slightly for our comparison, most significantly by adding the criterion of invariance under the addition of insignificant variables. We include two relatively recent methods, namely the median success rule [1] and the population step size adaptation [12]. For simplicity and clarity we perform our analysis for an ES without CMA mechanism (fixing C to the identity matrix).

The paper is organized as follows. In the next section we introduce the simple ES with step size adaptation. Then we formulate a list of desirable properties for step size adaptation methods (section 3). In section 4 we review a variety of existing SA methods and list their properties as far as they can be derived analytically. This analysis is enriched with

Table 1: Constants used in the ES.

constant	value
λ	$4 + \lfloor 3 \log(d) \rfloor$
w_i	$\dfrac{\max\{0, \log(\lambda/2+1/2) - \log(i)\}}{\sum_{j=1}^{\lambda} \max\{0, \log(\lambda/2+1/2) - \log(j)\}}$
σ_0	$\dfrac{1}{\sqrt{d}}$

empirical data in section 5. The results obtained in sections 4 and 5 culminate in a discussion (section 6), from which we extract our conclusions (section 7).

2. EVOLUTION STRATEGIES

Throughout this paper we consider the following ES. At the beginning of each iteration t it samples a new offspring population $\{x_{t,1}, \ldots, x_{t,\lambda}\}$ of size λ from its Gaussian search distribution with density

$$p_t(x) = \frac{1}{\sqrt{2^d \pi^d \sigma_t^d}} \exp\left(-\frac{\|x - m_t\|^2}{2\sigma_t^2}\right) ,$$

which is parameterized by the current mean m_t and the step size (standard deviation) σ_t. In the next step it computes the function values $f(x_{t,i})$ and sorts the offspring by fitness, so that $f(x_{t,i}) \leq f(x_{t,i+1})$. The next mean m_{t+1} is obtained as a convex combination of the offspring using weights w_i with $\sum_{i=1}^{\lambda} w_i = 1$

$$m_{t+1} = \sum_{i=1}^{\lambda} w_i x_{t,i} .$$

Truncation selection is encoded by giving non-zero weights only to the first $\mu = \lambda/2$ points. Finally a step size adaptation (SA) algorithm computes σ_{t+1}. Even though σ_t appears only in the sampling of offspring points it is a crucial parameter since it governs the length of the step $\mu_{t+1} - \mu_t$. For the parameters λ and w_i we use the default values of CMA-ES [8], which are given in Table 1.

3. REQUIREMENTS FOR SA METHODS

The prime measure of performance of an optimization algorithm operating on a continuous domain is its rate of convergence. However, the convergence rate can be measured in different ways, e.g., based on distance in search and objective space. In the following, we will focus our discussion on scale invariant functions, that is functions for which hold $f(a * x) = g(a) \cdot f(x)$, $x \in \mathbb{R}^d$, $a \in \mathbb{R}$. On these functions, most evolution strategies exhibit convergence to the isolated optimum x^* at a linear rate, which is defined in accordance with [7] as[2]

$$r = \lim_{t \to \infty} \exp\left(\frac{1}{2t} \log\left(\frac{f(x_t) - f(x^*)}{f(x_1) - f(x^*)}\right)\right) . \quad (1)$$

Comparing SA methods empirically based on the achieved rate of convergence is hard since their performance depends crucially on their tuning parameters. In practice, the heuristics are tuned on a set of benchmark functions to show good

---

[2]In contrast to the ES, this definition is not invariant under monotonic transformations of fitness values. However, it is well-defined for quadratic objective functions, which are used in the experimental evaluation.

average or worst case performance. What is missing is an assessment of whether the tuning makes sense or whether it is a byproduct of over-fitting to the chosen benchmark functions.

The primary example is an SA algorithm that naturally adapts the step sizes to too small values. Honest tuning of the algorithm might result in hyperparameter settings that slow down the adaptation so much that the observed step sizes are on the right scale. It is obvious that the tuning result is fragile and may yield sub-optimal step sizes on other problems. Thus, severe flaws of an SA method can be hidden and the chosen parameters might only work reasonably well on the given set of benchmark functions, while the performance on on unseen functions might be much worse. In the example above, if a new function is chosen so that the optimizer can approach the optimum only slowly, then the step size has more time to adapt and thus the SA method will select a too small step size. This could be observed, e.g., when tuning on the Sphere function and testing the tuned SA algorithm on an Ellipsoid function.

One way of dealing with this problem is to require tuning on an extensive predefined set of objective functions. However, this makes tuning even harder, and new methods have to compete with well-known and thus well tuned algorithms. Also the benefit of this approach can be disputed since even an extensive set of benchmark functions might not give us a deep understanding of the method.

Therefore we follow a different route proposed in [7]: step size adaptation methods are judged according to whether and to which degree they fulfill a set of requirements. The properties we consider in this paper are:

1. **Mean Progress**. The mean m_t is the ES's best current estimate of the optimum, hence it should improve over time. The SA should optimize this progress by maximizing (1). This means that the optimal step sizes found by the algorithm should be close to the one that optimizes progress in each single step and that this estimate is reliable over different problems.

2. **Fixed Point dynamics** of σ. We require that for a properly tuned algorithm the realized step sizes are close to the fixed-point dynamics of the step size adaptation algorithm. This entails that the fixed point is a meaningful estimate of the optimal step size and thus the learning rates merely govern how fast and how well the algorithm tracks it.

3. Invariance to **Constant Dimensions**. The step size should be independent of the addition of variables in which the objective function values are constant (i.e., the function does not depend on these variables). This is important in a black-box setting in which we cannot find a reparameterization that would remove an irrelevant subspace.

Checking these requirements makes it easier to compare algorithms and, more importantly, to judge whether a given empirical comparison is fair or not. For example, comparing an algorithm fulfilling the requirement of the quality of the stationary distribution to one that does not, might not be fair since the latter could be tuned to a small set of benchmark functions while the former is inherently stable across a larger set of problems.

In addition to these requirements Hansen et al. [7] consider the following goals: on a random or flat fitness $\log(\sigma_t)$ should perform an unbiased random walk, σ_t should grow exponentially fast on a linear function, and the algorithm should be invariant under translation and rotation of the search space. We are not testing these since the desired behavior on a random or flat fitness is debatable, and in our setup all considered algorithms grow σ_t at an exponentially rate on a linear function and fulfill the invariance properties by design.

4. ALGORITHMS

In this section we introduce seven different step size adaptation (SA) algorithms and analyze them in terms of the requirements listed in section 3.

4.1 Cumulative Step Size Adaptation (CSA)

Cumulative Step Size Adaptation (CSA) is the current state-of-the-art used in the CMA-ES algorithm. It is based on the assumption that when the step size is well adapted, steps taken will become uncorrelated [15] on average. The CSA computes an evolution path, a long-term average of previous steps, and compares its length with the length expected for uncorrelated steps. When samples are drawn from a normal distribution with mean m_t and covariance matrix C_t, the update of the evolution path $p_{\sigma,t}$ is given by

$$p_{\sigma,t+1} = (1 - c_p)p_{\sigma,t} + \sqrt{c_\sigma(1 - c_p)\mu_{\text{eff}}} C_t^{-1/2} \frac{m_{t+1} - m_t}{\sigma_t} .$$

Here, $\mu_{\text{eff}} = \left(\sum_{i=1}^{\lambda} w_i^2\right)^{-1}$ is the effective sample size of the weighted individuals, c_p is a hyperparameter, and $C_t^{-1/2}$ is the matrix square root. The term $C_t^{-1/2} \frac{m_{t+1} - m_t}{\sigma_t}$ is the last step of the mean transformed into a coordinate system which is independent of σ_t and C_t, and $\sqrt{c_\sigma(1 - c_\sigma)\mu_{\text{eff}}}$ is a normalization term ensuring $p_{\sigma,t} \sim \mathcal{N}(0, I_d)$ assuming $\sqrt{\mu_{\text{eff}}} C_t^{-1/2} \frac{m_{t+1} - m_t}{\sigma_t} \sim \mathcal{N}(0, I_d)$. Thus, $\|p_\sigma\|$ can be compared with the expected length of a sample from the standard normal distribution. If it is longer (shorter), then the step size in increased (decreased) in an exponential manner. The resulting update reads

$$\sigma_{t+1} = \sigma_t \exp\left(\frac{c_\sigma}{d_\sigma}\left(\frac{\|p_{\sigma,t+1}\|}{\chi_d} - 1\right)\right) ,$$

where d_σ is another damping factor and χ_d is the expectation of the χ distribution with d degrees of freedom.

The CSA method is not invariant w.r.t. the addition of constant dimensions because all individuals and hence the mean take on random values in these components, which adds noise to the path vector. The fixed point dynamics of the CSA is not independent of its hyperparameters, as the learning rate of the evolution path changes how correlation is measured. In the extreme case $c_\sigma = 1$ correlation is ignored completely and only the length of the current step is taken into account.

4.2 xNES SA

The exponential Natural Evolution Strategy (xNES) algorithm [5, 18] is an instance of the information geometric optimization (IGO) method [14]. The xNES algorithm applies multi-variate Gaussian distributions with mean m and covariance matrix C. The square root $\sigma = \sqrt[2d]{\det(C)}$ of the geometric mean of the eigenvalues of C is interpreted as the

method's global step size parameter, and xNES allows to control the learning rate for this scale parameter independent of the learning rates for the shape of the distribution.

The IGO framework treats all parameters of the search distribution the same, irrespective of their role. Hence there is no dedicated mechanism for the adaptation of the step size, instead the parameter is adapted just like the mean and the remaining covariance parameters. The update rule is derived from stochastic natural gradient descent on the statistical manifold spanned by the search distribution parameters, where the offspring population serves as a Monte Carlo sample. For details we refer the interested reader to [5, 14].

The simplistic step size adaptation rule of the xNES algorithm can be extracted as a standalone method, subsequently referred to as xNES SA. The update rule reads

$$\sigma_{t+1} = \sigma_t \cdot \exp\left(\frac{c_\sigma}{\sqrt{d}} \cdot \sum_{i=1}^{\lambda} w_i \cdot \left[\left\|C_t^{-1/2}\frac{x_{t,i} - m_t}{\sigma_t}\right\|^2 - d\right]\right) ,$$

where $c_\sigma > 0$ is a hyperparameter. The rule is based solely on the immediate offspring $x_{t,i}$, which enter the stateless exponential update term as standardized samples. The squared norms of these samples are compared to their expectation (the dimension d). If highly weighted offspring correspond to steps longer than the expectation, then the argument of the exponential is positive and the step size is increased. If successful steps are shorter, the step size is decreased.

4.3 mean-xNES SA

In a variant of xNES SA we replace the samples by the actual step taken. This leads to an update similar to the CSA without an evolution path

$$\sigma_{t+1} = \sigma_t \cdot \exp\left(\frac{c_\sigma}{d} \cdot \left[\mu_{\text{eff}}\left\|C_t^{-1/2}\frac{m_{t+1} - m_t}{\sigma_t}\right\|^2 - d\right]\right) .$$

We call this the mean-xNES SA. In contrast to the xNES SA, we scale the χ^2-statistic by d^{-1}, not $d^{-1/2}$, motivated by our experimental findings in Section 6. The difference in scaling factor does not matter in most cases as it can be compensated by the learning rate. However, when changing the learning rate this scaling turns out to be more stable across different dimensions.

4.4 xNES SA with Log-normal Prior

One disadvantage of xNES SA and mean-xNES SA is that they do not compare a-priori defined step sizes, but only a-posteriori observed step sizes, which are not invariant under the addition of constant dimensions. We can expand the xNES approach by introducing a prior probability distribution on σ and amend the ES by sampling individuals as $p_t(x) = p_t(x|\sigma)p_t(\sigma)$ by sampling $\sigma_{t,i} \sim p_t(\sigma)$ and $x_{x,i} \sim p_t(x|\sigma_{t,i})$, for $i = 1, \ldots, \lambda$. We choose $p_t(\sigma)$ as the log-normal distribution with density

$$p_t(\sigma) = \frac{1}{\sigma\beta\sqrt{2\pi}} \exp\left(-\frac{(\log(\sigma) - \log(\sigma_t))^2}{2\beta}\right)$$

and $p_t(x|\sigma)$ as a normal distribution with mean m_t and standard deviation σ. Applying the same derivation as in the xNES SA on σ_t we arrive at the update

$$\sigma_{t+1} = \sigma_t^{1-c_\sigma} \exp\left(c_\sigma \sum_{i=1}^{\lambda} w_i \log(\sigma_{t,i})\right)$$

with learning rate c_σ. The update can be interpreted as a geometric update of the old step size using the weighted geometric mean of the current iteration. The hyperparameters are the learning rate c_σ and the variance parameter β of the log-normal distribution. This update is close to the update rule of the CMSA [3] with $c_\sigma = 1$ and exchanging the geometric average of $\sigma_{t,i}$ by an arithmetic average. The geometric average leads to an unbiased estimate of the mean on a flat or random function and therefore to random walk behaviour.

The xNES SA and the mean-xNES SA are not invariant w.r.t. the addition of constant dimensions due to the variability of $x_{t,i}$ in these dimensions. This defect is fixed by the introduction of a prior, because the step size $\sigma_{t,i}$ is independent of the actual step.

4.5 Median Rule

The Median Rule was proposed in [1] as a way to adapt Rechenberg's 1/5-rule [16] to non-elitist algorithms. The idea is to compare the objective function values $f(x_{t,1}) \leq \cdots \leq f(x_{t,\lambda})$ of the current iteration to a chosen quantile of the function values $f(x_{t-1,1}) \leq \cdots \leq f(x_{t-1,\lambda})$ of the previous iteration. Let κ be the rank of the individual in the previous generation that represents the threshold $f(x_{t-1,\kappa})$. Then we estimate the probability that a newly sampled point has a smaller function value as

$$u_t = \frac{1}{\lambda} \sum_{i=1}^{\lambda} \mathbb{1}\left\{ f(x_{t,i}) \leq f(x_{t-1,\kappa}) \right\} \ .$$

The rank κ is a hyperparameter. It is chosen so that with an optimal step size the probability that a currently sampled point has a smaller function value than $f(x_{t-1,\kappa})$ is $1/2$ on the Sphere function. Normalizing the values of u_t to $[-1, 1]$ so that a success rate of $1/2$ transforms to 0 we define the time averaged statistic

$$z_{t+1} = (1 - c_z)z_t + c_z(2u_t - 1)$$

and σ_t is updated in an exponential fashion according to

$$\sigma_{t+1} = \sigma_t \exp\left(\frac{z_{t+1}}{d_\sigma}\right) \ ,$$

where d_σ is a damping factor controlling the speed of adaptation.

4.6 Population SA

This algorithm has recently been introduced as part of the Limited Memory CMA-ES [12] as an improvement to the Median-Rule, motivated by the need to overcome the runtime complexity problems of CSA. This success-based rule increases the step size when the new samples are more successful than the previous ones. The measure of success is based on a Whitney-U rank sum statistic.

Let $r_{t,i}$ be the rank of the point $x_{t,i}$ and $o_{t,i}$ the rank of the individual $x_{t-1,i}$ in the combined set $\{f(x_{t-1,1}), \ldots, f(x_{t-1,\lambda}), f(x_{t,1}), \ldots, f(x_{t,\lambda})\}$. We define the rank-sum

$$u_t = \frac{1}{\lambda^2} \sum_{i=1}^{\lambda} (o_{t,i} - r_{t,i}) \in [-1, 1] \ .$$

When $u_t > 0$ then the current population is more successful than the previous one. A target success rate $b > 0$ is subtracted and the statistic is time averaged by $z_{t+1} =$ $(1 - c_z)z_t + c_z(u_t - b)$. The update of σ_t is then again performed in an exponential fashion

$$\sigma_{t+1} = \sigma_t \exp\left(\frac{z_{t+1}}{d_\sigma}\right)$$

with damping factor d_σ.

The bias b serves two roles: It corrects for the fact that any successful step of the mean m_t will improve the sampled points compared to the previous iterations and thus setting $b = 0$ would increase the step size until no progress can be seen any more. The second role is to force the algorithm to shrink its step size once the progress seen is smaller than the expected value.

Median Rule and Population SA are perfectly invariant w.r.t. the addition of constant dimensions. This is because they rely solely on function values $f(x_{t,i})$, not on the underlying vectors $x_{t,i}$, where random fluctuation in these components would show. On the other hand, they rely on the assumption that the optimal step size is coupled to a fixed success rate. This assumption is fragile, as the optimal success rate is problem independent. For example, on an ill-conditioned ellipsoid, the success rate will be very small unless individuals are sampled with small variance. Thus a fixed target success rate might entail small steps.

4.7 Two-point Step Size Adaptation (TPA)

The Two-point Step Size Adaptation (TPA) is one of the most simple adaptation rules. It was introduced in [17], adopted in [6] and reformulated in [7]. Its idea can be viewed as a simplified line-search approach. The version we use here is closer to [6], as [7] is incompatible with the ES defined in section 2. We further deviate from [6] by using the step size proposal from [17] since it showed better results in our experiments. Further improvements can be obtained by swapping the order of updating σ_t and x_t in the ES, which is more in line with the line-search motivation and closer to the approach in [17].

After a step in direction s_t is performed with the current step size σ we are at the point $m_{t+1} = m_t + \sigma_t s_t$. We want to know whether it would have been beneficial to have taken a longer or shorter step. In a non-black-box method we could check the sign of the derivative $d = s_t^T \frac{\partial}{\partial m_{t+1}} f(m_{t+1})$. A positive (negative) value indicates that a shorter (longer) step would have made more progress. Hence we should decrease (increase) the step size.

In a black-box setting we cannot compute derivatives, but we can estimate the sign numerically simply by comparing two points created by making the step shorter and longer. We choose to decrease the step size by a factor $\alpha < 1$ and increase it by a factor $\beta > 1$, evaluate $f_{t,\alpha} = f(x_t + \alpha\sigma s_t)$ and $f_{t,\beta} = f(x_t + \beta\sigma s_t)$, and estimate the sign as $\mathrm{sign}(d) = \mathrm{sign}(f_{t,\beta} - f_{t,\alpha})$. We compute the time-average

$$z_{t+1} = (1 - c_z)z_t + c_z \log(\alpha)\mathbb{1}\{f_{t,\alpha} < f_{t,\beta}\}$$
$$+ c_z \log(\beta)\mathbb{1}\{f_{t,\alpha} \geq f_{t,\beta}\}$$

and finally perform the exponential update

$$\sigma_{t+1} = \sigma_t \exp\left(\frac{z_{t+1}}{d_\sigma}\right) \ .$$

Analog to [17] we choose $\beta = \frac{1}{\alpha}$ in our experiments. This amounts to increasing or decreasing $\log(\sigma)$ by the same value $|\log(\alpha)| = |\log(\beta)|$.

Table 2: Theoretical and empirical properties of the studied algorithms as described in section 3.

Algorithm	Mean Progress	Fixed Point	Const. Dim.
Cumulative SA	yes	yes	no
Median SA	no	no	yes
Population SA	no	no	yes
xNES SA	no	no	no
prior-xNES SA	no	no	yes
mean-xNES SA	yes	yes	no
Two-point SA	yes	yes	yes

The two-point method is completely invariant under the addition of constant dimensions.

In this study, we considered the original variant of two-point step size adaptation, which uses two additional function evaluations per generation. This makes it the only method in our comparison that requires additional evaluations of the objective function. However, newer variants of two-point step size adaptation do not suffer from this drawback [7]. If the step size adaptation is delayed by one generation, the individuals used for the two-point method can be part of the next offspring population, for details and further enhancements of the two-point method we refer to [7].

5. EXPERIMENTS

While properties like invariance under the addition of constant dimensions (and the need for additional function evaluations) can be determined from the algorithm description, this is not (always) the case for the progress of the mean and steady state stability. Therefore these properties are investigated experimentally in the following.

For all our experiments we utilize the family of quadratic functions

$$f_y(x) = \sum_{i=1}^{d} y_i x_i^2 \ .$$

This family of functions has the property of scale invariance, i.e., all (non-optimal) level sets share the same shape up to scaling. For the quadratic functions above this is ensured by the relation $f(ax) = a^2 f(x)$. For any given point x, setting $a = \frac{1}{\sqrt{f(x)}}$, we can always "normalize" the algorithm state to the unit level set $f(ax) = 1$.

A special case of this family is the Sphere function $f_s(x) = \|x\|^2$, which is distinguished in this study for exhibiting the same symmetries as the Gaussian search distribution. In addition we consider the Ellipsoid

$$f_{\text{ell},k}(x) = \sum_{i=1}^{d} k^{i/d} x_i^2$$

and the sphere function with $d - \tilde{d}$ constant dimensions ("Constant Sphere")

$$f_{\text{cs}}(x) = \sum_{i=1}^{\tilde{d}} x_i^2 \ .$$

We set $\tilde{d} = 4$ in all of our experiments. The ill-conditioned Ellipsoid problem is well known to be difficult to solve with isotropic search distributions, which poses a challenge to SA methods. The Constant Sphere function should be no harder to optimize than the Sphere function, provided that the SA method is invariant under the addition of constant dimensions.

Well-tuned default values are available for the various SA methods, usually from the papers where they were originally proposed. However, tuning can be performed aggressively or conservatively, on different benchmark suits and problem dimensions, and with different goals. The resulting optimization performance can differ significantly [13].

Therefore, in order to remove possible biases and to make our comparison fair, we first tuned all algorithms with the same setup. All parameters were tuned on the Sphere function at varying dimensionality for optimal performance. In many cases, the parameters found were close to those published in earlier literature, often only differing by a constant factor which lead to less conservative, larger learning rates. In subsequent experiments the algorithms are analyzed with the pre-tuned parameters. The parameters we found are summarized in Table 3. The experiments can be reproduced with the source code provided as supplementary material.

Experiment 1: Optimization Performance.

In this experiment we measured the performance of all tuned algorithms on the Sphere function. We varied the dimensionality $d \in \{4, 8, 16, 32, 64, 128\}$ and measured the number of function evaluations until reaching the target objective value of 10^{-14}. We report median and lower and upper quantiles over 100 trials.

We repeated this experiment on the Constant Sphere function to asses how the algorithms are affected by meaningless variables. We performed this experiment in two variants: firstly, we set the learning rates exactly as on the Sphere function with ambient dimension d, and secondly, we set the values as for dimension $d = \tilde{d} = 4$, which makes the results comparable to the underlying 4-dimensional Sphere problem. In the latter experiment, an algorithm that is completely invariant to constant dimensions must show identical performance.

Experiment 2: Distribution of Step Sizes.

In our second experiment we compare the realized (normalized) step sizes of the different algorithms to the optimal step size. This provides first insights into why an algorithm performs well or not. Scale invariance of the objective function as well as the algorithms under consideration implies that the algorithm state given by m_t, σ_t and other state variables such as evolution paths and stored function values from previous iterations, normalized by the scaling factor $\frac{1}{\sqrt{f(m_t)}}$, forms a Markov chain, the stationary distribution of which gives rise to its long-term behavior [4]. Hence the normalized step size $\sigma_t/\sqrt{f(m_t)}$ can be estimated by the mean or median over a large number of iterations. Numerically more stable results are achieved by instead re-normalizing the algorithm state after each iteration.

In all experiments we first perform $50,000$ iterations to let the algorithm converge to its long term behavior and then compute the median normalized step size over the next $50,000$ iterations. We again analyze problem dimensions $d \in \{4, 8, 16, 32, 64, 128\}$ and report the results on Ellipsoid functions of various difficulties with $k \in \{1, 10, 100\}$.

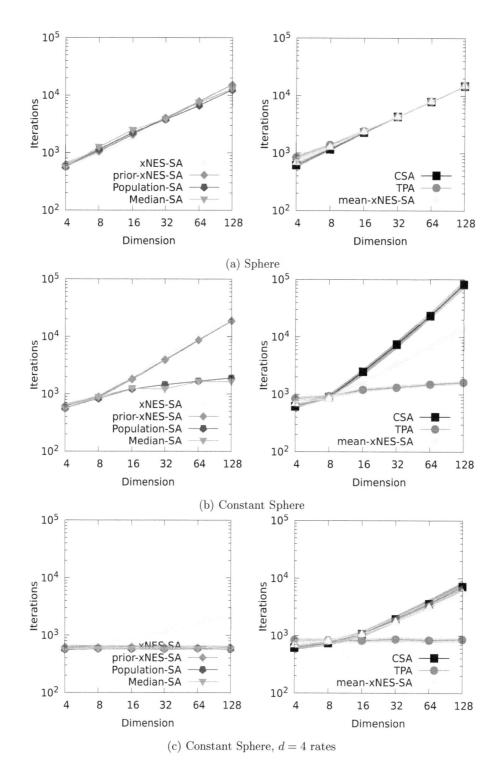

(a) Sphere

(b) Constant Sphere

(c) Constant Sphere, $d = 4$ rates

Figure 1: Number of iterations needed by the different algorithms to reach the target threshold at varying dimensionality. From top to bottom: Sphere, Sphere with $d - 4$ constant dimensions, and Sphere with $d - 4$ constant dimensions and learning rates of $d = 4$. The shaded areas depict the 25% and 75% percentile. Note that due to the tuning all curves are largely overlapping on Sphere.

This experiment reveals the realized normalized step sizes while approaching the optimum. On scale invariant functions, the realized step sizes will on average overestimate the value obtained at the fixed point, as the update step of σ_t will update it in direction of the *current* true unnormalized step size, while with every successful step the true unnormalized step size will shrink. To obtain the fixed point, we perform the same re-normalization as in the previous experiment, but do not re-normalize σ_t. As the renomalization normalizes to the $f(m_t) = 1$ iso-surface, this allows the algorithm to let its value of σ_t converge to the value of the normalized step size at its fixed-point.

We estimated the optimal normalized step size by performing a grid search over $\sigma/\sqrt{f(m)}$ for maximal convergence rate. We used a two stage grid (coarse to fine), first obtaining the best $\hat{\sigma}_0^* \in \{10^{-3+\frac{3}{20}i} \mid i = 1, \ldots, 20\}$ and then finding the best $\sigma_0^* \in \{\hat{\sigma}_0^* 10^{-\frac{1}{5}+\frac{2}{5}\frac{i}{30}} \mid i = 1, \ldots, 30\}$.

6. RESULTS AND DISCUSSION

When interpreting the experimental results we are primarily interested in identifying sub-optimal behavior, and we focus in particular on how and why different SA mechanisms break. We intend to provide insights and potential starting points for improving SA mechanisms in the future.

The results of the first experiment are illustrated in Figure 1. On Sphere (Figure 1, left) all algorithms performed essentially the same. This is of course an artifact of tuning on this very function. More interestingly, on Sphere with constant dimensions (Figure 1, middle) we see large differences between algorithms. While xNES SA, prior-xNES SA, and mean-xNES SA performed the same as on the Sphere function, CSA required more iterations, while the remaining algorithms required less. When setting learning rates and population size to the values of the four-dimensional Sphere problem (Figure 1, right), we saw that CSA performance improved to the level of mean-xNES SA and xNES SA, while for the remaining algorithms the number of iterations became independent of the ambient problem dimension.

These results can be explained as follows. CSA, xNES SA, and mean-xNES SA compare lengths of vectors (either steps or a path) to the expected length under random selection. In this case only four dimensions are relevant for selection, hence the ES performs a random walk in the orthogonal subspace. The squared norm of the vectors in the orthogonal subspace follows the χ^2_{d-4} distribution with variance $2(d-4)$. Thus, to keep the algorithms stable, the learning rate must be scaled to reduce the overall variance in the update of the step size. This is achieved by the factor $1/d$ or $1/\sqrt{d}$ in the update rules of the algorithms, which slows down learning of the meaningful dimensions for $d \gg 4$.

The results of the second experiment are given in Figure 2. Since all algorithms were tuned on Sphere ($k = 1$, left column), the realized step sizes were close to optimal. Still, the fixed-point step sizes of xNES SA and prior-xNES SA were underestimating the optimal step size.

On the Ellipsoid problem, the gap between the optimal and the realized step size increased with increasing conditioning k. For xNES SA and prior-xNES SA the gap increased further as they converged to their fixed-point. Also, the fixed points of Population SA and Median SA were clearly inferior to CSA and TPA, where CSA was superior to TPA for large conditioning numbers k. We observe that for large k algorithms relying on a statistic on the mean (CSA, TPA and mean-xNES SA) outperformed xNES SA relying on the length of individual steps and the population-based variants relying purely on ranking information.

The biggest difference between xNES SA and prior-xNES SA on the one hand and CSA and TPA on the other hand

Table 3: Parameters used by the algorithms in the experiments after tuning on Sphere.

constant	value
CSA	
c_p	$\dfrac{\mu_{\text{eff}} + 2}{d + \mu_{\text{eff}} + 5}$
d_σ	$\dfrac{1}{4}\left(1 + c_p + 2\max\left\{0, \sqrt{\dfrac{\mu_{\text{eff}} - 1}{d + 1}} - 1\right\}\right)$
Median-Rule	
κ	$\left\lfloor 1 + \dfrac{\mu_{\text{eff}}}{\lambda}\dfrac{1}{d}\right\rfloor$
c_z	0.4
d_σ	1
Population SA	
c_z	0.4
b	0.4
d_σ	1
xNES SA	
c_σ	$\dfrac{\mu_{\text{eff}}}{2\log(d)\sqrt{d}}$
mean-xNES SA	
c_σ	1
prior-xNES SA	
β	$\dfrac{\log 2}{\sqrt{d}\log(d)}$
c_σ	$\dfrac{9\mu_{\text{eff}}}{10\sqrt{d}}$
Two-point SA	
α	0.7
c_z	0.5
d_σ	1

is that the former are based on distances of sampled points from the mean, while the latter consider the lengths of steps of the mean. This is an important difference, as it is improbable to create a sample in the optimal direction, while the mean of the selected samples is a much more stable estimate of this direction. However, when the direction is not optimal, then the optimal step size in this direction will very likely be smaller than in the optimal direction, which holds especially true on Ellipsoid with large k. This results in a bias towards smaller step sizes, which is pronounced for methods relying on properties of selected individuals.

The population-based algorithms Median-Rule and Population SA suffer from their definition of success. With increasing k the probability to draw a point that is better than the current median decreases. Thus the distributions of ranks overlap more and more. Therefore, for optimal performance, with growing k the success rates or percentiles would need to be adapted to smaller values.

The algorithms CSA, TPA, and mean-xNES SA suffered the least losses in performance on the Ellipsoid. Although for $k = 10$ they were close to the optimal learning rate, there was still a relevant loss in performance. This is because the Euclidean length of a step gives less information than on Sphere about how much progress was made. For CSA there is another problem. Samples are selected more aggressively in some directions than in others, thus the distribution of the observed noise is not as expected and the noise level of uncorrelated steps changes. TPA suffers from a similar problem because it adapts the step size based on the expected success probability of a larger or smaller step. This leads to a more conservative choice of the step size in cases where the probability of success is small but the gain of a successful step is large.

7. CONCLUSION

We have analyzed the behavior of a set of step size adaptation (SA) algorithms based on a predefined set of requirements. Some of the requirements can be checked based on obvious properties of the SA methods. Others required an empirical investigation, which could be limited to a small set of easy to analyze benchmark functions found in many of the current benchmark sets.

We focus on the following aspects: Is the algorithm invariant to the addition of constant dimensions or does its performance suffer? Does the normalized step size converge to a reasonable fixed-point on scale invariant functions? And is this fixed point close to optimal across different objective functions?

We argue that an algorithm can only be competitive on a wide range of black-box functions if it fulfills (at least) these requirements, since otherwise its performance will depend crucially on the tuning of its parameters.

It turns out that only one of the analyzed algorithms, the two-point adaptation method TPA, fulfills all these requirements. This makes the new variant of TPA, which does not require additional objective function evaluations, an interesting alternative to CSA in the CMA-ES [7], also because it should work seamlessly with the novel efficient covariance matrix update scheme proposed in [11, 10].

We show that algorithms that are based on information geometric optimization (natural gradients) under-estimate the step size, an effect that gets even worse for ill-conditioned problems. This explains the conservatively tuned learning rates of the xNES algorithm, which has significantly smaller default learning rates than all of its competitors. We argue that this is the case because most offspring are not sampled in the direction towards the optimum, but instead more and more orthogonal with growing problem dimension. Thus the step size adaptation mechanisms take steps into account which the overall algorithm does not take. As in these directions successful steps are typically smaller, this results in a too small step size. We showed that this is indeed the case by implementing a new algorithm that performs the update using the actual step taken. This leads to a competitive algorithm, which is however not derived from information geometry, but instead closely resembles CSA without temporal integration.

While present SA methods work quite satisfactory in many situations, it is still easy to construct problems resulting in far from optimal step sizes. In this paper we have systematically investigated the weak spots of the underlying adaptation mechanisms. The currently available algorithms differ quite widely in their working principles and also in their relative strengths and weaknesses. We therefore believe that there is room for developing techniques that combine the strengths of all present SA algorithms.

Acknowledgements

Oswin Krause acknowledges support from the Danish National Advanced Technology Foundation through the project "Personalized breast cancer screening".

8. REFERENCES

[1] O. Ait Elhara, A. Auger, and N. Hansen. A median success rule for non-elitist evolution strategies: Study of feasibility. In *Proceedings of the Genetic and Evolutionary Computation Conference (GECCO)*, pages 415–422. ACM, 2013.

[2] A. Auger. Convergence results for the $(1, \lambda)$-SA-ES using the theory of φ-irreducible Markov chains. *Theoretical Computer Science*, 334(1–3):35–69, 2005.

[3] H.-G. Beyer and B. Sendhoff. Covariance matrix adaptation revisited–the CMSA evolution strategy. In *Parallel Problem Solving from Nature (PPSN)*, pages 123–132. Springer, 2008.

[4] A. Chotard, A. Auger, and N. Hansen. Markov chain analysis of evolution strategies on a linear constraint optimization problem. In *Evolutionary Computation (CEC), 2014 IEEE Congress on*, pages 159–166. IEEE, 2014.

[5] T. Glasmachers, T. Schaul, Y. Sun, D. Wierstra, and J. Schmidhuber. Exponential natural evolution strategies. In *Proceedings of the Genetic and Evolutionary Computation Conference (GECCO)*, 2010.

[6] N. Hansen. CMA-ES with two-point step-size adaptation. *arXiv N. arXiv:0805.0231*, 2008.

[7] N. Hansen, A. Atamna, and A. Auger. How to assess step-size adaptation mechanisms in randomised search. In *Parallel Problem Solving from Nature (PPSN)*, pages 60–69. Springer, 2014.

[8] N. Hansen and A. Ostermeier. Completely derandomized self-adaptation in evolution strategies. *Evolutionary Computation*, 9(2):159–195, 2001.

[9] C. Igel, T. Suttorp, and N. Hansen. A computational efficient covariance matrix update and a $(1+1)$-CMA for evolution strategies. In *Proceedings of the Genetic and Evolutionary Computation Conference (GECCO)*, pages 453–460. ACM, 2006.

[10] O. Krause, D. R. Arbonès, and C. Igel. CMA-ES with optimal covariance update and storage complexity. In *Advances in Neural Information Processing Systems (NIPS)*, 2016.

[11] O. Krause and C. Igel. A more efficient rank-one covariance matrix update for evolution strategies. In J. He, T. Jansen, G. Ochoa, and C. Zarges, editors, *Foundations of Genetic Algorithms (FOGA 2015)*, pages 129–136. ACM Press, 2015.

[12] I. Loshchilov. A computationally efficient limited memory CMA-ES for large scale optimization. In *Proceedings of the Genetic and Evolutionary Computation Conference (GECCO)*, pages 397–404. ACM, 2014.

[13] I. Loshchilov, M. Schoenauer, M. Sebag, and N. Hansen. Maximum likelihood-based online adaptation of hyper-parameters in cma-es. In *Parallel Problem Solving from Nature (PPSN)*, pages 70–79. Springer, 2014.

[14] Y. Ollivier, L. Arnold, A. Auger, and N. Hansen. Information-geometric optimization algorithms: a unifying picture via invariance principles. *arXiv preprint arXiv:1106.3708v3*, 2014.

[15] A. Ostermeier, A. Gawelczyk, and N. Hansen. Step-size adaptation based on non-local use of

selection information. In *Parallel Problem Solving from Nature (PPSN)*, pages 189–198. Springer, 1994.

[16] I. Rechenberg. *Evolutionsstrategie: Optimierung technischer Systeme nach Prinzipien der biologischen Evolution*. Frommann-Holzboog, 1973.

[17] R. Salomon. Evolutionary algorithms and gradient search: similarities and differences. *IEEE Transactions on Evolutionary Computation*, 2(2):45–55, 1998.

[18] D. Wierstra, T. Schaul, T. Glasmachers, Y. Sun, J. Peters, and J. Schmidhuber. Natural Evolution Strategies. *Journal of Machine Learning Research*, 15:949–980, 2014.

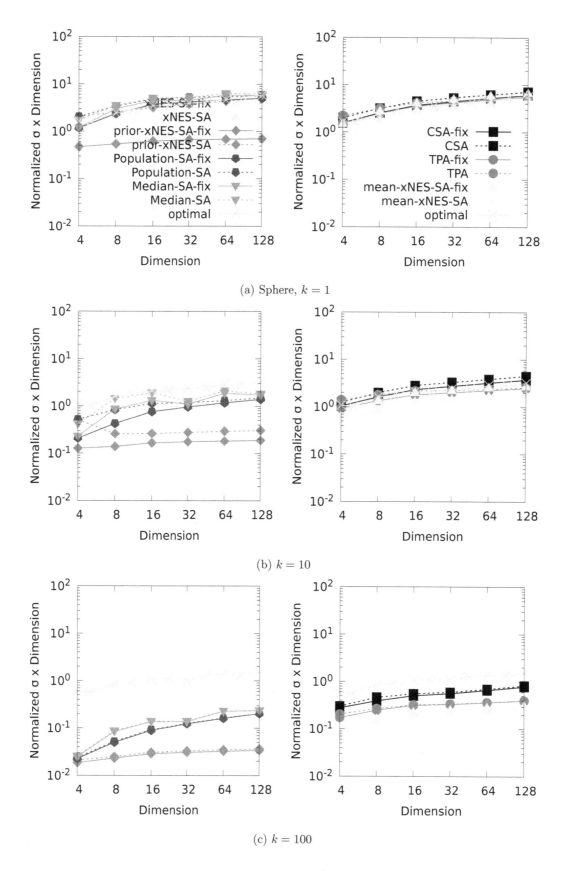

(a) Sphere, $k = 1$

(b) $k = 10$

(c) $k = 100$

Figure 2: Normalized step sizes times dimensions obtained by the algorithms on the ellipsoid function, with growing difficulty $k \in \{1, 10, 100\}$ from top to bottom. The plots compare the progress of the fixed-point of the step size adaptation(dashed lines) and the progress of the step size of the optimization dynamics to the progress with optimal step size. Note that for large k fixed-point and normal dynamics are overlapping.

Linearly Convergent Evolution Strategies via Augmented Lagrangian Constraint Handling

Asma Atamna
Inria
Centre Saclay–Île-de-France
LRI, Université Paris-Saclay
atamna@lri.fr

Anne Auger
Inria
Centre Saclay–Île-de-France
LRI, Université Paris-Saclay
auger@lri.fr

Nikolaus Hansen
Inria
Centre Saclay–Île-de-France
LRI, Université Paris-Saclay
hansen@lri.fr

ABSTRACT

We analyze linear convergence of an evolution strategy for constrained optimization with an augmented Lagrangian constraint handling approach. We study the case of multiple active linear constraints and use a Markov chain approach—used to analyze randomized optimization algorithms in the unconstrained case—to establish linear convergence under sufficient conditions. More specifically, we exhibit a class of functions on which a homogeneous Markov chain (defined from the state variables of the algorithm) exists and whose stability implies linear convergence. This class of functions is defined such that the augmented Lagrangian, centered in its value at the optimum and the associated Lagrange multipliers, is positive homogeneous of degree 2, and includes convex quadratic functions. Simulations of the Markov chain are conducted on linearly constrained sphere and ellipsoid functions to validate numerically the stability of the constructed Markov chain.

Keywords

Augmented Lagrangian, constrained optimization, evolution strategies, Markov chain, randomized optimization algorithms

1. INTRODUCTION

Randomized (or stochastic) optimization algorithms are robust methods widely used in industry for solving continuous real-world problems. Among them, the covariance matrix adaptation (CMA) evolution strategy (ES) [12] is nowadays recognized as the state-of-the art method. It exhibits linear convergence on wide classes of functions when solving unconstrained optimization problems. However, many practical problems come with constraints and the question of how to handle them properly to particularly preserve the linear convergence is an important one [2]. Recently, an augmented Lagrangian approach to handle constraints within ES algorithms was proposed with the motivation to design an algorithm converging linearly [2]. The algorithm was analyzed theoretically and sufficient conditions for linear convergence, posed in terms of stability conditions of an underlying Markov chain, were formulated [3]. In those works, however, only the case of a single linear constraint was considered.

FOGA '17, January 12 - 15, 2017, Copenhagen, Denmark

© 2017 Copyright held by the owner/author(s). Publication rights licensed to ACM.
ISBN 978-1-4503-4651-1/17/01...$15.00

DOI: http://dx.doi.org/10.1145/3040718.3040732

Markov chain theory [14] provides useful tools to analyze the linear convergence of adaptive randomized optimization algorithms and particularly evolution strategies. In a nutshell, for the case of unconstrained optimization, on scaling-invariant functions—a class of functions that includes all convex-quadratic functions—for adaptive ESs satisfying certain invariance properties (typically translation and scale-invariance), the stability analysis of an appropriate Markov chain can lead to linear convergence proofs of the original algorithm [7]. This general approach was exploited in [5] to prove the linear convergence of the $(1, \lambda)$-ES with self-adaptation on the sphere function and in [6] to prove the linear convergence of the $(1 + 1)$-ES with $1/5$th success rule. This general methodology to prove linear convergence in the case of unconstrained optimization was generalized to constrained optimization, in the case where a single constraint is handled via an adaptive augmented Lagrangian approach [3]. The underlying algorithm being a $(1 + 1)$-ES.

In this work, we generalize the study in [3] to the case of multiple linear inequality constraints. We analyze a $(\mu/\mu_w, \lambda)$-ES with an augmented Lagrangian constraint handling approach in the case of active constraints. The analyzed algorithm is an extension of the one analyzed in [3], where we generalize the original update rule for the penalty factor in [2] to the case of multiple constraints. We construct a homogeneous Markov chain for problems such that the corresponding augmented Lagrangian, centered at the optimum of the problem and the corresponding Lagrange multipliers, is positive homogeneous of degree 2, given some invariance properties are satisfied by the algorithm. Then, we give sufficient stability conditions on the Markov chain such that the algorithm converges to the optimum of the constrained problem as well as to the associated Lagrange multipliers. Finally, the stability of the constructed Markov chain is investigated empirically.

The rest of this paper is organized as it follows: we present augmented Lagrangian methods in Section 2 and give an overview on how the Markov chain approach is used to prove linear convergence in the unconstrained case in Section 3. We formally define the studied optimization problem, as well as the considered augmented Lagrangian in Sections 4 and 5 respectively. In Section 6, we present the studied algorithm and discuss its invariance properties. In Section 7, we present the constructed Markov chain and deduce linear convergence given its stability. Finally, we present our empirical results in Section 8 and conclude with a discussion in Section 9.

Notations

The notations that are not explicitly defined in the paper are presented here. We denote $\mathbb{R}^+$ the set of positive real numbers, $\mathbb{R}^+_>$ the set of strictly positive real numbers, and $\mathbb{N}_>$ the set of natural numbers without 0. $\mathbf{x} \in \mathbb{R}^n$ is a column vector, $\mathbf{x}^\intercal$ is its transpose, and $\mathbf{0} \in \mathbb{R}^n$ is the zero vector. $\|\mathbf{x}\|$ denotes the Euclidean norm of $\mathbf{x}$, $[\mathbf{x}]_i$ its ith element, and $[\mathbf{M}]_{ij}$ the element in the ith row and jth column of matrix $\mathbf{M}$. $\mathbf{I}_{n \times n} \in R^{n \times n}$ denotes the identity matrix, $\mathcal{N}(\mathbf{0}, \mathbf{I}_{n \times n})$ the multivariate standard normal distribution, and $\sim$ the equality in distribution. The symbol $\circ$ is the function composition operator. The derivative with respect to $\mathbf{x}$ is denoted $\nabla_\mathbf{x}$ and the expectation of a random variable $X \sim \pi$ is denoted E_π.

2. AUGMENTED LAGRANGIAN METHODS

Augmented Lagrangian methods are constraint handling approaches that combine penalty function methods with the Karush-Kuhn-Tucker (KKT) necessary conditions of optimality. They were first introduced in [13, 16] to overcome the limitations of penalty function methods—in particular quadratic penalty methods—which suffer from ill-conditioning as the penalty parameters need to tend to infinity in order to converge [15].

Similarly to penalty methods, augmented Lagrangian methods transform the constrained problem into one or more unconstrained problems where an augmented Lagrangian, consisting in a Lagrangian part and a penalty function part, is optimized. The Lagrangian is a function $\mathcal{L} : \mathbb{R}^n \times \mathbb{R}^m \to \mathbb{R}$ defined as

$$\mathcal{L}(\mathbf{x}, \gamma) = f(\mathbf{x}) + \sum_{i=1}^m \gamma^i g_i(\mathbf{x}) , \qquad (1)$$

for a function f subject to m constraints $g_i(\mathbf{x}) \le 0$. The vector $\gamma = (\gamma^1, \cdots, \gamma^m)^\intercal \in \mathbb{R}^m$ represents the Lagrange factors. An important property of $\mathcal{L}$ is the so-called KKT stationarity condition which states that, given some regularity conditions (constraint qualifications) are satisfied, if $\mathbf{x}^* \in \mathbb{R}^n$ is a local optimum of the constrained problem, then there exists a vector $\gamma^* = (\gamma^{*1}, \cdots, \gamma^{*m})^\intercal \in (\mathbb{R}^+)^m$ of Lagrange multipliers γ^{*i}, $i = 1, \cdots, m$, such that

$$\nabla_\mathbf{x} \mathcal{L}(\mathbf{x}^*, \gamma^*) = \nabla_\mathbf{x} f(\mathbf{x}^*) + \sum_{i=1}^m \gamma^{*i} \nabla g_i(\mathbf{x}^*) = \mathbf{0} ,$$

if we assume f and g_i, $i = 1, \cdots, m$, are differentiable at $\mathbf{x}^*$.

Remark 1. Given the gradients $\nabla_\mathbf{x} f(\mathbf{x}^*)$ and $\nabla_\mathbf{x} g_i(\mathbf{x}^*)$, $i = 1, \cdots, m$, exist, the first-order necessary conditions of optimality (KKT conditions) ensure the existence of at least one vector γ^* of Lagrange multipliers. However, if the constraints satisfy the linear independence constraint qualification (LICQ), that is, the set of constraint normals is linearly independent, the vector γ^* of Lagrange multipliers is unique [15].

The Lagrangian $\mathcal{L}$ is combined to a penalty function, which is a function of the constraints g_i, to construct the augmented Lagrangian h. Examples of augmented Lagrangians are given in (9) and (10), where $\omega = (\omega^1, \cdots, \omega^m)^\intercal \in (\mathbb{R}_>^+)^m$ is the vector of penalty factors ω^i. More generally, the augmented Lagrangian can be defined as

$$h(\mathbf{x}, \gamma, \omega) = f(\mathbf{x}) + \sum_{i=1}^m \varphi(g_i(\mathbf{x}), \gamma^i, \omega^i) , \qquad (2)$$

where φ is chosen such that a local optimum $\mathbf{x}^*$ of the constrained problem is a stationary point of h, that is for all $\omega \in (\mathbb{R}_>^+)^m$,

$$\nabla_\mathbf{x} h(\mathbf{x}^*, \gamma^*, \omega) = \mathbf{0} ,$$

assuming the gradients at $\mathbf{x}^*$ are defined. The augmented Lagrangian h is minimized for given values of γ and ω instead of the initial objective function f.

In adaptive augmented Lagrangian approaches, γ is adapted to approach the Lagrange multipliers and ω is adapted to guide the search towards feasible solutions. A proper adaptation mechanism for ω helps preventing ill-conditioning since, with an augmented Lagrangian approach, the penalty factors ω^i do not need to tend to infinity to achieve convergence [15].

There exist in the literature some examples where augmented Lagrangian approaches are used in the context of evolutionary algorithms. In [17], the authors present a coevolutionary method for constrained optimization with an augmented Lagrangian approach, where two populations (one for the parameter vector and one for Lagrange factors) are evolved in parallel, using an evolution strategy with self-adaptation. The approach is tested on four non-linear constrained problems, with a fixed value for the penalty parameter.

In [9], the authors present an augmented-Lagrangian-based genetic algorithm for constrained optimization. Their algorithm requires a local search procedure for improving the current best solution in order to converge to the optimal solution and to the associated Lagrange multipliers.

More recently, an augmented Lagrangian approach was combined with a $(1 + 1)$-ES for the case of a single linear constraint [2]. An update rule was presented for the penalty parameter and the algorithm was observed to converge on the sphere function and on a moderately ill-condition ellipsoid function, with one linear constraint. This algorithm was analyzed in [3] using tools from the Markov chain theory. The authors constructed a homogeneous Markov chain and deduced linear convergence under the stability of this Markov chain. In [4], the augmented Lagrangian constraint handling mechanism in [2] is implemented for CMA-ES and a general framework for building a general augmented Lagrangian based randomized algorithm for constrained optimization in the case of one constraint is presented.

3. MARKOV CHAIN ANALYSIS AND LINEAR CONVERGENCE

Randomized or stochastic optimization algorithms are iterative methods where—most often—the state of the algorithm is a Markov chain. For a certain class of algorithms obeying proper invariance properties, Markov chain theory can provide powerful tools to prove the linear convergence of the algorithms [8, 7, 5]. We illustrate here on a simple case the general methodology to prove linear convergence of an adaptive randomized algorithm using Markov chain theory. We assume for the sake of simplicity the minimization of the sphere function $\mathbf{x} \mapsto f(\mathbf{x}) = \frac{1}{2}\mathbf{x}^\intercal \mathbf{x}$ with, without loss of generality, the optimum in zero. We assume that the state of the algorithm at iteration t is given by the current estimate $\mathbf{X}_t$ of the optimum and a positive factor, the step-size σ_t. From this state, λ new candidate solutions are sampled according to

$$\mathbf{X}_{t+1}^i = \mathbf{X}_t + \sigma_t \mathbf{U}_{t+1}^i, \ i = 1, \ldots, \lambda ,$$

where $\mathbf{U}_{t+1}^i$ are independent identically distributed (i.i.d.) standard multivariate normal distributions (with mean zero and covariance matrix identity). The state of the algorithm is then updated via two deterministic update functions $\mathcal{G}_\mathbf{x}$ and $\mathcal{G}_\sigma$ according to

$$\mathbf{X}_{t+1} = \mathcal{G}_\mathbf{x}((\mathbf{X}_t, \sigma_t), \varsigma * \mathbf{U}_{t+1}) , \qquad (3)$$

$$\sigma_{t+1} = \mathcal{G}_\sigma(\sigma_t, \varsigma * \mathbf{U}_{t+1}) , \qquad (4)$$

where $\mathbf{U}_{t+1} = [\mathbf{U}_{t+1}^1, \cdots, \mathbf{U}_{t+1}^\lambda]$ is the vector of i.i.d. random vectors $\mathbf{U}_{t+1}^i$ and

$$\varsigma = Ord(f(\mathbf{X}_t + \sigma_t \mathbf{U}_{t+1}^i)_{i=1, \cdots, \lambda})$$

is the permutation that contains the indices of the candidate solutions $\mathbf{X}_t + \sigma_t \mathbf{U}_{t+1}^i$ ranked according to their f-value. That is, the ordering is done using the operator Ord such that, given λ real numbers $z_1, \cdots, z_\lambda$, $\varsigma = Ord(z_1, \cdots, z_\lambda)$ satisfies

$$z_{\varsigma(1)} \leq \cdots \leq z_{\varsigma(\lambda)} \ . \tag{5}$$

In (3) and (4), the operator '*' applies the permutation ς to $\mathbf{U}_{t+1}$ and

$$\varsigma * \mathbf{U}_{t+1} = [\mathbf{U}_{t+1}^{\varsigma(1)}, \cdots, \mathbf{U}_{t+1}^{\varsigma(\lambda)}] \ . \tag{6}$$

It has been shown that if the update functions $\mathcal{G}_\mathbf{x}$ and $\mathcal{G}_\sigma$ satisfy the following conditions [7]:

(i) for all $\mathbf{x}, \mathbf{x}_0 \in \mathbb{R}^n$, for all $\sigma > 0$, for all $\mathbf{y} \in (\mathbb{R}^n)^\lambda$

$$\mathcal{G}_\mathbf{x}((\mathbf{x} + \mathbf{x}_0, \sigma), \mathbf{y}) = \mathcal{G}_\mathbf{x}((\mathbf{x}, \sigma), \mathbf{y}) + \mathbf{x}_0 \ ,$$

(ii) for all $\mathbf{x} \in \mathbb{R}^n$, for all $\alpha, \sigma > 0$, for all $\mathbf{y} \in (\mathbb{R}^n)^\lambda$

$$\mathcal{G}_\mathbf{x}((\mathbf{x}, \sigma), \mathbf{y}) = \alpha \mathcal{G}_\mathbf{x}\left(\left(\frac{\mathbf{x}}{\alpha}, \frac{\sigma}{\alpha}\right), \mathbf{y}\right) \ ,$$

(iii) for all $\alpha, \sigma > 0$, for all $\mathbf{y} \in (\mathbb{R}^n)^\lambda$

$$\mathcal{G}_\sigma(\sigma, \mathbf{y}) = \alpha \mathcal{G}_\sigma\left(\frac{\sigma}{\alpha}, \mathbf{y}\right) \ ,$$

then the algorithm is translation-invariant and scale-invariant. As a consequence, $(\mathbf{Y}_t)_{t \in \mathbb{N}}$, with $\mathbf{Y}_t = \frac{\mathbf{X}_t}{\sigma_t}$, is a homogeneous Markov chain that can be defined independently of $(\mathbf{X}_t, \sigma_t)$, given $\mathbf{Y}_0 = \frac{\mathbf{x}_0}{\sigma_0}$, as

$$\mathbf{Y}_{t+1} = \frac{\mathcal{G}_\mathbf{x}((\mathbf{Y}_t, 1), \varsigma * \mathbf{U}_{t+1})}{\mathcal{G}_\sigma(1, \varsigma * \mathbf{U}_{t+1})} \ ,$$

where $\varsigma = Ord(f(\mathbf{Y}_t + \mathbf{U}_{t+1}^i)_{i=1,\cdots,\lambda})$ [7, Proposition 4.1] (this result is true for the sphere function but more generally for a scaling-invariant objective function). Let consider now the following definition of linear convergence:

Definition 1. We say that a sequence $(\mathbf{X}_t)_{t \in \mathbb{N}}$ of random vectors $\mathbf{X}_t$ converges linearly almost surely (a.s.) to $\mathbf{x}_{\text{opt}}$ if there exists $CR > 0$ such that

$$\lim_{t \to \infty} \frac{1}{t} \ln \frac{\|\mathbf{X}_t - \mathbf{x}_{\text{opt}}\|}{\|\mathbf{X}_0 - \mathbf{x}_{\text{opt}}\|} = -CR \text{ a.s.}$$

The constant CR is called the convergence rate.

Using the property of the logarithm, the quantity $\frac{1}{t} \ln \frac{\|\mathbf{X}_t\|}{\|\mathbf{X}_0\|}$ ($\mathbf{x}_{\text{opt}} = \mathbf{0}$ here) can be expressed as a function of $\mathbf{Y}_t$ according to

$$\frac{1}{t} \ln \frac{\|\mathbf{X}_t\|}{\|\mathbf{X}_0\|} = \frac{1}{t} \sum_{k=0}^{t-1} \ln \frac{\|\mathbf{X}_{k+1}\|}{\|\mathbf{X}_k\|}$$

$$= \frac{1}{t} \sum_{k=0}^{t-1} \ln \frac{\|\mathbf{X}_{k+1}\|}{\|\mathbf{X}_k\|} \frac{\sigma_k \mathcal{G}_\sigma(1, \varsigma * \mathbf{U}_{k+1})}{\sigma_{k+1}}$$

$$= \frac{1}{t} \sum_{k=0}^{t-1} \ln \frac{\|\mathbf{Y}_{k+1}\|}{\|\mathbf{Y}_k\|} \mathcal{G}_\sigma(1, \varsigma * \mathbf{U}_{k+1}) \ , \tag{7}$$

where we have successively artificially introduced $\sigma_{k+1} = \sigma_k \mathcal{G}_\sigma(1, \varsigma * \mathbf{U}_{k+1})$ and then used that $\mathbf{Y}_k = \mathbf{X}_k / \sigma_k$ and $\mathbf{Y}_{k+1} = \mathbf{X}_{k+1} / \sigma_{k+1}$. In (7), we have expressed the term whose limit we are interested in as the empirical average of a function of a Markov chain. However, we know from Markov chain theory that if some sufficient stability conditions—given for instance in Theorem 17.0.1 from [14]—are satisfied by $(\mathbf{Y}_t)_{t \in \mathbb{N}}$, then a law of large numbers (LLN) for

Markov chains can be applied to the right-hand side of the previous equation. Consequently,

$$\lim_{t \to \infty} \frac{1}{t} \ln \frac{\|\mathbf{X}_t\|}{\|\mathbf{X}_0\|} = \lim_{t \to \infty} \frac{1}{t} \sum_{k=0}^{t-1} \ln \frac{\|\mathbf{Y}_{k+1}\|}{\|\mathbf{Y}_k\|} \mathcal{G}_\sigma(1, \varsigma * \mathbf{U}_{k+1})$$

$$= \int \ln \|\mathbf{y}\| \pi(d\mathbf{y}) - \int \ln \|\mathbf{y}\| \pi(d\mathbf{y})$$

$$+ \underbrace{\int E(\ln(\mathcal{G}_\sigma(1, \varsigma * \mathbf{U}_{t+1})) | \mathbf{Y}_t = \mathbf{y}) \pi(d\mathbf{y})}_{-CR} \ ,$$

where π is the invariant probability measure of the Markov chain $(\mathbf{Y}_t)_{t \in \mathbb{N}}$. Hence, assuming that a law of large number holds for the Markov chain $(\mathbf{Y}_t)_{t \in \mathbb{N}}$, the algorithm described by the iterative sequence $(\mathbf{X}_t, \sigma_t)_{t \in \mathbb{N}}$ will converge linearly at the rate expressed as minus the expected log step-size change (where the expectation is taken with respect to the invariant probability measure of $(\mathbf{Y}_t)_{t \in \mathbb{N}}$). This methodology to prove the linear convergence of adaptive algorithms (including many evolution strategies) in the unconstrained case holds on scaling-invariant functions (that include particularly functions that write $g \circ f$, where g is a 1-D strictly increasing function and f is positively homogeneous, typically f can be a convex-quadratic function). It provides the *exact* expression of the convergence rate that equals the expected log step-size change with respect to the stationary distribution of a Markov chain. This illustrates that Markov chains are central tools for the analysis of convergence of adaptive randomized optimization algorithms. Remark that the convergence rate can be easily simulated to obtain quantitative estimates and dependencies with respect to internal parameters of the algorithm or of the objective functions.

We see that there are two distinct steps for the analysis of the linear convergence:

(i) Identify on which class of functions the algorithms we study can exhibit a Markov chain whose stability will lead to the linear convergence of the underlying algorithm (in the example above, the Markov chain equals $\mathbf{Y}_t = \mathbf{X}_t / \sigma_t$).

(ii) Prove the stability of the identified Markov chain.

The second step is arguably the most complex one. So far, it has been successfully achieved for the analysis of the linear convergence of self-adaptive evolution strategies [5] and for the $(1+1)$-ES with one-fifth success rule [6] in the unconstrained case. The main tools to prove the stability rely on Foster-Lyapunov drift conditions [14]. In this paper, we will focus on the first step. Particularly, the Markov chain for step-size adaptive randomized search optimizing scaling-invariant functions (i.e. unconstrained optimization) was identified in [7]. In addition, in the constrained case, the Markov chain has been identified for the $(1 + 1)$-ES with an augmented Lagrangian constraint handling in the case of one linear inequality constraint [3]. We consider here the extension to more than one constraint and a more general algorithm framework.

4. OPTIMIZATION PROBLEM

We consider throughout this work the problem of minimizing a function f subject to m linear inequality constraints $g_i(\mathbf{x}) \leq 0$, $i = 1, \cdots, m$. Formally, this writes

$$\min_\mathbf{x} f(\mathbf{x})$$

$$\text{subject to } g_i(\mathbf{x}) \leq 0, \ i = 1, \cdots, m \ , \tag{8}$$

where $f : \mathbb{R}^n \to \mathbb{R}$, $g_i : \mathbb{R}^n \to \mathbb{R}$, and $g_i(\mathbf{x}) = \mathbf{b}_i^\mathsf{T} \mathbf{x} + c_i$, $\mathbf{b}_i \in \mathbb{R}^n$, $c_i \in \mathbb{R}$.

We assume this problem to have a unique global optimum $\mathbf{x}_{\text{opt}}$. We also assume the constraints to be active at $\mathbf{x}_{\text{opt}}$, that is, $g_i(\mathbf{x}_{\text{opt}}) = 0$, $i = 1, \cdots, m$. This constitutes the most difficult case. Indeed, if the constraint is not active, when close enough to the optimum, the algorithm will typically not see the constraint such that it will behave as in the unconstrained case. In terms of theoretical analysis, the unconstrained case—for a general class of step-size adaptive algorithms—is well understood in the case of scaling-invariant functions [7]. Additionally, we assume that the gradients at $\mathbf{x}_{\text{opt}}$, $\nabla_{\mathbf{x}} f(\mathbf{x}_{\text{opt}})$ and $\nabla_{\mathbf{x}} g_i(\mathbf{x}_{\text{opt}})$, $i = 1, \cdots, m$, are defined and that the constraints satisfy the linear independence constraint qualification (LICQ) [15] at $\mathbf{x}_{\text{opt}}$. We denote γ_{opt} the (unique) vector of Lagrange multipliers associated to $\mathbf{x}_{\text{opt}}$.

5. CONSIDERED AUGMENTED LAGRANGIAN

A practical augmented Lagrangian for the optimization problem in (8) is given in the following equation

$$h(\mathbf{x}, \gamma, \omega) = f(\mathbf{x})$$
$$+ \sum_{i=1}^{m} \underbrace{\begin{cases} \gamma^i g_i(\mathbf{x}) + \frac{\omega^i}{2} g_i(\mathbf{x})^2 & \text{if } \gamma^i + \omega^i g_i(\mathbf{x}) \geq 0 \\ -\frac{\gamma^{i2}}{2\omega^i} & \text{otherwise} \end{cases}}_{\varphi_1(g_i(\mathbf{x}), \gamma^i, \omega^i)} . \quad (9)$$

The use of a different penalty factor for each constraint is motivated by the fact that the penalization should depend on the constraint violation—which might be different for different constraints. The quality of a solution $\mathbf{x}$ is evaluated by adding $f(\mathbf{x})$ and either (i) $\gamma^i g_i(\mathbf{x}) + \frac{\omega^i}{2} g_i(\mathbf{x})^2$ if $g_i(\mathbf{x})$ is larger than $-\frac{\gamma^i}{\omega^i}$ or (ii) $-\frac{\gamma^{i2}}{2\omega^i}$ otherwise, for each constraint function g_i.

The augmented Lagrangian in (9) is constructed such that (i) the fitness function h remains unchanged when far in the feasible domain and (ii) h is "smooth" in that it is differentiable with respect to g_i. Therefore, (9) is the recommended augmented Lagrangian in practice. For the analysis, however, we consider a simpler augmented Lagrangian (equation below) so that we can construct a Markov chain.

$$h(\mathbf{x}, \gamma, \omega) = f(\mathbf{x}) + \sum_{i=1}^{m} \underbrace{\gamma^i g_i(\mathbf{x}) + \frac{\omega^i}{2} g_i(\mathbf{x})^2}_{\varphi_2(g_i(\mathbf{x}), \gamma^i, \omega^i)} . \quad (10)$$

The difference is that in the previous formulation the penalization is a constant and hence inconsequential for $g_i(\mathbf{x}) < -\gamma^i/\omega^i$. Since we focus in our study on problems where the constraints are active at the optimum, the augmented Lagrangians in (9) and (10) are equivalent in the vicinity of $\mathbf{x}_{\text{opt}}$, as illustrated in Figure 1 for one constraint. Inactive constraints are covered in that the analysis remains valid when these constraints are removed, in which case we recover the original equation (9) up to adding a constant to the f-value. Therefore, conducting the analysis with (10) gives insight into how a practical algorithm using (9) would perform close to the optimum.

6. ALGORITHM

In this section, we present a general ES (Algorithm 1) with comma-selection and weighted recombination (denoted $(\mu/\mu_{\text{w}}, \lambda)$-ES) for constrained optimization, where the constraints are handled using an augmented Lagrangian approach.

First, λ i.i.d. vectors $\mathbf{U}_{t+1}^i$ are sampled in Line 3 of Algorithm 1 according to a normal distribution of mean $\mathbf{0}$ and covariance matrix

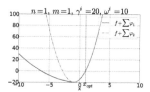

Figure 1: Left: $\varphi_j(g_i(\mathbf{x}), \gamma^i, \omega^i)$ for $j = 1$ (blue) and $j = 2$ (red), as a function of g_i. Right: Augmented Lagrangians, $f(\mathbf{x}) + \sum_{i=1}^{m} \varphi_j(g_i(\mathbf{x}), \gamma^i, \omega^i)$, for $j = 1$ (blue) and $j = 2$ (red), in $n = 1$ with $m = 1$. $f(x) = \frac{1}{2} x^2$, $g_1(x) = x - 1$, and $x_{\text{opt}} = 1$.

the identity. They are used to create λ candidate solutions $\mathbf{X}_{t+1}^i$ according to

$$\mathbf{X}_{t+1}^i = \mathbf{X}_t + \sigma_t \mathbf{U}_{t+1}^i , \quad (11)$$

where $\mathbf{X}_t$ is the current estimate of the optimum and σ_t is the step-size. The candidate solutions are then ranked according to their fitness, determined by their h-value. This is done in Line 4 with the operator Ord defined in (5), where ς is the permutation that contains the indices of the ordered candidate solutions.

Later on, we will make explicit the dependency of ς on the objective function, the current solution, and the current step-size, where needed (this would read $\varsigma_{(\mathbf{X}_t, \sigma_t)}^{h(\cdot, \gamma_t, \omega_t)}$ here). The solution $\mathbf{X}_{t+1}$ at the next iteration is computed by recombining the μ best candidate solutions—or parents—in a weighted sum according to Line 5, where w_i, $i = 1, \cdots, \mu$, are the weights associated to the parents and the operator '$*$' applies the permutation ς to the vector $\mathbf{U}_{t+1}$ of the sampled vectors $\mathbf{U}_{t+1}^i$ as defined in (6).

The step-size is adapted in Line 6 using a general update function $\mathcal{G}_\sigma$. For the sake of simplicity, we consider that $\mathcal{G}_\sigma$ is a function of the current step-size σ_t and the ranked vector $\varsigma * \mathbf{U}_{t+1}$ of the sampled vectors $\mathbf{U}_{t+1}^i$.

The Lagrange factors are adapted in Line 7. As a result of this update rule, a Lagrange factor γ_t^i is increased if $g_i(\mathbf{X}_{t+1})$ is positive and decreased otherwise. A damping factor d_γ is used to attenuate the change in the value of γ_t^i.

Each penalty factor ω_t^i is adapted according to Line 8. This update is a generalization to the case of many constraints of the original update proposed in [2] for the case of a single constraint. A penalty factor ω_t^i is increased in two cases: the first one is given by the first inequality in Line 8 and corresponds to the case where (i) the change in h-value due to changes in γ_t^i and ω_t^i is smaller than the change in h-value due to the change in $\mathbf{X}_t$. Indeed

$$\omega_t^i g_i(\mathbf{X}_{t+1})^2 \approx |h(\mathbf{X}_{t+1}, \gamma_t + \Delta_i \gamma, \omega_t + \Delta_i \omega) - h(\mathbf{X}_{t+1}, \gamma_t, \omega_t)| ,$$

where $\Delta_i \gamma = (0, \cdots, \Delta \gamma^i, \cdots, 0)^{\mathsf{T}}$ and $\Delta_i \omega = (0, \cdots, \Delta \omega^i, \cdots, 0)^{\mathsf{T}}$. By increasing the penalization, we prevent premature stagnation [2]. The parameter ω_t^i is also increased if (ii) the change in the corresponding constraint value $|g_i(\mathbf{X}_{t+1}) - g_i(\mathbf{X}_t)|$ is significantly smaller than $|g_i(\mathbf{X}_t)|$ (second inequality in Line 8). In this case, increasing the penalization allows approaching the constraint boundary ($g_i(\mathbf{x}) = 0$) more quickly. However, increasing ω_t^i increases the ill-conditioning of the problem at hand, therefore, in all other cases, ω_t^i is decreased (second case in Line 8). Similarly to the update of the Lagrange factors, we use a damping factor d_ω to moderate the changes in ω_t^i.

Algorithm 1 is a randomized adaptive algorithm that can be defined in an abstract manner as follows: given the state variables $(\mathbf{X}_t, \sigma_t, \gamma_t, \omega_t)$ at iteration t, a transition function $\mathcal{F}^{(f, \{g_i\}_{i=1, \cdots, m})}$, and the vector $\mathbf{U}_{t+1} = [\mathbf{U}_{t+1}^1, \cdots, \mathbf{U}_{t+1}^\lambda]$ of i.i.d. normal vectors

Algorithm 1 $(\mu/\mu_{\mathrm{w}}, \lambda)$-ES with Augmented Lagrangian Constraint Handling

0 **given** $n \in \mathbb{N}_>$, $\chi, k_1, k_2, d_\gamma, d_\omega \in \mathbb{R}_>^+, \lambda, \mu \in \mathbb{N}_>, 0 \le w_i < 1$,
$\sum_{i=1}^{\mu} w_i = 1$

1 **initialize** $\mathbf{X}_0 \in \mathbb{R}^n$, $\sigma_0 \in \mathbb{R}_>^+$, $\gamma_0 \in \mathbb{R}^m$, $\omega_0 \in (\mathbb{R}_>^+)^m$, $t = 0$

2 **while** stopping criterion not met

3 $\quad \mathbf{U}_{t+1}^i = \mathcal{N}(\mathbf{0}, \mathbf{I}_{n \times n}), i = 1, \cdots, \lambda$

4 $\quad \varsigma = Ord(h(\mathbf{X}_t + \sigma_t \mathbf{U}_{t+1}^i, \gamma_t, \omega_t)_{i=1,\cdots,\lambda})$

5 $\quad \mathbf{X}_{t+1} = \mathbf{X}_t + \sigma_t \sum_{i=1}^{\mu} w_i[\varsigma * \mathbf{U}_{t+1}]_i, \mathbf{U}_{t+1} = [\mathbf{U}_{t+1}^1, \cdots, \mathbf{U}_{t+1}^\lambda]$

6 $\quad \sigma_{t+1} = \mathcal{G}_\sigma(\sigma_t, \varsigma * \mathbf{U}_{t+1})$

7 $\quad \gamma_{t+1}^i = \gamma_t^i + \dfrac{\omega_t^i}{d_\gamma} g_i(\mathbf{X}_{t+1}), i = 1, \cdots, m$

8 $\quad \omega_{t+1}^i = \begin{cases} \omega_t^i \chi^{1/(4d_\omega)} & \text{if } \omega_t^i g_i(\mathbf{X}_{t+1})^2 < k_1 \times \\ & \dfrac{|h(\mathbf{X}_{t+1}, \gamma_t, \omega_t) - h(\mathbf{X}_t, \gamma_t, \omega_t)|}{n} \\ & \text{or } k_2|g_i(\mathbf{X}_{t+1}) - g_i(\mathbf{X}_t)| < |g_i(\mathbf{X}_t)| \\ \omega_t^i \chi^{-1/d_\omega} & \text{otherwise}, i = 1, \cdots, m \end{cases}$

9 $\quad t = t + 1$

$\mathbf{U}_{t+1}^i$, compute the state at iteration $t + 1$ according to

$$(\mathbf{X}_{t+1}, \sigma_{t+1}, \gamma_{t+1}, \omega_{t+1}) =$$
$$\mathcal{F}^{(f, \{g_i\}_{i=1,\cdots,m})}((\mathbf{X}_t, \sigma_t, \gamma_t, \omega_t), \mathbf{U}_{t+1}),$$

where the superscript indicates the objective function to minimize, f, and the constraint functions, g_i. The deterministic transition function $\mathcal{F}^{(f, \{g_i\}_{i=1,\cdots,m})}$ is defined by the following general update rules for $\mathbf{X}_t, \sigma_t, \gamma_t$, and ω_t:

$$\mathbf{X}_{t+1} = \mathcal{G}_\mathbf{x}((\mathbf{X}_t, \sigma_t), \varsigma * \mathbf{U}_{t+1}) \ , \tag{12}$$

$$\sigma_{t+1} = \mathcal{G}_\sigma(\sigma_t, \varsigma * \mathbf{U}_{t+1}) \ , \tag{13}$$

$$\gamma_{t+1}^i = \mathcal{H}_\gamma^{g_i}(\gamma_t^i, \omega_t^i, \mathbf{X}_{t+1}), i = 1, \cdots, m \ , \tag{14}$$

$$\omega_{t+1}^i = \mathcal{H}_\omega^{(f, g_i)}(\omega_t^i, \gamma_t^i, \mathbf{X}_t, \mathbf{X}_{t+1}), i = 1, \cdots, m \ , \tag{15}$$

where $\varsigma, \mathcal{G}_\mathbf{x}, \mathcal{H}_\gamma$, and $\mathcal{H}_\omega$ are given in Lines 4, 5, 7, and 8 of Algorithm 1 respectively. These notations are particularly useful for defining the notions of translation and scale-invariance in the next subsection. They also make the connection between the constructed homogeneous Markov chain and the original algorithm clearer.

Comparing (12), (13), (14), and (15) to (3) and (4), it is easy to see that Algorithm 1 is built by taking an adaptive algorithm for unconstrained optimization and changing its objective function to an adaptive one—the augmented Lagrangian—where the parameters of the augmented Lagrangian are additionally adapted every iteration. This idea was already put forward in [4] for the case of a single constraint, and we generalize it here to the case of m constraints.

6.1 Invariance

Invariance with respect to transformations of the search space is a central property in randomized adaptive algorithms. In the unconstrained case, it is exploited to demonstrate linear convergence [7, 6]. In this subsection, we discuss translation-invariance and scale-invariance of Algorithm 1. We first recall the definition of a group homomorphism and introduce some notations.

Definition 2. Let $(G_1, .)$ and $(G_2, *)$ be two groups. A function $\Phi : G_1 \to G_2$ is a group homomorphism if for all $x, y \in G_1$, $\Phi(x.y) = \Phi(x) * \Phi(y)$.

We denote $\mathcal{S}(\Omega)$ the set of all bijective transformations from a set Ω to itself and $\mathrm{Homo}((\mathbb{R}^n, +), (\mathcal{S}(\Omega), \circ))$ (respectively $\mathrm{Homo}((\mathbb{R}_>^+, .), (\mathcal{S}(\Omega), \circ)))$ the set of group homomorphisms from $(\mathbb{R}^n, +)$ (respectively from $(\mathbb{R}_>^+, .)$) to $(\mathcal{S}(\Omega), \circ)$.

Translation-invariance informally translates the non-sensitivity of an algorithm with respect to the choice of its initial point, that is the algorithm will exhibit the same behavior when optimizing $\mathbf{x} \mapsto f(\mathbf{x})$ or $\mathbf{x} \mapsto f(\mathbf{x} - \mathbf{x}_0)$ for any $\mathbf{x}_0$. More formally, an algorithm is translation-invariant if we can find a state-space transformation such that optimizing $\mathbf{x} \mapsto f(\mathbf{x})$ or $\mathbf{x} \mapsto f(\mathbf{x} - \mathbf{x}_0)$ is the same up to the state-space transformation. In the next definition, which is a generalization to the constrained case of the definition given in [7], we ask that the set of state-space transformations is given via a group homomorphism from the group acting on the function to transform the functions, that is $(\mathbb{R}^n, +)$, to the group of bijective state-space transformations. Indeed this group homomorphism naturally emerges when attempting to prove invariance. More formally, we have the following definition of translation-invariance.

Definition 3. A randomized adaptive algorithm with transition function $\mathcal{F}^{(f, \{g_i\}_{i=1,\cdots,m})} : \Omega \times \mathbb{U}^\lambda \to \Omega$, where f is the objective function to minimize and g_i are the constraint functions, is translation-invariant if there exists a group homomorphism $\Phi \in \mathrm{Homo}((\mathbb{R}^n, +), (\mathcal{S}(\Omega), \circ))$ such that for any objective function f, for any constraint g_i, for any $\mathbf{x}_0 \in \mathbb{R}^n$, for any state $\mathbf{s} \in \Omega$, and for any $\boldsymbol{u} \in \mathbb{U}^\lambda$,

$$\mathcal{F}^{(f(\mathbf{x}), \{g_i(\mathbf{x})\}_{i=1,\cdots,m})}(\mathbf{s}, \boldsymbol{u})$$
$$= \Phi(-\mathbf{x}_0) \left(\mathcal{F}^{(f(\mathbf{x}-\mathbf{x}_0), \{g_i(\mathbf{x}-\mathbf{x}_0)\}_{i=1,\cdots,m})}(\Phi(\mathbf{x}_0)(\mathbf{s}), \boldsymbol{u}) \right) \ .$$

Similarly for scale-invariance, the set of state-space transformations comes from a group homomorphism between the group where the scaling factors acting to transform the objective functions are taken from, that is the group $(\mathbb{R}_>^+, .)$ and the group of bijective state-space transformations.

Definition 4. A randomized adaptive algorithm with transition function $\mathcal{F}^{(f, \{g_i\}_{i=1,\cdots,m})} : \Omega \times \mathbb{U}^\lambda \to \Omega$, where f is the objective function to minimize and g_i are the constraint functions, is scale-invariant if there exists a group homomorphism $\Phi \in \mathrm{Homo}((\mathbb{R}_>^+, .), (\mathcal{S}(\Omega), \circ))$ such that for any objective function f, for any constraint g_i, for any $\alpha > 0$, for any state $\mathbf{s} \in \Omega$, and for any $\boldsymbol{u} \in \mathbb{U}^\lambda$,

$$\mathcal{F}^{(f(\mathbf{x}), \{g_i(\mathbf{x})\}_{i=1,\cdots,m})}(\mathbf{s}, \boldsymbol{u}) =$$
$$\Phi(1/\alpha) \left(\mathcal{F}^{(f(\alpha\mathbf{x}), \{g_i(\alpha\mathbf{x})\}_{i=1,\cdots,m})}(\Phi(\alpha)(\mathbf{s}), \boldsymbol{u}) \right) \ .$$

The next proposition states translation-invariance of Algorithm 1.

PROPOSITION 1. *Algorithm 1 is translation-invariant and the associated group homomorphism Φ is given by*

$$\Phi(\boldsymbol{x}_0)(\boldsymbol{x}, \sigma, \gamma, \omega) = (\boldsymbol{x} + \boldsymbol{x}_0, \sigma, \gamma, \omega) \ , \tag{16}$$

for all $\boldsymbol{x}_0, \boldsymbol{x} \in \mathbb{R}^n$, for all $\sigma \in \mathbb{R}$, and for all $\gamma, \omega \in \mathbb{R}^m$.

The proof of this proposition is given in Appendix A.1. In the next proposition we state the scale-invariance of Algorithm 1 under scale-invariance of the transition function $\mathcal{G}_\sigma$.

153

PROPOSITION 2. *If the update function $\mathcal{G}_\sigma$ of the step-size satisfies the following condition*

$$\mathcal{G}_\sigma(\sigma_t, \varsigma * U_{t+1}) = \alpha \mathcal{G}_\sigma(\sigma_t/\alpha, \varsigma * U_{t+1}) \ , \qquad (17)$$

for all $\alpha > 0$, then Algorithm 1 is scale-invariant and the associated group homomorphism Φ is defined as

$$\Phi(\alpha)(\boldsymbol{x}, \sigma, \gamma, \omega) = (\boldsymbol{x}/\alpha, \sigma/\alpha, \gamma, \omega) \ , \qquad (18)$$

for all $\alpha > 0$, for all $\boldsymbol{x} \in \mathbb{R}^n$, for all $\sigma \in \mathbb{R}$, and for all $\gamma, \omega \in \mathbb{R}^m$.

The proof of the proposition is given in Appendix A.2.

In the next section, we illustrate how translation and scale-invariance induce the existence of a homogeneous Markov chain whose stability implies linear convergence.

7. ANALYSIS

In this section, we demonstrate the existence of an underlying homogeneous Markov chain to Algorithm 1, given the augmented Lagrangian in (10) satisfies a particular condition. To construct the Markov chain, we exploit invariance properties of Algorithm 1, as well as the updates of the Lagrange factors and the penalty factors.

As stated in Section 4, we assume that the optimization problem admits a unique global optimum $\mathbf{x}_{\text{opt}}$ and that the constraints g_i, $i = 1, \cdots, m$, satisfy the LICQ at $\mathbf{x}_{\text{opt}}$, hence that the vector γ_{opt} of Lagrange multipliers is unique. Once we have the Markov chain, we show how its stability leads to linear convergence of (i) the current solution $\mathbf{X}_t$ towards the optimum $\mathbf{x}_{\text{opt}}$, (ii) the vector of Lagrange factors γ_t towards the vector of Lagrange multipliers γ_{opt}, and (iii) the step-size σ_t towards 0.

7.1 Homogeneous Markov Chain

We start by recalling the definition of positive homogeneity.

Definition 5. [Definition 4 from [3]] A function $p : X \to Y$ is positive homogeneous of degree $k > 0$ with respect to $\mathbf{x}^* \in X$ if for all $\alpha > 0$ and for all $\mathbf{x} \in X$,

$$p(\mathbf{x}^* + \alpha \mathbf{x}) = \alpha^k p(\mathbf{x}^* + \mathbf{x}) \ . \qquad (19)$$

Example 1. Our linear constraint functions, $g_i(\mathbf{x}) = b_i^\intercal \mathbf{x} + c_i$, are positive homogeneous of degree 1 with respect to any $\mathbf{x}^* \in \mathbb{R}^n$ that satisfies $g_i(\mathbf{x}^*) = 0$. Indeed,

$$\begin{aligned} g_i(\mathbf{x}^* + \alpha \mathbf{x}) &= b_i^\intercal(\mathbf{x}^* + \alpha \mathbf{x}) + c_i = \alpha(b_i^\intercal \mathbf{x} + c_i) + \alpha b_i^\intercal \mathbf{x}^* \\ &= \alpha g_i(\mathbf{x}^* + \mathbf{x}) \ , \text{ for all } \alpha > 0. \end{aligned} \qquad (20)$$

The following theorem gives sufficient conditions under which the sequence $(\Phi_t)_{t \in \mathbb{N}}$, with $\Phi_t = (\boldsymbol{Y}_t, \Gamma_t, \omega_t)$, is a homogeneous Markov chain, where the random variables $\boldsymbol{Y}_t$ and Γ_t are defined in (21) below.

THEOREM 1. *Consider the $(\mu/\mu_{\text{w}}, \lambda)$-ES with augmented Lagrangian constraint handling minimizing the augmented Lagrangian h in (10), such that the step-size update function $\mathcal{G}_\sigma$ satisfies the condition in (17). Let $(\boldsymbol{X}_t, \sigma_t, \gamma_t, \omega_t)_{t \in \mathbb{N}}$ be the Markov chain associated to this ES and let $(\boldsymbol{U}_t)_{t \in \mathbb{N}}$ be a sequence of i.i.d. normal vectors. Let $\bar{\boldsymbol{x}} \in \mathbb{R}^n$ such that $g_i(\bar{\boldsymbol{x}}) = 0$ for all $i = 1, \ldots, m$, and let $\bar{\gamma} \in \mathbb{R}^m$. Let*

$$\boldsymbol{Y}_t = \frac{\boldsymbol{X}_t - \bar{\boldsymbol{x}}}{\sigma_t} \text{ and } \Gamma_t = \frac{\gamma_t - \bar{\gamma}}{\sigma_t} \ . \qquad (21)$$

Then, if the function $\mathcal{D}h_{\bar{\boldsymbol{x}}, \bar{\gamma}, \omega} : \mathbb{R}^{n+m} \to \mathbb{R}$ defined as

$$\mathcal{D}h_{\bar{\boldsymbol{x}}, \bar{\gamma}, \omega}(\boldsymbol{x}, \gamma) = h(\boldsymbol{x}, \gamma, \omega) - h(\bar{\boldsymbol{x}}, \bar{\gamma}, \omega) \qquad (22)$$

is positive homogeneous of degree 2 with respect to $[\bar{\boldsymbol{x}}, \bar{\gamma}]$, then the sequence $(\Phi_t)_{t \in \mathbb{N}}$, where $\Phi_t = (\boldsymbol{Y}_t, \Gamma_t, \omega_t)$, is a homogeneous Markov chain that can be defined independently of $(\boldsymbol{X}_t, \sigma_t, \gamma_t, \omega_t)$ as $\boldsymbol{Y}_0 = (\boldsymbol{X}_0 - \bar{\boldsymbol{x}})/\sigma_0$, $\Gamma_0 = (\gamma_0 - \bar{\gamma})/\sigma_0$ and for all t

$$\boldsymbol{Y}_{t+1} = \mathcal{G}_{\boldsymbol{x}}((\boldsymbol{Y}_t, 1), \varsigma * \boldsymbol{U}_{t+1})/\mathcal{G}_\sigma(1, \varsigma * \boldsymbol{U}_{t+1}) \ , \qquad (23)$$

$$\Gamma_{t+1}^i = \mathcal{H}_\gamma^{g_i(\cdot + \bar{\boldsymbol{x}})}(\Gamma_t^i, \omega_t^i, \tilde{\boldsymbol{Y}}_{t+1})/\mathcal{G}_\sigma(1, \varsigma * \boldsymbol{U}_{t+1}) \ , \qquad (24)$$

$$\omega_{t+1}^i = \mathcal{H}_\omega^{(f(\cdot + \bar{\boldsymbol{x}}), g_i(\cdot + \bar{\boldsymbol{x}}))}(\omega_t^i, \Gamma_t^i + \bar{\gamma}^i, \tilde{\boldsymbol{Y}}_{t+1}) \ , \qquad (25)$$

with

$$\varsigma = Ord(h(\boldsymbol{Y}_t + \boldsymbol{U}_{t+1}^i + \bar{\boldsymbol{x}}, \Gamma_t + \bar{\gamma}, \omega_t)_{i=1,\cdots,\lambda}) \ , \quad (26)$$

$$\tilde{\boldsymbol{Y}}_{t+1} = \mathcal{G}_{\boldsymbol{x}}((\boldsymbol{Y}_t, 1), \varsigma * \boldsymbol{U}_{t+1}) \ , \qquad (27)$$

where the Ord operator extracts the permutation of ordered candidate solutions (see (5)).

The proof of Theorem 1 is given in Appendix A.3. The key idea in the proof is that when $\mathcal{D}h_{\bar{\boldsymbol{x}}, \bar{\gamma}, \omega_t}$ is positive homogeneous of degree 2 with respect to $[\bar{\boldsymbol{x}}, \bar{\gamma}]$, the same permutation ς is obtained when ranking candidate solutions $\boldsymbol{X}_t + \sigma_t \boldsymbol{U}_{t+1}^i$ on $h(., \gamma_t, \omega_t)$ than when ranking candidate solutions $\boldsymbol{Y}_t + \boldsymbol{U}_{t+1}^i$ on $h(. + \bar{\boldsymbol{x}}, \Gamma_t + \bar{\gamma}, \omega_t)$, i.e.,

$$\varsigma_{(\boldsymbol{X}_t, \sigma_t)}^{h(., \gamma_t, \omega_t)} = \varsigma_{(\boldsymbol{Y}_t, 1)}^{h(. + \bar{\boldsymbol{x}}, \Gamma_t + \bar{\gamma}, \omega_t)} = \varsigma \ .$$

Scale-invariance of Algorithm 1, induced by the property of $\mathcal{G}_\sigma$ in (17), is also used explicitly in the proof while translation-invariance is used implicitly.

Theorem 1 holds for any $\bar{\boldsymbol{x}} \in \mathbb{R}^n$ such that $g_i(\bar{\boldsymbol{x}}) = 0$, for all $i \in \{1, \cdots, m\}$, and for any $\bar{\gamma} \in \mathbb{R}^m$. In particular, it holds for the optimum $\mathbf{x}_{\text{opt}}$ of our constrained problem and the associated vector γ_{opt} of Lagrange multipliers.

The following corollary states that on convex quadratic functions, $(\Phi_t)_{t \in \mathbb{N}}$ (defined in Theorem 1) is a homogeneous Markov chain for $\bar{\boldsymbol{x}} = \mathbf{x}_{\text{opt}}$ and $\bar{\gamma} = \gamma_{\text{opt}}$.

COROLLARY 1. *Let $(\boldsymbol{X}_t, \sigma_t, \gamma_t, \omega_t)_{t \in \mathbb{N}}$ be the Markov chain associated to the $(\mu/\mu_{\text{w}}, \lambda)$-ES in 1 optimizing the augmented Lagrangian h in (10), with f convex quadratic defined as*

$$f(\boldsymbol{x}) = \frac{1}{2}\boldsymbol{x}^T \boldsymbol{H} \boldsymbol{x} \ , \qquad (28)$$

where $\boldsymbol{H} \in \mathbb{R}^{n \times n}$ is a symmetric positive-definite matrix. Let $\boldsymbol{Y}_t = \frac{\boldsymbol{X}_t - \boldsymbol{x}_{opt}}{\sigma_t}$ and $\Gamma_t = \frac{\gamma_t - \gamma_{opt}}{\sigma_t}$, where x_{opt} is the optimum of the constrained problem and γ_{opt} is the vector of the associated Lagrange multipliers. Then $(\Phi_t)_{t \in \mathbb{N}}$, with $\Phi_t = (\boldsymbol{Y}_t, \Gamma_t, \omega_t)$, is a homogeneous Markov chain defined independently of $(\boldsymbol{X}_t, \sigma_t, \gamma_t, \omega_t)$ as in (23), (24), (25), (26), and (27) by taking $\bar{\boldsymbol{x}} = \boldsymbol{x}_{opt}$ and $\bar{\gamma} = \gamma_{\text{opt}}$.

We prove the corollary by showing that the function $\mathcal{D}h_{\mathbf{x}_{\text{opt}}, \gamma_{\text{opt}}, \omega}$ defined in (22) is positive homogeneous of degree 2 with respect to $[\mathbf{x}_{\text{opt}}, \gamma_{\text{opt}}]$ for $f(\mathbf{x}) = \frac{1}{2}\mathbf{x}^\intercal \mathbf{H} \mathbf{x}$. For the proof (see Appendix A.4), we use the following elements:

- The definitions of the gradients of f and g_i, $\nabla_{\mathbf{x}} f(\mathbf{y}) = \mathbf{y}^\intercal \mathbf{H}$ and $\nabla_{\mathbf{x}} g_i(\mathbf{y}) = b_i^\intercal$, respectively.

- The KKT stationarity condition at the optimum $\mathbf{x}_{\text{opt}}$

$$\nabla_{\mathbf{x}} f(\mathbf{x}_{\text{opt}}) + \sum_{i=1}^m \gamma^i \nabla_{\mathbf{x}} g_i(\mathbf{x}_{\text{opt}}) = \mathbf{0} \ . \qquad (29)$$

Remark 2. For a convex quadratic objective function f and linear constraints g_i, $i = 1, \cdots, m$, KKT conditions are sufficient conditions for optimality. That is, a point that satisfies KKT conditions is also an optimum of the constrained problem (see [15, Theorem 16.4]). The optimization problem we consider is unimodal, therefore $\mathbf{x}_{opt}$ is the only point satisfying the KKT conditions.

7.2 Sufficient Conditions for Linear Convergence

In the sequel, we investigate linear convergence of Algorithm 1. There exist many definitions—not always equivalent—of linear convergence. We consider here the almost sure linear convergence whose definition is given in Definition 1. We will also briefly discuss another definition of linear convergence that considers the expected log-progress $\ln \frac{\|\mathbf{X}_{t+1} - \mathbf{x}_{opt}\|}{\|\mathbf{X}_t - \mathbf{x}_{opt}\|}$.

We start by giving the definitions of an invariant probability measure and positivity [14]. We consider a Markov chain $(\mathbf{X}_t)_{t \in \mathbb{N}}$ that takes its values in a set $\mathcal{X} \subset \mathbb{R}^n$ equipped with its Borel σ-algebra $\mathcal{B}(\mathcal{X})$. The transition probabilities are given by the transition probability kernel P such that for $\mathbf{x} \in \mathcal{X}$ and $B \in \mathcal{B}(\mathcal{X})$

$$P(\mathbf{x}, B) = \Pr(\mathbf{X}_{t+1} \in B \mid \mathbf{X}_t = \mathbf{x}) .$$

Definition 6. Let π be a probability measure on $\mathcal{X}$ and let $\mathbf{X}_t \sim \pi$. We say that π is invariant if

$$\pi(B) = \int_{\mathcal{X}} \pi(d\mathbf{x}) P(\mathbf{x}, B) .$$

We say that a Markov chain is positive if there exists an invariant probability measure for this Markov chain.

Harris-recurrence [14] is related to the notion of irreducibility. Informally, a Markov chain is φ-irreducible if there exists a nonzero measure φ on $\mathcal{X}$ such that all φ-positive sets (that is, sets $B \in \mathcal{B}(\mathcal{X})$ such that $\varphi(B) > 0$) are reachable from anywhere in $\mathcal{X}$. In such a case, there exists a maximal irreducibility measure ψ that dominates other irreducibility measures [14].

Definition 7. Let $(\mathbf{X}_t)_{t \in \mathbb{N}}$ be a ψ-irreducible Markov chain. A measurable set $B \in \mathcal{B}(\mathcal{X})$ is Harris-recurrent if

$$\Pr(\sum_{t \in \mathbb{N}_>} \mathbf{1}_{\{\mathbf{X}_t \in B\}} = \infty \mid \mathbf{X}_0 = \mathbf{x}) = 1 ,$$

for all $\mathbf{x} \in B$. By extension, we say that $(\mathbf{X}_t)_{t \in \mathbb{N}}$ is Harris-recurrent if all ψ-positive sets are Harris-recurrent.

We can now recall Theorem 17.0.1 from [14] that gives sufficient conditions for the application of a LLN for Markov chains.

THEOREM 2 (THEOREM 17.0.1 FROM [14]). *Let $\mathbf{Z}$ be a positive Harris-recurrent chain with invariant probability π. Then the LLN holds for any function q such that $\pi(|q|) = \int |q(\mathbf{z})| \pi(d\mathbf{z}) < \infty$, that is, for any initial state $\mathbf{Z}_0$, $\lim_{t \to \infty} \frac{1}{t} \sum_{k=0}^{t-1} q(\mathbf{Z}_k) = \pi(q)$ almost surely.*

Consider now Algorithm 1 minimizing the augmented Lagrangian h in (10) corresponding to the optimization problem in (8), such that the function $\mathcal{D}h_{\mathbf{x}_{opt}, \gamma_{opt}, \omega_t}$ defined in (22) is positive homogeneous of degree 2 with respect to $[\mathbf{x}_{opt}, \gamma_{opt}]$. By virtue of Theorem 1, $(\Phi_t)_{t \in \mathbb{N}}$ is a homogeneous Markov chain. The following theorem gives sufficient conditions under which Algorithm 1 converges to the optimum $\mathbf{x}_{opt}$ of the constrained problem, as well as to the corresponding Lagrange multiplier γ_{opt}.

THEOREM 3. *Let $(\mathbf{X}_t, \sigma_t, \gamma_t, \omega_t)_{t \in \mathbb{N}}$ be the Markov chain associated to Algorithm 1 optimizing the augmented Lagrangian h such that the function $\mathcal{D}h_{\mathbf{x}_{opt}, \gamma_{opt}, \omega_t}$ defined in (22) is positive homogeneous of degree 2 with respect to $[\mathbf{x}_{opt}, \gamma_{opt}]$, where $\mathbf{x}_{opt}$ is the optimum of the constrained problem (8) and γ_{opt} is the corresponding Lagrange multiplier. Let $(\Phi_t)_{t \in \mathbb{N}}$ be the Markov chain defined in Theorem 1 and assume that it is positive Harris-recurrent with invariant probability measure π, that $E_\pi(|\ln \|[\phi]_1\||) < \infty$, $E_\pi(|\ln \|[\phi]_2\||) < \infty$, and $E_\pi(\mathcal{R}(\phi)) < \infty$, where*

$$\mathcal{R}(\phi) = E\big(\ln(\mathcal{G}_\sigma(1, \varsigma * U_{t+1}))|\Phi_t = \phi\big) . \tag{30}$$

Then for all $\mathbf{X}_0$, for all σ_0, for all γ_0, and for all ω_0,

$$\lim_{t \to \infty} \frac{1}{t} \ln \frac{\|\mathbf{X}_t - \mathbf{x}_{opt}\|}{\|\mathbf{X}_0 - \mathbf{x}_{opt}\|} = \lim_{t \to \infty} \frac{1}{t} \ln \frac{\|\gamma_t - \gamma_{opt}\|}{\|\gamma_0 - \gamma_{opt}\|} = \lim_{t \to \infty} \frac{1}{t} \ln \frac{\sigma_t}{\sigma_0}$$
$$= -CR \ a.s. ,$$

where

$$-CR = \int \mathcal{R}(\phi) \pi(d\phi) .$$

The proof idea is similar to the one discussed in Section 3 for the unconstrained case, where the quantities $\frac{1}{t} \ln \frac{\|\mathbf{X}_t - \mathbf{x}_{opt}\|}{\|\mathbf{X}_0 - \mathbf{x}_{opt}\|}$, $\frac{1}{t} \ln \frac{\|\gamma_t - \gamma_{opt}\|}{\|\gamma_0 - \gamma_{opt}\|}$, and $\frac{1}{t} \ln \frac{\sigma_t}{\sigma_0}$ are expressed as a function of the Markov chain Φ_t. The detailed proof of Theorem 1 is given in Appendix A.5.

While in the previous theorem we have presented sufficient conditions on the Markov chain Φ_t for the almost sure linear convergence of the algorithm, other sufficient conditions can allow to derive the geometric convergence of the expected log-progress. Typically, assuming we have proven a so-called geometric drift for the chain Φ_t, plus some assumptions ensuring that the conditional log-progress is dominated by the drift function (see for instance [7, Theorem 5.4]), then

$$\sum_t r^t |E_{\Phi_0} \ln \frac{\|\mathbf{X}_{t+1} - \mathbf{x}_{opt}\|}{\|\mathbf{X}_t - \mathbf{x}_{opt}\|} - (-CR)| \le RV(\Phi_0) , \tag{31}$$

where $r > 1$, R is a positive constant and $V \ge 1$ is the drift function. Equation (31) also holds when replacing $\ln \frac{\|\mathbf{X}_{t+1} - \mathbf{x}_{opt}\|}{\|\mathbf{X}_t - \mathbf{x}_{opt}\|}$ by $\ln \frac{\|\gamma_{t+1} - \gamma_{opt}\|}{\|\gamma_t - \gamma_{opt}\|}$ and $\ln \frac{\sigma_{t+1}}{\sigma_t}$.

8. EMPIRICAL RESULTS

We describe here our experimental setting and discuss the obtained results.

8.1 Step-Size Adaptation Mechanism

We test Algorithm 1 with cumulative step-size adaptation (CSA) [12]. The idea of CSA consists in keeping track of the successive steps taken by the algorithm in the search space. This is done by computing an evolution path, p_t, according to

$$p_{t+1} = (1 - c_\sigma)p_t + \sqrt{\frac{c_\sigma(2 - c_\sigma)}{\sum_{k=1}^\mu w_k^2}} \sum_{k=1}^\mu w_k \mathbf{U}_{t+1}^{\varsigma(k)} , \tag{32}$$

where $0 < c_\sigma \le 1$ and $p_0^\sigma = \mathbf{0}$. The constant $\sqrt{\frac{c_\sigma(2-c_\sigma)}{\sum_{k=1}^\mu w_k^2}}$ is a normalization factor that is chosen such that under random selection, if p_t is normally distributed ($p_t \sim \mathcal{N}(\mathbf{0}, \mathbf{I}_{n \times n})$), then p_{t+1} is identically distributed [10, 11]. The evolution path is used to adapt the step-size σ_t according to the following rule.

$$\sigma_{t+1} = \sigma_t \exp^{\frac{c_\sigma}{d_\sigma}} \left(\frac{\|p_{t+1}\|}{E\|\mathcal{N}(\mathbf{0}, \mathbf{I}_{n \times n})\|} - 1 \right) . \tag{33}$$

The norm of the evolution path is compared to the expected norm of a standard normal vector by computing the ratio $\frac{\|p_{t+1}\|}{E\|\mathcal{N}(\mathbf{0}, \mathbf{I}_{n \times n})\|}$ and the step-size is updated depending on this ratio: if $\frac{\|p_{t+1}\|}{E\|\mathcal{N}(\mathbf{0}, \mathbf{I}_{n \times n})\|} \geq 1$, σ_t is increased as this suggests that the progress is too slow. Otherwise, σ_t is decreased. d_σ is a damping factor whose role is to moderate the changes in σ_t values.

In order for this adaptation mechanism to be compliant with our general adaptation rule $\mathcal{G}_\sigma(\sigma_t, \varsigma * \mathbf{U}_{t+1})$ (see (13)), we take $c_\sigma = 1$, that is, we consider CSA without cumulation. In this case, (32) becomes

$$p_{t+1} = \sqrt{\frac{1}{\sum_{k=1}^{\mu} w_k^2} \sum_{k=1}^{\mu} w_k \mathbf{U}_{t+1}^{\varsigma(k)}} \ .$$

For the damping factor, we use

$$d_\sigma = 2 + 2 \max\left(0, \sqrt{\frac{1/\sum_{k=1}^{\mu} w_k^2 - 1}{n+1}} - 1\right) \ ,$$

which is the default value recommended in [11] with $c_\sigma = 1$.

8.2 Simulations of the Markov Chain and Single Runs

We test Algorithm 1 on two convex quadratic functions, as a particular case of Corollary 1: the sphere function, f_{sphere}, and the ellipsoid function, $f_{\text{ellipsoid}}$, with a moderate condition number. They are defined according to (28) by taking (i) $\mathbf{H} = \mathbf{I}_{n \times n}$ for f_{sphere} and (ii) $\mathbf{H}$ diagonal with diagonal elements $[\mathbf{H}]_i = \alpha^{\frac{i-1}{n-1}}$, $i = 1, \cdots, n$, for $f_{\text{ellipsoid}}$ and with a condition number $\alpha = 10$.

We choose $\mathbf{x}_{\text{opt}}$ to be at $(10, \cdots, 10)^\mathsf{T}$ and construct the (active) constraints following the steps below:

- For the first constraint, $\mathbf{b}_1 = -\nabla_{\mathbf{x}} f(\mathbf{x}_{\text{opt}})^\mathsf{T}$ and $c_1 = -\mathbf{b}_1^\mathsf{T} \mathbf{x}_{\text{opt}}$,

- For the $m-1$ remaining constraints, we choose the constraint normal $\mathbf{b}_i$ as a standard normal vector ($\mathbf{b}_i \sim \mathcal{N}(\mathbf{0}, \mathbf{I}_{n \times n})$) and $c_i = -\mathbf{b}_i^\mathsf{T} \mathbf{x}_{\text{opt}}$. We choose the point $\nabla_{\mathbf{x}} f(\mathbf{x}_{\text{opt}})^\mathsf{T} = -\mathbf{b}_1$ to be feasible, along with $\mathbf{x}_{\text{opt}}$. Therefore, if $g_i(\nabla_{\mathbf{x}} f(\mathbf{x}_{\text{opt}})^\mathsf{T}) > 0$, we modify $\mathbf{b}_i$ and c_i according to: $\mathbf{b}_i = -\mathbf{b}_i$ and $c_i = -c_i$.

With the construction above, the constraints satisfy the LICQ (see Remark 1) with probability one. In such a case, the unique vector of Lagrange multipliers associated to $\mathbf{x}_{\text{opt}}$ is $\gamma_{\text{opt}} = (1, 0, \cdots, 0)^\mathsf{T}$.

As for the parameters of Algorithm 1, we choose the default values in [11] for both λ and μ. We set the weights w_i, $i = 1, \cdots, \mu$, according to [1], where they are chosen to be optimal on the sphere function in infinite dimension. We take $d_\gamma = d_\omega = 5$, $\chi = 2^{1/n}$, $k_1 = 3$, and $k_2 = 5$.

We run Algorithm 1 and simulate the Markov chain $(\Phi_t)_{t \in \mathbb{N}}$ (defined in Theorem 1) in $n = 10$ on f_{sphere} and $f_{\text{ellipsoid}}$ with $m = 1, 2, 5, 9$ constraints. For each problem, we test three different initial values of the penalty vector $\omega_0 = (1, \cdots, 1)^\mathsf{T}, (10^3, \cdots, 10^3)^\mathsf{T}, (10^{-3}, \cdots, 10^{-3})^\mathsf{T}$. In all the tests, $\mathbf{X}_0$ and $\mathbf{Y}_0$ are sampled uniformly in $[-5, 5]^n$, $\sigma_0 = 1$, and $\gamma_0 = \Gamma_0 = (5, \cdots, 5)^\mathsf{T}$.

Figures 2-5 show simulations of the Markov chain on f_{sphere} (left column) and $f_{\text{ellipsoid}}$ (right column) subject to 1, 2, 5, and 9 constraints respectively. Displayed are the normalized distance to $\mathbf{x}_{\text{opt}}$, $\|\mathbf{Y}_t\|$ (red), the normalized distance to γ_{opt}, $\|\Gamma_t\|$ (green), and the norm of the vector of penalty factors, $\|\omega_t\|$ (blue) in log-scale, for $\omega_0 = (1, \cdots, 1)^\mathsf{T}$ (first row), $\omega_0 = (10^3, \cdots, 10^3)^\mathsf{T}$ (second row), and $\omega_0 = (10^{-3}, \cdots, 10^{-3})^\mathsf{T}$ (third row). We observe an overall convergence to a stationary distribution, independently of ω_0, after a certain number of iterations. For $\omega_0 = (10^3, \cdots, 10^3)^\mathsf{T}$,

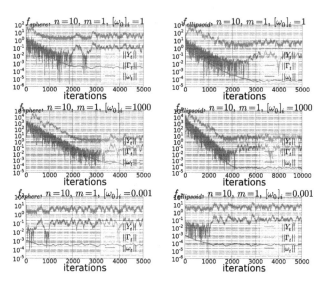

Figure 2: Simulations of the Markov chain on f_{sphere} (left) and $f_{\text{ellipsoid}}$ (right) with $m = 1$ in $n = 10$.

the adaptation phase before reaching the stationary state is longer than with $\omega_0 = (1, \cdots, 1)^\mathsf{T}$ or $\omega_0 = (10^{-3}, \cdots, 10^{-3})^\mathsf{T}$ on both f_{sphere} and $f_{\text{ellipsoid}}$. It also increases with increasing m: it takes approximately 4×10^3 iterations on f_{sphere} and $f_{\text{ellipsoid}}$ with $m = 1$ (Figure 2) and approximately 6×10^3 iterations with $m = 9$ (Figure 5). Indeed, the problem becomes more difficult for large m (as shown below with single runs). We also observe from Figures 2-5 that $\|\omega_t\|$ stabilizes around a larger value as m increases (approximately 4×10^{-4} and 6×10^{-5} on f_{sphere} and $f_{\text{ellipsoid}}$ respectively with $m = 1$ versus approximately 1 and 4 with $m = 9$).

Figures 6-9 show single runs of Algorithm 1 on the same constrained problems described previously. Results on constrained f_{sphere} and constrained $f_{\text{ellipsoid}}$ are displayed in left and right columns respectively. The displayed quantities are (i) the distance to the optimum, $\|\mathbf{X}_t - \mathbf{x}_{\text{opt}}\|$ (red), (ii) the distance to the Lagrange multipliers, $\|\gamma_t - \gamma_{\text{opt}}\|$ (green), (iii) the norm of the penalty vector, $\|\omega_t\|$ (blue), and (iv) the step-size, σ_t (purple), in log-scale. Linear convergence occurs after an adaptation phase whose length depends on the accuracy of the choice of the initial parameters: for $m = 1$ and $\omega_0 = (10^{-3}, \cdots, 10^{-3})^\mathsf{T}$ (Figure 6, third row), linear convergence occurs after only around 30 iterations because ω_0 is already close to a stationary value (see Figure 2). On f_{sphere} with $m = 2$ (Figure 7, left column), the algorithm reaches a distance to $\mathbf{x}_{\text{opt}}$ of 10^{-4} after around 750 iterations with $\omega_0 = (1, \cdots, 1)^\mathsf{T}$, compared to around 2500 iterations with $\omega_0 = (10^3, \cdots, 10^3)^\mathsf{T}$ and around 1300 iterations with $\omega_0 = (10^{-3}, \cdots, 10^{-3})^\mathsf{T}$. The reason is that $\omega_0 = (1, \cdots, 1)^\mathsf{T}$ is closer to the stationary value in this case (Figure 3, left column). As the number of constraints increases (Figures 8 and 9), the number of iterations needed to reach a given precision increases: it takes more than 2 times longer to reach a distance from the optimum of 10^{-4} on both f_{sphere} and $f_{\text{ellipsoid}}$ with $m = 9$ and $\omega_0 = (1, \cdots, 1)^\mathsf{T}$ (Figure 9, first row) than with $m = 1$ (Figure 6, first row). These results are consistent with the simulations of the Markov chain in that the observed stability of the Markov chain leads to linear convergence (or divergence) of the algorithm—as stated in Theorem 3.

9. DISCUSSION

In this work, we investigated linear convergence of a $(\mu/\mu_{\text{w}}, \lambda)$-ES with an augmented Lagrangian constraint handling on the lin-

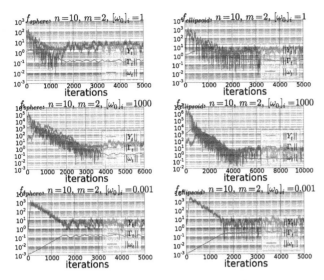

Figure 3: Simulations of the Markov chain on f_{sphere} (left) and $f_{\mathrm{ellipsoid}}$ (right) with $m = 2$ in $n = 10$.

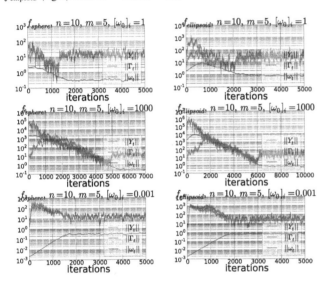

Figure 4: Simulations of the Markov chain on f_{sphere} (left) and $f_{\mathrm{ellipsoid}}$ (right) with $m = 5$ in $n = 10$.

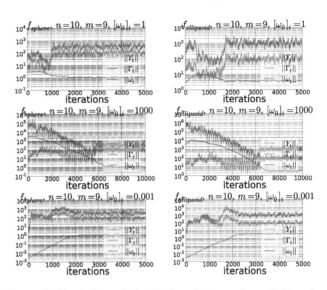

Figure 5: Simulations of the Markov chain on f_{sphere} (left) and $f_{\mathrm{ellipsoid}}$ (right) with $m = 9$ in $n = 10$.

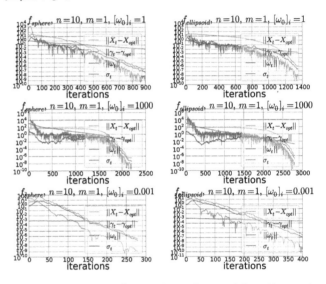

Figure 6: Single runs on f_{sphere} (left) and $f_{\mathrm{ellipsoid}}$ (right) with $m = 1$ in $n = 10$, with three different values of ω_0.

early constrained problem where all the constraints are active. We adopted a Markov chain approach and exhibited a homogeneous Markov chain on problems where the associated augmented Lagrangian, centered in the optimum and the corresponding Lagrange multipliers, is positive homogeneous of degree 2. We gave sufficient stability conditions which, when satisfied by the Markov chain, lead to linear convergence to the optimum as well as to the Lagrange multipliers. Simulations of the Markov chain on linearly constrained convex quadratic functions (as a particular case of the exhibited class of functions) show empirical evidence of stability for the tested parameter setting. We draw attention, however, to the fact that the observed stability may depend on the chosen parameter setting—in particular the damping factors for the Lagrange factors and the penalty factors—and proper parameter values are necessary to observe stability, especially in larger dimensions and for large numbers of constraints.

The conducted analysis gives insight into the behavior of the practical $(\mu/\mu_{\mathrm{w}}, \lambda)$-ES obtained when optimizing the augmented Lagrangian presented in (9). Indeed, we focus our study on the most difficult case in practice, where all the constraints are active at the optimum.

Finally, this work illustrates how the Markov chain approach—which is already applied to prove linear convergence of randomized optimization algorithms in the unconstrained case—can be extended to the constrained case.

Acknowledgments

This work was supported by the grant ANR-2012-MONU-0009 (NumBBO) from the French National Research Agency.

10. REFERENCES

[1] D. V. Arnold. Optimal weighted recombination. In *Foundations of Genetic Algorithms*, pages 215–237. Springer, 2005.

[2] D. V. Arnold and J. Porter. Towards an Augmented Lagrangian Constraint Handling Approach for the

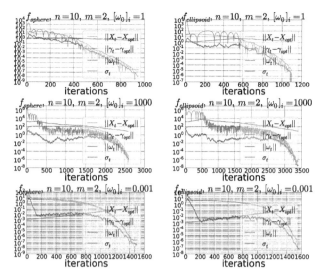

Figure 7: Single runs on f_{sphere} (left) and $f_{\text{ellipsoid}}$ (right) with $m = 2$ in $n = 10$, with three different values of ω_0.

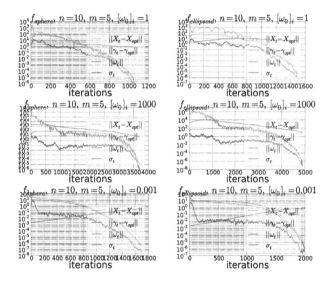

Figure 8: Single runs on f_{sphere} (left) and $f_{\text{ellipsoid}}$ (right) with $m = 5$ in $n = 10$, with three different values of ω_0.

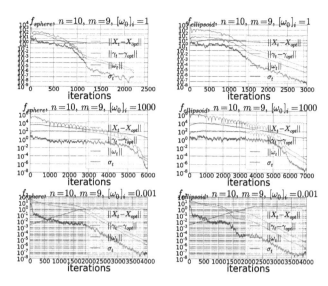

Figure 9: Single runs on f_{sphere} (left) and $f_{\text{ellipsoid}}$ (right) with $m = 9$ in $n = 10$, with three different values of ω_0.

$(1 + 1)$-ES. In *Genetic and Evolutionary Computation Conference*, pages 249–256. ACM Press, 2015.

[3] A. Atamna, A. Auger, and N. Hansen. Analysis of Linear Convergence of a $(1 + 1)$-ES with Augmented Lagrangian Constraint Handling. In *Genetic and Evolutionary Computation Conference*, pages 213–220. ACM Press, 2016.

[4] A. Atamna, A. Auger, and N. Hansen. Augmented Lagrangian Constraint Handling for CMA-ES—Case of a Single Linear Constraint. In *Parallel Problem Solving from Nature*, pages 181–191. Springer, 2016.

[5] A. Auger. Convergence Results for the $(1, \lambda)$-SA-ES Using the Theory of φ-Irreducible Markov Chains. *Theoretical Computer Science*, 334(1-3):35–69, 2005.

[6] A. Auger and N. Hansen. Linear Convergence on Positively Homogeneous Functions of a Comparison Based Step-Size Adaptive Randomized Search: the $(1 + 1)$ ES with

Generalized One-Fifth Success Rule. Submitted for publication, 2013.

[7] A. Auger and N. Hansen. Linear Convergence of Comparison-Based Step-Size Adaptive Randomized Search via Stability of Markov Chains. *SIAM Journal on Optimization*, 26(3):1589–1624, 2016.

[8] A. Bienvenüe and O. François. Global Convergence of Evolution Strategies in Spherical Problems: Some Simple Proofs and Difficulties. *Theoretical Computer Science*, 306(1–3):269–289, 2003.

[9] K. Deb and S. Srivastava. A Genetic Algorithm Based Augmented Lagrangian Method for Constrained Optimization. *Computational Optimization and Applications*, 53(3):869–902, 2012.

[10] H. Hansen, D. V. Arnold, and A. Auger. Evolution strategies. In J. Kacprzyk and W. Pedrycz, editors, *Handbook of Computational Intelligence*, chapter 44, pages 871–898. Springer, 2015.

[11] N. Hansen. The CMA Evolution Strategy: A Tutorial. http://arxiv.org/pdf/1604.00772v1.pdf, 2016.

[12] N. Hansen and A. Ostermeier. Completely Derandomized Self-Adaptation in Evolution Strategies. *Evolutionary Computation*, 9(2):159–195, 2001.

[13] M. R. Hestenes. Multiplier and Gradient Methods. *Journal of Optimization Theory and Applications*, 4(5):303–320, 1969.

[14] S. P. Meyn and R. L. Tweedie. *Markov Chains and Stochastic Stability*. Springer-Verlag, 1993.

[15] J. Nocedal and S. J. Wright. *Numerical Optimization*. Springer, 2nd edition, 2006.

[16] M. J. D. Powell. A Method for Nonlinear Constraints in Minimization Problems. In R. Fletcher, editor, *Optimization*, pages 283–298. Academic Press, 1969.

[17] M.-J. Tahk and B.-C. Sun. Coevolutionary Augmented Lagrangian Methods for Constrained Optimization. *IEE Transactions on Evolutionary Computation*, 4(2):114–124, 2000.

APPENDIX

A. PROOFS

A.1 Proof of Proposition 1

For Algorithm 1, the state $\mathbf{s}_t = (\mathbf{X}_t, \sigma_t, \gamma_t, \omega_t)$. Let

$$(\mathbf{X}'_{t+1}, \sigma'_{t+1}, \gamma'_{t+1}, \omega'_{t+1}) = $$
$$\mathcal{F}^{(f(.-\mathbf{x}_0), \{g_i(.-\mathbf{x}_0)\}_{i=1,\cdots,m})}(\Phi(\mathbf{x}_0)(\mathbf{X}_t, \sigma_t, \gamma_t, \omega_t), \mathbf{U}_{t+1}) .$$

Given the definition of $\Phi(\mathbf{x}_0)$ in (16) and the update functions $\mathcal{G}_\mathbf{x}$, $\mathcal{G}_\sigma$, $\mathcal{H}_\gamma$, and $\mathcal{H}_\omega$ in (12), (13), (14), and (15) respectively, we have

$$\mathbf{X}'_{t+1} = \mathcal{G}_\mathbf{x}((\mathbf{X}_t + \mathbf{x}_0, \sigma_t), \varsigma^{h(.-\mathbf{x}_0, \gamma_t, \omega_t)}_{(\mathbf{X}_t+\mathbf{x}_0, \sigma_t)} * \mathbf{U}_{t+1})$$

$$= \mathbf{X}_t + \mathbf{x}_0 + \sigma_t \sum_{i=1}^{\mu} w_i [\varsigma^{h(.-\mathbf{x}_0, \gamma_t, \omega_t)}_{(\mathbf{X}_t+\mathbf{x}_0, \sigma_t)} * \mathbf{U}_{t+1}]_i ,$$

$$\sigma'_{t+1} = \mathcal{G}_\sigma(\sigma_t, \varsigma^{h(.-\mathbf{x}_0, \gamma_t, \omega_t)}_{(\mathbf{X}_t+\mathbf{x}_0, \sigma_t)}) .$$

On the other hand, we have

$$\varsigma^{h(.-\mathbf{x}_0, \gamma_t, \omega_t)}_{(\mathbf{X}_t+\mathbf{x}_0, \sigma_t)} = Ord(h(\mathbf{X}_t + \mathbf{x}_0 + \sigma_t \mathbf{U}^i_{t+1} - \mathbf{x}_0, \gamma_t, \omega_t)_{i=1,\cdots,\lambda})$$
$$= \varsigma^{h(., \gamma_t, \omega_t)}_{(\mathbf{X}_t, \sigma_t)} .$$

It follows that

$$\mathbf{X}'_{t+1} = \mathcal{G}_\mathbf{x}((\mathbf{X}_t, \sigma_t), \varsigma^{h(., \gamma_t, \omega_t)}_{(\mathbf{X}_t, \sigma_t)} * \mathbf{U}_{t+1}) + \mathbf{x}_0$$
$$= \mathbf{X}_{t+1} + \mathbf{x}_0 , \tag{34}$$
$$\sigma'_{t+1} = \mathcal{G}_\sigma(\sigma_t, \varsigma^{h(., \gamma_t, \omega_t)}_{(\mathbf{X}_t, \sigma_t)}) = \sigma_{t+1} .$$

Using (34), we obtain

$$\gamma'^i_{t+1} = \mathcal{H}^{g_i(.-\mathbf{x}_0)}_\gamma(\gamma^i_t, \omega^i_t, \mathbf{X}'_{t+1}) = \gamma^i_t + \frac{\omega^i_t}{d_\gamma} g_i(\mathbf{X}'_{t+1} - \mathbf{x}_0)$$
$$= \mathcal{H}^{g_i}_\gamma(\gamma^i_t, \omega^i_t, \mathbf{X}_{t+1}) = \gamma^i_{t+1}, \quad i = 1, \cdots, m ,$$

$$\omega'^i_{t+1} = \mathcal{H}^{(f(.-\mathbf{x}_0), g_i(.-\mathbf{x}_0))}_\omega(\omega^i_t, \gamma^i_t, \mathbf{X}_t + \mathbf{x}_0, \mathbf{X}'_{t+1})$$

$$= \begin{cases} \omega^i_t \chi^{1/(4d_\omega)} & \text{if } \omega^i_t g_i(\mathbf{X}'_{t+1} - \mathbf{x}_0)^2 < \\ & k_1 \frac{|h(\mathbf{X}'_{t+1} - \mathbf{x}_0, \gamma_t, \omega_t) - h(\mathbf{X}_t + \mathbf{x}_0 - \mathbf{x}_0, \gamma_t, \omega_t)|}{n} \\ & \text{or } k_2|g_i(\mathbf{X}'_{t+1} - \mathbf{x}_0) - g_i(\mathbf{X}_t + \mathbf{x}_0 - \mathbf{x}_0)| < \\ & |g_i(\mathbf{X}_t + \mathbf{x}_0 - \mathbf{x}_0)| \\ \omega^i_t \chi^{-1/d_\omega} & \text{otherwise}, \quad i = 1, \cdots, m \end{cases}$$
$$= \mathcal{H}^{(f, g_i)}_\omega(\omega^i_t, \gamma^i_t, \mathbf{X}_t, \mathbf{X}_{t+1}) = \omega^i_{t+1}, \quad i = 1, \cdots, m .$$

Therefore,

$$(\mathbf{X}_{t+1} + \mathbf{x}_0, \sigma_{t+1}, \gamma_{t+1}, \omega_{t+1}) = $$
$$\mathcal{F}^{(f(.-\mathbf{x}_0), \{g_i(.-\mathbf{x}_0)\}_{i=1,\cdots,m})}(\Phi(\mathbf{x}_0)(\mathbf{X}_t, \sigma_t, \gamma_t, \omega_t), \mathbf{U}_{t+1}) . \tag{35}$$

By applying the inverse transformation $\Phi(-\mathbf{x}_0)$ to (35), we recover $\mathcal{F}^{(f, \{g_i\}_{i=1,\cdots,m})}(\mathbf{X}_t, \sigma_t, \gamma_t, \omega_t)$.

A.2 Proof of Proposition 2

The state at iteration t is $\mathbf{s}_t = (\mathbf{X}_t, \sigma_t, \gamma_t, \omega_t)$. Let

$$(\mathbf{X}'_{t+1}, \sigma'_{t+1}, \gamma'_{t+1}, \omega'_{t+1}) = $$
$$\mathcal{F}^{(f(\alpha.), \{g_i(\alpha.)\}_{i=1,\cdots,m})}(\Phi(\alpha)(\mathbf{X}_t, \sigma_t, \gamma_t, \omega_t), \mathbf{U}_{t+1}) .$$

By definition, we have

$$\varsigma^{h(\alpha., \gamma_t, \omega_t)}_{(\mathbf{X}_t/\alpha, \sigma_t/\alpha)} = Ord(h(\alpha(\mathbf{X}_t/\alpha + \sigma_t/\alpha \mathbf{U}^i_{t+1}), \gamma_t, \omega_t)_{i=1,\cdots,\lambda})$$
$$= \varsigma^{h(., \gamma_t, \omega_t)}_{(\mathbf{X}_t, \sigma_t)} .$$

Using the definition of $\Phi(\alpha)$ in (18), (12), (13), (14), (15), and the equation above, it follows

$$\mathbf{X}'_{t+1} = \mathcal{G}_\mathbf{x}((\mathbf{X}_t/\alpha, \sigma_t/\alpha), \varsigma^{h(., \gamma_t, \omega_t)}_{(\mathbf{X}_t, \sigma_t)} * \mathbf{U}_{t+1})$$
$$= \frac{\mathbf{X}_t}{\alpha} + \frac{\sigma_t}{\alpha} \sum_{i=1}^{\mu} w_i [\varsigma^{h(., \gamma_t, \omega_t)}_{(\mathbf{X}_t, \sigma_t)} * \mathbf{U}_{t+1}]_i$$
$$= \frac{1}{\alpha} \mathcal{G}_\mathbf{x}((\mathbf{X}_t, \sigma_t), \varsigma^{h(., \gamma_t, \omega_t)}_{(\mathbf{X}_t, \sigma_t)} * \mathbf{U}_{t+1}) = \frac{\mathbf{X}_{t+1}}{\alpha} , \tag{36}$$

and $\sigma'_{t+1} = \mathcal{G}_\sigma(\sigma_t/\alpha, \varsigma^{h(., \gamma_t, \omega_t)}_{(\mathbf{X}_t, \sigma_t)} * \mathbf{U}_{t+1})$. Using the scale-invariance property of $\mathcal{G}_\sigma$ (see (17)), we obtain

$$\sigma'_{t+1} = \frac{1}{\alpha} \mathcal{G}_\sigma(\sigma_t, \varsigma^{h(., \gamma_t, \omega_t)}_{(\mathbf{X}_t, \sigma_t)} * \mathbf{U}_{t+1}) = \frac{\sigma_{t+1}}{\alpha} .$$

Finally, using (36) we get

$$\gamma'^i_{t+1} = \mathcal{H}^{g_i(\alpha.)}_\gamma(\gamma^i_t, \omega^i_t, \mathbf{X}'_{t+1}) = \gamma^i_t + \frac{\omega^i_t}{d_\gamma} g_i(\alpha \mathbf{X}'_{t+1})$$
$$= \mathcal{H}^{g_i}_\gamma(\gamma^i_t, \omega^i_t, \mathbf{X}_{t+1}) = \gamma^i_{t+1}, \quad i = 1, \cdots, m ,$$

and

$$\omega'^i_{t+1} = \mathcal{H}^{(f(\alpha.), g_i(\alpha.))}_\omega(\omega^i_t, \gamma^i_t, \mathbf{X}_t/\alpha, \mathbf{X}'_{t+1})$$

$$= \begin{cases} \omega^i_t \chi^{1/(4d_\omega)} & \text{if } \omega^i_t g_i(\alpha \mathbf{X}'_{t+1})^2 < \\ & k_1 \frac{|h(\alpha \mathbf{X}'_{t+1}, \gamma_t, \omega_t) - h(\alpha \mathbf{X}_t/\alpha, \gamma_t, \omega_t)|}{n} \\ & \text{or } k_2|g_i(\alpha \mathbf{X}'_{t+1}) - g_i(\alpha \mathbf{X}_t/\alpha)| < \\ & |g_i(\alpha \mathbf{X}_t/\alpha)| \\ \omega^i_t \chi^{-1/d_\omega} & \text{otherwise}, \quad i = 1, \cdots, m \end{cases}$$
$$= \mathcal{H}^{(f, g_i)}_\omega(\omega^i_t, \gamma^i_t, \mathbf{X}_t, \mathbf{X}_{t+1}) = \omega^i_{t+1}, \quad i = 1, \cdots, m .$$

Therefore,

$$\left(\frac{\mathbf{X}_{t+1}}{\alpha}, \frac{\sigma_{t+1}}{\alpha}, \gamma_{t+1}, \omega_{t+1}\right) = $$
$$\mathcal{F}^{(f(\alpha.), \{g_i(\alpha.)\}_{i=1,\cdots,m})}(\Phi(\alpha)(\mathbf{X}_t, \sigma_t, \gamma_t, \omega_t), \mathbf{U}_{t+1}) . \tag{37}$$

By applying the inverse transformation $\Phi(1/\alpha)$ to (37), we obtain $\mathcal{F}^{(f, \{g_i\}_{i=1,\cdots,m})}(\mathbf{X}_t, \sigma_t, \gamma_t, \omega_t)$.

A.3 Proof of Theorem 1

We have

$$\mathbf{Y}_{t+1} = \frac{\mathbf{X}_{t+1} - \bar{\mathbf{x}}}{\sigma_{t+1}} = \frac{\mathcal{G}_\mathbf{x}((\mathbf{X}_t, \sigma_t), \varsigma * \mathbf{U}_{t+1}) - \bar{\mathbf{x}}}{\mathcal{G}_\sigma(\sigma_t, \varsigma * \mathbf{U}_{t+1})} .$$

Using translation-invariance and scale-invariance of Algorithm 1, it follows

$$\mathbf{Y}_{t+1} = \frac{\mathcal{G}_\mathbf{x}((\mathbf{Y}_t, 1), \varsigma * \mathbf{U}_{t+1})}{\mathcal{G}_\sigma(1, \varsigma * \mathbf{U}_{t+1})} ,$$

with

$$\varsigma = \varsigma^{h(., \gamma_t, \omega_t)}_{(\mathbf{X}_t, \sigma_t)} = \varsigma^{h(\sigma_t. + \bar{\mathbf{x}}, \gamma_t, \omega_t)}_{(\mathbf{Y}_t, 1)} = \varsigma^{h(\sigma_t. + \bar{\mathbf{x}}, \sigma_t \Gamma_t + \bar{\gamma}, \omega_t)}_{(\mathbf{Y}_t, 1)}$$
$$= Ord(h(\sigma_t(\mathbf{Y}_t + [\mathbf{U}_{t+1}]_i) + \bar{\mathbf{x}}, \sigma_t \Gamma_t + \bar{\gamma}, \omega_t)_{i=1,\cdots,\lambda})$$
$$= Ord(\mathcal{D}h_{\bar{\mathbf{x}}, \bar{\gamma}, \omega_t}(\sigma_t(\mathbf{Y}_t + [\mathbf{U}_{t+1}]_i) + \bar{\mathbf{x}}, \sigma_t \Gamma_t + \bar{\gamma})_{i=1,\cdots,\lambda}) ,$$

where $\mathcal{D}h_{\bar{\mathbf{x}},\bar{\gamma},\omega_t}$ is defined in (22) and $\mathbf{Y}_t$ and Γ_t in (21). By positive homogeneity of $\mathcal{D}h_{\bar{\mathbf{x}},\bar{\gamma},\omega_t}$, it follows

$$
\begin{aligned}
\varsigma &= Ord(\sigma_t{}^2 \mathcal{D}h_{\bar{\mathbf{x}},\bar{\gamma},\omega_t}(\mathbf{Y}_t + [\mathbf{U}_{t+1}]_i + \bar{\mathbf{x}}, \Gamma_t + \bar{\gamma})_{i=1,\cdots,\lambda}) \\
&= Ord(\mathcal{D}h_{\bar{\mathbf{x}},\bar{\gamma},\omega_t}(\mathbf{Y}_t + [\mathbf{U}_{t+1}]_i + \bar{\mathbf{x}}, \Gamma_t + \bar{\gamma})_{i=1,\cdots,\lambda}) \\
&= Ord(h(\mathbf{Y}_t + [\mathbf{U}_{t+1}]_i + \bar{\mathbf{x}}, \Gamma_t + \bar{\gamma}, \omega_t)_{i=1,\cdots,\lambda}) \\
&= \varsigma_{(\mathbf{Y}_t,1)}^{h(\cdot+\bar{\mathbf{x}},\Gamma_t+\bar{\gamma},\omega_t)} \ .
\end{aligned}
$$

On the other hand, we have

$$
\begin{aligned}
\Gamma_{t+1}^i &= \frac{\gamma_{t+1}^i - \bar{\gamma}^i}{\sigma_{t+1}} = \frac{\mathcal{H}_\gamma^{g_i}(\gamma_t^i, \omega_t^i, \mathbf{X}_{t+1}) - \bar{\gamma}^i}{\mathcal{G}_\sigma(\sigma_t, \varsigma * \mathbf{U}_{t+1})} \\
&= \frac{\gamma_t^i + \frac{\omega_t^i}{d_\gamma} g_i(\mathbf{X}_{t+1}) - \bar{\gamma}^i}{\sigma_t \mathcal{G}_\sigma(1, \varsigma * \mathbf{U}_{t+1})} = \frac{\Gamma_t^i + \frac{\omega_t^i}{d_\gamma \sigma_t} g_i(\mathbf{X}_{t+1})}{\mathcal{G}_\sigma(1, \varsigma * \mathbf{U}_{t+1})} \ .
\end{aligned}
$$

Using positive homogeneity of g_i with respect to $\bar{\mathbf{x}}$ (see (20)) and the definition of $\tilde{\mathbf{Y}}_{t+1}$ in (27), we have

$$
\begin{aligned}
g_i(\mathbf{X}_{t+1}) &= g_i(\sigma_{t+1}\mathbf{Y}_{t+1} + \bar{\mathbf{x}}) \\
&= \sigma_t g_i(\underbrace{\mathcal{G}_\sigma(1, \varsigma * \mathbf{U}_{t+1})\mathbf{Y}_{t+1}}_{\mathcal{G}_\mathbf{x}((\mathbf{Y}_t,1),\varsigma*\mathbf{U}_{t+1})=\tilde{\mathbf{Y}}_{t+1}} + \bar{\mathbf{x}}) \ . \quad (38)
\end{aligned}
$$

Therefore,

$$
\Gamma_{t+1}^i = \frac{\Gamma_t^i + \frac{\omega_t^i}{d_\gamma} g_i(\tilde{\mathbf{Y}}_{t+1} + \bar{\mathbf{x}})}{\mathcal{G}_\sigma(1, \varsigma * \mathbf{U}_{t+1})} = \frac{\mathcal{H}_\gamma^{g_i(\cdot+\bar{\mathbf{x}})}(\Gamma_t^i, \omega_t^i, \tilde{\mathbf{Y}}_{t+1})}{\mathcal{G}_\sigma(1, \varsigma * \mathbf{U}_{t+1})} \ ,
$$

for $i = 1, \cdots, m$. Finally,

$$
\begin{aligned}
\omega_{t+1}^i &= \mathcal{H}_\omega^{(f,g_i)}(\omega_t^i, \gamma_t^i, \mathbf{X}_t, \mathbf{X}_{t+1}) \\
&= \begin{cases} \omega_t^i \chi^{1/(4d_\omega)} & \text{if } \omega_t^i g_i(\mathbf{X}_{t+1})^2 < \\ & \quad k_1 \frac{|h(\mathbf{X}_{t+1},\gamma_t,\omega_t) - h(\mathbf{X}_t,\gamma_t,\omega_t)|}{n} \\ & \quad \text{or } k_2 |g_i(\mathbf{X}_{t+1}) - g_i(\mathbf{X}_t)| < \\ & \quad\quad |g_i(\mathbf{X}_t)| \\ \omega_t^i \chi^{-1/d_\omega} & \text{otherwise, } i = 1, \cdots, m \end{cases} \\
&= \begin{cases} \omega_t^i \chi^{1/(4d_\omega)} & \text{if } \omega_t^i g_i(\tilde{\mathbf{Y}}_{t+1} + \bar{\mathbf{x}})^2 < \\ & \quad k_1 \frac{|h(\tilde{\mathbf{Y}}_{t+1}+\bar{\mathbf{x}},\Gamma_t+\bar{\gamma},\omega_t) - h(\mathbf{Y}_t+\bar{\mathbf{x}},\Gamma_t+\bar{\gamma},\omega_t)|}{n} \\ & \quad \text{or } k_2 |g_i(\tilde{\mathbf{Y}}_{t+1} + \bar{\mathbf{x}}) - g_i(\mathbf{Y}_t + \bar{\mathbf{x}})| < \\ & \quad\quad |g_i(\mathbf{Y}_t + \bar{\mathbf{x}})| \\ \omega_t^i \chi^{-1/d_\omega} & \text{otherwise} \end{cases} \\
&= \mathcal{H}_\omega^{(f(\cdot+\bar{\mathbf{x}}),g_i(\cdot+\bar{\mathbf{x}}))}(\omega_t^i, \Gamma_t^i + \bar{\gamma}^i, \mathbf{Y}_t, \tilde{\mathbf{Y}}_{t+1}) \ ,
\end{aligned}
$$

for $i = 1, \cdots, m$, where we used (20), along with (38), and positive homogeneity of $\mathcal{D}h_{\bar{\mathbf{x}},\bar{\gamma},\omega_t}$ with respect to $[\bar{\mathbf{x}}, \bar{\gamma}]$ to deduce that

$$
\begin{aligned}
h(\mathbf{X}_{t+1}, \gamma_t, \omega_t) - h(\mathbf{X}_t, \gamma_t, \omega_t) &= \sigma_t^2(\mathcal{D}h_{\bar{\mathbf{x}},\bar{\gamma},\omega_t}(\tilde{\mathbf{Y}}_{t+1} + \bar{\mathbf{x}}, \sigma_t\Gamma_t + \bar{\gamma}) \\
&\quad - \mathcal{D}h_{\bar{\mathbf{x}},\bar{\gamma},\omega_t}(\mathbf{Y}_{t+1} + \bar{\mathbf{x}}, \sigma_t\Gamma_t + \bar{\gamma})) \\
&= \sigma_t^2(h(\tilde{\mathbf{Y}}_{t+1} + \bar{\mathbf{x}}, \Gamma_t + \bar{\gamma}, \omega_t) - h(\mathbf{Y}_t + \bar{\mathbf{x}}, \Gamma_t + \bar{\gamma}, \omega_t)) \ .
\end{aligned}
$$

$\Phi_{t+1} = (\mathbf{Y}_{t+1}, \Gamma_{t+1}, \omega_{t+1})$ is a function of only $\mathbf{Y}_t, \Gamma_t, \omega_t$, and i.i.d. vectors $\mathbf{U}_{t+1}$. Therefore, $(\Phi_t)_{t\in\mathbb{N}}$ is a homogeneous Markov chain.

A.4 Proof of Corollary 1

By definition, we have

$$
\begin{aligned}
h(\mathbf{x}_{\text{opt}} + \alpha\mathbf{x}, \gamma_{\text{opt}} + \alpha\gamma, \omega) &= \underbrace{f(\mathbf{x}_{\text{opt}} + \alpha\mathbf{x})}_{A} \\
&+ \underbrace{\sum_{i=1}^m (\gamma_{\text{opt}}^i + \alpha\gamma^i) g_i(\mathbf{x}_{\text{opt}} + \alpha\mathbf{x})}_{B} + \underbrace{\sum_{i=1}^m \frac{\omega^i}{2} g_i(\mathbf{x}_{\text{opt}} + \alpha\mathbf{x})^2}_{C} \ .
\end{aligned}
$$

By developing A, B, and C, we obtain

$$
A = \alpha^2 f(\mathbf{x}_{\text{opt}} + \mathbf{x}) + (1 - \alpha^2) f(\mathbf{x}_{\text{opt}}) + \alpha(1 - \alpha) \underbrace{\mathbf{x}_{\text{opt}}^\mathsf{T}\mathbf{H}}_{\nabla_\mathbf{x} f(\mathbf{x}_{\text{opt}})} \mathbf{x} \ ,
$$

$$
B = \sum_{i=1}^m \alpha^2 (\gamma_{\text{opt}}^i + \gamma^i) g_i(\mathbf{x}_{\text{opt}} + \mathbf{x}) + \alpha(1 - \alpha) \gamma_{\text{opt}}^i \underbrace{\mathbf{b}^i}_{\nabla_\mathbf{x} g_i(\mathbf{x}_{\text{opt}})} \mathbf{x} \ ,
$$

$$
C = \alpha^2 \sum_{i=1}^m \frac{\omega^i}{2} g_i(\mathbf{x}_{\text{opt}} + \mathbf{x})^2 \ .
$$

The constraints being active at $\mathbf{x}_{\text{opt}}$, $h(\mathbf{x}_{\text{opt}}, \gamma_{\text{opt}}, \omega) = f(\mathbf{x}_{\text{opt}})$ for all $\omega \in (\mathbb{R}_>^+)^m$. It follows that

$$
\begin{aligned}
&\mathcal{D}h_{\mathbf{x}_{\text{opt}},\gamma_{\text{opt}},\omega}(\mathbf{x}_{\text{opt}} + \alpha\mathbf{x}, \gamma_{\text{opt}} + \alpha\gamma) \\
&= \alpha^2 \Big(f(\mathbf{x}_{\text{opt}} + \mathbf{x}) + \sum_{i=1}^m (\gamma_{\text{opt}}^i + \gamma^i) g_i(\mathbf{x}_{\text{opt}} + \mathbf{x}) + \frac{\omega^i}{2} g_i(\mathbf{x}_{\text{opt}} + \mathbf{x})^2 \\
&\quad - f(\mathbf{x}_{\text{opt}})\Big) + \alpha(1 - \alpha) \underbrace{\Big(\nabla_\mathbf{x} f(\mathbf{x}_{\text{opt}}) + \sum_{i=1}^m \nabla_\mathbf{x} g_i(\mathbf{x}_{\text{opt}})\Big)}_{0} \mathbf{x} \ .
\end{aligned}
$$

The KKT stationarity condition in (29) is satisfied for $\mathbf{x}_{\text{opt}}$ and γ_{opt}. Therefore,

$$
\begin{aligned}
&\mathcal{D}h_{\mathbf{x}_{\text{opt}},\gamma_{\text{opt}},\omega}(\mathbf{x}_{\text{opt}} + \alpha\mathbf{x}, \gamma_{\text{opt}} + \alpha\gamma) \\
&\quad\quad = \alpha^2 \mathcal{D}h_{\mathbf{x}_{\text{opt}},\gamma_{\text{opt}},\omega}(\mathbf{x}_{\text{opt}} + \mathbf{x}, \gamma_{\text{opt}} + \gamma) \ .
\end{aligned}
$$

Consequently, $(\Phi_t)_{t\in\mathbb{N}}$ is a homogeneous Markov chain with f convex quadratic.

A.5 Proof of Theorem 3

We express $\frac{1}{t} \ln \frac{\|\mathbf{X}_t - \mathbf{x}_{\text{opt}}\|}{\|\mathbf{X}_0 - \mathbf{x}_{\text{opt}}\|}$, $\frac{1}{t} \ln \frac{\|\gamma_t - \gamma_{\text{opt}}\|}{\|\gamma_0 - \gamma_{\text{opt}}\|}$, and $\frac{1}{t} \ln \frac{\sigma_t}{\sigma_0}$ as a function of the homogeneous Markov chain $(\Phi_t)_{t\in\mathbb{N}}$ defined in Theorem 1. Using the property of the logarithm, we have

$$
\begin{aligned}
\frac{1}{t} \ln \frac{\|\mathbf{X}_t - \mathbf{x}_{\text{opt}}\|}{\|\mathbf{X}_0 - \mathbf{x}_{\text{opt}}\|} &= \frac{1}{t} \sum_{k=0}^{t-1} \ln \frac{\|\mathbf{X}_{k+1} - \mathbf{x}_{\text{opt}}\|}{\|\mathbf{X}_k - \mathbf{x}_{\text{opt}}\|} \\
&= \frac{1}{t} \sum_{k=0}^{t-1} \ln \frac{\|\mathbf{Y}_{k+1}\|}{\|\mathbf{Y}_k\|} \mathcal{G}_\sigma(1, \varsigma * \mathbf{U}_{k+1}) \\
&= \frac{1}{t} \sum_{k=0}^{t-1} \ln \|\mathbf{Y}_{k+1}\| - \frac{1}{t} \sum_{k=0}^{t-1} \ln \|\mathbf{Y}_k\| \\
&\quad + \frac{1}{t} \sum_{k=0}^{t-1} \ln \mathcal{G}_\sigma(1, \varsigma * \mathbf{U}_{t+1}) \ . \quad (39)
\end{aligned}
$$

$(\Phi)_{t\in\mathbb{N}}$ is positive Harris-recurrent with an invariant probability measure π and $E_\pi(|\ln\|[\phi]_1\||) < \infty$, $E_\pi(|\ln\|[\phi]_2\||) < \infty$, and $E_\pi(\mathcal{R}(\phi)) < \infty$. Therefore, we can apply Theorem 2 to the right-hand side of (39). We obtain

$$\lim_{t \to \infty} \frac{1}{t} \ln \frac{\|\mathbf{X}_t - \mathbf{x}_{\mathrm{opt}}\|}{\|\mathbf{X}_0 - \mathbf{x}_{\mathrm{opt}}\|} = \lim_{t \to \infty} \frac{1}{t} \sum_{k=0}^{t-1} \ln \|\mathbf{Y}_{k+1}\|$$

$$- \lim_{t \to \infty} \frac{1}{t} \sum_{k=0}^{t-1} \ln \|\mathbf{Y}_k\| + \lim_{t \to \infty} \frac{1}{t} \sum_{k=0}^{t-1} \ln \mathcal{G}_\sigma(1, \varsigma * \mathbf{U}_{t+1})$$

$$= \int \ln \|[\phi]_1\| \pi(d\phi) - \int \ln \|[\phi]_1\| \pi(d\phi) + \int \mathcal{R}(\phi) \pi(d\phi)$$

$$= -\mathrm{CR} \ .$$

We proceed similarly with $\frac{1}{t} \ln \frac{\|\gamma_t - \gamma_{\mathrm{opt}}\|}{\|\gamma_0 - \gamma_{\mathrm{opt}}\|}$ and $\frac{1}{t} \ln \frac{\sigma_t}{\sigma_0}$.

$$\frac{1}{t} \ln \frac{\|\gamma_t - \gamma_{\mathrm{opt}}\|}{\|\gamma_0 - \gamma_{\mathrm{opt}}\|} = \frac{1}{t} \sum_{k=0}^{t-1} \ln \|\Gamma_{k+1}\| - \frac{1}{t} \sum_{k=0}^{t-1} \ln \|\Gamma_k\|$$

$$+ \frac{1}{t} \sum_{k=0}^{t-1} \ln \mathcal{G}_\sigma(1, \varsigma * \mathbf{U}_{t+1}) \ , \qquad (40)$$

$$\frac{1}{t} \ln \frac{\sigma_t}{\sigma_0} = \frac{1}{t} \sum_{k=0}^{t-1} \frac{\sigma_{k+1}}{\sigma_k}$$

$$= \lim_{t \to \infty} \frac{1}{t} \sum_{k=0}^{t-1} \ln \mathcal{G}_\sigma(1, \varsigma * \mathbf{U}_{t+1}) \ . \qquad (41)$$

By applying Theorem 2 to the right-hand side of (40) and (41), we obtain

$$\lim_{t \to \infty} \frac{1}{t} \ln \frac{\|\gamma_t - \gamma_{\mathrm{opt}}\|}{\|\gamma_0 - \gamma_{\mathrm{opt}}\|} = \lim_{t \to \infty} \frac{1}{t} \ln \frac{\sigma_t}{\sigma_0} = -\mathrm{CR} \ .$$

161

Author Index

Akimoto, Youhei 111

Atamna, Asma 149

Auger, Anne 111, 149

Covantes Osuna, Edgar 55

Friedrich, Tobias 25, 37, 45

Glasmachers, Tobias 139

Hansen, Nikolaus 111, 149

Igel, Christian 139

Imada, Ryo 95

Ishibuchi, Hisao 95

Kötzing, Timo 25, 45

Krause, Oswin 139

Krejca, Martin S. 65

Lagodzinski, Gregor 45

Mühlenthaler, Moritz 13

Neumann, Frank 37, 45

Nojima, Yusuke 95

Paixão, Tiago 3

Pérez Heredia, Jorge 3

Pourhassan, Mojgan 37

Quinzan, Francesco 25

Raß, Alexander 13

Schirneck, Martin 45

Schmitt, Manuel 13

Setoguchi, Yu 95

Sheppard, John W. 81

Shir, Ofer M. 127

Siegling, Andreas 13

Strasser, Shane 81

Sudholt, Dirk 55

Sutton, Andrew M. 25

Thorup, Mikkel 1

Wanka, Rolf 13

Witt, Carsten 65

Yehudayoff, Amir 127